"Wayne Grudem is one of the outstanding biblical scholars in America. He's going to handle very well any subject he tackles. I particularly appreciate his work in this area, because he looks at the relationship between religion and politics through a biblical lens. Too often we confuse ideology with revealed truth. There are sections of this book that are uncannily timely, particularly on medical ethics, the rule of the courts, and the purpose of government. This can be a wonderful resource as we face growing tensions from an ever more powerful state."

—CHUCK COLSON, Founder, Prison Fellowship

"Wayne Grudem's call for men and women of faith to be engaged in the public life of our great country is precisely and exactly the call the rising generation needs to hear. Our duty as Christians is to recognize the vital differences between the city of God and the city of man, and to be involved in the public life of our great country."

—TIMOTHY GOEGLEIN, Vice President, External Relations, Focus on the Family

"If you read this year only one Christian book on politics, read *Politics—According to the Bible*. Wayne Grudem shows how we should approach more than fifty specific issues. His biblically-based good sense overwhelms the nostrums of Jim Wallis and the evangelical left. Wayne also shows why those seeking a vacation from politics need to rise up and go to work."

—MARVIN OLASKY, editor-in-chief, *World*, and provost, The King's College, New York City

Conservative and hard-hitting both biblically and culturally, Grudem's treatise is essentially a giant tract for the times, covering the whole waterfront of America's political debate with shrewd insight and strong argument. This book will be a valued resource for years to come, and right now no Christian can afford to ignore it. An outstanding achievement!

—JAMES I. PACKER, Board of Governors' Professor of Theology, Regent College, Vancouver

Zondervan Books and Products by Wayne Grudem

Systematic Theology

Bible Doctrine

Christian Beliefs

Systematic Theology Laminated Sheet

Are Miraculous Gifts for Today? 4 Views (General Editor)

Politics—According to the Bible

POLITICS
ACCORDING TO THE BIBLE

A COMPREHENSIVE RESOURCE FOR
UNDERSTANDING MODERN POLITICAL ISSUES IN
LIGHT OF SCRIPTURE

WAYNE GRUDEM

ZONDERVAN®

ZONDERVAN.com/
AUTHORTRACKER
follow your favorite authors

ZONDERVAN

Politics—According to the Bible
Copyright © 2010 by Wayne A. Grudem

This title is also available as a Zondervan ebook.
Visit www.zondervan.com/ebooks.

This title is also available in a Zondervan audio edition.
Visit www.zondervan.fm.

Requests for information should be addressed to:

Zondervan, *Grand Rapids, Michigan 49530*

Library of Congress Cataloging-in-Publication Data

Grudem, Wayne A.
        Politics—according to the Bible : a comprehensive resource for understanding modern political
    issues in light of scripture / Wayne Grudem.
            p. cm.
        Includes bibliographical references.
        ISBN 978-0-310-33029-5 (hardcover, printed)
        1. Politics in the Bible. 2. Bible and politics. 3. Christianity and politics. 4. Church and social
    problems. I. Title.
        BS680.P45G78 2010
        261.7—dc22   201002252

Cover design: Rob Monacelli
Cover photography: SuperStock / Masterfile
Interior design: Matthew VanZomeren

Printed in the United States of America

10 11 12 13 14 15 /DCI/ 28 27 26 25 24 23 22 21 20 19 18 17 16 15 14 13 12 11 10 9 8 7 6 5

CONTENTS

Part 2

SPECIFIC ISSUES

Part 3
CONCLUDING OBSERVATIONS

PREFACE

I have not written this book from the perspective of a lawyer or journalist or professional politician, but from the perspective of a professor with a Ph.D. in New Testament studies and twenty-eight years of experience in teaching the Bible at the M.Div. and (sometimes) the Ph.D. level. I wrote this book because I was convinced that God intended the Bible to give guidance to every area of life—including how governments should function!

I support political positions in this book that would be called more "conservative" than "liberal." That is because of my conclusions about the Bible's teaching on the role of government and a biblical worldview (see chaps. 3 and 4). It is important to understand that I see these positions as *flowing out of the Bible's teachings* rather than positions that I hold prior to, or independently of, those biblical teachings. And I do not hesitate to criticize Republican policies where I differ with them (for instance, in the endorsement of runaway government spending and the continual expansion of the federal government even under conservative Republican presidents). My primary purpose in the book is not to be liberal or conservative, or Democratic or Republican, but to explain a biblical worldview and a biblical perspective on issues of politics, law, and government.

I also want to say something at the outset about Barack Obama, who is the President of the United States as I am writing this book. Because of the conservative political conclusions in this book, at several points I end up criticizing some policies of President Obama and the current Democratic leadership in the US Congress. Although I disagree with many of the President's policies, I also find him to be articulate, poised, highly intelligent, and a remarkably effective speaker. And I think it was a wonderful thing for the United States that an African-American man was elected as President. I rejoice that our nation has been able to overcome its previous history of racial discrimination to such a degree that we could elect our first black President. This has been a significant milestone in American history, and for this, even those of us who did not vote for him can and should be thankful.

But I also want to point out that not all black Americans hold the liberal political views of President Obama. Politically conservative black leaders who have risen to high government positions include Supreme Court Justice Clarence Thomas, former

Secretary of State Condoleezza Rice, former Secretary of State Colin Powell (a Republican though he endorsed Barack Obama), former Secretary of Education Roderick Paige, Chairman of the Republican National Committee Michael Steele (the former Lieutenant Governor of Maryland), former Ohio Secretary of State Ken Blackwell, Judge Janice Rogers Brown of the District of Columbia Court of Appeals, and former member of Congress and chair of the House Republican Conference J. C. Watts Jr. And one of the most influential conservative economists in the United States is Thomas Sowell. These leaders and many others remind us that black Americans can strongly advocate conservative political positions as well as liberal ones. So one of my hopes for this book is that many black Christians who accept the Bible as the Word of God and supported President Obama in 2008 will consider my arguments from the Bible and perhaps decide that they, too, will support the conservative positions that I argue for in these pages.

I wish to thank a number of friends who helped me with this book, especially Craig Osten, vice president of research at Alliance Defense Fund, whose remarkable research skills in fact-checking and documentation provided me with exactly the information I needed again and again. Craig's input has improved the content of nearly every chapter of the book, and I don't think I could have written this book without his excellent help. David Payne, economist at the US Department of Commerce, provided valuable information and several helpful corrections to chapter 9 on economic policies. Cal Beisner, national spokesman for the Cornwall Alliance for the Stewardship of Creation and (in my estimation) the world's leading expert on a Christian perspective on uses of the environment, provided valuable information and corrections for chapter 10 on the environment and, at my request, also wrote the first draft of the entire section on global warming, which I then revised and incorporated into this manuscript. Daniel Heimbach, ethics professor at Southeastern Baptist Theological Seminary and former Deputy Assistant Secretary of the Navy for Manpower, provided valuable comments for the material on national defense and just war in chapter 11. (Dr. Heimbach brings real-life experience to this topic, because while working as a staff member in the White House, he drafted the just war framework that President George H. W. Bush used in leading coalition forces against Iraq in the Persian Gulf War in 1991.)

Joe Infranco, Jordan Lorence, and Jeff Ventrella of the Alliance Defense Fund gave me helpful advice on specific topics in the book, and Jeff also invited me to present parts of it for some Alliance Defense Fund litigation seminars. Madison Trammel also provided several helpful suggestions about the manuscript. Greg Forster read the manuscript and gave me several helpful suggestions from his far greater expertise in matters of governmental theory and history of ideas. John Hayward called my attention to several British books on these topics. My friend Barry Asmus gave me helpful counsel in the economics section, and Craig Shultz helped me to understand another perspective in my section on tort reform. In addition, my adult Bible class at Scottsdale Bible Church has been a great encouragement and corrected several mistakes as I taught through this material in the class over several months. The students in my class "Biblical Theology of Law, Politics, and Government" at Phoenix Seminary also provided helpful feedback.

Sharon Hoshiwara quickly and accurately typed most of the book, often on short deadlines. Anne Boyd then carefully typed some of the final sections. Dan Julian helped me with computer setup and troubleshooting and with additional research, and Joshua D. Brooks also helped me with research. Sarah McCurley compiled a detailed table of contents and provided secretarial help in other ways at various times. Sean Reynolds and Joshua D. Brooks carefully compiled the indexes for the book. Joshua and Alyssa Brooks both helped with proofreading.

I am also grateful to President Darryl DelHousaye and the members of the board at Phoenix Seminary, who have graciously allowed me to teach on a half-time basis, which enabled me to complete this book rather quickly. The partners of Marketplace One in Phoenix provided significant support that has increased my writing productivity in many ways.

I am deeply grateful for all of this help, and I hope all of these people will understand that they too have had a significant role in the production of this book.

I have dedicated this book to three people who, in the providence of God, were most responsible for leading me to write it. Alan Sears and Ben Bull of the Alliance Defense Fund first approached me several years ago with the interesting idea of writing a book like this. They were also able to provide helpful funding for some aspects of the research and editorial work, although the range of topics in the book ended up going far beyond their initial suggestions. Then Cathi Herrod, president of the Center for Arizona Policy, encouraged me in this project from the beginning, gave wise suggestions, and gave me opportunities to present and promote some of this material to various audiences. I do not even know if these three friends would agree with all that I write here, but I am most grateful for their encouragement in the overall project.

Above all, I am thankful to Margaret, my wonderful wife of forty years, who encouraged me daily as I was writing, quietly brought meals to my study, regularly prayed for me, kept me from accepting too many other obligations, made me laugh countless times with her wonderful sense of humor, brought joy to my heart again and again, and served as a wise and loving counselor to me on countless occasions as we would talk over my progress on the book and the events of life in general.

I hope that Christians who take the Bible as a guide for life will find these discussions encouraging. I believe that God's perspective on politics is joyful "good news," just as the rest of the Bible is good news for all areas of life! I believe the Bible's teachings about politics will bring hope and beneficial change to people in every nation where they are put into practice. When these teachings are put into practice in a nation, it will be good news for those who are oppressed, good news to those who long for justice, good news to those who long for peace, good news for young and old, weak and powerful, rich and poor—good news for everyone who will follow the wonderful paths of freedom and sound government that are taught in the pages of the Bible. The prophet Isaiah extolled the beautiful sound of the feet of a messenger who came running with good news from God himself:

> How beautiful upon the mountains are the feet of him who brings good news, who publishes peace, who brings good news of happiness, who publishes salvation, who says to Zion, "Your God reigns" (Isa. 52:7).

Therefore I hope that as people and nations follow these principles for government, they will begin to see a reversal of the continual decline in peace, civility, liberty, and civic goodness that we have seen in recent decades in our societies, and instead we will begin to see regular progress toward increasingly good, pleasant, productive, low-crime, free, and happy civil societies in which we can live.

I am well aware that the Bible is not an American book, for it was finished nearly 1,700 years before the United States existed! The principles and teachings in the Bible contain wisdom that is helpful for *all* nations and all governments. Therefore I have tried to keep in mind that people in other nations might read this book and find it useful for formulating their own positions on the political issues that they face in their own nations. Yet in my examples and my choice of political issues, I focus primarily on the United States, because that is the country I know best, the country I am proud to be a citizen of, and the country I deeply love.

What about readers who don't believe the Bible to be from God or who may not be sure what they think about the Bible? I hope they will still consider the arguments in this book on their own merits and find them useful—perhaps even persuasive—in formulating their own opinions. If not, their right to disagree with me is still very important to any government that follows the principles in this book. I believe there should be strong protections for freedom of religion in every nation (see chap. 1), and I earnestly desire to protect each person's freedom to make decisions about religious belief for himself or herself, totally without any compulsion from government. I want to protect other people's right to disagree with me and to express that disagreement publicly in any nation.

Finally, I encourage readers to skip around in this book and perhaps go directly to the topics they find most interesting. There is no need to read it from beginning to end, because most of the chapters are self-contained. However, the foundational material is in chapters 1–4, and perhaps readers will want at least to read those chapters first.

Wayne Grudem, Ph.D.

February 2010

INTRODUCTION

Should churches exert any influence in politics?

Should pastors preach about political questions?

Is there only one "Christian" position on political issues?

Does the Bible teach anything about how people should vote?

I think there are some clear answers to these questions, but we have to recognize at the outset that dozens of other books and articles have already given their own answers to such questions. These books range from saying that the Bible gives outright support for many liberal Democratic positions to saying that the Bible supports conservative Republican positions.[1] Some books argue that Christians have simply become far too entangled in political activities, while another important book argues that Christians have a biblical mandate to be involved in politics.[2] Another widely influential book gives many real-life examples of remarkable Christian influence on laws and governments.[3] One book that has received wide consideration in the United Kingdom proposes a rethinking of major political questions in light of the Bible's priority of personal relationships.[4]

There have been a few recent books by theologians and biblical scholars dealing at a more theoretical level with the question of Christian perspectives on politics.[5]

---

1. A book supporting mostly Democratic positions would be Jim Wallis, *God's Politics: Why the Right Gets It Wrong and the Left Doesn't Get It* (New York: HarperSanFrancisco, 2005); one supporting mostly Republican positions would be D. James Kennedy and Jerry Newcombe, *How Would Jesus Vote? A Christian Perspective on the Issues* (Colorado Springs: Waterbrook, 2008).

2. John MacArthur, *Why Government Can't Save You: An Alternative to Political Activism* (Nashville: Word, 2000), and Cal Thomas and Ed Dobson, *Blinded by Might: Why the Religious Right Can't Save America* (Grand Rapids: Zondervan, 1999), are two examples of works that espouse caution and much restraint in Christian involvement in politics (and especially, for Thomas and Dobson, the church's involvement in politics). On the other hand, Tom Minnery's thoughtful and challenging book *Why You Can't Stay Silent* (Wheaton, IL: Tyndale House, 2001) calls believers to become much more involved in political issues of the day.

3. See Charles W. Colson, *God and Government: An Insider's View on the Boundaries between Faith and Politics* (Grand Rapids: Zondervan, 2007; previously published as *Kingdoms in Conflict*).

4. See Michael Schluter and John Ashcroft, eds., *Jubilee Manifesto* (Leicester: Inter-Varsity Press, 2005).

5. Several of these books address the larger theoretical questions about law and government with far more wisdom and erudition than I can offer; see especially D. A. Carson, *Christ and Culture Revisited* (Grand Rapids: Eerdmans, 2008); see also

In this book I start out by explaining what seem to me to be five clearly wrong (and harmful) views about Christians and politics: (1) "government should compel religion," (2) "government should exclude religion," (3) "all government is evil and demonic," (4) "the church should do evangelism, not politics," and (5) "the church should do politics, not evangelism." As an alternative, I argue for what I think to be the correct view: (6) "significant Christian influence on government."

But what exactly does the Bible itself say about civil government? In chapter 3 I survey the Bible's teachings about the purpose of government and the characteristics of good government and bad government.

Before turning to specific political issues, I attempt in chapter 4 to lay a foundation concerning the main components of a Christian worldview: What does the Bible say about God as Creator, about the earth he created, about us as men and women created in his image, about sin, and about God's purpose for putting human beings on the earth in the first place? I lay this broad foundation so as to avoid a common mistake of using Bible verses out of context to support nearly any position on current political disputes.

This foundation of a Christian worldview is necessary in order to "see the parts in light of the whole" and thus to understand individual verses correctly from within the overall framework of the Bible's primary teachings. I put this material at the beginning of the book because basic worldview differences have profound implications for many matters of government policy. In fact, differences over worldview questions explain many of the disagreements between "liberals" and "conservatives" in politics today.

In the rest of the book I examine about sixty specific current issues. I attempt to analyze them from the standpoint of that biblical understanding of civil government and that biblical worldview and also with reference to specific teachings of the Bible that pertain to each issue.

Do I think that everyone who tries to follow the Bible will agree with my understanding of these issues? No. In a book that covers sixty political topics, many readers will agree with me in some sections and disagree with me in others. Many Christian readers who accept the authority of the Bible might argue for alternative positions that they think are better supported from the overall teaching of the Bible. That is fine with me, for I think we grow in our understanding by discussing and reasoning with one another (in a civil manner!). "Where there is no guidance, a people falls, but in an abundance of counselors there is safety" (Prov. 11:14).

I also want to say that I do not hold with equal confidence every position I support in this book. On some issues I think the overall teaching of the Bible is *clear, direct, and decisive*, such as the idea that civil governments are set up by God to punish evil and

Richard Bauckham, *The Bible in Politics: How to Read the Bible Politically* (London: SPCK, 1989); Chris Green, ed., *A Higher Throne: Evangelicals and Public Policy* (Nottingham: Apollos, 2008); Gordon McConville, *God and Earthly Power: An Old Testament Political Theology* (London: T. & T. Clark, 2006); Oliver O'Donovan, *The Desire of the Nations: Rediscovering the Roots of Political Theology* (Cambridge: Cambridge University Press, 1996); and Nick Spencer and Jonathan Chaplin, eds., *God and Government* (London: SPCK, 2009). An older book is Robert Culver, *Toward a Biblical View of Civil Government* (Chicago: Moody Press, 1974).

reward good (chap. 3) or the idea that laws in a nation should protect people's lives, particularly the lives of preborn children (chap. 6).

There is a second set of issues where I depend on *arguments from broader principles*. One example is my view that some kind of democracy is a preferable form of government (chap. 3). In this case I have reasoned not from direct, specific biblical teaching on the topic but from broader biblical principles (such as the equality of all people in the image of God and the importance of limitations on the power of human government). That kind of argument from broader principles requires wise judgment in applying those principles correctly to a modern situation, and thus there is a greater possibility of making a mistake or failing to balance the principle with other principles that might modify one's conclusions.

Then I have used a third type of argument: *an appeal to facts in the world*. In some sections (such as chap. 9, on economics), much of my argument depends on one's evaluation of the *actual results* of certain policies (for instance, do lower taxes lead to greater economic growth or not?). Such arguments are different from arguments from *direct biblical statements*, and they are different from arguments from *broader biblical principles*, for they depend not on the Bible but on *an evaluation of the relevant facts* in the world today.

For example, arguments about the environment and the current state of natural resources in the world are in large measure based on appeals to actual facts in the world. To take one specific issue, the argument about global warming is almost entirely an argument about climate facts. It would be impossible to write about political issues today without appealing to a large number of facts in the world.

But a different evaluation of the facts might lead someone to a different conclusion about a certain policy. I am certainly *not* claiming that the Bible also supports all the *facts* I cite about the world today. Readers are free to evaluate and search out evidence about those factual question themselves. What I am doing in each chapter, however, is to say that if my understanding of these facts is correct, then the teachings of the Bible seem to me to lead to one conclusion or another about the specific issue under discussion.

I have not distinguished these three types of argument in the pages that follow. I have not made explicit where I am depending on *direct teachings of the Bible*, where I am depending on *broader biblical principles*, where I am depending on an *evaluation of facts* in the world today, and where I am depending on some combination of these three. But I hope readers will be able to make those distinctions for themselves as they weigh the arguments that I present. And in the end, I hope that most readers will find themselves persuaded by the book.

Part 1

BASIC PRINCIPLES

Chapter 1

FIVE WRONG VIEWS ABOUT CHRISTIANS AND GOVERNMENT

Before explaining my own understanding of the proper role of Christians in politics, I need to examine what I think are five wrong views on this question—sadly mistaken views that have been propagated by many writers throughout history. Then in the following chapter I propose what I think is a better, more balanced solution.

A. GOVERNMENT SHOULD COMPEL RELIGION

The first wrong view (according to my judgment) is the idea that civil government should compel people to support or follow one particular religion.

Tragically, this "compel religion" view was held by many Christians in previous centuries. This view played a large role in the Thirty Years' War (1618–48) that began as a conflict between Protestants and Roman Catholics over control of various territories, especially in Germany. There were many other "wars of religion" in Europe, particularly between Catholics and Protestants, in the sixteenth and seventeenth centuries. Also in the sixteenth century, the Reformed and Lutheran Protestants persecuted and killed thousands from the Anabaptist groups in Switzerland and Germany who sought to have churches for "believers only" and practiced baptism by immersion for those who made a personal profession of faith.

Over the course of time, more and more Christians realized that this "compel religion" view is inconsistent with the teachings of Jesus and inconsistent with the nature of faith itself (see discussion below). Today I am not aware of any major Christian group that still holds to the view that government should try to compel people to follow the Christian faith.[1]

---

1. There is a small, fringe movement called Christian Reconstructionism that advocates government enforcement of Old Testament laws today (see discussion, pp. 65–66), but most or all recognized leaders in the evangelical movement in the United States have clearly distanced themselves from this position regarding civil laws.

But other religions still promote government enforcement of their religion. This is seen in countries such as Saudi Arabia, which enforces laws compelling people to follow Islam and where those who fail to comply can face severe penalties from the religious police. The law prohibits any public practice of any religion other than Islam and prohibits Saudis from converting to other religions. Islamic advocate Bilal Cleland writes at the pro-Islamic web site *Islam for Today*, "Legislation contained in the Quran becomes the basic law of the state."[2]

The "compel religion" view is also used by violent groups around the world to justify persecution of Christians, such as the burning by Muslims of an entire Christian village in Pakistan, killing six Christians in early August 2009,[3] or the warfare waged by Islamic militant groups against Christians in Nigeria, Sudan, and other sub-Saharan African countries. The "compel religion" view has also led to the violent persecution of Christians by some Hindu groups in India. In 1999 it was reported that fifty-one Christian churches and prayer halls were burned to the ground in the western state of Gujarat. An Australian missionary, Graham Staines, and his two young sons were burned to death in their jeep by a Hindu mob in Orissa state on the eastern coast of India.[4] In 2007 it was reported by the Associated Press that Hindu extremists set fire to nearly a dozen churches.[5]

But it must be noted that other Muslims and other Hindus also favor democracy and allowing varying degrees of freedom of religion.

In the early years of the United States, support for freedom of religion in the American colonies increased both because of a need to form a united country with people from various religious backgrounds (such as Congregational, Episcopalian, Presbyterian, Quaker, Baptist, Roman Catholic, and Jewish) and because many of the colonists had fled from religious persecution in their home countries. For example, the New England Pilgrims had fled from England where they had faced fines and imprisonment for failing to attend services in the Church of England and for conducting their own church services.

In 1779, just three years after the Declaration of Independence, Thomas Jefferson drafted the Virginia Act for Establishing Religious Freedom, which demonstrated the increasing support for religious freedom in the United States. Jefferson wrote:

> Be it therefore enacted by the General Assembly, That no man shall be compelled to frequent or support any religious worship, place, or ministry whatsoever, nor shall be enforced, restrained, molested, or burdened in his body or goods, nor shall otherwise suffer on account of his religious opinions or belief; but that all men shall be free to profess, and by argument to maintain, their

2. Bilal Cleland, "Islamic Government," *Islam for Today*. www.islamfortoday.com/cleland04.htm.

3. Ben Quinn, "Six Christians Burned Alive in Pakistan Riots," *guardian.co.uk* (Aug. 2, 2009). www.guardian.co.uk/world/2009/aug/02/christians-burned-alive-pakistan.

4. Ramola Talwar Badam, "Christians, Hindus Clash in India," Associated Press (Oct. 30, 1999). www.washingtonpost.com/wp-srv/aponline/19991030/aponline111427_000.htm.

5. Gabin Rabinowitz, "Hindus, Christians Clash in India," Associated Press (Dec. 27, 2007). www.foxnews.com/printer_friendly_wires/2007Dec27/0,4675,IndiaChurchesAttacked,00.html.

opinions in matters of religion, and that the same shall in nowise diminish, enlarge, or affect their civil capacities.[6]

Several teachings of the Bible show that "government should compel religion" is an incorrect view, one that is contrary to the teachings of the Bible itself.

1. Jesus distinguished the realms of God and of Caesar

The first biblical argument against the "compel religion" view comes from Jesus' teachings in Matthew 22. Jesus' Jewish opponents were trying to trap him with the question, "Is it lawful to pay taxes to Caesar, or not?" (Matt. 22:18). To say "yes" to Roman taxes ran the risk of appearing to support the hated Roman government. To say "no" to Roman taxes would make Jesus sound like a dangerous revolutionary against Rome's power. Taking his opponents by surprise, Jesus said, "Show me the coin for the tax," and "they brought him a denarius" (v. 19). After that, here is how the teaching unfolded:

> And Jesus said to them, "Whose likeness and inscription is this?" They said, "Caesar's." Then he said to them, "Therefore render to Caesar the things that are Caesar's, and to God the things that are God's" (Matt. 22:20–21).

This is a remarkable statement because Jesus shows that there are to be *two different spheres of influence*, one for the government and one for the religious life of the people of God. Some things, such as taxes, belong to the civil government ("the things that are Caesar's"), and this implies that the church should not try to control these things. On the other hand, some things belong to people's religious life ("the things that are God's"), and this implies that the civil government should not try to control those things.

Jesus did not specify any list of things that belong to each category, but the mere distinction of these two categories had monumental significance for the history of the world. It signaled the endorsement of a different system from the laws for the nation of Israel in the Old Testament. With regard to Old Testament Israel, the whole nation was a "theocracy" in that God was the ruler of the people, the laws were directly given to Israel by God (rather than being decided upon by the people or a human king), and *the whole nation* was considered "God's people." Therefore everyone in the nation was expected to worship God, and the laws of Israel covered not only what we today would consider "secular matters" such as murder and theft, but also "religious matters" such as animal sacrifices and punishments for worshiping other gods (see Lev. 21–23; Deut. 13:6–11).

In Jesus' statement about God and Caesar, he established the broad outlines of a new order in which "the things that are God's" are *not* to be under the control of the civil government (or "Caesar"). Such a system is far different from the Old Testament theocracy that was used for the people of Israel. Jesus' new teaching implies that all civil governments—even today—should give people freedom regarding the religious faith

---

6. "The Virginia Act for Establishing Religious Freedom," drafted by Thomas Jefferson in 1779, passed by the Virginia General Assembly in 1786.

they follow or choose not to follow and regarding the religious doctrines they hold and how they worship God. "Caesar" should not control such things, for they are "the things that are God's."

2. Jesus refused to try to compel people to believe in him

Another incident in Jesus' life also shows how he opposed the "compel religion" view, for he rebuked his disciples when they wanted instant punishment to come to people who rejected him:

> And he sent messengers ahead of him, who went and entered a village of the Samaritans, to make preparations for him. But the people did not receive him, because his face was set toward Jerusalem. And when his disciples James and John saw it, they said, "Lord, do you want us to tell fire to come down from heaven and consume them?" (Luke 9:52–54).

The disciples apparently thought they had an excellent way to convince people to come to hear Jesus in the next village. If fire came down from heaven and wiped out the Samaritan village that had rejected Jesus, then word would get around and Jesus and the disciples would have 100% attendance in the next village. What a persuasive method to "compel religion"!

But Jesus would have nothing to do with this idea. The next verse says, "But he turned and rebuked them" (Luke 9:55). Jesus directly refused any attempt to try to force people to believe in him or follow him.

3. Genuine faith cannot be forced

The nature of genuine faith fits with Jesus' condemnation of any request for "fire from heaven" to compel people to follow him. The underlying reason is that *true faith in God must be voluntary*. If faith is to be genuine, it can never be compelled by force. This provides another reason why governments should never try to compel adherence to any particular religion.

A clear respect for people's individual will and voluntary decisions is seen throughout the ministry of Jesus and the apostles. They always *taught* people and *reasoned* with them and then *appealed* to them to make a personal decision to follow Jesus as the true Messiah (see Matt. 11:28–30; Acts 28:23; Rom. 10:9–10; Rev. 22:17).

Genuine religious belief cannot be compelled by force, whether by fire from heaven or by the force of civil government, and Christians should have no part in any attempt to use government power to *compel* people to support or follow Christianity or any other religion.

But what about the laws God gave to Israel in the Old Testament, especially in the books of Exodus, Leviticus, Numbers, and Deuteronomy? Those laws required people to give tithe money to support the Jewish priesthood and temple services, and they required people to make certain specified sacrifices to the Lord every year (see Lev. 23).

They even ordered severe punishments for anyone who tried to teach another religion (see Deut. 13:6–11). But these laws *were only for the nation of Israel for that particular time*. They were never imposed on any of the surrounding nations. They were part of the Old Testament system that came to an end when Jesus established a "new covenant" for God's people in the New Testament. Such a system was ended by Jesus' teaching that some areas of life were "things that belong to Caesar" and some areas of life were "things that belong to God." Such Old Testament laws enforcing religion were never intended for people after Jesus established his "new covenant," or for any time after that.

4. Not a worldly kingdom

In another incident, just after Jesus had been captured by Roman soldiers near the end of his life, he told the Roman governor, Pontius Pilate,

> "My kingdom is not of this world. If my kingdom were of this world, my servants would have been fighting, that I might not be delivered over to the Jews. But my kingdom is not from the world" (John 18:36).

Jesus refused to have his disciples fight with swords and military power, because *he was not attempting to establish an earthly kingdom like the Roman Empire* or the various other nations in the history of the world. Earthly kingdoms are established by armies and military power, but Jesus' kingdom would be established by the power of the Gospel changing people's hearts, bringing people to trust in him and obey him.

This does not mean that Jesus' kingdom has no effect on the world. Indeed, it transforms and overcomes the world (1 John 3:8; 5:4–5), but it does so by changing people's hearts and their deep convictions, not by military power. The power of government should never be used to compel a certain kind of religious belief or adherence to any specific religion, whether the Christian faith or any other faith.

In summary, the "compel religion" view is contrary to the Bible, and it is simply wrong.

5. Practical implications of rejecting the "compel religion" view

What are the practical implications of rejecting the "compel religion" view? One implication is that governments should never attempt to force people to follow or believe in one specific religion, but should guarantee freedom of religion for followers of all religions within the nation.

Another implication is that Christians in every nation should support freedom of religion and oppose any attempt by government to compel any single religion. In fact, *complete freedom of religion* should be the first principle advocated and defended by Christians who seek to influence government.

Sometimes non-Christians express a fear that if Christians get too much power in government, they will try to force Christianity on everyone. This is a common argument made by groups such as Americans United for Separation of Church and State, the Center for American Progress, and the Freedom from Religion Foundation. Some critics even suggest that right-wing Christians are trying to establish a theocracy in the United States by incremental means. Michelle Goldberg writes, "The Christian nation is both the goal of the religious right and its fundamental ideology, the justification for its attempt to overthrow the doctrine of separation of church and state.... Right now ... is high tide for theocratic fervor."[7] To counter this kind of false accusation, it is important for Christians involved in politics to affirm again and again their commitment to complete religious freedom in America (and in every other country).

A third implication has to do with governments giving direct financial support to one church as an established "state church." Such government support is a more benign form of the "compel religion" view, but it is still one that I do not think is right. This support occurs in some countries where the civil government uses tax money and privileged status to support one single religion or denomination as the "state church." Such action was prohibited to the US government by the First Amendment—"Government shall make no law respecting an establishment of religion"—where an "establishment of religion" meant giving governmental support for only one church, the "established church."

An established church does still exist in some countries. For example, in the United Kingdom today the Church of England is still the state church;[8] in Scandinavian countries such as Norway and Sweden the Lutheran Church is the state church;[9] and in many countries with a highly Catholic populace such as Spain, the Roman Catholic Church is the state-supported church. In Germany, church taxes are accessed on Catholic, Protestant, and Jewish wage-earners, up to 8 or 9% of their total income. The state then disperses these funds to the churches to be used for social services.[10]

I recognize that some Christians in these countries argue that the benefits that come from having such a state church outweigh the negative effects, but I still cannot see sufficient warrant for it in the New Testament. I see no evidence that government tax money, rather than the donations of individual Christians, should be used to support the religious activities of a church. In addition, the historical pattern seems to be that direct government support weakens a church rather than strengthening it. (Notice the extremely low church attendance at state-sponsored Lutheran churches in Germany or Sweden, for example.)

6. What about giving some tax benefits to churches?

If the government gives some tax benefits to religious organizations, is that another example of the "compel religion" view? For example, in the United States, churches do not pay property taxes on the land and buildings they own, and individuals do not have to pay income taxes on the amount of their income that they donate to churches or other charities.

7. Michelle Goldberg, *Kingdom Coming: The Rise of Christian Nationalism* (New York: Norton, 2007), 27–28. See also Kevin Phillips, *American Theocracy* (New York: Viking Adult, 2006).
8. John L. Allen Jr., "In Europe, 'Church Taxes' Are Not Unusual," *National Catholic Reporter* (Jan. 29, 2009). www.natcath.com/NCR_Online/archives/012999/012999f.htm.
9. Ibid.
10. Ibid.

I do not object to these policies because I do not think they are *compelling* religion in any meaningful sense. No specific denomination or religion is given preferential treatment. Baptist churches receive these benefits, but so do Buddhist temples, Jewish synagogues, Roman Catholic churches, and Muslim mosques. The reason for this preferential tax treatment for churches and other charities is that the society has decided that, in general, charitable organizations such as churches do much good for the society as a whole. In the classic wording of the preface to the US Constitution, they "promote the general welfare." Therefore it is entirely reasonable for a society to decide to give churches some tax benefits that are open to all religions equally. This is not compelling support of any one religion; it is not giving any government funds directly to any religious group; and it is certainly not contrary to the original meaning and intention of the First Amendment. Giving such tax benefits is not compelling religion.

7. The spiritual influence behind the "compel religion" view

There is an invisible spiritual power with a hidden goal behind this "compel religion" viewpoint, and it can be seen in its results. By compelling religious belief, this viewpoint tends to destroy true Christian faith in two ways. If it compels people *to follow a non-Christian religion* (such as Hinduism in India or Islam in many other nations), then it often leads to violently suppressing Christians and aims at driving Christianity out of a nation. On the other hand, if it attempts to compel people *to become Christians*, then it also tends to drive out true Christianity because the opportunity to choose freely to become a Christian is removed from people's lives. A few people will have genuine faith, but most will not. The result is that the entire society will be "Christian," but in name only. In addition, such a church will then be governed by "Christians" who are not really Christians at all because they do not have genuine faith. And a church governed primarily by non-Christians will quickly become a spiritually dead and ineffective church.

Therefore it should not be difficult for Christians, who believe the teachings of the Bible, to discern the real spiritual influence behind the "compel religion" view. It is an influence that is completely opposed to the teachings of the Bible and to genuine Christian faith. It is an influence that seeks to destroy true Christianity.

B. GOVERNMENT SHOULD EXCLUDE RELIGION

The opposite error from the "compel religion" view is the view that says we should completely exclude religion from government and politics. According to this view, religious beliefs should never be mentioned in governmental functions or on government property and should never play a role in the decision-making process in politics or government.

This second view is the one effectively promoted by the American Civil Liberties Union (ACLU), Americans United for Separation of Church and State, and much of the rest of secular society today. According to this view, religious belief should be kept at home and kept quiet. There should be no influence from religious groups in the political process.

Examples of this view are seen when people object to prayers being given at the beginning of a city council meeting or at a legislative session.[11] Other examples are seen when groups demand that the Ten Commandments be removed from any public places or crosses be removed from government seals and veterans' memorials,[12] or demand that student Bible studies, prayers before a sports event,[13] a prayer at a graduation ceremony,[14] or a valedictorian talking about his or her faith at graduation[15] should be prohibited from public high schools.

For example, after ACLU threats, the cross was removed from the Los Angeles County seal[16] and a high school valedictorian in Las Vegas, Nevada, was told she had to remove all references to Christ from her speech. She chose to keep them in and had the sound cut off by the school principal in the middle of her address.[17]

The "exclude religion from government" view was seen when a judge threw out the death sentence in a murder trial in Colorado because it was discovered that some of the jurors had quoted Bible verses during the jury's deliberations. This was considered juror misconduct.[18]

The most troubling example of this view was seen in the 1996 Supreme Court decision *Romer v. Evans*. The case concerned a constitutional amendment that had been passed by the citizens of Colorado. The amendment prohibited giving special legal rights to homosexuals, and the result of the amendment would be that homosexuals would be treated the same as everyone else in society, not given special rights and protections simply because they were homosexuals. The Supreme Court struck down this amendment because the majority of the court held that the amendment "lacks a rational relationship to legitimate state interests" and that the citizens of Colorado had shown "animosity towards homosexuals" when they voted for the amendment.[19]

This "exclude religion" view has had a strong influence in recent campaigns to persuade the courts to legalize same-sex "marriage." When the Iowa Supreme Court decided to impose same-sex "marriage" on the state of Iowa (in the case *Varnum v. Brien*, April 3, 2009), it noted that only 28.1% of Iowans supported it.[20] The court then observed that "much of society rejects same-sex marriage due to sincere, deeply ingrained—even

11. See *ACLU of Kentucky v. Mercer County, Kentucky*, U.S. Court of Appeals for the 6th Circuit, No. 03–5142. Argued: April 27, 2004. Decided and Filed: Dec. 20, 2005; and numerous other cases.

12. John Antczak, "ACLU Demands Removal of Cross from Los Angeles County Seal," Associated Press (May 25, 2004); Peter J. Smith, "City of 'Las Cruces' Sued to Remove 3 Crosses from Emblem," *LifeSite.com* (Aug. 8, 2006), and David Asman, "Battle to Tear Down a Tribute," *Fox News* (June 2, 2005).

13. Adam Nossiter, "ACLU Asks Jail for Tangipahoa School Officials," Associated Press (May 18, 2005), and "High School's Pre-Game Prayer Called 'Un-American and Immoral,'" *WKYC.com* (April 6, 2005).

14. "West VA School District Ends Graduation Prayer Policy; Student's Lawsuit 'Educated' Officials," *ACLU Press Release* (Aug. 14, 2002).

15. Nisha N. Mohammed, "Victory: Federal Court Again Rules That High School Valedictorian Silenced for Referencing Christ

Should Have Day in Court" (June 22, 2007). www.rutherford.org/articles_db/press_release.asp?article_id=671; and Nathan Burchfiel, "Valedictorian Silenced over Her Christian Faith Will Go to Court," *CNSNews.com* (Dec. 19, 2006).

16. Antczak, "ACLU Demands Removal of Cross from Los Angeles County Seal."

17. Burchfiel, "Valedictorian Silenced over Her Christian Faith Will Go to Court."

18. The 2005 death sentence of Robert Harlan was eventually changed to life in prison as a result of a decision by the Colorado Supreme Court. See "Colorado's Death Row," Coloradans Against the Death Penalty. www.coadp.org/thedeathrow/RobertHarlan.html.

19. *Romer v. Evans*, No. 94–1039, Decided by the United States Supreme Court, May 20, 1996. www.law.cornell.edu/supct/html/94–1039.ZO.html.

20. *Varnum v. Brien*, 763 N.W.2d 862 (Iowa Supreme Court, 2009), 64, n. 29.

fundamental—religious belief." But such views should not be taken into account, said the court, because the Iowa constitution says, "The general assembly shall make no law respecting an establishment of religion."[21] In other words, limiting marriage to one man and one woman would be equivalent to "establishing" a religion.

The same kind of argument was made in California. David Boies, a prominent lawyer challenging Proposition 8 (a California constitutional amendment that limits marriage to one man and one woman), argued that, while people may have "genuine religious beliefs" that marriage should be between a man and a woman, still "the other half of the First Amendment, the Establishment Clause ... says that a majority is not entitled to impose its religious beliefs on a minority."[22] In other words, even though 52% of Californians voted to define marriage as between one man and one woman, they were wrongly "establishing" a religion.

There are several reasons why the "exclude religion from government" view is wrong.

1. It fails to distinguish the reasons for a law from the content of the law

Such "exclude religion" arguments are wrong because marriage is not a religion! When voters define marriage, they are not establishing a *religion*. In the First Amendment, "Congress shall make no law respecting an establishment of religion, or prohibiting the free exercise thereof," the word "religion" refers to the church that people attend and support. "Religion" means being a Baptist or Catholic or Presbyterian or Jew. It does not mean being married. These arguments try to make the word "religion" in the Constitution mean something different from what it has always meant.

These arguments also make the logical mistake of failing to distinguish the *reasons* for a law from the *content* of the law. There were *religious reasons* behind many of our laws, but these laws do not "establish" a religion. All major religions have teachings against stealing, but laws against stealing do not "establish a religion." All religions have laws against murder, but laws against murder do not "establish a religion." The campaign to abolish slavery in the United States and England was led by many Christians, based on their religious convictions, but laws abolishing slavery do not "establish a religion." The campaign to end racial discrimination and segregation was led by Dr. Martin Luther King Jr., a Baptist pastor, who preached against racial injustice from the Bible. But laws against discrimination and segregation do not "establish a religion."

If these "exclude religion" arguments succeed in court, they could soon be applied against evangelicals and Catholics who make "religious" arguments against abortion. Majority votes to protect unborn children could then be invalidated by saying these voters are "establishing a religion." And, by such reasoning, *all the votes of religious citizens* for almost *any* issue could be found invalid by court decree! This would be the direct opposite of the kind of country the Founding Fathers established, and the direct opposite of what they meant by "free exercise" of religion in the First Amendment.

---

21. Ibid., 64–65.
22. "Prop. 8 Defenders Say Plaintiffs Attacked 'Orthodox Religious Beliefs,'" *Wall Street Journal* (online blog, Feb. 10, 2010).

http://blogs.wsj.com/law/2010/02/10/prop-8-defenders-accuse-plaintiffs-of-attacking-orthodox-religious-beliefs/tab/print/.

2. It overrides the will of the people

In Colorado, supporters of the constitutional amendment mentioned above included many thousands of Christians whose views on homosexual conduct were influenced by the teachings of the Bible and traditional Judeo-Christian moral values. But such a religious viewpoint, said the court, could not be said to have "a rational relationship to legitimate state interests."[23] In other words, religious or moral reasons that were sincerely held by the citizens of Colorado were not "rational" reasons. Their votes did not count because they used religious reasons to decide their vote. So their 52% vote was overturned by the Supreme Court.[24] This kind of decision is the natural outcome of the "exclude religion from government" view, and it simply overrides the will of the people in amending their state's constitution (as was the case also in Iowa and California, mentioned above).

3. It changes freedom of religion into freedom from religion

From the perspective of American history, another reason that "exclude religion" is a wrong viewpoint is that it twists the positive ideal of "freedom *of* religion" to mean "freedom *from* all religious influence"—which is something entirely different and something the signers of the Declaration of Independence and the framers of the US Constitution never intended.

In fact, the "exclude religion from politics" view would invalidate the very reasoning of the Declaration of Independence, on which the United States of America was first founded. The first two sentences mention God twice in order to say that God's laws authorize this independence from Great Britain in 1776 and that God is the one who gives human beings the rights that governments seek to protect:

> When in the Course of human events, it becomes necessary for one people to dissolve the political bands which have connected them with another, and to assume among the Powers of the earth, the separate and equal station to which the Laws of Nature *and of Nature's God* entitle them, a decent respect to the opinions of mankind requires that they should declare the causes which impel them to the separation.
>
> We hold these truths to be self-evident, that all men are created equal, that they are *endowed by their Creator* with certain unalienable Rights, that among these are Life, Liberty, and the pursuit of Happiness. That to secure these rights, Governments are instituted among Men....

In other words, the fifty-six signers of the Declaration of Independence proclaimed that both the laws of nature *and God himself* gave our country the right to become an independent nation. They are claiming *divine authorization* for the very existence of the United States of America!

---

23. *Varnum v. Brien.*
24. Ibid.

Then the signers say that the entire purpose of government is to protect the rights that are given to people by God. The second sentence states "that all Men are created equal" and "are *endowed by their Creator* with certain unalienable Rights, that among these are Life, Liberty, and the pursuit of Happiness." Then the signers add that "Governments are instituted among Men" in order to protect or "secure" these rights. In other words, these most basic of human rights are given *by God* ("endowed by their Creator"), and the purpose of government is to protect those God-given rights, according to the Declaration of Independence upon which the country was founded. The "exclude religion from government" view is wrong when it implies the illegitimacy of statements like these found in the very basis of our existence as a nation. Using religious *reasons* to support a secular law is not *establishing a religion*.

The First Amendment to the Constitution then declared: "Congress shall make no law *respecting an establishment of religion*, or *prohibiting the free exercise thereof*; or abridging the freedom of speech." What they meant by "an establishment of religion" was an established state church, a government-sponsored or government-endorsed denomination or specific religion. The First Amendment therefore prohibited the United States from having a state church such as the Church of England, from which many of the original colonists had fled in order to gain their religious freedom.

In fact, the now-famous "separation of church and state" letter that Thomas Jefferson wrote back in 1802 to the Danbury Baptists of Connecticut dealt with this issue. The Danbury Baptists had written to the new President expressing their concern over their home state of Connecticut designating the Congregational Church as the official state church. In his response, Jefferson pointed out that the meaning of the First Amendment was to keep government out of the affairs of the church, not to keep the church out of the affairs of government. Jefferson argued that when government left the church alone and did not compel its citizens to be members of an official state church, religious freedom could flourish.[25]

The First Amendment was never intended to guarantee that government should be free from religion or religious influence. The only "freedom of religion" that was intended was freedom from government sponsorship of one particular religion or denomination.

4. It wrongly restricts freedom of religion and freedom of speech

The First Amendment also excluded any law "prohibiting the free exercise" of religion. Therefore the First Amendment is directly opposed to the "exclude religion from government" view, which actually seeks to *prohibit* Christians and Jews and many from other religious backgrounds from exercising their religious freedom when arguing for an amendment to the Colorado constitution, or when arguing for a certain jury verdict,

---

25. Thomas Jefferson, letter to Danbury Baptists (Jan. 1, 1802), www.loc.gov/loc/lcih/9806/danpre.html; see also Daniel Dreisbach, *Thomas Jefferson and the Myth of Separation* (New York: New York University Press, 2002), 29; Joseph LoConte, "The Wall Jefferson Almost Built" (Dec. 27, 2001), www.heritage.org/Press/Commentary.ed122701c.cfm.

or when speaking or giving a prayer at a public event. Their free exercise of religion is taken away from them.

This view also wrongly restricts individual freedom of speech. Why should a high school valedictorian not be free to express her own viewpoint in her graduation speech? Why should Christian citizens not be free to campaign for or against a certain polity based on their moral convictions—convictions that are derived from their religious faith? *Speaking* a religious opinion in public is not *compelling* people to accept that viewpoint!

The nature of a free society requires that people should be able to base their political convictions on whatever reasoning process and whatever authority they prefer, and they should be free to attempt to persuade others that their reasoning is correct. We should protect people's freedom to base their moral and political convictions on the dialogues of Plato if they want, or the teachings of Confucius or the Bible or the Jewish Talmud—or, I suppose, even a song by Bob Dylan if that is what they find persuasive. And if other voters choose to accept the reasoning put forth by the followers of Plato or Confucius or the Bible (or Bob Dylan!), then the Supreme Court should not take it upon itself to say that the reasons that voters used are not "rational" reasons. It is not up to the Supreme Court to decide that some people's votes are legitimate and some people's votes are illegitimate.

5. It was never adopted by the American people

The "exclude religion" view was never adopted by the American people through any democratic process, but it is being imposed on our nation by the exercise of "raw judicial power" by our courts, and especially by the Supreme Court. This has been an increasing problem for the last several decades in America.

The Supreme Court decision *Lemon v. Kurtzman* (1971) was especially significant. In that case the court said that government actions "must not have the primary effect of advancing or inhibiting religion."[26] It did not say "advancing or inhibiting *one particular religion*" but "religion" in general.

In fact, the court's tendency to exclude government actions that brought benefit *to religions generally* had first found expression in the 1947 decision *Everson v. Board of Education*, in which the majority opinion opposed aid to "all religions."

> The "establishment of religion" clause of the First Amendment means at least this: Neither a state nor the Federal Government can set up a church. Neither can pass laws which aid one religion, *aid all religions*, or prefer one religion over another.... *The First Amendment has erected a wall between church and state.* That wall must be kept high and impregnable. We could not approve the slightest breach. New Jersey has not breached it here.[27]

---

26. *Lemon v. Kurtzman*, 403 U.S. 602 (1971). Majority opinion written by Chief Justice Warren Earl Burger.

27. *Everson v. Board of Education*, 330 U.S. 1 (1947), italics added.

Although subsequent decisions have not applied the *Lemon* guideline stringently, when it is understood broadly it results in excluding *all* religious expression from the public square. It is an extreme example of the "exclude religion" view, never adopted or approved by the American people but simply decreed by our Supreme Court, taking to itself powers it never legitimately had.

6. It removes from government God's teaching about good and evil

The Bible says that a government official is "God's servant for your good" (Rom. 13:4), but how can government officials effectively serve God if no one is allowed to tell them what they believe God expects of them? The Bible says that government officials are sent "to punish those who do evil and to praise those who do good" (1 Peter 2:14), but how can they do that if no spokesmen from any of the world's religions are allowed to give them counsel on what is "good" and what is "evil"?

Such a viewpoint has to assume that there is no God, or if there is, we cannot know his moral standards.

7. Biblical examples of God's people giving counsel to rulers

The Bible gives several examples of faithful believers who gave clear witness to government officials about how they should govern. The prophet Daniel told King Nebuchadnezzar of Babylon, the most powerful ruler in the world in about 600 BC:

> "O king, let my counsel be acceptable to you: break off your sins by practicing righteousness, and your iniquities by showing mercy to the oppressed, that there may perhaps be a lengthening of your prosperity" (Dan. 4:27).

In the New Testament, John the Baptist rebuked Herod the Tetrarch (a civil governor under the Roman Empire) "for Herodias, his brother's wife, and for all the evil things that Herod had done" (Luke 3:19). Certainly John's rebuke of "all the evil things" included many acts that Herod had done as a governmental ruler.

Later, the apostle Paul reasoned with the Roman governor Felix "about righteousness and self-control and the coming judgment" (Acts 24:25). It is likely that Paul was calling Felix to account for his conduct as a government official under the Roman Empire, and "Felix was alarmed" and sent Paul away (v. 25). In addition, many Old Testament prophets spoke to foreign nations about their sins. One can read these prophetic rebukes in Isaiah 13–23; Jeremiah 46–51; Ezekiel 25–32; Amos 1–2; Obadiah (to Edom); Jonah (to Nineveh); Nahum (to Nineveh); Habakkuk 2; and Zephaniah 2.

Therefore the Bible does not support the "exclude religion from government" view.

8. The spiritual basis for the "exclude religion" view

It should not be hard for Christians to discern a deep spiritual basis underlying the "exclude religion" view. This is because the final goal of the "exclude religion" view is to make government completely secular and then, by extension, to make society completely secular. This view would remove from government any sense of accountability to God for its actions. And since government has such a huge influence on all people's lives, it would tend to remove from the nation in general any sense of accountability to God, especially as all religious viewpoints are removed from the entire system of public education of children.

Moreover, since all *absolute* moral standards are in some way based on religious convictions and a sense of moral accountability to God, this view would *tend to remove from the entire nation any sense of absolute moral standards* or any sense that there is any clear way of knowing right from wrong. Therefore the ultimate goal of this viewpoint is not only the destruction of all *belief in God*, but also the *complete moral disintegration* of a society. For Christians who believe the Bible, it should not be hard to discern the ultimate spiritual force behind this viewpoint.

C. ALL GOVERNMENT IS EVIL AND DEMONIC

According to this third view, all use of government power is deeply infected by evil, demonic forces. The realm of government power is the realm of Satan and his forces, and therefore all governmental use of "power over" someone is "worldly" and is not the way of life that Jesus taught.

Those who hold this view also usually favor military pacifism. They argue that since Jesus told us to turn the other cheek (Matt. 5:39), the best way to resolve disputes—even among nations—is *never* to use military force, but *always* to negotiate and build friendships and act in a Christlike way, showing love to other nations.

1. Support from Luke 4:6

This viewpoint has been strongly promoted by Minnesota pastor Greg Boyd in his influential book *The Myth of a Christian Nation* (Grand Rapids: Zondervan, 2005). Boyd's views in this book have had a large impact in the United States, especially on younger evangelical voters.[28]

Boyd says that all civil government is "demonic" (p. 21). Boyd's primary evidence is Satan's statement to Jesus in Luke 4:

> And the devil took him up and showed him all the kingdoms of the world in a moment of time, and said to him, "To you I will give all this authority and their glory, *for it has been delivered to me*, and I give it to whom I will. If you, then, will worship me, it will all be yours" (Luke 4:5–7).

Boyd emphasizes Satan's claim that all the authority of all the kingdoms of the world "has been delivered to me" and then says that Jesus "doesn't dispute the Devil's claim

---

28. For example, echoes of Boyd's writing can be seen at various places in Shane Claiborne and Chris Haw, *Jesus for President* (Grand Rapids: Zondervan, 2008).

to own them. Apparently, the authority of all the kingdoms of the world has been given to Satan."[29]

Boyd goes on to say, "Functionally, Satan is the acting CEO of all earthly governments."[30] This is indeed a thoroughgoing claim!

2. The mistake of depending on Luke 4:6

Greg Boyd is clearly wrong at this point. Jesus tells us how to evaluate Satan's claims, for he says that Satan "has nothing to do with the truth" because

> "there is *no truth in him*. When he lies, he speaks out of his own character, for he is a liar and the father of lies" (John 8:44).

Jesus didn't need to respond to *every* false word Satan said, for his purpose was to resist the temptation itself, and this he did with the decisive words, "It is written, 'You shall worship the Lord your God, and him only shall you serve'" (Luke 4:8).

In evaluating Boyd's claim that "the authority of all the kingdoms of the world has been given to Satan," we have a choice: Do we believe *Satan's words* that he has the authority of all earthly kingdoms, or do we believe *Jesus' words* that Satan is a liar and the father of lies? The answer is easy: Satan wanted Jesus to believe a lie, and he wants us to believe that same lie, that he is the ruler of earthly governments.[31]

By contrast, there are some very specific verses in the Bible that tell us how we should think of civil governments. These verses do not agree with Satan's claim in Luke 4:6 or with Boyd's claim about Satan's authority over all earthly governments. Rather, these verses where *God* (not Satan) is speaking portray civil government as a gift from God, something that is subject to God's rule (not Satan) and used by God for his purposes. Here are some of those passages:

> "*The Most High rules the kingdom of men* and gives it to whom he will and sets over it the lowliest of men" (Dan. 4:17).

> Let every person be subject to the governing authorities. For *there is no authority except from God, and those that exist have been instituted by God*. Therefore whoever resists the authorities resists what God has appointed, and those who resist will incur judgment. For rulers are not a terror to good conduct, but to bad. Would you have no fear of the one who is in authority? Then do what is good, and you will receive his approval, for *he is God's servant for your good*. But if you do wrong, be afraid, for he does not bear the sword in vain. For *he is the servant of God, an avenger who carries out God's wrath on the wrongdoer*. Therefore one must be in subjection, not only to avoid God's wrath but also for the sake of conscience. For the same reason you also pay taxes, for the *authorities are the ministers of God*, attending to this very thing (Rom. 13:1–6).

---

29. Greg Boyd, *The Myth of a Christian Nation* (Grand Rapids: Zondervan, 2005), 21.

30. Ibid., 22.

31. Boyd also quotes some other verses in *Myth of a Christian Nation*, 21–22, but none of them refer specifically to civil governments, so they do not prove his point.

Be subject for the Lord's sake to every human institution, whether it be to the emperor as supreme, or to governors as sent by him to punish those who do evil and to praise those who do good (1 Peter 2:13–14).

At this point it is interesting that both Paul (in Romans) and Peter see civil government as doing the *opposite* of what Satan does: civil governments are established by God "to *punish* those who do evil," but Satan *encourages* those who do evil! Civil governments are established by God "to *praise* those who do good," but Satan *discourages and attacks* those who do good. In addition, it would not make sense for Peter to say, "Be subject for the Lord's sake to every institution in which Satan is the CEO." Peter would not want Christian citizens to be subject to Satan's control and direction.

The point is that Satan wants us to believe that all civil government is under his control, but that is not taught anywhere in the Bible. (Of course, Satan can *influence* some individuals in government, but he is not in control.) The only verse in the whole Bible that says Satan has authority over all governments is spoken by the father of lies, and we should not believe it. Greg Boyd is simply wrong in his defense of the view that "all government is demonic."

3. But where did Jesus ever teach us to use force?

In supporting his position, Boyd often appeals to the teachings of Jesus rather than the teachings of the whole Bible. For example, "Jesus didn't come to give us the Christian answer to the world's many socio-political quandaries"[32] Boyd also says that the "just war" theory is "something that Christ never taught or hinted at"[33] (quoting George Zabelka with approval).

But this form of argument fails to recognize that the *whole Bible* was given to us by God. We have no right to restrict our views to the teachings of Jesus in the four Gospels. If the main teaching on civil government in the Bible is found in Genesis 9:5–6, and in the historical narratives and laws in Exodus to Deuteronomy and Judges to 2 Chronicles, and in Romans 13, and in 1 Peter 2:13–14, then getting Christians to neglect those passages gets them to misunderstand what the Bible says about civil government. That is exactly what Boyd is doing when he asks, "Where did Jesus ever act or talk like this?"[34] The answer is that *the whole Bible* comes with the authority of God and the authority of Jesus Christ, and our position on government should be based on the teaching of the whole Bible. (Also, Jesus did seem to authorize the use of a sword for self-defense and protection against robbers in Luke 22:36–38; see discussion below on pp. 201–3.)

4. Support from Homer's Iliad and Odyssey

One other argument used by Boyd depends on the Greek writer Homer in his epic poems *Iliad* and *Odyssey*. Boyd says that

---

32. Ibid., 59.
33. Ibid., 168.

34. Ibid., 91.

in Homer "the gods" are always involved in the affairs of humans.... For Homer, the inevitability of war is not just the result of conflicting passions—it has a supernatural dimension. And all the while, Zeus sits on Mount Olympus, amused by the sport of it all.[35]

Boyd says that if we understand these Greek "gods" to be demonic forces, then

Homer was also right about the gods.... Our tribal, territorial, and ideological passions have a demonic dimension to them.... From a scriptural perspective, these fallen gods are behind and involved in the conflict that occurs between nations. And all the while, Satan, the ultimate single "power over" god of this age, watches the bloodshed with a demonic sense of amusement.[36]

5. This view leads to a "moral equivalence" between good and evil governments

There are two problems with Boyd's analysis here: (1) Homer is not the Bible, nor did he write (in the eighth century BC) from a biblical worldview, and we should be suspicious of any worldview that is derived from ancient Greek mythology rather than from the Bible. (2) In Homer (as interpreted by Boyd) the motivating factors of the governments on the two different sides in a war *are both demonic.*

This leads Boyd to adopt a "moral equivalence" view of various conflicts between nations: both sides are following Satan. (Although Boyd does not explicitly say it, this view would imply that Adolf Hitler was following Satan, for example, and England and the United States were also following Satan in sending armies to defeat Hitler!) Boyd does apply his "moral equivalence" view to the modern conflict between American forces and terrorists in Iraq, and specifically the terrorists' beheading of an American civilian, Nicholas Berg. Boyd says this to his American readers:

Your yearning for justice is, of course, natural. But this rage is exactly what led the terrorists to cut off Mr. Berg's head in the first place. You probably passionately believe that our cause is just, and theirs is evil, but the terrorists passionately believe that their cause is just and ours is evil. Your passion for American justice is mirrored by their passion for Islamic justice.[37]

How could Boyd come to the point where he sees Islamic beheading of innocent civilians as *morally equivalent* to America defending itself against terrorist attacks? How could he believe that a nation that *never* intentionally targets innocent civilians is *morally the same* as a terrorist movement that *makes it a conscious policy* to target, torture, and kill innocent civilians?

Boyd reaches this conclusion because he follows this wrongful "all government is demonic" view. Boyd sees *committing* horrible terrorist acts and *defending* against

35. Ibid., 23.
36. Ibid., 24.

37. Ibid., 25.

terrorists as morally equivalent because he believes Satan's lie in Luke 4:6 that all the authority in the earth's kingdoms has been given to him, and he believes Homer's false Greek mythology that the "gods" (which Boyd sees as demons) motivate *both sides* in human conflicts. Boyd believes these errors from Satan and Homer rather than fully believing the Bible when it says that the civil government "is the servant of God, an avenger who carries out God's wrath on the wrongdoer" (Rom. 13:4).

Thus Boyd's "all government is demonic" view makes him unable to see the truth, namely, that terrorists who attack innocent civilians (as at 9/11) are evil, and the American military, when it pursues and kills terrorists who are attacking innocent civilians, is working as "God's servant for your good" and "is the servant of God, an avenger who carries out God's wrath on the wrongdoer" (Rom. 13:4). Boyd simply fails to realize that carrying out terrorist murders of innocent civilians is evil and defending a nation against such terrorists is good. But his position is the logical consequence of the "all government is demonic" view.

6. Boyd's rejection of all governmental "power over" as "worldly"

There is yet a deeper reason behind Boyd's "all government is demonic" view. The deeper reason is that Boyd rejects what he calls governmental "power over" others as worldly and not part of the kingdom of God. Boyd says,

> Wherever a person or group exercises *power over* others ... there is a version of the kingdom of the world. While it comes in many forms, the kingdom of the world is in essence a "power over" kingdom.... There have been democratic, socialist, communist, fascist, and totalitarian versions of the kingdom of the world, but they all share this distinctive characteristic: they exercise "power over" people.[38]

Boyd explains that this *power over* people is sometimes called "the power of the sword." He says, "The power of the sword is the ability to coerce behavior by threats and to make good on those threats when necessary: if a law is broken, you will be punished."[39] While Boyd admits that this exercise of "power over" others is "not altogether bad,"[40] because Romans 13 explains that God uses this power of government "to keep law and order in the world,"[41] he immediately returns to his main emphasis on Satan's authority over all the kingdoms of the world[42] and concludes that "even the best political ideology lies under the influence of a 'power over' cosmic ruler who is working at cross-purposes to God."[43]

By contrast, Boyd thinks people should recognize the contrast "between the 'power over' kingdom of the world and the 'power under' kingdom of God," which is the same as "Lion power" versus "Lamb power."[44] He says, "The kingdom God advances by people lovingly placing themselves *under* others, in service to others, at cost to themselves."[45]

---

38. Ibid., 18, italics added.
39. Ibid.
40. Ibid., 19.
41. Ibid.

42. Ibid., 21.
43. Ibid., 22.
44. Ibid., 31.
45. Ibid.

Boyd says that "coming under others has a power to do what laws and bullets and bombs can never do—namely, bring about transformation in an enemy's heart."[46] He then says,

> Obviously, when hearts and motives are transformed, behavior is eventually transformed as well—but without "power over" threats. Similarly, where the rule of God is established, law and order are established—but without "power over" force.... Do you trust "power over" or "power under"? Do you trust the power of the sword, the power of external force, or do you trust the influential but non-coercive power of Calvary-like love?[47]

7. Boyd says Christians should not even fight to defend their wives and children or their country

This rejection of governmental "power over" other people leads Boyd to say that a person totally conformed to the image of Jesus Christ should not even use physical violence to defend against an attacker who "threatened to kill you, your wife, or your children."[48] Plus, the rejection of the "power over" kingdom also leads him to say that Christians should never serve in combat situations in the military:

> I find it impossible to reconcile Jesus' teaching (and the teaching of the whole New Testament) concerning our call to love our enemies and never return evil with evil with the choice to serve (or not resist being drafted) in the armed forces in a capacity that might require killing someone.[49]

He also says, "I honestly see no way to condone a Christian's decision to kill on behalf of any country—or for any other reason."[50]

So at the heart of Boyd's teaching is *a fundamental opposition to the use of superior force to restrain evil,* even an evil criminal who attacks one's wife and children. Boyd's "all government is demonic" view leads him to advocate an absolute, total pacifism for those who wish to follow Christ.

8. God has established both evangelism and the power of government to restrain evil

The problem with Boyd's view here is that he fails to distinguish the task of *evangelism* from the task of *civil government.* Of course God has not told us to spread the Gospel of Christ by using the "power of the sword" or the power of government. We spread the Gospel by the proclamation of the Word of God (see Rom. 10:17). But God *has* told us that we should restrain evil by the power of the sword and by the power of civil government (as in the teaching of Romans 13:1–6, quoted above, p. 37).

---

46. Ibid.
47. Ibid., 32–33.
48. Ibid., 162, 166.

49. Ibid., 166–67.
50. Ibid., 173.

If the power of government (such as a policeman) is not present in an emergency, when great harm is being done to another person, then my love for the victim should lead me to use physical force to prevent any further harm from occurring. If I found a criminal attacking my wife or children, I would use all my physical strength and all the physical force at my disposal against him, not to persuade him to trust in Christ as his Savior, but to immediately stop him from harming my wife and children! I would follow the command of Nehemiah, who told the men of Israel, "Remember the Lord, who is great and awesome, and fight for your brothers, your sons, your daughters, your wives, and your homes" (Neh. 4:14; see also Genesis 14:14–16, where Abraham rescued his kinsman Lot who had been taken captive by a raiding army).

Boyd has wrongly taken *one* of the ways that God restrains evil in this world (changing hearts through the Gospel of Christ) and decided that it is the *only* way that God restrains evil (thus neglecting the valuable role of civil government). Both means are from God, both are good, and both should be used by Christians.

This is why Boyd misunderstands Jesus' statement, "If anyone slaps you on the right cheek, turn to him the other also" (Matt. 5:39). When this verse is rightly understood (see below, p. 82), we see that Jesus is telling individuals not to take revenge for a personal insult or a humiliating slap on the cheek.[51] But this command for individual kindness is not the same as the instructions that the Bible gives to governments, who are to "bear the sword" and be a "terror" to bad conduct and are to carry out "God's wrath on the wrongdoer" (Rom. 13:3–4). The verses must be understood rightly in their own contexts. One is talking about individual conduct and personal revenge. The other is talking about the responsibilities of government. We should not confuse the two passages.

9. Could more pacifism have stopped slavery or stopped Hitler?

Near the end of his book Boyd responds to the objection that war was necessary to end slavery in the United States (in the Civil War) and to stop Hitler's campaign to take over the entire world (in World War II). Didn't the use of military force bring about good in those cases?

Boyd's response is to say that if Christians had been better pacifists, history would have been different: "Had professing Christians been remotely like Jesus in the first place, there would have been no slavery or war for us to wonder about what *would have happened* had Christians loved their enemies and turned the other cheek."[52] With regard to the US Civil War, Boyd says, "A kingdom person should rather wonder what might have happened had more kingdom people been willing to live out the call of the radical kingdom."[53]

But this is just an elegant way of saying, "If history was different, it would prove my case." And that is another way of saying, "If the facts were different, they would prove my case." That is not a valid argument. It is appealing to wishful thinking rather than facts.

51. See explanation of this verse in *ESV Study Bible*, p. 1830; see also pp. 2554–55.

52. Boyd, *Myth of a Christian Nation*, 174.
53. Ibid., 177.

Boyd is simply saying that if the world were different, the world would be different. But that proves nothing. History is what it is, and history shows that both the evil of American slavery and the evil of Adolf Hitler were only stopped by the power of superior military force. That is the task that God has assigned to governments when they "bear the sword" (Rom. 13:4).

10. The more ominous implications of the "all government is demonic" view

I am concerned about the influence of Boyd's position because his mistake is not simply a harmless failure to distinguish the task of evangelism from the task of government. There is a much more serious problem with his position, namely, that it tends to persuade Christians *to oppose all governmental power over evil*. Although we cannot discuss the biblical passages in detail until later chapters, at many places in the Bible God approves the use of governmental power over evildoers: see, for example, Genesis 9:5–6; the narratives concerning Moses and other righteous judges and kings in the Old Testament; Romans 13:1–6; and 1 Peter 2:13–14. God establishes civil government and authorizes it to use its power to restrain evil, "to *punish* those who do evil and to praise those who do good" (1 Peter 2:14).

But what would happen if more and more Christians agreed with Greg Boyd that the use of "power over" evildoers by government is serving Satan as "CEO" and Christians should have no part in it?

On the world scene, it would mean less and less support for a strong military and more and more insistence on endless conversations with aggressive nations who would attack us and our allies. It would mean more and more of the kind of appeasement that led Prime Minister Neville Chamberlain of England to sign the Munich Agreement of 1938, giving Hitler a large section of Czechoslovakia with no objection from Britain, only in exchange for Hitler's (empty) promise of peace. This view would today result in increasing objection to the use of military power to oppose evil aggressors anywhere in the world. And that, in turn, would result in increased aggression by Islamic terrorists as well as by countries such as Russia, North Korea, Iran, Venezuela, Cuba, and any others who realize that no act of aggression would be answered by American military force anywhere in the world.

At the local level, this rejection of all governmental "power over" evil would mean more and more opposition to the use of superior force by local police, for Boyd's ideal way of opposing all evildoers is "by people lovingly placing themselves *under* others, in service to others, at cost to themselves."[54] Because Boyd's approach neglects God's appointed way of using governmental power to restrain evil, the result would be the unrestrained growth of violent crime in every community.

At this point, discerning Christians should be able to see a more ominous spiritual component at the heart of Boyd's position. Who would ultimately profit from persuading Christians that *all government power over evil is wrong and demonic*? Who would

---

54. Ibid., 31.

ultimately want to eliminate all use of power over evil by those who are followers of Jesus Christ? It would ultimately be Satan himself, who wants no force for good to restrain his evil deeds in the world.

Therefore, at the heart of Greg Boyd's position is *an exact reversal of the role of God and Satan with regard to civil government.* Boyd says that when government exercises power over evil, this itself is demonic and evil. But the Bible tells us that the ruler who exercises power to restrain and punish evil is doing "good" and is "God's servant" (Rom. 13:4).

The "all government is demonic and evil" view is a third wrong view.

D. DO EVANGELISM, NOT POLITICS

A fourth wrong view about Christians and politics is promoted by evangelicals who essentially say, "We should just preach the Gospel, and that is the only way Christians can hope to change people's hearts and change our society." I call this the "do evangelism, not politics" view. It claims that the church is only called to "preach the Gospel," not to preach about politics.

I hear this view expressed quite often in personal conversations. But are there any evangelical authors who actually advocate this view? There are some authors whose writings tend in this direction, even if it is qualified by statements that of course *some* political influence by the church is appropriate—but it will not do any spiritual or eternal good! Consider some statements by Cal Thomas and John MacArthur, two writers for whom (on other topics) I have great appreciation.

Nationally syndicated columnist Cal Thomas has written:

> No matter how hard they try to protect the gospel from corruption, ministers who focus on politics and politicians as a means of redemption must minimize their ultimate calling and message. The road to redemption does not run through Washington, D.C. Politicians can't redeem themselves from the temptations of Washington. What makes anyone think they can redeem the rest of us?[55]

John MacArthur, in *Why Government Can't Save You*, wrote the following:

> It is all right occasionally to support legitimate measures designed to correct a glaring social or political wrong.... A certain amount of healthy and balanced concern about current trends in government and the community is acceptable, as long as we realize that *such interest is not vital to our spiritual lives, our righteous testimony or the advancement of the kingdom of Christ.* Above all, the believer's political involvement should never displace the priority of preaching and teaching the gospel because *the morality and righteousness that God seeks is the result of salvation and sanctification.*[56]

55. Cal Thomas, "Pulpit Bullies," Tribune Media Services (Oct. 3, 2008). See www.calthomas.com/index.php?news=2381. A "do evangelism, not politics" view is also promoted by Greg Boyd's book, *The Myth of a Christian Nation*, which I discussed in the previous section.

56. John MacArthur, *Why Government Can't Save You: An Alternative to Political Activism* (Grand Rapids: Zondervan, 2000), 8, italics added.

[Jesus] did not come to earth to make the old creation moral through social and governmental reform but to make new creatures (His people) holy through the saving power of the gospel and the transforming work of the Holy Spirit.[57]

1. Too narrow an understanding of "the Gospel" and the kingdom of God

While I agree with Thomas and MacArthur on many other things, I cannot agree with their disparagement of the value of Christian political involvement for God's purposes on this earth. I think it represents too narrow an understanding of the work of God's kingdom and of the nature of the Christian gospel message.

"The Gospel" in the New Testament is not just "trust Jesus and be forgiven of your sins and grow in holiness and go to heaven" (though that is certainly true, and that is the heart of the Gospel and its foundational message). No, the Gospel is God's *good news* about all of life! Jesus said,

> "Go therefore and make disciples of all nations, baptizing them in the name of the Father and of the Son and of the Holy Spirit, *teaching them to observe all that I have commanded you*" (Matt. 28:19–20).

The phrase "all that I have commanded you" means more than John 3:16, as wonderful as that verse is. *All* that Jesus commanded includes everything that he taught as recorded in the four Gospels. This is because Jesus promised his disciples not only that the Holy Spirit would "bring to your remembrance all that I have said to you" (John 14:26), but also that the Holy Spirit "will teach you all things" (v. 26) and will "guide you into all the truth" (16:13).

That is why the apostle Peter could say that "the commandment of the Lord and Savior" came "through your apostles" (2 Peter 3:2), and Paul could say, "The things I am writing to you are a command of the Lord" (1 Cor. 14:37). Their epistles are also things that Jesus now commands us! Both the Gospels *and the Epistles* in the New Testament come to us with Jesus' authority, and he wants us to teach these things to our churches.

What about the Old Testament? Since Jesus and the apostles repeatedly relied on the Old Testament as the Word of God, we also receive the Old Testament Scriptures on the authority of Jesus and his apostles. Therefore, understood in a broad sense, "teaching them to observe all that I have commanded you" means that we should faithfully teach the *entire Bible* to those who become disciples of Jesus. Preaching "the whole Gospel" must also include preaching what the Bible says about civil government. That means that Christians will learn from the Bible how to influence governments for good. And since these things are taught in the Bible, God must count them important for the advance of his kingdom and his purposes on the earth.

Does Christian political activism do any spiritual good? A short answer is that if it is part of what God teaches us in Scripture, then of course it does spiritual good, because it is something that pleases God. "This is the love of God, that we keep his commandments"

57. Ibid., 11–12.

(1 John 5:3)—therefore, following his teachings regarding government is one way of showing love to him.

Another answer is provided by Tom Minnery, who looks to the example of Jesus' life. Jesus did not only forgive people's sins; he also healed their physical diseases. Jesus was concerned both about people's spiritual life and about the well-being of their actual physical life in this world. Healing people's physical bodies was doing spiritual good, in God's eyes. Minnery applies this pattern to any social activity we do to improve the state of people's lives:

> Social activity not only follows evangelism as its consequence and aim, and precedes it as a bridge, but also accompanies it as its partner. In His own ministry, Jesus went about teaching and preaching, and also doing good and healing. Both were expressions of his compassion for people, and both should be ours.[58]

I cannot therefore agree with John MacArthur's statement about the effect of good and bad governments:

> The ideal human government can ultimately do nothing to advance God's kingdom, and the worst, most despotic worldly government in the end cannot halt the power of the Holy Spirit or the spread of God's Word.[59]

I think of the difference between North Korea and South Korea. Even if the dictatorial, oppressive government of North Korea has not *completely* halted the spread of God's Word, its severe persecution has hindered it so much that millions of North Koreans are born, live, and die without ever hearing of Jesus Christ, and North Korea sends out zero missionaries. By contrast, the church in South Korea, where the government has allowed freedom, is growing, thriving, and sending missionaries around the world. Or compare the relatively small, repressed church in Cuba, which is unable to send out any missionaries anywhere, with the growing, thriving churches throughout many Latin American countries that have more freedom. Governments do make a difference to the work of God's kingdom. This is why Paul urged that prayers be made "for kings and all who are in high positions, that we may lead a peaceful and quiet life, godly and dignified in every way" (1 Tim. 2:2). That is, good governments help people to live a "peaceful" and "godly" life, and bad governments hinder that.

Governments can allow churches to meet freely and evangelize or they can prevent these things by force of law (as in Saudi Arabia and North Korea). They can hinder or promote literacy (the latter enabling people to read a Bible). They can stop murderers and thieves and drunk drivers and child predators or allow them to terrorize society and destroy lives. They can promote and protect marriages or hinder and even destroy them. Governments do make a significant difference for the work of God in the world, and we are to pray and work for good governments around the world.

58. Tom Minnery, *Why You Can't Stay Silent: A Biblical Mandate to Shape Our Culture* (Wheaton, IL: Tyndale House, 2001), 49.

59. MacArthur, *Why Government Can't Save You*, 7.

2. The "whole Gospel" includes a transformation of society

A second reason that "do evangelism, not politics" is a wrong view is that the whole Gospel includes transformation of society. Yes, forgiveness of sins is absolutely wonderful, and it is the central message of the Gospel. *Of course* we must proclaim forgiveness of sins through faith in Christ alone. *Of course* this is the only way that people's hearts will be *truly* transformed.

But forgiveness of sins is not the only message of the Gospel. That is because Jesus is looking for transformed lives and through them a transformed world. "The reason the Son of God appeared was to destroy the works of the devil" (1 John 3:8). The good news of the Gospel will result in changed lives, but Jesus wants that to result in *changed families* as well. And when the Gospel changes lives, it should also result in *changed neighborhoods.* And *changed schools.* And *changed businesses.* And *changed societies.* So shouldn't "the Gospel" also result in *changed governments* as well? Of course it should!

And should churches teach their people what the Bible says about God's will for families? About God's will for business? About God's will for educating children? Certainly they should. But then, shouldn't churches also teach about God's will for human government? Of course they should! And some Christians are called to implement that teaching in actually influencing governments for good.

It seems to me that the "do evangelism, not politics" view has a mistaken understanding of what is important to God, as if only spiritual (nonmaterial, other-worldly) things matter to him and not the actual circumstances of people's physical life in this world. That is a philosophical view akin to Platonism, and it is similar to an ancient deviation from Christianity called Gnosticism—but it is not the view of the Bible.

3. Which parts of the Bible should the church not preach about?

A third response to those who say, "The church should just do evangelism and not get involved in politics," is to ask this question: "What parts of the Bible have you decided not to preach about because you are 'just going to preach the Gospel'?" Have you decided that you won't preach on Romans 13:1–7? Or that you won't preach on 1 Peter 2:13–14? What about Genesis 9:5–6? Or what about the narratives of the Old Testament kings and their good and evil deeds? Are you not going to preach about Daniel's influence on the government of Babylon? Or on Isaiah's prophecies to the other nations in Isaiah 13–23? Are you not going to preach on the prophecies to the other nations in Amos 1–2? What parts of the Bible are left out of your preaching by the idea that you're going to "just preach the Gospel"?

4. God leaves Christians here on earth both to do evangelism and to do good for others

The fourth reason that the "do evangelism, not politics" view is wrong is that it misunderstands the reason why God left Christians on the earth. Think about this for a minute: When people trust in Christ as their Savior and have their sins forgiven, why does God not snatch them up to heaven immediately? Why does he leave them here on earth? Is it *only* so that they would preach the Gospel to others? Well then, what are *those people* supposed to do after they trust in Christ as Savior? Is their *only* purpose on earth to preach the Gospel to others, or does Jesus want us to do some other things, such as loving our neighbors as ourselves (see Matt. 22:39)?

Clearly, if we are here on earth to glorify God, we will glorify him (in part at least) by obeying the command, "You shall love your neighbor as yourself" (Matt. 22:39). But that means that I should seek the good of my neighbors in all parts of society. "You shall love your neighbor as yourself" means that I should seek *good laws* that will protect preborn children. It means that I should seek *good laws* that protect marriages and families. It means I should seek *good laws* that protect children from the corrupting moral influences that want to use the classroom to teach that all kinds of sexual experimentation outside of marriage are just fine and that there is nothing wrong with pornography.

One reason why Jesus left us here on earth is that we should glorify him *by doing good to other people in all areas of life*. "So then, as we have opportunity, let us do good to everyone, and especially to those who are of the household of faith" (Gal. 6:10). Certainly that means that we should do good to others, as we have opportunity, by being a good influence on laws and government and by having a good influence on the political process. Paul says this about Christians:

> For we are his workmanship, created in Christ Jesus for good works, which God prepared beforehand, that we should walk in them (Eph. 2:10).

Jesus left us here on earth in part because he wants to allow our lives to give glory to him in the midst of a fallen and sinful world: "Let your light shine before others, *so that they may see your good works* and give glory to your Father who is in heaven" (Matt. 5:16).

So, should churches teach their people how to do "good works" in hospitals and in schools, and in businesses and in neighborhoods, but not in government? Why should that area of life be excluded from the influence of the "good works" of believers that will "give glory to your Father who is in heaven"?

I conclude that Jesus' command that "you shall love your neighbor as yourself" means that I should seek the good of my neighbors in every aspect of society, *including seeking to bring about good government and good laws*.

5. God established both the church and the government to restrain evil

A fifth reason that the "do evangelism, not politics" view is wrong is that it overlooks the fact that God gave both the church and the government to restrain evil in this age. I agree that *one* significant way that God restrains evil in the world is through changing people's hearts when they trust in Christ as their Savior (see 2 Cor. 5:17). But we should not turn this *one way* into the *only way* that God restrains evil in this age. God also uses civil government to restrain evil, and there is much evil that can only be restrained by the power of civil government, for there will always be many who do not trust in Christ as their Savior and many who do not fully obey him.

For example, why do we need laws against drunk driving? Someone might say, "We really don't need laws against drunk driving. The influence of the Gospel should be enough to change society. If Christians were *really* doing their job of witnessing to others, and if Christians were *really* being a good example of sober driving, that would be enough to eliminate all drunk driving in the United States."

Of course, that is a foolish position. We recognize that in this present age there are many people who do not accept the Gospel. (And sadly, even some of those who do trust in Christ continue to do things as foolish as driving while intoxicated.) Until Christ returns there will always be drunk drivers who will not be persuaded by the Christian Gospel or by their conscience or by the example of others or by common sense. They will still get themselves drunk and then drive on our streets unless there is some other means of restraining this evil than just preaching the Gospel.

The way that God has established to stop drunk drivers in this age is the power of civil government. Government has been "instituted by God" so that it would be "not a terror to good conduct, but to bad" (Rom. 13:1, 3). The *primary* means God uses to stop drunk driving today is for civil government to take away these drunk drivers' liberty to drive. If they persist in driving anyway, they will go to jail. God restrains drunk driving not merely by preaching the Gospel, but also by the power of the civil government. Government is sent "to punish those who do evil and to praise those who do good" (1 Peter 2:14).

To take another example, when did people in the United States stop owning slaves? It was not when the Gospel had been preached throughout the South, but after the US government made it illegal through the Emancipation Proclamation in 1863. That happened when many Christian abolitionists influenced the government of the United States to change its laws (see discussion below).

6. Christians have influenced governments positively throughout history

Historian Alvin Schmidt points out how the spread of Christianity and Christian influence on government was primarily responsible for outlawing infanticide, child abandonment, and abortion in the Roman Empire (in AD 374);[60] outlawing the brutal battles-to-the-death in which thousands of gladiators had died (in 404);[61] outlawing the cruel punishment of branding the faces of criminals (in 315);[62] instituting prison reforms such as the segregating of male and female prisoners (by 361);[63] stopping the practice of human sacrifice among the Irish, the Prussians, and the Lithuanians as well as among other nations;[64] outlawing pedophilia;[65] granting of property rights and other protections to women;[66] banning polygamy (which is still practiced in some Muslim nations today);[67] prohibiting the burning alive of widows in India (in 1829);[68] outlawing the painful and crippling practice of binding young women's feet in China

---

60. Alvin Schmidt, *How Christianity Changed the World* (Grand Rapids: Zondervan, 2004; formerly published as *Under the Influence*, 2001), 51, 53, 59.
61. Ibid., 63.
62. Ibid., 65.
63. Ibid.
64. Ibid., 65–66.
65. Ibid., 87–88.
66. Ibid., 111.
67. Ibid., 115.
68. Ibid., 116–17.

(in 1912);[69] persuading government officials to begin a system of public schools in Germany (in the sixteenth century);[70] and advancing the idea of compulsory education of all children in a number of European countries.[71]

During the history of the church, Christians have had a decisive influence in opposing and often abolishing slavery in the Roman Empire, in Ireland, and in most of Europe (though Schmidt frankly notes that a minority of "erring" Christian teachers have supported slavery in various centuries).[72] In England, William Wilberforce, a devout Christian, led the successful effort to abolish the slave trade and then slavery itself throughout the British Empire by 1840.[73]

In the United States, though there were vocal defenders of slavery among Christians in the South, they were vastly outnumbered by the many Christians who were ardent abolitionists, speaking, writing, and agitating constantly for the abolition of slavery in the United States. Schmidt notes that two-thirds of the American abolitionists in the mid-1830s were Christian clergymen,[74] and he gives numerous examples of the strong Christian commitment of several of the most influential of the antislavery crusaders, including Elijah Lovejoy (the first abolitionist martyr), Lyman Beecher, Edward Beecher, Harriet Beecher Stowe (author of *Uncle Tom's Cabin*), Charles Finney, Charles T. Torrey, Theodore Weld, William Lloyd Garrison, "and others too numerous to mention."[75] The American civil rights movement that resulted in the outlawing of racial segregation and discrimination was led by Martin Luther King Jr., a Christian pastor, and supported by many Christian churches and groups.[76]

There was also strong influence from Christian ideas and influential Christians in the formulation of the Magna Carta in England (1215)[77] and of the Declaration of Independence (1776) and the Constitution (1787)[78] in the United States. These are three of the most significant documents in the history of governments on the earth, and all three show the marks of significant Christian influence in the foundational ideas of how governments should function. These foundations for British and American government did not come about as a result of the "do evangelism, not politics" view.

Schmidt also argues that several specific components of modern views of government also had strong Christian influence in their origin and influence, such as individual human rights, individual freedom, the equality of individuals before the law, freedom of religion, and separation of church and state.[79]

As for the present time, Charles Colson's insightful book *God and Government*[80] (previously published as *Kingdoms in Conflict*) reports dozens of encouraging narratives

69. Ibid., 119.

70. Ibid., 179.

71. Ibid., 179–80. Although this is not a matter of merely influencing laws, Schmidt also points out the immense influence of Christians on higher education: By the year 1932 there were 182 colleges and universities in the United States, and of that number, 92 percent had been founded by Christian denominations (p. 190).

72. Ibid., 274–76.

73. Ibid., 276–78.

74. Ibid., 279.

75. Ibid., 279–90.

76. Ibid., 287–89.

77. Ibid., 251–52.

78. Ibid., 253–58.

79. Ibid., 258–70.

80. Charles W. Colson, *God and Government: An Insider's View on the Boundaries between Faith and Politics* (Grand Rapids: Zondervan, 2007).

of courageous, real-life Christians who in recent years, in causes large and small, have had significant impact for good on laws and governments around the world.

Therefore I cannot agree with John MacArthur when he says, "God does not call the church to influence the culture by promoting legislation and court rulings that advance a scriptural point of view."[81] When I look over that list of changes in governments and laws that Christians incited, I think God *did* call the church and thousands of Christians within the church to work to bring about these momentous improvements in human society throughout the world. Or should we say that Christians who brought about these changes were *not* doing so out of obedience to God? That these changes made *no difference* to God? This cannot be true.

MacArthur says, "Using temporal methods to promote legislative and judicial change … is not our calling—and has no eternal value."[82] I disagree. I believe those changes listed above were important to the God who declares, "Let justice roll down like waters, and righteousness like an ever-flowing stream" (Amos 5:24). God *cares* how people treat one another here on earth, and these changes in government listed above *do* have eternal value in God's sight.

If the Christian church had adopted the "do evangelism, not politics" view throughout its history, it would never have brought about these immeasurably valuable changes among the nations of the world. But these changes did happen, because Christians realized that if they could influence laws and governments for good, they would be obeying the command of their Lord, "Let your light shine before others, so that they *may see your good works* and give glory to your Father who is in heaven" (Matt. 5:16). They influenced governments for good because they knew that "we are his workmanship, created in Christ Jesus *for good works*, which God prepared beforehand, that we should walk in them" (Eph. 2:10).

7. Doesn't the Bible say that persecution is coming?

Sometimes people ask me, "Why should we try to improve governments when the Bible tells us that persecution is coming in the end times before Christ returns? Doesn't that mean that we should expect governments to become more and more anti-Christian?" (They have in mind passages like Matt. 24:9–12, 21–22; 2 Tim. 3:1–5.)

The answer is that we cannot know when Christ will return or when the events preceding his coming will occur (see Matt. 24:36; 25:13). What we do know is that while we have opportunity, God tells us not to give up but to go on preaching "the whole counsel of God" (Acts 20:27) and doing "good works" (Eph. 2:10) and loving our neighbors as ourselves (Matt. 22:39). That means we should go on *trying to influence governments for good* as long as we are able to do so.

If all the Christians who influenced governments for good in previous centuries had just given up and said, "Persecution is coming and governments will become more evil,

---

81. MacArthur, *Why Government Can't Save You*, 130.
82. Ibid., 15.

so there is nothing we can do," then none of those good changes in laws would have come about. There would still be human sacrifice and burning of widows alive and slavery and racial discrimination protected by law. That mentality would have been a defeatist, fatalistic attitude, and it would have led Christians to disobey many of God's commands for how we are to live our lives during this present age. Instead of giving in to such a hopeless attitude, courageous Christians in previous generations sought to do good for others and for governments, and God often blessed their efforts.

8. But won't political involvement distract us from the main task of preaching the Gospel?

At this point someone may object that while political involvement may have *some* benefits and may do *some* good, it can so easily distract us, turn unbelievers away from the church, and cause us to neglect the main task of pointing people toward personal trust in Christ. John MacArthur writes, "When the church takes a stance that emphasizes political activism and social moralizing, it always diverts energy and resources away from evangelization."[83]

Yet the proper question is not, "Does political influence take resources away from evangelism?" but, "Is political influence something God has called us to do?" If God has called some of us to some political influence, then those resources would not be blessed if we diverted them to evangelism—or to the choir, or to teaching Sunday School to children, or to any other use.

In this matter, as in everything else the church does, it would be healthy for Christians to realize that God may call *individual Christians* to different emphases in their lives. This is because God has placed in the church "varieties of gifts" (1 Cor. 12:4) and the church is an entity that has "many members" but is still "one body" (v. 12).

Therefore God might call someone to devote almost all of his or her time to the choir, someone else to youth work, someone else to evangelism, someone else to preparing refreshments to welcome visitors, and someone else to work with lighting and sound systems. "But if Jim places all his attention on the sound system, won't that distract the church from the main task of preaching the Gospel?" No, not at all. That is not what God has called Jim to emphasize (though he will certainly share the Gospel with others as he has opportunity). Jim's exclusive focus on the church's sound system means he is just being a faithful steward in the responsibility God has given him.

In the same way, I think it is entirely possible that God called Billy Graham to emphasize evangelism and say nothing about politics and also called James Dobson to emphasize a radio ministry to families and to influencing the political world for good. Aren't there enough Christians in the world for us to focus on more than one task? And does God not call us to thousands of different emphases, all in obedience to him?

But *the whole ministry of the church* will include both emphases. And the teaching ministry from the pulpit should do nothing less than proclaim "the whole counsel of

---

83. Ibid., 14.

God" (Acts 20:27). It should teach, over the course of time, on all areas of life and all areas of Bible knowledge. That certainly must include, to some extent, what the Bible says about the purposes of civil government and how that teaching should apply to our situations today.

This means that in a healthy church we will find that some people emphasize influencing the government and politics, others emphasize influencing the business world, others emphasize influencing the educational system, others entertainment and the media, others marriage and the family, and so forth. When that happens, it seems to me that we should encourage, not discourage, one another. We should adopt the attitude toward each other that Paul encouraged in the church at Rome:

> Why do you pass judgment on your brother? Or you, why do you despise your brother? For we will all stand before the judgment seat of God.... So then each of us will give an account of himself to God. Therefore let us not pass judgment on one another any longer, but rather decide never to put a stumbling block or hindrance in the way of a brother (Rom. 14:10–13).

For several different reasons, then, I think the view that says the church should just "do evangelism, not politics" is incorrect.

E. DO POLITICS, NOT EVANGELISM

The fifth view says that the church should just try to change the laws and the culture and should not emphasize evangelism. I do not know of any responsible evangelical leaders or prominent Christian groups today who hold this view or say that Christians should just "do politics, not evangelism." But this was a primary emphasis of the Social Gospel movement in the late nineteenth and early twentieth centuries, with its campaigns to get the church to work aggressively to overcome poverty, slums, crime, racial discrimination, and other social evils. These were good causes in themselves, but this movement placed little emphasis on the need for individuals to place personal trust in Christ as Savior or the need to proclaim the entire Bible as the Word of God and worthy of our belief. The Social Gospel movement gained followers primarily among liberal Protestants rather than among more conservative, evangelical Protestant groups.

Some writers accuse Christians who emphasize political involvement of holding this "do politics, not evangelism" view. They say some conservative Christians seem to think that voting Republican will save the nation or that we should trust government to save us rather than trusting in God, or they make some similar allegation.

But these seem to me to be attacks against a straw man, a hypothetical opponent that does not really exist. So far as I know, this view has not been advocated by leaders at Focus on the Family, the Christian Coalition, the Family Research Council, the 700 Club, Concerned Women for America, the Alliance Defense Fund, the American Center for Law and Justice, or previous organizations such as Jerry Falwell's Moral Majority. No responsible leader that I know in those or similar organizations advocates seeking to change government instead of doing evangelism. In fact, many of the evangelical leaders who are involved in seeking to influence government have been active evangelists, such as the late D. James Kennedy, who preached regularly on biblical perspectives on political issues and whose *Evangelism Explosion*[84] book and program provided much encouragement to personal evangelism among many thousands of evangelicals.

Not once have I heard any Christian in any of these groups say, "Good government will save us" or "If we just win this election we do not have to pray or do evangelism or seek change in people's hearts." Not once have I heard anyone say, "We should trust government and not God"!

Yet Christians who encourage greater Christian involvement in politics need to hear an important word of caution: If we (and I include myself here) ever begin to think that *good laws alone* will solve a nation's problems or bring about a righteous and just society, we will have made a huge mistake. Unless there is simultaneously an inner change in people's hearts and minds, good laws alone will only bring about grudging, external compliance with the minimum level of obedience necessary to avoid punishment. Good government and good laws can prevent much evil behavior, and they can teach people what society approves, but they cannot by themselves produce good people. Cal Thomas and Ed Dobson rightly caution, "But we who are Christians are deluded if we think we will change our culture solely through political power."[85]

Genuine, long-term change in a nation will only happen (1) if people's *hearts* change so that they seek to do good, not evil; (2) if people's *minds* change so that their moral convictions align more closely with God's moral standards in the Bible; and (3) if a nation's *laws* change so that they more fully encourage good conduct and punish wrong conduct. Item 1 comes about through personal evangelism and the power of the Gospel of Jesus Christ. Item 2 takes place both through personal conversation and teaching and through public discussion and debate. Item 3 comes about through Christian political involvement. All three are necessary.

Whether it comes from the liberal Social Gospel movement or perhaps from evangelicals who might be tempted to think that political victories will solve everything, this "do politics, not evangelism" view is certainly wrong. The church must above all proclaim that "the wages of sin is death, but the free gift of God is eternal life in Christ Jesus our Lord" (Rom. 6:23). People definitely have a change in their hearts when they believe in Christ: "Therefore, if anyone is in Christ, he is a new creation. The old has passed away; behold, the new has come" (2 Cor. 5:17).

What then? Is there a correct view that is different from these five wrong views? The view I propose in the next chapter is "significant Christian influence on government." "Significant Christian influence on government" is not *compulsion* (view 1), it is not *silence* (view 2), and it is not *dropping out of the process* (views 3 and 4), nor is it thinking *the government can save people* (view 5). It is different from each of these wrong views, and I think it is much closer to the actual teaching of the Bible.

84. D. James Kennedy, *Evangelism Explosion* (Wheaton, IL: Tyndale House, 1977).

85. Cal Thomas and Ed Dobson, *Blinded By Might: Why the Religious Right Can't Save America* (Grand Rapids: Zondervan, 1999), 51.

Chapter 2

A BETTER SOLUTION: SIGNIFICANT CHRISTIAN INFLUENCE ON GOVERNMENT

In the previous chapter I examined five incorrect views about Christian involvement in civil government. In this chapter I propose what I think is a better solution: "significant Christian influence" on civil government.

The "significant influence" view says that Christians *should* seek to influence civil government according to God's moral standards and God's purposes for government as revealed in the Bible (when rightly understood). But while Christians exercise this influence, they must simultaneously insist on protecting freedom of religion for all citizens. In addition, "significant influence" does not mean angry, belligerent, intolerant, judgmental, red-faced, and hate-filled influence, but rather winsome, kind, thoughtful, loving, persuasive influence that is suitable to each circumstance and that always protects the other person's right to disagree, but that is also uncompromising about the truthfulness and moral goodness of the teachings of God's Word.

A. UNDERSTANDING THE BIBLE RIGHTLY

Someone might immediately object, "But who can understand the Bible rightly? And who is to decide what is a right interpretation?"

My response is that it is not impossible to understand the Bible rightly. Of course there are some areas where Christians have legitimate disagreement about the meaning of the Bible, but *among responsible evangelical interpreters of the Bible there are vastly more areas of widespread agreement than disagreement, both today and throughout history,* regarding the main teachings of the Christian faith and the methods of proper interpretation.

For example, among interpreters who take the whole Bible to be the trustworthy Word of God (that is, among mainstream evangelical interpreters at least, as well as among many conservative Roman Catholic interpreters), there is no significant disagreement over the fact that, according to the Bible, murder is morally wrong (Exod. 20:13), adultery is morally wrong (v. 14), stealing is morally wrong (v. 15), and bearing "false witness against your neighbor" is morally wrong (v. 16). There is also widespread agreement about the fact that God established civil government for our benefit, in order to restrain evil and promote good (Rom. 13:1–6; 1 Peter 2:13–14; also Gen. 9:5–6), and that there should be a distinction between those things that are governed by the church and those that are under the authority of civil government (Matt. 22:21). Other elements of a biblical worldview and its implications for civil government could be mentioned, but these should be enough to show that there is widespread consensus throughout the world among evangelical interpreters regarding the most significant principles that affect a person's view of the Bible and politics.

Of course, there are also areas where Christians disagree about the meaning of the Bible as it applies to government. There are disagreements, for example, over the theory of a "just war," disagreements over the death penalty, and disagreements over the specific responsibilities of government with respect to poverty and wealth. But even these disagreements are healthy when they can be pursued in open public forums (both spoken and written) in which different sides have opportunity to argue from the Bible in favor of their positions. As such respectful arguments continue over time, eventually one viewpoint or another has the more persuasive arguments and then the majority of pastors, seminary professors, parachurch leaders, and other opinion leaders, and then the vast majority of evangelical believers, come to be persuaded about that viewpoint, and the opposing viewpoint is marginalized and persists, if at all, among only a small minority of Christians. I saw this process happen regarding the question of abortion, for example, in the 1960s and 1970s. To take two earlier examples, consensus gradually developed throughout the sixteenth to eighteenth centuries with regard to the validity of charging interest ("usury") and the validity of the civil government allowing freedom of religion.

In fact, in much of the rest of this book, I argue on the basis of verses in the Bible for precisely that reason: *I am attempting to persuade others who believe the Bible* that the points I am making can in fact be substantiated from a responsible use of the Bible. Others who disagree have the right to publish arguments opposing what I say, and in that kind of healthy dialogue, Christians who read both sides often come to deeper understanding of the important issues.

B. LIBERAL DISTORTIONS OF THE BIBLE

One word of caution is appropriate at this point, however: Theologically liberal critics of the Bible are not a good guide to right interpretation of the Bible. (By "theologically liberal" I mean the viewpoint that holds that the Bible is not the divinely authoritative and entirely truthful and trustworthy Word of God, but that it consists of merely human writings with many mistakes and contradictions.) Sometimes liberal religion writers in the secular media mock anyone who claims to say "what the Bible teaches," and they do this by tossing out a rapid list of verses taken out of context and questions that seem to make it impossible to follow the Bible at all.

For example, British author A. N. Wilson, in criticizing American Southern Baptists, wrote this in the *New York Times*:

> It seems ... as impractical as it is undesirable to try to recreate the ethics and behavioral patterns of a vanished age.... [do] Southern Baptists condone slavery (as Paul does in his Epistle to Philemon)? Do the Southern Baptists pool all their property and hold everything in common, as the first Christians did? Do they condemn giving money upon usury ... and if so, how do they manage to invest in the stock market, put savings into pensions or even have a bank account?... How many Christian fundamentalists in America today keep the Jewish dietary laws? How many of them would approve of stoning adulteresses?... Yet *all these things are part of "Biblical morality."* ... Paul ... advised his followers not to marry at all. The early church was consistently hostile to family life.... A true Biblical faith recognizes that the Bible is not a book of answers. It's the story of the human race getting it wrong, over and over and over again. Even Saint Paul frequently contradicts himself....[1]

Here I count six things that Wilson says "are part of 'Biblical morality'": (1) slavery, (2) communal property, (3) forbidding the collection of interest on loans ("usury"), (4) Jewish dietary laws, (5) stoning people for adultery, and (6) discouraging marriage.

Yet I have taught and written on biblical ethics for more than thirty years, and I *do not teach that the Bible requires any of those things*, nor do any of the leading evangelical denominations and parachurch organizations advocate these things, nor do any of the commonly used ethics textbooks in evangelical colleges and seminaries.[2] Wilson is simply distorting and misrepresenting the Bible.

My point is that, as with any written document, it is always possible for a hostile reader to lift biblical statements unfairly out of their contexts and announce that "this is what the Bible teaches," but this is done with no attention to responsible principles of interpretation and no awareness of the place of specific verses within the broad sweep of historical development throughout the Bible. Wilson's objections are designed to lead people to conclude that "nobody can obey the Bible today," but they can all be answered, one at a time, by saying, "You are interpreting the Bible incorrectly at this point, and here are the reasons why."[3]

---

1. A. N. Wilson, "The Good Book of Few Answers," *New York Times*, op-ed page (June 16, 1998), emphasis added.

2. Here are some of the most commonly used textbooks for evangelical ethics: John Jefferson Davis, *Evangelical Ethics*, 3d ed. (Phillipsburg, NJ: P & R, 2004); John Feinberg and Paul Feinberg, *Ethics for a Brave World* (Wheaton, IL: Crossway, 1993); John Frame, *The Doctrine of the Christian Life* (Phillipsburg, NJ: P & R, 2008); Scott Rae, *Moral Choices*, 3rd ed. (Grand Rapids: Zondervan, 2009). Another one, from a pacifist perspective, is Glen Stassen and David Gushee, *Kingdom Ethics* (Downers Grove, IL: InterVarsity Press, 2003).

3. A recent one-volume Bible interpretation resource with contributions from ninety-five evangelical scholars is the *ESV Study Bible* (Wheaton, IL: Crossway, 2008). The interpretative notes at the passages Wilson refers to give far different and (I think) far more responsible answers to the issues Wilson raises. See also the topical essays on biblical ethics and on interpreting the Bible on pages 2535–65 of that volume. The ethics textbooks mentioned in the previous footnote also provide responsible, academically competent treatments of these issues.

Today there are hundreds of millions of evangelical Christian believers throughout the world who earnestly seek to obey the Bible, rightly understood, in all areas of life. They take the Bible as the Word of God, as their reliable, divinely authoritative guide to all of life, just as Christians have done throughout the centuries. And although they are aware of their own shortcomings, they find that seeking to follow the Bible daily is not at all impossible, but rather—when the Bible is understood rightly and obeyed wholeheartedly—it leads to a joyful, fulfilling pattern of life that knows frequent blessing from God.

I think that this applies to the Bible's teachings on civil government as well. These teachings can be understood, and to the extent that they are followed, they will bring many benefits to nations that follow them. That is why I am writing this book.

C. BIBLICAL SUPPORT FOR SIGNIFICANT CHRISTIAN INFLUENCE

1. Old Testament examples

The Bible shows several examples of believers in God who influenced secular governments.[4]

For instance, the Jewish prophet Daniel exercised a strong influence on the secular government in Babylon. Daniel said to Nebuchadnezzar,

> "Therefore, O king, let my counsel be acceptable to you: *break off your sins* by *practicing righteousness*, and your iniquities by *showing mercy to the oppressed*, that there may perhaps be a lengthening of your prosperity" (Dan. 4:27).

Daniel's approach is bold and clear. It is the opposite of a modern multicultural approach that might say something like this:

> "O King Nebuchadnezzar, I am a Jewish prophet, but I would not presume to impose my Jewish moral standards on your Babylonian kingdom. Ask your astronomers and your soothsayers! They will guide you in your own traditions. Then follow your own heart! It would not be my place to speak to you about right and wrong."

No, Daniel boldly told the king, "*Break off your sins* by practicing righteousness, and your iniquities by showing mercy to the oppressed."

Did Daniel specify in more detail what "sins" and "iniquities" needed to be changed in Nebuchadnezzar's reign? Did he tell the world's most powerful ruler how the God of the entire universe wanted him to act as king? The context suggests that he did.

At that time Daniel was a high official in Nebuchadnezzar's court. He was "ruler over the whole province of Babylon" and "chief prefect over all the wise men of Babylon"

---

4. A number of these passages were also mentioned but not developed earlier on page 35 with regard to view 2, "exclude religion."

(Dan. 2:48). He was regularly "at the king's court" (v. 49). Therefore it seems that Daniel had a significant advisory role to the king. This leads to a reasonable assumption that Daniel's summary statement about "sins" and "iniquities" and "showing mercy to the oppressed" (Dan. 4:27), was probably followed by a longer conversation in which Daniel named specific policies and actions of the king that were either good or evil in the eyes of God.

Daniel is an Old Testament example of a believer exercising "significant influence" on a civil government, and one ruled by a pagan king at that.

The counsel that Jeremiah proclaimed to the Jewish exiles in Babylon also supports the idea of believers having influence on laws and government. Jeremiah told these exiles, "*Seek the welfare of the city* where I have sent you into exile, and pray to the LORD on its behalf, for in its welfare you will find your welfare" (Jer. 29:7). But if believers are to seek to bring good to such a pagan society, that must include seeking to bring good to its government (as Daniel did). The true "welfare" of such a city will be advanced through governmental laws and policies that are consistent with God's teaching in the Bible, not by those that are contrary to the Bible's teachings.

Other believers in God had high positions of governmental influence in non-Jewish nations. Joseph was the highest official after Pharaoh, king of Egypt, and had great influence in the decisions of Pharaoh (see Gen. 41:37–45; 42:6; 45:8–9, 26). Later, Moses boldly stood before the Pharaoh and demanded freedom for the people of Israel, saying, "Thus says the LORD, 'Let my people go'" (Exod. 8:1). Nehemiah was "cupbearer to the king" (Neh. 1:11), a position of high responsibility before King Artaxerxes of Persia.[5] Mordecai "was second in rank to King Ahasuerus" of Persia (Esth. 10:3; see also 9:4). Queen Esther also had significant influence on the decisions of Ahasuerus (see Esth. 5:1–8; 7:1–6; 8:3–13; 9:12–15, 29–32).

In addition, there are several passages in the Old Testament prophets that address the sins of foreign nations around Israel: see Isaiah 13–23; Jeremiah 46–51; Ezekiel 25–32; Amos 1–2; Obadiah (addressed to Edom); Jonah (sent to Nineveh); Nahum (addressed to Nineveh); Habakkuk 2; Zephaniah 2. These prophets could speak to nations outside of Israel because the God who is revealed in the Bible is the God of *all peoples* and *all nations* of the earth. He is their Creator, and they will one day stand before him in judgment. Therefore the moral standards of God as revealed in the Bible are the moral standards to which God will hold all people accountable. This includes more than the way people conduct themselves in their marriages and families, in their neighborhoods and schools, and in their jobs and businesses. It also concerns the way people conduct themselves *in government offices*. Believers have a responsibility to bear witness to the moral standards of the Bible by which God will hold all people accountable, including those people in public office.

---

5. "The position of cupbearer to the king was a high office and involved regular access to the king," *ESV Study Bible* (Wheaton, IL: Crossway, 2008), 825.

2. New Testament examples

A New Testament example of influence on government is found in the life of John the Baptist. During his lifetime the ruler of Galilee (from 4 BC to AD 39) was Herod Antipas, a "tetrarch" who had been appointed by the Roman emperor and was subject to the authority of the Roman Empire. Herod was not from the people of Israel but was an Idumean (from Edom, a neighboring nation). Matthew's Gospel tells us that John the Baptist had been rebuking Herod the tetrarch for a specific personal sin in his life:

> For Herod had seized John and bound him and put him in prison for the sake of Herodias, his brother Phillip's wife, because John had been saying to him, "It is not lawful for you to have her" (Matt. 14:3–4).

But then Luke's Gospel adds more detail:

> [John the Baptist] preached good news to the people. But Herod the tetrarch, who had been reproved by him for Herodias, his brother's wife, *and for all the evil things that Herod had done*, added this to them all, that he locked up John in prison (Luke 3:18–20).

Certainly "all the evil things that Herod had done" included many evil actions that he had carried out as a governing official in the Roman Empire. John the Baptist rebuked him *for all of them*. He boldly spoke to officials of the empire about the moral right and wrong of their governmental policies. In doing this, John was following in the steps of Daniel and many Old Testament prophets (see above). The New Testament portrays John the Baptist's actions as those of "a righteous and holy man" (Mark 6:20). He is an excellent example of a believer who had what I call "significant influence" on the policies of a government (though it cost him his life: see Mark 6:21–29).

Yet another example is the apostle Paul. While Paul was in prison in Caesarea, he stood trial before the Roman governor Felix. Here is what happened:

> After some days Felix came with his wife Drusilla, who was Jewish, and he sent for Paul and heard him speak about faith in Christ Jesus. And *as he reasoned about righteousness and self-control and the coming judgment*, Felix was alarmed and said, "Go away for the present. When I get an opportunity I will summon you" (Acts 24:24–25).

While Luke does not give us any more details, the fact that Felix was "alarmed" and that Paul reasoned with him about "righteousness" and "the coming judgment" indicates that Paul was talking about moral standards of right and wrong and the ways in which Felix, as an official of the Roman Empire, had obligations to live up to the standards that are given by God. Paul no doubt told Felix that he would be accountable for his actions at "the coming judgment," and this was what led Felix to be "alarmed." When Luke tells us that Paul "reasoned" with Felix about these things, the word (Greek *dialegomai*) indicates a back-and-forth conversation or discussion. It is not difficult to suppose that Felix asked Paul, "What about this decision that I made? What about this policy? What about this ruling?" It would be an artificial restriction on the meaning of the text to suppose that Paul *only* spoke with Felix about his "private" life and not about his actions as a Roman governor. Paul is thus an excellent example of attempting to exercise "significant Christian influence" on civil government.

Therefore if we as Christians attempt to bring "significant Christian influence" to bear on civil governments and government leaders, we have many positive examples in the narrative history of the Bible, including Joseph, Moses, Daniel, Nehemiah, Mordecai, and Esther. We also have as examples the written prophecies of Isaiah, Jeremiah, Ezekiel, Amos, Obadiah, Jonah, Nahum, Habakkuk, and Zephaniah. In the New Testament we have the courageous examples of John the Baptist and the apostle Paul. Such influences on governments are no minor examples in obscure portions of the Bible, but are found in Old Testament history from Genesis all the way to Esther (the last historical book), in the canonical writing prophets from Isaiah to Zephaniah, and in the New Testament in both the Gospels and the Epistles. And those are just the examples of God's servants bringing "significant influence" to pagan kings who gave no allegiance to the God of Israel or to Jesus in the New Testament times. If we add to this list the many stories of Old Testament prophets bringing counsel and encouragement and rebuke to the good and evil kings of Israel as well, then we would include the histories of all the kings and the writings of all the prophets—nearly every book of the Old Testament. And we could add in several passages from Psalms and Proverbs that speak of good and evil rulers. Influencing government for good on the basis of the wisdom found in God's own words is a theme that runs through the entire Bible.

3. Romans 13 and 1 Peter 2

In addition to these examples, the mere existence of *specific Bible passages that teach about government* is an argument for "significant Christian influence" on government. Why do we think God put Romans 13:1–7 and 1 Peter 2:13–14 and other related passages (as in Psalms and Proverbs) in the Bible? Are they in the Bible simply as a matter of intellectual curiosity for Christians who will read them privately but never use them to speak to government officials about how God understands their roles and responsibilities? Does God intend this material to be *concealed* from people in government and *kept secret* by Christians who read it and silently moan about "how far government has strayed from what God wants it to be"?

Certainly God put them there not only to inform Christians about how *they* should relate to civil government, but also in order that *people with governmental responsibilities* could know what God himself expects from them. This also pertains to other passages in the Bible that instruct us about God's moral standards, about the nature and purpose of human beings made in God's image, about God's purposes for the earth, and about principles concerning good and bad governments. All of these teachings are relevant for those who serve in governmental office, and we should speak and teach about them when we have opportunity to do so.

4. The responsibility of citizens in a democracy to understand the Bible's teaching

There is another argument for "significant Christian influence" on government that applies to anyone who lives in a democracy, because in a democracy a significant portion of the ruling power of government is entrusted to the citizens generally, through the ballot box. To be able to vote is to have a share of ruling power. Therefore all citizens who are old enough to vote have a *responsibility* before God to know what God expects of civil government and what kind of moral and legal standards he wants government to follow. But *how can citizens learn what kind of government God is seeking?* They can learn this only if churches teach about government and politics from the Bible.

I realize that pastors will differ in the degree of detail they wish to teach with regard to specific political issues facing a nation (for example, whether to teach about issues such as abortion, euthanasia, care for the poor, the military and national defense, use and care of the environment, or the nature of marriage). But surely it is a responsibility of pastors to teach on *some* of these specific policies in ways that go beyond the mere statement, "You all have a responsibility to vote intelligently."

After all, who else is going to teach these Christians about *exactly how* the Bible applies to specific political issues? Would pastors think it right to leave their congregations with such vague guidance in other areas of life? Would we say, "You have a responsibility to bring up your children according to Christian principles," and then never explain to them what those Christian principles are? Would we think it right to say to people in the business world, "You have a responsibility to work in the business world according to Christian principles," and then never give them any details about what these Christian principles are? No, the responsibility of pastors is to give wise biblical teaching, *explaining exactly how the teachings of the Bible apply to various specific situations in life*, and that should certainly include instruction about some policy matters in government and politics. (That is what I am attempting to do in the remainder of this book.)

D. HISTORICAL EXAMPLES OF CHRISTIAN INFLUENCE ON SECULAR GOVERNMENTS

An examination of the history of the Christian church throughout almost two thousand years shows an amazing pattern of positive influence on secular governments. We must readily admit that the church made some mistakes, sometimes very harmful ones, especially as it forgot Jesus' teaching about the distinction between "the things that are Caesar's" and "the things that are God's" (Matt. 22:21). When it forgot this distinction, the church too often fell into the mistake of wrong view #1 that I mentioned earlier, the "government should compel religion" view (see pp. 23–29). But in spite of these mistakes, there are many examples of excellent results that came from significant Christian influence on governments.

As I mentioned in some detail in the previous chapter (see pp. 49–51), the Christian church throughout history has been largely responsible for persuading governments to place much greater value on individual human rights, individual freedom, freedom of religion, equality before the law, and separation of church and state. Significant Christian influence can be traced in the Magna Carta, the US Declaration of Independence, and the US Constitution. Moreover, Christian influence led to the abolition of evils such as abortion, infanticide, gladiatorial contests, human sacrifice, polygamy, the burning alive of widows, and slavery, as well as the granting of property rights, voting rights, and other protections to women.

The biblical teaching that all human beings are created in the image of God and therefore have equal status before God had a significant influence on the thinking of the Founding Fathers of the United States and their bold declaration that "all men are created equal." This stood in clear contrast to the prior assumption in many European nations that there was a special group of human beings known as "royalty" who had the hereditary right to rule over ordinary people. In many nations, this conviction of the equality of all people led to the spread of democracy and, even in nations that preserved a monarchy, this conviction led to the limitation of the role of the monarch to mostly ceremonial and symbolic functions, and to a role of leadership by example for promoting a nation's exemplary behavioral standards and the best of its cultural heritage (for example, in the United Kingdom or in Norway, both of which still have a monarchy).

In the twentieth century, the Christian convictions of Martin Luther King Jr. had a significant influence in the outlawing of racial segregation and discrimination in the United States. More recently, tens of thousands of committed Christians have formed the backbone of the pro-life movement that continues to work for the prohibition of abortion (except to save the life of the mother) in the United States.

Many more examples could be given, but these should be sufficient to demonstrate that the entire history of the Christian church gives significant support to show that there should be "significant Christian influence" on governments and that this influence brings beneficial results to a nation.

Here is a common objection to my position: When I talk about "significant Christian influence" on government, some people are quick to raise the issue of Prohibition in America, which was a period from 1920 to 1933 in which a constitutional amendment outlawed making or selling alcoholic beverages in the United States. People explain that this was a failure, and from that they conclude, "You can't legislate morality."

But I think the example of Prohibition proves something else entirely and actually supports my position. The history is this: In 1919, the United States adopted the Eighteenth Amendment to the Constitution (effective Jan. 16, 1920), which prohibited "the manufacture, sale, or transportation of intoxicating liquors … for beverage purposes." But this law was widely disobeyed, and many people had their own breweries and distilleries. The law was impossible to enforce effectively. Finally, in 1933, the Twenty-first Amendment to the Constitution was passed, which said "the 18th Article of Amendment to the Constitution of the United States is hereby repealed." (However, it allowed for states to regulate alcohol usage and sale according to their own laws.)

What does this experience prove? It proves that it is impossible to enforce moral standards on a population *when those moral standards are more strict than the standards found in the Bible itself.* Although the Bible contains frequent warnings against drunkenness (see Eph. 5:18), it does not prohibit moderate use of alcoholic beverages, and the apostle Paul even tells his associate Timothy, "No longer drink only water, but use a little wine for the sake of your stomach and your frequent ailments" (1 Tim. 5:23). Therefore the absolute prohibition on alcoholic beverages was a law that did not find an echo in the hearts of people generally, because it did not reflect the moral standards of God that he has written on all people's hearts (see Rom. 2:15).

I do not think, therefore, that Prohibition in the United States was an experiment in attempting to enforce biblical standards of conduct on the nation. I think it was an experiment that proved the impossibility of trying to enforce standards that went beyond what the Bible required. And I think Prohibition was rightly repealed.

E. IS THE UNITED STATES A CHRISTIAN NATION?

When I begin to explain that I think there should be "significant Christian influence" on government, sometimes people ask me if I think the United States is "a Christian nation."

The question cannot be answered with a simple "yes" or "no" until we define more carefully what we mean by "a Christian nation." That is one reason why people sometimes become so upset about this question—different people have different meanings in mind for the phrase "a Christian nation," and therefore they can end up talking about different things but using the same words and just misunderstanding one another.

Here are several meanings one can attach to the phrase "a Christian nation," together with an answer to the question that varies according to each meaning:

(1) *Is Christian teaching the primary religious system that influenced the founding of the United States?* Yes, it is.

(2) *Were the majority of the Founding Fathers of the United States Christians who generally believed in the truth of the Bible?* Yes, they were.

(3) *Is Christianity (of various sorts) the largest religion in the United States?* Yes, it is.

(4) *Did Christian beliefs provide the intellectual background that led to many of the cultural values still held by Americans today?* (These would include things such as respect for the individual, protection of individual rights, respect for personal freedom, the value of hard work, the need for a strong national defense, the need to show care for the poor and weak, the value of generosity, the value of giving aid to other nations, and respect for the rule of law.) Yes, Christian beliefs have provided much of the intellectual background for many of these and other cultural values.

(5) *Was there a Supreme Court decision at one time that affirmed that the United States is a Christian nation?* Yes, there was, but that wasn't the issue that was under dispute in the case. It was in an 1892 decision, *Church of the Holy Trinity v. the United States*, 143 US 457 (1892). The ruling established that a church had the right to hire a minister from a foreign nation (England), and thus the church was not in violation of an 1885 law that had prohibited hiring "foreigners and aliens ... to perform labor in the United States." The court's argument was that there was so much evidence showing the dominant

"Christian" character of this nation that Congress could not have intended to prohibit churches from hiring Christian ministers from other countries.

It seems to me that here the Supreme Court was arguing that the United States is a "Christian nation" according to meanings (3) and (4) above. There is a long history of significant Christian influence on the United States.

(6) *Are a majority of people in the United States Bible-believing, evangelical, born-again Christians?* No, I do not think they are. Estimates range from 18 to 42% of the US population who are evangelical Christians, and I suspect a number around 20% is probably more nearly correct. In a 2005 poll, Gallup, after doing a survey designed to find how many Americans had true evangelical beliefs, came up with a figure of 22%.[6] In addition, there are many conservative Roman Catholics who take the Bible plus the official teachings of the Catholic Church as a guide for life, and a significant number of them have a personal trust in Jesus Christ as their Savior. But even if these groups are added together, it does not constitute a majority of people in the United States.

(7) *Is belief in Christian values the dominant perspective promoted by the United States government, the media, and universities in the United States today?* No, it is not.

(8) *Does the United States government promote Christianity as the national religion?* No, it does not.

(9) *Does a person have to profess Christian faith in order to become a US citizen or to have equal rights under the law in the United States?* No, certainly not. This has never been true. In fact, the Constitution itself explicitly prohibits any religious test for public office:

> No religious test shall ever be required as a qualification to any office or public trust under the United States (Article VI, section 3).

In conclusion, how can we answer the question, "Is the United States a Christian nation?" It all depends on what someone means by "a Christian nation." In five possible meanings, the answer is yes. In four other possible meanings, the answer is no. Because there are that many possible meanings in people's minds (and possibly more that I have not thought of), I do not think the question is very helpful in current political conversations. It just leads to arguments, misunderstanding, and confusion. The same points that a speaker wants to make with this claim can be made more clearly, without causing confusion, in terms of one or more of the expanded meanings that I have listed above.

F. WHAT ABOUT OLD TESTAMENT LAWS? (THE QUESTION OF THEONOMY)

There is a view among a few Christians in the United States today called "Theonomy." It is also called "Christian Reconstructionism" and sometimes "Dominion Theology."

---

6. Albert L. Winseman, "U.S. Evangelicals: How Many Walk the Walk?" *Gallup.com* (May 31, 2005). www.gallup.com/poll/16519/US-Evangelicals-How-Many-Walk-Walk.aspx.

Critics have labeled it "Dominionism" (which has echoes of "Jihadism"). I will use the term "Theonomy," which is the general term used in theological critiques of this movement.

Theonomists argue that the Old Testament laws that God gave to Israel in the Mosaic covenant should be the pattern for civil laws in nations today. This would include carrying out the death penalty for such things as blasphemy or adultery or homosexual conduct!

The error of Theonomists is that they misunderstand the unique place that these laws for Israel had in the history of the whole Bible, and they misunderstand the New Testament teaching of the distinction between the realm of the church and the realm of the state that Jesus established when he said, "Render to Caesar the things that are Caesar's, and to God the things that are God's" (Matt. 22:21). (See further discussion of the unique status of the Mosaic laws in chap. 3, pp. 83–85.)

The primary defenders of Theonomy have been Rousas John Rushdoony (1916–2001)[7] and Greg Bahnsen (1948–1995).[8] Critiques of Theonomy have been written by Vern Poythress[9] and John Frame.[10]

Some secular critics of Christian influence on politics and government have attempted to claim that *evangelical Christians generally* seek to follow Theonomy or "Dominion Theology," and they accuse Christians of wanting to enforce these extreme Theonomist views in the United States: see Michelle Goldberg, *Kingdom Coming: The Rise of Christian Nationalism.*[11] But these accusations are based on careless scholarship and guilt by association. I am aware of no Christian today who has significant influence in the evangelical world or the political world who holds to the small minority viewpoints of Theonomy or Christian Reconstructionism regarding modern civil government enforcement of such Old Testament laws.

G. SHOULD CHRISTIANS ONLY VOTE FOR CHRISTIAN CANDIDATES?

When I speak about "significant Christian influence" on government, I want to be very clear that *I do not mean that Christians should only vote for Christian candidates for office,* or even that Christians should generally prefer an evangelical candidate over others who are running.

To take one example, President Jimmy Carter was a Southern Baptist who taught a Sunday school class at his home church in Georgia, and media reports made much of Carter's profession of faith as a "born-again" Christian. But many politically conservative evangelical Christians decided to vote for Ronald Reagan in 1980 instead of Carter, based on differences with President Carter's policies (regarding national defense and economic policy, for example). (Reagan also professed Christian faith, but he was not so publicly identified as an evangelical Christian as Carter was.)

---

7. Rousas John Rushdoony, *The Institutes of Biblical Law* (Phillipsburg, NJ: Presbyterian & Reformed, 1973).

8. Greg Bahnsen, *Theonomy in Christian Ethics* (Nutley, NJ: Craig Press, 1979).

9. Vern Poythress, *The Shadow of Christ in the Law of Moses* (Phillipsburg, NJ: P & R Publishing, 1991), 311–61.

10. John Frame, *The Doctrine of the Christian Life* (Phillipsburg, NJ: P & R Publishing, 2008), especially 217–24, 957–76.

11. Michelle Goldberg, *Kingdom Coming: The Rise of Christian Nationalism* (New York: W. W. Norton, 2007).

To take another example, I personally wrote an endorsement for Mitt Romney, a Mormon candidate, during the Republican presidential primary campaign in 2007. I did this because I agreed with Romney's policies, especially on economics and national defense, more than with those of other candidates, even Mike Huckabee, a Southern Baptist candidate who is a winsome, articulate representative of evangelical Christian faith. I strongly differed with Romney's theological beliefs but agreed with his political views and thought him to be well qualified. Here is what I wrote:

What about his religion? Romney is a Mormon, and I strongly disagree with a significant number of Mormon *theological beliefs*, which I find to be inconsistent with the Bible and with historic Christian teachings. But many Mormon teachings on *ethics and values* are similar to those in the Bible, and those teachings support Romney's conservative political values.

Can evangelicals support a candidate who is politically conservative but not an evangelical Christian? Yes, certainly. In fact, it would demonstrate the falsehood of the liberal accusation that evangelicals are just trying to make this a "Christian nation" and only want evangelical Christians in office. For evangelicals to support a Mormon candidate would be similar to supporting a conservative Jewish candidate—someone we don't consider a Christian but who comes from a religious tradition that believes in absolute moral values very similar to those that Christians learn from the Bible. Here in Arizona a few years ago I voted for Matt Salmon, a Mormon candidate for governor. He lost, but his policies would have been much more conservative than those of Janet Napolitano, who has now vetoed dozens of pro-life, pro-family bills.

Or have we come to the point where evangelicals will only vote for people they consider Christians? I hope not, for nothing in the Bible says that people have to be born again Christians before they can be governmental authorities who are used greatly by God to advance his purposes. God used Pharaoh, King of Egypt, to raise Joseph to a position of authority over the whole country, so he could save his people from famine (Genesis 41:37–57). God used Nebuchadnezzar, King of Babylon, to protect and raise up Daniel and his Jewish friends to positions of high authority over Babylon (Daniel 2:46–49). God used Cyrus, King of Persia, to restore the Jewish exiles to their homeland (Isaiah 45:16; Ezra 1:1–4), and used Darius, King of Persia, to protect the Jewish people as they rebuilt the temple in Jerusalem (Ezra 6:1–12). God used Ahasuerus, King of Persia, to raise up Esther as Queen and to give Mordecai high authority and honor in his kingdom (Esther 6:10–11; 8:1–2, 7–15). In the New Testament age, God used the peace enforced by the secular Roman Empire, the *Pax Romana*, to enable the early Christians to travel freely and spread the Gospel throughout the Mediterranean world.

Here in the United States, God used not only Founding Fathers who were strong Christians, but also Deists such as Benjamin Franklin and Thomas Jefferson, to build the foundation of our nation. Jefferson even became our third President in 1801, a demonstration of the wisdom of Article 6 of the

Constitution, which says, "no religious test shall ever be required as a qualification to any office or public trust under the United States."

The Bible tells us to pray not just for Christians who happen to have government offices, but *"for kings and all who are in high positions, that we may lead a peaceful and quiet life, godly and dignified in every way"* (1 Timothy 2:2). It is not just Christians in government but all governing authorities who are "instituted by God" (Romans 13:1) and whom Paul can call "God's servant for your good" (Romans 13:4).[12]

Looking back now from the perspective of two years, though I still have great appreciation and respect for Romney, I can see that when I wrote that endorsement of Romney I did not realize how deep the anti-Mormon sentiment was among evangelical Christians, especially in the South, so that Romney did not carry even the evangelical vote in states such as South Carolina, placing fourth in the primary there with only 15% of the vote.[13] And the political reality is that a Republican candidate who cannot carry the evangelical vote in the South simply cannot win the presidency. In addition, the health care system that Romney successfully advocated in Massachusetts costs far more than was predicted and has lost much of its initial appeal. Therefore I do not know if I would support Romney or some other candidate in the future.

But the principle remains: I think Christians should support the candidate who best represents moral and political values consistent with biblical teaching, no matter what his or her religious background or convictions.

H. WITHOUT CHRISTIAN INFLUENCE, GOVERNMENTS WILL HAVE NO CLEAR MORAL COMPASS

Try to imagine what a nation and its government would be like *if all Christian influence on government were suddenly removed.* Imagine what it would be like if all the churches and all the Christians in a society stopped seeking to have any kind of influence on laws or on government. What would such a government and such a society look like?

Within a few years very few people would have any moral absolutes beyond their individual moral sentiments and moral intuitions, which can be so unreliable. Most people would have no moral authority beyond that of individual human opinion. Therefore, how could a nation find any moral guidance?

Consider how many political issues that now face the United States (and that face other nations) have significant moral components to them. For example, here are some of the issues:

(a) *War:* Is it right to use military power to protect one's own nation against aggressors from without? Or is it right to use military power to help a weaker nation defend itself against a much stronger aggressor?

12. Wayne Grudem, "Why Evangelicals Should Support Mitt Romney," at *Townhall.com* (Oct. 18, 2007).

13. Results: South Carolina. www.cnn.com/ELECTION/2008/primaries/results/state/#SC.

(b) *Same-sex "marriage":* Should state governments or a national government give the privileges and benefits of marriage to couples of the same sex? Should a society, through its laws, give its approval and encouragement to such relationships?

(c) *Abortion:* Is abortion the murder of another human being, and if so, should governments enact laws against abortion?

(d) *Pornography:* What is pornography, and what should governments do about it? Should there be any restrictions on materials available in public libraries or available to children?

(e) *Poverty:* What is the government's responsibility to the poor in a society? What are the best solutions to poverty? Should government money be given to religious organizations that help the poor?

(f) *Care for the environment:* What government regulations should be enacted to protect the environment? Is "untouched nature" the ideal, or does God want us to "subdue" the earth in some ways? Is there anything wrong with nature as it now exists?

(g) *Capital punishment:* Does God authorize or require civil governments to carry out the death penalty? Should retribution be part of the purpose of the punishment that is imposed by the courts?

(h) *Education:* Who has the primary responsibility to decide what children are taught in public schools? Should it be the parents? Or should it be agencies appointed by the local or national government?

(i) *Moral standards:* What moral standards should be taught in public schools? Or should none be taught to children?

There are many other issues like these, but this list should be sufficient to demonstrate that the United States at the present time (as well as many other nations) has a tremendous need for moral guidance. I am convinced that there is a great need for Christians to study and discuss and then speak publicly about these issues.

But if pastors and church members say, "I'll let somebody else speak about that," where will a nation's moral standards come from?

To put it another way, *if Christians do not speak publicly about moral and ethical issues facing a nation, who will? Where will people learn about ethics? Where will a nation learn how to tell right from wrong?* Perhaps from Hollywood movies? From their friends at work or at the local bar? From their professional counselors? From their elementary school teachers? But where do *these* people learn about right and wrong?

The simple fact is that if Christians do not speak publicly about what the Bible teaches regarding issues of right and wrong, there aren't many other good sources for finding any transcendent source of ethics, any source outside of ourselves and our own subjective feelings and consciences.

This is a matter of utmost importance for any nation: *If Christians are silent about such moral and ethical issues, then where will moral standards come from?*

As Christians, we need to remember that the entire world is locked in a tremendous spiritual battle. There are demonic forces, forces of Satan, that seek to oppose God's purposes and bring evil and destruction to every human being that God created in his own image. They are seeking to bring destruction to every human society and every nation. "We know that we are from God, and the whole world lies in the power of the evil one" (1 John 5:19).

Therefore if pastors and church members say, "I'm going to be silent about the moral and ethical issues that we face as a nation," that will leave a moral vacuum, and it will not be long until the ultimate adversaries of the Gospel—Satan and his demons—will rush in and influence every decision in a way contrary to biblical standards. And if that happens, then governments around the world will increasingly use their tremendous power to silence the church. Governments will in effect say to Christians and to churches, "Keep your homophobic, misogynist, oppressive, fear-inducing, intolerant, militarist, hate-mongering Christianity out of our lives, and out of our schools, and off our college campuses, and off our radio and TV stations, and out of any part of government, and out of our quiet suburbs where you are never going to get permission to build any more churches; and keep your hate-mongering Christian religion locked up in the privacy of your own home!"

That is where moral standards will come from if Christians remain silent.

(I read the previous paragraph aloud in a graduate classroom where I was discussing these things, and one seminary student immediately responded, "Isn't that too alarmist? Surely people aren't going to use that kind of inflammatory language in opposing Christians!" Then someone else in the class who had been involved for several years in attempting to bring Christian influence on civil government immediately responded, "That sounds exactly like the emails I receive on a regular basis." Recently, when a student at Los Angeles City College gave a speech about his Christian faith and his support for marriage as the union between one man and one woman, his professor stopped the speech and told the student, before the entire class, that he was a "fascist bastard." He then refused to grade the speech, telling the student, "Ask God what your grade is." When the student complained to the dean, the professor tried to have him expelled from the school.)[14]

For several reasons, then, I am convinced that it is right for Christians to seek to bring "significant Christian influence" to bear on civil governments. It is right for Christians to speak publicly and say, "This is what the Bible says about the purpose of government," and "This is what the Bible says about moral standards for human conduct."

When that happens, sometimes other Christians will answer, "No, I understand the teachings of the Bible to have a different view on the question of war" (or laws concerning abortion or same-sex marriage, etc.). And then a healthy discussion will follow, which is an excellent thing in a free society. Eventually a growing consensus will emerge among evangelical Christians, sometimes rather quickly and sometimes over a period of time. Then others in the society, who may or may not be Christians, will have to decide

---

14. Complaint filed in *Lopez v. Candaele*, U.S. District Court for the Central District of California, February 11, 2009. See www.alliancedefensefund.org/UserDocs/LopezComplaint.pdf.

whether they think such a Christian position (for example, regarding the protection of preborn children) is persuasive or not.

This kind of dialogue is healthful in a free society. Christians may not be able to persuade a majority of the society in every case—they will no doubt win some arguments and lose others. But over the course of time, the "significant Christian influence" view will eventually result in many positive changes in societies and governments. It has always been that way, and Christian influence has led to wonderful changes such as the abolition of slavery, the emphasis on universal literacy, universal education, laws that protected children and protected people working in factories, and laws that protected women from abuse.

To repeat the main point one more time: This kind of "significant Christian influence" on government is not (1) compulsion, it is not (2) silence, it is not (3) withdrawal from government, it is not (4) doing evangelism only, and it is not (5) trusting the government for salvation. It is simply being faithful to the biblical teaching on how Christians should have a positive influence on civil government.

I. THE RESPONSIBILITY OF PASTORS TO TEACH ON POLITICAL ISSUES

At this point some pastors reading this material might think, "Okay, I can see the need for *some* Christians to speak out publicly in these things, especially those who feel God calling them to be involved in the political process. But that doesn't mean that I'm actually going to *preach* about such issues from the pulpit! That would be too controversial, and, in addition, I know that I have both Democrats and Republicans in my congregation and I just don't want to alienate any of them! Preaching on politics is just too divisive!"

Here is my response:

1. I appreciate such a pastor's recognition that God calls people to different tasks in the overall work of his kingdom. I think God calls some people to be involved *heavily* in the political process, perhaps even running for office. He calls others to *moderate* political involvement, such as devoting time to writing and campaigning for various issues and candidates. He calls still others to form parachurch organizations, which have much more freedom than churches to devote most of their effort (if they wish) to certain political issues (such as pro-life and pro-marriage stands).

God calls still others to *minimal* political involvement because he wants them instead to sing in a church choir, help sponsor a youth group, teach a Sunday school class, or lead a home fellowship group, and so forth. We need to recognize that God calls people to give themselves to a wide variety of ministries as Christians. (See 1 Corinthians 12:12–31, where Paul compares the different gifts of people in the church to the different parts of the human body such as the hand or the foot or the eye or the ear, all of which have different functions but all of which are essential to the proper functioning of the body.) Christians who give a lot of time to politics and Christians who give little time to politics need to respect and be thankful for each other's gifts and callings. We can all do good in different areas of life.

2. But I still believe that pastors have a special responsibility to preach and teach from God's Word on at least *some* issues affecting laws and government and politics. After all, these topics are a part of the teaching of God's Word.

I realize that some of these topics are "controversial." I want to emphasize that *pastors will need much wisdom* to distinguish between political topics where they can say, "There is a clear biblical position on this issue" (for example, protecting the lives of preborn children) and other topics where they should wisely say, "I realize that Christians may legitimately have differences of viewpoint on this issue" (for example, leading evangelicals a few years ago differed publicly over whether the United States should grant China "most favored nation" trading status). There will also be some topics where a pastor says, "We should all agree on the *goal* (for example, helping the poor), but we have freedom to differ on *the best means to reach that goal* (such as what mix we should have of government welfare, job training programs, different tax policies, private charities, and incentives for businesses)." On still other issues, the pastor may say, "People disagree on this issue, not because they disagree about the *result* we should seek (for example, preserving an earth that is a good place for human beings to live), but because they disagree over the *relevant facts* (for example, whether human activity is contributing significantly to differences in the earth's temperature)."

Even such simple sentences from a pastor can actually help people understand the other side and place the issues in a context where further healthy dialogue can occur. And the pastor can also help the congregation talk privately about these things in ways that show respect for the other person and preserve friendships even when there are political differences. Pastors should regularly pray for God's guidance and seek counsel from their elders (or deacons, or church board) rather than simply surprising a congregation on these matters or rushing into an ill-considered and unwise sermon about a political issue.

Yet I want to emphasize this: The mere fact that something is "controversial" does not excuse pastors from the responsibility to preach about it and (sometimes) the responsibility of a church to take a stand on it. The apostle Paul did not think it enough to preach on only *some* of the teaching of God's Word. He didn't think it enough to preach on the easy topics and avoid the controversial topics. Rather, he thought he was accountable before God *to preach on everything that the Bible teaches.* When Paul met with the elders of the church in Ephesus and summarized his three-year ministry among them, he said,

> "I testify to you this day that I am innocent of the blood of all of you, *for* I did not shrink from declaring to you the whole counsel of God" (Acts 20:26–27).

Paul was saying that he had faithfully discharged his responsibility before God. He had not shrunk back from teaching on any topic simply because it was unpopular. And the word "for" in Paul's statement to these elders indicates that his blameless standing before God regarding what he taught depended on not shrinking back from unpopular topics.

If Paul had been fearful and therefore had failed to teach the church at Ephesus about biblical standards showing that adultery or premarital sex or homosexual conduct is wrong, and if young people growing up in the church had become involved in some of those sins because of Paul's failure to teach about them, then he could not have said, "I am innocent of the blood of all of you." He would have had some responsibility before God for the sin of those people—confused people that he had failed to teach.

If the teachings of the Bible about civil government and God's moral standards are part of "the whole counsel of God," then it seems clear that pastors have a responsibility to teach their churches about these things.

3. As for the question of "divisiveness," pastors will need wisdom to distinguish between clear biblical issues, where people who disagree with him simply don't agree with the Bible's teachings, and more difficult issues, where people who disagree with him simply evaluate the relevant facts and Bible teachings differently.

I can think of two recent examples. In November 2008, Arizona had a ballot measure that would amend the state constitution to say that marriage may only be between one man and one woman. Our pastor, from the pulpit, explained the issue briefly and told the people, "You should vote for this amendment." If someone had disagreed on that, it would probably have been because the person disagreed about the biblical definition of marriage. I don't think that kind of disagreement should make a pastor think he had preached something that was wrong.

On the other hand, there are topics where a pastor should not take a public position. For example, a current issue in the Untied States concerns what rate of interest the Federal Reserve Board should set for loaning money to banks and how that rate affects inflation, economic growth, and the exchange rate of the dollar against foreign currencies. The issue mostly turns on the results that will come from different policies, not on any teaching of Scripture. I surely don't think a pastor should advocate a particular interest rate from the pulpit!

Good judgment is required for each issue along with an ability to distinguish between the clear teachings of Scripture and disputed areas of relevant, present-day facts. On some issues the correct application of Scripture may not be very clear, and the pastor may decide not to preach on that issue at all.

In all cases, however, the decisive question should not be, "Will people disagree with me?" but rather, "What does Scripture teach, and how can I faithfully teach that to my congregation?" The question is faithfulness to God and his Word, not simply avoiding divisions in the church at all costs.

4. Pastors need to avoid placing excessive emphasis on politics. Christians come to church with hearts that are hungry for worship and fellowship and spiritual nourishment. They need to hear the pastor teach on "the whole counsel of God" (Acts 20:27). That should include some sermons about the Bible and key political issues, but it has to include the teachings of the rest of the Bible as well! If a pastor feels that God is calling him to devote most of his professional time to political matters, then he should consider working for a Christian parachurch organization that focuses exclusively on politics and let somebody else serve the church as its pastor.

J. THE OBLIGATIONS OF ALL CHRISTIAN CITIZENS

1. The obligation to be informed and to vote

I believe that every Christian citizen who lives in a democracy has at the very least a minimal obligation to be well-informed and to vote for candidates and policies that are most consistent with biblical principles. The opportunity to help select the kind of government we will have is a *stewardship* that God entrusts to citizens in a democracy, a stewardship that we should not neglect or fail to appreciate. That at least means that Christians are responsible to learn enough about the important issues to be able to vote intelligently.

One good way to become better informed is to discuss some key political issues in a church small group. A helpful new resource for this, including quotations of key Bible passages, statements from well-known political leaders of the past and present, and questions for discussion, is a book by Hugh Hewitt, *The Good and Faithful Servant: A Small Group Study on Politics and Government for Christians.*[15]

2. Is there an obligation to do more than vote?

Beyond this, I ask every Christian in the United States to consider whether he or she has a higher obligation than merely voting. (A similar question could be asked of Christians in other countries.) The question is whether someone thinks it is morally right *to receive great benefits from a nation but to give almost nothing in return.* The great freedoms that citizens have in the United States came only as a result of great sacrifice on the part of millions of others. The original signers of the Declaration of Independence knew that they were publicly declaring themselves to be guilty of treason against Britain, and they knew they would be subject to the death penalty and to confiscation of their property if the British caught them or defeated them.[16] Nor could they have any great confidence that they would win a war against the most powerful nation on earth at that time. Therefore the last line in the Declaration of Independence says this:

> And for the support of this declaration, with a firm reliance on the protection of divine Providence, we mutually pledge to each other our lives, our fortunes, and our sacred honor.[17]

Independence from Britain did not come cheaply. In the War of Independence, approximately 4,500 Americans died. Later wars were even more costly. In the Civil War, although the nation was preserved as a Union, 550,000 Americans died. Approximately 116,000 died in World War I, 405,000 in World War II, 36,000 in the Korean War, and 58,000 in the Vietnam War. Just over 4,000 died in the Iraq War, and more than 550

15. Hugh Hewitt, *The Good and Faithful Servant: A Small Group Study on Politics and Government for Christians* (Nashville: Townhall Press, 2009).

16. Pauline Maier, *American Scripture: Making the Declaration of Independence* (New York: Alfred A. Knopf, 1998), 59, 118, 125, 147, 152.

17. Declaration of Independence, adopted July 4, 1776. www.archives.gov/national_archives_experience/charters/declaration_transcript.html.

in the Afghanistan War (up to mid-2008).[18] Many others, equal to or more than those killed, were wounded in those wars.

These hundreds of thousands of men (and many women as well) *sacrificed their lives* to protect their nation and preserve the freedoms we enjoy today. *Is it right that we simply enjoy these freedoms while giving back to our nation nothing in return?* Should we not rather give heed to the challenge with which Abraham Lincoln ended his Gettysburg Address in 1863, as he surveyed the battlefield on which more than 6,650 soldiers had died and more than 29,000 were wounded?[19] His challenge in light of their sacrifice was this:

> It is rather for us to be here dedicated to the great task remaining before us—that from these honored dead we take increased devotion to that cause for which they gave the last full measure of devotion—that we here highly resolve that these dead shall not have died in vain—that this nation, under God, shall have a new birth of freedom—and that government of the people, by the people, and for the people, shall not perish from the earth.[20]

If so many have given *their very lives* to protect and preserve our nation, then do the rest of us who receive such great benefits from these sacrifices not have an obligation to do something more than merely voting? Should we not participate at least at some level in giving money or giving time to support specific candidates and issues? Or writing letters or helping to distribute literature? Or even running for office or volunteering to serve in the military? Is it not right that all of us at least do *something* more than merely voting to preserve and protect this nation?

K. CHURCHES AND THE INTERNAL REVENUE SERVICE (IRS) GUIDELINES

In the Unites States, since 1954 the Internal Revenue Service has had regulations that prohibit pastors or churches from explicitly saying that they support or oppose any candidates by name (though they are still allowed to take positions on moral issues that are part of an election campaign). I discuss this policy below (see pp. 509–12), and I also discuss a recent initiative designed to challenge the IRS policy as an unconstitutional violation of freedom of speech and freedom of religion.

But however that controversy is resolved, pastors in the United States today can easily teach on the moral issues that are at stake in any election without naming any specific candidate or even naming any political party, but simply saying that "Party A (or Candidate A) holds this view," and "Party B (or Candidate B) holds this view" and leaving it to the congregation to read and discover which party holds which view.[21]

---

18. "Fact Sheet: America's Wars," Department of Veterans Affairs (Nov. 2008). www1.va.gov/opa/fact/amwars.asp.

19. See http://gburginfo.brinkster.net/Casualties.htm.

20. Gettysburg Address, delivered by Abraham Lincoln, November 19, 1863.

21. For one example of a sermon that I preached just prior to the 2004 presidential election, discussing six issues but not mentioning the name of any candidate or the name of any political party, see "The Bible and the Election (2004)" at www.phoenixseminary.edu/, under Wayne Grudem—Publications.

L. CONCLUSION

For many reasons, then, it seems apparent that pastors have some responsibility to preach and teach about the significant moral issues that are at stake in each election. They should use wisdom (and seek the wisdom of their elders or church board) in deciding which issues are addressed by the moral teachings of Scripture and by the teachings of Scripture on civil government, and then they should faithfully instruct their congregations in these issues.

In addition, individual Christians have at least an obligation to be well-informed and to vote intelligently. And I believe that Christians should also seriously consider whether God is calling them to do more—perhaps to sacrifice a significant portion of their time, effort, or money to help influence the government of the nation for good.

Chapter **3**

BIBLICAL PRINCIPLES CONCERNING GOVERNMENT

Before we can examine specific political questions in light of the teachings of the Bible, it is necessary to study what the entire Bible teaches about civil government. Where did the idea of government come from? What should be the purpose of government? How should governments be chosen? What kind of government is best? What are the responsibilities of governmental rulers?

These are the kinds of questions that I seek to answer in this chapter. The first several sections show that God himself established civil government to bring multiple benefits to human societies. The sections after that show the limitations on governments and some specific values that governments should promote.

A. GOVERNMENTS SHOULD PUNISH EVIL AND ENCOURAGE GOOD

1. The Old Testament foundation

a. Genesis 9:5–6

The first indication of God's establishment of civil government in human society is found in the early history of Genesis, just after the flood, when Noah and his family came out of the ark. At this point God says that he will require payment ("a reckoning") for the crime of murder, and that he requires this to be carried out by other human beings:

And for your lifeblood I will require a reckoning: from every beast I will require it and from man. From his fellow man *I will require a reckoning* for the life of man.

"Whoever sheds the blood of man,
by man shall his blood be shed,
for God made man in his own image" (Gen. 9:5–6).

Here God indicates that the crime of murder (expressed by the biblical image of "shedding blood") would be repaid by the forfeiture of the criminal's own life: "by man shall his blood be shed." (See further discussion of this passage on pp. 186–88.)

No further details are given here regarding civil government. But in speaking these words to Noah, God establishes the obligation to carry out the most severe punishment (the taking of a human life) in retribution for the most horrible crime (the murder of another human being). *Once this principle is established*, then the imposition of *lesser* penalties for *lesser* crimes is also validated, since if a government has the right to carry out the most severe kind of punishment, then it certainly has the right to carry out lesser punishments for lesser crimes as well. (For example, various kinds of punishments were established for the government of the people of Israel in the laws found in Exodus to Deuteronomy.)

This command given to Noah is significant for our purposes in the twenty-first century because that event took place long before the establishment of the people of Israel as descendants of Abraham (beginning in Genesis 12) or the establishment of the nation of Israel as a distinct nation (beginning with the exodus from Egypt in Exodus 12:33–42, the crossing of the Red Sea in Exodus 14, and the assembly of the nation at Mount Sinai in Exodus 19–20). The commands to Noah in Genesis 9 were given *at the beginning of the reestablishment of human society* after God destroyed all but Noah's family in the waters of the flood. Therefore careful biblical interpretation would not limit the principles in Genesis 9:5–6 to the time of the Old Testament only or to the nation of Israel only, for neither limitation is supported by the context in which these statements are found. These principles have relevance for the whole human race for all time.

b. Anarchy is a highly destructive evil

Another section of the Old Testament reinforces this need for government to restrain evil, for it shows that when there is no government, or the government is so weak that it cannot enforce its laws, there are terribly destructive results. The stories in Judges 18–25 include some of the most horrible sins recorded anywhere in the Bible. These passages teach us the dreadful results of *anarchy*, a situation when there is no effective government at all, for "in those days there was no king in Israel. Everyone did what was right in his own eyes" (Judg. 17:6; cf. 18:1; 19:1; 21:25).

This tragic narrative in Judges shows in gruesome detail why civil government is so badly needed among sinful human beings. Where there is no ruler, sinful people make up their own morality and soon begin to do terrible things to one another. If there is no governmental authority to stop evil people, evil simply increases.

c. Governments should execute justice and defend the weak

Another way of speaking about punishing evil and rewarding good is to speak of "enforcing justice," where "justice" means ruling according to the just standards of God's laws. If a king executes justice, he brings punishment against those who have done wrong and protects and rewards those who have done right.

In the book of Psalms, one psalm says it this way when it shows God speaking to earthly rulers:

> How long will you judge unjustly and show partiality to the wicked?... *Give justice to the weak and the fatherless*; maintain the right of the afflicted and the destitute. Rescue the weak and the needy; deliver them from the hand of the wicked (Ps. 82:2–4).

This statement emphasizes that (1) rulers must judge with fairness and righteousness, and not "show partiality" but judge only according to the law and the facts in the case; (2) they must pay special attention to defending "the weak and the fatherless" and by implication others who have little power to defend themselves; and (3) they are to use their power to stop "the wicked" from harming others, particularly those who are "weak" and "needy."

A similar passage in Daniel teaches the same thing, for Daniel's counsel to King Nebuchadnezzar is that God wants him to practice "righteousness" and to show "mercy to the oppressed" (Dan. 4:27).

d. Governments should execute swift punishment as a deterrent to crime

A passage in Ecclesiastes reinforces the importance of civil punishment in restraining evil in society:

> Because the sentence against an evil deed is not executed speedily, the heart of the children of man is fully set to do evil (Eccl. 8:11).

2. Similar New Testament teaching

a. Romans 13:1–7

The New Testament supplements and reinforces what we found in Genesis 9 about the authority to punish evil. The longest passage is in Romans 13:1–7:

> Let every person be subject to the governing authorities. For *there is no authority except from God, and those that exist have been instituted by God.* Therefore whoever resists the authorities resists what God has appointed, and those who resist will incur judgment. For rulers are not a terror to good conduct, but to bad. Would you have no fear of the one who is in authority? Then do what is good, and you will receive his approval, for *he is God's servant for your good.* But if you do wrong, be afraid, for he does not bear the sword in vain. For *he is the servant of God, an avenger who carries out God's wrath on the wrongdoer.* Therefore one must be in subjection, not only to avoid God's wrath but also for the sake of

conscience. For the same reason you also pay taxes, for the authorities are ministers of God, attending to this very thing. Pay to all what is owed to them: taxes to whom taxes are owed, revenue to whom revenue is owed, respect to whom respect is owed, honor to whom honor is owed.

This passage tells us several things about government:

(1) God has appointed the authorities who have governmental power (vv. 1–2). This idea is also supported by Jesus' statement to Pilate, "You would have no authority over me at all unless it had been given you from above" (John 19:11).

(2) Civil rulers are a "terror to bad conduct" (cf. v. 3), which means they restrain evil by the threat of punishment for wrongdoing. This is consistent with what is taught in Genesis 9:5–6.

(3) They give "approval" or praise (Greek *epainos*, "approval, recognition, praise") to those who do what is good (v. 3). In addition, the ruler "is God's servant for your good." These verses indicate that government has a role in promoting the common good of a society. It should not only punish wrongdoing but also encourage and reward good conduct, conduct that contributes to the good of society.

Some examples of government supporting the common good would include tax-supported playgrounds and parks where families can picnic and sports teams can practice and compete. This responsibility to promote what is good would also provide a justification for giving tax-free status to churches on the understanding that churches generally are good for a society and promote the well-being of citizens. The same principle would also provide support for government promoting marriage through certain legal privileges and economic benefits.

(4) Governmental officials serve God. Paul says that the ruler "is *God's servant* for your good" and that "he is *the servant of God*" (v. 4). He also says "the authorities are *ministers of God*" (v. 6).

This means that we should think of government officials as serving God when they punish evil and promote what is good, whether or not they realize it. This is a strong passage in support of the idea that we should view civil government as a gift from God, something that brings us great benefits. Although individual people and individual governments can do evil, *the institution of civil government* in itself is something very good, a benefit that flows to us from God's infinite wisdom and love.

(5) Government officials are doing "good" as they carry out their work. Paul says the official is God's servant "for your *good*" (v. 4). This means that, in general, we should view the activities of government when it rewards good and punishes evil as something that is "good" according to God's Word. This is an additional reason to give thanks to God for civil government.

But this does not mean that we should think of *everything* that a ruler does as good! John the Baptist rebuked Herod "for all the *evil things* that Herod had done" (Luke 3:19). Daniel told Nebuchadnezzar, "Break off your *sins* by practicing righteousness" (Dan. 4:27). Old Testament history contains many stories of kings who "did what was evil in the sight of the LORD" (1 Kings 11:6 et al.). Therefore we should say that governmental rulers do "good" when they carry out their responsibilities in a just and fair way, following God's principles for government.

(6) Government authorities execute God's wrath on wrongdoers and thereby carry out a task of *retribution*. This is explicit in Paul's statement that the ruler "does not bear the sword in vain," but as "the servant of God" he functions as "an *avenger* who carries out God's wrath on the wrongdoer" (v. 4). The Greek word translated "avenger" is *ekdikos*, meaning "agent of punishment." This idea is reinforced by the other uses of this word (as in 1 Thess. 4:6) and the related verb *ekdikeō* ("inflict appropriate penalty for wrong done, punish, take vengeance for," as in Rev. 6:10; 19:2) as well as the related noun *ekdikēsis* ("vengeance, punishment," as in Acts 7:24; Rom. 12:19; 2 Thess. 1:8; Heb. 10:30).

This indicates that the purpose of civil punishment is *not only to prevent further wrongdoing*, but also *to carry out God's wrath on wrongdoing*, and that this will include bringing actual *punishment*—that is, some kind of pain or hardship to the wrongdoer, a punishment that is appropriate to the crime committed. That is why Paul can say that the government authority is "an avenger *who carries out God's wrath* on the wrongdoer" (v. 4).

This is significant especially in connection with Romans 12:19, which is only three verses before Paul's discussion of civil government beginning in Romans 13:1. (In the Greek text as Paul wrote it, there were no chapter or verse divisions, so this verse is very close to what we now refer to as Romans 13.) Paul says this:

> Beloved, *never avenge yourselves*, but *leave it to the wrath of God*, for it is written, "Vengeance is mine, I will repay," says the Lord (Rom. 12:19).

While Paul tells Christians not to take *personal vengeance* when wrong has been done to them, he tells them they should rather allow the wrongdoer to be punished by "the wrath of God." Then just a few sentences later (in Rom. 13:4) he explains that "God's wrath" against wrongdoers is carried out by civil government when it inflicts punishment on them. This means that it is often right for Christians to turn to the civil government to ask for justice to be done when they have suffered wrong at the hands of others. The civil government, in this life, is the means that God has established to carry out justice in such cases.

b. 1 Peter 2:13–14

Peter has a similar view of the role of government in his epistle:

> Be subject for the Lord's sake to every human institution, whether it be to the emperor as supreme, or to the governors as sent by him to punish those who do evil and to praise those who do good. (1 Peter 2:13–14)

Peter, like Paul, begins with a command to "be subject" to human institutions such as the emperor or governors. He also says that they are to restrain bad conduct and give praise and encouragement to good conduct, for they are "to *punish those who do evil* and to *praise those who do good*" (v. 14). The idea of the government being established by God is not made explicit, but it is hinted at when Peter says that Christians are to be subject "for the Lord's sake" to every human institution (v. 13). And Peter explicitly includes the idea of retribution against wrongdoers when he says that governors are sent "to punish those who do evil." ("Punish" is the Greek noun *ekdikēsis,* related to *ekdikos,* as we saw in Romans 13:4.) And the idea that they should "praise those who do good" gives additional support to the goal of promoting the common good of society.

c. What about "turning the other cheek" as in Matthew 5:39?

Some Christians today strongly object to the idea that government should punish wrongdoers. They say government should instead try to correct the *causes* that led a person to commit a crime—blaming the society much more than the person who did the wrong. Such people will often appeal to Jesus' statement in Matthew 5:39:

> "But I say to you, Do not resist the one who is evil. But if anyone slaps you on the right cheek, turn to him the other also."

Does this prohibit even government from executing punishment on wrongdoers? Not if it is rightly understood.

This "turn the other cheek" verse should be understood within its proper context. Here Jesus is not talking about the *responsibilities of government,* but is giving principles for *individual personal conduct.* In addition, in this section of Matthew Jesus is not giving absolute requirements that must be followed in every instance, but is rather giving specific, concrete *illustrations* of what personal conduct will often look like in the life of a Christian.

To take another example, it would be disobedient to the rest of Scripture to obey in every situation the command that comes just three verse later, "Give to the one who begs from you, and do not refuse the one who would borrow from you" (Matt. 5:42). If that were an absolute requirement, then any one beggar could bankrupt any Christian simply by repeatedly asking for more and more! But the Bible *also* requires Christians to be good stewards of their resources. (See Luke 16:10, "One who is faithful in a very little is also faithful in much," and 1 Corinthians 4:2, "It is required of stewards that they be found trustworthy;" and the parable of the talents in Matthew 25:14–30.)

For these reasons, therefore, Jesus' command to turn the other cheek is not a persuasive argument against governmental use of force or retributive punishment on wrongdoers, which are responsibilities of government that are explicitly taught in several other passages of Scripture.

d. There would be civil governments even in a sinless world

Is government only required because there is evil in the world? No, I do not think that conclusion follows. Even if there were no evil in the world, I think there would still be some need for government. This would include doing things that *promote the common good* of society, such as (in a modern society at least) the building and regulation of roads, the establishment of standard weights and measures, the maintenance of public records, the establishment of laws for safety (such as speed limits and standards for building materials), the standardization of electrical power, and the establishment of a certain currency to be used as money for legal exchange within a nation. Such activities promote the common good. They would fall in the category of what the US Constitution calls "promote the general welfare."

B. WHAT ABOUT THE DETAILED LAWS FOR ISRAEL GIVEN IN EXODUS–DEUTERONOMY?

If it is true that governments are responsible before God to punish evil and encourage good, then should we not look to the extensive laws that God gave to the nation of Israel in the Old Testament to find out in more detail how governments are to function?

We cannot do this directly, and we can only do it with much difficulty, because of the special place those laws occupy in the scope of the whole Bible. Here is an overview of why that creates a problem for interpreters today:

The Old Testament books of Exodus, Leviticus, Numbers, and Deuteronomy record many laws that God gave specifically for the nation of Israel. These laws belong to what is called the "Mosaic covenant" because God gave the laws to Moses and Moses gave them to the people. (A "covenant" in the Bible is a legally defined relationship between God and his people, and the laws of the Mosaic covenant defined that relationship from the time of Moses onward.) Understanding exactly how *Israel's* laws might possibly be relevant to *secular civil governments today* is one of the most complex questions in biblical interpretation, for several reasons:

(1) *The place of Israel*: Proper interpretation of Israel's laws requires a mature understanding of the place of the nation of Israel in the history of the Bible and God's purposes for Israel in the history of the world.

(2) *Israel as a theocracy*: Proper interpretation of Israel's laws also requires a realization that Israel was unique because it was to be for God "a kingdom of priests and a holy nation" (Exod. 19:6). It was a *theocracy* ruled by God himself, and therefore *the laws of Israel governed the religious life of God's people* (such as their sacrifices and festivals, and their worship of the one true God) as well as matters that ordinarily belong to all civil governments in all ages of history.

(3) *God's end-time judgment breaking into current history*: Proper interpretation of Israel's laws requires an understanding of some unusual examples of God's judgment suddenly "breaking in" to human history. In fact, even before the establishment of Israel as a nation, there were some examples of God's judgment suddenly breaking into history to bring swift retribution to extreme human sinfulness. The story of the flood and Noah's ark (Gen. 6–9) is one example of such judgment. The story of Sodom and Gomorrah (see Gen. 19:24–28), in which God destroyed theses cities with sulfur and fire from heaven, is another. And the story of the destruction of the cities of Canaan by the people of Israel is still another example, a unique event carried out under God's direction (see Deut. 20:16–18; contrast vv. 10–15, where such a war of divine judgment was forbidden in other cases). This war of the conquest and destruction of Canaan was carried out at the specific command of God and was part of his plan for establishing his people in the land he had promised to them. It also foreshadowed God's ultimate final judgment on the whole earth. But it should never provide the pattern for civil governments to imitate today. It was historically unique.

(4) *Extensive application of the death penalty*: Proper interpretation of Israel's laws requires understanding of another unique aspect of the laws of Israel, namely, the

imposition of the death penalty, not only for murder (as in Gen. 9:5–6), but also for promoting a false religion (see Exod. 22:18, 20; Lev. 20:22; Deut. 13:6–17), for rebellion against family authority (see Exod. 21:15, 17; Deut. 21:18–21), and for sexual sin (see Lev. 20:10–14). These and other examples of the death penalty were part of Israel's identity as a "holy nation" (Exod. 19:6) before God, but that does not mean that nations today, which do not exist as theocracies or as "holy nations" before God, should ever attempt to follow these examples. In fact, the Old Testament historical narrative shows that such severe laws and penalties could not create a truly holy people, because the laws did not change people's hearts (see Jer. 31–33; Rom. 8:3–4; Gal. 3:21–24). Such severe penalties for religious infractions, family rebellion, and sexual sin should not be used as a pattern for governments today.

(5) *Conclusion*: If these distinctions are kept in mind, the laws that God gave to Israel can still provide useful information for understanding the purposes of government and the nature of good and bad government. In the following chapters, I will seek to use that material thoughtfully with just such attention to the unique historical context in which it occurs. And we must still remember that, by comparison with the laws and customs of the surrounding nations of the ancient near east, the laws that God gave to Israel were an amazing model of how justice, fairness, compassion for the poor and oppressed, and genuine holiness of life can work out in daily life. In fact, Moses said to the people of Israel, "And what great nation is there, that has statutes and rules so righteous as all this law that I set before you today?" (Deut. 4:8).[1]

Although the specific provisions of the Mosaic law in Exodus–Deuteronomy were intended to apply directly only to Israel at that time, some other sections of the Old Testament are not addressed specifically to the Jewish people but speak in general terms about governments and kings. For example, the book of Proverbs alone has thirty-two verses that mention a king. Psalms and Ecclesiastes add more. These verses give additional wisdom about civil government that we will use at specific points in subsequent chapters.

But what about the Sabbath command? When I talk about "Christian influence on government," sometimes people ask whether governments today should enforce the command against working on the Sabbath that is found in the Ten Commandments in Exodus:

> "Remember the Sabbath day, to keep it holy. Six days you shall labor, and do all your work, but the seventh day is a Sabbath to the LORD your God. On it you shall not do any work ..." (Exod. 20:8–10).

Christians have had honest differences over the application of this commandment for several hundred years. Some think it is a requirement that Christians should still observe today, and they believe it would be sinning against God to work on Sunday. My own viewpoint, however, is that the Sabbath commandment is different from the other

---

1. For further discussion see Christopher Wright, *Old Testament Ethics for the People of God* (Downers Grove, IL: InterVarsity Press, 2004); Walter C. Kaiser, *Toward Old Testament Ethics* (Grand Rapids: Zondervan, 1991); Gordon Wenham, *Story as Torah: Reading Old Testament Narrative Ethically* (Grand Rapids: Baker, 2000).

nine commandments in that it was *a summary of all the ceremonial laws* that God gave to Israel, including the Sabbath year, the Jubilee year, and all the sacrifices and offerings that the people of Israel were required to make to God. Consider these teachings of Paul:

> Therefore let no one pass judgment on you in questions of food and drink, or with regard to a festival or a new moon *or a Sabbath.* These are a shadow of the things to come, but the substance belongs to Christ (Col. 2:16–17).

> You observe *days* and months and seasons and years! I am afraid I may have labored over you in vain (Gal. 4:10–11).

Therefore, my own conclusion is that the Sabbath requirement to refrain from work was a "ceremonial law" like the laws about animal sacrifices that we no longer have to obey. Therefore I would not be in favor of having government laws requiring that businesses stay closed on Sunday.

Does this mean that I think people should work seven days a week? No. God's wisdom and love regarding his people were reflected in his generous gift of one day in seven when the people of Israel did not have to work in Old Testament times. So it seems to me to be *a wise practice* if Christians in this New Testament age set up a pattern of life in which they also refrain from work one day in seven. (Perhaps this will be Sunday, but for pastors and others who work on Sunday, it could be another day of the week.) It is wise for employers to give workers some days off from work as well, at least one day in seven (and often two, since other personal "work" often takes up a whole day). But this is a question of biblically informed human wisdom, not a matter of sinning or not sinning or an absolute rule that can never be broken.

Other Christians disagree with me on this and hold that God still requires them not to work on Sunday, ever. I respect their courage and faith, and I realize that their convictions have led some of them to keep their businesses closed on Sundays. (In the United States, Chick-Fil-A and Hobby Lobby are two large retail sales companies that are closed on Sundays, for example.) But I do not think that every Christian is required to do this, nor would I support laws requiring Sunday closing of all retail businesses (as there used to be in many parts of the United States).

Probably regarding a similar issue, the apostle Paul writes this in the letter to the Romans:

> One person esteems one day as better than another, while another esteems all days alike. Each one should be fully convinced in his own mind (Rom. 14:5–6).

C. GOD IS SOVEREIGN OVER ALL NATIONS, AND ALL PEOPLE ARE ACCOUNTABLE TO HIM

The extensive sections of prophecies to pagan nations in several of the Old Testament prophets show that God also holds unbelieving nations accountable for their actions (see Isa. 13–23; Jer. 46–51; Ezek. 25–32; Amos 1–2; Obadiah—written to Edom; Jonah—sent to Nineveh; Nahum—written to Nineveh; Hab. 2; Zeph. 2).

A number of other passages teach God's sovereignty over the selection and establishment of governmental rulers. Through Moses, God said to Pharaoh, "For this purpose *I have raised you up*, to show you my power, so that my name may be proclaimed in all the earth" (Exod. 9:16).

God also predicts, through Isaiah, the establishment of Cyrus, king of Persia, about 150 years before his life:

> Who says of Cyrus, "He is my shepherd, and he shall fulfill all my purpose."...
> Thus says the LORD to his anointed, to Cyrus, whose right hand I have grasped, to subdue nations before him ... (Isa. 44:28–45:1).[2]

The idea of God's appointment of rulers is expressed in a general way in Psalm 75:

> For not from the east or from the west and not from the wilderness comes lifting up, but it is God who executes judgment, putting down one and lifting up another (vv. 6–7).

Daniel also affirms this about God: "he removes kings and sets up kings" (Dan. 2:21), and "the Most High rules the kingdom of men and gives it to whom he will" (Dan. 4:25; see also vv. 17, 32).

D. GOVERNMENTS SHOULD SERVE THE PEOPLE AND SEEK THE GOOD OF THE PEOPLE, NOT THE RULERS

If the civil government is to be "God's servant for your good" (Rom. 13:4), then government exists for the good of the people, not for the good of the king or the emperor or the president. In the Old Testament, Samuel illustrated this principle well during his service as judge. At the end of his judgeship, he said to the people of Israel,

> "Here I am; testify against me before the LORD and before his anointed. Whose ox have I taken? Or whose donkey have I taken? Or whom have I defrauded? Whom have I oppressed? Or from whose hand have I taken a bribe to blind my eyes with it? Testify against me and I will restore it to you."
>
> They said, "You have not defrauded us or pressed us or taken anything from any man's hand" (1 Sam. 12:3–4).

In contrast to his own conduct as judge, Samuel warned the people that a king would abuse his power and take from the people for the benefit of himself and his family:

> "These will be the ways of the king who will reign over you: he will *take* your sons and appoint them to his chariots and to be his horsemen and to run before his chariots ... and some to plow his ground and to reap his harvest.... He will

---

2. When Isaiah prophesied (about 740–681 BC), the Assyrian empire was dominant in the Ancient Near East. But Assyria was defeated by forces of the Babylonian empire in 612 BC. Then Babylon fell to the Persians in 539 BC. Cyrus became king of Persia in 538 BC. Therefore Isaiah, under the inspiration of God, predicted Cyrus by name, a ruler who would come after two empires and about 150 years after Isaiah prophesied.

take your daughters to be perfumers and cooks and bakers. He will *take* the best of your fields and vineyards and olive orchards and give them to his servants. He will *take* the tenth of your grain and of your vineyards.... He will *take* your male servants and female servants.... He will *take* the tenth of your flocks, and you shall be his slaves" (1 Sam. 8:11–17).

This use of government power for self enrichment of the leader and his family and friends betrays the fundamental purpose of government to serve the people. It is repeatedly condemned in the Old Testament (see Deut. 16:19; Ps. 26:10; Prov. 15:27; 17:23; Isa. 33:15; Ezek. 22:12; Amos 5:12; Hab. 1:2–4).

Sadly, the more unchecked power a government has, and the less public accountability it has to the people, the more likely a ruler is to forget this principle and to "take" more and more to himself, just as Samuel warned that the king would do.

A tragic example of such abuse of power was seen in the life of Omar Bongo, who ruled the African nation of Gabon for forty-one years. When he died in 2009, the *Daily Telegraph* of London reported that Bongo "considered everything inside [Gabon] to be his personal property and elevated corruption to a method of government." Taking for himself a large share of Gabon's oil wealth, he "owned 33 properties in Paris and Nice," and an additional £86 million [$138 million] were in accounts in New York, and "these discoveries were probably only the tip of the iceberg: Bongo's fortune certainly ran into the hundreds of millions of dollars and may have reached the billions."[3] Unfortunately, among countries where governments have no effective separation of powers, stories like this could be repeated many times.

E. CITIZENS SHOULD BE SUBJECT TO THE GOVERNMENT AND OBEY THE LAWS OF THE GOVERNMENT (EXCEPT IN CERTAIN CIRCUMSTANCES)

1. The general obligation to be subject to the civil government

Because God has established the government to restrain evil and do good for the nation, citizens should, in general, be subject to the government and obey its laws. Paul writes:

Let every person be subject to the governing authorities. For there is no authority except from God, and those that exist have been instituted by God. Therefore whoever resists the authorities resists what God has appointed (Rom. 13:1–2).

Similarly, Peter tells Christians, "Be subject for the Lord's sake to every human institution, whether it be to the emperor as supreme, or to governors as sent by him to punish those who do evil and to praise those who do good" (1 Peter 2:13–14).

---

3. *The Daily Telegraph* (June 9, 2009), 29.

These passages teach that people in general, and Christians in particular, have an obligation to obey the civil government.

2. When is it right to disobey the civil government?

God does not hold people responsible for obeying the civil government, however, when obedience would mean directly disobeying a command of God himself. This principle is indicated by a number of passages in the narrative sections of the Bible.

One clear example occurs in the early days of the Christian church. After Jesus had commanded the early apostles to preach the Gospel (see Matt. 28:19–20), the Jewish governing authority, the Sanhedrin, arrested some of them and commanded them "not to speak or teach at all in the name of Jesus" (Acts 4:18). But the apostles Peter and John answered, "We cannot but speak of what we have seen and heard" (Acts 4:20), and later Peter proclaimed, "We must obey God rather than men" (5:29). This is a clear affirmation of the principle that *God requires his people to disobey the civil government if obedience would mean directly disobeying God.*

Other passages also establish this. In Daniel 3:13–27, King Nebuchadnezzar commanded three Jewish men—Shadrach, Meshach, and Abednego—to bow down and worship a golden statue that he had erected. But they refused and said, "We will not serve your gods or worship the golden image that you have set up" (v. 18). God showed his approval of their actions by rescuing them from the burning fiery furnace (vv. 19–30).

When Pharaoh commanded the Egyptian midwives to put newborn Hebrew baby boys to death, they disobeyed, and God approved of their disobedience (see Exod. 1:17, 21). When it was against the law for anyone to come into the presence of King Ahasuerus without being invited, Esther disobeyed the law and risked her own life to save her people, the Jews (see Esth. 4:16). Daniel, likewise, disobeyed a law that prohibited him from praying to God (see Dan. 6:10). In addition, when Herod the king had commanded the wise men to return and tell him where the newborn king of the Jews was to be found, they were warned by an angel not to obey this command, so they disobeyed King Herod and "departed to their own country by another way" (see Matt. 2:8, 12).

3. Is it ever right to attempt to overthrow the existing government or obtain freedom from an existing government?

Sometimes people raise the question of whether it was right for the early American colonies to declare their independence from Great Britain. Was this not showing a failure to be subject to the governing authorities, and was this not therefore an act of disobedience to God's command in Romans 13?

Some Christian writers have argued for this position. For instance, John MacArthur argues that rebelling against the British government and declaring independence was "contrary to the clear teachings and commands of Romans 13:1–7." Therefore, MacArthur says, "The United States was actually born out of a violation of New Testament principles, and any blessings that God has bestowed on America have come in spite of that disobedience by the Founding Fathers."[4]

At the time of the American Revolution, a number of Christians agreed with the position that MacArthur states here. Some left the American colonies and returned to England to be subject to the British crown rather than participate in the American Revolution.

But I disagree with this viewpoint. I am convinced, after studying the historical situation and the principles of Scripture, that the American Revolution was morally justified in the sight of God.

The reason that a number of early Americans thought it was justified to rebel against the British monarchy is that *it is morally right for a lower government official to protect the citizens in his care from a higher official* who is committing crimes against these citizens.

This thinking in Protestant circles goes back as far as John Calvin. In his *Institutes of the Christian Religion* (1559) he argued as follows about "magistrates" (lower government officials):

> If there are now any magistrates of the people, appointed to restrain the willfulness of kings ... if they wink at kings who violently fall upon and assault the lowly common folk, I declare that ... they dishonestly betray the freedom of the people, of which they know that they have been appointed protectors by God's ordinance.[5]

Other Lutheran and Reformed thinkers made similar statements, and the right to rebel against tyrants is also found in the words of Roman Catholic philosopher Thomas Aquinas (c. 1225–74) and many other Christian writers. According to Greg Forster, a scholar with expertise in the history of governmental theory, one common argument among Christian writers was that a tyrannical "government" is "not really a government at all but a criminal gang masquerading as a government, and is therefore not entitled to the obedience that governments (properly so called) can claim."[6] Another argument was that "the principle of the rule of law ... implies the right to rebellion."[7]

Therefore the leaders who founded the United States and declared its independence thought of themselves as doing something that was *morally right and even necessary, for they were protecting those citizens in their care from the evil attacks of King George III of England*, who had repeatedly acted as a "tyrant." Those citizens needed protection from King George just as much as they would need protection from a thief or murderer who would attack people from within the country, and just as much as they would need protection from a hostile army that would invade it from another country.

The Declaration of Independence in fact contains a long statement of grievances against England that made it "necessary for one people to dissolve the political bands which connect them with another." They wrote that they had patiently endured much suffering, seeking other solutions:

4. John MacArthur, *Why Government Can't Save You: An Alternative to Political Activism* (Nashville: Word, 2000), 6–7.

5. John Calvin, *Institutes of the Christian Religion*, 4.20.31.

6. Greg Forster, personal email to me, Jan. 21, 2010.

7. Ibid.

> Prudence, indeed, would dictate that governments long established should not be changed for light and transient causes; and accordingly all experience has shown that mankind are more disposed to suffer, while evils are sufferable, than to right themselves by abolishing the forms to which they are accustomed.

But then the Declaration's signers essentially said that they could suffer the abuses of the king no longer:

> But when a long train of abuses and usurpations, pursuing invariably the same object, evinces a design to reduce them under absolute despotism, it is their right, it is their duty, to throw off such government, and to provide new guards for their future security.... The history of the present King of Great Britain is a history of repeated injuries and usurpations, all having in direct object the establishment of an absolute tyranny over these states. To prove this, let facts be submitted to a candid world.

What follows is a long and detailed list of the intolerable abuses of government power that the king of England had inflicted on the colonies of the United States.

Then the signers concluded the Declaration with the indication that they were not doing this as isolated individuals, but as

> Representatives of the United States of America, in General Congress, assembled, appealing to the Supreme Judge of the world for the rectitude of our intentions.

Finally, these representatives of the various states declared,

> That these United Colonies are, and of right ought to be free and independent states; that they are absolved from all allegiance to the British Crown, and that all political connection between them and the state of Great Britain is, and ought to be, totally dissolved.... And for the support of this Declaration, with a firm reliance on the protection of Divine Providence, we mutually pledge to each other our lives, our fortunes and our sacred honor.

(See the full text of the Declaration of Independence, including the long list of grievances, in the appendix to this chapter, pp. 113–15).

Another argument for seeking to change a government or obtain freedom from an existing government is the general principle that *the Bible does not ever say that it is wrong to change an existing government*. For example, Christians who live in a democracy regularly vote to elect leaders, and sometimes they vote to elect different leaders from those currently in office. They are trying to change the government through an election. Could it ever be right to seek to change the government by other means (such as declaring one's independence, and then defending that independent status against attack)?

The Bible says that ruling officials have been "appointed" by God, but *God certainly works through human actions* to appoint *different* leaders at different times. The whole history of Israel shows how God worked again and again through many significant events to remove one king from office and establish another.

A third reason why it is sometimes right to attempt to change the existing government is that *the Bible gives some examples where God raised up leaders to deliver his people from the rule of tyrants*, such as Moses leading his people out of Egypt and out of the rule of Pharaoh (see Exod. 1–14). The book of Judges records many stories showing how foreign rulers oppressed the people of Israel but then God delivered them through judges whom he had appointed: "The LORD raised up judges, who saved them out of the hand of those who plundered them" (2:16).

In the New Testament, one author speaks of some Old Testament heroes "who through faith *conquered kingdoms*" (Heb. 11:33), which meant that by military action they overthrew governments and established other ruling powers.

Many of the Founding Fathers of the United States were aware of these biblical examples of overthrowing tyrants. In fact, Benjamin Franklin's remarkable proposal for a design of the Great Seal of the United States (which was not ultimately adopted) was this (the proposal of which still exists in Franklin's own handwriting):

> Moses standing on the Shore, and extending his Hand over the Sea, thereby causing the same to overwhelm Pharaoh who is sitting in an open Chariot, a Crown on his Head and a Sword in his Hand. Rays from a Pillar of Fire in the Clouds reaching to Moses, to express that he acts by Command of the Deity. Motto, Rebellion to Tyrants is Obedience to God.[8]

In conclusion, the Declaration of Independence, like the American War of Independence, was morally justified and was actually necessary in order to free the nation from the tyranny under which it was suffering because of King George III of England.

F. GOVERNMENTS SHOULD SAFEGUARD HUMAN LIBERTY

Liberty in a nation is of utmost importance because it allows people to have freedom to choose to obey or disobey God and to serve him or not to serve him, according to their best judgment. The Bible consistently places a high value on individual human freedom and responsibility to choose one's actions. Beginning from the origin of the human race, when he put Adam and Eve in the garden of Eden, God gave people freedom of choice (see Gen. 2:16–17). Such freedom to choose is one of the highest manifestations of excellence in the human beings that God has created, and it is one of the ways in which mankind is more like God than any of the animals or plants that God has made.

1. Biblical arguments for human liberty

Several arguments from the Bible support the idea that governments should protect human liberty. The first consideration is the fact that *slavery and oppression are*

---

8. Cited from www.greatseal.com/committees/firstcomm/ (accessed Nov. 13, 2009).

always viewed negatively in Scripture, while *freedom is viewed positively*. When God gives the Ten Commandments to the people of Israel, he begins by saying, "I am the LORD your God, who brought you out of the land of Egypt, *out of the house of slavery*" (Exod. 20:2).

When the people of Israel turned against the Lord, he gave them into the hand of oppressors who enslaved them and took away their freedom (see Deut. 28:28–29, 33; Judg. 2:16–23). Loss of freedom was a judgment, not a blessing.

That is why one blessing promised by the Messianic prophecy in Isaiah 61 is that a deliverer would come who would free the people from such oppression by their enemies, for he would come "to proclaim liberty to the captives" (Isa. 61:1).

Individual liberty was also prized, for although people in Israel would sometimes sell themselves into slavery as a solution to severe poverty, the Jubilee year would come once every fifty years to set free those who had been thus enslaved:

> And you shall consecrate the fiftieth year, and *proclaim liberty throughout the land to all its inhabitants*. It shall be a jubilee for you, when each of you shall return to his property and each of you shall return to his clan (Lev. 25:10).

Freedom of individual choice is viewed favorably again and again in Scripture. It is a component of full human personhood and is ultimately a reflection of God's own attribute of "will," his ability to approve and bring about various actions as he pleases. Therefore we have not only God's testing of Adam and Eve in the garden of Eden, but also statements such as this:

> I have set before you life and death, blessing and curse. Therefore *choose* life, that you and your offspring may live (Deut. 30:19).

> "*Choose* this day whom you will serve" (Josh. 24:15).

> "*Come to me*, all who labor and are heavy laden, and I will give you rest" (Matt. 11:28).

> The Spirit and the Bride say, "*Come*." And let the one who hears say, "*Come*." And let the one who is thirsty come; let the one who desires take the water of life without price (Rev. 22:17).

Throughout the Bible, from the beginning of Genesis to the last chapter of Revelation, God honors and protects human freedom and human choice. Liberty is an essential component of our humanity. Any government that significantly denies people's liberty exerts a terribly dehumanizing influence on its people.

2. Governments should protect human liberty

Therefore God is pleased when governments protect basic human liberties and thereby allow people much freedom to decide how to use their time and their resources, according to what they think is best. Such liberty in any nation will lead to incredible diversity of choices in schooling, occupations, friendships and associations, religious beliefs, charitable activities, use of money, use of time, recreational activities, music, art, and thousands of other things. Freedom in a society allows people to decide what they want to do from among many good uses of their time and resources. Many people will devote their free time to caring for other family members or members of the community, or helping to coach children's sport teams, or doing volunteer work in a church or on a mission trip, or helping a relief agency, or doing volunteer work at a hospital or a school, or pouring time into starting and growing a new business, or pursuing hundreds upon hundreds of other worthwhile activities. A government that maximizes human freedom (while still punishing evildoers) will often find that its citizens do an amazing amount of good for others and for the world.

What human freedoms should be protected by civil government? The basic freedoms protected in the US Constitution are freedom of religion, freedom of speech, freedom of the press, freedom of assembly, and freedom to petition the government (see First Amendment to the Constitution). Other freedoms mentioned in the Bill of Rights are "the right of the people to keep and bear arms" (Second Amednment), "the right of the people to be secure in their persons, houses, papers, and effects, against unreason-able searches and seizure" (Fourth Amendment), freedom from self-incrimination in court, and a guarantee not to be "deprived of life, liberty, or property, without due process of law" (Fifth Amendment). Later, the Thirteenth Amendment in 1865 guaranteed freedom from "slavery" and "involuntary servitude."[9]

This requirement to protect human liberty implies that citizens and governments should agree to restrictions on human freedom only reluctantly and only where there is a significant need to do so. Totalitarian governments that control all aspects of life (as in several modern-day Muslim countries or in modern-day North Korea) are contrary to the Bible's emphasis on the high value of human liberty. In the Untied States, the slavery (or "involuntary servitude") that was allowed in some states until the Emancipation Proclamation of 1863 was another kind of wrongful denial of human liberty to those who were enslaved (see 1 Tim. 1:10 in the ESV, where "enslavers" are listed among vari-ous kinds of sinners before God).

In founding the United States, the authors of the Declaration of Independence understood the importance of liberty, for they affirmed at the outset not only that "all men are created equal" but also "that they are endowed by their Creator with certain unalienable rights, that among these are life, *liberty*, and the pursuit of happiness." The unalienable right to "liberty" was listed right next to the unalienable right to "life." The next sentence declared that it was the purpose of government to protect these rights such as life and liberty: "That *to secure these rights*, governments are instituted among men, deriving their just powers from the consent of the governed." Protecting human liberty was seen as one of the most important and most basic of all the functions of government.

---

9. "The Thirteenth Amendment: The Abolition of Slavery." See www.law.umkc.edu/faculty/projects/ftrials/conlaw/thir-teenthamendment.html.

3. How much restriction of liberty is necessary?

While liberty is to be highly valued, it cannot be an absolute right in light of other biblical teachings about the role of government. Government of necessity sometimes infringes on people's "liberty" to do wrong, as when it prohibits murder and thus infringes on someone's "liberty" to murder another person. Governmental regulation of speed limits on highways necessarily limits a person's "liberty" to drive at whatever speed he wants—but most people think this is appropriate because of the need to protect the life and welfare of others.

What worries me is that in recent years political debates show almost no awareness of the huge value of liberty and the great loss that comes when it is restricted. I agree that governments should restrict human liberty to the limited extent necessary to carry out the legitimate functions of the government, such as punishing evil and rewarding what is good. However, governments too often attempt to restrict human liberty in ways that are much more extensive and intrusive and that prohibit not only the doing of things that are clearly evil, but also doing things that are morally neutral or good but not favored by the government.

I do not have space here to discuss exactly how much government regulation is necessary or wise in multiple situations (see later chapters), but it is important to note here that *every incremental increase in governmental regulation of life is also an incremental removal of some measure of human liberty.* When small losses of liberty occur again and again over a period of years, people can become essentially slaves to a government without ever realizing what is happening.

Here are some small examples: If my local government would prohibit grocery stores from providing plastic bags, as San Francisco did in 2007, it would force me to use paper bags.[10] This deprives me of my liberty to choose which kind of bag I want. But I cannot carry nearly as many paper bags as plastic bags from the car to the house, because the paper bags break and tear more easily. Therefore every trip to the grocery store will now require some additional trips between the car and the house, an incremental loss of human liberty for every citizen. The paper bags also take more storage room and don't work as well for certain other tasks, so there is another small loss of liberty. Perhaps some people think this insignificant, and perhaps others think there is an environmental benefit that comes from avoiding plastic bags, and that is worth the price of depriving the citizens a small amount of liberty in this way. I do not. But my point is simply to note that my freedom to use my time as I wish has been eroded a bit, and no one seems to notice that this has happened.

Almost all of the really fun playground equipment that I loved as a boy growing up in Jim Falls, Wisconsin, has disappeared from playgrounds across America. There are much fewer merry-go-rounds or teeter-totters or high slides or high swings. Because of the threat of bankrupting lawsuits (and the lack of laws that place commonsense limitations

---

10. Charlie Goodyear, "S.F.: First City to Ban Plastic Shopping Bags," *San Francisco Chronicle* (March 28, 2007). www. sfgate.com/cgi-bin/article.cgi?file=/c/a/2007/03/28/MNG-DROT5QN1.DTL.

on liability and damages for injuries), everything is padded and "safe," and children are growing fat and timid and lazy, and they have lost the excitement of that great adventure of testing your courage and strength and balance and endurance against the playground equipment and against everyone else playing on it. Because of our nation's failure to have some commonsense legal reforms, our children have lost much of their freedom (and health!), and nobody seems to notice or care.[11]

Another loss of freedom happens with the longer time spent in security lines at airports—and hence the need to allow at least thirty minutes more check-in time than one did before the bombings of 9/11. I personally think such security measures are an unfortunate necessity, and they are a small price to pay for freedom from terrorist bombs, but the fact remains that a measure of liberty has been lost.

Government-compelled sorting of waste into various kinds of recyclable trash, to be put out on a separate day from other trash, is another erosion of liberty in people's use of time. (Is it worthwhile? Perhaps some is, I don't know—the calculations are complex, especially because there are other alternatives, with good results. My only point is that at least the discussion must recognize not only that the cost is monetary but that mandatory recycling also includes a *very real cost* in loss of human liberty, one small bit at a time.) Recently the US government required that all incandescent light bulbs (that fully light instantly) have to be discontinued by 2014.[12] We have started to switch to cheaper energy-efficient bulbs, but when I walk in to the closet or the kitchen pantry and turn on the light, it now takes several seconds until the room is fully lighted. So I wait, and another tiny bit of my liberty has been eroded—liberty to choose the kind of light bulb I prefer for each room, and liberty to use those few seconds of time as I wish. Another incremental loss of human liberty, right in my own home.

By far the largest loss of liberty by government action is through taxation, for if I have to pay an additional $100 in taxes, then (a) I have lost the freedom to decide for myself how I want to spend that $100, and (b) I have to work that much longer simply to have the same amount of money to spend before I had to pay the tax. Therefore every additional tax dollar collected from me takes away one more small amount of my freedom as well as (often) one more small amount of my time, which is one more small amount of my life. These "small amounts" can become enormous, so that people in some countries work over half of their time just to pay taxes to the government! They have become like medieval serfs, bound not to the feudal lord but to the national government, living half their lives in servitude.[13] Taxes have robbed them of huge portions of their lives. Incremental loss of our human liberty is incremental loss of our lives.

---

11. Manhattan lawyer Philip K. Howard documents dozens of examples of mindless government laws and regulations that incrementally diminish people's ability to live freely and enjoy their lives: see his book *The Death of Common Sense* (New York: Random House, 1994). Reprinted by permission

12. Paul Davidson, "It's Lights Out for Traditional Light Bulbs,"

USA Today (Dec. 16, 2007). www.usatoday.com/money/industries/energy/environment/2007–12–16-light-bulbs_N.htm.

13. For a classic description of how freedom is lost incrementally to government, see F. A. Hayek, *The Road to Serfdom*, Fiftieth Anniversary Edition (Chicago: University of Chicago Press, 1994).

G. GOVERNMENT CANNOT SAVE PEOPLE OR FUNDAMENTALLY CHANGE HUMAN HEARTS

1. Personal salvation is a work of God, not government

It is important to remember that there are tasks that government cannot do, tasks that God has entrusted to the church and to the Holy Spirit working through the Bible, which is the Word of God.

The civil government—even a very good one—cannot save people from their sins, for that can come about only through personal faith in Jesus Christ. "For by grace you have been saved through faith. And this is not your own doing; it is the gift of God, not the result of works, so that no one may boast" (Eph. 2:8–9). It is only God who can promise, "I will give you a new heart, and a new spirit I will put within you" (Ezek. 36:26). It is God who can say, "I will put my laws into their minds, and write them on their hearts, and I will be their God, and they shall be my people" (Heb. 8:10).

Therefore Christians should never place their ultimate hope in any government for changing human hearts or making a nation of sinful people into a nation of holy and righteous people before God. That is the work of God alone, and it is carried out through the church as it proclaims the Gospel of Jesus Christ and as people personally put their trust in Christ and find that "If anyone is in Christ, he is a new creation. The old has passed away; behold, the new has come" (2 Cor. 5:17).

This is important for Christians who work to influence government. We must remember that *the primary need of every society is the Gospel of Jesus Christ*, a Gospel that is made known through the church, not through the government. Jesus is "the way, and the truth, and the life" (John 14:6). The Bible says that in Christ "are hidden all the treasures of wisdom and knowledge" (Col. 2:3). Through Jesus Christ alone can people truly know God and lead lives pleasing to God.

2. Inwardly transformed people are necessary for a transformed society

Christians who seek to influence government must also remember that inwardly transformed people are needed if we are ever going to see a transformed society. Merely passing good laws and having good government will never be enough to change a society. The people of Israel in the Old Testament had good laws from God himself, but those laws did not keep people from going astray and eventually bringing God's judgment on themselves.

Therefore we must constantly remember that *winning elections is not enough to change a nation.* Christians could (in theory at least) gain enough influence to overturn the Supreme Court decision about abortion in *Roe v. Wade,* pass pro-life laws that protect the preborn, and pass defense-of-marriage laws, yet all of that will not be able to stop people from having premarital sex or getting abortions somehow or committing homosexual acts, unless there is a change of people's hearts and minds as well.

Laws work best when they govern a people who have good moral character and moral convictions. If an entire society is corrupt, laws will only be able to restrain the most egregious examples of sin and will leave the rest untouched. As John Adams, one of the principal Founding Fathers, said, "Our Constitution was made only for a moral and righteous people. It is wholly inadequate for the governance of any other."[14]

Unless a country has transformed people, it is unlikely that it will be able to pass very good laws or elect very good leaders. No candidate can win elections campaigning on "moral values in government" if the population as a whole lacks those moral values. (Think of what elections would have been like in Sodom and Gomorrah!) Therefore it is important that the church continue in its task of proclaiming the Gospel of Jesus Christ to change people's hearts and minds one at a time. And once people become Christians, it is important to teach them about moral principles from the Bible, including not only principles of conduct for their individual lives but also principles concerning the roles and responsibilities of civil government.

Nevertheless, if we stopped at this point, we would only have part of the truth from the Bible.

3. Governments significantly influence people's moral convictions and behavior and the moral fabric of a nation

The other part of the truth is to say that governments have an immense influence on the conduct of people in a society. The psalmist knows that there are "wicked rulers" who "frame injustice by statute" (Ps. 94:20)—that is, they pass laws to enable wrongdoing! Isaiah says, "Woe to those who decree *iniquitous decrees*, and the writers who keep writing oppression" (Isa. 10:1). Another psalm implies that evil rulers can influence people toward wrongdoing, because it implies that if "the scepter of wickedness" (a symbol of authority held by wicked rulers) ever would "rest on the land allotted to the righteous," then there is much greater likelihood that the righteous would "stretch out their hands to do wrong" (Ps. 125:3). Sometimes governments can pass laws that authorize horribly evil deeds, as when Haman persuaded King Ahasuerus to sign a decree that all the people in the kingdom of Persia could "annihilate all Jews, young and old, women and children, in one day" and then "plunder their goods" (Esth. 3:13).

This is one reason why Paul encouraged Christians to pray "for kings and all who are in high positions," so that Christian believers "may lead a peaceful and quiet life, godly and dignified in every way" (1 Tim. 2:2). Once again, the implication is that *good* rulers can influence a nation toward *good* conduct, while *evil* rulers can encourage and promote all sorts of *evil* conduct among their people.

In part, the influence of government comes by *personal example*. For many generations, school children were taught about the upright and heroic moral conduct of leaders such as George Washington and Abraham Lincoln, in order that they might imitate this conduct in their own lives. (I remember such teaching in my elementary school in Wis-

14. John Adams, *The Works of John Adams, Second President of the United States*, ed. Charles Francis Adams (Boston: Little, Brown, 1854), IX:229 (Oct. 11, 1798).

consin.) By contrast, one reason the people of the United States—from both parties—felt such profound disappointment in President Bill Clinton's sexual misconduct in office was the poor example it set for adolescent children and, indeed, for all the rest of society.

Another reason that government influences conduct is that *laws have a teaching function*. For many or perhaps most of the people in a society, if the government passes laws that say something is legal, people will also think that it is morally right. If the government says that something is illegal, then many people will think that it is morally wrong. This is especially true for people who do not seek moral guidance from the Bible, but it can also be true for Christian believers.

The teaching function of law is one reason why there are still so many abortions in the United States, for example. Many people take the easy way out and reason that if the government allows something, society must think that it is morally right or at least morally permissible. So they decide to have an abortion, perhaps even going against the quiet inward voice of their conscience. But if there were laws prohibiting people from taking the lives of preborn children, then many of these same people would find that their conscience agrees with the law and would support it and think that it is right.

To take another example, my own conversations in the state of Arizona (where I live) suggest to me that the large majority of evangelical Christians there would think it perfectly natural and morally right for Christians to own a gun for purposes of self-defense in case of an emergency. But I suspect that a similarly large majority of evangelical Christians in England (where I have stayed many times for study or for teaching) would think it morally wrong for Christians to do this. I do not find this surprising, since the laws of England make it nearly impossible for private citizens to own guns, but the laws and customs in Arizona make it very easy for private citizens to do so. The laws have a teaching function, and they influence people's ideas of right and wrong.

The same considerations apply to people's attitudes about same-sex "marriage," the proper grounds for divorce, the age at which it is appropriate for children to drink alcoholic beverages (compare laws in the United States with much more liberal laws in Europe), the place of secular religious speech in public activities, and so forth. Laws have a teaching function with respect to the general population.

In addition to this, what the government considers legal or illegal affects what is taught in schools to the children in any society. Recent court actions that legalized same-sex "marriage" in Massachusetts, Iowa, and Connecticut will give added incentive for schools to teach that homosexual conduct is to be considered normal and morally right, and to attempt to silence anyone who would express the view that homosexual conduct is morally wrong.[15] This influence on the children in a society will have a profound influence on their sense of moral right and wrong and their future sexual conduct.

15. See "Federal Court Mulls Classroom Gay Subject Matter," Associated Press (Feb. 7, 2007); "First-graders attend lesbian wedding," United Press International (Oct. 11, 2008); Bob Unruh, "Judge orders 'gay' agenda taught to Christian children," *WorldNetDaily.com* (Feb. 24, 2007); Carol Innerst, "Lessons on homosexuality taking hold in U.S. schools," *Washington Times* (Nov. 25, 1997); and Diana Jean Schemo, "Lessons on homosexuality Move into the Classroom," *New York Times* (Aug. 15, 2007).

Therefore the laws and policies of a government have enormous impact on the conduct of people in a society. Christians should care about this, first, because sin destroys people's lives and Christians are commanded, "You shall love your neighbor as yourself" (Matt. 22:39), and, second, because the entire course of a nation is set by the moral conduct of its individual citizens, and "righteousness exalts a nation, but sin is a reproach to any people" (Prov. 14:34). While it is true, then, that government cannot save people or fundamentally change human hearts, whenever we say this, we must simultaneously affirm that government policy and laws do have an immense influence on a nation for good or for evil.

H. PRINCIPLES FOR A RIGHT RELATIONSHIP BETWEEN CHURCH AND STATE

As I argued in chapter 1, when Jesus said, "Render to Caesar the things that are Caesar's, and to God the things that are God's" (Matt. 22:21), he established the principle that there is one realm of activity under the authority of civil government and another realm of activity under the direct authority of God. This distinction leads us to two principles:

1. The church should not govern "the things that are Caesar's"

This principle means that *there should be no church control on the actions of civil government.* Here is a matter on which liberals and conservatives, both Democrats and Republicans, agree in the United States today.

Another support for this idea is the fact that in the New Testament there is no indication that the elders in local churches have any responsibility in local government or provincial or empire-wide government. Those governmental officials are always distinct from the elders of the New Testament churches.

In fact, at one point in his ministry, Jesus himself refused to assume any governmental role. Someone came to him asking that he decide a dispute over an inheritance, and he refused:

> Someone in the crowd said to him, "Teacher, tell my brother to divide the inheritance with me." But he said to him, "Man, who made me a judge or an arbitrator over you?" (Luke 12:13–14).

Jesus refused to take authority in a realm of civil government that had not been assigned to him.

If the church should not govern the state, this implies that various popes in the Middle Ages were wrong to attempt to assert authority over kings and emperors, or even to claim a right to select the emperor. These things came about as a result of failing to appreciate the distinction that Jesus made between "the things that are Caesar's" and "the things that are God's."

2. The civil government should not govern "the things that are God's"

This principle implies that every nation should allow freedom of religion, by which every person is free to follow whatever religion he or she chooses. The principle, it seems to me, is rightly protected in the First Amendment to the US Constitution, which says, "Congress shall make no law respecting an establishment of religion, or prohibiting the free exercise thereof."

Further support for the idea that government should not control the church (or synagogue or mosque) is found in the selection of church officers in the New Testament. The first apostles were chosen by Jesus, not by any Roman official (see Matt. 10:1–4). The early church, not any government official, chose "seven men of good repute" to oversee the distribution of food to the needy (Acts 6:3). Paul gave qualifications for elders and deacons that would have been evaluated by those within the church (see 1 Tim. 3:1–13; Titus 1:3–9). There was clearly no involvement by the civil government, neither by local officials nor by the Roman Empire, in any selection of officers in the early church.

This is because, contrary to the nation of Israel in the Old Testament, *the government of the church and the government of the state are different systems of government*, and they have authority over different groups of people, for different purposes. The civil government should not rule the church or infringe on the church's right to govern itself.

3. Civil government should support and encourage churches and bona-fide religious groups in general

While civil government should not rule over the church and should not promote any one religion above another, it is an entirely separate question to ask, should government give support to churches and to religion *in general?* One example of such support (though it is not direct support or funding) would be the granting of tax-exempt status to churches, so that churches would not pay tax on their property or on the income and contributions they receive. Another example would be government support for chaplains in the military and in US prisons.

These actions seem to me to be appropriate for government. They flow from the government's responsibility to "promote the general welfare" (in the words of the US Constitution), or to promote the good of the nation as a whole (see above, pp. 80, 86). As long as the opportunity is available for *any religious group* to take advantage of these benefits, it does not seem that the government is inappropriately favoring one religion over another.

Sadly, some segments of American society have lost sight of the idea that churches are healthy for a society and should be encouraged. An ominous trend is appearing in municipal zoning whereby it is increasingly difficult for churches to obtain zoning approval to build churches or buy buildings to use as churches in many areas.

4. The most difficult church/state questions arise when people disagree over whether something belongs to the realm of the church or to the realm of the state

Most of the really difficult questions regarding the relationship between church and state arise when there is a conflict over whether something belongs to "the things that belong to Caesar" or "the things that belong to God." In the ancient church, the civil government thought that bowing down to a statue of Caesar and swearing allegiance to him as a god was an appropriate thing for the government to require of every person. Bowing down to Caesar was something that "belonged to Caesar"! But the early Christians thought this was forcing them to commit idolatry, and they thought it was one of "the things that belong to God." Many of the early Christians died for the sake of that conviction (which I think was the right conviction—the government has no rightful authority to command anyone to worship any person or supposed god).

In the United States, it seems to me that most of these God versus Caesar disputes in hard cases have been settled correctly. For instance, Jehovah's Witnesses have traditionally objected to blood transfusions, claiming that this is a *religious* belief. But the civil government, in a number of cases, has forcibly imposed blood transfusions to save the life of a young child over the objections of Jehovah's Witness parents, reasoning that the *protection of a child's life* is not a matter of worship or church activities but is rightly the domain of civil government (and I agree).[16] In another case, a Brazilian religion in New Mexico claimed that the use of hallucinogenic tea in worship services was part of their traditional religious practice.[17] The Supreme Court (rightly, it seems to me) allowed them to continue this religious practice as an element of their worship, but when a new religious group in California claimed that its recently invented religion required them to grow and use marijuana as part of their "worship," a federal district court (again rightly, I think) prohibited this, saying that there was no historic tradition establishing this as a genuine religious belief.[18]

In still another case, Sultanna Freeman, a Muslim woman in Orlando, Florida, claimed the right to be veiled except for a thin slit for her eyes when getting her driver's license photo. She claimed this to be a "sincerely held religious belief." The state made a reasonable effort to accommodate her, saying that she could be photographed in a private setting with only women present, but she was not satisfied with this solution. Finally, the Florida Circuit Court, on June 6, 2003, ruled that if she wanted a driver's license, the state did have a "compelling interest" in requiring her to have a photo taken without a veil.[19] Once again, I think the decision was correct and the requirement of an identifiable photo for a driver's license is not among "the things that belong to God" but rather is "among the things that belong to Caesar." Freedom of religion does not release people from the obligation to obey the ordinary and morally good laws that are required of all members of a society.

I. GOVERNMENTS SHOULD ESTABLISH A STRONG AND CLEAR SEPARATION OF POWERS

Because of the presence of sin in every human heart (see below, pp. 119–22), and because of the corrupting influence of power, there should be a clear separation of powers at every

---

16. For example, see Catherine Philip, "Babies Seized after Jehovah's Witness Mother Refuses Blood for Sextuplets," *Times Online* (Feb. 23, 2007).

17. *Gonzales v. O Centro Espirita Beneficiente Uniao Do Vegetal*, United States Supreme Court, Docket No. 04–1084, Decided February 21, 2006.

18. *Kiczenski v. Ashcroft*, U.S. District Court for Eastern District of California, Decided February 24, 2006.

19. "U.S. Muslim Ordered to Lift Veil," *BBC News* (June 6, 2003).

level of civil government. The phrase "separation of powers" means that government power should be divided among several different groups or persons, not concentrated in only one person or group.

Several parts of Scripture give support to the idea of separation of powers in a governing authority. The Old Testament narratives give many examples of kings who had unchecked power and abused it. Saul repeatedly put his own interests first rather than those of the people. David misused his royal authority in his sin with Bathsheba (see 2 Sam. 11). Solomon wrongfully accumulated "700 wives, princesses, and 300 concubines. And his wives turned away his heart" (1 Kings 11:3–4). In addition, he had excessive silver and gold even though that had been prohibited (Deut. 17:17). During the divided monarchy, most kings abused their power and did evil (see 1–2 Kings; 1–2 Chronicles). Many other examples of unchecked power throughout human history confirm the idea that when power is combined with sin in the human heart, it has a corrupting influence on people and is easily misused.

The prophet Samuel warned against just this thing, saying that a king would abuse his power and "take" and "take" again and again from the people (see 1 Sam. 8:11–18).

But what is the solution that can prevent abuse of power by those in government? The best safeguard against the abuse of power is divided power, so that one person or group within a government provides "checks" on the use of power by the other group. When power is divided among several groups, then different people in different parts of government all struggle to be sure that no one part of government has too much power (because they tend to protect their own turf).

The Bible contains a number of positive examples of various kinds of divided power, reflecting the wisdom of God in protecting against the abuse of power by one person. In the Old Testament, the king had *some* checks on his power because of the existence of the offices of prophet and priest (even though the king often disregarded them). In the New Testament it is noteworthy that Jesus established not *one* apostle with authority over the church, but *twelve* apostles (see Matt. 10:1–4; Acts 1:15–26). Although Peter at first served as spokesman for the apostles (see Acts 2:14; 3:12; 15:7), James later seems to have assumed that role (see Acts 15:13; 21:18; Gal. 1:19; 2:9, 12). Moreover, the Jerusalem Council in Acts 15 made its decision not based on the authority of the apostles alone, but on a decision that "seemed good to the apostles and the elders, *with the whole church*" (Acts 15:22). Every indication of the form of government that was followed by local churches in the New Testament shows that they were not governed by a single *elder* but by plural *elders* (see Titus 1:5; James 5:14).

Separation of powers in a government can be accomplished in many ways, and different nations have adopted different structures. The example I know best is the United States, where the power of the national government is divided among three branches: the legislative (Congress), the executive (the President and everyone under his authority), and the judicial (the courts). The legislative power itself is divided between a House (with members elected every two years), and a Senate (with members elected every six years). New legislation must be passed by both houses and signed by the President.

There are other ways that power is divided in the United States. Power is allocated in portions to the national government, to the fifty state governments, and to county and local city governments, with each level retaining authority over some areas. The power of the army is under the authority of the President and a civilian Secretary of Defense (who is not a member of the armed forces but has authority over all of them). Funding for the military has to be approved by Congress. The power of the United States army is itself limited, for the army is prohibited by law from exercising civilian police functions within the United States. In addition, each of the individual states has a national guard not under the authority of the US Army or the President or any branch of the Federal Government but under the authority of the governor of that state.

Local police forces are accountable only to the city or county government for whom they work. This means that no one could take over the United States simply by assuming control of the army (as can happen in some nations), for the army has no authority over the hundreds of thousands of local police forces that answer only to the citizens in their own cities and towns.

As a further safeguard against a tyranny imposed from the top, the Founding Fathers incorporated in the Second Amendment to the Constitution "the right of the people to keep and bear arms." An armed citizenry provides an additional level of defense against a potential tyrant and provides further separation of power in a nation. (Switzerland provides another example of this principle, with its requirement that all men in the nation be armed and trained in the use of firearms.)

Another kind of separation of power has to do with the dissemination of information. For this reason the First Amendment to the Constitution also prohibits "abridging the freedom of speech, or of the press; or the right of the people peaceably to assemble, and to petition the Government, for redress of grievances." This guarantees that there will be public knowledge of the workings of government and accountability to the people. It guarantees that opposition political parties cannot be outlawed or persecuted, but must be given rights and protected. In this way, freedom of speech, freedom of the press, and freedom of assembly are essential elements in protecting against governmental abuse of power.

This principle of the separation of powers to guard against the abuse of power is at the heart of the current controversy in the United States over the nature of the Supreme Court and its decisions. The principle is that judges who *interpret* the laws should not also be the people who *make* the laws, for this would concentrate power wrongfully in one branch of government and would violate the principle of separation of powers. In my own understanding, the "activist" Supreme Court justices and judges in lower courts who create new policies and laws that have never been approved by the people or by any legislature violate this rule (see chap. 5 below for further discussion).

J. THE RULE OF LAW MUST APPLY EVEN TO THE RULERS IN A NATION

In a nation with good government, the law rules over the rulers, not the rulers over the law. This principle was established in the nation of Israel and was reinforced by the requirement that a new king was to write a copy of the Mosaic law for himself, so that he would understand it and remember to be subject to it:

> And when he sits on the throne of his kingdom, *he shall write for himself in a book a copy of this law*, approved by the Levitical priests. And it shall be with him, *and he shall read in it all the days of his life*, that he may learn to fear the LORD his God by keeping all the words of this law and these statutes, and doing them, that his heart may not be lifted up above his brothers, and that he may not turn aside from the commandment, either to the right hand or to the left, so that he may continue long in his kingdom, he and his children, in Israel (Deut. 17:18–20).

In actual practice, the principle of "rule of law" means that no king or president or prime minister would have unchecked power. The king would not be *above* the law, but would be *subject* to the law (as dramatically illustrated by Nathan the prophet when he came and rebuked King David in 2 Samuel 12 for disobeying God's laws). Other kings were also rebuked by the prophets for disobeying the words of God (such as Saul in 1 Samuel 13:13–14 and Ahab in 1 Kings 18:18). In the early church, even the apostle Peter was rebuked by Paul when he strayed from the principles of the Word of God and the teachings of Christ (see Gal. 2:11–12).

This principle that even rulers are not above the law is illustrated in the United States every time a sitting US governor or senator or representative is convicted in court for using his or her office for personal gain or for taking bribes to influence a decision.

The principle of rule of law is violated, however, whenever any person or group in a society has unchecked power and can disobey the law without fear of punishment. This is the case with dictators and their friends and family in many smaller countries, or with criminal mobs that repeatedly violate the law in Russia, or with government-supported monopolies that have unchecked power (as with the telecommunications companies controlled by Mr. Slim in Mexico),[20] or with the "checkpoints" that extort payments from trucks attempting to travel highways in Cameroon and other African countries.[21] The rule of law is also violated in countries where the government has a media monopoly and can publish lies or cover up government misconduct with no fear of consequence (as in the "trials" of many house-church leaders in China, or in the silencing of opposition journalists in Russia).

---

20. David Luhnow, "The Secrets of the World's Richest Man," *Wall Street Journal* (Aug. 4, 2007).

21. US Department of State Report on Cameroon (March 11, 2008). See www.state.gov/g/drl/rls/hrrpt/2007/100470.htm. See also Robert Guest, *The Shackled Continent* (Oxford: Macmillan, 2004). Guest reports that he accompanied a large truck carrying a cargo of Guinness beer from the brewery in Douala, the main port city in Cameroon, to Bertoua, a town 500 kilometers (about 300 miles) away. The trip was supposed to take eighteen hours but instead took four days. The problem was forty-seven "checkpoints" consisting of a board across the road with nails protruding upward, and a self-appointed "inspector" who would assess "fines" for all sorts of invented-on-the-spot violations of some rule or other. The driver had to pay multiple bogus "fines" before the roadblocks were removed (172–76). By such robbery and extortion, commerce within the nation is crippled and consumers have to pay higher prices for everything. The entire nation pays the price for such an absence of the rule of law.

K. THE BIBLE GIVES INDIRECT BUT SIGNIFICANT SUPPORT TO THE IDEA THAT GOVERNMENT SHOULD BE CHOSEN BY THE PEOPLE (SOME KIND OF DEMOCRACY)

The Bible does not explicitly command or directly teach that governments should be chosen by a democratic process, and in fact there are no commands telling how God wants governments to be chosen.[22] There are actually many historical examples of *hereditary kings* throughout the Old Testament, and there are a Roman emperor and governors sent by him in the New Testament. These rulers are *recorded* in the Bible's history, but that does not mean their form of government is *endorsed* or *commanded*. There is no explicit teaching that other governments in other nations should take these forms.

If we look beyond these mere historical examples to biblical principles regarding government and the nature of human beings, a rather strong biblical argument can be made in support of the idea that *some form of government chosen by the people* is preferable to other kinds of government (at least during this present age, until the return of Christ).

Several concepts taught in Scripture support this idea:

(1) The first support for some kind of democracy is the concept of *the equality of all people in the image of God.* "So God created man *in his own image,* in the image of God he created him; male and female he created them" (Gen. 1:27; this applies also to the whole human race descended from Adam and Eve. Other passages of Scripture also affirm that all human beings are in the image of God: see Gen. 9:6; James 3:9). To be "in the image of God" means to be like God and to represent him on earth—the highest status given to anything God made.

But if *all people* share equally in the high privilege of being in the image of God, then what reason can there be for any family to think that they have a special right to act as "royalty" or rule over others without their consent? Far from endorsing anything like a "divine right of kings," this foundational principle taught in the first chapter of the Bible is one of equality of all human beings descended from Adam and Eve, equality in the image of God.

---

22. The word "democracy" can have either a broad or a narrow meaning. In a broad sense, "democracy" means "government by the people, exercised either directly or through elected representatives" (meaning 1 in *The American Heritage Dictionary* [Boston: Houghton Mifflin, 1996]), 497). In this sense, the United States is clearly a democracy: it is not a monarchy or an oligarchy or a dictatorship, but is government "by the people ... through elected representatives."

But sometimes people try to inform me, "The United States is a republic, not a democracy." They are using the word "democracy" in a more narrow sense that just means "majority rule," and they understand the word to refer only to a pure

democracy, as in an ancient city-state where all decisions were made by a vote of all the citizens. They understand the precise word "republic" to be the only proper term to describe a government by elected representatives.

My response to these people is that, yes, the United States is a *republic,* but it is *also* a *democracy,* because I am not using the word "democracy" in the narrow sense of "pure democracy." I am simply using the word "democracy" to mean a system of government where the rulers are elected by the people. That is the most common sense of the word today, and that is what it means in ordinary conversational and written English.

This rejection of any hereditary right of any "royal family" to rule over others was the background that led to the statement in the second paragraph of the US Declaration of Independence:

> We hold these truths to be self-evident, that all men are created equal, that they are endowed by their creator with certain unalienable rights....[23]

(2) Another reason in favor of some form of democracy is that *accountability of rulers to the people* helps prevent a misuse of their power. As I argued above (see pp. 101–3), if there is a separation of powers in government, it tends to prevent abuse. Perhaps the most effective separation of powers is the separation between the power given to government and the power reserved for the people, which is evident in free elections. *The need to gain and maintain consent from those who are governed*, through elections at periodic intervals, is probably the single greatest protection against the abuse of power and the single greatest guarantee of accountability on the part of rulers. Rulers who become corrupt and abuse their power regularly abolish free elections, imprison or murder political opponents, intimidate voters, and rig elections so that they "win" because their cronies control the ballots, the counting of votes, and the media reports of the election results. (Recent rigged "elections" in Russia,[24] Zimbabwe,[25] and Venezuela[26] are notorious examples, as is the nullified election of Aung San Suu Kyi in Myanmar/Burma.[27])

How can we know if a country is actually functioning as a democracy? Former Soviet dissident Natan Sharansky, in his book *The Case for Democracy*, provides "the town square test" to determine whether a particular society is what he calls a "free society" (and thus a genuine democracy) or a "fear society":

> Can a person walk into the middle of the town square and express his or her views without fear of arrest, imprisonment, or physical harm? If he can, then that person is living in a free society, not a fear society.[28]

(3) The purpose of government also argues for democracy. *If government is to serve for the benefit of the people* (to be "God's servant for *your good*," Rom. 13:4), this means that the government does not exist ultimately for the good of the *king* or the good of the *emperor* or the good of the *ruling council*, but for the good of the people themselves.

23. Declaration of Independence, adopted July 4, 1776. www.archives.gov/national_archives_experience/charters/declaration_transcript.html.

24. "The election was not fair and failed to meet standards for democratic elections," concluded the Organisation for Security and Co-operation in Europe (OSCE) and the Council of Europe in a joint statement. See "Russia's Fraudulent Election," *The Economist* (Dec. 3, 2007). www.economist.com/world/europe/displaystory.cfm?story_id=10238268.

25. Peta Thorneycraft, "Police 'Rigged' Ballot in Zimbabwe Election," *Theage.com.au* (April 12, 2008). www.theage.com.au/news/world/police-rigged-ballot-in-zimbabwe-election/2008/04/11/1207856835491.html.

26. Christopher Toothaker, "Efforts to dispel claims of vote-rigging in Venezuela's recall vote suffer a setback," Associated Press (Aug. 18, 2004). www.signonsandiego.com/news/world/20040818-1544-venezuela-recall.html.

27. Meghan Dunn, "U.N. Chief Urges Myanmar to Hold 'Fair' Election," *CNN.com* (July 14, 2009). www.cnn.com/2009/WORLD/asiapcf/07/13/myanmar.un.elections/index.html; and "Myanmar Junta Dismisses Sui Kyi Victory," Associated Press/*USA Today* (July 6, 2008). www.usatoday.com/news/world/2008-07-06-3081463627_x.htm.

28. Natan Sharansky, *The Case for Democracy: The Power of Freedom to Overcome Tyranny and Terror* (New York: Public Affairs, 2004), 40–41.

The next question that follows from that is this: Who is best suited to decide what is best for the people? Shouldn't the people as a whole have the right to decide what kind of leaders best advance the good of the people and the good of the nation? Of course, the people as a whole can make mistakes, just as any elite group of rulers could make mistakes about what is best for the people. But ultimately the people who are *supposed* to benefit from the rule of government should be the ones who can best decide what is *actually* for their benefit and what is not. (Rulers can delude themselves into thinking that their policies are "for the people's good," but it is hard to believe this if they have to rig elections and imprison political opponents and silence dissent.)

(4) A number of narrative examples in Scripture indicate that *government seems to work best with the consent of those who are governed.* Even though Moses had been appointed by God, he sought the assent of the elders and the people of Israel (Exod. 4:29–31), as did Samuel when he stood before all the people in his role as judge (1 Sam. 7:5–6), and Saul after he had been anointed as king (see 1 Sam. 10:24).

When David became king over Judah, he gained the public consent of all the people: "The men of Judah came, and there they anointed David king over the house of Judah" (2 Sam. 2:4). When Zadok the priest anointed Solomon as king, then "All the people said, 'Long live King Solomon!'" (1 Kings 1:39; see also 12:1).

In the New Testament, the apostles asked for the consent of the congregation in selecting leaders to oversee the distribution of food to the needy: "Therefore, brothers, *pick out from among you* seven men of good repute, full of the Spirit and of wisdom, whom we will appoint to this duty" (Acts 6:3).

By contrast, there are negative examples in Scripture where tyrants did not gain the consent of the people but ruled harshly in opposition to the people's consent. "So the king [Rehoboam] did not listen to the people" (1 Kings 12:15), and as a result the ten northern tribes rebelled against the king: "And when all Israel saw that *the king did not listen to them*, the people answered the king, 'What portion do we have in David? ... To your tents, O Israel!'" (v. 16). Israel was divided into the northern and southern kingdoms from that day onward.

In a similar way, the Old Testament contains several examples of oppressive rulers who subjected the people of Israel to slavery and who certainly did not rule by the consent of those over whom they ruled, whether this be Pharaoh as king in Egypt (Exod. 3:9–10) or the Philistines who ruled harshly over Israel during the time of the Judges (Judg. 14:4) or Nebuchadnezzar and other foreign kings who conquered and eventually carried the people off into exile (2 Kings 25:1–21). These events are all viewed negatively in the biblical narrative.

In the New Testament, under the Roman government, Herod the Great and his successors were also oppressive rulers, ruling without the consent of the Jewish people, and ruling harshly over them (see Matt. 2:16–17; Luke 13:1; Acts 12:1–2).

Therefore, substantial biblical arguments can be given in support of the idea of some form of government chosen by the people themselves (that is, in general terms, a democracy). Such a government seems to be preferable to all other forms of government such as dictatorship or hereditary monarchy or government by a hereditary or self-perpetuating aristocracy. (Several democracies today, such as the United Kingdom and Norway, have retained a monarchy that functions in a largely ceremonial and symbolic function, but they are democracies because the real governing power rests with the elected representatives of the people.)

There is, however, one King for whom the Bible gives unlimited approval, and that is Jesus Christ, who will one day return to the earth to reign as "King of kings and Lord of lords" (Rev. 19:16). There will be no injustice or abuse of power in his domain, for he will reign in perfect righteousness. The book of Daniel prophesies about his reign:

> And to him was given dominion and glory and a kingdom, that all peoples, nations, and languages should serve him; his dominion is an everlasting dominion, which shall not pass away, and his kingdom one that shall not be destroyed (Dan. 7:14).

But until Christ returns to reign, some form of democracy seems to be the best form of government, based on the principles above.

In the early history of the United States, when the pilgrims established the Mayflower Compact in 1620, and thereby established a form of self-government, they did so with a strong biblical knowledge influenced by many of these passages and principles of Scripture mentioned above. They also had vivid memories of oppression by the monarchy in England. As a result, the Mayflower Compact established a government *by the consent of the governed,* and this would set a pattern for the subsequent colonies and for the United States as a whole in later years. They declared that they were forming a "civil body politik" that would enact "laws" for the general good of the colony, and then they said, "unto which we promise all due submission and obedience."[29] This was a voluntary submission to a government that they themselves had created. It was not imposed on them from without by a king or some other conquering force. It was setting up a government to function with the consent of the governed—a kind of democracy.

These same principles found fuller expression in the US Declaration of Independence:

> We hold these truths to be self-evident, that all men are created equal, that they are endowed by their Creator with certain unalienable Rights, that among these are Life, Liberty, and the pursuit of Happiness. That to secure these rights, Governments are instituted among Men, *deriving their just powers from the consent of the governed.*

Although there were some forms of democratic government in local areas in ancient and medieval history (such as ancient Athens), when the United States began as a representative democracy in 1776, it could be called the "American experiment," because there were at that time no other functioning national democracies in the world. But after the founding of the United States, and especially in the twentieth century, the number of functioning national democracies grew remarkably. The World Forum on Democracy

29. See www.mayflowerhistory.com/PrimarySources/MayflowerCompact.php and www.historyplace.com/unitedstates/revolution/mayflower.htm.

reports that in 1950 there were 22 democracies accounting for 31% of the world population and a further 21 states with restricted democratic practices, accounting for 11.9% of the globe's population. Since the turn of the century, electoral democracies now represent 120 of the 192 existing countries and constitute 58.2% of the world's population.[30]

Therefore, when people today complain to me that they don't want to get involved in politics because they think that politicians are too corrupt (or arrogant, greedy, power-hungry, and other forms of being "unspiritual"), I want to remind them that although democracy is messy, it still works quite well, and all the alternative forms of government are far worse. We should be thankful for those who are willing to be involved in it, often at great personal sacrifice.

L. NATIONS SHOULD VALUE PATRIOTISM

What should the attitude of citizens be toward the nation in which they live? Because any nation can have rulers who are evil, or basically good rulers who still do wrong things from time to time, a Christian view of government would never endorse a kind of "blind patriotism" according to which a citizen would never criticize a country or its leaders. In fact, a *genuine patriotism,* which always seeks to promote the good of the nation, would honestly criticize the government and its leaders when they do things contrary to biblical moral standards.

But is patriotism a virtue *at all*? My conclusion is that the Bible gives support to a genuine kind of patriotism in which citizens love, support, and defend their own country.

1. Biblical reasons for patriotism

Biblical support for the idea of patriotism begins with a recognition that *God has established nations on the earth.* Speaking in Athens, Paul says that God "made from one man every *nation* of mankind to live on all the face of the earth, having determined allotted periods and the boundaries of their dwelling place" (Acts 17:26).

One example of this is found in God's promise to make the descendants of Abram (later Abraham) into a distinct nation:

> "And I will make of you a great *nation,* and I will bless you and make your name great, so that you will be a blessing" (Gen. 12:2).

Later God says to Abraham, "In your offspring shall *all the nations* of the earth be blessed" (Gen. 22:18).

The ancient origin of many nations on earth is recorded in the Table of Nations descended from Noah in Genesis 10, which concludes, "These are the clans of the sons of Noah, according to their genealogies, *in their nations,* and from these the nations spread abroad on the earth after the flood" (v. 32).

---

30. "List of Electoral Democracies," World Forum on Democracy, June 25–27, 2000. www.fordemocracy.net/2007/ electoral-democracies.html.

In the ongoing progress of history, Job says that God *"makes nations great, and he destroys them; he enlarges nations, and leads them away"* (Job 12:23).

The sense of what a "nation" meant in the Bible is not different in any substantial way from what we mean by a nation today—a group of people living under the same government that is sovereign and independent in its relationship to other nations.

In the modern age, and for purposes of this book, a "nation" is ordinarily a relatively large group of people living under an independent government, although in a few cases today there are nations that aren't very large, such as Monaco and Luxembourg, and in some cases there are nations that are only partially independent from a larger, more dominant nation.

The existence of many independent *nations* on the earth should be considered a blessing from God.

One benefit of the existence of nations is that *they divide and disperse government power throughout the earth*. In this way they prevent the rule of any one worldwide dictator, which would be more horrible than any single evil government, both because it would affect everyone on earth and because there would be no other nation that could challenge it. History has shown repeatedly that rulers with unchecked and unlimited power become more and more corrupt.

The signers of the US Declaration of Independence realized that they were establishing themselves as a *separate nation*, as indicted in the first sentence:

> When in the course of human events it becomes necessary for one people to dissolve the political bands which have connected them with another, and to assume among the powers of the earth, *the separate and equal station* to which the Laws of Nature and of Nature's God entitle them, a decent respect to the opinions of mankind requires that they should declare the causes which impel them to the separation.

The Bible teaches Christians to obey and honor the leaders of the nation in which they live. Peter tells Christians to "honor the emperor" (1 Peter 2:17) and to

> Be subject for the Lord's sake to every human institution, whether it be to the emperor as supreme, or to governors ... (vv. 13–14).

Paul likewise encourages not only obedience but also honor and appreciation for civil rulers when he writes to the Romans, "Let every person be subject to the governing authorities" (Rom. 13:1) and says that the ruler is "God's servant for your good" (v. 4). He concludes this section by implying that Christians should not only pay taxes but also give respect and honor, at least in some measure, to rulers in civil government:

> Pay to all what is owed to them: taxes to whom taxes are owed, revenue to whom revenue is owed, *respect to whom respect is owed, honor to whom honor is owed* (v. 7).

These commands follow a pattern found in the Old Testament as well, as the following verses indicate:

My son, fear the LORD and the king, and do not join with those who do otherwise (Prov. 24:21).

Even in your thoughts, do not curse the king, nor in your bedroom curse the rich (Eccl. 10:20).

Thus says the LORD of Hosts, the God of Israel, to all the exiles whom I have sent into exile from Jerusalem to Babylon.... Seek the welfare of the city where I have sent you into exile, and pray to the LORD on its behalf, for in its welfare you will find your welfare (Jer. 29:4–7).

God's establishment of individual nations, the benefits that come to the world from the existence of nations, and the biblical commands that imply that one should give appreciation and support to the government leaders where one lives, all tend to support the idea of patriotism in a nation.

2. The benefits of patriotism in a nation

With these factors in mind, I would define genuine patriotism as including at least the following factors:

(1) A *sense of belonging* to a larger community of people, which provides one aspect of a person's sense of identity and his obligation to others.

(2) *Gratitude* for the benefits that a nation provides, such as the protection of life, liberty, and property, the existence of laws to deter wrongdoing and encourage good, the establishment of a monetary system and economic markets, and the establishment of a common language or languages.

(3) A *shared sense of pride in the achievements of other individuals* to whom one "belongs" as fellow citizens of the same nation (including pride in athletic, scientific, economic, artistic, philanthropic, or other endeavors).

(4) A *sense of pride for the good things that a nation has done*, something that is developed by a proper understanding of the nation's history and a sense of belonging to a group of people that includes previous generations within that nation.

(5) A *sense of security* with respect to the future, because of an expectation that the larger group—that is, everyone in the nation—will work for the good of the nation and therefore will defend each person in the nation from attacks by violent evildoers, whether from within or outside its borders.

(6) A *sense of obligation to serve the nation* and do good for it in various ways, to defend it from military attack or from unfair criticism by others, to protect the existence and character of the nation for future generations, and to improve the nation in various ways where possible, even through helpful criticism of things that are done wrong within the nation.

(7) A *sense of obligation to live by and to transmit to newcomers and succeeding generations a shared sense of moral values and standards* that are widely valued by those within the nation. Such a sense of obligation to shared moral standards is more likely to happen within a nation than within the world as a whole, because a person can act as a

moral agent and be evaluated by others within the context of an entire nation, but very seldom does anyone have enough prominence to act with respect to the entire world. Another reason is that values and standards can readily spread to most of the citizens of one nation (especially where most speak a common language), but the world is so large and diverse that it is difficult to find many moral values and standards that are shared throughout all nations, or any awareness in one nation of what values are held in other nations. Within an individual nation, if a nation to is to have such moral values and national ideals preserved and transmitted, it is usually necessary to share a common sense of the origins of the nation and its history.

By contrast, the opposite of patriotism is an attitude of dislike or even scorn or hatred for one's nation, accompanied by continual criticism of one's country. Rather than sharing in gratitude for the benefits provided by the country and pride in the good things it has done, those opposed to patriotism will repeatedly emphasize any negative aspect of the country's actions, no matter how ancient or how minor compared with the whole of its history. They will not be proud of the nation or its history, and they will not be very willing to sacrifice for it or to serve it or to protect and defend it. Such anti-patriotic attitudes will continually erode the ability of the nation to function effectively and will eventually tend to undermine the very existence of the nation itself. In such cases, a healthy but limited criticism of the wrongs of a nation becomes exaggerated to the point where reality is distorted and a person becomes basically opposed to the good of the nation in general.

To take a modern example, a patriotic citizen of Iran in 2010 might well say, "I love my country and its great traditions and ideals and history, but I'm deeply saddened by the oppressive and evil nature of the current totalitarian government." A patriotic citizen of North Korea might say something similar. A patriotic citizen of Iraq under the regime of Saddam Hussein might have said similar things as well.

To take another example, a patriotic citizen of Germany might say, "I love my nation and I'm proud of its great historical achievements in science, literature, music, and many other areas of human thought, though I am deeply grieved by the evils perpetrated under the leadership of Adolf Hitler, and I am glad that we were finally liberated from his oppressive rule."

I give these examples to illustrate the fact that even citizens of countries with evil rulers can retain a genuine patriotism that is combined with sober and truthful criticism of current or past leaders. But such patriotism will still include the valuable components mentioned above, such as a sense of belonging to that particular nation, gratitude for the benefits it gives, shared pride in its achievements, a sense of security, a sense of obligation to serve and protect it (and hopefully to change any evil leadership), and a sense of obligation to follow and transmit shared values and ideals that represent the best of the country's history.

If such things can be true of even these examples of bad governments, then certainly patriotism can be a value inculcated in all the other nations of the world as well. In this sense, a Christian view of government encourages and supports genuine patriotism within a nation.

DECLARATION OF INDEPENDENCE

In Congress July 4, 1776
The Unanimous Declaration of The Thirteen United States of America

When in the course of human Events, it becomes necessary for one People to dissolve the Political Bands which have connected them with another, and to assume among the Powers of the Earth, the separate and equal Station to which the Laws of Nature and of Nature's God entitle them, a decent Respect to the Opinions of Mankind requires that they should declare the causes which impel them to the Separation.

We hold these Truths to be self-evident, that all Men are created equal, that they are endowed by their Creator with certain unalienable Rights, that among these are Life, Liberty, and the pursuit of Happiness. —That to secure these Rights, Governments are instituted among Men, deriving their just Powers from the Consent of the Governed. —That whenever any Form of Government becomes destructive of these Ends, it is the Right of the People to alter or abolish it, and to institute a new Government, laying its Foundation on such Principles, and organizing its Powers in such Form, as to them shall seem most likely to effect their Safety and Happiness. Prudence, indeed, will dictate that Governments long established should not be changed for light and transient Causes; and accordingly all Experience hath shewn, that Mankind are more disposed to suffer, while Evils are sufferable, than to right themselves by abolishing the Forms to which they are accustomed. But when a long Train of Abuses and Usurpations, pursuing invariably the same Object, evinces a Design to reduce them under absolute Despotism, it is their Right, it is their Duty, to throw off such Government, and to provide new Guards for their future Security. Such has been the patient Sufferance of these Colonies; and such is now the Necessity which constrains them to alter their former Systems of Government. The History of the Present King of Great-Britain is a History of repeated Injuries and Usurpations, all having in direct Object the Establishment of an absolute Tyranny over these States. To prove this, let Facts be submitted to a candid World.

He has refused his Assent to Laws, the most wholesome and necessary for the public Good.

He has forbidden his Governors to pass Laws of immediate and pressing Importance, unless suspended in their Operation till his Assent should be obtained; and when so suspended, he has utterly neglected to attend to them.

He has refused to pass other Laws for the Accommodation of large Districts of People; unless those People would relinquish the Right of Representation in the Legislature, a Right inestimable to them, and formidable to Tyrants only.

He has called together Legislative Bodies at Places unusual, uncomfortable, and distant from the Depository of their public Records, for the sole Purpose of fatiguing them into Compliance with his Measures.

He has dissolved Representative Houses repeatedly, for opposing with manly Firmness his Invasions on the Rights of the People.

He has refused for a long Time, after such Dissolutions, to cause others to be elected; whereby the Legislative Powers, incapable of Annihilation, have returned to the People at large for their exercise; the State remaining in the mean time exposed to all the Dangers of Invasion from without, and Convulsions within.

He has endeavoured to prevent the Population of these States; for that Purpose obstructing the Laws for Naturalization of Foreigners; refusing to pass others to encourage their Migrations hither, and raising the Conditions of new Appropriations of Lands.

He has obstructed the Administration of Justice, by refusing his Assent to Laws for establishing Judiciary Powers.

He has made Judges dependent on his Will alone, for the Tenure of their Offices, and Amount and Payment of their Salaries.

He has erected a Multitude of new Offices, and sent hither Swarms of Officers to harass our People, and eat out their Substance.

He has kept among us, in Times of Peace, Standing Armies, without the consent of our Legislature.

He has affected to render the Military independent of and superior to the Civil Power.

He has combined with others to subject us to a Jurisdiction foreign to our Constitution, and unacknowledged by our Laws; giving his Assent to their Acts of pretended Legislation:

For quartering large Bodies of Armed Troops among us:

For protecting them, by a mock Trial, from Punishment for any Murders which they should commit on the Inhabitants of these States:

For cutting off our Trade with all Parts of the World:

For imposing taxes on us without our Consent:

For depriving us, in many Cases, of the Benefits of Trial by Jury:

For transporting us beyond Seas to be tried for pretended Offences:

For abolishing the free System of English Laws in a neighbouring Province, establishing therein an arbitrary Government, and enlarging its Boundaries, so as to render it at once an Example and fit Instrument for introducing the same absolute Rule in these Colonies:

For taking away our Charters, abolishing our most valuable Laws, and altering fundamentally the Forms of our Governments:

For suspending our own Legislatures, and declaring themselves invested with Powers to legislate for us in all Cases whatsoever.

He has abdicated Government here, by declaring us out of his Protection and waging War against us.

He has plundered our Seas, ravaged our Coasts, burnt our Towns, and destroyed the Lives of our People.

He is, at this Time, transporting large Armies of foreign Mercenaries to compleat the Works of Death, Desolation, and Tyranny, already begun with circumstances of Cruelty and Perfidy, scarcely paralleled in the most barbarous Ages, and totally unworthy the Head of a civilized Nation.

He has constrained our fellow Citizens taken Captive on the high Seas to bear Arms against their Country, to become the Executioners of their Friends and Brethren, or to fall themselves by their Hands.

He has excited domestic Insurrections among us, and has endeavoured to bring on the Inhabitants of our Frontiers, the merciless Indian Savages, whose known Rule of Warfare, is an undistinguished Destruction, of all Ages, Sexes and Conditions.

In every stage of these Oppressions we have Petitioned for Redress in the most humble Terms: Our repeated Petitions have been answered only by repeated Injury. A Prince, whose Character is thus marked by every act which may define a Tyrant, is unfit to be the Ruler of a free People.

Nor have we been wanting in Attentions to our British Brethren. We have warned them from Time to Time of Attempts by their Legislature to extend an unwarrantable Jurisdiction over us. We have reminded them of the Circumstances of our Emigration and Settlement here. We have appealed to their native Justice and Magnanimity, and we have conjured them by the Ties of our common Kindred to disavow these Usurpations, which, would inevitably interrupt our Connections and Correspondence. They too have been deaf to the Voice of Justice and of Consanguinity. We must, therefore, acquiesce in the Necessity, which denounces our Separation, and hold them, as we hold the rest of Mankind, Enemies in War, in Peace, Friends.

We, therefore, the Representatives of the United States of America, in General Congress, Assembled, appealing to the Supreme Judge of the World for the Rectitude of our Intentions, do, in the Name, and by the Authority of the good People of these Colonies, solemnly Publish and Declare, That these United Colonies are, and of Right ought to be, Free and Independent States; that they are absolved from all Allegiance to the British Crown, and that all political Connection between them and the State of Great-Britain, is and ought to be totally dissolved; and that as Free and Independent States, they have full Power to levy War, conclude Peace, contract Alliances, establish Commerce, and to do all other Acts and Things which Independent States may of right do. And for the support of this Declaration, with a firm Reliance on the Protection of the divine Providence, we mutually pledge to each other our Lives, our Fortunes, and our sacred Honor.

[Connecticut:] Samuel Huntington, Roger Sherman, William Williams, Oliver Wolcott

[Delaware:] Thomas McKean, George Read, Caesar Rodney

[Georgia:] Button Gwinnett, Lyman Hall, George Walton

[Maryland:] Charles Carroll, Samuel Chase, William Paca, Thomas Stone

[Massachusetts:] John Adams, Samuel Adams, Elbridge Gerry, John Hancock, Robert Treat Paine

[New Hampshire:] Josiah Bartlett, Matthew Thornton, William Whipple

[New Jersey:] Abraham Clark, John Hart, Francis Hopkinson, Richard Stockton, John Witherspoon

[New York:] William Floyd, Francis Lewis, Philip Livingston, Lewis Morris

[North Carolina:] Joseph Hewes, William Hooper, John Penn

[Pennsylvania:] George Clymer, Benjamin Franklin, Robert Morris, John Morton, George Ross, Benjamin Rush, Jason Smith, George Taylor, James Wilson

[Rhode Island:] William Ellery, Stephen Hopkins

[South Carolina:] Thomas Heyward, Jr., Thomas Lynch, Jr., Arthur Middleton, Edward Rutledge

[Virginia:] Carter Braxton, Benjamin Harrison, Thomas Jefferson, Francis Lightfoot Lee, Richard Henry Lee, Thomas Nelson, Jr., George Wythe

Chapter 4

A BIBLICAL WORLDVIEW

Before examining specific political issues it is important that we begin with an overall Christian worldview. There are several basic, fundamental truths about God and his relationship to the world, and about human beings, that will affect nearly every political policy decision in one way or another. It is crucial for Christians to understand these components of a biblical worldview and also to realize that many non-Christians in society today hold positions that are far different from these basic principles.

A. GOD CREATED EVERYTHING

The very first sentence of the Bible tells us the most important building block of a Christian worldview:

In the beginning, God created the heavens and the earth (Gen. 1:1).

The first chapter of Genesis goes on to explain how God created the plants and trees (v. 11), and birds and fish (vv. 20–21). Then it says, "And God made the beasts of the earth according to their kinds and the livestock according to their kinds, and everything that creeps on the ground according to its kind. And God saw that it was good" (v. 25).

After this, we read that God created man:

So God created man in his own image,
in the image of God he created him;
male and female he created them (v. 27).

The first element in a Christian worldview, then, is that God is the Creator and every-thing that exists has been created by him. Although Christian interpreters have differed about some of the details (such as how many different kinds of animals God created from nothing, or how long he took to complete the creation process), there should be no disagreement about the basic fact that God created all of it and therefore the entire creation belongs to him, and he is the rightful Lord over all creation.

Here is one immediate application: When the fact of God's creation of the universe is excluded from our nation's educational system, *the most fundamental fact in the entire universe is concealed from children in schools.* Just *how* this should be taught and *when* and in *what form*, are questions over which there can be legitimate differences, but there should be no disagreement over the fact that the Bible presents this as something that is *true*, something that happened in space-time history. We should also recognize that a secular educational system that systematically denies this truth is at odds with the Christian worldview.

The fact that God is Creator also means that he deserves the obedience and worship of his creatures. The elders around God's throne in heaven have it right when they sing,

> "Worthy are you, our Lord and God,
> to receive glory and honor and power,
> for you created all things,
> and by your will they existed and were created" (Rev. 4:11).

Another implication of God's creation of the universe is that he has planted some indications of his existence and character in the world that he made:

> The heavens declare the glory of God,
> and the sky above proclaims his handiwork (Ps. 19:1).

In addition, Paul says in Romans, "His invisible attributes, namely, his eternal power and divine nature, *have been clearly perceived*, ever since the creation of the world, *in the things that have been made*" (Rom. 1:20).

B. THE ONE TRUE GOD REVEALS HIMSELF AND HIS MORAL STANDARDS CLEARLY IN THE BIBLE

The true knowledge about God that results in genuine faith comes through what is writ-ten in the Bible: "Faith comes from hearing, and hearing through the Word of Christ" (Rom. 10:17). This is because "All Scripture is breathed out by God and profitable for teaching, for reproof, for correction, and for training in righteousness" (2 Tim. 3:16). It is the "sacred writings" of the Bible that are "able to make you wise for salvation through faith in Christ Jesus" (2 Tim. 3:15). Regarding the words of the Old Testament prophets, Peter says that "men spoke from God as they were carried along by the Holy Spirit" (2 Peter 1:21). Jesus could refer to the words of the Bible as "every word that comes from the mouth of God" (Matt. 4:4). These verses teach that in the words of the Bible God speaks to us and gives us a clear and truthful revelation of himself.

When God first established the people of Israel as a nation at Mount Sinai, he gave them the Ten Commandments (Exod. 20:1–17) so that they could know how to live in obedience to him. Therefore the Old Testament can proclaim that to walk in obedience to the law of the Lord is to be "blameless" before God:

> Blessed are those whose way is *blameless,*
> who walk in the law of the Lord! (Ps. 119:1).

How can people learn what God thinks is right and what is wrong? By reading his words in the Bible: "How can a young man keep his way pure? By guarding it *according to your Word*" (Ps. 119:9).

The moral standards that God reveals in the Bible are not simply moral standards for one particular church or one particular religion, but are the moral standards for which the one true God, the Creator and Lord of the entire universe, will hold every single person accountable at the last judgment. When Peter writes to Christians living in a hostile non-Christian culture, he tells them that their non-Christian neighbors "are surprised when you do not join them in the same flood of debauchery, and they malign you; *but they will give account* to him who is ready to judge the living and the dead" (1 Peter 4:4–5).

This fact does not change even when people do not believe the Bible or do not think that it contains God's moral standards. It still *is true*, and it still *does* contain his moral standards for all people, for all time. A Christian worldview affirms that there is only one true God over the whole world, and the moral standards that he has given in the Bible are the ones by which he will judge every single human being—even the unbelievers who were opposing the early Christians to whom Peter was writing. Similarly, in speaking to the pagan Greek philosophers in Athens, Paul said that the God "who made the world and everything in it" (Acts 17:24) is the same God who

> commands all people everywhere to repent, because he has fixed a day in which *he will judge the world in righteousness* by a man whom he has appointed; and of this he has given assurance to all by raising him from the dead (vv. 30–31).

Despite the fact that these Greek philosophers did not believe in or accept the Bible or the words of the Old Testament as God's words, Paul still told them that *they would be judged by God and they would be held accountable by him.* This is the case for every human being who has ever lived, according to the biblical worldview.

This truth has significant implications for how Christians understand political questions that involve right and wrong. For example, if God says that murder is wrong (Exod. 20:13), and if it is determined that the command not to murder applies to preborn children and to those who are elderly or very ill, it clearly affects how one views laws regarding abortion and euthanasia. To take another example, if the Bible views homosexual conduct as morally wrong (see below, pp. 217–19), then that has a significant influence on how one views laws that would give government approval and encouragement to homosexual "marriage."

C. THE ORIGINAL CREATION WAS "VERY GOOD"

When God first completed his work of creation, he "saw everything that he had made, and behold, *it was very good*" (Gen. 1:31). This was a world in which there was no disease and no "thorns and thistles" (see Gen. 3:18) to harm human beings. It was a world of great abundance and beauty, far beyond anything we can imagine today. Moreover, Adam and Eve were included in the pronouncement "very good," so they were perfectly free from sin. In addition, they were not subject to disease or aging or death (see Rom. 5:12; also Eccl. 7:29).

But even in this perfect world, God gave Adam and Eve work to do in caring for the garden: "The LORD God took the man and put him in the Garden of Eden *to work it and keep it*" (Gen. 2:15). God also set before Adam and Eve the entire creation and told them to develop it and make it useful, with the implication that they would enjoy it and give thanks to him: "And God said to them, 'Be fruitful and multiply and fill the earth *and subdue it and have dominion* over the fish of the sea and over the birds of the heavens and over every living thing that moves on the earth' " (Gen. 1:28).

This implies that productive work is not in itself an evil thing or something to be avoided, but *work is something good and part of the purpose for which God made human beings*. And this implies that "ideal" life for human beings is not one of perpetual inactivity and laziness—on a tropical island, for example—but one of meaningful, productive activity, filled with some kind of work that is pleasing to God.

D. BECAUSE ADAM AND EVE SINNED, THERE IS MORAL EVIL ("SIN") IN THE HEART OF EVERY HUMAN BEING

A Christian worldview must include the idea that there is a measure of moral evil (what the Bible calls "sin") in the heart of every human being who lives on the face of the earth. In addition, the Bible shows that this moral evil in human beings must be defined in comparison to an *external standard* of right and wrong, a standard that comes *not* from within the human race but from God himself. This one idea, that human beings are viewed as sinful before the absolute moral standards of the one true God, has *immense* implications for numerous policy differences between Republicans and Democrats (as will be seen in the chapters that follow).

Here is the narrative from the beginning chapters of the Bible that explains the origin of evil in the human race:

> And the LORD God commanded the man, saying, "You may surely eat of every tree of the garden, but of the tree of the knowledge of good and evil you shall not eat ..." (Gen. 2:16–17).

However, Adam and Eve disobeyed this command:

> So when the woman saw that the tree was good for food, and that it was a delight to the eyes, and that the tree was to be desired to make one wise, she

took of its fruit and ate, and she also gave some to her husband who was with her, and he ate (Gen. 3:6).

After this event God confronted Adam and Eve and imposed punishment on them (see Gen. 3:8–24). In addition, the entire human race was affected for all subsequent generations. In the New Testament, Paul wrote:

> Sin came into the world through one man, and death through sin, and so death spread to all men because all sinned.... One trespass led to condemnation for all men.... *By the one man's disobedience the many were made sinners"* (Rom. 5:12, 18–19).

After Adam and Eve's sin, their inward moral nature was sinful. They had a tendency to sin more. And this tendency to sin was passed on to all later generations, to every human being on earth: see Romans 3:23, "All have sinned and fall short of the glory of God."

This first sin by Adam and Eve at the beginning of human history has several implications that affect a person's worldview and ultimately a person's view of many political questions:

1. There are moral standards external to the human race

Human conduct today (even the best conduct) is not the true standard of right and wrong. It cannot be, according to the Bible, because all people are sinful and fall short of what God requires. This means that our standards of what is "right" and "wrong" *should not be determined merely by observing current human experience.* When God told Adam and Eve not to eat of a certain tree, *the standard of right and wrong came from outside themselves.* And when God gave the human race other commands, the moral standards came from outside the human race as well.

In contrast to this idea, many people in society today adopt an entirely man-centered approach to moral standards. Much of society assumes that *human beings are basically good* and that *moral standards can only come from observing human conduct and considering human opinions* about right and wrong. They reject the idea that there can be any absolute moral standard external to the human race or that anyone can know what God's moral standards are. Therefore these people tend to advocate moral relativism, thinking that differences in people's sexual behavior (for example) are *just different personal choices* that people have made and cannot be measured by standards of right and wrong. Beginning with this secular assumption, people will come to entirely different opinions on matters of law and politics that have to do with whether we can know that some things are right and others are wrong.

2. Human nature is not basically good

All human beings have both good and evil tendencies in their hearts. They have a sinful tendency (or sinful nature) from Adam and Eve, but they also have a conscience that often reflects God's moral laws. Paul says, "The work of the law is written on their hearts, while their conscience also bears witness, and their conflicting thoughts accuse or even excuse them" (Rom. 2:15). People also retain many elements of likeness to God, for they are created in his image, and by what is called "common grace," God still gives them many blessings in this life that they do not actually deserve, including a sense of right and wrong. Therefore people's individual conduct can be either good or evil and is often some mixture of both. People choose between the good and evil tendencies in their own hearts, so that the ultimate human reason why someone does good or evil is that person's own choice:

> Let no one say when he is tempted, "I am being tempted by God," for God cannot be tempted with evil, and he himself tempts no one. But *each person is tempted when he is lured and enticed by his own desire*. Then desire when it has conceived gives birth to sin, and sin when it is fully grown brings forth death (James 1:13–15).

This biblical principle means that *evil does not come merely from the influence of society on a person*, and *those who do evil are not merely victims of external influences* that they have experienced. Certainly there are evil influences on people, and society should try to remove those influences where possible. Nevertheless, *doing evil things is still a result of a person's evil choices, and people therefore should be held accountable for the evil that they do.*

By contrast to this viewpoint, a secular perspective would tend to believe that human beings are basically good and therefore when they do wrong the primary reason must be because *something in society* has harmed them and has caused them to act in wrong ways. Thus, some part of *society* will be mostly blamed for the wrong, and the wrong-doer himself will more likely be viewed primarily as a "victim," not a wrongdoer. This difference accounts for many political differences regarding responses to crime and to the threat of international terrorism.

3. Human responsibility

The implication of the previous section is that people should be held responsible for their actions, because their actions come from their decisions to follow tendencies toward good or evil that are found in their own hearts. By contrast, much of secular society tends to want to avoid holding people responsible for their wrong actions, because they think that wrongdoing is to be blamed on *societal* influences, not on evil in the human heart.

4. Some violent, irrational evil

The Bible recognizes that in some people the tendency to do evil becomes exceptionally strong and violent, and in these cases it must be restrained by superior force (that is, by the government) in order to protect society from harm. That is why Paul can say, "For rulers are not a terror to good conduct, but to bad" (Rom. 13:3). Some examples of such violent evil would be Adolf Hitler in Germany (who was only stopped by foreign armies), or terrorists, or serial murderers and rapists.

Some who hold a purely secular viewpoint and believe in the basic goodness of all human hearts would reject the idea that the best way to deal with such people is the use of superior force by the government. They would still hope for change through more talking and reasoning with even the most evil people and through trying to address the "causes" of their behavior (such as poverty or a violent childhood or oppression by a more powerful country). But a biblical viewpoint would say that in some people evil is so strong that these people have become irrational and violent, and they can only be stopped by police or military power, for they will not respond to reason:

> But if you do wrong, be afraid, for he does not bear the sword in vain. For he is the servant of God, an avenger who carries out God's wrath on the wrongdoer (Rom. 13:4).

The idea that there is violent, irrational evil in some human beings—evil that can only be stopped by a more powerful authority—also has significant implications for several political questions, concerning not only national defense but also punishment and deterrence of crime and even discipline of children in a family and in schools (see the following chapters).

E. BECAUSE ADAM AND EVE SINNED, GOD PLACED A CURSE ON THE ENTIRE NATURAL WORLD

A Christian worldview also includes the idea that the current state of the "natural world" is not the way God created it. After Adam and Eve sinned, one punishment he imposed was to change the functioning of the natural world so that it was no longer an idyllic garden of Eden, but was a much more dangerous and difficult place for human beings to live. God told Adam this about the ground: *"Cursed is the ground because of you*; in pain you shall eat of it all the days of your life; *thorns and thistles it shall bring forth for you"* (Gen. 3:17–18).

Here the expression "thorns and thistles" functions as a kind of poetic image, a specific, recognizable example that represents a multitude of things—such as hurricanes, floods, droughts, earthquakes, poisonous plants, poisonous snakes and insects, and hostile wild animals—that make the earth a place in which its natural beauty and usefulness are constantly mixed with other elements that bring destruction, sickness, and even death.

Therefore, *what we think of as "natural" today is not always good*. We must build floodwalls and levies to protect against hurricanes, for example. We heat our homes in winter and air-condition them in summer rather than living all the time in "natural" temperature. We irrigate fields to grow crops where "nature" did not decide to grow them. We put screens on windows or spray insect repellant to keep "natural" mosquitoes from biting us. Fallen nature today is not exactly the garden of Eden!

The fact that nature is not now perfect today has many other implications, which I will explore in chapter 10.

F. GOD WANTS HUMAN BEINGS TO DEVELOP THE EARTH'S RESOURCES AND TO USE THEM WISELY AND JOYFULLY

The final component of a biblical worldview regarding political questions has to do with God's purpose for placing human beings on the earth. At the very beginning of human history, immediately after God created Adam and Eve,

> God blessed them. And God said to them, "Be fruitful and multiply and fill the earth *and subdue it and have dominion* over the fish of the sea and over the birds of the heavens and over every living thing that moves on the earth" (Gen. 1:28).

This responsibility to "subdue" the earth and "have dominion" over it implies that God expected Adam and Eve and their descendants to explore and develop the earth's resources in such a way that they would bring benefit to themselves and other human beings.

However, these commands to subdue the earth and have dominion over it *do not mean that we should use the earth in a wasteful or destructive way* or intentionally treat animals with cruelty, for "whoever is righteous has regard for the life of his beast" (Prov. 12:10). God also told the people of Israel to take care to protect fruit trees during a time of war (see Deut. 20:19–20). In addition, the command "You shall love your neighbor as yourself" (Matt. 22:39) implies a responsibility to think of the needs of other people, even those who will come in future generations. Therefore we should not use the earth in such a way that we destroy its resources or make them unable to be used in the future. *We should use the resources of the earth wisely, as good stewards*, not wastefully or abusively.

Another implication of this component of a Christian worldview is that *we should view the development and production of goods from the earth as something morally good*, not merely an evil kind of "materialism." God placed in the earth resources that would enable man to develop much more than food and clothing. There are resources that enable the construction of beautiful homes, automobiles, airplanes, computers, and millions of other consumer goods. While these things can be misused, and while people's hearts can have wrongful attitudes about them (such as pride, jealousy, and coveting), *the things in themselves* should be viewed as *morally good* because they are part of God's intention in placing us on the earth.

God's command to subdue the earth and have dominion over it also implies that *it is not his intention for all human beings to live in abject poverty or to live as subsistence farmers barely surviving from crop to crop*. His intention is rather that all human beings should enjoy the abundance of the earth's resources with thanksgiving to him. This implies that it is *morally right* for us to seek to overcome poverty wherever it is found. It is *morally right* also for us to help the poor have the ability to develop and enjoy the earth's good resources in abundance, as others already do.

I will explain what this means in much more detail in chapters 9 (on economic questions) and 10 (on the environment).

Chapter 5

THE COURTS AND THE QUESTION OF ULTIMATE POWER IN A NATION

A. ULTIMATE POWER: WHO WILL HAVE IT?

The most basic issue regarding any system of government is this: Who will have the ultimate power to control the nation, and how will such persons be selected?

Throughout human history, different countries have given different answers to that question. The most common answer has probably been a *monarchy*, in which the king has ultimate power and is chosen by hereditary right. Other countries have been ruled by *dictators* who placed themselves in office by overthrowing the previous government through military conquest. Other countries have had *a prime minister or a president* either elected directly by the people or chosen by some group such as a national congress. And some countries, at least for a time, have had nobody in authority but have lived under *anarchy*, perhaps with marauding bands killing and stealing at will.

When the United States was founded, it answered that question with a different kind of solution. The highest authority in the nation would not be any human person at all, but rather a *document* (the Constitution). This Constitution could only be changed with great difficulty, and all officials and all laws were to be subject to it. Here is a simple diagram of such a system:

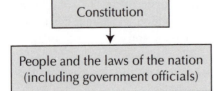

Figure 5.1:

GOVERNMENT UNDER A CONSTITUTION AS THE HIGHEST AUTHORITY

In this paradigm, no human ruler has ultimate power over the nation.

Government with such a constitution as the highest authority is unlike a system in which a king or dictator or president is the highest law in himself, can make up policies and laws however he wants, and is himself "above the law." Such a system would look like this:

Figure 5.2:

GOVERNMENT UNDER A KING AS THE HIGHEST AUTHORITY

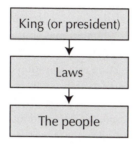

Under such a system, even if the highest official is "elected" by a popular vote, the temptation to abuse the power of government is so great that the election will seldom be fair, and in any case, a corrupt, oppressive government will result. This is because, with sinful human beings—as the British parliamentarian Lord Acton famously said— "Power tends to corrupt, and absolute power corrupts absolutely."[1]

To guard against such a tyranny of a human ruler with too much power (whether one ruler or a small group), the system of government designed by the US Founding Fathers prohibited any one person or group of persons from gaining such ultimate power and made everyone subject to the Constitution. In this way the nation was founded on a "rule of law" as opposed to a "rule of men."

Such a system bears significant similarities to the system of government in ancient Israel that is found in the Bible (see the discussion on "rule of law" in chap. 3, pp. 103–4). All the governmental officials in Israel were to be subject to an external law, namely, the law of God. In fact, when a new king took office, the law of God given through Moses required that the king would "write for himself in a book a copy of this law" (Deut. 17:18) and that "he shall read in it all the days of his life, that he may learn to fear the LORD his God by keeping all the words of this law and these statutes, and doing them" (v. 19). The king was to be subject to the laws that God had given to Israel.

This was illustrated dramatically in the tragic story of David and Bathsheba. Although David was the greatest king in the history of Israel, when he committed adultery with Bathsheba and then arranged to have her husband killed (see 2 Sam. 11:1–27), the

1. Lord Acton, British member of Parliament and Cambridge professor of history, in *Letter to Bishop Mandell Creighton* (April 3, 1887). http://oll.libertyfund.org/index.php?option=com_content&task=view&id=1354&Itemid=262.

prophet Nathan came and rebuked David and pronounced judgment on him (see 2 Sam. 12:1–15). Not even the greatest king in Israel was above the law that God had given. It was *God's law* that ultimately ruled over the nation, *not the king*.

However, in establishing a "rule of law" system of government in the United States, another problem faced the Founding Fathers: How could they guarantee that some powerful group would not take over the government, violate the Constitution at will, and refuse to be subject to its requirements? Their solution was a separation of powers, so that the power of government would be divided among various groups. Each group, protecting its own interests, would have some authority to provide a "check" on the power of other groups and thus there would be a "balance" between the various groups that held power. This system of "checks and balances" was designed to protect the nation from any powerful person or groups that might arise and abuse their power. This also was consistent with biblical teachings that apply to government, and it included multiple kinds of separation of powers (see the section on separation of powers in chap. 3, pp. 101–3).

With respect to the separation of powers between the legislatures and the courts, the United States was set up to have a system by which one group would *make the laws* (namely, the national Congress, and the state and local legislatures and boards), and another group would *interpret and apply the laws* (the courts), and would also decide if the laws were consistent with the Constitution. In this way the courts would judge the individual laws that were made. Such a system looks like this:

Figure 5.3:

MAKING LAWS SEPARATED FROM INTERPRETING AND APPLYING LAWS IN THE UNITED STATES

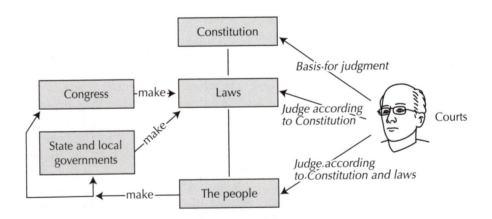

In this system, the judges *interpret* and *apply* the Constitution and the laws, but they do not *make* laws, and they certainly do not change the Constitution. In fact, as the US

Constitution was originally set up, judges had absolutely no role in making any new laws, nor did they have any role whatsoever in the difficult process of amending the Constitution.

Was this a good plan for the government of the United States? I believe it was an excellent plan. Particularly with respect to the courts, there are several benefits to having a government with such a plan:

(1) *Separation of powers*: There is a clear separation of powers: some groups make the laws, and other groups judge the laws to see if they conform to the Constitution. Thus, the Congress can *pass* laws but it cannot *judge* the laws to see if they are constitutional. If they did this, it would be similar to a student grading his or her own exam, or an ice skating competitor scoring his or her own performance. There would be no impartiality in judging, because the Congress would be judging its own work.

For a similar reason, according to this system established by the Constitution, the courts do not *write* new laws, but *judge* them. If they both wrote the laws and judged them, once again they would be judging their own work, and there would be no impartiality and no separation of powers or check against the abuse of power. The principle is that those who *judge* the laws should not be those who also *make* the laws.

(2) *Accountability for those who make laws*: Those who make the laws are most accountable to the people. The Congress and the state legislatures and the local city councils and county boards that make laws are the officials who are directly elected by the people, and they are the officials who are closest to the people at every level of government. This guarantees that the nation will function as a democracy rather than a dictatorship or an oligarchy unresponsive to the needs and desires of the people. The people do have ultimate authority in the nation (for they elect the government officials), but they do so through elected representatives and under the Constitution.

(3) *Rule of law:* The highest authority in the nation is not any person or group of persons, but a document. There is a "higher law" above the lawmakers, and therefore even the lawmakers are to be subject to the rule of law. Amending the Constitution itself is possible, but it is very difficult and it has rarely been done. (Amendments require a 2/3 vote of both houses of Congress and then ratification by the legislatures of 3/4 of the states. An alternative method is a constitutional convention requested by the legislatures of 2/3 of the states, with changes then ratified by the legislatures of 3/4 of the states. Only 27 amendments have ever been made to the U.S. Constitution, and 10 of those were in the original Bill of Rights. The most recent amendment was the 27th, ratified in 1992, which prohibits any law that increases or decreases the salary of members of the Congress from taking effect until the beginning of the next set of terms of office.[2]

2. See www.archives.gov/exhibits/charters/constitutional_ amendments_11–27.html.

(4) *Protection from fundamental change:* This system protects the nation from becoming fundamentally different than what it started out to be, both by ensuring that the Constitution will be enforced, and by making it extremely difficult to change the Constitution.

(5) *Protection from a hasty majority:* This system protects the nation from a tyranny of a majority of people who may be swept away by the urgent needs of a particular crisis, thereby making decisions that would erode or destroy some of the pillars on which the nation was founded.

But has this system worked? Is it still working today? Before we can answer that question, it is appropriate to examine what the Bible says about the role of judges in a government.

B. ACCORDING TO THE BIBLE, WHAT SHOULD JUDGES DO?

1. The essential role of judges is to judge according to a law external to themselves

In the Bible, judges were expected to judge according to a set of laws external to themselves. For example, God told Ezekiel that the priests would act as judges:

> In a dispute they shall take their stand to judge; they shall *judge it according to My laws and My statutes.* (Ezek. 44:24 NASB).

The "ordinances" that God had given provided the standard by which judges were to decide a dispute. They were not to make up their own laws or regulations, but were to evaluate the accused person's conduct in light of the established laws of God that were fixed and known and were external to the judges themselves.

In the New Testament, when Paul was on trial before the Jewish Sanhedrin, one of the members of this Jewish council ordered Paul to be struck on the mouth for what he had said. Paul responded,

> "God is going to strike you, you whitewashed wall! Are you sitting *to judge me according to the law,* and yet contrary to the law you order me to be struck?" (Acts 23:3).

Paul appealed to a standard external to the council: the established, recognized law, by which he should be judged.

It is interesting that this principle of judging according to a law external to the judges was also recognized by a pagan king, Artaxerxes of Persia. In his decree in which he sent Ezra and others to Jerusalem, he said:

> "And you, Ezra, according to the wisdom of your God that is in your hand, appoint magistrates and *judges who may judge all the people* in the province Beyond the River, all *such as know the laws of your God.* And those who do not know them, you shall teach. Whoever will not obey the law of your God and the law of the king, let judgment be strictly executed on him" (Ezra 7:25–26).

It was necessary for the judges to know the laws of God in order to judge the people rightly. Those who did not know these laws had to be taught by Ezra. Once again, these judges are to judge according to a standard of law *external to themselves*, the laws that had been given by God. In the narrative of Ezra this is viewed as something good that Artaxerxes did under God's sovereign direction. In fact, in the very next verse, Ezra writes, "Blessed be the LORD, the God of our fathers, who put such a thing as this into the heart of the king, to beautify the house of the Lord that is in Jerusalem" (Ezra 7:27).

2. Judges are not to show partiality or take bribes, for this would be using some other basis for judgment than the established law

Moses told the people of Israel,

> "You shall appoint judges and officers in all your towns that the LORD your God is giving you, according to your tribes, *and they shall judge the people with righteous judgment.* You shall not pervert justice. *You shall not show partiality,* and *you shall not accept a bribe,* for a bribe blinds the eyes of the wise and subverts the cause of the righteous. Justice, and only justice, you shall follow, that you may live and inherit the land that the LORD your God is giving you" (Deut. 16:18–20).

For example, suppose a man had stolen a sheep from his neighbor and sold it. The theft is discovered, and he is brought before the judge. In such a case, the law is clear: not only does it say, "You shall not steal" (Exod. 20:15), but it also prescribes a specific penalty:

> "If a man steals an ox or a sheep, and kills it or sells it, he shall repay five oxen for an ox, and four sheep for a sheep" (Exod. 22:1).

The duty of a judge in such a case was clear: If he decided that the man was guilty, *he was to order him to repay four sheep* for the one sheep that he had stolen. This case functions like the following diagram:

Figure 5.4

But what if, the night before the trial, the accused man had secretly gone to the judge and given him a generous "gift"—that is, a bribe. On the next day, coming into the court, the neighbor whose sheep had been stolen did not know that the judge had been bribed, and yet, in spite of honest witnesses and clear evidence of wrongdoing, the judge said, "Not guilty." In this case, the judge was dishonest and did not judge fairly according to what the law said. Instead of using the clear standard in the law "You shall not steal," the judge substituted a different standard: "You shall not steal, unless you give the judge a bribe—then you may steal." This case may be put in a diagram as follows:

Figure 5.5

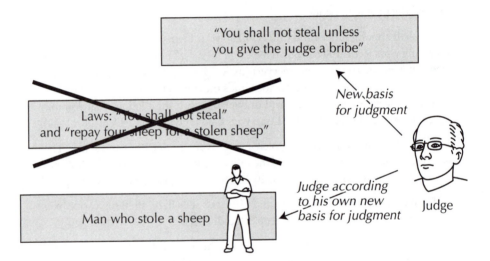

In such a case, justice has not been done. The judge has abandoned the established, external standard that was in the law and has let his personal greed and desires create *a new standard that is internal to himself*, a standard that he himself has created and that has no basis in the established law. This was exactly what was prohibited in Deuteronomy 16:19–20: "You shall not pervert justice. You shall not show partiality, and you shall not accept a bribe ... justice, and only justice, you shall follow."

The same consideration would apply if the man who stole the sheep was a friend of the judge. In that case the judge could show partiality and let his friend get off without paying a penalty. Then the standard is no longer "You shall not steal" but rather "You shall not steal, unless you are a friend of the judge—then you may steal."

If a judge were to show partiality to wealthy people, his new standard would be "You shall not steal, unless you are rich and powerful—then you may steal," but that is not what the law commanded.

If a judge shows partiality to the poor, then his standard would be "You shall not steal, unless you are poor—then you may steal." But once again, this would not be judging according to the established law. It would be distorting the law and failing to carry out justice.

The Old Testament laws emphasized that such distortions of justice were not to be carried out in Israel:

Nor shall you be *partial to a poor man* in his lawsuit (Exod. 23:3).

You shall not *pervert the justice due to your poor* in his lawsuit (Exod. 23:6, prohibiting favoritism to those who are wealthy or powerful).

And *you shall take no bribe*, for a bribe blinds the clear-sighted and subverts the cause of those who are in the right (Exod. 23:8).

You shall do no injustice in court. *You shall not be partial to the poor or defer to the great*, but in righteousness shall you judge your neighbor (Lev. 19:15).

And I charged your judges at that time, "Hear the cases between your brothers, and judge righteously between a man and his brother or the alien who is with him. You shall not be partial in judgment. You shall hear the small and the great alike. *You shall not be intimidated by anyone*, for the judgment is God's" (Deut. 1:16–17).

He appointed judges in the land in all the fortified cities of Judah, city by city, and said to the judges, "Consider what you do, for you judge not for man but for the Lord. He is with you in giving judgment. Now then, let the fear of the Lord be upon you. Be careful what you do, for there is no injustice with the Lord our God, or partiality or taking bribes" (2 Chron. 19:5–7).

How long will you judge unjustly and show partiality to the wicked?… Give justice to the weak and the fatherless; maintain the right of the afflicted and the destitute. Rescue the weak and the needy; deliver them from the hand of the wicked (Ps. 82:2–4, addressing human government).

To impose a fine on a righteous man is not good, nor to strike the noble for their uprightness (Prov. 17:26).

3. Conclusion

The role of judges in the Bible is clear. They were to evaluate and judge cases fairly *according to an established standard of law external to themselves*. They were not to change the law or to use any other basis for judgment than the law that was clearly established, a law that was external to themselves.

C. WHAT HAS ACTUALLY HAPPENED IN THE UNITED STATES?

For most of the history of the United States, the system established by the Constitution worked quite well. The courts would decide cases according to the laws that had been passed and according to the Constitution. There were not only federal courts dealing with cases of laws for the whole United States, but also state and local courts dealing with their own laws. Difficult cases could be appealed to a higher court and eventually to the Supreme Court.

The courts also evaluated laws that were passed, to see whether they conformed to the Constitution. If someone thought a new law was unconstitutional, he could file suit in a US district court, asking the court to overturn the new law. In such cases, the losing party could appeal to a higher court, one of twelve US Courts of Appeal. Above them was the Supreme Court. So the system looked like this:

Figure 5.6

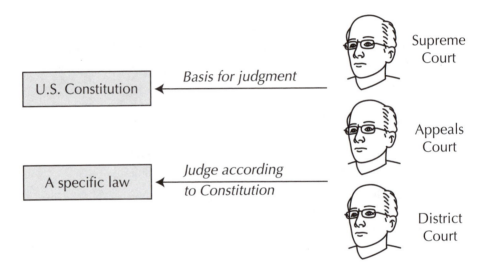

1. The gradual discovery that the Supreme Court could have unlimited power

However, there was a weakness in the system that the justices on the Supreme Court discovered over time. (Judges on the Supreme Court are called "justices" rather than simply "judges.") If a case came to the Supreme Court and *the Constitution did not say something that the Supreme Court justices wanted it to say, or thought it should say,* they could claim to "discover" new principles in the Constitution, and no one would have power to overrule them. Whenever they thought it was important, *they could simply create a new law* and call it an "interpretation" of some part of the Constitution, and suddenly it would become the highest law of the land! In this way the Supreme Court justices discovered that they could become the most powerful rulers in the entire country.

---

3. *Roe v. Wade,* 410 U.S. 113 (1973).

One example of this happened on January 22, 1973, when the Supreme Court announced its decision regarding abortion in the case *Roe v. Wade*.[3] This decision overturned the laws that restricted or prohibited abortion in all fifty states. The decision gave women an unrestricted right to abortion up to the point of "viability" (the point at which the preborn child could live outside the womb, about twenty-eight weeks), but allowed for abortion to protect a woman's "health" even after that point. Since "health" was then defined broadly enough to include *mental health and well-being*, the actual result of the decision was to permit an unrestricted right to abortion throughout the entire forty weeks of pregnancy. (See discussion of *Doe v. Bolton* on p. 164.)

The decision was by a 7–2 majority.[4] But how could the justices claim that the *Constitution* guaranteed a woman a right to abortion when *the Constitution said nothing at all about abortion?* And how could they discover this new meaning specifically in the Fourteenth Amendment to the Constitution when *laws restricting or prohibiting abortion* had been in existence in thirty-six states and territories at the very time that the Fourteenth Amendment was adopted?[5]

The justices claimed that they found this right to abortion contained in a "right to privacy" that they saw in the Fourteenth Amendment to the Constitution, particularly in the "due process" provision of that amendment. That due process clause says this:

> Nor shall any State deprive any person of life, liberty, or property, *without due process of law* (emphasis added).

Where is a "right to privacy" contained in those words? It is simply not there. The Fourteenth Amendment had been ratified in 1868, and its primary purpose was to guarantee that slaves and their descendants would have all the rights of citizenship and equal protection to all other citizens under the law.

But where does the Fourteenth Amendment say anything or imply anything *about abortion*? It does not. Had the laws restricting abortion in each of the fifty states been passed according to the normal process of approving laws in these states? Presumably so. Were these states then depriving any one of "life, liberty, or property, without due process of law"? Certainly not, at least *not according to the intention of those who wrote and ratified this amendment*, nor according to *the ordinary, publicly known meanings of the words used at the time that they were written*. The Fourteenth Amendment was never intended to have anything to do with abortion.

But by a 7–2 majority the Supreme Court found that *the right to abortion was contained in the Fourteenth Amendment!* And because the Supreme Court said so, it became the law of the land and has remained so since that day. There was nothing anyone in the nation could do about it.

---

4. Ibid. Justices Warren Earl Burger, Harry A. Blackmun, William O. Douglas, William J. Brennan Jr., Potter Stewart, Thurgood Marshall, and Lewis F. Powell Jr. were in the majority, with William H. Rehnquist and Byron White dissenting.

5. In his dissent to *Roe v. Wade*, then-Associate Justice William Rehnquist wrote: "To reach its result, the Court necessarily has had to find within the scope of the Fourteenth Amendment a right that was apparently completely unknown to the drafters of the Amendment.

In a strongly worded dissent, Justice Byron White wrote as follows:

> I find *nothing in the language or history of the Constitution* to support the Court's judgment. The Court simply fashions and announces a new constitutional right for pregnant mothers and, with scarcely any reason or authority for its action, invests that right with sufficient substance to override most existing state abortion statutes.... As an exercise of raw judicial power, the Court perhaps has authority to do what it does today; but, in my view, its judgment is an improvident and extravagant exercise of the power of judicial review that the Constitution extends to this Court.[6]

White went on to say, "I find no constitutional warrant for imposing such an order of priorities on the people and legislatures of the states.... This issue, for the most part, should be left with the people and to the political processes the people have devised to govern their affairs."[7]

Justice William Rehnquist also dissented strongly from *Roe v. Wade*. He wrote:

> To reach its result, the Court necessarily has had to find within the scope of the Fourteenth Amendment *a right that was apparently completely unknown to the drafters of that Amendment*.... By the time of the adoption of the Fourteenth Amendment in 1868, there were at least thirty-six laws enacted by state or territorial legislatures limiting abortion.... There apparently was no question concerning the validity of [the Texas law under dispute] ... nor any of the other state statutes when the Fourteenth Amendment was adopted. The only conclusion possible from this history is that the drafters did not intend that the Fourteenth Amendment withdraw from the states the power to legislate with respect to this matter.[8]

2. The Supreme Court thus became the most powerful group in the nation

As the Supreme Court issued more and more decisions of this nature—*decisions not grounded in any law* that had been passed by any Congress or any state legislature, *and that were not part of what the Constitution originally meant*—it became, in actual functioning, the highest governing authority in the nation. The justices discovered that they had the freedom to make up new constitutional doctrines whenever they could get a majority of five persons to do so, and they could always claim to "discover" the new doctrine in some vague principle of the Constitution or another.

This has happened so often in the last several decades that many people in the United States simply *assume* this is what should happen, that this is the kind of government we are *supposed* to have as a nation. But in fact it is far different from the government as originally established. In contrast with the diagram in figure 5.3, the current functioning of the government of the United States is as follows:

---

6. Justice Byron White, dissent, in *Doe v. Bolton*, announced together with *Roe v. Wade* on Jan. 22, 1973 (emphasis added).

7. Ibid.

8. Justice William Rehnquist, dissent, in *Roe v. Wade* (1973) (emphasis added).

Figure 5.7

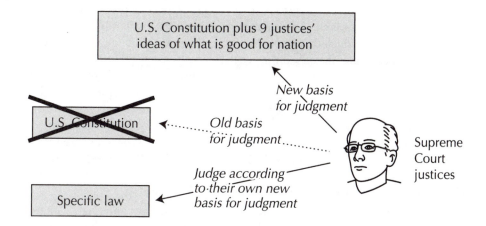

Notice the difference between this diagram and the original plan for the United States government (see figure 5.3 above). The Supreme Court would now appear at two points in that earlier diagram. It not only *interprets* the laws and *judges* according to the laws, but also *makes new laws* in the sense of new provisions it claims to find in the Constitution, based on what it thinks is good for the nation. As former Chief Justice Charles Evans Hughes said, "We are under a Constitution, but the Constitution is what the judge says it is."[9]

No person or group or government agency has any authority over the Supreme Court. It can simply *invent* new provisions that it claims are now part of the Constitution (such as the right to an abortion), and no one but the court itself can call into question or overrule or change its decisions.

Since Supreme Court justices are appointed for life, they are accountable to no one. New justices can be appointed by the President with the consent of the US Senate, but justices can stay on the court for thirty years or more, and no one can overrule them as long as they are in office.

There is another significant difference today from the government that was set up in the Constitution. Now the most important laws in the land—those that decide the most fundamental issues facing our society—are not made by officials who are closest to the people and *accountable to the people* (the Congress and state and local governments), but are made by a group of justices *who have never been elected by the people* and have *no accountability whatsoever to the people of the nation.*

This is a system that is completely opposite from the wise system designed by the Founding Fathers. They had decided that laws would be made by the people through

9. Charles Evans Hughes, quoted by Craig R. Ducat and Harold W. Chase, *Constitutional Interpretation* (St. Paul: West Publishing Co., 1974, 1983), 3.

their elected representatives (passed by Congress and signed by the President, all of whom were elected by the people). As the Constitution was written, judges were to have *absolutely no role* in the process of making laws or in the difficult process of amending the Constitution. They were to judge according to a standard of laws *outside of themselves*, a standard over which they would have no influence at all. But now the system is reversed so that they have the only influence that can ultimately prevail.

This new power of the Supreme Court has not merely affected the question of whether a woman has a right to get an abortion. It has affected hundreds of other issues, which is why the decisions announced by the Supreme Court are so important in the direction of the nation. The *Roe v. Wade* decision was one of the most blatant exercises of "raw judicial power," but it was just one example of a policy that has been followed by the courts and Supreme Court in many other areas.

a. Supreme Court changes regarding freedom of religion

With regard to freedom of religion, the First Amendment says only that "Congress shall make no law respecting an establishment of religion, or prohibiting the free exercise thereof." At the time of the First Amendment, this was simply intended to prohibit the establishment of a state church, such as the Church of England or the Lutheran Church in Scandinavian countries. Its purpose was to prevent the government from "establishing" a certain denomination as the official religion of the national government.

The First Amendment was never intended to remove the people's right to religious speech or writing in public places, at government functions, or even on government buildings (as abundant evidence from historical documents will indicate).[10] But in 1971, in the decision *Lemon v. Kurtzman*, the Supreme Court decided that a government action "must not have the primary effect of either advancing or inhibiting *religion*."[11] This meant that government could now do nothing that would give support to religious viewpoints or religious beliefs *in general*. Far from prohibiting the favoring of *one particular religion*, the Supreme Court decided that government could no longer favor *religion at all*, and in this and similar decisions, the Supreme Court has thus excluded religious speech from more and more areas of life, whether public monuments, displays of the Ten Commandments, prayer at school events, or even a "moment of silence" for students in public schools. (See further in chap. 14, pp. 503–7.)

No matter what one thinks about these individual issues, the important point is the *process* by which they were decided. *None of these restrictions had first been passed by*

---

10. A large amount of such material has been extensively documented by David Barton and his WallBuilders organization. See, for example, David Barton, *America's Godly Heritage* (Aledo, TX: Wallbuilders Press, 1993), and David Barton, *Separation of Church and State* (Aledo, TX: Wallbuilders Press, 2007).

11. *Lemon v. Kurtzman*, 403 U.S. 602 (1971). In fact, the basis of the court's tendency to exclude government actions that brought benefit to religions generally had actually found expression earlier in the 1947 decision *Everson v. Board of Education*, in which the majority opinion said, "The 'establishment of religion' clause of the First Amendment means at least this: Neither a state nor the Federal Government can set up a church. Neither can pass laws which aid one religion, *aid all religions*, or prefer one religion over another.... The First Amendment has erected *a wall between church and state*. That wall must be kept high and impregnable. We could not approve the slightest breach. New Jersey has not breached it here."

state or local representatives who are accountable to the people whom they serve. The decision about whether an opening prayer should be allowed in a graduation ceremony or a football game, or whether a copy of the Ten Commandments or some other moral quote should be posted in the hallways of a school, should be made by officials of the local school district, who are most accountable to the citizens of that community.

Asking a Roman Catholic priest or a Jewish rabbi to give an opening prayer at a football game is a far cry from "establishing" Roman Catholicism or Judaism as the official religion in the country. These two things bear no significant similarity to each other. In fact, allowing *a diversity of religious opinions* to be expressed actually protects freedom of religion for everyone. Allowing such diversity of expression in such settings (as was the custom in the United States prior to these restrictions by the Supreme Court decisions) *enhances* freedom of religion and does not suppress it. It shows that many different religions are allowed and protected in America. In addition, the restrictions on religious expression that the Supreme Court has imposed simply go contrary to the original intention of the First Amendment when it said that Congress could make no law "*prohibiting* the free exercise thereof," that is, prohibiting the free exercise of religion. But now the "free exercise of religion" is severely restricted in public places.

The exclusion of statements about religion from the public square also means that schools are now prohibited from teaching the most fundamental fact in the universe, namely, that God created it. And they are prevented from teaching that God created human beings. They are prevented from teaching that God exists, though that belief is held by more than 90% of the people in the nation.[12] But the views of that overwhelming majority do not matter to the members of the Supreme Court, for it has issued its decrees and has excluded this viewpoint from public schools—all on the basis of a theory of "separation of church and state" that was no part of the meaning of the First Amendment when it was adopted.[13]

Moreover, even if 90 or 100% of the people in a local school district believe that children should be taught the moral values in the Ten Commandments, that viewpoint means nothing to the Supreme Court, for it has ruled that such teaching must be excluded from public schools (other than as a matter of historical interest that certain people believed these things at a certain time in history). No longer are parents or citizens allowed to decide what teaching about divine moral standards is best for their children, for that decision has been made for them by the Supreme Court.

b. Taking private property for private development

In 2005, in the case *Kelo v. City of New London*, the Supreme Court decided by a 5-to-4 majority that the city of New London, Connecticut, could use the power of eminent domain to transfer private land to another *private owner* and that this could be consid-

---

12. Brian Braiker, "90% Believe in God," *Newsweek* (March 31, 2007).

13. Examples include *Engel v. Vitale* (1962), *Abington Town-* *ship v. Schempp* (1963), *Epperson v. Arkansas* (1968), *Wallace v. Jaffrey* (1985), and *Lee v. Weisman* (1992).

ered *"public use"* under the Fifth Amendment.[14] ("Eminent domain" is a legal principle by which the government can take private land without the owner's consent and pay the owner just compensation, as is sometimes necessary to build a highway or airport when one or more stubborn landowners could otherwise prevent the highway from being built.)

The Fifth Amendment to the Constitution assumed this right but restricted it:

> Nor shall private property be taken for public use without just compensation.

The distinction between "private property" and "public use" had historically been understood to mean that governments could take private property (with fair compensation given to the owner) for the purpose of building such things as roads, railroads, and public utilities—those were *public use* in contrast to *private use*.

But in the *Kelo* case, the city claimed the right to take a *private* home (that of Susette Kelo), so it could be used for an urban redevelopment plan that was being carried out by a *private developer,* making the land financially more profitable. The city argued that "public use" should include the "public purpose" of urban renewal for private profit.

Once again, the question is not whether someone agrees or disagrees with what the city of New London did. The deeper question is whether the *original intent* of the Constitution or its authors or signers was that governments can take property from *one private person* and give it to *another private person*, against the will of the first party. That was not the original sense of "public use," but the Supreme Court in this decision (and in an earlier string of related decisions) discovered this new right in the Constitution. (The majority opinion was written by John Paul Stevens and joined by Anthony Kennedy, David H. Souter, Ruth Bader Ginsburg, and Stephen G. Breyer.)

As a sad follow-up to that case, four years after the decision, the *Wall Street Journal* reported, "The wrecked and condemned neighborhood still stands vacant, without any of the touted tax benefits or job creation," and the developer—pharmaceutical giant Pfizer Inc.—decided to close its entire nearby corporate facility and move away.[15]

There was a strong dissent by the minority on the Supreme Court (O'Connor, Rehnquist, Scalia, and Thomas). Writing for the minority, Justice Sandra Day O'Connor wrote, "Any property may now be taken for the benefit of another private party, but the fall-out from this decision will not be random. The beneficiaries are likely to be those citizens with disproportionate influence and power in the political process, including large corporations and development firms."[16]

In a separate dissent, Justice Clarence Thomas argued that the court's decision was completely unrelated to the meaning of "public use" in the Fifth Amendment. He wrote:

> If such "economic development" takings are for "public use," any taking is, and the court has erased the Public Use Clause from our Constitution, as Justice O'Connor powerfully argues in dissent.... I do not believe that this Court can eliminate liberties expressly enumerated in the Constitution, and

14. *Kelo v. New London*, 545 U.S. 469 (2005).

15. "Pfizer and *Kelo's* Ghost Town," *Wall Street Journal* (Nov. 11, 2009), A20.

16. *Kelo v. New London,* dissent by Associate Justice Sandra Day O'Connor.

therefore joined her dissenting opinion. Regrettably, however, the court's error runs deeper than this. Today's decision is simply the latest in a string of cases construing the Public Use Clause to be a virtual nullity, without the slightest nod to its original meaning. In my view, the Public Use Clause, originally understood, is a meaningful limit on the government's eminent domain power.[17]

But the Supreme Court had ruled, and their decision was now the law of the land. The Constitution had not originally allowed governments to take private property and sell it to a wealthy developer, and no amendment had ever been passed adding that power to the government, but five justices on the Supreme Court had decided that it would be a good idea if government had such power, so they just told the nation that *that is now the new meaning of the Constitution*, and the matter was settled. They had the ultimate power in the nation. Like King Ahab, who unjustly took Naboth's vineyard through the misuse of governmental power (see 1 Kings 21), the Supreme Court has now given local governments the right to take any private property they want, as long as they think it to be for the public good (as they determine that good).

c. Four votes to change laws regarding acceptance of homosexual conduct

In the 2000 decision *Boy Scouts of America et al. v. Dale*, the Supreme Court came within one vote of declaring that people have a constitutional right to engage in homosexual conduct, even though the Constitution says absolutely nothing about homosexual conduct.

The background to that case is that James Dale was an assistant scoutmaster in New Jersey while he was a student at Rutgers University. He also became president of the Lesbian/Gay Student Alliance and published an interview in which he stated that he was a homosexual. When officials of the Boy Scouts read the interview, he was dismissed from his position as a scoutmaster and expelled from the Boy Scouts. But the New Jersey Supreme Court ruled that the Boy Scouts of America had to readmit him to his position because the Boy Scouts were a "public accommodation" and could not place restrictions on who can or can't be a leader.[18]

A five-member majority of the US Supreme Court (Rehnquist, O'Connor, Scalia, Kennedy, and Thomas) overturned the New Jersey Supreme Court decision (Stevens, Souter, Ginsburg, and Breyer dissented). The close majority held that the Boy Scouts, as a private organization, are allowed to exclude a person from membership on the basis of the constitutional right to freedom of association, which also implies the freedom *not* to associate with certain people.[19] This right not to associate is especially strong when such association would hinder the organization's ability to communicate a message representing certain values. In this case, the Boy Scouts had an official position against homosexual relationships, and forcing them to hire a homosexual scoutmaster would contradict that message.

---

17. Ibid., dissent by Associate Justice Clarence Thomas.

18. "New Jersey Appeals Court Rules Boy Scouts Can't Ban Gays," Associated Press (March 3, 1998).

19. *Boy Scouts of America v. Dale*, 540 U.S. 640 (2000).

What is troubling about this decision is that if only one justice had voted differently, the Supreme Court would have decreed that private organizations like the Boy Scouts cannot decide to exclude someone or refuse to hire someone based on the person's homosexual conduct. That ruling could have set a legal precedent that could be used against any Christian ministry that opens its doors to the public. *Four* of the justices thought it was right for the Supreme Court to require the Boy Scouts to hire homosexual scoutmasters who would presumably then go camping with young boys.

Had the citizens of the United States voted to approve such a requirement for the Boy Scouts and similar organizations? No. Had the representatives of the people in state legislatures voted to approve such a requirement? No. But even so, four members of the Supreme Court thought they had the right to impose such a requirement on the entire United States.

What would such a decision have meant for youth pastors or other employees in local churches? It is hard to predict. Some trends in other countries are quite troubling in this regard. For instance, on February 8, 2008, an employment tribunal in Cardiff, Wales, awarded £47,000 (approximately $94,000 in US dollars) to John Reaney, a homosexual man who had been turned down when he applied for a job as a youth worker in a local diocese (a church district) of the Church of England. The tribunal ruled that Mr. Reaney had been discriminated against "on the grounds of sexual orientation."[20]

The larger question is this: Did the founders of the United States and the original authors and signers of the Constitution ever intend that the Supreme Court would have *the right to decide for the entire nation* what is appropriate and protected sexual conduct and what is not? Why should such a question of monumental significance to a nation be decided by nine unelected judges (actually, just by a majority of five unelected judges) *rather than by the people as a whole* through their elected representatives?

The very fact that people in the United States simply *assume* that the Supreme Court can decide such things means that we have long since abandoned the essence of the nation as it was founded, that is, the right of the people as a whole, through democratic processes and their elected representatives, to decide the most important issues facing the nation.

d. State laws regarding same-sex marriage

Following the pattern of the US Supreme Court, many state supreme courts have invented further "constitutional rights" that they suddenly discover in their state constitutions. So at the state level, the supreme courts also become the most powerful body in the state, surpassing the state legislatures and governors.

For example, the Massachusetts Supreme Judicial Court in 2003 decided, by a 4-to-3 majority, that the commonwealth's constitution required that same-sex couples be given the right to marry (the case was *Goodridge v. Department of Public Health*).[21] Did the citizens of Massachusetts or their elected representatives decide this question? No, it was four

---

20. "Tribunal Decision Is Mixed Blessing for Church," Diocese of Hereford Press Release (July 18, 2007). www.hereford. anglican.org/pages/news_press releae.php?tribunal.txt.

21. *Goodridge v. Department of Health*, SJC–08860 (2003).

members of the Massachusetts Supreme Judicial Court, appointed by various governors but not elected by any public vote, who decided this for the whole state. The constitution of Massachusetts (whose primary author was Founding Father John Adams) says nothing about same-sex marriage, and such a legal "right" would have been thought preposterous and immoral by the original authors and signers of the state constitution. But this sweeping change in the laws of a state was simply imposed by a state supreme court.

The Iowa Supreme Court enacted a similar decision in the case *Varnum v. Brien* on April 3, 2009, when it ruled (unanimously) that same-sex marriages must be allowed in Iowa and that a state law limiting civil marriage to a union between one man and one woman was unconstitutional. In a key passage in that decision, the court said, "A statute inconsistent with the Iowa constitution must be declared void, even though it may be supported by strong and deep-seated traditional beliefs and popular opinion"[22] (section III, p. 13).

But how was the requirement that marriage be between one man and one woman "inconsistent with the Iowa constitution"? There was not a word in the Iowa constitution about same-sex marriage. The truth is that requiring marriage to be limited to one man and one woman *was inconsistent with the Iowa Supreme Court judges' new ideas of what the Iowa constitution should say,* including their argument that "equal protection" of the law must now mean that same-sex couples could marry. The laws passed by the Iowa legislature did not matter. The "strong and deep-seated traditional beliefs and popular opinion" of the people of Iowa did not matter. The plain historical meanings of the words in the Iowa constitution did not matter—for when the Iowa constitution was written and adopted, it would have been unthinkable that "equal protection" under law meant a "protection" for a man to marry a man in plain *violation* of the marriage law of the state. But the original meaning of the constitution did not matter. Nothing mattered except the new, liberal opinions of the judges on the Iowa Supreme Court, who suddenly imposed their new standards on the state by the exercise of raw judicial power. And thereby an entire state's understanding of marriage was transformed in a single stroke.

e. Laws giving special legal rights to homosexuals

Prior to 1992, Denver, Boulder, and Aspen in Colorado had passed laws banning discrimination against homosexuals in those cities. At first such laws sounded reasonable to people—who wants to be in favor of "discrimination"? The United States already has such laws forbidding discrimination against people because of race, gender, or age, for example.

But on further reflection, when such laws include homosexuals, then will a Christian photographer be forced to take the job if asked to photograph a homosexual "wedding"? This happened in New Mexico, when a young photographer named Elaine Hugenin had a complaint filed against her by a lesbian couple because she respectfully declined to photograph their same-sex "commitment" ceremony. The New Mexico Human Rights Commission ordered Elaine and her husband to pay nearly $7,000 in attorney fees to the

---

22. *Varnun v. Brien,* No. 07–1499 (2009).

couple, even though same-sex "marriage" isn't even legal in New Mexico.[23] The Alliance Defense Fund has appealed her case to the New Mexico trial court.[24]

Will a church be forced to rent its facilities to homosexuals for a homosexual "wedding"? This occurred in New Jersey when the Ocean Grove Camp Meeting Association of the United Methodist Church declined to rent its worship pavilion to two lesbian couples for a "civil union" ceremony. The lesbians filed a complaint with the state civil rights commission, and the association lost its tax-exempt status for the pavilion. The Alliance Defense Fund filed a lawsuit against the state of New Jersey to defend the ministry's right to not be forced to rent its property for activities contrary to its beliefs.[25] The tax-exempt status was subsequently restored, at least until the case is concluded.

Will a Christian couple who own a private guest house or a bed-and-breakfast be forced to rent a room to a homosexual couple? Will a Christian bookstore or Christian radio station be forced to hire a qualified homosexual who applies for a job? Or will *any* owner of a small business be forced to hire a homosexual who applies for a job, out of fear of being hit with an antidiscrimination lawsuit, even if he thinks that homosexual conduct is harmful or wrong? And will elementary schools then be forced to teach children that homosexual conduct is a morally good choice for those who want to choose it? (This has already happened in California, where Governor Arnold Schwarzenegger signed S.B. 777,[26] which redefines a student's sex as his or her "gender identity," relying on a student's feelings rather than biology as to whether the student is male or female.) Will parents be forced to keep their students in school for such instruction, since this is now the position of the law?

Previously, homosexuals were protected by the same laws that protect everyone else in society, but these new laws went further and made homosexuals a special class of people who were given special privileges under the law and special protections. These laws gave homosexual behavior a privileged position under the law and began to make it increasingly difficult for people who thought homosexuality was destructive to society and/or morally wrong to express their viewpoint, conduct their businesses, and raise their children in a way consistent with their viewpoint.

Because of such considerations, a number of Colorado citizens disagreed with such "gay rights laws" that had been passed in the cities mentioned, and they proposed an amendment to the Colorado constitution that would prevent such laws anywhere in the state. This amendment to the state constitution passed with a vote of 53.4% on November 3, 1992.[27] The amendment prohibited the state or local governments in Colorado

23. *Willock v. Elane Photography,* Human Rights Commission, State of New Mexico (April 9, 2008). www.telladf.org/UserDocs/ElaneRuling.pdf.

24. "ADF to appeal N.M. commission's ruling against Christian photographer" (April 9, 2008). www.alliancedefensefund.org/news/pressrelease.aspx?cid=4467.

25. "N.J. ministry sues to prevent state from forcing church to violate its religious beliefs" (Aug. 13, 2007). www.alliancedefensefund.org/news/pressrelease.aspx?cid=4206.

26. Jill Tucker, "Uproar in Alameda Over Lessons About Gays," *San Francisco Chronicle* (May 16, 2009). www.sfgate.com/cgi-bin/article.cgi?f=/c/a/2009/05/15/BA9C17LD8G.DTL. Also see Text of California Senate Bill 777, introduced by Senator Shiela Kuehl, http://info.sen.ca.gov/pub/07–08/bill/sen/sb_0751–0800/sb_777_bill_20070223_introduced.html. "ADF: Calif. law eliminates 'gender' roles, creates safety hazard for women and children" (Nov. 27, 2007). www.alliancedefensefund.org/news/story.aspx?cid=4311.

27. *Romer v. Evans,* 517 U.S. 620 (1996).

from passing laws that gave special protection to "homosexual, lesbian or sexual orientation, conduct, practices, or relationships" or entitled such persons to have a claim to "any minority status, quota preferences, protected status or claim of discrimination."[28]

But Amendment Two was challenged in the courts and appealed all the way to the US Supreme Court. In the case *Romer v. Evans,* announced on May 20, 1996, by a 6-to-3 majority, the Supreme Court overturned this amendment to the Colorado constitution.[29]

Once again, it is important to observe what happened. The question about whether homosexuals should be given *special rights and protections under the law* is a decision of great significance to any society. The citizens of Colorado decided not to give such special protections, by a statewide vote in a democratic process. (Homosexuals were always protected by all the other laws of the state, as were all other citizens, so the only question was whether to make them a class deserving of special protection.) But the US Supreme Court decreed that the citizens of Colorado did not have the right to make that decision by themselves. Instead, the court made the decision for them and overturned the democratic process of deciding this matter.

Once again, nothing in the US Constitution says anything about giving special rights to homosexuals. But the Supreme Court "discovered" this right, supposedly in the Constitution.

Even more troubling is the reasoning the court used. Writing for the majority, Justice Anthony Kennedy said of the amendment, "Its sheer breadth is so discontinuous with the reasons offered for it that the amendment seems inexplicable by anything but animus toward the class it affects: it lacks a rational relationship to legitimate state interests."[30]

Many of the supporters of Amendment Two were Christian voters who held to traditional moral values regarding sexual conduct. They were attempting to uphold traditional standards of sexual morality. But Justice Kennedy ruled that the amendment "lacks a rational relationship to legitimate state interests." Apparently the Supreme Court was saying that traditional moral standards, to say nothing of Christian moral values, lack any "rational relationship to legitimate state interests."[31]

So we should ask, did the Constitution or its authors or signers ever intend that traditional moral values should be *excluded* as a basis for state laws? No. Did the Constitution ever say anything guaranteeing that homosexuals would be considered a special class, accorded special protections under the law? No. These are new policies imposed on the nation by six justices of the Supreme Court.

Not surprisingly, Justice Antonin Scalia (joined by Rehnquist and Thomas) strongly dissented from this decision. Scalia said that Amendment Two was "a modest attempt by seemingly tolerant Coloradans to preserve traditional sexual mores against the efforts of a politically powerful minority to revise those mores through use of the laws." He added, "Since the Constitution of the United States says nothing about this subject, it is left to be resolved by normal democratic means, including the democratic adoption of

28. Ibid.
29. Ibid.
30. Ibid., majority opinion by Associate Justice Anthony Kennedy.

31. Ibid.

provisions in state constitutions.... I think it no business of the courts (as opposed to the political branches) to take sides in this culture war. But the court today has done so, not only by inventing a novel and extravagant constitutional doctrine to take the victory away from traditional forces, but even by verbally disparaging as bigotry adherence to traditional attitudes."[32]

Justice Scalia concluded as follows:

> Today's opinion has no foundation in American constitutional law, and barely pretends to. The people of Colorado have adapted an entirely reasonable provision which does not even disfavor homosexuals in any substantive sense, but merely denies them preferential treatment. Amendment Two is designed to prevent piecemeal deterioration of the sexual morality favored by a majority of Coloradans, and is not only an appropriate means to that legitimate end, but a means that Americans have employed before. Striking it down is an act, not of judicial judgment, but of political will. I dissent.[33]

But the Supreme Court's decision was 6–3, and it was then the law of the land. Because of the power of the Supreme Court, there was now nothing that any citizen, or any majority of citizens in any state, or any majority of citizens in the entire nation, could do to change it. The issue was decided, not by the people of the United States, but by the court.

f. Other cases, including capital punishment

There are numerous other examples of the Supreme Court creating new laws that were never passed by any elected body of officials and were not part of the US Constitution, but were "discovered" there by the justices of the court.[34] In addition, many federal district courts and courts of appeals have similarly created new laws out of their own reasoning, and their decisions have been upheld by the US Supreme Court. Many state supreme courts have also taken a similar approach to their state constitutions and have "created" new rights and new laws that have not been passed by any legislature.

One further example can be mentioned. From 1972 to 1976 the Supreme Court outlawed all capital punishment in the United States in its decision *Furman v. Georgia* (1972). It found that the death penalty was "cruel and unusual punishment" and thus violated the Eighth Amendment to the US Constitution, which prohibited "cruel and unusual punishments."[35] But this was clearly not the original meaning of the US Constitution, for capital punishment had been carried out hundreds of times in the country prior to and subsequent to the adoption of the Constitution. In fact, the Constitution itself assumes the right of capital punishment in more than one place. The Fifth Amendment says, "... nor shall any person be subject for the same offence to be twice put in jeopardy of *life* or limb," assuming that people could be put to death for some crimes. The same

---

32. Ibid., dissent by Associate Justice Antonin Scalia.

33. Ibid.

34. For discussion of twelve key cases, see Robert Levy and William Mellor, *The Dirty Dozen: How Twelve Supreme Court Cases Radically Expanded Government and Eroded Freedom* (New York: Sentinel, 2008). See also Alan Sears and Craig Osten, *The ACLU vs. America* (Nashville: Broadman & Holman, 2005), 22–26.

35. *Furman v. Georgia,* 408 U.S. 238 (1972).

amendment also required "indictment of a Grand Jury" in a "capital ... crime," where "capital" means "subject to capital punishment," that is, the death penalty.

Then in 2008, in *Kennedy v. Louisiana*, the Supreme Court prohibited the death penalty for *any* crime against an individual "where the victim's life was not taken."[36] However, this still allows capital punishment in the case of certain "offenses against the state," for things such as treason or espionage. (The decision in *Kennedy v. Louisiana* was again 5–4, with Kennedy providing the swing vote, this time siding with Stevens, Souter, Ginsburg, and Breyer, while the "originalist" justices Scalia, Thomas, John G. Roberts Jr., and Samuel A. Alito Jr. dissented from the opinion.)

Once again the question is this: Should the issue of capital punishment be decided by the citizens of the United States through their elected representatives? Within individual states, should it be left to the elected representatives to decide? Or should the matter of capital punishment be left to a simple majority of nine unelected judges sitting on the Supreme Court? The original plan of the Constitution was to leave such questions to the people themselves, to be decided through their elected representatives, but that is no longer how such matters are decided.

It is important to realize how broad the powers of the court have become. *All* the important legal issues of our time are now decided by a small group of nine judges, *none of whom has ever been elected by any group of voters in the United States*, and none of whom is accountable to any group of voters in the entire Untied States. They are unelected, unaccountable, and they decide nearly all the important issues of our nation today.

Is this the kind of government we want to have? Is this really what a democracy is supposed to be? Is this how our nation was set up to function? Certainly not.

g. What if citizens want to change these decisions?

What happens if the citizens of the nation decide that they want to change the laws that have been created by the Supreme Court? What if citizens decide they do not think that abortion should be allowed at every point during a woman's pregnancy or that they want to allow an opening prayer at a high school graduation ceremony or before a high school football game?

The simple fact is that the citizens of the United States have *absolutely no power* to overcome these rulings. It would not matter if the Congress itself and all fifty state legislatures passed laws restricting a woman's right to have an abortion in certain circumstances. It would not matter, because the Supreme Court has ruled that such laws are not "constitutional." The people of the nation are no longer allowed to make the decision for themselves. The Supreme Court makes such decisions for the people, and all the people are able to do is submit to that decision.

3. Liberal politicians uphold this process of judges making new laws

At this point a reader may ask, when all of this power was being usurped by the Supreme Court and taken away from the Congress and the state and local legislative bodies,

---

36. *Kennedy v. Louisiana*, 554 U.S. 36 (2008).

why didn't the system of checks and balances work to correct the mistake? Why didn't the President (the executive branch) and Congress (the legislative branch) step in and *appoint new justices* (the judicial branch) when others died or retired, so as to replace these "activist" judges who were taking so much power to themselves?[37] Why didn't the executive branch and legislative branch *defend themselves* against the judicial branch's distortion of the original system?

The answer is that many liberal politicians in the other two branches began to realize that the goals they had for remaking the United States could be accomplished simply through the rulings of the courts rather than by taking the hard path of getting the people and their representatives to approve the changes. For example, many liberal politicians were delighted at the *Roe v. Wade* decision that legalized abortion in the United States. This was a much quicker and easier solution than trying to persuade each of the fifty states to overturn its laws restricting or prohibiting abortions.

Therefore, rather than acting as a "check and balance" against the Supreme Court, many in Congress decided that they would *support* the court's usurpation of power and would *support* judges at the federal district level and at the appeals court level who would also uphold this judicial activism. More liberal Presidents (such as President Clinton) appointed justices to the Supreme Court (such as Ruth Bader Ginsburg and Stephen Breyer) who would promote this judicial activism. In other words, rather than each of the three branches of government working to protect its own rights, influential members of the legislative and executive branches *joined with and supported* the Supreme Court in its wrongful usurpation of power. Once that happened, the system of checks and balances was broken.

What this meant in the actual events of history is that a number of politicians began to attempt to take over the means of selecting justices for the Supreme Court and other judges for the lower courts. This was for the purpose of imposing their convictions on the whole nation.

This process came into clear focus in the national controversy over President Reagan's nomination of Robert Bork as a Supreme Court justice in 1987. Bork had been a highly respected judge from 1982 to 1988 in the most influential court in the United States except for the Supreme Court, namely, the United States Court of Appeals for the District of Columbia Circuit. He had also served from 1973 to 1977 as Solicitor General of the United States (the person who represents the Government of the United States in cases before the Supreme Court), and he was a professor at Yale Law School in 1972–75 and again in 1977–81. At the time of his nomination, he had been called the most able constitutional scholar in the United States.

But many liberal senators, led by the late Senator Ted Kennedy of Massachusetts, strongly opposed his nomination. They realized that if Bork's nomination were confirmed, a majority on the Supreme Court would oppose and probably overturn the *Roe v. Wade* decision regarding abortion. This would mean that questions about the legality

---

37. Some have even suggested that another remedy was possible, to impeach such justices and remove them from office. But the Constitution makes this very difficult, authorizing it only for "treason, bribery, or other high crimes and misdemeanors" (United States Constitution, Article II, Section 4: Impeachment).

of abortion would return once again to the democratic process and would be decided by the laws of the various states and of the United States itself as passed by Congress. Within forty-five minutes of Bork's nomination, Kennedy issued a strong condemnation of Bork in a nationally televised speech on the floor of the US Senate.[38] Senator Joe Biden was head of the Senate Judiciary Committee at that time and, with Senator Kennedy, led the opposition to Bork.[39]

The Reagan administration was unprepared for the massive public relations campaign that liberal causes launched against Judge Bork, and they failed to respond effectively to it. Many of the more conservative Southern Democrats in the Senate who had been expected to support President Reagan's nomination eventually voted against Bork, as did six of the more liberal Republican senators.[40] In the final vote, Bork's nomination was rejected by a vote of 58–42. Eventually the vacant seat to which he had been nominated was filled by Anthony Kennedy. That single vote in the US Senate tragically changed the course of history in the United States for decades to come.

Since the defeat of his nomination in 1987, Bork has been a strong advocate for "originalism," the idea that the original public meaning of the Constitution should be the guiding principle in interpretation of the Constitution, not the personal views of the justices as to what is necessary or right for the nation.

Three years after his nomination, in 1990, Judge Bork published a bestselling book, *The Tempting of America: The Political Seduction of the Law*. The book is a significant critique of the usurping of power by the courts. In it Judge Bork clearly articulates just what is at stake:

> In the past few decades American institutions have struggled with the temptations of politics. Professions and academic disciplines that once possessed a life of their own have steadily succumbed, in some cases almost entirely, to *the belief that nothing matters beyond politically desirable results, however achieved.* In this quest, *politics invariably tries to dominate another discipline*, to capture and use it for politics' own purposes, while the second subject—law, religion, literature, economics, science, journalism, or whatever—struggles to maintain its independence. But retaining a separate identity and integrity becomes increasingly difficult as more and more areas of our culture, including the life of the intellect, perhaps especially the life of the intellect, become politicized. *It is coming to be denied that anything counts, not logic, not objectivity, not even intellectual honesty, that stands in the way of the "correct" political outcome.*
>
> The process by which this is accomplished may vary from field to field.... *In law, the moment of temptation is the moment of choice, when a judge realizes that in the case before him his strongly held view of justice, his political and moral imperative, is not embodied in a statute or in any provision of the Constitution.* He must then choose between *his version of justice* and *abiding by the American*

38. James Reston, "Kennedy and Bork," *New York Times* (July 5, 1987).

39. Tony Mauro, "Joe Biden and the Judges," *Law.com* (Sept. 8, 2008).

40. The Republican senators who voted against Bork were John Chafee (RI), Bob Packwood (OR), Arlen Specter (PA), Robert Stafford (VT), John Warner (VA), and Lowell P. Weicker (CT).

form of government.... To give in to temptation, this one time, solves an urgent human problem, and a faint crack appears in the American foundation. A judge has begun to rule where a legislator should.[41]

The clash over my nomination was simply one battle in this long-running war for control of our legal culture.... *In the larger war for control of the law, there are only two sides. Either the Constitution and statutes are law,* which means that their principles are known and control judges, *or they are malleable texts that judges may rewrite to see that particular groups or political causes win....* The Constitution ... is the highest prize, and control of the selection of judges is the last step on the path to that prize. Why? Because the Constitution is the trump card in American politics, and judges decide what the Constitution means. When the Supreme Court invokes the Constitution, whether legitimately or not, as to that issue the democratic process is at an end.[42]

The foundation of American freedoms is in the structure of our Republic. The major features of that structure are the separation of the powers of the national government and the limitation of national power to preserve a large degree of autonomy in the states. Both are mandated in the Constitution.... The phrase "separation of powers," as briefly put, means that Congress has "All legislative Powers," as those are defined in article I of the Constitution, while the President possesses "The executive Power," which is outlined in article II, and article III sets forth the elements of "the judicial Power." ... *There is no faintest hint in the Constitution, however, that the judiciary shares any of the legislative or executive power.* The intended function of the federal courts is to apply the law as it comes to them from the hands of others. The judiciary's great office is to preserve the constitutional design....

The Constitution preserves our liberties by providing that all of those given the authority to make policy are directly accountable to the people through regular elections. Federal judges, alone among our public officials, are given life tenure precisely so that they will not be accountable to the people.... But if judges are, as they must be to perform their vital role, unelected, unaccountable, and unrepresentative, who is to protect us from the power of judges? *How are we to be guarded from our guardians? The answer can only be that judges must consider themselves bound by law that is independent of their own views of the desirable.* They must not make or apply any policy not fairly to be found in the Constitution or a statute.[43]

What does it mean to say that a judge is bound by law? It means that he is bound by the only thing that can be called law, *the principles of the text,* whether Constitution or statute, *as generally understood at the enactment.*[44]

---

41. Robert Bork, *The Tempting of America: The Political Seduction of the Law* (New York: Simon & Schuster, 1990), 1 (emphasis added in this and the following quotations from this book). Reprinted and edited with the permission of the Free Press, a Division of Simon & Schuster, Inc., copyright © 1990 by Robert H. Bork. All rights reserved.

42. Ibid., 2–3.
43. Ibid., 4–5.
44. Ibid., 5.

Judges are by definition members of the intellectual class.... Like most people, judges tend to accept the assumptions of the culture that surrounds them.... If they can be persuaded to abandon the idea of original understanding, they are quite likely to frame constitutional rules that reflect the assumptions of modern liberal culture.

That has happened repeatedly in the past few decades. It probably explains... the fact that the Supreme Court has approved reverse discrimination on the basis of sex and race under a statute that clearly forbids it, found a right to abortion in the Constitution without explaining even once how that right could be derived from any constitutional materials, and came within one vote of finding a constitutional right to engage in homosexual conduct. For a few years the Court even abolished the death penalty, though the Constitution several times explicitly assumes that penalty to be a matter of legislative choice. My point is not that these choices are necessarily morally or politically wrong; my point is simply that, under the Constitution, *these are questions left for the people and their elected representatives, not for courts, to decide.*

It seems significant that every departure from the original understanding on that list ... resulted in the judicial enactment, or attempted enactment, of an item on the modern liberal agenda ... the principles of a liberal culture that cannot achieve those results democratically. This difference about the proper role of courts is what the battle over my confirmation was about.... The opposition knew they were fighting over more than one judge. They were fighting for control of the legal culture.[45]

The battle was ultimately about whether intellectual class values, which are far more egalitarian and socially permissive, which is to say left-liberal, than those of the public at large and so cannot carry elections, were to continue to be enacted into law by the Supreme Court.[46]

4. The rise of originalism in constitutional interpretation

During the entire time that the Supreme Court was increasing its power and creating new laws from the bench, others critiqued this process quite strongly. Many of these critiques have been found in the dissenting opinions written by the minority justices. The term "originalism" has commonly been used to refer to the viewpoint that cases before the Supreme Court should be decided on the basis of the "original meaning" of the law at the time it was written.

In the case *Roe v. Wade* in 1973, only one justice of the Supreme Court, William Rehnquist (who had taken his seat on the court in 1972), was an advocate of originalism. In 2010, four justices have clearly held to originalism: Chief Justice Roberts as well as Justices Scalia, Thomas, and Alito. Justice Kennedy sides with these four in some cases and votes against them in other cases.

---

45. Ibid., 8–9.　　　　　　　　　　　　46. Ibid., 337.

These justices have again and again said that the Supreme Court should not be deciding these issues of major importance to the nation, but should send them back to the people to decide through their elected representatives at the national, state, and local levels. This is the way that the nation was originally established to function and the way the Constitution specifies it should function. The first section of Article One of the Constitution says, "All legislative powers herein granted shall be vested in a Congress of the United States, which shall consist of a Senate and House of Representatives."

D. LIMITING THE POWER OF THE COURTS BY APPOINTING "ORIGINALIST" JUDGES IS THE MOST IMPORTANT ISSUE FACING THE NATION TODAY

1. Democrats and Republicans differ strongly over this issue

I believe that the battle for control of the judicial system is now the single most important issue for the future of the United States. On the one side of this issue are liberal judges who insist that they will continue to make and uphold new laws as they think best, calling them "interpretations" of the Constitution, and also liberal politicians, who are determined to support the actions of these activist judges. In individual states, Democratic governors appoint state supreme court judges who hold this activist view of the power of the courts. On a national level, Democratic candidates for President and Democratic members of the Senate have done everything they can to protect and preserve this process of new court-made laws by opposing most originalists who are nominated to Supreme Court or Appeals Court positions, and by Democratic Presidents appointing strong "activist" justices (such as Ginsburg, Breyer, and now apparently Sonia M. Sotomayor) who favor the idea that the Constitution is a "living document" in which justices can discover new rights and new laws.

On the other side of this issue are those on the more conservative end of the political spectrum, including many judges who have decided that their task is *only to interpret and apply* the Constitution and the laws of the nation and the states *according to the original intent* of those documents at the time they were written. Most Republican governors, Republican candidates for President, and Republican senators have supported such candidates for judicial positions. (Although Justice John Paul Stevens was appointed by Republican President Gerald Ford in 1975 and had a reputation as a moderately conservative judge at that time, for most of his tenure he consistently sided with the liberal or activist wing of the court.)

"What is wrong with our nation?" many people ask. "Why have we moved so far away from traditional moral values and practices?" One of the primary reasons has been the Supreme Court's takeover of the right to make decisions in all the important political questions facing the United States. Consider the following areas that have been pushed constantly leftward by decisions of the US Supreme Court and state supreme courts:

(1) Abortion
(2) Homosexuality and homosexual marriage

(3) Removal of religion from public events and public places

(4) The legitimacy of religious convictions as reasons to influence public actions

(5) As a result of (3) and (4), the removal from public schools of any teaching of accountability to God for one's actions or of any absolute moral standards, resulting in widespread moral erosion

(6) The undermining of personal sexual morality through the nullification of all but the most mild restraints on pornography

(7) Promoting the use of international law to interpret the US Constitution, and thereby undermining American sovereignty.

2. The current status of the Supreme Court

The makeup of the Supreme Court in 2010 is almost evenly balanced between liberal "activist" justices and conservative "originalist" justices, according to the following division:

Usually liberal:

Stephen Breyer (born 1938; serving 1994–) (appointed by President Clinton)

Ruth Bader Ginsburg (born 1933; serving 1993–) (appointed by President Clinton)

Sonia Sotomayor (born 1954; serving 2009–) (appointed by President Obama)

Elena Kagan (born 1960; serving 2010–) (appointed by President Obama)

"Swing" vote, often siding with "originalist" justices:

Anthony Kennedy (born 1936; serving 1988–) (appointed by President Reagan)

Consistently ruling according to the original meaning of the Constitution:

Samuel Alito (born 1950; serving 2006–) (appointed by President George W. Bush)

John Roberts (born 1955; serving 2005–) (appointed by President George W. Bush)

Antonio Scalia (born 1936; serving 1986–) (appointed by President Reagan)

Clarence Thomas (born 1948; serving 1991–) (appointed by President George H. W. Bush)

This situation cannot last forever. Five of the current nine justices (as I write this) are at least seventy years old. Whenever one retires or dies, the current President nominates a replacement, and that person must be confirmed by the US Senate.

This is why the election every four years of a President, and the elections of US senators, are going to decide the direction of the Supreme Court and the direction that the nation will take in this most crucial issue.

If the four liberal justices were to be replaced by four more "originalist" justices, then they would consistently send cases back to the Congress and back to the individual states for the elected representatives of the people to decide the important issues facing the nation. The United States would again become a functioning democracy rather than a nation ruled by unelected judges. The United States would once again function in the way that its founders intended, and the system of checks and balances between the legislative, executive, and judicial branches of government would be restored.

But if one or more of the conservative justices were to be replaced by a more liberal one, then by a majority of five to four the liberal justices could move aggressively to impose more and more of the liberal agenda that they desire on the entire nation. And there would be nothing that we could do to stop it.

At present, Anthony Kennedy is in effect deciding, by himself, many of the important issues facing our nation. He can side with whichever group he chooses, and they will have the majority. Therefore many of the important issues facing the nation are decided by one man who was never elected to office.

This is anything but a democracy. This is anything but the constitutional republic that was given to us by the Founding Fathers. This is anything but the system of government that our forefathers fought and died to establish. This is anything but a government "of the people, by the people, and for the people." This is government now effectively ruled by one unelected man, and it is a system gone horribly wrong.

The leaders of both political parties are deeply aware of this reality. And they are deeply aware that the ability to appoint justices to the Supreme Court is at present the ultimate prize in the American political system.

In addition, because the Supreme Court only decides very few cases each year, the twelve US Courts of Appeals have an immense amount of power. That is why, when Democrats gained control by one vote of the United States Senate after the 2006 elections, they were able to block nearly all of President Bush's nominees for appeals court positions. By having a fifty-one-vote majority in the Senate, Democrats gained control of all the Senate committees. Once that happened, Senator Patrick Leahy of Vermont, the chairman of the Judiciary Committee, simply refused to hold hearings on many of President Bush's nominations for appeals court positions and lower district court positions. Many of the nominees waited for two years or more and were given no hearings, with no expectation of any hearings. This was a blatant violation of the responsibility of the Senate either to approve or disapprove of the nominees of the President to these court positions and of the right of the President to appoint judges to these positions.

When President Bush left office, there were ten nominees for appeals court positions who had been given no hearings[47] and seventeen district court nominees who had been given no hearings.[48] This far exceeded the total for any previous Senate regarding presidential nominees.

3. Relevant biblical principles that apply to the issue of the Supreme Court

Is there a clear biblical position on this question? It seems to me that a Christian worldview should lead us to support judges who rule according to the "original intent" of the Constitution or the law that they are considering, for several reasons:

---

47. Congressional Research Service Report for Congress: Nominations to Article III Lower Courts by President George W. Bush During the 110th Congress, Updated Oct. 20, 2008, 5.

www.fas.org/sgp/crs/misc/RL33953.pdf.
48. Ibid.

(1) Romans 13:1 says, "Let every person be subject to the governing authorities." In the system of government established in the United States, the highest "governing authority" is a document, the Constitution itself. When justices enact rulings that are not fairly based on the original meaning of the Constitution, or are even contrary to the original meaning of the Constitution, then they are not being "subject to the governing authorities" under which we live, namely, the Constitution as the highest authority in the nation. These justices are not being subject to the system of government that they have sworn to uphold. It seems to me that when they do this, they are disobeying the clear principle established in Romans 13.

(2) The biblical argument that it is wise to have a separation of powers in human government argues strongly against the concentration of so much power in the hands of only one small group. (See chap. 3, pp. 101–3, regarding separation of powers.) The best safeguard against the abuse of power is divided power, as was the case in the Old Testament in the government of Israel and as was the case in the plurality of apostles and plurality of elders in the New Testament church.

(3) The principle that people should be accountable for their actions (a principle inherent in every governing structure established in the Bible) implies that it is wrong for those who *judge the laws* (the Supreme Court justices) to be the exact same people who actually *make the laws* (the new laws invented by the court when what they decide is not legitimately based in any statute or any provision of the Constitution). Nor should the people who make the most important laws be unelected and unaccountable to the people. With the present Supreme Court, there is no accountability for the justices' actions, and their power is easily abused.

(4) Any Christian can look at the anti-Christian results in such areas as the exclusion of God from the public square, the prevalence of pornography, the erosion of moral standards in many other areas of life, the prohibition against teaching in public schools that God even exists(!) and that he created the world, the unrestricted right to abortion, the increasing rights given to homosexual conduct, and the erosion of many other personal freedoms. These all indicate significant results from the current activist judiciary, results that are contrary to biblical principles.

4. Individual votes for Democrats or Republicans will decide the future of the nation on this issue

The one practical way that individual Christians can influence this issue is by voting. Every Christian citizen who votes helps one side or the other on this issue in every election.

Unfortunately, the two political parties in the United States have now adopted completely opposite approaches to this issue, with Democrats supporting liberal, activist judges who will use the courts to advance a liberal agenda, and (most, but not all) Republicans supporting "originalist" judges and justices who will rule according to the original meaning of the Constitution. Therefore, *every vote for every candidate* at the state and national level will tend to strengthen one party or the other and will tend to perpetuate either a liberal, activist system of judges or a conservative, originalist system of judges.

If Democrats are elected to the US Senate, they will tend to perpetuate the system of activist judges. If Democrats are elected to the US House or to state offices, some of them will advance to positions in the US Senate or to the Presidency. At the state level, Democratic governors will appoint justices who follow these activist tendencies, and Democrats in state legislatures will generally support this trend as well.

On the other hand, Republicans (not entirely, but for the most part) have sought to support judges at both state and national levels who hold to the original intent of the Constitution and the laws that have been passed. Therefore voting for Republican candidates for state and national positions is the best way—in fact, the only way known to me—to bring about a change and break the rule of unaccountable judges over our society.

I believe this is the most important issue facing the nation, for it will decide who will rule the nation. It will decide whether we will once again become a nation with a government "of the people, by the people, and for the people" or whether we will forever be ruled by nine unelected, lifetime justices on the Supreme Court.

Part 2

SPECIFIC ISSUES

Chapter 6

THE PROTECTION OF LIFE

A. ABORTION

1. The issue

With regard to the question of abortion, the political question is this:

Should governments make laws to protect the lives of preborn children?

If the answer to that question is yes, then there are more specific questions, such as:

Should the preborn child be protected from the moment of conception to the moment of birth, or only from some later point in pregnancy?

What should the preborn child be called—a "fetus," a "preborn child," an "unborn child," or a "baby"?

What kind of penalties should attach to taking the life of a preborn child?

Even for those who do not think governments should make laws protecting the lives of preborn children, other policy questions remain:

Should governments pay for women to have abortions?

Should physicians and other health-care providers who think abortion is morally wrong be compelled to perform abortions?

Should government policies promote or discourage abortions? (This would include educational policies, policies regarding aid to other nations, and so forth.)

2. Relevant biblical teaching

a. The preborn child should be treated as a person from the moment of conception

Several passages in the Bible suggest that a preborn child should be thought of as a person from the moment of conception. For example, before the birth of John the Baptist, when his mother, Elizabeth, was in about her sixth month of pregnancy, she was visited by her relative, Mary, who was to become the mother of Jesus. Luke reports:

> And when Elizabeth heard the greeting of Mary, the baby leaped in her womb. And Elizabeth was filled with the Holy Spirit, and she exclaimed with a loud cry,... "Behold, when the sound of your greeting came to my ears, *the baby in my womb leaped for joy*" (Luke 1:41–44).

Under the influence of the Holy Spirit, Elizabeth calls the preborn child in the sixth month of pregnancy a "baby" (Greek *brephos*, "baby, infant"). This is the same Greek word that is used for a child after it is born, as in Luke 2:16, where Jesus is called a "baby [*brephos*] lying in a manger" (see also Luke 18:15; 2 Tim. 3:15). Elizabeth also says that the baby "leaped for joy," which attributes personal human activity to him. He was able to hear Mary's voice and somehow, even prior to birth, feel joyful about it. (Note that modern medical research shows that preborn children can distinguish and become familiar with the voices of their father, mother, or other family members.)

King David sinned with Bathsheba and then was rebuked by Nathan the prophet. Afterward, David wrote Psalm 51, in which he pleads with God, "Have mercy on me, O God, according to your steadfast love" (v. 1). Amidst confessing his sin, he writes,

> Behold, I was brought forth in iniquity, and *in sin did my mother conceive me* (Ps. 51:5).

David thinks back to the time of his birth and says that he was "brought forth" from his mother's womb as a sinner. In fact, his sinfulness as a person extended back even prior to his birth, for David, under the direction of the Holy Spirit says, "In sin did my mother conceive me."

He is not talking about his mother's sin in any of the preceding verses, but is talking about the depth of *his own sinfulness* as a human being. Therefore, in this verse he is talking about himself as well. He is saying that from the moment of conception he had a sinful nature. This means that *he thought of himself as a distinct human being, a distinct person, from the moment of conception*. He was not merely part of his mother's body, but was distinct in his personhood. And this goes all the way back to the point of conception.

David also thinks of himself as a person while he was growing in his mother's womb, for he says,

> You formed my inward parts; you knitted *me* together in my mother's womb (Ps. 139:13).

Here also he speaks of himself as a distinct person ("me") when he was in his mother's womb. The word translated "inward parts" is Hebrew *kilyah*, literally "kidneys," but in contexts such as this one, it refers to the innermost parts of a person, including his deepest inward thoughts and emotions (see its uses in Pss. 16:7; 26:2; 73:21; Prov. 2:16; Jer. 17:10).

In an earlier example, Rebekah, the wife of Isaac, was pregnant with the twins who were to be named Jacob and Esau. We read:

> The children [Hebrew *banim*, plural of *ben*] struggled together within her, and she said, "If it is thus, why is this happening to me?" So she went to inquire of the LORD. And the LORD said to her, "Two nations are in your womb, and two peoples from within you shall be divided; the one shall be stronger than the other, the older shall serve the younger" (Gen. 25:22–23).

Once again, the preborn children are viewed as "children" within her womb. (Hebrew *ben* is the ordinary word used more than 4,900 times in the Old Testament for "son" or—plural—"children.") These twins are viewed as already struggling together. Before the point of birth they are thought of as distinct persons, and their future is being predicted.

For the question of abortion, perhaps the most significant passage of all is found in the specific laws God gave Moses for the people of Israel during the time of the Mosaic covenant. One particular law spoke of the penalties to be imposed in case the life or health of a pregnant woman or her preborn child was endangered or harmed:

> When men strive together and hit a pregnant woman, so that her children come out, *but there is no harm*, the one who hit her shall surely be fined, as the woman's husband shall impose on him, and he shall pay as the judges determine. But *if there is harm*, then you shall pay life for life, eye for eye, tooth for tooth, hand for hand, foot for foot, burn for burn, wound for wound, stripe for stripe (Exod. 21:22–25).[1]

This law concerns a situation when men are fighting and one of them accidentally hits a pregnant woman. Neither one of them intended to do this, but as they fought they were not careful enough to avoid hitting her. If that happens, there are two possibilities:

1. If this causes a premature birth but *there is no harm to the pregnant woman or her preborn child*, there is still a penalty: "The one who hit her shall surely be fined" (v. 22). The penalty was for carelessly endangering the life or health of the pregnant woman and her child. We have similar laws in modern society, such as when a person is fined for drunken driving, even though he has hit no one with his car. He recklessly endangered human life and health, and he deserved a fine or other penalty.

---

1. The phrase "so that her children come out" is a literal translation of the Hebrew text, which uses the plural of the common Hebrew word *yeled*, "child," and another very common word, *yātsā'*, which means "go out, come out." The plural "children" is probably the plural of indefiniteness, allowing for the possibility of more than one child. Other translations render this as "so that she gives birth prematurely," which is very similar in meaning (so NASB, from 1999 editions onward; similarly: NIV, TNIV, NET, HCSV, NLT, NKJV).

2. But *"if there is harm"* to either *the pregnant woman or her child*, then the penalties are quite severe: "Life for life, eye for eye, tooth for tooth …" (vv. 23–24). This means that both the mother and the preborn child are given equal legal protection. The penalty for harming the preborn child is just as great as for harming the mother. Both are treated as persons, and both deserve the full protection of the law.[2]

This law is even more significant when we put it in the context of other laws in the Mosaic covenant. In other cases in the Mosaic law where someone *accidentally* caused the death of another person, there was no requirement to give "life for life," no capital punishment. Rather, the person who accidentally caused someone else's death was required to flee to one of the "cities of refuge" until the death of the high priest (see Num. 35:9–15, 22–29). This was a kind of "house arrest," although the person had to stay within a city rather than within a house for a limited period of time. It was a far lesser punishment than "life for life."

This means that God established for Israel a law code *that placed a higher value on protecting the life of a pregnant woman and her preborn child than the life of anyone else in Israelite society.* Far from treating the death of a preborn child as *less significant* than the death of others in society, this law treats the death of a preborn child or its mother as *more significant* and worthy of more severe punishment. And the law does not place any restriction on the number of months the woman was pregnant. Presumably it would apply from a very early stage in pregnancy, whenever it could be known that a miscarriage had occurred and her child or children had died as a result.

Moreover, this law applies to a case of *accidental* killing of a preborn child. But if *accidental* killing of a preborn child is so serious in God's eyes, then surely *intentional* killing of a preborn child must be an even worse crime.

The conclusion from all of these verses is that the Bible teaches that we should think of the preborn child as a person from the moment of conception, and we should give to the preborn child legal protection at least equal to that of others in the society.

Additional note: It is likely that many people reading this evidence from the Bible, perhaps for the first time, will already have had an abortion. Others reading this will have encouraged someone else to have an abortion. I cannot minimize or deny the moral

---

2. Some translations have adopted an alternative sense of this passage. The NRSV translates it, "When people who are fighting injure a pregnant woman so that there is a miscarriage, and yet no further harm follows …" (RSV is similar, as was NASB before 1999). In this case, causing a miscarriage and the death of a preborn child results only in a fine. Therefore, some have argued, this passage treats the preborn child as *less worthy* of protection than others in society, for the penalty is less. But the arguments for this translation are not persuasive. The primary argument is that this would make the law similar to a provision in the law code of Hammurabi (about 1760 BC in ancient Babylon). But such a supposed parallel should not override the meanings of the actual words in the Hebrew text of Exodus. The moral and civil laws in the Bible often differed from those of the ancient cultures around Israel. In addition, there is a Hebrew word for a miscarriage (*shakal*, Gen. 31:38; see also Exod. 23:26; Job 21:20; Hosea 9:14), but that word is not used here, nor is *nēphel*, another term for "miscarriage" (see Job 3:16; Ps. 58:8; Eccl. 6:3). However, the word that is used, *yātsā'*, is ordinarily used to refer to the live birth of a child (see Gen. 25:26; 38:29; Jer. 1:5). Finally, even on this (incorrect) translation, a *fine* is imposed on the person who accidentally caused the death of the preborn child. This implies that *accidentally* causing such a death is still considered morally wrong. Therefore, *intentionally* causing the death of a preborn child would be much more wrong, even on this translation.

wrong involved in this action, but I can point to the repeated offer of the Bible that God will give forgiveness of sins to those who repent of their sin and trust in Jesus Christ for forgiveness: "If we confess our sins, he is faithful and just to forgive us our sins and to cleanse us from all unrighteousness" (1 John 1:9). Although such sin, like all other sin, deserves God's wrath, Jesus Christ took that wrath on himself as a substitute for all who would believe in him: "He himself bore our sins in his body on the tree, that we might die to sin and live to righteousness. By his wounds you have been healed" (1 Peter 2:24).

b. Scientific information on the distinct personhood of the preborn child

Dr. Dianne Irving, a biochemist and biologist and professor at Georgetown University, writes:

To begin with, scientifically something very radical occurs between the processes of gametogenesis and fertilization—the change from a simple *part* of one human being (i.e., a sperm) and a simple *part* of another human being (i.e., an oocyte—usually referred to as an "ovum" or "egg"), which simply possess "human life," to a new, genetically unique, newly existing, individual, whole living human being (a single-cell embryonic human zygote). That is, upon fertilization, parts of human beings have actually been transformed into something very different from what they were before; they have been changed into a single, whole human being. During the process of fertilization, the sperm and the oocyte cease to exist as such, and a new human being is produced.

To understand this, it should be remembered that each kind of living organism has a specific number and quality of chromosomes that are characteristic for each member of a species. (The number can vary only slightly if the organism is to survive.) For example, the characteristic number of chromosomes for a member of the human species is 46 (plus or minus, e.g., in human beings with Down's or Turner's syndromes). Every somatic (or, body) cell in a human being has this characteristic number of chromosomes. Even the early germ cells contain 46 chromosomes; it is only their mature forms—the sex gametes, or sperms and oocytes—which will later contain only 23 chromosomes each. Sperms and oocytes are derived from primitive germ cells in the developing fetus by means of the process known as "gametogenesis." Because each germ cell normally has 46 chromosomes, the process of "fertilization" can not take place until the total number of chromosomes in each germ cell is cut in half. This is necessary so that after their fusion at fertilization the characteristic number of chromosomes in a single individual member of the human species (46) can be maintained—otherwise we would end up with a monster of some sort.

To accurately see why a sperm or an oocyte are considered as only possessing human life, and not as living human beings themselves, one needs to look at the basic scientific facts involved in the processes of **gametogenesis** and of **fertilization**. It may help to keep in mind that the products of gametogenesis and fertilization are very different. The products of gametogenesis are mature sex gametes with only 23 instead of 46 chromosomes. The product of fertilization is a living human being with 46 chromosomes. Gametogenesis refers to the maturation of germ cells, resulting in gametes. Fertilization refers to the initiation of a new human being.[3]

c. Objections regarding the personhood of the preborn child

Some objections may be raised against the idea that the preborn child should be treated as a person from the moment of conception.

(1) Unable to interact and survive on its own: One objection is that the preborn child is unable to talk or interact with other people or perform moral actions. In addition, it is unable to survive without its mother.

But these factors do not mean that the preborn child is not a person. For instance, a newborn is still unable to talk or perform moral actions. This is also true for a person in a coma due to a serious accident. Moreover, a newborn infant is surely unable to survive without its mother. (In fact, some people would say that most junior high students are unable to survive without their mother!) Such an objection is not persuasive.

(2) Birth defects: Another objection concerns preborn children who are known to have birth defects. Should parents not have the right to abort such children, thus saving themselves much hardship and saving the child from a life of suffering?

But the relevant question here is this: Would we think it right to put such a child to death *after* it is born?

If we have already established that the preborn child should be treated as a person from the moment of conception, then being born or not yet being born should make no difference in assessment of the child's personhood. If we would not think it right to kill such a child after it is born, then we should not think it right to kill the child *before* it is born.

Moreover, prior to birth the "possible" or "probable" diagnosis of birth defects can be in error. Sometimes children can be perfectly normal even though there was a diagnosis of a "possible" or "probable" birth defect. Many birth defects can be very small and not have significant impact on the child's life. And even when the birth defect is quite significant (for example, Down syndrome) the child can still lead a happy life and bring much joy and blessing to his or her own family and to many others. In such cases Christians should be encouraged to trust in God's wise providence and his sovereign direction of their lives. The Lord said to Moses, "Who has made man's mouth? Who makes him mute, or deaf, or seeing, or blind? Is it not I, the LORD?" (Exod. 4:11). When Jesus saw a man who had been blind from birth,

> his disciples asked him, "Rabbi, who sinned, this man or his parents, that he was born blind?" Jesus answered, "It was not that this man sinned, or his parents, but that the works of God might be displayed in him" (John 9:2–3).

---

3. Dianne Irving, Ph.D., "When Do Human Beings Begin? 'Scientific' Myths and Scientific Facts," http://catholiceducation.org/articles/abortion/ab0027.html. Dr. Irving is a former career-appointed bench research biochemist/biologist (NIH, NCI, Bethesda, MD), an M.A. and Ph.D. philosopher (Georgetown University, Washington, DC), and Professor of the History of Philosophy and of Medical Ethics.

Randy Alcorn quotes an example of a medical school professor who told about the following case study and asked students what they would do:

> The father had syphilis and the mother had tuberculosis. Of four previous children, the first was blind, the second died, the third was both deaf and dumb, and the fourth had tuberculosis. What would you advise the woman to do when she finds she is pregnant again?

One student answered, "I would advise an abortion." Then the professor said, "Congratulations.... You have just killed Beethoven."[4]

(3) Pregnancies resulting from rape or incest: If a child has been conceived through rape or incest, we must recognize the genuine pain and hardship experienced by the mother, who is involuntarily pregnant and perhaps pregnant at a very young age. Christians who know of such situations should be ready to give encouragement and support in many ways.

But once again the question must be asked, would we think it right to kill a baby conceived through rape or incest *after* it is born? Most people would say, certainly not. Such a child does not lose its right to live because of the circumstances of its conception. But then we should not think it right to kill the child *before* it is born either. The rape that occurred is not the fault of the child, and the child should not be put to death because of someone else's crime. "Fathers shall not be put to death because of their children, nor shall children be put to death because of their fathers. Each one shall be put to death for his own sin" (Deut. 24:16; compare Ezek. 18:20). In addition, such instances are quite rare, constituting at most 1% of all abortions,[5] but probably much less than that.

Alcorn points out that well-known Gospel singer Ethel Waters was born as a result of pregnancy that occurred when her mother was raped at age twelve.[6] There are no doubt other people today who lead useful, productive, fulfilling lives, even though their birth was the result of the horrible crime of rape. We should not justify taking the life of the preborn child in such cases.

(4) Abortion to save the life of the mother: According to the Centers for Disease Control, abortion carried out to save the life of the mother is extremely rare (less than 0.118% of all abortions).[7] Such a situation is different from the others we considered above, because here the choice is between the loss of one life (the baby's) and the loss of two lives (both the baby's and the mother's). I cannot see a reason to say this would be morally wrong, and in fact, I believe it would be morally right for doctors to save the life that can be saved and take the life of the preborn child. This is significantly different from the other cases, because removing the preborn child from the mother's body (for example from the Fallopian tube in the case of an ectopic pregnancy) results from

4. Randy Alcorn, *ProLife Answers to ProChoice Arguments* (Portland, OR: Multnomah, 1992), 175.

5. A. Torres and J. Forest, "Why Do Women Have Abortions?" *Family Planning Perspectives* 20:4 (July/Aug. 1988), 169–76; still the best source of US data according to A. Bankole et al., "Reasons Why Women Have Induced Abortions: Evidence from 27 Countries," *Family Planning Perspectives* 24:3 (Aug. 1998), 117–25, 152.

6. Alcorn, *ProLife Answers,* 179.

7. Jeani Chang et al., "Pregnancy-Related Mortality Surveillance—United States, 1991–1999," Centers for Disease Control, *Morbidity and Mortality Weekly Report* (Feb. 21, 2003). www.cdc.gov/mmwr/preview/mmwrhtml/ss5202a1.htm.

directly intending to save the life of the mother, not from *directly intending to take the child's life.* If the medical technology exists to save the child's life in such cases, then of course the child's life should also be saved. But if abortion is necessary to save the mother's life, this would seem to be the only situation in which abortion is morally justified.

Therefore it seems right to me that all mainstream pro-life proposals for legal restrictions on abortion have included an exception to save the life of the mother.

But in politics, proponents of "abortion rights" too often lump together "life" and "health" and declare that they are willing to restrict abortion "except to save the life or health of the mother." Then in actual practice, "health" becomes defined so broadly in legal precedents that it also includes "mental health," including freedom from excessive distress; thus, "except to save the life *or health* of the mother" in practice means abortion is allowed whenever the mother wants to obtain one.

In fact, *Doe v. Bolton,* the companion case to *Roe v. Wade,* defined maternal "health" as "all factors—physical, emotional, psychological, familial, and the woman's age—relevant to the well-being of the patient." These factors are so vague and open-ended that almost any reason can be cited to allow an abortion in the second and third trimesters. Therefore, abortion is legal—and cannot be prohibited—in the fourth, fifth, sixth, seventh, eighth, or ninth month of pregnancy if any one of these reasons is invoked.[8]

3. Arguments from reason and evidence apart from the Bible

When talking about abortion with people who do not think of the Bible as God's Word, a case for the personhood of the preborn child can still be argued in several ways. Medical evidence about the distinct genetic identity and distinct DNA of the child can be used to show that the preborn child is far different (in every single cell of its body!) from any other part of the mother's own body. Modern ultrasound technology can give highly realistic images of the preborn child—images that look so much like a real human person that they have great persuasive force. For that reason, many abortion advocates try to discourage pregnant women from seeing such vivid images. Nancy Keenan, president of NARAL Pro-Choice America in Washington, DC, said, "Politicians should not require a doctor to perform a medically unnecessary ultrasound, nor should they force a woman to view an ultrasound against her will."[9] Abortion advocate William Saletan, writing in *Slate* magazine, said, "Ultrasound has exposed the life in the womb to those of us who didn't want to see what abortion kills. The fetus is squirming, and so are we."[10]

As of February 2009, eleven states were considering ultrasound laws, requiring that a woman be given an opportunity to view an ultrasound of her preborn child prior to having an abortion (Connecticut, Indiana, Kansas, Maryland, Missouri, Nebraska, New York, South Carolina, Texas, Virginia, and Wyoming).[11] At present, three states (North

8. *Doe v. Bolton,* 41 U.S. 179, 192 (1973).

9. Jennifer Parker, "Bill Would Mandate Ultrasound before Abortion," *ABCNews.com* (March 16, 2007). http://abcnews.go.com/US/story?id=2958249&page=1&CMP=OTC-RSS-Feeds0312.

10. William Saletan, "Sex, Lies, and Videotape," *Slate.com* (April 28, 2007). www.slate.com/id/2165137/.

11. "More States Considering Mandating Ultrasounds before Abortions," *USA Today* (Feb. 8, 2009). www.usatoday.com/news/nation/2009-02-08-abortion-laws_N.htm.

Dakota, South Dakota, and Utah) mandate that a woman be given an opportunity to view an ultrasound when seeking abortion.[12]

In addition, the arguments from how we would treat a child after it is born can have significant persuasive force. (For example, would we think it right for our laws to allow a parent to kill a child simply because the parent does not want the child or finds the child a difficult burden?)

Another argument against abortion is the incalculable loss to the nation from the deaths of more than one million babies per year. Since the 1973 Supreme Court decision *Roe v. Wade*, nearly 50 million children have been put to death through abortion.[13] Some of those would now be thirty-seven years old. Others would be thirty-six, and thirty-five, and so on, down to 1,200,000 of them who would be in their first year of life.[14] Many of them by now would be scientists and doctors, engineers and business leaders, entrepreneurs, artists, electricians, poets, carpenters, musicians, sports figures, political leaders, and so forth. Many of them would be mothers taking care of their own children and fathers helping to raise their children. They would be contributing to society in all areas of life—but they never had the chance to be born. They never had the chance to contribute in a positive way to this world.

A further argument can be made simply from the instinctive sense a pregnant woman has that what is growing in her womb is not a piece of tissue or merely a part of her body, but is in fact *a baby*. (Such an instinct is given even to unbelievers by God himself, for the Bible tells us, with respect to Gentiles "who do not have the Law," that "the work of the Law is *written on their hearts*, while their *conscience* also bears witness, and their conflicting thoughts accuse or even excuse them" [Rom. 2:14–15].) This gives us some hope that arguments showing the personhood of the preborn child will eventually be persuasive to the majority of people in a society.

4. Objections

Here are some objections that people have raised against the idea of prohibiting abortions.

a. A wrongful restriction of freedom

Some people will argue that a law prohibiting abortions is a wrongful restriction on individual human freedom. Shouldn't the decision about whether to carry a baby to full term and give birth be a decision made by the mother herself? How can it be right to say that the law should force a woman to endure a pregnancy and bear a child that she does not want? Isn't individual freedom a foundational principle of this country? Sometimes people will say, "I am personally opposed to abortion, but I think that's a decision that should be up to the mother and her doctor."

---

12. Alan Guttmacher Institute, "State Policies in Brief: Requirements for Ultrasound" (Sept. 1, 2009). www.guttmacher.org/statecenter/spibs/spib_RFU.pdf.

13. As of September 2009, National Right to Life calculates the total number of abortions since *Roe v. Wade* to be 49,551,703. www.nrlc.org/abortion/facts/abortionstats.html.

14. Recent statistics show current rate of 1.2 million abortions per year, down from a peak of 1.6 million per year in 1990. From 1980 to 1992 the average was over 1.5 million per year, but it has been declining slightly ever since then. See ibid.

For example, US Vice President Joe Biden has repeatedly said, "My position is that I am personally opposed to abortion, but I don't think I have a right to impose my view on the rest of society."[15] In 2004, then-presidential candidate John Kerry was asked about his position on abortion on *Meet the Press*. He said, "I don't want abortion. Abortion should be the rarest thing in the world. I am actually personally opposed to abortion. But I don't believe that I have a right to take what is an article of faith to me and legislate it to other people."[16] In the meantime, the 2004 Democratic platform that he ran under read, "Because we believe in the privacy and equality of women, we stand proudly for a woman's right to choose, consistent with Roe v. Wade, and regardless of her ability to pay. We stand firmly against Republican efforts to undermine that right."[17]

In response, individual freedom is of course important and should be protected. But the real question is not freedom in the abstract but what appropriate restrictions the law should place on individual freedom. The law already restricts freedom in many ways that people agree on. The law does not allow me the freedom to drive while intoxicated or steal my neighbor's car or beat up on someone I don't like or fire a gun inside the city limits—and surely it does not allow parents to put their living children to death. So the question is not human freedom, but whether the law should allow people *freedom to take their child's life*. If the preborn child is considered a human person, the question is whether the government should allow people to commit murder against their own children. Certainly it should not.

b. All children should be wanted children

This is another popular phrase used by politicians who advocate abortion. For example, New Jersey Democratic Senator Robert Menendez says on his website, "I support women's reproductive rights, including the right to preventative options and family planning options. Regardless of a person's position on contraception and choice, I think that we can all agree that the ultimate goal is to ensure that all children are wanted children."[18] The benefit of allowing abortions, some people say, is that it gives mothers the freedom not to bear children they really don't want, children that might grow up to be neglected and abused and poorly cared for in any case. Why not allow abortions, so that only mothers who really *want* their children will have them?

But if we consider the preborn child to be a person, then this argument is merely another way of saying that people should be allowed to kill other people that they do not want to care for. In particular, parents should be able to kill the children that they do not want to care for.

Once a child is born, would we say that a parent who does not "want" to care for that child any longer should have the right to put him or her to death because "all children

15. Scott Richert, "Where Do Barack Obama and Joe Biden Stand on Abortion?" *About.com*, http://catholicism.about.com/od/thechurchintheworld/p/Dem_Abortion.htm.

16. Carla Marinucci, "Dems Give Abortion Foes Space," *San Francisco Chronicle* (Feb. 7, 2005). www.sfgate.com/cgi-bin/article.cgi?f=/c/a/2005/02/07/ABORTION.TMP&type=printable.

17. "Strong at Home, Respected in the World," 2004 Democratic Party Platform, www.democrats.org/pdfs/2004platform.pdf.

18. See http://menendez.senate.gov/issues/reproductiver-ights.cfm.

should be wanted children"? Surely not. This is a horrible thought, but it is simply the logical conclusion of the "all children should be wanted children" argument. This is really a bankrupt moral argument, one that so devalues human life that it values a mother's desire for convenience more highly than the right to life of a child made in the very image of God.

c. "I'm personally against abortion, but I just don't support laws against abortion"

This argument is made by a number of politicians who do not want to appear to be *supporting* the idea of killing preborn children, but still are committed to protecting the *legal* right of women to have an abortion if they choose. Presumably, if they were asked for advice by a pregnant woman, they would tell her that they would *personally recommend* that she not get an abortion. But the decision, of course, is still up to her.

This argument fails to understand the difference between personal moral persuasion and governmental laws. If we really believe that an action is taking innocent human lives, then we will not be content to depend on moral influence to stop it. This position would be similar to saying, "I'm *personally opposed* to drunk driving, and I wouldn't *personally recommend* drunk driving, but I don't support having laws against it, because I think *individual drivers should have the right to decide for themselves* whether to drive when drunk." The fact of the matter is that, apart from legal enforcement by the government, many people will foolishly decide to drive while intoxicated and will actually kill other people through their wrongful choices. Government is instituted by God to protect us from such wrongdoing by others.

This argument is, in fact, a subtle attempt at changing the subject. The whole subject under dispute is not *personal preferences* of individuals, but what *the laws of a government* should prohibit. Just as we would not say, "I'm personally opposed to murder, but I don't think there should be any laws against murder," so it seems naïve and, I think, misleading to say, "I'm personally opposed to abortion, but I don't think that there should be laws against abortion."

d. "We should reduce the causes of abortion but not have laws against abortion"

A similar position to "I'm personally against abortion, but I don't support laws against abortion" is that of Jim Wallis, in his book *God's Politics*. Wallis says that "the abortion rate in America is much too high for a good and healthy society that respects both women and children," and he recommends "really targeting the problems of teen pregnancy and adoption reform, which are so critical to reducing abortion, while offering real support for women, especially low-income women, at greater risk for unwanted pregnancies."[19]

---

19. Jim Wallis, *God's Politics: Why the Right Gets It Wrong and the Left Doesn't Get It* (New York: HarperSanFransisco, 2005), 299–300.

But this is just changing the subject. The subject under discussion is *laws* about abortion. The specific question is *what should the laws about abortion be?* Should laws prohibit abortion (with certain exceptions) or not? Saying we should try to reduce teen pregnancy in order to stop abortion is like saying we should support Alcoholics Anonymous in order to stop drunk driving, or we should support job creation to stop stealing, or we should support anger management clinics to stop murders. Those are helpful social programs, but they alone will not stop those crimes.

This comes back to the question of the worldview assumptions that we discussed in chapter 4 (see pp. 119–22). Is the ultimate cause of wrongdoing something in society (and therefore we should just give more support to low-income women who become pregnant), or is it that people make evil choices (to kill their preborn children), so laws should hold people accountable for those choices?

What Jim Wallis refuses to say in *God's Politics* is that we should have *laws* that prevent women from taking the lives of their preborn children. Our laws should protect human life. The main difference between conservatives and liberals on abortion is how they answer this question: *Should it be against the law to kill your preborn child?* I believe it should be against the law (except to save the mother's life). Certainly we *also* should give support to low-income women who are pregnant, but both sides agree on this. The solution is "both-and"—both maternal support and laws. But Wallis and most of his fellow Democrats will not say "both-and." When the question is asked about *what the laws should be*, they simply change the subject to maternal support. They will not support laws to prohibit abortion, and most Democrats actively oppose such laws. (On Wallis's claim to a "consistent ethic of life," see discussion below, pp. 176–77.)

e. "Christians should not try to impose their moral standards on other people"

People who make this objection would usually say that it's fine for Christians to think that abortion is wrong for themselves, but they have no right to try to force that conviction on others who do not have a Christian viewpoint.

In response, it must be said that many of our laws are based on moral convictions that are held by the vast majority of the population. The laws against murder are based on a moral conviction that murder is wrong. The laws against stealing are based on the moral conviction that stealing is wrong. Laws against polygamy and incest are based on moral convictions that those things are wrong. Laws against sexual harassment, or adults having sex with minors, are based on convictions that those things are wrong. We could multiply examples by the thousands from all areas of the law.

So the question is not whether laws should be based on *some* moral convictions, but whether laws about abortion should be based on *these* moral convictions.

Which moral standards support laws against abortions? There are two: (1) People should not be allowed to murder other people; (2) the preborn child should be considered a human person and should be protected as a human person. No doubt almost everyone would agree on the first point. So the question really involves the second point, whether the preborn child should be considered a human person worthy of legal protection.

In our system of government, Christians cannot *impose* their moral convictions on anyone. But everyone in the nation is free to attempt to *persuade* others about the moral convictions that should be the basis for various laws. So a more accurate way of phrasing this objection is not that "Christians should not try to impose their moral standards on others," but rather, "Christians should not try to persuade others that the preborn child is a human person and deserves the legal protections due to human persons." Of course, when the objection is stated that way, hardly anyone would agree with it. Surely our nation was founded on the ability of citizens *to speak freely about their convictions and try to persuade others* and thereby try to influence laws. In fact, the First Amendment *guarantees* freedom of speech and freedom of the press, assuring us that people of all persuasions are free to argue and attempt to persuade others about what kinds of laws should be made.

Finally, Christians should not view these convictions about the personhood of the preborn child as "*our* moral convictions." We did not make them up out of our own minds, but found them written in the Bible. And the Bible presents these as not mere human opinion, but the moral standards of God himself, by which he holds all people in every nation accountable (see discussion above, chap. 4, pp. 117–18).

It does seem right for Christians to attempt to persuade others that the moral standards found in the Bible are correct and should be used in human government. It was on the basis of this conviction that Paul could reason with the Roman governor, Felix, "about righteousness and self-control and the coming judgment" (Acts 24:25). It was on this basis that John the Baptist "reproved" Herod the Tetrarch "for all the evil things that Herod had done" (Luke 3:19). And in the Old Testament, Daniel warned King Nebuchadnezzar of Babylon about his "sins" and "iniquities" (Dan. 4:27), and Jonah warned the entire city of Nineveh to repent (see Jonah 3:4; see also the discussion of Christian influence on government in chap. 2, pp. 58–61).

5. Recommendations for Political Policies

a. Governments should enact laws prohibiting abortions except to save the life of the mother

One of the fundamental responsibilities of a government is to protect the lives of the people it governs, for if government is to punish those who do evil and to prevent them from harming the innocent (see chap. 3, pp. 77–82), then a government certainly must protect its people from the ultimate harm of being killed (see discussion of Gen. 9:5–6 on pp. 77–78, 186–88). If preborn children are considered persons, then surely government should protect their lives. In fact, it is *especially* the weak and helpless, those without other means of protection, who should be the objects of governmental protections:

> Give justice to the weak and fatherless; maintain the right of the afflicted and the destitute. Rescue the weak and needy; deliver them from the hand of the wicked (Ps. 82:3–4).

If laws are eventually made to prevent abortions, what penalties should be given to those who perform an abortion? That question should be left to individual state legislatures to decide through a normal political process, just as penalties are determined for all other violations of the law. In a democracy, laws can only be passed with support from a majority of the elected representatives of the people, and ultimately this means that—in ordinary circumstances anyway—laws can only be passed and sustained with the support of the majority of the citizens covered by a law. Therefore, in determining an appropriate penalty for performing an abortion, it would be foolish for pro-life representatives to insist on penalties so severe that they would not gain assent from a reasonable majority of the population or their elected representatives, for then no law would be passed at all. (Prior to *Roe v. Wade*, most state penalties were against the doctor who performed the abortion rather than the woman who got the abortion.)

What if a "compromise" law were proposed that would prohibit abortions except to save the life of the mother or in cases of rape or incest? I think that Christians should support such legislation, since it would still prohibit probably 99 percent of the abortions that are occurring today. After such a law is passed, perhaps further modifications could be made to the law in the future, if public sentiment would support it. But even such a law would do a tremendous amount of good in protecting the lives of the vast majority of preborn children who today are being put to death.

b. No government policies should promote or fund abortions

No government money should be given to pay the medical costs of abortions (while they are still legal). Nor should any government money be given to promote abortions (supporting proabortion groups such as Planned Parenthood, for example). Nor should foreign aid be given for the purpose of "population control," which involves paying for abortions in other countries. If abortion is the wrongful taking of a human life, and if civil government is given by God "to punish those who do evil and to praise those who do good" (1 Peter 2:14), then government should surely do nothing to encourage such wrongdoing.

Democratic and Republican presidents have clearly differed on this question. Republican President Ronald Reagan instituted what has become known as the "Mexico City Policy," which forbade government funds going to international "family planning groups" that provide abortions. This ban was lifted by Democratic President Bill Clinton in 1993 and reinstituted by Republican President George W. Bush in 2001. Democratic President Barack Obama lifted the ban again in 2009.[20]

c. No government policy should compel people to participate in abortions or to dispense drugs that cause abortions

In the current situation in the United States, abortions are still legal. This gives women freedom to choose whether or not they will have an abortion. In such a situation it is

---

20. See Jake Tapper, "Obama Overturns 'Mexico City Policy' Instituted by Reagan," *ABCNews.com* (Jan. 23, 2009). http://abc-news.go.com/Politics/International/story?id=6716958&page=1.

essential that doctors (as well as nurses and other medical workers) have the freedom to choose whether or not to participate in abortions, both in medical school as part of their training and then in their practice of medicine. It is also essential that pharmacists be allowed to choose not to dispense drugs that cause abortions (such as Mifepristone or RU–486, also otherwise known as the "morning-after" pill). Sadly, some laws and governmental regulations have attempted to deny people freedom of conscience on whether they participate in abortions or dispense such drugs.[21] This is a blatant violation of freedom of conscience, and it is ironic that it is promoted by those who call themselves "pro-choice." They are for anything *but* choice on the part of these doctors and pharmacists.

In Washington state, the pro-life owner of a local pharmacy declined to stock or dispense the morning-after pill and soon found himself in violation of the state law mandating that all pharmacists make the drug available, regardless of their religious beliefs. Attorneys with the Alliance Defense Fund filed a lawsuit on his behalf against the law. On May 2, 2008, the US Court of Appeals for the Ninth Circuit ruled that Washington pharmacists' rights of conscience will be protected while an appeal by state officials who oppose those rights moves forward.[22]

A pro-life nurse at Mount Sinai Hospital in New York was forced in 2009 to participate in a late-term abortion or face loss of her job and nursing license, even though the hospital had known since 2004 that she requested to not be involved in abortions. Hospital administrators threatened senior nurse Cathy Cenzon-DeCarlo with disciplinary measures if she did not honor a last-minute summons to assist in a scheduled late-term abortion. The patient was not in crisis at the time of the surgery, yet the hospital insisted on the nurse's participation in the procedure on the grounds that it was an "emergency" even though the procedure was not classified as such. Again, attorneys with the Alliance Defense Fund have filed suit on her behalf to protect not only her right of conscience, but that of other pro-life medical professionals.[23]

In response to this kind of increasing pressure in society, on November 20, 2009, several Christian leaders released the Manhattan Declaration, which was eventually signed by more than 400,000 people from Roman Catholic, Orthodox, and evangelical Protestant backgrounds. (I thought the statement was excellent, and I was one of the original signers.) Part of this declaration said:

> Because the sanctity of human life, the dignity of marriage as a union of husband and wife, and the freedom of conscience and religion are foundational

21. In January 2009, Alliance Defense Fund attorneys, along with attorneys from the Christian Legal Society, filed motions to intervene in three lawsuits that seek to invalidate a federal regulation protecting medical professionals from discrimination because they refuse to participate in abortions. Abortion advocates are challenging a regulation enacted by the Department of Health and Human Services in December 2008 that prohibits recipients of federal grants from forcing medical professionals to participate in abortions. The regulation requires that grantees certify compliance with existing laws protecting rights of conscience in order to receive government funds.

22. "9th Circuit thwarts Wash. state's attempt to stall conscience rights," *ADF News Release* (May 24, 2008). Copy of the order is available at www.telladf.org/UserDocs/StormansWin.pdf.

23. "NY nurse threatened, forced to assist in late-term abortion," *ADF News Release* (July 22, 2009). Copy of complaint is available at www.telladf.org/UserDocs/Cenzon-DeCarloComplaint.pdf.

principles of justice and the common good, we are compelled by our Christian faith to speak and act in their defense....

We are Christians who have joined together across historic lines of ecclesial differences to affirm our right—and, more importantly, to embrace our obligation—to speak and act in defense of these truths. We pledge to each other, and to our fellow believers, that no power on earth, be it cultural or political, will intimidate us into silence or acquiescence....

Because we honor justice and the common good, we will not comply with any edict that purports to compel our institutions to participate in abortions, embryo-destructive research, assisted suicide and euthanasia, or any other anti-life act.... We will fully and ungrudgingly render to Caesar what is Caesar's. But under no circumstances will we render to Caesar what is God's.[24]

d. No funding or support should be given to the process of creating human embryos for the purpose of destroying them in medical research.

The term "embryo" is applied to preborn children from the moment of conception until the eighth week of pregnancy.

If the Bible encourages us to treat the preborn child as a person from the moment of conception (see arguments above), then the argument here is whether we should create the beginnings of little babies simply to harvest their stem cells and then put them to death. The biblical arguments given above on the personhood of the preborn child would argue against the validity of this action.

The argument in favor of such research is that such stem cells taken from such embryos might be used to grow all sorts of different kinds of useful organs that could be transplanted into people to overcome various diseases and disabilities.

But it is doubtful that such stem cells need to be taken from human embryos, for there are other excellent sources of stem cells being discovered every year. These stem cells can be taken from human adults and used in research with apparently as much potential for medical benefits as embryonic stem cells. Why should we take stem cells from embryos and destroy tiny human lives instead of taking stem cells from other human tissue so that we destroy no human lives?

For example, UCLA stem cell scientists reprogrammed human skin cells into cells with the same unlimited properties as embryonic stem cells, and they did it without using embryos or eggs. The researchers used genetic alteration to turn back the clock on human skin cells and create cells that are nearly identical to human embryonic stem cells, which have the ability to become every cell type found in the human body. According to the researchers:

The implications for disease treatment could be significant. Reprogramming adult stem cells into embryonic stem cells could generate a potentially limitless

---

24. See the Manhattan Declaration at http.//manhattan-declaration.org/home.aspx.

source of immune-compatible cells for tissue engineering and transplantation medicine. A patient's skin cells, for example, could be reprogrammed into embryonic stem cells. Those embryonic stem cells could then be prodded into becoming various cell types—beta islet cells to treat diabetes, hematopoetic cells to create a new blood supply for a leukemia patient, motor neuron cells to treat Parkinson's disease.[25]

From this perspective, President George W. Bush's decision in 2001 that he would not allow government funding for the creation of *new* embryos to begin *new* stem cell lines was certainly the correct decision.[26] He allowed government funding to *continue* on stem cell research where the stem cells had already been taken from embryos and the embryos has already been destroyed. But he did not allow government funding to be used for the intentional creation of and destruction of new embryos. His decision *only involved government funding*. It did not affect ongoing research in the *private* sector, nor did it do anything to prohibit *private* research companies from using embryonic stem cells.

However, President Bush's actions (and subsequent vetoes of embryonic stem cell research bills) were widely misrepresented and misreported in the media as "preventing" research. Liberal pundit Michael Kinsley called Bush's actions "cynical," writing:

> The week-old embryos used for stem-cell research are microscopic clumps of cells, unthinking and unknowing, with fewer physical human qualities than a mosquito. Fetal-tissue research has used brain cells from aborted fetuses, but this is not that. Week-old, lab-created embryos have no brain cells.... None of this matters if you believe that a microscopic embryo is a human being with the same human rights as you and me. George W. Bush claims to believe that, and you have to believe something like that to justify your opposition to stem-cell research.... If he's got both his facts and his logic wrong—and he has—Bush's alleged moral anguish on this subject is unimpressive. In fact, it is insulting to the people (including me) whose lives could be saved or redeemed by the medical breakthroughs Bush's stem-cell policy is preventing.[27]

e. The ban on partial-birth abortions

The term "partial-birth abortion" (also known in medical literature by other terms such as "intact dilation and extraction") is a procedure in which the preborn child is partially extracted from the mother's womb, starting with the feet and then delivering the baby as far as the neck. Then the head is crushed and the brain is sucked out of the baby, and the dead child is removed completely from its mother's womb. This horrible

---

25. "Human Skin Cells Reprogrammed Into Embryonic Stem Cells," *ScienceDaily.com* (Feb. 12, 2008). www.sciencedaily.com/releases/2008/02/080211172631.htm.

26. "President's Remarks on Stem Cell Research," The White House (Aug. 9, 2001). http://usgovinfo.about.com/blwh-release16.htm.

27. Michael Kinsley, "Taking Bush Personally," *Slate.com* (Oct. 23, 2003).

procedure is most frequently used in late-term abortions, up to and including the ninth month of pregnancy.

Efforts to produce legislation prohibiting this procedure began in 1995. One bill, written under the leadership of Florida Congressman Charles Canady (a graduate of Yale Law School), was passed in October 1996 by Congress, but it was vetoed by President Clinton.[28] It was passed again in October 1997 by both houses of Congress, but was once again vetoed by President Clinton.[29] Republicans who supported the bill did not have enough votes to override President Clinton's veto in either case.[30] Then, in the 2002 congressional elections Republicans increased their majority in the House and gained a fifty-one-seat majority in the Senate.[31] This enabled them to pass the Partial-Birth Abortion Ban Act in the House October 2, 2003,[32] and in the Senate October 21, 2003.[33] President George W. Bush signed it into law on November 5, 2003.[34]

Pro-abortion forces challenged the ban in several different federal district courts (California, New York, and Nebraska).[35] All three ruled the ban unconstitutional, and the federal courts of appeal (in the Ninth Circuit, Second Circuit, and Eighth Circuit, respectively) affirmed those rulings.[36] At that point the partial-birth abortion ban could still not take effect because, even though it had been passed by Congress and signed by the President, and even though nothing in the Constitution said a word about this procedure or anything related to it, these federal courts had ruled that the law was "unconstitutional."

The three cases were all appealed to the US Supreme Court and were consolidated into one case, *Gonzales v. Carhart.* By a five-to-four majority the Supreme Court upheld the law as constitutional, declaring its decision on April 18, 2007.[37] (Supporting the law were Justices Roberts, Kennedy, Thomas, Scalia, and Alito. Dissenting were Justices Ginsburg, Stevens, Souter, and Breyer.) Therefore, after twelve years of effort, this extremely limited restriction on the right to abortion, applying only to a very tiny percentage of cases, finally became the law of the land.

Although this law applies to all hospitals and medical facilities under *federal* jurisdiction, many *states* still do not have such laws applying to medical facilities under state jurisdiction. Several other states do have such laws.

28. "Clinton Vetoes Partial-Birth Abortion Ban," *AllPolitics. com* (April 10, 1996). www.cnn.com/ALLPOLITICS/1996/news/9604/10/abortion/index.shtml.

29. "Clinton Again Vetoes Abortion Ban," *AllPolitics.com* (Oct. 10, 1997). www.cnn.com/ALLPOLITICS/1997/10/10/lateterm.abortion/.

30. "Presidential Vetoes, 1989–2000," www.senate.gov/reference/resources/pdf/presvetoes.pdf.

31. See www.cnn.com/ELECTION/2002/pages/senate/index.html.

32. "House Passes Ban on Abortion Method," *Washington Times* (Oct. 2, 2003).

33. "Partial-Birth Abortion Ban Heads to President's Desk," *Online News Hour Update* (Oct. 21, 2003).

34. "Bush Signs Ban on Partial-Birth Abortions," *Fox News* (Nov. 5, 2003).

35. "Supreme Court to Take Up Partial-Birth Abortion Issue," *USA Today* (Feb. 21, 2006). www.usatoday.com/news/washington/2006–02–21-abortion_x.htm.

36. Ibid.

37. *Gonzales v. Carhart* and *Gonzales v. Planned Parenthood*, 550 U.S. (2007). www.supremecourtus.gov/opinions/06pdf/05–380.pdf.

f. The most important legal goal regarding abortion is appointing Supreme Court justices who will overturn *Roe v. Wade* because no significant restriction on abortions can be made at either the state or national level until the Supreme Court overturns the *Roe v. Wade* decision

I do not think that many Christians understand how the key to this entire matter is the appointment of "originalist" Supreme Court justices who will vote to overturn *Roe v. Wade.* Until that Supreme Court decision is changed, the highest law of the land (the US Constitution, as "interpreted" by the Supreme Court) declares that all women in the United States have a *constitutional right* to an abortion at any time in their pregnancy.[38]

Therefore the US Congress *has no power* to pass a law prohibiting abortions at any stage of pregnancy. The fifty state legislatures *have no power* to pass any law prohibiting abortion. (The prohibition on partial-birth abortion is the only exception, as discussed above.) This is because every law prohibiting abortion has been struck down by the Supreme Court as "unconstitutional" because they say it violates the Constitution's guarantee of a right to abortion! And this is the decision of the court even though the Constitution itself says nothing about abortion.

But will the Supreme Court overturn *Roe v. Wade*? The court now is almost evenly divided between four justices who would always vote to uphold *Roe v. Wade* and four justices who would probably vote to overturn that decision, with one justice in the middle.

Figure 6.1

Would keep *Roe v. Wade*	Often in middle (perhaps would overturn?)	Would probably overturn *Roe v. Wade*
Stephen Breyer	Anthony Kennedy	John Roberts
Ruth Ginsburg		Samuel Alito
Sonia Sotomayor		Antonin Scalia
Elena Kagan		Clarence Thomas

This is why the election of a President and the elections of US senators are so important to the future of this issue. If a liberal, pro-choice President such as President Obama is allowed to appoint some replacements for the four conservative members of the Supreme Court (when they retire or die), it would solidify a majority in support of upholding *Roe v. Wade* for many years to come. And a Democratic Senate would confirm such appointments. But if a pro-life President (such as Ronald Reagan or George W. Bush)

---

38. Under *Roe* and the companion case *Doe v. Bolton,* the Supreme Court allowed abortion for the mother's health, including emotional and psychological health, which effectively allows abortion at any time in the nine months of pregnancy (see discussion earlier in this chapter, p. 164).

would be allowed to appoint any replacements for the four more liberal justices or for Justice Kennedy (through death or retirement of any one of them), and if there was a Republican majority in the Senate to confirm such justices, then it is likely that a test case would be brought and *Roe v. Wade* would be overturned.

Until such a change comes about in the Supreme Court, no major changes can be made in the law. States can (and should) pass laws requiring parental notification prior to abortion or requiring certain kinds of informed consent, but they cannot pass any laws that prohibit people who want abortions from getting them.

If the *Roe v. Wade* decision were to be overturned by the Supreme Court, what would happen? Then the democratic process could function once again regarding this issue. Members of Congress and the elected representatives of the legislatures of the fifty states would have to consider and decide what laws they would pass regarding abortion. It is difficult to predict in advance what the outcome of those discussions would be, and what laws would result. But at least decisions would be made as they should be in a nation that believes in democracy—by the people themselves and their elected representatives, not by nine unelected and unaccountable justices in the Supreme Court.

Unfortunately, abortion has become a major dividing line—perhaps the principal dividing line—between the Democratic and Republican parties in the United States at this time, at least at a national level. The Democratic leadership is united in supporting abortion rights and, above all, in seeking to appoint activist justices to the Supreme Court who will uphold *Roe v. Wade*, which is by itself keeping the entire abortion industry in place and protecting it from legal interference. But Republicans have consistently nominated pro-life candidates for President and Vice President, and most Republican senators and representatives have supported a pro-life position.

g. What about a "consistent ethic of life"?

How can some evangelicals still vote for Democratic candidates for the US Senate or for President? One approach is to change the subject from discussing laws about abortion to saying we should give more support to women who are pregnant, and so reduce abortion (see discussion above, pp. 167–68). Another common approach is the argument of Jim Wallis. He says that Christians should support "a consistent ethic of life," but *neither party* is satisfactory in this area. He defines this ethic as including "the life issues" of "abortion, euthanasia, capital punishment, nuclear weapons, poverty, and racism." He calls these "critical components of a consistent ethic of life."[39] Then he says,

> The tragedy is that in America today, one can't vote for a consistent ethic of life. Republicans stress some of the life issues, Democrats some of the others, while both violate the seamless garment of life on several vital matters....[40]

In other words, no party agrees with "a consistent ethic of life" (according to Wallis) on all of these issues, and therefore people shouldn't think that they should vote for

---

39. Jim Wallis, *God's Politics*, 300–301.
40. Ibid., 301.

Republicans because of the abortion issue, because there are other "life" issues where the Democratic position is better.

But Christians should understand what Wallis is doing here. He is changing the subject from laws prohibiting abortion to laws about a whole range of things and is claiming that a *truly Christian* pro-life position would include things like opposition to capital punishment, opposition to nuclear weapons, and increased government help for the poor (as he explains elsewhere in his book). The effect of this argument by Wallis is to downplay the importance of the abortion issue by saying these are all "life" issues.

I agree that it is important to consider all the issues that Republicans and Democrats stand for before deciding how to vote. But it is hard to see how any issue could have more importance than stopping the wrongful murder of more than 1,000,000 innocent preborn children every year, year after year after year. I think Wallis is wrong to diminish this issue by lumping it with a whole basket of other controversial and complicated questions.

In addition, many Christians sincerely disagree with Wallis about capital punishment, national defense, and solutions to poverty (see discussions below). Wallis's phrase "a consistent ethic of life" is a misleading slogan that attempts to make people think that his pacifist views on capital punishment and war, his support for government redistribution of wealth, and his own solutions to racial discrimination are the truly "pro-life" positions. This confuses the argument about the biblical teaching against abortion by changing the subject to many other disputed issues. This sleight-of-hand argument should not blind us to the plain fact that every vote for every Democratic candidate for President or Congress undeniably has the effect of continuing to protect 1,000,000 abortions per year in the United States.

6. The importance of this issue

The Old Testament contains sober warnings to a nation that allowed people to put their children to death. In imitation of the practices of other nations, some of the people of Israel had begun "to burn their sons and their daughters in the fire" (Jer. 7:31), which referred to putting their live children into a fire to sacrifice them to Molech and other pagan gods. For allowing this practice to continue, God issued a severe warning of judgment through the prophet Jeremiah:

> For the sons of Judah have done evil in my sight, declares the LORD.... And they have built the high places of Topheth, which is in the Valley of the Son of Hinnom, *to burn their sons and their daughters in the fire*, which I did not command, nor did it come into my mind. Therefore, behold, the days are coming, declares the LORD, when it will no more be called Topheth, or the Valley of the Son of Hinnom, but the Valley of Slaughter; for they will bury in Topheth, because there is no room elsewhere. And the dead bodies of this people will be food for the birds of the air, and for the beasts of the earth, and none will frighten them away. And I will silence in the cities of Judah and in the streets of Jerusalem the voice of mirth and the voice of gladness, the voice of the bridegroom and the voice of the bride, *for the land shall become a waste* (Jer. 7:30–34).

The troubling question with regard to the United States elections of 2008 concerns the direction the nation has willingly chosen. The nation freely elected a president who is a strong supporter of abortion "rights." The White House website states, "President Obama has been a consistent champion of reproductive choice and believes in preserving women's rights under *Roe v. Wade*."[41] The nation elected a sizable Democratic majority (sixty) in the Senate, and they strongly support abortion "rights" in the United States. This sets the stage for the appointment of additional fairly young liberal justices to the Supreme Court, such as Justice Sotomayor (and, more recently, Elena Kagan as a replacement for Justice Stevens).

The nation has willingly chosen to be represented by people with these convictions. What will God's evaluation of our nation be in light of this decision? Or do we not think that God is still sovereign over the affairs of nations?

7. For further reading

Bibliography on abortion:

Randy Alcorn, *ProLife Answers to ProChoice Arguments* (Portland, OR: Multnomah, 1992); Francis Beckwith, *Politically Correct Death: Answering Arguments for Abortion Rights* (Grand Rapids: Baker, 1992); John Jefferson Davis, *Evangelical Ethics*, 3rd ed. (Phillipsburg, NJ: P & R, 2004), 137–65; John Feinberg and Paul Feinberg, *Ethics for a Brave New World* (Wheaton, IL: Crossway, 1993), 47–72; John Frame, *The Doctrine of the Christian Life* (Phillipsburg, NJ: P & R, 2008), 717–32; Richard Ganz, ed., *Thou Shalt Not Kill: The Christian Case against Abortion* (New Rochelle, NY: Arlington House, 1978); Michael J. Gorman, *Abortion and the Early Church* (Eugene, OR: Wipf and Stock, 1982); Randall Hekman, *Justice for the Preborn* (Ann Arbor, MI: Servant Books, 1984); Jeff Hensley, *The Zero People: Essays on Life* (Ann Arbor, MI: Servant Books, 1983); Scott Rae, *Moral Choices*, 3rd ed. (Grand Rapids: Zondervan, 2009), 121–43.

B. EUTHANASIA

1. The issue

The word "euthanasia" is derived from the Greek words *eu* ("good") and *thanatos* ("death"), and therefore people sometimes understand it to mean "good death," a rather misleading understanding of the term. This procedure is also popularly called "mercy killing," another term that is misleading in portraying such an action in a positive way. It simply means the act of putting to death an elderly person or one who is terminally ill.

The issue in the question of euthanasia is this:

> Should governments make laws against intentionally taking the lives of elderly or dying persons?

---

41. See www.whitehouse.gov/issues/women/.

This issue often comes to focus in the case of terminally ill patients who are experiencing chronic pain and who no longer want to live and who may even wish that they could be put to death. It also is a question in the case of people who have lost much or most of their mental capacities because of a coma or severe dementia, or patients who through severe injury or illness appear to have no reasonable human hope of recovery. What should the law do in such cases?

2. The relevant biblical teaching

a. The command against murder

The primary biblical teaching in this regard is found in the Ten Commandments:

> "You shall not murder" (Exod. 20:13).

This commandment, which is affirmed in the New Testament in Matthew 18:19 and Romans 13:9, applies to all human beings created in the image of God. It does not say, "You shall not murder, except when a person is more than eighty or ninety years old," or "You shall not murder, except when a very ill person wants to be murdered."

Just as the command against murder prohibits abortion in the very early stages of human life, so the command against murder also prohibits intentionally taking the life of a person in the final stages of human life.

The word translated "murder" in Exodus 20:13 includes both premeditated murder (which is implied by the English word "murder") and also any accidental causing of another person's death. The term is always applied to the murder of human beings, not of animals.

Therefore this biblical command prohibits the action of taking the life of another person, even an elderly or terminally ill person, or a person in great pain.

One other passage of special significance is 2 Samuel 1:1–16. King Saul had recently died in battle, in effect making David king. A few days after the battle where Saul had died, a man came to David and claimed that he had found Saul gravely wounded and that Saul had begged for the man to kill him, and the man had done so. In several ways this was an act of "euthanasia." Yet David's response was to order capital punishment for the man who had done this. Here is the story:

> After the death of Saul, when David had returned from striking down the Amalekites, David remained two days in Ziklag. And on the third day, behold, a man came from Saul's camp, with his clothes torn and dirt on his head. And when he came to David, he fell to the ground and paid homage. David said to him, "Where do you come from?" And he said to him, "I have escaped from the camp of Israel." And David said to him, "How did it go? Tell me." And he answered, "The people fled from the battle, and also many of the people have fallen and are dead, and Saul and his son Jonathan are also dead." Then David said to the young man who told him, "How do you know that Saul and his son Jonathan are dead?" And the young man who told him said, "By chance I happened to be on Mount Gilboa, *and there was Saul leaning on his spear, and behold, the chariots and the horsemen were close upon him.* And when he looked

behind him, he saw me, and called to me. And I answered, 'Here I am.' And he said to me, 'Who are you?' I answered him, 'I am an Amalekite.' And he said to me, '*Stand beside me and kill me, for anguish has seized me*, and yet my life still lingers.' *So I stood beside him and killed him, because I was sure that he could not live after he had fallen*. And I took the crown that was on his head and the armlet that was on his arm, and I have brought them here to my lord."

Then David took hold of his clothes and tore them, and so did all the men who were with him. And they mourned and wept and fasted until evening for Saul and for Jonathan his son and for the people of the LORD and for the house of Israel, because they had fallen by the sword. And David said to the young man who told him, "Where do you come from?" And he answered, "I am the son of a sojourner, an Amalekite." David said to him, "How is it you were not afraid to put out your hand to destroy the LORD's anointed?"

Then David called one of the young men and said, "*Go, execute him.*" *And he struck him down so that he died.* And David said to him, "Your blood be on your head, for your own mouth has testified against you, saying, 'I have killed the LORD's anointed'" (2 Sam. 1:1–16).

This situation had several similarities to modern examples where people might say euthanasia is justified:

(1) The patient (Saul) appeared to be terminally ill, with no reasonable human hope of recovery. (He had fallen on his own sword in an attempt to commit suicide: see 1 Sam. 31:4–5.)

(2) The patient was in extreme pain, and if he did not die, he faced the prospect of even more suffering.

(3) The patient clearly requested, even begged, that someone else would actively put him to death.

(4) This request was also a command from the head of government at that time, because Saul was still the king.

But David, who at that time is clearly portrayed as a man after God's "own heart" (1 Sam. 13:14; cf. Acts 13:22), declares that this man is worthy of capital punishment. In other words, the person who carried out euthanasia is *guilty of murder*.

Three objections may be brought against this interpretation:

(a) This story about the Amalekite messenger killing Saul is not mentioned in 1 Samuel 31:3–6, where Saul's death is first reported. Therefore the Amalekite messenger may be making up this story to show David that he had killed Saul, who was David's enemy.

However, this idea does not nullify the force of this narrative, because even if the story is not true, *David accepts it as true and passes judgment on the man based on the story*. David condemns him based on his own confession of guilt. And thus the narrative of Scripture portrays the decision of this wise king, a man after God's own heart, as *an appropriate and morally right judgment* on the man who has carried out euthanasia. In addition, the Amalekite messenger actually had the crown and the armlet that Saul had been wearing, and he knew that Saul had fallen on his own sword, so it is quite certain that the man was there in the very vicinity of Saul when Saul was dying. Therefore it is certainly possible that it is entirely true and it simply was not included in the summary of Saul's death in 1 Samuel 31. Verse 4 of that chapter does not specify that Saul killed himself, but that he tried to do so: "Saul took his own sword and fell upon it." The next verse says that at some later point Saul's armor-bearer "saw that Saul was dead," but it allows for the Amalekite to end Saul's life before that. In any case, the events probably occurred very quickly in the heat of battle.

(b) Another objection is that this case is unique because Saul was king, and David refers to him as "the Lord's anointed" (2 Sam. 1:14). Therefore this case should not be used to establish a general principle that euthanasia is wrong, but only the specific application that assassination of a king is wrong.

However, this objection is not persuasive, because the wrongfulness of murder does not depend on the status or rank of the victim. Murder is wrong in the Bible because God prohibits it (Exod. 20:13), and more specifically because it is the taking of the life of a person made in the image of God (see Gen. 9:5–6). A king does not possess a greater share of the image of God than others who do not happen to be king! All human beings share equally in the status of being "created in the image of God" (cf. Gen. 1:27). Therefore, if it is wrong to kill a terminally ill king who requests it, then it is also wrong to kill anyone else who requests it.

(c) A final objection is that the sin of the Amalekite messenger was not murder, but rebellion against the king who was "God's anointed." However, this interpretation does not match the actual words of the text, for David does not put the man to death for rebellion, but for killing the king (vv. 14, 16). And in fact, at the time this happened, the Amalekite was not rebelling against the king, but was actually obeying what the king commanded. The sin was murder, and David punished it accordingly.

Therefore this narrative gives significant confirmation of the rightness of applying "you shall not murder" to the question of euthanasia.

The conclusion is that both Exodus 20:13 and 2 Samuel 1:1–16 indicate that it is morally wrong to actively take the life of a terminally ill person.

b. Killing versus letting die

A clear distinction must be made between "killing" and "letting die." *Killing* is actively doing something to a patient that hastens or causes the person's death. On the other hand, *letting die* is passively allowing someone to die from other causes, without interfering with that process. In the first case, the cause of death is the action taken by another person. In the second case, the cause of death is the disease or injury or aging process that has already been occurring in the person who dies. While the Bible prohibits actively killing someone, in the case of letting someone die the decision is more complex.

We should intervene and try to help a person recover, and *not* passively allow the person to die, when (a) there is a reasonable human hope of recovery, and (b) we are able to help. This would be obeying Jesus' teaching, "You shall love your neighbor as yourself" (Matt. 22:39), and his command, "So whatever you wish that others would do to you, do also to them, for this is the Law and the Prophets" (Matt. 7:12). Moreover, in the Parable of the Good Samaritan, Jesus implicitly condemned the priest and the Levite who neglected to do what they could to help a badly injured man (see Luke 10:30–37).

On the other hand, in cases where (a) there is no reasonable human hope of recovery (sometimes called a situation of "futility"), and (b) it is the patient's wish to be allowed to die, and/or (c) we are unable to help (such as a person trapped in a burning car, or where we could not afford the extraordinary expense of some elaborate medical treatments), *then it may be right to allow the person to die.* This is morally distinct from actively murdering a person.

Allowing someone to die may include not starting a medical life-support system (such as an artificial respirator) or stopping an artificial life-support system. Sometimes in Scripture we see examples of people realizing that their death is near, and they trust God and yield their lives into his hands (see Luke 23:46; Acts 7:59; also Gen. 49:33; Heb. 2:15; and 1 Cor. 15:55–57).

In addition, modern medicine should be used to alleviate the pain and suffering of a terminally ill patient (see Matt. 7:12 and 22:39). In the vast majority of cases today (perhaps in all cases), modern medicines, such as morphine or what are known as opioids, are available that will protect people from ongoing, extreme suffering as they near death.[42]

3. Arguments from reason and evidence apart from the Bible

Most people have a conviction that it is wrong to murder another human being. An argument can be made from this general conviction to the specific application that it is wrong to murder elderly or terminally ill persons. Is murder not murder whether the victim is young or old, strong or weak, in good health or suffering? None of these considerations should change the moral status of the person as a human being.

Moreover, concerns about a "slippery slope" in public policy have some persuasive force. If euthanasia is allowed for *some* patients who are suffering, then how can we prevent it from being applied to *more and more* patients who are suffering? And with the increasing cost of health care for elderly and extremely ill patients, there will likely be a tendency to put pressure on people to ask that their lives be taken. In fact, "nations that have allowed for physician-assisted suicide find that a society can quickly move from merely *allowing* 'the right to die' to the belief that there is 'an *obligation* to die' on the part of the elderly and the very ill people who are 'draining resources' from the society. In such situations it becomes likely that a number of elderly people will be put to death against their will."[43]

The situation in the Netherlands has become particularly notorious,[44] where a number of elderly people have been put to death against their will. According to the Netherlands' "adult euthanasia vetting commissions," approximately 2,000 people per year are euthanized through a mix of sedatives and a lethal dose of muscle relaxant.[45] Wesley Smith, an attorney for the International Anti-Euthanasia Task Force, has written that the amount is actually much higher:

42. U.S. Institute of Health, "Last Days of Life." www.cancer.gov/cancertopics/pdq/supportivecare/lasthours/Patient/page2#Keypoint7.

43. *ESV Study Bible,* "The End of Life," p. 2543.

44. A concise summary of the Netherlands' euthanasia law can be read at www.internationaltaskforce.org/hollaw.htm.

45. "Dutch to Set Guidelines for Euthanasia of Babies," Associated Press (Sept. 29, 2005).

The evidence of decades demonstrates that such involuntary euthanasia is rampant. Indeed, in its 1997 ruling refusing to create a constitutional right to assisted suicide (*Washington* v. *Glucksberg*) the United States Supreme Court quoted a 1991 Dutch government study finding that in 1990 doctors committed "more than 1000 cases of euthanasia without an explicit request" and "an additional 4,941 cases where physicians administered lethal morphine overdoses without the patients' explicit consent." That means in 1990, nearly 6,000 of approximately 130,000 people who died in the Netherlands that year were involuntarily euthanized—approximately 4 percent of all Dutch deaths. So much for "choice."[46]

Euthanasia advocate Dr. Phillip Nitschke invented the so-called "peaceful pill" to induce suicide, and he also conducted "how to commit suicide" clinics. He said that his personal position is that if we believe that there is a right to life, then we must accept that people have a right to dispose of that life whenever they want."[47] He continued:

Many people I meet and argue with believe that human life is sacred. I do not.... If you believe that your body belongs to God and that to cut short a life is a crime against God, then you will clearly not agree with my thoughts on this issue. I do not mind people holding these beliefs and suffering as much as they wish as they die. For them, redemptive suffering may well pry open heaven's door that little bit wider, and if that is their belief they are welcome to it, but I strongly object to having those views shoved down my neck. I want my belief—that human life is not sacred—accorded the same respect.[48]

The slippery slope has also extended into infant euthanasia. In September 2005 the Dutch government announced its intention to expand its euthanasia policy to allow doctors to end the lives of infants with the parents' consent. Under the "Gronican Protocol," euthanasia would be allowed when it is decided that a child is terminally ill with no prospect of recovery and suffering great pain.

Christine Rosen, author of *Preaching Eugenics*, says:

The Netherlands' embrace of euthanasia has been a gradual process aided by the growing acceptance (in a much more secular Europe) that some life is "unworthy of life." Indeed, Europe is doing just that. According to the Associated Press, 73 percent of French doctors have admitted to using drugs to end an infant's life, with between 2 and 4 percent of doctors in the United Kingdom, Italy, Spain, Germany, and Sweden confessing the same.[49]

---

46. Wesley Smith, "Going Dutch," *National Review Online* (Dec. 18, 2000). www.nationalreview.com/comment/comment121800d.shtml.

47. Kathryn Jean Lopez, "Euthanasia Sets Sail: An interview with Philip Nitschke, the other 'Dr. Death,'" *National Review Online* (June 5, 2001). www.nationalreview.com/interrogatory/interrogatory060501.shtml.

48. Ibid.

49. Christine Rosen, *Preaching Eugenics: Religious Leaders and the American Eugenics Movement* (Oxford: Oxford University Press, 2004): cited in Kathryn Jean Lopez, "Mercy!" *National Review Online* (March 30, 2005). www.nationalreview.com/lopez/lopez200503300755.asp.

A final argument against euthanasia comes from personal narratives and testimonies from people who were apparently terminally ill or had life-threatening injuries and then have recovered, as well as from elderly people who are still living happy, productive lives.

One recent example of this is Jesse Ramirez of Mesa, Arizona. In May 2007, then–36-year-old Jesse was in a horrific automobile accident while he and his wife were engaged in an argument.[50] Barely ten days after the accident, Jesse's food, water, and antibiotics were withdrawn at the request of his wife. He was then transferred to hospice, where he would have died, but Alliance Defense Fund attorneys, at the behest of Jesse's sister, were successful in restoring food, water, and treatment. While he did go without food and water for six days until it was restored, Jesse recovered and walked out of the hospital in October 2007 and continued his recovery at home.[51] In 2008 the state of Arizona passed "Jesse's Law," which closed a loophole in the decision-making process for patients who are physically unable to communicate their wishes regarding medical care.[52]

4. Objections

The primary objections to the position outlined above emphasize (1) the value of protecting human freedom, even individual freedom to choose to end one's own life, and (2) the need to alleviate pain and frustration felt by the terminally ill patient.

In response, if it is morally wrong to actively murder another person, then the fact that a person would choose to be murdered does not nullify this moral argument. There are many cases where someone might so despair of life that he or she would say, "I want to die." But should we then say that it is right to murder such a person? If it is morally wrong, then even the person who wants to be murdered cannot make it morally right, for it is still taking a human life. A person's right to life does not depend on the person himself wanting to live.

As for pain and frustration, these are not sufficient reasons for overcoming the moral prohibition against murder. A better solution is to alleviate the pain and do what can be done to overcome the person's frustration.

A final argument is this: (3) Since money and medical resources are limited, we should put to death elderly or very ill people so they do not waste money or medical resources. This is not the question of allocating a scarce resource (say, a kidney transplant) to a younger or healthier person. Rather, it is the argument that older or very ill people should not be using so much medical care *at all*.

But this argument, phrased another way, essentially says that it is right to *kill* people who are costing us too much to care for. Since more money can always buy more

50. Dennis Wagner, "Injured Man's Awakening Called 'Miracle,'" *USA Today* (June 27, 2007). www.usatoday.com/news/nation/2007–06–26-comatose_N.htm?csp=34.

51. Rick Dubek, "Comatose Mesa Man Walks Out of Hospital," *AZCentral.com* (Oct. 19, 2007). www.azcentral. com/12news/news/articles/jesseramirezwalks10192007-CR. html.

52. "ADF Commends Signing of 'Jesse's Law,'" *ADF Press Release* (June 25, 2008). www.telladf.org/news/story. aspx?cid=4583.

medical resources, in the end this argument is simply a way of saying, "We don't have enough money to care for these elderly and terminally ill people." But is that a justification for taking another person's life? This would change the commandment "You shall not murder" into a different commandment: "You shall not murder unless you do so to spend your money on something else." This objection is hardly acceptable on moral grounds.

It is important to realize that all three of these objections are based on a viewpoint that is contrary to a Christian worldview. These three objections do not value human life as something sacred, something that uniquely carries the image of God in this world. And they do not give full weight to the moral force of God's command, "You shall not murder."

5. Recommendation for political policies

a. Governmental laws against murder should continue to be applied to cases of euthanasia

In most states in the United States, euthanasia is still prohibited and laws against murder apply to it. However, Oregon voters enacted the "Death with Dignity Act," what is called physician-assisted suicide, in 1994,[53] and this was upheld by the US Court of Appeals for the Ninth Circuit in 1997. The US Supreme Court subsequently denied an appeal to the law.[54] In a subsequent challenge involving the federally controlled substance acts, the court ruled 6-to-3 in the law's favor.[55] In November 2008 the citizens of Washington state also legalized physician-assisted suicide.[56] On the other hand, in 1999, Dr. Jack Kevorkian, a physician in Michigan, was convicted for assisting someone to commit suicide in an act that was displayed on television and that violated current Michigan law.[57]

6. The importance of this issue

The direction a society takes on the question of euthanasia is a reflection of how highly it values human life and how highly it values God's command not to murder. In societies where physician-assisted suicide becomes legal, this will set the stage for a further erosion of the protection of human life. Some people will be thought "too old" to deserve medical treatment. Compassion and care for the elderly will diminish, and they will be more and more thought of as burdens to care for, rather than valuable members of the society.

And, unless we experience premature death, all of us reading this chapter will ourselves one day be those "elderly" people who need care and support from others.

53. Death with Dignity Act. www.oregon.gov/DHS/ph/pas/.
54. See www.oregon.gov/DHS/ph/pas/about_us.shtml.
55. *Gonzales v. Oregon,* 546 U.S. 243 (2006).
56. "Washington State to Allow Assisted Suicide," *USA Today* (March 2, 2009). www.usatoday.com/news/nation/2009-03-01-washington-assisted_N.htm.
57. "Kevorkian Gets 10 to 25 Years in Prison," *CNN.com* (April 13, 1999). www.cnn.com/US/9904/13/kevorkian.03/.

7. For further reading

Bibliography on euthanasia:

Davis, *Evangelical Ethics,* 167–201; Feinberg and Feinberg, *Ethics for a Brave World,* 99–126; Frame, *The Doctrine of the Christian Life,* 732–38; John Kilner, Arlene Miller, and Edmund Pellegrino, eds., *Dignity and Dying: A Christian Appraisal* (Grand Rapids: Eerdmans, 1996); Joni Eareckson Tada, *When Is It Right to Die?* (Grand Rapids: Zondervan, 1992).

C. CAPITAL PUNISHMENT

1. The issue

The question with regard to capital punishment (also called the death penalty) is this:

> Should the government take the life of a person who has been convicted of certain crimes?

The crimes for which capital punishment (or execution) is specified as the penalty usually include premeditated murder and treason. Other crimes that are sometimes thought to deserve capital punishment include an attempt to use weapons of mass destruction, espionage that results in loss of life of a country's citizens, and crimes such as aggravated rape, aggravated kidnaping, aircraft hijacking, or perjury that leads to a person's death. (An aggravated crime is one where the intent or actual circumstances add significantly to the guilt of the criminal or the harm to the victim.)

But the primary question is whether governments should have the right to carry out capital punishment *at all.*

2. The relevant biblical teaching

a. Genesis 9:5–6 provides the foundation for human government

In the early history of the human race, Genesis 6–9 relates that God brought a massive flood on the earth, destroying all human beings except the eight who were rescued in the ark: Noah, his wife, his three sons, and their wives.

When the flood ended, Noah and his family came out of the ark and started human society all over again. At that point God gave them instructions regarding the life they were about to begin. Among those instructions is the following passage, which provides the foundation for human government:

> And for your lifeblood I will require a reckoning: from every beast I will require it and from man. From his fellow man I will require a reckoning for the life of man.
>
> > "Whoever sheds the blood of man,
> > by man shall his blood be shed,
> > for God made man in his own image" (Gen. 9:5–6).

The verb "shed" in this statement translates the Hebrew verb *shāphak*, which means "to pour out in large amount, causing death." Therefore, "In this verse, 'shedding blood' refers to the violent, unjustified taking of human life (cf. Gen. 37:22; Num. 35:33; 1 Kings 2:31; Ezek. 22:4)."[58] This law says that when someone murders another person, the murderer himself should be put to death: "by man shall his blood be shed" (v. 6).

This execution of the murderer was not going to be carried out directly by God, but by a human agent, "by man." Yet this was not to be seen as human vengeance, but as carrying out God's own requirement of justice, for it explains what God means when he says, "from his fellow man *I will require a reckoning* for the life of man" (v. 5).

The reason God gives for this is the immense value of human life: "*For* God made man in his own image" (v. 6). To be in the image of God is the highest status and highest privilege of anything in all creation, and only human beings share in that status (see Gen. 1:27). To be in God's image means that human beings are more like God than anything else on the earth, and it also means that human beings are God's representatives on the earth (for they are like him and thus can best represent him). Therefore, to murder a human being is to murder someone who is more like God than any other creature on the earth. The murder of another human being is therefore a kind of attack against God himself, for it is an attack against his representative on the earth, an attack against the "image" that he has left of himself on the earth.

In order to give just punishment for such a serious crime, God decrees that the murderer will pay the ultimate price: he will forfeit his own life as a punishment. The punishment will fit the crime: "Whoever sheds the blood of man, *by man shall his blood be shed*, for God made man in his own image" (Gen. 9:6).

This verse therefore lays the foundational principles for all human governmental authority. At the very beginning of human society after the flood destroyed the earth, God establishes that he will delegate to human beings the authority to carry out punishment on wrongdoers ("by man shall his blood be shed"). Therefore the authority to execute punishment on wrongdoing has not simply been invented by human beings on their own. Rather, it is an authority that has been delegated to human beings by God, and through this authority God carries out his righteous justice on wrongdoers, for he says this is the way in which he "will require a reckoning for the life of man" (v. 5). Therefore the authority to punish wrongdoing (presumably through some form of government that would be established) is given by God to human government. And such authority to punish wrongdoing also implies that human governments will have to decide (a) what wrongdoing is worthy of punishment, (b) what punishment is appropriate for each wrongdoing, and (c) whether or not an individual is guilty of that wrongdoing.

As I explained in chapter 3 (see pp. 77–78), this passage comes long before the establishment of the nation of Israel (at the exodus from Egypt) or the giving of the laws of the Mosaic covenant (in Exodus, Leviticus, Numbers, and Deuteronomy). Therefore the application of this passage is not limited to the nation of Israel for a specific period of time, but is intended to apply to all people, for all time. It is important to recognize

---

58. *ESV Study Bible*, p. 2552.

that when the New Testament speaks of the "Old Covenant" (see 2 Cor. 3:14), it always refers to the covenant established through Moses with the nation of Israel. (See also Jer. 31:31–32; Luke 22:20; 1 Cor 13:11; 2 Cor. 3:4–16; and Heb. 8–10). But the covenant God made with Noah after the flood is nowhere called the "Old Covenant," and it is nowhere said to be abolished or no longer in effect. The covenant with Noah applies to all human beings on the earth, for all generations:

> "When the bow is in the clouds, I will see it and remember the *everlasting covenant* between God and *every living creature* of all flesh that is on the earth" (Gen. 9:16).

What we conclude from this passage is that God gave to human government the authority to carry out capital punishment and that this is the foundational authority of all governments of the earth.

One objection to this understanding of Genesis 9 is to say that it is a "proverb" and not an actual command from God about how human beings should act. Glen Stassen and David Gushee say this about Genesis 9:6: "As it stands in Genesis, it does not command the death penalty but gives wise advice based on the likely consequence of your action: if you kill someone, you will end up being killed."[59]

But this interpretation is not persuasive, for three reasons.

(1) When verse 5 is connected to verse 6, it shows that execution of the murderer is the way that *God himself will carry out justice in human society*: God says, "from his fellow man *I will require a reckoning* for the life of man" (Gen. 9:5). But Stassen and Gushee say nothing about verse 5.

(2) The last clause of verse 6 (which Stassen and Gushee also fail to mention) gives an *explanation* for the command. The death penalty is to be carried out for murder *because* man is in the image of God. This shows why the crime is so serious. But in Stassen and Gushee's view, this reason would make no sense. They understand this "proverb" to mean, in effect, "If you do something wrong (murder), another wrong will be done to you (another murder)." But how can our creation in God's image be a reason for wrongdoing? This is like saying (on their view that capital punishment is wrong), "People will do wrong to each other because they are made in God's image." That ends up saying that God's image is the reason why people do wrong!

(3) Later passages in the Old Testament show that God himself did institute the death penalty for the crime of murder (see Num. 35:16–34).

Because of these three reasons, Stassen and Gushee's interpretation is not persuasive.

b. Romans 13:1–7 is the first of two primary New Testament passages that teach about civil government

I have already discussed Romans 13:1–7 in some detail in chapter 3 (see pp. 79–81). But two specific details deserve comment at this point. Here is the passage once again:

---

59. Glen Stassen and David Gushee, *Kingdom Ethics* (Downers Grove, IL: InterVarsity Press, 2003), 202.

Let every person be subject to the governing authorities. For there is no authority except from God, and those that exist have been instituted by God. Therefore whoever resists the authorities resists what God has appointed, and those who resist will incur judgment. For rulers are not a terror to good conduct, but to bad. Would you have no fear of the one who is in authority? Then do what is good, and you will receive his approval, for he is God's servant for your good. But if you do wrong, be afraid, for he does not bear the sword in vain. For *he is the servant of God, an avenger who carries out God's wrath on the wrongdoer.* Therefore one must be in subjection, not only to avoid God's wrath but also for the sake of conscience. For the same reason you also pay taxes, for the authorities are ministers of God, attending to this very thing. Pay to all what is owed to them: taxes to whom taxes are owed, revenue to whom revenue is owed, respect to whom respect is owed, honor to whom honor is owed (Rom. 13:1–7).

First, Paul says, the agent of government is "the servant of God, an avenger [Greek *ekdikos*, "one who carries out punishment"] who carries out God's wrath on the wrongdoer" (v. 4). This is consistent with the teaching of Genesis 9 that God requires a reckoning for wrongdoing and that this will be carried out through human agents.

Second, Paul says, the civil government "does not bear the sword in vain" (v. 4). The Greek word for "sword" is *macharia*, which is used in several other verses to speak of the instrument by which people are put to death. Here are some examples:

Acts 12:2: He killed James the brother of John with the *sword*.

Acts 16:27: [The Philippian jailer] drew his *sword* and was about to kill himself, supposing that the prisoners had escaped.

Hebrews 11:37: They were stoned, they were sawn in two, they were killed with the *sword*.

Revelation 13:10: If anyone is to be slain with the *sword*, with the sword must he be slain.

A number of verses in the Septuagint (the Greek translation of the Old Testament) also use the word in this way, such as these:

Deuteronomy 13:15: You shall surely put the inhabitants of that city to the *sword*, devoting it to destruction.

Deuteronomy 20:13: And when the LORD your God gives it into your hand, you shall put all its males to the *sword*.

Therefore the idea, suggested by some, that the sword here is simply a symbol of governmental authority is hardly persuasive. When Paul says that civil government in general is authorized to "bear the sword," he means that it has been given authority from God to use the sword for the purpose for which people used it in the first century, and that is to put people to death.

c. First Peter 2:13–14 is the second primary passage on civil government in the New Testament

> Be subject for the Lord's sake to every human institution, whether it be to the emperor as supreme, or to governors as sent by him *to punish those who do evil and to praise those who do good.*

The expression translated "to punish" in verse 14 is *eis ekdikēsis,* using the same word that Paul used for "vengeance" that belongs to God (Rom. 12:19) and a word from the same root that Paul uses to say that the civil government is *"an avenger* who carries out God's wrath" (Rom. 13:4). In both Romans 13 and 1 Peter 2 the New Testament teaches that government has a responsibility not only to deter crime, but also actually to bring God's punishment to the wrongdoer. This is consistent with Genesis 9:5–6.

d. But is it right to desire that government punish a criminal?

Sometimes Christians may think that if a loved one has been murdered, or if they themselves have been robbed or beaten or severely injured by a drunk driver, they should merely forgive the person and never seek that the wrongdoer be punished by the courts. But that is not the solution Paul gives in Romans 12:19. He does not say, "Beloved, never avenge yourselves, but simply forgive everyone who has done wrong to you." Rather, he tells them to give up any desire to *seek revenge themselves* and instead give it over to the civil government, for after he says, "Beloved, never avenge yourselves," he says, "*but leave it to the wrath of God.*" Then he goes on to explain that the civil government is "the servant of God, an avenger who carries out *God's wrath* on the wrongdoer" (Rom. 13:4).

In other words, people should not seek to take *personal revenge* when they have been wronged, but they should seek that *justice be done* through the workings of the civil government. Letting the civil government carry out justice frees the believer to do good even to those who have wronged him. As Paul says, "If your enemy is hungry, feed him; if he is thirsty, give him something to drink" (Rom. 12:20). In that way they will "overcome evil with good" (v. 21), and that good comes not only through giving food and water but also through the justice system of the civil government, which is "God's servant for your good" (Rom. 13:4).[60]

But, someone might object, isn't it wrong for a Christian to *desire* vengeance? It depends on what kind of vengeance is desired. If we seek and desire to take *personal vengeance* (to harm the wrongdoer ourselves), then that is disobeying Romans 12 and 13; but if we desire that the government carry out *God's just vengeance* on the wrongdoer, then we are doing exactly what Paul says in 12:19 and are leaving vengeance "to the wrath of God." We are leaving it to the proper purpose of government, who is "the servant of God" when it "carries out God's wrath on the wrongdoer" (13:4). It cannot be wrong for us to desire that God's justice be carried out in this manner, for it is another way how God demonstrates the glory of his attribute of justice on the earth. (Jim Wallis

---

60. There were no chapter or verse divisions in the earliest Greek manuscripts, and the connection between what we now know as the end of chapter 12 and the beginning of chapter 13 would have been even clearer to Paul's original readers.

fails to make this distinction between wrongful personal vengeance and a rightful desire for God's vengeance to come through government when he opposes capital punishment, saying it "just satisfies revenge."[61] No, it satisfies God's requirement of justice.)

Therefore it does not seem to me to be wrong when Christians both (1) show personal kindness to and pray for the salvation and eternal forgiveness of those who have done them wrong, and (2) simultaneously pursue justice through the civil courts and desire that the wrongdoer be justly paid back for the wrong that he has done. In fact, I have spoken with more than one believer who had a friend or loved one murdered, and who deeply longed for the courts to carry out punishment on the murderer. It seemed to me that this reflected a deep-seated sense of God's justice that he has put in our human hearts and that was crying out for wrong to be punished and for justice to be done.

Another passage that gives confirmation to this is Revelation 6:9–10:

> When he opened the fifth seal, I saw under the altar the souls of those who had been slain for the word of God and for the witness they had borne. They cried out with a loud voice, "O Sovereign Lord, holy and true, *how long before you will judge and avenge* [Greek *ekdikeō*, "punish, take vengeance"] *our blood on those who dwell on the earth?*"

The significant point about this passage is that these "souls" are now completely free from sin, and this means that there is no trace of sinful desire left in their hearts. Yet they are crying out for God to avenge their murderers, to take vengeance on those who had murdered them, "on those who dwell on the earth" (v. 10). Therefore such a desire cannot be seen as morally wrong, nor is it inconsistent with forgiving others and continually committing judgment into the hands of God, even as Jesus did when he was on the cross (see 1 Peter 2:23 and Luke 23:34). In fact, it is exactly this action of committing judgment into the hands of God that allows us to give up the desire to seek it for ourselves and that gives us freedom to continue to show acts of personal mercy to them in this life.

e. What crimes are worthy of capital punishment?

Are any other crimes besides murder also worthy of capital punishment? The Bible does not give us explicit directions on that question, though some principles from it can inform our reasoning process. The main question is whether other crimes are *similar enough to murder in the degree of evil they involve*, so that they deserve capital punishment.

The final decision about which crimes deserve capital punishment should be made by each state or nation, ideally as the will of the people finds expression through the laws enacted by their elected representatives. (I certainly do not think this is a question that a democracy should allow to be decided by nine unelected justices on a Supreme Court, as now happens in the United States—see the discussion in chapter 5, pp. 144–45.)

---

61. Jim Wallis, *God's Politics*, 303.

Christopher Wright points out a significant feature of Old Testament law: "No property offense in normal legal procedure was punishable by death."[62] That is, *people* could not be put to death for stealing *things*, but some kind of monetary retribution had to be made instead. This seems to be a wise principle that should prevent the death penalty from even being considered for crimes involving only property.

However, one word of caution is in order: I do *not* think it right to appeal to the *many kinds of crimes subject to the death penalty* in the laws in the Mosaic covenant (in Exodus, Leviticus, Numbers, and Deuteronomy) to say that those crimes should receive capital punishment today. Those laws were only intended for the people of Israel at that particular time in history. Many of those laws reflected the unique status of Israel as a people for God's own possession who were required to worship him and not allow any hint of allegiance to other gods. There is no suggestion in the rest of the Bible that those particular uses of the death penalty in the Mosaic covenant should ever be applied by civil governments today.

As far as modern governments are concerned, I think that capital punishment should be the penalty for *some other crimes* that were intended to or actually did lead to the death of other people. Some examples might include perjury that resulted in the wrongful death of a falsely accused person, or espionage that resulted in the deaths of some of the citizens of a country. Other examples would be "crimes against the state" such as treason or plotting to use weapons of mass destruction, both of which could result in the deaths of many thousands of people. It also seems to me that a crime such as kidnapping along with brutal rape and beating of another person that did not result in death but resulted in permanent disability to the victim could also fall into the category of a crime worthy of capital punishment. (However, the US Supreme Court took away the right of any state to decide to impose such a death penalty in *Kennedy v. Louisiana*, announced on June 25, 2008, a case involving the brutal rape of a child. In that case the court also ruled out the death penalty for any crime against an individual "where the victim's life was not taken.")[63]

f. Conclusion

God gives to civil government the right and the responsibility to carry out capital punishment for certain crimes, at least for the crime of murder (which is specified in Genesis 9:6).

3. Arguments from reason and evidence apart from the Bible

Many private advocacy groups have advanced persuasive arguments for capital punishment based on the fact that it does in fact deter violent crime, that it can be fairly administered, that adequate safeguards can be taken to prevent innocent people from being executed, and that a widespread human sense of justice acknowledges that the crime of premeditated murder can only be adequately punished through taking the life of the

---

62. Christopher J. H. Wright, *Old Testament Ethics for the People of God* (Downers Grove, IL: InterVarsity Press, 2004), 308.

63. *Kennedy v. Louisiana*, 554 U.S. 36 (2008).

murderer. Christians should not be surprised that even unbelievers have an inward sense of the requirements of justice in such a case, because the Bible says that "the work of the law is written on their hearts, while their conscience also bears witness" (Rom. 2:15). This indicates that God has put in the hearts of all people a sense of right and wrong that reflects much of his moral law, and that would include also a sense of a need for justice to be carried out when a wrong has been committed.

4. Objections

a. Objections from the Bible

Some writers have raised objections to the idea that I have presented here, that governments have a right and responsibility to carry out capital punishment at least for premeditated murder. They have based their objections on other passages found in the Bible.[64]

(1) Exodus 20:13

Some have argued that Exodus 20:13, "You shall not murder," prohibits the death penalty. They claim that not even a government should "murder" a criminal.

But that interpretation misunderstands the sense of the Hebrew verb *rātsakh*, which is here translated "murder." This verb is used elsewhere in the Old Testament to refer to what we would call "murder" (in a criminal sense) today (see Num. 35:20). But the word *rātsach* is *not* the ordinary word that refers to judicial execution; that is Hebrew *muth*, along with other expressions. Thus Numbers 35:16 says, "The murderer [*rātsach*] shall be put to death [*muth*]," using a different verb for capital punishment.[65]

Therefore Exodus 20:13 should not be used as an argument against capital punishment, for that is not the sense in which the original readers would have understood it. (This also means that the RSV and KJV are misleading when they translate the verse, "You shall not kill," which could be taken by people to mean all sorts of killing, a much broader sense than what is intended by the Hebrew verb.)

In addition, God himself commanded that the death penalty be carried out in the actual laws that he gave for the Mosaic covenant (see, for example, Num. 35:16–21, 30–34). It would not be consistent to think that in Exodus 21:13 God prohibited what he commanded in Numbers 35.

(2) Matthew 5:38–39

This Scripture passage says, "You have heard that it was said, 'An eye for an eye and a tooth for a tooth.' But I say to you, Do not resist the one who is evil. But if anyone slaps you on the right cheek, turn to him the other also."

---

64. Several of these objections are taken from the extensive argument against the death penalty found in Stassen and Gushee, *Kingdom Ethics*, 197–203.

65. Out of forty-nine instances of *rātsach* in the Old Testament, it is only used once to apply to judicial execution, and that is in a proverbial or axiomatic saying that does not represent the ordinary use of the word, even in the context of that verse: "If anyone kills a person, the murderer [*rātsach*] shall be put to death [*rātsach*] on the evidence of witnesses. But no person shall be put to death [*muth*] on the testimony of one witness" (Num. 35:30).

However, in this verse Jesus is speaking to *individual persons* and talking about how they should be relating to other individuals. It is similar to Romans 12:19, where Paul prohibits personal vengeance. Jesus is not talking about the responsibility of governments or telling governments how they should act with regard to the punishment of crime. We need to pay attention to the context of passages and apply them to the situations they are addressing; Matthew 5 is addressing personal conduct (see pp. 42, 82, 201–2), while Romans 13 explicitly addresses the responsibilities of governments.

(3) Matthew 22:39

Here Jesus says, "You shall love your neighbor as yourself." Does this command prohibit putting a murderer to death? Is it possible to love one's neighbor, in obedience to this command, and at the same time put him to death for murder? How can these be consistent with each other? And shouldn't this command of Jesus take precedence over the Old Testament commands about executing the death penalty?

But this objection, if it pits Jesus' command against some Old Testament commands about the death penalty, clearly misunderstands the context from which Jesus took these words. Jesus is actually quoting from the Old Testament, from Leviticus 19:18, where God commanded the people, "You shall not take vengeance or bear a grudge against the sons of your own people, but *you shall love your neighbor as yourself*: I am the Lord." In that same context, God also commanded the death penalty for certain crimes (see Lev. 20:2, 10). Therefore it must have been consistent for God to command love for one's neighbor *and also* command the death penalty, for example, for people who put their children to death in sacrificing to idols (see 20:2). Love for one's neighbor does not nullify the requirement to carry out God's justice on wrongdoers.

(4) Matthew 26:52

When Jesus was being arrested, Peter drew his sword and struck the servant of the high priest, thinking to defend Jesus against attack. But Jesus said to him, "Put your sword back into its place. For all who take the sword will perish by the sword" (Matt. 26:52). Does this argue against the death penalty?

This verse should not be taken as a command to people serving as agents of a government. That interpretation would fail to take account of who Peter was and what his role was at that point. Jesus was not saying that no soldiers or policemen should ever have weapons; rather, he was telling Peter not to attempt to resist those who were arresting Jesus and would lead him to crucifixion. Jesus did not want to begin a civil uprising among his followers, and he certainly did not want Peter to be killed at that time for attempting to defend and protect him.

But it is also interesting that Peter, who had been traveling with Jesus regularly for three years, was carrying a sword! People carried swords at that time for self-defense against robbers and others who would do them harm, and Jesus apparently had not taught them that it was wrong to carry a sword for self-defense. (He seems to authorize swords for this very purpose in Luke 22:38.) In addition, Jesus did not tell Peter to give his sword away or throw it away, but, "Put your sword back into its place" (Matt. 26:52).

It was apparently right for Peter to continue carrying his sword, just not to use it to prevent Jesus' arrest and crucifixion. In that context, "all who take the sword will perish by the sword" must mean that those who take up the sword *in an attempt to do the spiritual work of advancing the kingdom of God* will not succeed in that work, and if Jesus' followers attempted to overthrow the Roman government as a means of advancing the kingdom of God at that time, they would simply fail and perish by the sword.

(5) John 8:2–11

The Old Testament had commanded the death penalty for the crime of adultery (see Deut. 22:23–24), but in the New Testament story of the woman caught in adultery, Jesus first said, "Let him who is without sin among you be the first to throw a stone at her" (John 8:7), and then, when all the accusers had left, he said, "Neither do I condemn you; go, and from now on sin no more" (8:11). Does this imply that Jesus no longer wanted people to enforce the death penalty?

There are several reasons why this passage should not be used as an argument against the death penalty. First, even if this text is used to argue against using the death penalty *for adultery,* which was taught in the Mosaic covenant (see Deut. 22:23–24), it is not a story about a murderer and it cannot be used to apply to the use of the death penalty *for murder,* which was established in God's covenant with Noah long before the time of the covenant with Moses.

Second, the historical context of this passage explains more about Jesus' answer: He did not allow himself to be drawn into a trap in which he would tell the Jewish leaders to carry out the death penalty, whereas the Roman government had prohibited anyone from carrying out the death penalty except the Roman officials themselves.

Third, the entire story is contained in John 7:53–8:11, a passage of doubtful origin, as is plain from the explanatory notes in any modern Bible translation. Although the passage is retained in many Bibles today, it is usually with double brackets or other marks showing that it almost certainly was not a part of the original manuscript of John's gospel. Thus the authority of this text itself is doubtful.

Therefore, on several levels the text does not provide a persuasive objection to the death penalty with respect to crimes such as murder.

(6) "We should follow the teachings of Jesus"

Sometimes opponents of the death penalty say that we should follow the teachings of Jesus on this matter rather than other verses in the Bible, especially some Old Testament passages. Stassen and Gushee, for example, say, "One way to study the biblical teaching on the death penalty is to begin with Jesus Christ as Lord, and with the commitment to be followers of Jesus.... Then we ask first what Jesus taught on the death penalty as a response to murder."[66] They contrast this approach with using as the key passage "not Jesus' teaching but Genesis 9:6."[67] This is similar to the objection from Greg Boyd that I discussed in chapter 1 (see p. 38).

---

66. Stassen and Gushee, *Kingdom Ethics,* 197.

67. Ibid., 199.

The primary biblical teaching about the responsibilities of civil government is found in passages such as Genesis 9, Romans 13, and 1 Peter 2 (see chap. 3 for other passages), but *Jesus himself* did not give much explicit teaching about civil government. Therefore, when someone says, "We should follow the teaching of Jesus" regarding civil government, he has ruled out most of the relevant teaching in the Bible about civil government! In another sense, however, *the whole Bible* comes with the authority of Jesus, and we should seek to follow all that it teaches on this topic. Finally, as explained with regard to passages from Matthew above, Stassen and Gushee incorrectly try to apply some of Jesus' teachings to the question of the death penalty as used by governments, a subject that these teachings were not intended to address.

(7) God spared some murderers such as Cain and King David

The final biblical argument against the death penalty is that God's own actions show that murderers should not be put to death, because God himself spared Cain, who murdered his brother Abel (Gen. 4:8–16), and also spared the life of King David when David caused the death of Bathsheba's husband, Uriah (see 2 Sam. 12:13).[68]

But this objection merely changes the subject from the *responsibility of civil government* to the *freedom of God* to pardon whomever he wishes. Of course, God can pardon some people until the day of final judgment and execute immediate judgment on others, according to his wise purposes. He is God! In other passages he executed immediate judgment that ended people's lives, as with the fire from heaven on Sodom and Gomorrah (Gen. 19:24–29), or the flood (Gen. 6–9), or Korah, Dathan, and Abiram (Num. 16:31–33), or Nadab and Abihu (Lev. 10:1–2), or Uzzah (2 Sam. 6:7). The simple truth is that God can pardon whom he will until the day of final judgment, and he can carry out immediate judgment on whom he will. But he is *not* telling us in these passages *what he wants civil governments to do!* He has established that clearly in Genesis 9:5–6, in Romans 13:1–7, in 1 Peter 2:13–14, and elsewhere. Where he tells us what he wants governments to do, governments should follow those teachings.

It is characteristic of the opponents of capital punishment that they continue to appeal to passages that *do not* speak explicitly about the subject of civil government, in order to use them to deny the teaching of those passages that *do* speak about civil government. This is hardly sound biblical interpretation.

(8) A "whole life ethic"

Some opponents of the death penalty have said that Christians should apply a "whole life ethic," in which they oppose all intentional taking of human life, including abortion, euthanasia, capital punishment, and war. (This view is sometimes called the "seamless garment" argument.) Jim Wallis takes this position in his book *God's Politics*.[69] Joseph

---

68. Stassen and Gushee also mention some other Old Testament examples; see their *Kingdom Ethics*, 200.

69. Jim Wallis, *God's Politics,* 300, 303–6. Wallis does not discuss any passages from the Bible in support of his view, but just his vague, general principle of a "consistent ethic of life."

Cardinal Bernardin of Chicago was an advocate of this view, stating, "The spectrum of life cuts across the issues of genetics, abortion, capital punishment, modern warfare and the care of the terminally ill."[70] Pope John Paul II also advocated this position in his *Evangelium Vitae*, writing,

> This is the context in which to place the problem of the death penalty. On this matter there is a growing tendency, both in the Church and in civil society, to demand that it be applied in a very limited way or even that it be abolished completely. The problem must be viewed in the context of a system of penal justice ever more in line with human dignity and thus, in the end, with God's plan for man and society. The primary purpose of the punishment which society inflicts is "to redress the disorder caused by the offence." Public authority must redress the violation of personal and social rights by imposing on the offender an adequate punishment for the crime, as a condition for the offender to regain the exercise of his or her freedom. In this way authority also fulfills the purpose of defending public order and ensuring people's safety, while at the same time offering the offender an incentive and help to change his or her behaviour and be rehabilitated.
>
> It is clear that, for these purposes to be achieved, the *nature and extent of the punishment* must be carefully evaluated and decided upon, and ought not go to the extreme of executing the offender except in cases of absolute necessity: in other words, when it would not be possible otherwise to defend society. Today however, as a result of steady improvements in the organization of the penal system, such cases are very rare, if not practically non-existent.[71]

In response, the proper approach to decide a biblical position on a topic is to take *the specific teaching of the Bible about that topic*, rather than fleeing to a vague cloud of generalities (such as "whole life ethic") that can then be used to support most any position the proponent wants. As I have argued above, the specific texts pertaining to abortion and euthanasia teach against these things, but the specific texts that pertain to capital punishment support it.

Another argument against this "whole life ethic" view is the fact that in Ezekiel 13:19 God says, "You have profaned me among my people …," and then he condemns both "putting to death souls who should not die and *keeping alive souls who should not live*" (emphasis added). ("Souls" here is used to mean "people.") Therefore the true biblical ethic is not "protect all human life in every case," but rather "protect the innocent and also punish the guilty, in proportion to the crime they have committed."

Rather than a "whole life ethic," Christians should adopt a "whole Bible ethic" and be faithful to the teaching of the entire Bible on this subject as well as on others.

70. Joseph Cardinal Bernardin: quoted in R. Kenneth Overberg, "A Consistent Ethic of Life," *Catholic Update,* St. Anthony's Press, 2009.

71. John Paul II, "*Evangelium vitae*: On the Value and Inviolability of Human Life," Paragraph 56 (March 25, 1995). www.vatican.va/edocs/ENG0141/_Index.htm.

b. Objections to the death penalty based on results and fairness

Most arguments about capital punishment *apart from* the teachings of the Bible have to do with the results of using or abolishing the death penalty. Those who argue against the death penalty say that (a) it does not deter crime; (b) innocent victims might be put to death; (c) violence by government provokes more violence in society; (d) it is unfairly administered, so that the poor and some ethnic minorities are much more likely to receive the death penalty; and (e) capital punishment historically has been used in cruel and oppressive ways, even by Christians.

In response, proponents of the death penalty argue the following:

(1) Is the death penalty a deterrent to murder? When overall statistics are examined, there is *a fairly clear inverse relationship* between the number of executions of murderers and the number of murders in the United States. When the number of executions goes down, the number of murders goes up, but when executions increase, murders drop. This is seen in the following chart from two professors at Pepperdine University:[72]

Figure 6.2

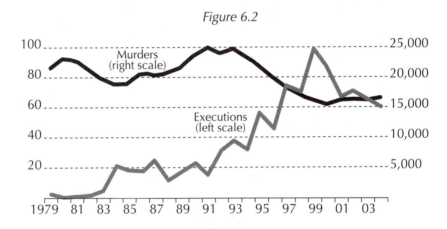

Some studies have shown that for each murderer executed, as many as fourteen to eighteen additional murders are deterred.[73]

This deterrence effect has been recognized even by researchers who oppose capital punishment. "I personally am opposed to the death penalty," said H. Naci Mocan, an economist at Louisiana State University and an author of a study finding that each execution saves five lives. "But my research shows that there is a deterrent effect."[74]

72. Roy D. Adler and Michael Summers, "Capital Punishment Works," *Wall Street Journal* (Nov. 2, 2007). http://online. wsj.com/article/SB119397079767680173.html. Reprinted by permission of Dr. Michael Summers, Pepperdine University.

73. Testimony of David B. Muhlausen, Ph.D., "The Death Penalty Deters Crime and Saves Lives," Heritage Foundation (Aug. 28, 2007). www.heritage.org/Research/Crime/tst082807a. cfm: citing Paul R. Zimmerman, "State Executions, Deterrence,

and the Incidence of Murder," *Journal of Applied Ecomomics* 7:1 (May 2004), 909–41.

74. H. Naci Mocan: quoted in Adam Liptak, "Does Death Penalty Save Lives? A New Debate," *New York Times* (Nov. 18, 2007). www.nytimes.com/2007/11/18/us/18deter.html?ei=512 4&en=fe19d37a68eea8b4&ex=1353042000&partner=deliciou s&exprod=delicious&pagewanted=all.

Similarly, anti-death penalty proponents Cass Sunstein of the University of Chicago and Adrian Vermeule of Harvard University wrote, "Capital punishment may well save lives." They added, "Those who object to capital punishment, and who do so in the name of protecting life, must come to terms with the possibility that the failure to inflict capital punishment will fail to protect life."[75]

This shows the inadequacy of the arguments from authors such as Wallis, who claims it is part of a "consistent ethic of life" to be against capital punishment.[76] My response is to say that when we support capital punishment, we show that we place *the highest possible value on human life*: for when life is wrongfully taken, society requires the greatest punishment, forfeiting the life of the murderer. These studies also show that Wallis is incorrect when he writes that "there is no real evidence that [capital punishment] deters murder; it just satisfies revenge."[77] (He quotes no data to support this.)

In addition, there is an argument from common sense: If a criminal knows he will possibly be put to death, will he be more likely or less likely to commit murder than if he knows he cannot be put to death? He will be less likely.

The current legal system in the United States allows appeals to drag on for a decade or more, so we have not been able to see in recent years a reliable evaluation of the deterrent effect if the death penalty were carried out more quickly when someone has clearly been determined to be guilty and reasonable appeals have been exhausted. The deterrent effect would no doubt be much greater than it is today. The Bible says, "Because the sentence against an evil deed is not executed speedily, the heart of the children of man is fully set to do evil" (Eccl. 8:11).

(2) Are innocent people put to death? With regard to the possibility of innocent victims being put to death, there has been (to my knowledge) *no known example* of an innocent person put to death in the United States since the resumption of the death penalty in 1976. A number of innocent death-row prisoners have been *released* due to DNA testing,[78] but that does not prove that any people have wrongfully been executed. Of course, the death penalty should be carried out only when guilt is established with extremely high standards of proof, but that is done in many murder convictions.

What is the result of failing to carry out the death penalty in the case of premeditated murder? Life imprisonment is also a cruel kind of punishment and is extremely expensive. Moreover, giving a murderer life in prison or a long-term sentence may lead to his committing other murders in prison or after he escapes or is pardoned. For example, in 1981 Glen Stewart Godwin was sentenced to twenty-five years in prison for the stabbing death of a drug runner and pilot named Kim Robert LeValley. Godwin stabbed LeValley twenty-six times. He escaped from Folsom (California) Prison and fled to Mexico, where he began a new life as a drug dealer. He was arrested there and killed a member of a Mexican drug cartel while in prison. Soon afterward, he broke out of prison again

---

75. Cass Sunstein and Adrian Vermeule, "Is Capital Punishment Morally Required? The Relevance of Life-Life Tradeoffs," *Stanford Law Review* 58:703 (2005): quoted in Liptak, "Does Death Penalty Save Lives?"

76. See Wallis, *God's Politics*, 300, 303.

77. Ibid., 303.

78. One example is Nicholas James Yarris, who was exonerated by DNA evidence in 2003 for the rape and murder of a suburban Philadelphia woman and was removed from death row. See Cindi Lash, "DNA Exonerates Death Row Inmate," *Pittsburgh Post-Gazette* (Dec. 10, 2003). www.post-gazette.com/localnews/20031210yarris1210p1.asp.

and (as of 2008) has remained a refugee from justice, with a $100,000 reward offered by the US Federal Bureau of Investigation (FBI) for information leading to his arrest.[79]

The fact remains that God gave the requirement for the death penalty in Genesis 9:6 at the beginning of human society after the flood, when methods of collecting evidence and the certainty of proof were far less reliable than they are today. Yet God still gave the command to fallible human beings, not requiring that they be omniscient to carry it out, but only expecting that they act responsibly and seek to avoid further injustice as they carried it out. Among the people of Israel, a failure to carry out the death penalty when God had commanded it was to "pollute the land" and "defile" it before God, for justice had not been done (see Num. 35:32–34).

(3) Does all violence beget more violence? The idea that "violence" by government (in capital punishment) "begets more violence" is simply wrong. It is contrary to the teachings of Genesis 9:5–6, Romans 13:4, and 1 Peter 3:12–13. In fact, exactly the opposite is true: Capital punishment actually has a deterrent effect and saves many innocent lives, as several studies have shown (see discussion above).

(4) Are there racial or economic disparities in the death penalty? If capital punishment is unfairly or disproportionately carried out among certain segments of a population *when compared with the number of murders committed by that segment of the population*, then the necessary legal steps should be taken to correct that imbalance. But that is not an argument against the death penalty in general. It is merely an argument that demonstrates that it should be carried out fairly, among rich and poor alike, and among members of every ethnic group, when crimes worthy of capital punishment have been committed. There should be no discrimination based on a person's social status or economic class or racial background.

(5) Has the death penalty been abused in past history? It is true that capital punishment has sometimes in history been used with horrible excess and for far lesser crimes than murder. There are tragic examples in the history of the church where people were put to death because of what the church considered to be the propagation of false doctrine. But these executions are *abuses* that should not be defended by anyone today; such abuses are not arguments against the rightful use of the death penalty.

5. Recommendations about laws and policies

In light of the previous discussion, I would make two specific recommendations:

a. *Governments should institute the death penalty for cases of premeditated murder.* The reasons for this have been discussed above (pp. 186–90).

b. *Societies and governments should use the normal decision-making processes established by their governments to decide whether any crimes other than murder are so similarly horrible that they are worthy of capital punishment.* Some factors relevant to that determination have been discussed above (pp. 190–93).

79. Melissa Underwood, "Glen Stewart Godwin Wanted for Murder, Escape From Prison," *Fox News* (Jan. 28, 2008). www.foxnews.com/story/0,2933,326034,00.html.

6. The importance of this issue

The issue of capital punishment is important for four reasons: (1) God in both the Old Testament and the New Testament teaches that governments should carry out this punishment at least for the crime of murder; (2) it satisfies a deep human sense that just punishment is required when a murder has been committed; (3) it satisfies God's requirement for the just punishment that he expects societies to carry out in such cases; (4) it acts as an important deterrent to the horrible crime of murder, especially in cases where the execution is carried out fairly and swiftly and with adequate safeguards against punishing innocent people.

7. For further reading

Bibliography on capital punishment:

Davis, *Evangelical Ethics*, 203–18; Feinberg and Feinberg, *Ethics for a Brave New World*, 127–48; Frame, *The Doctrine of the Christian Life*, 701–4; H. Wayne House and John Howard Yoder, eds., *The Death Penalty Debate: Two Opposing Views of Capital Punishment* (Waco, TX: Word, 1991); Erik Owens, John Carlson, and Eric Elshtian, eds., *Religion and the Death Penalty: A Call for Reckoning* (Grand Rapids: Eerdmans, 2004); Rae, *Moral Choices*, 209–24; Glen H. Stassen and David P. Gushee, *Kingdom Ethics* (Downers Grove, IL: InterVarsity Press, 2003), 194–214.

D. SELF-DEFENSE AND OWNERSHIP OF GUNS

The political question regarding gun ownership is this:

> Should governments prohibit private citizens from owning some or all kinds of guns?

1. The relevant biblical teaching

The biblical teaching that is relevant to the question of gun-control laws has to do, first, with the question of self-defense. Is it right to defend ourselves from physical attacks, and is it right ever to use a weapon in such self-defense? If self-defense is morally right, then the question of gun ownership is primarily a question of whether that is an appropriate kind of weapon to use for self-defense.

a. Is it right to defend ourselves and others from physical attacks when we are able to do so?

Sometimes people think that Jesus prohibited all self-defense when he told his disciples that they should turn the other cheek:

> "You have heard that it was said, 'An eye for an eye and a tooth for a tooth.' But I say to you, do not resist the one who is evil. But if anyone slaps you on the right cheek, turn to him the other also" (Matt. 5:38–39).

But Jesus is not prohibiting self-defense here. He is prohibiting individuals from taking personal vengeance simply to "get even" with another person. The verb "slaps" is the Greek term *rhapizō*, which refers to a sharp slap given in insult (a right-handed person would use the back of the hand to slap someone "on the right cheek").[80] So the point is not to hit back when someone hits you as an insult. But the idea of a violent attack to do bodily harm or even murder someone is not in view here.

Other passages of Scripture seem to show that it is right to try to avoid being harmed by a violent attacker. When King Saul threw a spear at David, David "eluded Saul, so that he struck the spear into the wall," and David fled from him (1 Sam. 19:10).

When King Aretas attempted to capture him in Damascus, Paul escaped by being let down in a basket through an opening in the wall (2 Cor. 11:32–33). Jesus also escaped from an angry crowd at Nazareth that was trying to throw him off a cliff (see Luke 4:29–30), and on another occasion Jesus hid himself in the temple and then escaped from hostile Jews who were seeking to harm him (see John 8:59; 10:39).

In none of these cases did the person who was attacked "turn the other cheek"—that is, David did not hand the spear back to Saul and say, "Try again!"

In the very context of Matthew 5:38–39, several of Jesus' other statements give *examples* of how Christlike conduct will look, but they are *not absolute commands* to be obeyed in every situation. For example, "Give to the one who begs from you, and do not refuse the one who would borrow from you" (Matt. 5:42, just three verses after the verse on turning the other cheek) cannot be obeyed in *every* situation, or a persistent beggar could bankrupt any Christian or any church just by asking.

In another passage Jesus seemed to encourage his disciples to have swords for self-defense:

> He said to them, "But now let the one who has a moneybag take it, and likewise a knapsack. And let the one who has no sword sell his cloak and buy one. For I tell you that this Scripture must be fulfilled in me: 'And he was numbered with the transgressors.' For what is written about me has its fulfillment." And they said, "*Look, Lord, here are two swords.*" And he said to them, "It is enough" (Luke 22:36–38).

People commonly carried swords at that time for protection against robbers, and apparently at least two of Jesus' disciples, who had been with him for three years, were still carrying swords, and Jesus had not forbidden this. Although some interpreters understand Jesus to be speaking about "swords" in a metaphorical way (meaning the disciples should be armed spiritually to fight spiritual enemies), this is not a persuasive interpretation, because in this very context the *moneybag* and *knapsack* and *sandals* (see vv. 35–36) are all literal, and *the swords that they showed him* were literal swords. The fact that Jesus was going to be crucified meant an increasing danger of people attacking the disciples as well. When Jesus says, "It is enough," it is immediately in response to the disciples showing him "two swords," so "enough" is best understood to mean "enough swords."

---

80. In rabbinic literature there is a parallel to this expression: see Mishnah, *Baba Kamma* 8.6.

In attempting to argue that this verse does not justify carrying a sword, some interpreters have said that Jesus means, "It is enough of this talk about swords." But that would make little sense, for Jesus himself was the one who first brought up the topic of a sword, and the disciples had simply answered him by showing him swords and making a very brief comment. He would not rebuke them ("Enough of this talk!") for merely answering him with one short sentence. When Jesus says, "It is enough," he means that two swords are enough, and this is an expression of approval of what they have just said and done. There is no hint of a rebuke. But that means that *Jesus is encouraging his disciples to carry a sword for self-defense*, and even to "buy one" (v. 36) if they do not have one.

Another argument in favor of self-defense is that God wants us to care for the health of our bodies, not to encourage actions that would harm them (see 1 Cor. 6:19–20).

Yet another argument is that failing to oppose a violent attack will often lead to even more harm and more wrongdoing. Therefore acting in love *both* toward the attacker *and* toward one's self would include seeking to stop the attack before harm is done.

It is true that later in Luke 22 Jesus rebuked Peter for cutting off the right ear of the servant of the high priest (with a literal sword—see Luke 22:50; John 18:10), but this was because he did not want his disciples to attempt to stop his crucifixion or to try to start a military uprising against Rome. This is also the meaning of Matthew 26:52: "All who take the sword will perish by the sword." Jesus did not want Peter to try to advance the kingdom of God by force. But in the very same verse, Jesus did not tell Peter to throw away his sword, but to keep it, for he said, "Put your sword back into its place" (Matt. 26:52). (See further discussion of this verse on pp. 194–95).

b. Is it right for a person to use a weapon for self-defense?

The verses discussed above (both Luke 22:36–38 and Matt. 26:52) give significant support for the idea that Jesus wanted his disciples to have an effective weapon to use in self-defense. Most of the time, merely carrying a sword would deter a criminal, who would not want to risk being harmed himself. The sword would also enable a person to defend someone else such as a woman or a child or an elderly person who might be under attack from someone stronger.

Another reason for carrying a weapon such as a sword is that it could overcome great inequalities in size or strength between an attacker and a victim. One of Jesus' disciples might be smaller or weaker, but if reasonably skilled in the use of a sword, he still could provide an effective defense against an attacker, who would not want to risk being harmed himself.

A third reason why people carried swords is that although the Roman officials and local police were able to enforce the peace in general, there simply would never be enough of them to be on the spot whenever a crime was being committed. The sword would provide protection against violent crime whenever a policeman or soldier was not in sight.

c. Is it right to use a gun for self-defense?

If the Bible authorizes the idea of self-defense in general, and if Jesus encouraged his disciples to carry a sword to protect themselves, then it seems to me that it is also morally right for a person to be able to use *other kinds of weapons* for self-defense. Today that would include the use of a gun (where the nation or state allows this) or the use of other weapons such as pepper spray that would deter an attacker.

One significant reason why people will choose a gun as a weapon for self-defense is that a gun is a great equalizer that offsets huge differences in physical strength. An eighty-year-old woman with a gun, living alone in her home at night, or a frail seventy-year-old shopkeeper in a high-crime area, would have an effective means of defense against a twenty-five-year-old, 280-pound athletic male intruder. No other kind of weapon would give a person that ability.

In the vast majority of cases, merely brandishing a handgun will cause an attacker to flee (the literature cited below contains references to hundreds of such stories), and in the next most common event, the intruder is wounded and disabled, the attack is thwarted, and the attacker fully recovers and stands trial. The requirement to act in love toward our neighbors, including even the intruder, implies that the least amount of force required to stop the attack should be used, resulting in the least amount of physical harm to the intruder himself.

2. In nations where there is already widespread possession of guns, the laws should allow private citizens to own guns for self-defense

From several personal conversations, I am aware that the attitudes of Christians regarding gun ownership tend to differ quite widely depending on the nation in which they live. For example, in the United Kingdom, private gun ownership has been quite rare for several generations, and current laws make it almost impossible for most private citizens to own a gun. Most policemen in the United Kingdom do not carry guns either. (Britain's Home Office says being unarmed is part of the "character of the police" there.)[81] The nationwide prohibition on gun ownership seems to have been so effective that a relatively small percentage of crimes are committed by criminals with guns. In such a situation, the long traditions of the nation, the generally law-abiding nature of its population, and the widespread popular disapproval of allowing any private ownership of guns all made it unlikely that any change in the law to allow gun ownership would gain enough support to be approved in the United Kingdom. I can understand the viewpoint of British Christians who would be opposed to any change in the current laws.

On the other hand, things are not as peaceful as they might seem. The recent situation is such that, surprisingly, the rate of violent crime (with or without guns) per capita in the United Kingdom is now about twice as large as the rate in the United States.[82] And gun crime itself is also increasing. In September 2009 it was reported that in the previous twelve months London saw a 17% rise in gun offenses, up from 1,484 to 1,737.[83] Bob

81. "For Some Bobbies, a Gun Comes with the Job," Associated Press (Oct. 23, 2009). www.cnbc.com/id/33448132.

82. John Lott Jr., "Banning Guns in the U.K. Has Backfired," *Wall Street Journal Europe* (Sept. 3, 2004), reprinted by American Enterprise Institute for Public Policy Research. www.aei.org/article/21136.

83. "For Some Bobbies, a Gun Comes with the Job," Associated Press.

Ayers, a London-based former US intelligence officer, said, "In the past the police were authority figures dealing primarily with people who respected the police. However, as terrorism and crime increases in the United Kingdom, the traditional icon of the Bobby on the beat is becoming incapable of dealing with terrorists and violent crime."[84]

Sometimes people have a popular perception of higher rates of violent crime in the United States, but these attitudes generally come not from official statistics but from anecdotal evidence stemming from a few highly publicized violent crimes as well as from movies and television shows that hardly paint a fair picture of the nation as a whole.

In the United States, official statistics estimate that 35% of American households own guns, but some people estimate that the actual number may be as high as 50% because government statistics count only documented ownership, not ownership that is not recorded on any government database. Some states and cities have enacted fairly strict restrictions on gun ownership, but the overall statistical pattern seems to be that where more strict laws *against gun ownership* are enacted, the rates of violent crime go up rather than down![85] A. L. Kellerman, writing in the *American Journal of Public Health*, said, "Gun control laws encourage the substitution of other weapons, which may be also quite dangerous if used by a criminal. In fact, such substitution may be even more dangerous like shoulder weapons, or increase the possibility of injury as knives."[86] This makes sense for two reasons: (a) If a law prohibiting guns is enacted in a city, the law-abiding citizens will tend to turn in their guns at a much higher rate than criminals, and (b) if the law-abiding citizens outnumber the criminals in the society, then taking away guns will mostly take away guns from law-abiding citizens who have been using them to prevent crimes from happening.

3. Do gun-control laws reduce gun crime?

My conclusion from reading statistics from a number of studies is that, in general, increasingly strict gun-control laws have not been shown to reduce gun crime, and in several places they seem to have led to an increase in crime. Some significant examples are seen in the experience of New Jersey, Hawaii, and Washington, DC:

New Jersey adopted what was described as the "most stringent gun law in America" in 1966, and two years later the homicide rate had increased 46% and the reported robbery rate had doubled.

After Hawaii adopted a series of increasingly restrictive measures on guns, its murder rate tripled from 2.4 per 100,000 in 1968 to 7.2 in 1977.

84. Ibid.
85. A. L. Kellerman, "Firearm Related Violence: What We Don't Know Is Killing Us," *American Journal of Public Health* 84 (1994): 541–42.
86. Ibid.

The District of Columbia enacted one of the most restrictive gun-control laws in the country, and the murder rate has increased 134% at the same time that the national murder rate decreased by 2%.[87]

A major study of the impact of gun-control laws by Florida State University criminologist Gary Kleck showed that in general they had no significant effect on decreasing rates of violent crime or suicide.[88]

A 2003 review of published studies on gun control released by the Centers for Disease Control and Prevention *could not find any statistically significant decrease in crime that came from such laws.*[89]

As a result of a massive study of state gun-control laws, author John Lott concluded that allowing citizens to carry concealed weapons clearly leads to a reduction in crime. This is because a potential criminal will not know whether a possible victim is carrying a gun or not, and this is a significant deterrence to crime. Rather than studying individual examples, Lott compared FBI crime statistics from all 3,054 counties in the United States. He found that:

- Concealed handgun laws reduced murder by 8.5%, rape by 5%, and severe assault by 7%.
- If right-to-carry laws prevailed throughout the country, there would be 1,600 fewer murders, 4,200 fewer rapes, and 60,000 fewer severe assaults over a fifteen-year period.[90]

Some people may imagine that most of the guns found in the United States will eventually be used to commit a crime. But it is interesting to compare the total number of guns with the total number of murders committed using a gun. For the nine-year period 1988–97 there were 233,251 homicides in the United States, of which 68% were committed using guns.[91] That means there were 158,611 homicides with guns over the course of nine years, or an average of 17,623 homicides per year.

How does that number compare with the total number of guns available in the United States? In 1993 there were approximately 223 *million* guns available.[92] This averages out to 12,654 guns for every murder committed with a gun. In other words, for every gun that is used for murder in the United States, there are 12,653 guns that are *not* used in a murder. And many of those guns, in fact, are used to prevent murders.

Nor do guns lead to a higher incidence of suicide. Studies of the relationship between gun ownership and total suicide rates have shown that if gun ownership is restricted, of

87. "Myth No. 2: Gun Control Laws Reduce Crime," National Center for Policy Analysis. www.ncoa.org/pub/st/st176/s176c.html.

88. Gary Kleck and E. Britt Patterson, "The impact of gun control and gun ownership levels on violence rates," *Journal of Quantitative Criminology* 9:3, 249–87.

89. "First Reports Evaluating the Effectiveness of Strategies for Preventing Violence: Firearms Laws," *Morbidity and Mortality Review,* Centers for Disease Control (Oct. 3, 2003). www.cdc.

gov/mmwr/preview/mmwrhtml/rr5214a2.htm.

90. John R. Lott, *More Guns, Less Crime* (Chicago: University of Chicago Press, 1998, 2000), 76–77.

91. National Center for Injury Prevention and Control, Centers for Disease Control and Prevention, Injury, mortality statistics. www.wonder.cdc.gov/mortICD9J.shtml.

92. Lott, *More Guns, Less Crime,* 76–77.

course the number of suicides *using guns* is diminished, but the total number of suicides apparently is unchanged, because about the same number of people will commit suicide by other means. Gary Kleck writes,

> … one reason that few suicides could be prevented by removing guns was that people who use guns in suicide typically have a more serious and persistent desire to kill themselves than suicide attempters using other methods. If denied guns, some or all of this group would substitute other methods and kill themselves anyway.[93]

Citing the US National Center for Health Statistics, Kleck reported that 57 percent of gun deaths in 1998 were suicides, and "most gun suicides would probably occur even if a gun was not available."[94] Contrary to popular myth, possession of a gun does not increase, but rather decreases, a person's likelihood of being injured in a crime. Studies by Kleck found that victims of a crime or attempted crime who defend themselves with a gun are in fact less likely to be injured or to lose property than victims who did not defend themselves, or attempted to defend themselves without a gun.[95] Kleck argues also that there is no evidence that using a gun for self-protection means that the attacker will take the gun away and use it against the victim.[96]

Some argue that ownership of a gun increases the likelihood of domestic violence. But the statistics used in this argument need to be examined carefully, because in many instances of gun violence occurring within a home that owns a gun, the situation involved either a case of self-defense by a weaker, abused victim against a much stronger abuser (and no criminal charges were brought), or else a gun was brought into the home by the criminal (in a violent area, and thus the gun that was already in the home was not used in the crime).

Statistics about the number of "children" killed by guns each year also need to be understood in light of who are the people counted as "children." Many of the aggregate statistics cited include deaths of *gang members up to the age of anywhere from eighteen to twenty-one*, depending on the state, where these persons are legally still considered "children" and not "adults." Actual numbers of fatal gun accidents involving *children age zero to fourteen* in the United States have shown a steady decline from 530 children per year in 1970 to 227 per year in 1991. Even these are tragic numbers, but they need to be understood in light of other statistics, such as more than 300 child deaths per year involving bicycles.[97] And all of these statistics need to be understood in light of the estimated 2.1 million crimes that are prevented every year through private ownership of guns.[98]

93. Gary Kleck, *Armed* (Amherst, NY: Prometheus Books, 2001), 182.

94. Ibid., 317: citing US National Center for Health Statistics, *Deaths: Final Data for 1998* (Washington DC: U.S. Government Printing Office), 71.

95. Ibid., 296, citing Albert J. Reiss and Jeffrey A. Roth, "Firearms and Violence," *Understanding and Preventing Violence* (Washington, DC: National Academy Press, 1993), 266.

96. Ibid., 301.

97. Statistics taken from David B. Kopel, *Guns: Who Should Have Them?* (Amherst, NY: Prometheus Books, 1995), 311–13.

98. Don B. Kates Jr., "Gun Control: Separating Reality from Symbolism," *Journal of Contemporary Law* (1994), 353–79.

4. The current legal situation in the United States and the Second Amendment

For many years a legal battle raged in the United States over the meaning of the Second Amendment to the Constitution, which says this:

> A well-regulated Militia, being necessary to the security of a free State, the right of the people to keep and bear Arms, shall not be infringed.

What is meant by "the right of the people to keep and bear Arms"? Does it refer to an *individual* right belonging to the citizens of the United States generally? Or should it be restricted (as some have argued) to those who have weapons as part of their membership in a military force or "a well-regulated Militia," which is mentioned in the first few words of the amendment? If the second interpretation is correct, then the amendment would only protect a right to own guns for people who belong to a branch of the military or to some kind of police force.

In a landmark decision announced June 26, 2008, the Supreme Court (by a 5-to-4 majority) held the following:

(1) "The Second Amendment protects an individual right to possess a firearm unconnected with service with a militia, and to use that arm for traditionally lawful purposes, such as self-defense within the home."[99]

So why does the amendment mention "a well-regulated Militia"? The Court's opinion noted that it was due to the fact that individual states feared that a standing army under the leadership of the federal government might seek to take control over the entire nation, and a prelude to this would be the federal government attempting to disarm the people of the individual states. The meaning of "Militia" at the time of the writing of the Constitution was "all males physically capable of acting in concert for the common defense."[100] The phrase therefore did *not* refer to the *actual military forces* organized by the government such as the army or navy (as is evident in Article 1, Section 8 of the Constitution, where "the militia" is distinguished from "armies" and "a navy" and also from that part of the militia "as may be employed in the service of the United States"). A "militia" meant armed male citizens.

(2) This does not mean that the Second Amendment *only* protects the right of people to own firearms for the purpose of defending themselves against the tyranny of a powerful federal government, but simply means that that purpose is the one that led to its being put into the Constitution. In the majority opinion, Justice Scalia wrote:

> It is therefore entirely sensible that the Second Amendment's prefatory clause announces the purpose for which the right was codified: to prevent elimination of the militia. The prefatory clause does not suggest that preserving the militia was the only reason Americans valued the ancient right; most

---

99. *District of Columbia v. Heller*, 554 U.S. __ (2008), 2 (syllabus Sect. 1, Item a). www.supremecourtus.gov/opinions/07pdf/07–290.pdf.

100. Ibid., 22, sec. 2a.

undoubtedly thought it even more important for self-defense and hunting. But the threat that the new Federal Government would destroy the citizens' militia by taking away their arms was the reason that right—unlike some other English rights—was codified in a written Constitution.[101]

In other words, the reason the Second Amendment was added to the Constitution was to provide another protection against tyranny—to make it harder for any potential dictator or would-be king to take control of the entire nation against the will of the people. Stated another way, it was one outworking of the idea that a separation of powers is the best protection against government misuse of power (see chap. 3, pp. 101–3), for it meant that the federal government could never become the only entity that had all the guns in the nation and thus all the effective power.

(3) The Second Amendment did not confer a new right but simply protected an ancient and basic human right: the right of self-defense. The majority opinion states:

> The Second Amendment was not intended to lay down a "novel principl[e]" but rather codified a right "inherited from our English ancestors," *Robertson v. Baldwin*, 165 US 275, 281 (1897).[102]

Scalia also noted that the central human right to self-defense, far from peripheral to the amendment, was the fundamental right underlying the amendment itself: "Self-defense had little to do with the right's *codification*; it was the *central component* of the right itself."[103]

Justice Scalia's extensive opinion traces the meanings of terms as they were used at the time of the adoption of the Constitution, and the history of interpretation of the Second Amendment, showing the correctness of this opinion. This was an argument based on the "original public meaning" of the words of the Constitution. In particular, the usage of the phrase "the people" elsewhere in the Constitution shows that it was meant to apply to *individual citizens* of the United States, not to organizations such as an organized state or federal military force. (Notice that the First Amendment speaks of "the right of *the people* peaceably to assemble," and the Fourth Amendment speaks of "The right of *the people* to be secure in their persons, houses, papers, and effects.")

(4) The requirement that any guns kept in a home be kept locked and unloaded "makes it impossible for citizens to use arms for the core lawful purpose of self-defense and is hence unconstitutional."[104]

(5) This decision does not invalidate most existing laws that prohibit felons and the mentally ill from possessing firearms, or forbid the carrying of firearms "in sensitive places such as schools and government buildings," or other sorts of reasonable conditions and qualifications on the sale and possession of arms. Nor does it invalidate laws that prohibit "dangerous and unusual weapons."[105] This means that existing laws that restrict the sale of machine guns for private use, for example, are still allowed under the Constitution.

---

101. Ibid., 25, sec. 3.
102. Ibid., 26, sec. 3.
103. Ibid., 26, sec. 3.

104. Ibid., 3 (syllabus, item 3).
105. Ibid., 2 (syllabus, sec. 2).

5. Objections

The primary objections against allowing gun ownership are arguments from *results*. That is, people argue that allowing gun ownership leads to more injuries and deaths from guns. These arguments have been included in the discussion of the results of gun-control laws (see sec. 3 above, pp. 205–7).

A second kind of objection comes from those who also oppose capital punishment and all use of "violence" in general. I have addressed these objections both in my response to Greg Boyd in chapter 1 (see pp. 36–44) and in the discussion of objections to capital punishment earlier in this chapter (see p. 200).

6. Recommendations about laws and policies

a. Laws should guarantee that citizens have the right to possess some kind of effective means of self-defense

The right to self-defense should be seen as a fundamental human right, and governments should protect that right. This is especially important for women, for the elderly, and for any others who might be less able to defend themselves from an attack or who might appear to be more vulnerable to an attack, but it is a right that should be available to all citizens.

Protecting this right will also tend to reduce crime in any segment of society, because potential attackers will be unable to know who will have an effective weapon to use in self-defense.

Tragic mass murders in which a lone gunman can hold at bay an entire restaurant or church full of people, for example, and begin killing one after the other, are much less likely to happen in states where a large number of people carry concealed weapons and would act to stop such a person.

John Lott reports an example of a lone shooter—Peter Odighizuwa—who opened fire and killed two adminsitrators and a student at Appalachian Law School in Virginia in 2002. Odighizuwa might have killed many more students except that two male students, Mikael Gross and Tracy Bridges, ran to their cars, got their guns, and came back pointing their guns at the shooter, who then threw his gun down and the attack was stopped. But worldwide media coverage, due to a bias against reporting any good use of guns, almost uniformly failed to even mention that Gross and Bridges used guns to subdue the shooter, as they clearly specified in their interviews with reporters.[106]

In December 2007 a gunman killed one person and wounded four others when he opened fire at New Life Church in Colorado Springs, Colorado, but was stopped from killing others when a church security officer shot and killed him. CNN reported that Chief Richard Myers called the Colorado Springs church security staffer "a courageous security staff member who probably saved many lives."[107]

---

106. John Lott, *The Bias against Guns* (Chicago: Regnery, 2003), 24–25.

107. "Gunman Killed After Opening Fire at Church," *CNN.*

com (Dec. 9, 2007). www.cnn.com/2007/US/12/09/church.shooting/index.html.

b. In the United States, the right of the citizens to own guns for the purpose of self-defense should be protected by the laws

A gun is the most effective means of defense in all kinds of threatening situations, especially against attackers who may be stronger or more numerous. Protection of the right to own a gun is especially important in areas of higher crime or more frequent violence.

Unfortunately, it is precisely in areas where the right to self-defense is most needed that some gun-control laws have been most restrictive. And when stricter gun-control laws are introduced in a state or city, the incidence of violent crime and murders tends to increase rather than decrease.[108] This is because most of the guns that are taken away by these laws, or rendered ineffective by laws stating that they have to be unloaded and locked up, are taken away from law-abiding citizens who believe they should conform to the new laws. But criminals who have been using guns or want to use guns to commit crimes are the least likely to turn them in. There is truth in the popular slogan, "If guns are outlawed, only outlaws will have guns."

c. Governments should place reasonable restrictions on gun ownership

It is appropriate for governments to prohibit convicted felons and the mentally ill from owning or possessing guns. It is also appropriate to prohibit the possession of guns in certain sensitive places, such as in courtrooms or on airplanes. (But we must remember that both of these situations are highly controlled areas with very low possibility of a violent attack by one person against another, and in the extremely rare occasions where an attack occurs, it is immediately subdued by the authorities present. Thus these situations are different from life in the general public where citizens have much more freedom.)

Other reasonable restrictions would include the prohibition of private ownership of certain types of weapons not needed for personal self-defense—for example, weapons such as a machine gun or an anti-tank rocket launcher or an anti-aircraft missile launcher that would only be needed in military conflict.

To guarantee compliance with such restrictions, a background check would seem appropriate when someone wants to buy a gun. But it should not become so difficult that it actually becomes a means of preventing gun ownership by legitimate, law-abiding citizens. (In the United States, a background check ordinarily requires a Social Security number, some states also require a driver's license, and the necessary approval can usually be obtained within about two minutes by a sales clerk working at a gun store.)[109]

d. What about countries other than the United States?

In countries where citizens face a danger of violent attack, the laws should allow private citizens to own and carry firearms for self-defense. Strict gun-control laws do not prevent

108. See "Myth No. 2: Gun Control Laws Reduce Crime," and Lott, *The Bias against Guns*, 50–96, 135–38.

109. "Guide to National Instant Check System," www.nraila.org/Issues/FactSheets/Read.aspx?id=82.

110. David B. Kopel, *The Samurai, the Mountie, and the Cowboy—Should America Adopt the Gun Controls of Other Democracies?* (Amherst, NY: Prometheus Books, 1992), 257–77.

criminal violence in such countries but probably result in an increase in violence. (Brazil and Jamaica[110] are two such examples.)

In countries where there exist almost no guns in the hands of either private citizens or criminals, and where police control and societal customs are strong enough that there is little risk of a citizen being physically attacked by someone else, citizens may decide it is best to leave the situation as it is rather than try to import guns when other means of self-defense and protection are functioning quite well. But if the number of physical attacks increases dramatically, then the laws need to allow responsible, law-abiding private citizens to obtain some effective weapon for use in self-defense. And the most effective weapon in such cases—especially for potential victims who are older, smaller, or weaker, or potentially outnumbered—is some kind of handgun.

e. But should an individual Christian own a gun?

This entire discussion does not address the question of whether individual Christians will decide that it is *wise* to own a gun themselves. There is room for Christians to differ about this question and for individuals to decide what is best in their own situation. Many Christians will live in areas where they think the need for any weapon of self-defense is so small that it is outweighed by the negative considerations of the cost and the potential danger of a gun being found and misused by a child or used in an accidental way. Those are matters of individual preference and personal decision.

7. The importance of this issue

In the United States, the gun-control issue is important for several reasons:

First, because it upholds the meaning of the Second Amendment to the Constitution as it was originally intended.

Second, and more fundamentally, because it effectively protects a basic human right, the right of self-defense.

Third, because the right of citizens to bear arms is a significant protection against tyranny. It is a protection against an oppressive, dictatorial regime taking control of the nation against the will of the vast majority of its citizens.

Fourth, because study after study has shown that where private citizens have the right to possess guns for self-defense, that is a significant deterrent to violent crime.

8. For further reading

Frame, *The Doctrine of Christian Life*, 692–93; Gary Kleck and Don B. Kates, *Armed: New Perspectives on Gun Control* (Amherst, NY: Prometheus, 2001); John R. Lott Jr., *More Guns, Less Crime* (Chicago: University of Chicago Press, 1998); John R. Lott Jr., *The Bias Against Guns: Why Almost Everything You've Heard about Gun-Control Is Wrong* (Washington, DC: Regnery, 2003); Stassen and Gushee, *Kingdom Ethics*, 189–91 (opposed to allowing gun ownership).

Chapter 7

MARRIAGE

Should government define and regulate marriage? And how should marriage be defined?

A. BIBLICAL TEACHING: MARRIAGE IS ONLY BETWEEN ONE MAN AND ONE WOMAN

Not surprisingly, the Bible contains clear and explicit teachings about marriage. Many of these teachings are relevant to our consideration of governmental laws and policies about marriage.

1. God created marriage at the beginning of the human race as a lifelong union between one man and one woman

In the first chapters of the Bible we read that God created Adam and Eve and told them that together they should bear children:

> So God created man in his own image, in the image of God he created him; male and female he created them. And God blessed them. And God said to them, "Be fruitful and multiply and fill the earth and subdue it ..." (Gen. 1:27–28).

But were Adam and Eve actually a married couple? Yes, because the next chapter calls them "the man and his wife" (Gen. 2:25).

The Bible actually views the relationship between Adam and Eve as *the pattern for all marriages to follow on the earth*. This is clear from the more detailed description of their creation that comes in chapter 2. We read that "the LORD God caused a deep sleep to fall upon the man, and while he slept took one of his ribs and closed up its place with flesh," and then, "The rib that the LORD God had taken from the man he made into a woman and brought her to the man" (vv. 21–22). At that point Adam exclaimed with great joy,

> "This at last is bone of my bones
> and flesh of my flesh;
> she shall be called Woman,
> because she was taken out of Man" (v. 23).

The very next sentence uses this union between Adam and Eve as the pattern for marriages generally, for it says,

> Therefore a man shall *leave his father and his mother* and *hold fast to his wife*, and they shall become one flesh (v. 24).

The phrase "a man shall leave his father and his mother" pictures a situation in which the man departs from the household of which he was a part, and it implies that a new household is being established. The phrase "hold fast to his wife" indicates that this new relationship, between a man and his wife, is the basis of the new household that is established. Therefore marriage in general is defined here as a union between "a man" and "his wife."

This is also Jesus' understanding of Genesis 1–2 when responding to a question from the Pharisees about divorce:

> Pharisees came up to him and tested him by asking, "Is it lawful to divorce one's wife for any cause?" He answered, "Have you not read that he who created them from the beginning made them male and female, and said, 'Therefore a man shall leave his father and his mother and hold fast to his wife, and the two shall become one flesh'? So they are no longer two but one flesh. What therefore God has joined together, let not man separate" (Matt. 19:3–6).

Jesus understands that the essence of marriage was established when God "created them from the beginning" and "made them male and female" and also said that "a man shall ... hold fast to his wife, and they shall become one flesh" (vv. 4–5). He also affirms that marriage is therefore an institution God creates between a man and a woman, because he calls marriage a relationship between two people whom "God has joined together" (v. 6).

Jesus also affirms that God intended marriage to be a lifelong relationship, not a mere temporary agreement, for he specifies, "What therefore God has joined together, let not man separate" (v. 6). This perspective is given further emphasis when the Pharisees ask him in response, "Why then did Moses command one to give a certificate of divorce and to send her away?" (v. 7). Jesus answered,

> "Because of your hardness of heart Moses allowed you to divorce your wife, but from the beginning it was not so" (v. 8).

In other words, God's purpose in marriage from the beginning was *a lifelong, committed, faithful relationship between one man and one woman* (though because of sin, God would later allow for some divorce).

In addition, it is clear that sexual faithfulness to one's partner is an essential component of marriage, for adultery is regularly viewed as a sin. In fact, the command "You shall not commit adultery" (Exod. 20:14) is one of the Ten Commandments, and it is reaffirmed several times in the New Testament (see Matt. 19:18; Rom. 2:22; 13:9; James 2:11).

2. God's definition of marriage was not for the Jewish people only, but was intended to apply to all people in all societies for all time

This establishment of marriage is not like a number of laws in the Old Testament that were intended only for the Jewish people and only for a particular time in their history, such as the laws about the sacrifices of animals and clean and unclean foods. All of those laws came after the Exodus of the people of Israel from Egypt (see Exod. 1–15). These laws were given in Exodus 20–40 and in Leviticus, Numbers, and Deuteronomy.

But the basic material about marriage comes *from the beginning of the human race*, at the time when Adam and Eve were created. It comes even before there was any evil or sin in the world (which came in Genesis 3). That is why Jesus says that these truths about marriage come "from the beginning" (Matt. 19:4) and they belong to the essence of God's creating us as "male and female."

Therefore this understanding of marriage as the lifelong union between one man and one woman is intended by God to be understood as the correct definition of marriage for all people on the earth, for all cultures and societies, and for all periods of history until the beginning of the new heaven and new earth.[1]

Thus God can bring judgment, for example, on the gentile (non-Jewish) cities of Sodom and Gomorrah because of their widespread practice of homosexual conduct (see Gen. 19:1–28, especially 19:5; also Jude 7). He can bring judgment against Pharaoh, king of Egypt, if he commits adultery with someone else's wife (see Gen. 12:17–20). The book of Proverbs, which contains much wisdom not merely for the people of Israel in the Old Testament but for the conduct of life generally, gives frequent warnings against adultery (see 2:16–19; 5:1–23; 6:20–35; 7:4–27; 23:27–28).

In the New Testament, John the Baptist rebuked Herod Antipas, an Idumean and not part of the people of Israel, for wrongfully committing incest by taking his brother's wife (Mark 6:17–18). Paul can say that Gentiles, who do not have the Jewish laws, are still guilty of violating God's moral standards regarding sexual conduct (see Rom. 1:26–27; 1 Cor. 5:9–10, 13; 6:9; cf. 1 Peter 4:3–5). The great city called "Babylon," which is the center of earthly rebellion against God, is judged in the end of the book of Revelation for many sins, and among them is "sexual immorality" (Rev. 18:3, 9). And those outside the heavenly city in Revelation 21 include "the sexually immoral" (v. 8).

Therefore, from Genesis to Revelation—from the beginning of the Bible to the end—God has established moral standards regarding the nature and conduct of

---

1. In Matthew 22:30 Jesus indicates that a significant change will occur after the final resurrection of believers: "For in the resurrection they neither marry nor are given in marriage, but are like angels in heaven." But that does not affect the legal or moral definition of marriage in this present age.

marriage, and he repeatedly indicates that he will hold *all people on the earth* accountable for disobedience to those standards.

Further evidence of this is seen in Leviticus 18, which states that the Canaanites were morally responsible before God for many kinds of sexual sin (specified in vv. 6–23): "For the people of the land, who were before you, did all of these abominations, so that the land became unclean" (v. 27). God held these Canaanites accountable for violating his standards regarding marriage, even though they did not have the written laws of Israel and were not part of the Jewish people. Yet they had God's moral standards written on their hearts, and they had their own consciences that bore witness to those standards, and therefore God rightly held them accountable (see Rom. 2:14–15).

For Christians who are thinking about what kind of definition of marriage a civil government should adopt, these passages indicate that *the definition of marriage as established by God in the Bible* (a lifelong union between one man and one woman) *should be the standard adopted by all governments.* (This does not mean that all divorce should be prohibited: Because of the advent of sin in the world, later teaching in the Bible specified some conditions under which God allowed for divorce to break the lifelong commitment of marriage; see below.) And this legal standard for marriage should apply to all people, not merely to Christians or those who personally happen to agree with the Bible's standards.

3. Marriage between a man and a woman is the most fundamental institution in any society

The establishment of marriage in Genesis 1–2 comes before the establishment of any other institution in human society. It comes immediately after the creation of man and woman.

It is significant that God establishes marriage before there is any establishment of cities, nations, courts of law, or any human laws. It certainly comes before any national government, state government, or city government. It comes before any establishment of schools and universities, or businesses and corporations, or churches and other nonprofit organizations. It comes before the establishment of *any institution* in any human society. And it is foundational to the establishment of any society.

Human societies have long recognized the need for some kind of normalization of a dependable, ongoing, faithful marriage relationship between men and women. So far as I know, every human nation on earth, every society of any size or permanence at all, has recognized and protected the institution of heterosexual marriage. (Though some have had polygamy as a recognized form of marriage, it is still heterosexual marriage.)

British anthropologist J. D. Unwin reached this conclusion after conducting exhaustive research to investigate the assertions made by Sigmund Freud. Unwin discovered that Freud's call for the liberation of sexual behavior had grave consequences for society. In his research Unwin chronicled the historical decline of eighty-six different cultures and found that "strict marital monogamy" was central to social energy and growth. Indeed, no society flourished for more than three generations without it. Unwin wrote,

"In human records there is no instance of a society retaining its energy after a complete new generation has inherited a tradition which does not insist on prenuptial and post-nuptial continence" (by which he meant abstinence from sex outside of marriage).[2]

B. INCEST, ADULTERY, AND HOMOSEXUALITY ARE PROHIBITED IN BIBLICAL ETHICS

When the moral standards regarding marriage are explained in more detail in other parts of the Old Testament, certain types of relationships are excluded from being accepted as valid marriages. Incest is prohibited in Leviticus 18:1–18; 20:11–20; Deuteronomy 22:30; and 1 Corinthians 5:1–2. And of course, adultery was regularly prohibited (Exod. 20:14), which would also prohibit marrying someone who was already married to someone else.

More specific biblical teaching on the question of homosexuality is found in the following passages:

You shall not lie with a male as with a woman; it is an abomination (Lev. 18:22).

If a man lies with a male as with a woman, both of them have committed an abomination; they shall surely be put to death; their blood is upon them (Lev. 20:13).

For this reason God gave them up to dishonorable passions. For their women exchanged natural relations for those that are contrary to nature [Greek *para physin*]; and the men likewise gave up natural relations with women and were consumed with passion for one another, men committing shameless acts with men and receiving in themselves the due penalty for their error (Rom. 1:26–27).

Or do you not know that the unrighteous will not inherit the kingdom of God? Do not be deceived: neither the sexually immoral, nor idolaters, nor adulterers, *nor men who practice homosexuality*, nor thieves, nor the greedy, nor drunkards, nor revilers, nor swindlers will inherit the kingdom of God. And such were some of you. But you were washed, you were sanctified, you were justified in the name of the Lord Jesus Christ and by the Spirit of our God (1 Cor. 6:9–11).

Understanding this, that the law is not laid down for the just but for the lawless and disobedient, for the ungodly and sinners, for the unholy and profane, for those who strike their fathers and mothers, for murderers, the sexually immoral, *men who practice homosexuality*, enslavers, liars, perjurers, and whatever else is contrary to sound doctrine (1 Tim. 1:9–10).

---

2. Joseph Daniel Unwin, *Sex and Culture* (London: Oxford University Press, 1934); *Sexual Regulations and Cultural Behavior* (London: Oxford University Press, 1935); and *Hopousia: Or the Sexual and Economic Foundations of a New Society* (London: George Allen and Unwin, 1940), cited by Daniel R. Heimbach, "Deconstructing the Family," The Howard Center for Family, Religion, and Society, *The Religion and Society Report* 22:7 (Oct. /Nov. 2005). www.profam.org/pub/rs/rs_2207.htm#endfn57.

Some pro-homosexual interpreers have objected that these passages do not say that all kinds of homosexual conduct are sinful, but only some specific kind of homosexuality, such as homosexual conduct between men and underage boys, or homosexual prostitution (where money is exchanged), or unfaithful homosexual relationships, or "unnatural" homosexual conduct by people who do not naturally have homosexual desires (as opposed to homosexual conduct by people who are said to be naturally homosexual or "born gay").

However, *none of these biblical passages makes any such distinction* or says anything indicating that it is only talking about certain types of homosexual conduct. And when no such distinction is made in the words or context of the passages, it is not a correct process of interpretation simply to claim that the passages have limited scope anyway. In other words, *the words themselves* as they are written apply to *all kinds* of homosexual conduct, so it is incorrect to say that they do not.

In addition, several ancient writers before or near the time of the New Testament viewed all homosexual conduct as wrong and used language very similar to Paul's language in Romans, 1 Corinthians, and 1 Timothy. The Greek philosopher Plato (c. 429–347 BC) wrote:

> When male unites with female for procreation, the pleasure experienced is held to be due to nature, but contrary to nature [Greek *para physin*, the same phrase used in Rom. 1:26] when male mates with male or female with female, and … those … guilty of such enormities were impelled by their slavery to pleasure.[3]

The Jewish philosopher Philo (c. 30 BC–c. AD 45), in writing about Lev. 18:22 and 20:13, condemned homosexual behavior. Philo wrote: "Much graver than the above is another evil, which has ramped its way into the cities, namely pederasty"[4] (the Greek term *paiderasteuō*, used here, refers to sexual activity between grown men and adolescent boys). Philo says this is a pleasure that is "contrary to nature" (*para physin*, the same phrase Paul used in Rom. 1:26), and says it is "worthy of death."[5]

In another place, Philo speaks of homosexual conduct in general in his writing *On Abraham*, where he says the homosexual conduct in Sodom was "corrupting the whole of mankind," so that God, in raining fire from heaven and destroying the city, "abominated and extinguished this unnatural and forbidden intercourse."[6]

The Jewish historian Josephus (AD 37–c. 100) wrote that the people of Elis and Thebes, in their homosexual conduct, practiced an "unnatural [*para physin*, the same expression found in Rom 1:26] vice," and in that context, he referred to "the practice of sodomy" (homosexual conduct) as "the monstrous and unnatural [*para physin* again] pleasures in which they … indulged."[7]

The Greek historian Plutarch (c. AD 50–c. 120) referred to homosexual conduct between men as "contrary to nature" [*para physin*] and "indecent."[8]

3. Plato, *Laws* 1.636C.
4. Philo, *Special Laws* 3:37.
5. Ibid., 3.38–39.
6. Philo, *On Abraham*, 136–37.
7. Josephus, *Against Apion* 2.273–75.
8. Plutarch, *Moralia, Dialogue on Love*, 751.D–E.

These quotations show that when the New Testament writers condemned homosexual conduct, they were using the same terminology that was commonly used in other Greek literature to condemn all kinds of homosexual conduct as something "contrary to nature" and morally wrong. The words of the New Testament do not allow these prohibitions to be limited, as homosexual advocates claim, to some narrowly defined particular type of homosexual conduct.

The conclusion, then, is that the Bible views homosexual conduct as morally wrong in all cases, something contrary to God's moral standards.

C. WHAT ABOUT POLYGAMY IN THE OLD TESTAMENT?

There are a number of examples of polygamy in the Old Testament. Does having more than one wife reflect God's pattern for marriage?

The answer is that God *temporarily allowed* polygamy to occur without giving explicit commands against it, even though it did not conform to his original purpose for marriage as indicated in Genesis 1–2. But we get some hints from the narrative passages, because in every example where a man has more than one wife, the situation leads to significant difficulty in the marriage relationship, and readers are left to draw their own conclusions from this. A helpful summary of the biblical material on polygamy is found in the *ESV Study Bible*:

> Why did God allow polygamy in the Old Testament? Nowhere in the Bible did God ever command polygamy or tell anyone to marry more than one wife. Rather, God temporarily allowed polygamy to occur (he did not give any general prohibition against it) without giving it any explicit moral approval. Nevertheless, in the OT narratives, whenever a man has two or more wives, it seems to lead to trouble (see Gen. 16; 29–31; 1 Sam. 1; 1 Kings 11; note also the prohibition in Deuteronomy 17:17). In addition, polygamy is horribly dehumanizing for women, for it does not treat them as equal in value to their husbands, and therefore it does not recognize that they share fully in the high status of being created "in the image of God" (Gen. 1:27), and of being worthy of honor as "heirs with you of the grace of life" (1 Pet. 3:7). The requirement "husband of one wife" (1 Tim. 3:2) would exclude polygamists from being elders.... This restriction would provide a pattern that would generally lead to the abolition of polygamy in a church in a generation or two.[9]

D. DIVORCE

In the laws that Moses gave to Israel it was assumed that divorce would occur in some cases, though it is difficult to determine exactly what constituted a valid reason for divorce, and subsequent rabbinic discussion varied widely in its interpretations. The

---

9. *ESV Study Bible*, p. 2544.

passages that assumed that some divorce will occur are found in Deuteronomy 24:1–4 and also Leviticus 21:7, 14 and Numbers 30:9.

In the New Testament, the most common understanding among Protestant interpreters since the time of the Reformation has been that Jesus allowed divorce for the physical act of adultery and also allowed remarriage in such cases:

> "And I say to you: whoever divorces his wife, *except for sexual immorality*, and marries another, commits adultery" (Matt. 19:9).

The implication is that if a man divorces his wife *for sexual immorality* and marries another, this action does not constitute adultery and it is not sin.

In addition, Paul allowed divorce in a case where an unbelieving spouse has deserted a believing partner:

> But if the unbelieving partner separates, let it be so. In such cases the brother or sister is not enslaved. God has called you to peace (1 Cor. 7:15).

There have been other interpretations of these passages. Some have held that Jesus allowed divorce but not remarriage. Others have held that even in the case of adultery, divorce was not allowed, in part because Jesus' words, "except for sexual immorality" (Matt. 19:9), are found in Matthew 5:32 but not in Mark 10:11 or Luke 16:18. But my own understanding of these passages, and the understanding of the majority of evangelical interpreters, is that the Bible allows (but does not require) divorce in the case of adultery or desertion, and it also allows remarriage to another person in such cases. Remarriage in these cases is not sin in God's sight.

What laws should governments make regarding divorce? If we believe that God intended marriage to be a lifelong commitment except in cases of serious defilement of the marriage, then laws should protect marriage by protecting spouses from both abandonment and harm. Protection from abandonment would include measures such as mandatory counseling and significant mandatory waiting periods prior to divorce, and especially the elimination of no-fault divorce, which makes divorce far too easy and trivializes the "commitment" that is made when a marriage begins. In no-fault divorce, the spouse seeking the divorce is not required to show any wrongdoing on the part of the other spouse, so a person can get a divorce simply because he or she no longer wants to be married. (Prior to no-fault divorce, the person seeking divorce had to prove that the spouse had committed a wrong that seriously violated the marriage, such as adultery, abuse, or abandonment. Thus there were far fewer divorces for more trivial reasons or just because one person wanted out of the marriage.) The first no-fault divorce law in the United States took effect January 1, 1970, in California, and all other states eventually adopted no-fault divorce laws, resulting in more frequent divorce throughout the country.

Laws to protect a spouse from harm would include serious penalties (such as mandatory jail time and rehabilitation) for spouses who commit physical abuse (the perpetrator is usually, but not always, the husband) and also more strict reinforcement of the obligations of financial support. To protect a spouse whose marriage has been deeply harmed or defiled, divorce should certainly be allowed in the case of adultery or desertion.

with signature required when returning products to us. **Store products from a *"Close Out Sale"* or *"Scratch & Dent Sales"* are non-returnable. Any College or Real Estate Course Book, or Computer Software or Books with CD-ROM's are not returnable under any circumstances.** Some products may carry a restocking fee.

Please note: Refund processing can take up to six weeks for merchant banks (your bank or credit card company) to apply credits. USPS Media Rate takes 4-14 business days' delivery time, and may take 21+ business days in some post office locations. Our company is not responsible for USPS *"Media Rate-Third Class Mail"* delivery times.

Damaged or Incorrect Products

If you receive a damaged or incorrect product, contact our office for a return authorization number during normal business hours. We will credit your account for USPS Media Rate ($2.30) return shipping and replace the product at our expense. We are here to fully support you.

Send All Returns to:
Pinson Logistics

ATTN: Product Returns # (your original order number here, plus include your packing slip back to us)
146 Dunbar Avenue, Suite B
Oldsmar, Florida 34677

Office Hours: Monday - Friday 9:00 AM - 4:30 PM EST
(813) 855-3663 / Fax (813) 855-5254 / Closed on holidays and weekends

Pinson Logistics is a division of Pinson Communications, Inc. (www.PinsonCommunications.com) that provides product drop ship and fulfillment services for third party retail organizations.

Our 100% Money Back Guarantee*

Product Returns Policy

Pinson Logistics provides drop ship and customer support services for third party specialty retail and Internet stores. We service many third party stores and their customers, so please be sure to reference your order identification number on your packing slip when contacting us. We strive toward your 100% satisfaction with your purchase. Please telephone us between 9:00 - 4:00 EST, Monday through Friday for support. Our support specialists will do everything possible to help you. We stand behind our quality guarantee and offer the highest personalized service. If for any reason you are not 100% satisfied with any product you have received from us, you may return the product within 30 days of your invoice date. Some return restrictions may apply.

*Return Restrictions (College, Real Estate and Audio Books)

College, Higher Education, Engineering, Real Estate Books, Computer Software, Audio tape or CD-ROM Books, or any book with a CD-ROM is non-returnable. **NOTE:** Non-returnable products that are returned to us are unauthorized returns and will not be credited or shipped back to the customer.

To Return a Product for Exchange, Credit, or Refund

Your Return Authorization Number (RMA) is your original Order Number at the top of the opposite side of this page. Indicate your preference for exchange, credit, or refund. Repack the item in its original packaging, with all other materials including your original packing slip. Special shopping bonus offers with the purchase must also be returned to receive proper credit. The Return Authorization Number must be clearly marked on the label and inside the box. Returns that are mailed more than 30 days after the original purchase order date will not be accepted. **Liability for lost or damaged returned items belongs to the customer.**

The product that is being returned must be in new condition and undamaged. Any marks, scratches, or dents in or on a book will disqualify the book for a refund. **Shipping and handling charges are not refundable at any time.** In order to provide prompt service to you, we process returns daily.

E. CIVIL GOVERNMENTS SHOULD DEFINE MARRIAGE FOR ALL CITIZENS

1. Defining and regulating marriage fits the purposes of government according to the Bible

Among the most important purposes of civil government, according to the Bible, are (1) to restrain evil, (2) to bring good to society, and (3) to bring order to society. (See the discussion of these purposes in chap. 3, pp. 77–82.) On all three of these grounds, a Christian should conclude that it is right for government to define and regulate marriage.

First, marriage restrains evil by promoting sexual faithfulness between a man and a woman, by establishing a legally binding commitment for parents to care for their children, by establishing a legally binding commitment for spouses to be financially responsible for and to care for one another, and by providing a legal protection to keep women from being exploited by men who might otherwise enjoy a sexual relationship for a time and then abandon a woman and any children she may have borne from that union.

Second, marriage brings good to society in multiple ways—in promoting social stability,[10] economic well-being,[11] educational and economic benefits for children,[12] the transmission of moral and cultural values to the next generation, and a stable social unit for interactions within society.[13] (These benefits are explained more fully in section F. 2 below.)

Third, the establishment of marriage brings order to society so that the general public will know who is married and who is not. Marital status can be established as a matter of public record, so that in various ways the society as a whole can honor and protect individual marriages and can know who is responsible for the care and protection and training of children, and for the care of spouses who have medical or financial or other needs. In this way, defining and regulating marriage gives stability and order to a society. It is an extremely important social good that government should encourage and protect.

2. Defining and regulating marriages is morally right

The definition of marriage as a lifelong faithful union between one man and one woman, as found in the Bible, provides a moral standard in which God tells us what is right to do. Defining and regulating and protecting marriage as this kind of institution is thus something that is morally right in God's eyes. It is not merely something that brings

---

10. James S. Coleman, "Social Capital in the Creation of Human Capital," *American Journal of Sociology* 94 (1988): S–95-S120: cited in Testimony of Barbara Dafoe Whitehead, Co-Director, National Marriage Project, Rutgers, the State University of New Jersey, before the Committee on Health, Education, Labor, and Pensions, Subcommittee on Children and Families, US Senate (April 24, 2008). http://marriage.rutgers.edu/Publications/Pub%20Whitehead%20Testimony%20Apr%2004.htm.

11. Mary Parke, "Are Married Parents Really Better for Chil-

dren?" *Center for Law and Social Policy* (May 2003), 7. www.clasp.org: cited in ibid.

12. Parke, 2–3; Robert I. Lerman, "Marriage and the Economic Well-Being of Families with Children: A Review of the Literature" (2002), www.urban.org/expert.cfm?ID=RobertLerman; and *Why Marriage Matters: Twenty-One Conclusions from the Social Sciences* (New York: Institute, 2002), www.marriagemovement.org: cited in ibid.

13. Coleman, "Social Capital in the Creation of Human Capital."

benefits to society, but also something that a society *should* do, according to God's own definition of right and wrong as given in the Bible.

F. ARGUMENTS ABOUT MARRIAGE FROM REASON AND EXPERIENCE APART FROM THE BIBLE

1. Governments should define and establish marriage because no other institution can do that for an entire society

Only a civil government is able to define a standard of what constitutes a marriage for a whole nation or whole society. No churches or denominations could do this, because they only speak for their own members. No voluntary societies could do this, because they don't include all the people in the society.

If no definition of marriage is given to an entire society, then chaos and much oppression of women and children will result. Stanley Kurtz of the Hudson Institute writes,

> In setting up the institution of marriage, society offers special support and encouragement to the men and women who together make children. Because marriage is deeply implicated in the interests of children, it is a matter of public concern. Children are helpless. They depend upon adults. Over and above their parents, children depend upon society to create institutions that keep them from chaos. Children cannot articulate their needs. Children cannot vote. Yet children *are* society. They are us, and they are our future. That is why society has the right to give special support and encouragement to an institution that is necessary to the well being of children—even if that means special benefits for some, and not for others. The dependence intrinsic to human childhood is why unadulterated libertarianism can never work.[14]

Without a governmentally established standard of what constitutes marriage, the result will be a proliferation of children born in relationships of incest and polygamy as well as in many temporary relationships without commitment, and many children born with no one having a legal obligation to care for them.

The consensus from nations all over the world from all of history is that the society as a whole, through its governing authorities, needs to define and regulate marriage for all its citizens. Aristotle said that the first duty of wise legislators is to define and regulate marriage. He wrote:

> Since the legislator should begin by considering how the frames of the children whom he is rearing may be as good as possible, his first care will be about marriage—at what age should his citizens marry, and who are fit to marry?[15]

---

14. Stanley Kurtz, "Deathblow to Marriage" (Feb. 5, 2004). www.nationalreview.com/kurtz/kurtz200402050842.asp.

15. Aristotle, "Politica," in William David Ross, ed., *The Works of Aristotle* 10:1334–35: cited in Lynn D. Wardle, "Is Preference for Marriage in Law Justified?" World Family Policy

Forum (1999). www.worldfamilypolicy.org/New%20Page/forum/1999/wardle.pdf. Lynn Wardle is a professor of law at Brigham Young University. Also see www.fordham.edu/halsall/ancient/aristotle-politics1.html.

Some people may argue that governments today no longer need to define marriage at all, but this is just saying that we can now hope to act contrary to the wisdom of the entire course of all societies in world history for all time.[16] Such a prospect does not encourage optimism for success.

Maggie Gallagher says,

> The purpose of marriage law is inherently normative, to create and to force others to recognize a certain kind of union: permanent, faithful, co-residential, and sexual couplings.[17]

2. Government should encourage and reward marriage between one man and one woman because it gives benefits to society that no other relationship or institution can give

Because marriage provides society with unique and immensely valuable benefits, society has an interest in protecting and encouraging marriage. This was the fundamental question at stake in the Mormon polygamy controversy in the United States from about 1845 to 1895. Although Utah territory, which was dominated by Mormons, applied for statehood seven times, beginning in 1849, Congress did not permit it to become a state until 1896, after Utah finally agreed to insert a ban on polygamy in the state constitution.[18] Thus Congress imposed on a state (as a condition of its becoming a state) *a national standard for marriage* that excluded polygamous relationships.

In responding to a challenge to this idea, the US Supreme Court in *Murphy v. Ramsey* (1885) said that "the idea of the family, as consisting in and springing from the union for life of one man and one woman" is "the sure foundation of all that is stable and noble in our civilization."[19]

In brief, the history of marriage laws in the United States shows that society has a strong interest in protecting and encouraging marriage between one man and one woman because of the great benefits that this institution gives to society in multiple ways, benefits that no other relationship or institution can give.

These benefits can be summarized in several points:

a. Marriage provides a better environment for having babies than any other relationship or institution. Providing a good environment for having babies is important because all societies need babies in order to survive beyond the lifetimes of the adults now living.

16. Even if there were short-lived periods of some societies where anarchy regarding marriage prevailed, such a situation would be inherently unstable and would soon result in some standardization of marriage or the dissolution of the society.

17. Maggie Gallagher, "(How) Will Gay Marriage Weaken Marriage as a Social Institution: A Reply to Andrew Koppelman," *University of St. Thomas Law Review*, 2, no. 1 (Fall 2004): 43.

18. "Utah's Struggle for Statehood," UtahPolicy.org (July 2, 2009), www.utahpolicy.com/featured_article/utahs-struggle-

statehood; and Edward Leo Lyman, *Political Deliverance: The Mormon Quest for Utah Statehood* (1986); Henry J. Wolfinger, "A Reexamination of the Woodruff Manifesto in Light of Utah Constitutional History," *Utah Historical Quarterly* 39 (Fall 1971); and Gustive Q. Larson, *The Americanization of Utah for Statehood* (1971): cited in http://historytogo.utah.gov/utah_chapters/statehood_and_the_progressive_era/struggleforstatehood.html.

19. *Murphy v. Ramsey*, 114 U.S. 45 (1885). http://supreme.justia.com/us/114/15/case.html.

When we compare the environment provided by marriage during the pregnancy and birth of a baby with the environment provided by a cohabiting couple with no legal commitment to marriage, or with the environment provided by a temporary sexual liaison with no ongoing relationship, or with the environment provided by a homosexual couple that lacks either a mother or a father, or with the environment provided by a single mother who bears a child through *in vitro* fertilization or surrogate motherhood, it is evident that the environment provided by a married couple provides for the baby far greater security and provides the baby with both a mother and a father who are committed to care and provide for it.

In addition, the environment is better for the mother, because marriage provides a far better guarantee that the baby's father will not abandon her to care for the child alone. And the environment provided by marriage is better for the father because it provides a strong legal and societal expectation that he will stay around and act responsibly with regard to the responsibilities formally associated with fatherhood.

All of these benefits provide an argument that society should encourage and reward marriage between a man and a woman. All societies need babies to survive, and marriage is the best environment for having babies. Societies should *encourage* an institution that provides this best kind of environment for raising babies.

b. Married couples raise and nurture children far better than any other human relationship or institution. The benefits that a married couple brings to their children are numerous:

(1) Children who live with their own two married parents have significantly higher educational achievement.[20]

(2) Children who live with their own two married parents are much more likely to enjoy a better economic standard in their adult lives and are much less likely to end up in poverty.[21]

(3) Children who live with their own two married parents have much better physical health and emotional health.[22]

(4) Children who live with their own two married parents are far less likely to commit crimes,[23] are less likely to engage in alcohol and substance abuse,[24] and are more likely to live according to higher standards of integrity and moral principles.[25]

20. Mary Parke, "Are Married Parents Really Better for Children?" *Center for Law and Policy* (May 2003), 2–3: cited in Testimony of Barbara Dafoe Whitehead, Co-Director, National Marriage Project, Rutgers, the State University of New Jersey, before the Committee on Health, Education, Labor, and Pensions, Subcommittee on Children and Families, US Senate (April 24, 2008). http://marriage.rutgers.edu/Publications/Pub%20Whitehead%20Testimony%20Apr%2004.htm.

21. Robert I. Lerman, "How Do Marriage, Cohabitation, and Single Parenthood Affect the Material Hardships of Families With Children?" (July 2002), and Robert I. Lerman, "Married and Unmarried Parenthood and Economic Well-Being: A Dynamic Analysis of a Recent Cohort" (July 2002). www.urban.org/expert.cfm?ID=RobertILerman: cited in ibid.

22. Frank F. Furstenburg and Andrew Cherlin, *Divided Families: What Happens to Children When Parents Part* (Cambridge,

MA: Harvard University Press, 1991), 56; and Paul R. Amato, "Children's Adjustment to Divorce: Theories, Hypothesis, and Empirical Support," *Journal of Marriage and the Family* 23 (1993): cited in Wardle, "Is Preference for Marriage in Law Justified?"

23. Cynthia Harper and Sarah McClanahan, "Father Absence and Youth Incarceration," *Journal of Research on Adolescence* 14 (2004): 369–97.

24. "Family Matters: Substance Abuse and the American Family," The National Center on Addiction and Substance Abuse at Columbia University (March 2005), 17. www.casacolumbia.org/absolutenm/articlefiles/380-Family%20Matters.pdf.; and Robert L. Flewelling and Karl E. Bauman, "Family Structure as a Predictor of Initial Substance Abuse and Sexual Intercourse in Adolescence," *Journal of Marriage and the Family* 52 (1990): 171–81.

25. Furstenburg and Cherlin, op cit.; and Amato, op.cit.: cited in Wardle, "Is Preference for Marriage in Law Justified?"

(5) Children who live with their own two married parents are less likely to experience physical abuse and are more likely to live in homes that provide support, protection, and stability for them.[26]

(6) Children who live with their own two married parents are more likely to establish stable families in the next generation.[27]

c. Marriage provides a guarantee of lifelong companionship and care far better than any other human relationship or institution.[28]

d. Marriage leads to a higher economic standard and diminished likelihood of ending up in poverty for men and women.[29]

e. Marriage provides women with protection against domestic violence and abandonment far better than any other human relationship or institution.[30]

f. Marriage encourages men to socially beneficial pursuits far better than any other human relationship or institution.[31]

g. Men and women in general have an innate instinct that values sexual faithfulness in intimate relationships, and marriage provides a societal encouragement of such faithfulness far better than any other relationship or institution.[32]

h. Marriage provides greater protection against sexually transmitted diseases than any other relationship or institution.[33]

i. The biological design of men's and women's bodies argues that sexual intimacy is designed to be enjoyed between only one man and one woman.

For all of these reasons, marriage is the basic building block of any stable society, and it is essential to the continuation of a healthy, stable society. All of these reasons argue that it is right that governments *encourage* and *reward* marriage between one man and one woman. This institution gives immeasurable benefits to a society that no other relationship or institution can provide. Therefore society has a high interest in protecting and encouraging marriage through its laws.

---

26. Patrick F. Fagan, Ph.D., "The Child Abuse Crisis: The Disintegration of Marriage, Family, and the American Community," *Heritage Foundation, Backgrounder #115* (May 15, 1997), www.heritage.org/Research/Family/BG1115.cfm; and E. Thompson, T. L. Hanson, and S. S. McLanahan, "Family Structure and Child Well-Being: Economic Resources versus Parental Behaviors," *Social Forces* 73: 221–42: cited in "The Verdict on Cohabitation vs. Marriage," www.marriageandfamilies.byu. edu/issues/2001/January/cohabitation.htm.

27. Patrick F. Fagan, Ph.D., "How Broken Families Rob Children of Their Chances for Future Prosperity," *Heritage Foundation, Backgrounder #1283* (June 11, 1999). www.heritage.org/Research/Family/BG1283.cfm.

28. Linda J. Waite and Maggie Gallagher, "The Case for Marriage: Why Married People are Happier, Healthier, and Better Off Financially" (New York: Doubleday, 2000): cited in "The Verdict on Cohabitation vs. Marriage," www.marriageandfamilies.byu.edu/issues/2001/January/cohabitation.htm.

29. David J. Eggebeen and Daniel T. Lichter, "Race, Family Structure, and Changing Poverty Among American Children," *American Social Review* 56: 801, 806: cited in Wardle, "Is Preference for Marriage in Law Justified?"

30. Patrick F. Fagan, Ph.D., and Kirk A. Johnson, Ph.D., "Marriage: The Safest Place for Women and Children," *Heritage Foundation, Backgrounder #1535* (April 10, 2002). www.heritage.org/Research/Family/BG1535.cfm.

31. Linda Waite, "Does Marriage Matter?" *Demographics* 32 (1995): 483: cited in Wardle, "Is Preference for Marriage in Law Justified?"

32. Robert T. Michael, John H. Gagnon, Edward O. Laumann, and Gina Kolata, *Sex in America: A Definitive Survey* (Boston: Little Brown, 1994), 105: cited in "What's Happening to Marriage?" *State of Our Unions 2009*, Rutgers University National Marriage Project. http://marriage.rutgers.edu/Publications/pubwhatshappening.htm#2.

33. Fagan and Johnson, "Marriage: The Safest Place for Women and Children."

But if the benefits that the laws now give to married couples are *also* given to other arrangements (such as polygamous marriages or same-sex marriages, or heterosexual relationships that lack the long-term commitment of marriage), then to that degree, marriage is not given these *special* benefits. To that degree, marriage between one man and one woman is *not encouraged by the government more than these other relationships*. To that degree, then, government no longer gives *special incentives* encouraging men and women to marry. And to that degree, society will begin to lose the benefits gained from giving special advantages to the relationship of marriage between one man and one woman.

Moreover, if the benefits that society now gives to marriage are also given to same-sex couples, then society is *encouraging* the *harmful consequences* to children and to men and women that are the opposite of these benefits that come from same-sex monogamous marriage. Rather than doing "good" for the nation, such changes in the laws will do harm for the nation. This is the opposite of what God intends government to do.

The damaging consequences of homosexual conduct are rarely mentioned in the mainstream press. However, Jeffrey Satinover, a psychiatrist who is a graduate of MIT, Harvard, and the University of Texas and has lectured at both Yale and Harvard, reports some of the medical harm that is typically associated with male homosexual practice:

- A twenty-five to thirty-year decrease in life expectancy
- Chronic, potentially fatal, liver disease—infectious hepatitis
- Inevitably fatal immune disease including associated cancers
- Frequently fatal rectal cancer
- Multiple bowel and other infectious diseases
- A much higher than usual incidence of suicide[34]

What is the reason for these medical conditions? Satinover explains that many are due to the common homosexual practice of anal intercourse:

> ... we are designed with a nearly impenetrable barrier between the bloodstream and the extraordinarily toxic and infectious contents of the bowel. Anal intercourse creates a breach in this barrier for the receptive partner, whether or not the insertive partner is wearing a condom. As a result, homosexual men are disproportionately vulnerable to a host of serious and sometimes fatal infections caused by the entry of feces into the bloodstream. These include hepatitis B and the cluster of otherwise rare conditions ... known as the "Gay Bowel Syndrome."[35]

Satinover also points out a significant contrast in the sexual behaviors of heterosexual and homosexual persons. Among heterosexuals, sexual faithfulness was relatively high: "90 percent of heterosexual women and more than 75 percent of heterosexual men have never engaged in extramarital sex." But among homosexual men the picture is far different:

---

34. Jeffrey Satinover, *Homosexuality and the Politics of Truth* (Grand Rapids: Baker, 1996), 51. (This is an excellent book on the medical harm and addictive nature of homosexual conduct and also the ability of homosexuals to change their behavior.)

35. Ibid., 67–68.

A 1981 study revealed that only 2 percent of homosexuals were monogamous or semi-monogamous—generously defined as ten or fewer lifetime partners.... A 1978 study found that 43 percent of male homosexuals estimated having sex with five hundred or more different partners.... Seventy-nine percent said that more than half of these partners were strangers.[36]

Such patterns of behavior need to be taken into account when voters decide whether to give societal encouragement and legal benefits to same-sex relationships.

One additional argument in favor of laws defining marriage as one man and one woman is that laws in any society also have a "teaching" function. The kinds of relationships that are approved by the law are more likely to be approved of and followed by the society as a whole. People will reason, "This is according to the law, therefore it must be right." Thus laws that limit marriage to one man and one woman will tend to encourage the society to think that this is the kind of marriage that is right and that should be supported by them and by others.

For all of the foregoing reasons, therefore, I differ with the viewpoint of Jim Wallis. In *God's Politics* he argues that different views on same-sex "marriage" should be allowed within churches. He says,

> The controversies over gay marriage and the ordination of gay bishops, and so on, should not be seen as "faith breakers." The church is going to have to learn to stay together and talk about these things until we find some resolutions together.... One could also argue that gay civil marriage is necessary under "equal protection." One could also argue for church blessings of gay unions. I think all those are strong points, even if the churches are unlikely to change their whole theology and sacrament of marriage itself.[37]

Wallis also speaks of "encouraging healthy, monogamous, and stable same-sex relationships—which religious conservatives should be careful not to pit themselves against, regardless of how such relationships are ultimately defined."[38] Wallis thus fails to uphold and defend the Bible's teaching on marriage for either the laws of society or the policies adopted by churches.

The Manhattan Declaration (which I gladly signed) stands in clear contrast to Jim Wallis's statements. This document, released November 20, 2009, declares:

> Because we honor justice and the common good, we will not ... bend to any rule purporting to force us to bless immoral sexual partnerships, treat them as marriages or the equivalent, or refrain from proclaiming the truth, as we know it, about morality and immorality and marriage and the family. We will fully and ungrudgingly render to Caesar what is Caesar's. But under no circumstances will we render to Caesar what is God's.[39]

36. Ibid., 55. Satinover points out, however, that "Lesbian sexual practices are less risky than gay marriage practices; and lesbians are not nearly so promiscuous as gay men" (52).

37. Jim Wallis, *God's Politics: Why the Right Gets It Wrong and the Left Doesn't Get It* (New York: HarperSanFrancisco, 2005), 334.

38. Ibid., 340.

39. The entire statement is found at http://manhattandeclaration.org/home.aspx.

G. LEGAL ARGUMENTS ABOUT MARRIAGE

1. Appeals courts in the United States have repeatedly held that the State has a legitimate interest in protecting marriage between one man and one woman[40]

The Indiana Court of Appeals in 2005 said this:

> The State of Indiana has a legitimate interest in encouraging opposite-sex couples to enter and remain in, as far as possible, the relatively stable institution of marriage for the sake of children who are frequently the natural result of sexual relations between a man and a woman. One commentator has put it succinctly as follows: "The public legal union of a man and woman is designed … to protect the children that their sexual union (and that type of sexual union alone) regularly produces."[41]

Similarly, the Arizona Court of Appeals said the following in 2003:

> Indisputably, the only sexual relationship capable of producing children is one between a man and a woman. The State could reasonably decide that by encouraging opposite-sex couples to marry, thereby assuming legal and financial obligations, the children born from such relationships will have better opportunities to be nurtured and raised by two parents within long-term, committed relationships, which society has traditionally viewed as advantageous for children. Because same-sex couples cannot by themselves procreate, the State could also reasonably decide that sanctioning same-sex marriages would do little to advance the State's interest in ensuring responsible procreation within committed, long-term relationships.[42]

Other appeals courts have reached similar conclusions.[43]

2. No right to polygamous marriages is found in the US Constitution

This was the decision of the United States in *Murphy v. Ramsey*, 114 US15 (1885) (cited above). To allow a "right" to a marriage of one man and two or more women would redefine marriage as it had been understood in all the laws of the United States and the individual states up to that point. Therefore it would not simply be granting a "right" to certain men and women involved in polygamy, but also actually be *changing the definition of marriage itself* for the entire society.

---

40. In this section I am indebted to Jordan Lorence of the Alliance Defense Fund for the collection of relevant legal material that is quoted here. Much of it is taken from his unpublished paper "Same-Sex 'Marriage' and Its Relatives," from January 2009, which he provided to me.

41. *Morrison v. Sadler,* 821 N.E.2d 15, 30–31 (Indiana Court of Appeals, 2005): citing Maggie Gallagher, *What is Marriage For? The Public Purposes of Marriage Law,* 62 La. L. Rev. 773, 782 (2002).

42. *Standhardt v. Superior Court,* 77 P.3d. 451, 462–63 (Ariz. App. Div. 1 2003).

43. Jordan Lorence, "Same-Sex 'Marriage' and Its Relatives" (Jan. 2009), 7–8. Lorence cites the decision of the New Jersey Court of Appeals in *Lewis v. Harris* (2005) and two New York appellate court decisions: *Hernandez v. Robles* (2005) and *Samuels v. New York Department of Health* (2006).

3. No right to "homosexual marriage" is found in the Constitution

To many people it will seem obvious that the US Constitution, which says nothing at all about homosexual marriage, cannot be claimed to support any "right" to homosexual marriage. The US Supreme Court has not ruled on this issue, but several state courts have issued rulings. Most notably the Massachusetts,[44] Connecticut,[45] and Iowa[46] supreme courts have now "found" a right to same-sex marriage in state constitutions that contained absolutely no mention at all of homosexual marriage. The California Supreme Court also created a "right" to same-sex marriage,[47] but that decision was overturned when the voters in November 2008 passed Proposition 8, a constitutional amendment that restored marriage as the union between one man and one woman.[48]

How could various courts "discover" same-sex "marriage" in their state constitutions? Or how could it ever be decreed by any federal court or by the US Supreme Court? Only if it were invented by the judges out of their own imaginations.

Judge Richard Posner, a widely respected judge on the US Court of Appeals for the Seventh Circuit, said this in a public interview:

> Nothing in the Constitution or its history suggests a constitutional right to homosexual marriage. If there is such a right, it will have to be manufactured by the justices out of whole cloth. The exercise of so freewheeling a judicial discretion in the face of adamantly opposed public opinion would be seriously undemocratic. It would be a matter of us judges, us enlightened ones, forcing our sophisticated views on a deeply unwilling population.[49]

Three states—Maine,[50] New Hampshire,[51] and Vermont[52]—have passed laws legalizing same-sex "marriage," and one state, New Jersey, has created "civil unions" that are the legal equivalent of marriage.[53] But on November 3, 2009, the people of Maine overruled the legislature and governor by enacting Question 1, restoring the definition of marriage as one man and woman in the state.[54]

---

44. *Goodridge et al. v. Department of Public Health* SJC–08860, Supreme Judicial Court of Massachusetts (Nov. 18, 2003).

45. *Kerrigan v. State of Connecticut,* SC 17716, Connecticut Supreme Court (Oct. 28, 2008).

46. *Varnum v. Brien,* No. 07–1499, Iowa Supreme Court (April 3, 2009).

47. *In re: Marriage Cases,* S147999, California Supreme Court (May 15, 2008).

48. Jessica Garrison, Cara Mia DiMassa, and Richard C. Paddock, "Voters Approve Proposition 8 Banning Same-Sex Marriages," *Los Angeles Times* (Nov. 5, 2008). www.latimes.com/news/local/la-me-gaymarriage5–2008nov05,0,1545381.story.

49. Richard Posner, "Wedding Bell Blues," *The New Republic Online* (Dec. 22, 2003).

50. "Baldacci signs same-sex marriage into law," *Portland Press-Herald* (May 6, 2009). http://pressherald.mainetoday.com/story.php?id=254850&ac=PHnws.

51. Eric Moskowitz, "New Hampshire Ties Gay-Marriage Knot," *Boston Globe* (June 4, 2009). www.boston.com/news/local/new_hampshire/articles/2009/06/04/nh_ties_gay_marriage_knot/.

52. "Abby Goodnough, Vermont Legalizes Same-Sex Marriage," *New York Times* (April 7, 2009). www.nytimes.com/2009/04/08/us/08vermont.html.

53. Jeff Zelevansky, "Gay Couples in New Jersey Line Up for Civil Unions," *USA Today* (Feb. 20, 2007). www.usatoday.com/news/nation/2007–02–18-nj-civil-unions_x.htm.

54. Susan Cover, "Mainers Vote Down Gay Marriage Law," *Kennebec Journal* (Nov. 4, 2009). http://pressherald.mainetoday.com/story.php?id=293976&ac=PHnws.

4. Restricting marriage to one man and woman does not violate anyone's fundamental rights

Sometimes advocates for same-sex marriage argue that the right to marry is a fundamental human right and that this is being denied to them as homosexuals.

But the answer is that when the law defines marriage as between one man and one woman, *it does not prohibit any homosexual person from marrying*. They would just have to marry in the same way that everyone else in society has to marry—namely, they would have to marry someone of the opposite sex. This right is extended *equally* to all unmarried adults in the society.

Yet, when homosexuals claim that they want to marry *another person of the same sex*, they are not simply claiming the right to marry that is available to everybody else in society. Rather, they are claiming *a new right* that had not previously been available to anyone in this society—namely, the right to marry someone *of the same sex*. Such a right has been denied to *everyone* in the society prior to this time, so it is not discriminating against them to say that this kind of right is denied to them.

This would be somewhat analogous to a man claiming that he wanted to marry his sister and that the law was wrongfully denying him a basic human right that everybody else had, the right to marry. But that would be an invalid argument. No man in this society has the legal right to marry his sister, and no woman has the legal right to marry her brother. The law prohibits such kinds of marriage. But if no man in a society has the right to marry his sister, then when the law denies him the right to marry his sister, it is not denying him anything that it does not deny to everybody else as well. When he claims that he should have a right to marry his sister, he is really claiming the right *to redefine marriage* according to his own desires and preferences. He is not just claiming a private right for himself, but *is claiming a right to change the definition of marriage that has been adopted by the whole society*. And the law is correct when it denies him the right to do this.

The same arguments would go for a woman who claimed that she should have the right to marry her son, or a man who claimed that he should have the right to marry his daughter. And the same kind of arguments would apply to a man who claimed he should have the right to marry a woman who was already married to someone else. Or to a man who claimed that he should have the right to marry more than one wife at the same time. All these would not simply be claims that an *individual* would make regarding a *private right* that would affect no one else. These are claims to be able to *redefine* the institution of marriage for the whole of a society.

Another argument sometimes raised by same-sex advocates is that laws limiting marriage to one man and one woman are unconstitutional "sex discrimination" because they use gender-based classifications.

However, both the US Supreme Court and various state supreme courts have rejected this argument. According to constitutional law expert Jordan Lorence, the US Supreme Court has held that marriage laws treat men and women equally and the court has ruled that uses of gender classifications in the law are not inherently discriminatory. In addition, Lorence asserts that, based on Supreme Court precedents in *Nguyen v. I.N.S.* and

Nordlinger v. Hahn, government programs to prevent breast cancer or prostate cancer are not discriminatory and that separate bathrooms for men and women are not "sex discriminatory." As a result, there is no disparate impact on men or women because marriage laws treat men and women the same.[55] In addition, the New York Court of Appeals said:

> By limiting marriage to opposite-sex couples, [the State] is not engaging in sex discrimination. The limitation does not put men and women in different classes, and give one class a benefit not given to the other. Women and Men are treated alike—they are permitted to marry people of the opposite sex, but not people of their own sex.[56]

The Maryland Court of Appeals and the Washington State Supreme Court have reached the same conclusion: Laws that limit marriage to one man and one woman are not unconstitutional sex discrimination. Lorence quotes from the Maryland court:

> The limitations on marriage effected by Family Law §2–201 do not separate men and women into discrete classes for the purpose of granting to one class of persons benefits at the expense of the other class. Nor does the statute, facially or in its application, place men and women on an uneven playing field. Rather, the statute prohibits equally both men and women from the same conduct.[57]

5. A marriage amendment to the US Constitution would be the most effective way to establish a uniform understanding of marriage once again in the United States

Some people have proposed an amendment to the US Constitution that would limit marriage to one man and woman. As of November 2008, thirty states had approved such amendments to their individual state constitutions.[58]

The wording of the 2004 Federal Marriage Amendment, as introduced in both the US Senate and the US House, was as follows:

> Marriage in the United States shall consist solely of the union of a man and a woman. Neither this Constitution, nor the constitution of any State, shall be construed to require that marriage or the legal incidents thereof be conferred upon any union other than the union of a man and a woman.[59]

55. Jordan Lorence, "Same-Sex Marriage and Its Relatives."

56. *Hernandez v. Robles,* 7 N.Y. 3d 388, 821 N.Y.S. 2d 770, 855 N.E. 2d 1, 6 (2006).

57. *Conaway v. Deane,* 401 Md. 219, 264, 932 A.2d 571, 598, Md. (2007).

58. The following states have passed constitutional amendments protecting marriage as the union between one man and one woman: Alabama, Alaska, Arizona, Arkansas, California, Colorado, Florida, Georgia, Hawaii, Idaho, Kansas, Kentucky, Louisiana, Michigan, Missouri, Mississippi, Montana, Nebraska, Nevada, North Dakota, Ohio, Oklahoma, Oregon, South Carolina, South Dakota, Tennessee, Texas, Utah, Virginia, and Wisconsin. www.domawatch.org/state-issues/index.html.

59. H.J. Res. 106, introduced September 23, 2004. www.congress.gov/cgi-bin/query/z?c108:H.J.RES.106.

In order to amend the Constitution, a two-thirds majority of both houses of Congress is required. The House took a vote on the amendment on September 30, 2004. The result was 227 yea votes (55%) to 186 nay votes (45 percent).[60] Republicans voted 191-to-27 *for* the amendment; Democrats voted 158–36 *against* it.[61] Therefore the amendment failed. A two-thirds majority would have been 290 votes.

The amendment failed in the Senate because of a filibuster by its opponents. On July 14, 2004, there was a cloture motion in the Senate that would have forced a vote on the amendment. It needed 60 votes to pass, but received only 48 yea votes to 50 nay votes, so it was 12 votes short of the supermajority needed to end debate and force the Senate to vote on the amendment. Forty-two Democrats voted against the motion, compared with eight Republicans.[62] Therefore there is not now strong enough support for such an amendment to pass by two-thirds majority in both houses of Congress. And even if it were to pass Congress, it would then have to be ratified by the legislatures of three-fourths (thirty-eight) of the states.

But political sentiment in the United States can change over time, and it may be that sometime in the future the sentiment of the people of the nation will be strong enough to support such a measure.

The benefits of such an amendment would be that (1) it would prevent the current US Supreme Court and all future US Supreme Courts from redefining marriage as the Massachusetts, Connecticut, and Iowa supreme courts have already done; (2) it would prevent individual state supreme courts from redefining marriages; and (3) it would give a uniform definition of marriage throughout the nation rather than allowing a hodge-podge of definitions to spring up in the various states.

Such an amendment would not wrongfully violate the constitutional separation of powers between the federal government and the state governments, because neither the Congress nor the Constitution itself has ever understood such separation of powers to mean that states could completely redefine marriage in this way. In fact, in the Mormon polygamy controversy, the nation affirmed that the United States has a strong national interest in establishing a uniform definition of marriage for the entire nation. This concern was also reiterated by Congress when it welcomed Arizona into the Union and simultaneously required that the constitution of Arizona similarly prohibit polygamous marriages.[63]

6. Objections

The primary objection brought against the view of marriage that I support in this chapter is that "Christians should not try to impose their moral standards on the rest of society."

The first response is that attempting to *persuade* people that these moral standards are right and beneficial to society is not the same as "imposing" them on others. Everyone

60. See www.congress.gov/cgi-bin/bdquery/z?d108:h.j.res.00106.

61. See http://clerk.house.gov/evs/2004/roll484.xml.

62. See www.senate.gov/legislative/LIS/roll_call_lists/roll_call_vote_cfm.cfm?congress=108&session=2&vote=00155.

63. "Modern History of Polygamy," *AZCentral.com* (May 30, 2008). www.azcentral.com/news/articles/2008/05/30/20080530centennial-timeline.html.

in a free society should have the right to attempt to persuade others to agree with his or her views, and that is what I am attempting to do here, arguing that for many reasons this one-man, one-woman standard is best for society.

The second answer is one I discussed in chapter 4 (pp. 117–18): The Bible presents these standards for marriage not as merely Christian standards but as the standards that come from the one true God, the Creator of the universe. They are the standards by which he will one day hold all people accountable. In that sense, I am arguing here that these moral standards regarding marriage *already are the true standards that God applies to the whole society in every nation*, whether or not everyone acknowledges that.

H. RECOMMENDATIONS ABOUT SPECIFIC LAWS AND POLICIES RELATED TO MARRIAGE

1. Marriage should continue to be defined by government for society as a whole.

I gave arguments in support of this policy in sections E and F above (pp. 221–23).

2. Laws should define marriage as a union between one man and one woman.

This would mean that laws should continue to exclude same-sex marriages and polygamous marriages, just as they have in the past.

3. Laws should make other restrictions on marriages that reflect historical and traditional standards. (These are standards that Christians also think reflect biblical moral standards.)

It is appropriate that marriage be restricted to those who have attained a certain age (eighteen in many states today) and who give their consent to be married. Marriage should also be restricted to those who are not already married, so as to protect the status of marriage as a union between one man and one woman and to prevent adulterous relationships from being considered marriage. Laws should also prohibit polygamous marriages—that is, a man who is already married to one woman would not be allowed to marry another woman at the same time.

In addition, the laws should prohibit incestuous relationships from being considered marriage. Therefore a person could not marry someone of the opposite sex in his or her immediate family, such as a brother or sister or a son or daughter. A person could not marry an aunt or uncle or niece or nephew or first cousin.

Such provisions not only reflect biblical moral standards, but also reflect the historical wisdom that such relationships are harmful rather than helpful to society.

4. Homosexual relationships should not be granted the status of "marriage."

If a society were to grant this status, it would give governmental encouragement and endorsement to a relationship that is contrary to the moral standards of the Bible and detrimental to the raising of children. No Christian should support such a proposal.

5. It is doubtful that domestic partner benefits should be given to homosexual relationships or that they should be normalized in any way as "civil unions."

Regarding "domestic partnership" benefits, the question is whether the society as a whole, through its government, wishes to give encouragement and endorsement to a relationship that is contrary to the moral standards of the Bible. If the members of a society wish to do this, they are of course free to do so, but it is not a proposal that Christians should support. Our standards of what is right and wrong for human conduct, and what is helpful or harmful to individuals and to society, should be taken from the Bible.

Nevertheless, if the majority of a society decides to grant such domestic partner benefits, they should not be limited to homosexual domestic partners, but should apply to *all people living together in long-term relationships where there is mutual commitment and obligation to care and support each other.* They should also certainly apply to an elderly sister and brother living together and caring for one another, or an adult child living with and caring for an elderly parent. These relationships should be allowed the same privileges and benefits that would be given to homosexual couples living together. And such benefits, if given, should be dependent on the couple making a legal commitment to some measure of obligation for mutual financial support and physical care if needed. Such a provision would guarantee that society receives some benefits in return for granting some privileges or benefits.

Of course, there are various kinds of "benefits" that might be granted. Domestic partner benefits with no significant financial costs to the taxpayers or to consumers are less controversial and would include things such as allowing hospital visitation rights and access to medical records. But other kinds of domestic partner benefits would involve substantial costs to taxpayers or consumers, such as coverage by a partner's health insurance plan at work, the right to a partner's pension plan, significant financial benefits in inheritance laws by which no tax penalty is incurred for inheriting an estate when a spouse dies, and access to a portion of Social Security benefits that have been earned by one spouse during his or her lifetime. Campaigns for this kind of benefit are primarily campaigns for monetary benefits.

The objections to giving such monetary benefits to same-sex relationships are the following: (1) These benefits were originally intended by society to encourage the bearing and raising of children in a heterosexual marriage, which is the only kind of sexual union that can produce children; (2) to give such benefits to homosexual relationships, which (by themselves) cannot produce new children, becomes a means by which *society encourages other types of relationships* that will not ordinarily produce children and will not raise them in the most beneficial way; (3) such benefits also confer a societal indication of *approval* on the relationships, but Christians should not support policies that give approval to relationships that the Bible disapproves of and considers morally wrong.

It is in fact this symbol of approval by society that is one of the major reasons behind the push by homosexuals to gain domestic partner benefits and ultimately to gain the status of marriage. To the extent that these benefits confer such endorsement and approval, and for that very reason, Christians should oppose and not support such proposals.

For the same reasons, other privileges related to marriage such as the right to adopt children should not be granted to homosexual relationships.

6. Known homosexuals should continue to be prohibited from military service.

Widespread evidence indicates that mixing active homosexual persons with non-homosexuals in the close quarters required in military service has a significantly detrimental effect on military morale and effectiveness. That alone is sufficient reason for maintaining the current policy of not allowing known homosexuals to serve in the military.

Campbell University Law Professor William A. Woodruff has stated,

> The American military does not fight an armed enemy sworn to destroy our way of life by showing how enlightened and progressive our popular culture is. The armed forces exist to project combat power as an arm of foreign policy and to protect our vital national interests. Anything, whether it is height, weight, IQ, character, physical fitness, medical condition, or any other condition that detracts from unit cohesion and combat effectiveness, disqualifies an otherwise patriotic American from serving in the military. The military is not popular culture. It is very different and must remain so to defend the freedoms that advance our popular culture.

Woodruff added,

> Those who favor personnel policies grounded in notions of fairness to the individual must be required to demonstrate beyond any doubt that military discipline, unit cohesion, and combat effectiveness will not be diminished one iota by adoption of their preferred policy. Otherwise, it elevates the individual over the mission, and that is the antithesis of military service.[64]

Brian Jones, a retired US Army Ranger, testified to Congress in 2008:

> As a US Army Ranger, I performed long-range patrols in severe cold weather conditions, in teams of 10, with only mission essential items on our backs. No comfort items. The only way to keep from freezing at night was to get as close as possible for body heat—which means skin to skin. On several occasions, in the close quarters that a team lives, any attraction to same sex teammates, real or perceived, would be known and would be a problem. The presence of openly gay men in these situations would elevate tensions and disrupt unit cohesion and morale.[65]

In an open letter to President Obama, more than one thousand flag and general officers of the military wrote:

> Our past experience as military leaders leads us to be greatly concerned about the impact of repeal [of the law] on morale, discipline, unit cohesion, and overall military readiness. We believe that imposing this burden on our men and women in uniform would undermine recruiting and retention, impact leadership at all levels, have adverse effects on the willingness of parents who

---

64. William A. Woodruff: quoted in Summary Statement of Elaine Donnelly, President, Center for Military Readiness House Armed Services Committee. Subcommittee on Personnel, in Support of Section 654, Title 10, the 1993 Law Stating that Homosexuals are not Eligible to Serve in the Military, Rayburn House Office Building, Washington, DC (July 23, 2008). http://cmrlink.org/fileuploads/HASC072308DonnellyShortStatement.pdf.

65. Statement of Brian Jones, Sergeant Major USA (Ret), CEO, Adventure Training Concepts. Subcommittee on Personnel. In Support of Section 654, Title 10, The 1993 Law Stating That Homosexuals Are Not Eligible to Serve in the Military. 2118 Rayburn House Office Building, Washington, DC (July 23, 2008).

lend their sons and daughters to military service, and eventually break the All-Volunteer Force.[66]

7. Private organizations such as the Boy Scouts should continue to be allowed to exclude homosexuals from employment as scoutmasters.

The US Supreme Court agreed with this position with its decision in *Boy Scouts of America et al. v. Dale* in 2000. A majority of the court (5-to-4) agreed that the First Amendment right of freedom of association "plainly presupposes a freedom not to associate."[67]

The concluding paragraph of the majority opinion was very explicit in this regard:

> We are not, as we must not be, guided by our views of whether the Boy Scouts' teachings with respect to homosexual conduct are right or wrong; public or judicial disapproval of a tenet of an organization's expression does not justify the State's effort to compel the organization to accept members where such acceptance would derogate from the organization's expressive message. "While the law is free to promote all sorts of conduct in place of harmful behavior, it is not free to interfere with speech for no better reason than promoting an approved message or discouraging a disfavored one, however enlightened either purpose may strike the government." *Hurley,* 515 US, at 579.

8. Should homosexuals be granted the legal status of a protected class?

Certain groups have a special legal status in society, the status of a protected class of persons. This is true, for example, regarding gender and race, so that discriminating on the basis of gender or race is illegal. Should homosexuals also be granted such a special status, so that discrimination on the basis of "sexual orientation" is considered illegal? This is the force of many "gay rights" ordinances and laws in various cities and twenty-one states.[68]

Christians should not support such ordinances, because they also have the force of giving governmental approval and encouragement to a relationship that is contrary to the moral standards of the Bible.

Deciding that homosexuals should *not* be considered a "protected class" in the law simply means they have *the same legal status everyone else does.* Homosexual men have the same status and protections as all other men in society. Homosexual or lesbian women have the same status and protections that every other woman has in society. They have these without designating them as a specially protected class in the law.

But if homosexuals are designated as a protected class, then it very quickly becomes against the law for Christians and others with similar moral standards to act in a way consistent with their beliefs. For example, if homosexuals are a protected class, then

---

66. "Concerns Regarding Recruiting, Retention, and Readiness." www.flagandgeneralofficersforthemilitary.com/.

67. *Roberts v. United States Jaycees,* 468 U.S. 609, 622 (1984): cited by Chief Justice William Rehnquist, *Boy Scouts of America v. Dale,* 530 U.S. 5 (2000).

68. State Nondiscrimination Laws in the US. www.thetask-force.org/downloads/reports/issue_maps/non_discrimination_7_09_color.pdf.

can a Christian wedding photographer decide not to provide photography services to a homosexual wedding or commitment ceremony (see above, pp. 141–42)? Or can a church refuse to rent an auditorium for the purpose of holding a homosexual marriage or civil union ceremony (see above, p. 142)?

In these and other cases, Christians are being put in the position of *lawbreakers* simply because they do not want to use their facilities or services to endorse a relationship that they consider morally wrong. In this way such gay rights ordinances *violate the freedom of conscience of individuals* in the society. Such ordinances, when they have this effect, are certainly wrong.

9. Should homosexual conduct itself be against the law?

Until 2003, some states had laws that prohibited private homosexual conduct. In fact, such "sodomy laws" existed at one point in many or all states in the United States.[69] In 1986, the US Supreme Court, in *Bowers v. Hardwick*, upheld the right of Georgia to have such a law.[70] In the majority opinion, then-Chief Justice Warren Burger wrote:

> Decisions of individuals relating to homosexual conduct have been subject to state intervention throughout the history of Western civilization. Condemnation of those practices is firmly rooted in Judeo-Christian moral and ethical standards ... To hold that the act of homosexual sodomy is somehow protected as a fundamental right would be to cast aside millennia of moral teaching."[71]

But seventeen years later, in 2003, the Supreme Court explicitly overruled *Bowers v. Hardwick* in the case *Lawrence v. Texas*. In that case, the Supreme Court held that consensual sexual activity between same-sex adults is an essential freedom protected by the idea of "due process" in the Fourteenth Amendment.[72]

Sodomy laws (that prohibited private homosexual conduct) were in several ways similar to the laws against fornication that had been on the books in various states for most of the history of the United States, *but had seldom or never been enforced.* And if laws prohibiting private consensual sexual acts between unrelated adults are never enforced, then it seems pointless to have such laws in the first place. As I will argue below in the discussion on laws regarding the viewing of pornography (see p. 242), there are some actions that are contrary to biblical morality but that nevertheless should not be prohibited or penalized by law. With regard to homosexual conduct, this also seems to be the consensus of a broad majority of American society at this time, probably out of a

---

69. See footnote 6 in *Bowers v. Hardwick*, 478 U.S. 186 (1986). Sodomy laws existed in all of the colonies and subsequent states. The first state repealing its law barring sodomy was Illinois in 1962.

70. *Bowers v. Hardwick* was decided by a 5–4 majority, with Burger, White, Powell, Rehnquist, and O'Connor in the majority and Blackmun, Brennan, Marshall, and Stevens dissenting.

71. *Bowers v. Hardwick*, 478 U.S. 186 (1986) concurring opinion by Chief Justice Warren Burger.

72. In *Lawrence v. Texas,* the majority of six justices included Kennedy, Stevens, Souter, Ginsburg, Breyer, and O'Connor,

while the minority of three justices in dissent included Scalia, Rehnquist, and Thomas. All three justices who dissented said they did so, not because they approved of laws against sodomy, but because they argued that it is not the right of the court to decide issues of law based on society's view of sexual morality, because this is a matter that should entirely be decided by the legislative processes in the nation and the states themselves. They argued that there is nothing in the Constitution itself that could provide a basis for the ruling of the majority in *Lawrence v. Texas*. (I think that they were correct in this dissent—see chapter 5 on the courts, pp. 131–50).

common realization that attempts at enforcement of such laws would inevitably involve *excessive government intrusion into people's private lives.*

In any case, since *Lawrence v. Texas,* it is now considered unconstitutional to have laws against sodomy (and probably, by implication, against fornication). I see no reason for Christians to argue that this conclusion should be overturned.

I. PORNOGRAPHY

1. The issue

Should governments restrict the production and distribution of pornography?

2. The relevant biblical teaching

The question of pornography must be analyzed within the broader framework of the Bible's teaching on marriage (see above). The Bible indicates that, for married persons, having sexual intercourse outside of marriage (that is, committing adultery) is morally wrong. The seventh commandment says, "You shall not commit adultery" (Exod. 20:14).

Having sexual intercourse outside of marriage is also viewed as morally wrong for unmarried persons. This was called "fornication" in older Bible translations and in legal statutes that dealt with this subject, but in more recent Bible translations other terms have been used, most commonly "sexual immorality."[73]

The prohibition against sex between unmarried persons is clear not only from the laws of Moses that penalized such conduct (see Exod. 22:16–17; Deut. 22:13–21), but also from the teachings of Jesus, who pointed out sin in the life of the woman at the well in Samaria by saying to her, "You have had five husbands, and the one you now have is not your husband" (John 4:18). Other verses that use the phrase "sexual immorality" (translating Greek *porneia*) in modern translations (such as Matt. 15:19; Gal. 5:19; Eph. 5:3) also show that sexual intercourse outside of marriage is sin. (See also John 8:41; Acts 15:20; 1 Cor. 6:18; 7:2, 9; 1 Thess. 4:3; note also the imagery in 2 Cor. 11:2.)

With regard to pornography, more can be said: The consistent teaching of the Bible is that God is concerned not merely with human *actions,* but also with the *attitudes of our hearts.* That is clear from the last of the Ten Commandments:

> "You shall not covet your neighbor's house; you shall not covet your neighbor's wife, or his male servant, or his female servant, or his ox, or his donkey, or anything that is your neighbor's" (Exod. 20:17).

The command not to "covet" means not to have a desire to take what belongs to someone else as your own. But the command not to covet "your neighbor's wife" therefore is

---

73. For example, in the English Standard Version (ESV), the New International Version (NIV), the New English Translation (NET), and the Holman Christian Standard Bible (HCSB).

a command not to *desire* to have her as your own or to have intercourse with her. This is made explicit, for example, in Proverbs 6:25, referring to an adulteress: "Do not desire her beauty in your heart."

Jesus brought out the intent of these Old Testament laws of sexual purity in his teaching on the Sermon on the Mount:

> "You have heard that it was said, 'You shall not commit adultery.' But I say to you that everyone who looks at a woman with lustful intent has already committed adultery with her in his heart" (Matt. 5:27–28).

In fact, one Old Testament prophet shows an example of a relationship between looking at pictures and lusting after what one sees, and then committing sinful actions. Speaking of the city of Jerusalem in a parable of a woman called Oholibah, Ezekiel says the following:

> But she carried her whoring further. She *saw* men portrayed on the wall, the images of the Chaldeans portrayed in vermilion, wearing belts on their waists, with flowing turbans on their heads, all of them having the appearance of officers, a likeness of Babylonians whose native land was Chaldea. When she saw them, she *lusted* after them and *sent* messengers to them in Chaldea. And the Babylonians came to her into the bed of love, and they defiled her with their whoring lust. And after she *was defiled* by them, she turned from them in disgust (Ezek. 23:14–17).

Here Ezekiel traces a progression of sexual sin. Oholibah saw, then she lusted, then she sent for those who were pictured, then she committed adultery with them.

The conclusion from all of these verses is that God's moral standards require that people avoid longing for sexual intercourse with someone apart from being married to that person (a relationship in which the Bible views sexual attraction and intimacy as a wholesome and wonderful gift from God).

The moral question about pornography, then, is the question of whether it is right to create, to distribute, to acquire, and to view photographs or videos, or written material, or audio material *whose primary purpose is to arouse in people sexual desires that are contrary to God's moral standards*. It seems clear that this is not a morally right thing to do and should be considered morally wrong.

3. Arguments from reason and experience apart from the Bible

From the standpoint of an appeal to ordinary common sense, one significant argument is that pornography attracts a person's affections and desires outside of one's marriage and away from one's spouse. A man who uses pornography is robbing his wife of emotional affection that should be hers and is turning his heart away from her and from desiring her affection. It will hinder his sexual relationship within marriage and will create harmful memories that will last for a long time and probably interfere with his marriage for several years to come. In addition, when a man uses pornography, his wife (or girlfriend) will often sense some impurity or moral uncleanness in the man even if she does not discover any facts about what he is doing.

An abundance of evidence from sociological studies is also available, showing the harmful effects of pornography on those who view it and then on those who are subsequently harmed by these people. The harmful results may be summarized in the following points by the National Coalition for the Protection of Children and Families in their report, "The Effects of Pornography and Sexual Messages."[74] The report says that

> research has shown that pornography and its messages are involved in shaping attitudes and encouraging behavior that can harm individual users and their families. Pornography is often viewed in secret, which creates deception within marriages that can lead to divorce in some cases. In addition, pornography promotes the allure of adultery, prostitution and unreal expectations that can result in dangerous promiscuous behavior.[75]

It continues:

> Young people growing up in our already overly sexualized culture are being exposed to sexually explicit material on a daily basis through network television, movies, music and the Internet. Children are being subjected to sexual material and messages before they are mentally prepared to understand or evaluate what they are viewing. In addition, the majority of sex education is taking place in the media, not in the home, church or school.[76]

According to the report, the following false messages are sent by our culture:

- Sex with anyone, under any circumstances, any way it is desired, is beneficial and does not have negative consequences.
- Women have one value—to meet the sexual demands of men.
- Marriage and children are obstacles to sexual fulfillment.
- Everyone is involved in promiscuous sexual activity, infidelity and premarital sex.[77]

The report goes on to deal with the issue of pornography and addiction. It states, "Not only is the pornography industry, as well as the mainstream media, filling consumers' heads with these false beliefs and attitudes, but studies have found that pornography can be highly addictive. In fact, Dr. Victor Cline, an expert on sexual addiction, found that there is a four-step progression among many who consume pornography."

1. **Addiction:** Pornography provides a powerful sexual stimulant or aphrodisiac effect, followed by sexual release, most often through masturbation.
2. **Escalation:** Over time addicts require more explicit and deviant material to meet their sexual "needs."

---

74. "The Effects of Pornography and Sexual Messages." www.nationalcoalition.org/effects.asp.
75. Ibid.
76. Ibid.
77. Ibid.

3. **Desensitization:** What was first perceived as gross, shocking and disturbing, in time becomes common and acceptable.

4. **Acting out sexually:** There is an increasing tendency to act out behaviors viewed in pornography.[78]

The report goes on to say that the National Council on Sexual Addiction Compulsivity estimates that 6-to-8% of Americans are sexual addicts.[79]

As for the negative ramifications of pornography on communities, the report states, "Sexually oriented businesses, such as strip clubs and massage parlors, attract crime to communities. In addition, the general content of pornography supports abuse and the rape myth (that women enjoy forceful sex) and serves as a how-to for sex crimes, primarily the molestation of children." Land Use Studies by the National Law Center for Children and Families show evidence of the correlation of adult businesses and crime. For example, in Phoenix neighborhoods where adult businesses were located, the number of sex offenses was 506% greater than in areas without such businesses. The number of property crimes was 43% greater, and the number of violent crimes, 4% greater. Dr. Mary Anne Layden, director of education for the University of Pennsylvania Health System, points out, "I have been treating sexual violence victims and perpetrators for 13 years. I have not treated a single case of sexual violence that did not involve pornography."[80]

Finally, with regard to the child pornography, the report says, "Most will agree on the amount of harm caused by child pornography, which consists of photographs, videos, magazines, books and films that show children engaged in sexual acts, all of which are illegal. All production of these materials is an illegal and permanent record of the abuse or exploitation of children. Material digitally doctored to look like child pornography was also illegal, until a Supreme Court decision in April 2002 that found the 'virtual' child porn law unconstitutional."[81] The report concludes:

> Child and adult pornography is frequently used by pedophiles to lure children. The typical child molester befriends the child, often through Internet chat rooms, and, after building "trust," exposes the child to pornography. This is done in attempt to make the child think that this behavior is acceptable and to lure him or her to participate. The experience of exploitation and abuse becomes a lifelong struggle for the victim and leaves them with the fear that their photos are still out there.[82]

Alan Sears, president and CEO of the Alliance Defense Fund and former director of then-Attorney General Edwin Meese III's Commission on Pornography, adds:

> The sexual union within marriage, between one man and one woman, is meant by the Creator to be an act of supreme love, giving and unity. It's a picture, if you will, of supreme selflessness. Virtually all advocates of secular sexual

---

78. Ibid.

79. Ibid.

80. Haven Bradford Gow, "Child Sex Abuse: America's Dirty

Little Secret," *MS Voices for Children* (March 2000): cited in ibid.

81. "The Effects of Pornography and Sexual Messages," op.cit.

82. Ibid.

behavior center on an "it's all about me" philosophy rather than mutual love and care for the other partner.... In years of public speaking since that time, I have repeatedly referred to pornography as the "true hate literature" of our age, because of its hatred and exploitation of the human person, regardless of size, shape, color or gender. It reduces human beings to valueless commodities to be ogled at and disposed of like used tissue.[83]

4. What laws should governments make regarding pornography?

The fact that something is morally wrong according to the Bible does not by itself mean that governments should have laws against it. For instance, there are no laws against private drunkenness or laziness or foolish and wasteful uses of money. For the entire history of the United States, either there were *no laws* against fornication (in the sense of private sexual intercourse between consenting unrelated, unmarried adults of the opposite sex), or else those laws were *never enforced*. Thus, for example, I don't think anyone should support the idea of laws against looking at pornographic material, however a person might obtain it.

But the question of *creating* and *distributing* such material to others is a different question. In that case a person is creating material that (from a biblical point of view) has a harmful effect on the moral standards of the society and specifically on the people who use the pornography and others to whom they relate in intimate ways.

Therefore, since pornography makes people more likely to commit violence against women or children or more likely to commit rape, a strong argument can be made for enacting laws against the production, distribution, and sale of pornographic materials.

5. The definition of pornography

The First Amendment was primarily intended to protect political speech, and not all kinds of speech are protected. Slander, libel, and incitement to riot are not protected, nor is consumer fraud or mail fraud, for example, and courts have rightly recognized this. The courts have also recognized that the First Amendment cannot rightly be used to claim protection for obscene material.

How, then, should pornography be defined? In the 1957 Supreme Court decision *Roth v. United States*, the standard established by the court was "whether to the average person, applying contemporary community standards, the dominant theme of the material taken as whole appeals to the prurient interest." (The word "prurient" means "inordinately interested in matters of sex.") Then, in the 1973 case *Miller v. California* the Supreme Court decided that a work is not considered obscene unless it "lacks serious literary, artistic, political, and scientific value."[84]

---

83. Interview with Alan Sears: "Pornography: the Degrading Behemoth," CitizenLink.org (Aug. 3, 2005). www.citizenlink.org/FOSI/pornography/A000000851.cfm.

84. *Miller v. California*, 413 U.S. 15.

These cases still provide a useful standard that can be used effectively in prosecutions of pornographers, provided that juries are allowed to give a commonsense meaning to the word "serious," so that the word is not robbed of its force by misleading jury instructions or undue deference to testimony by so-called experts brought in by lawyers defending pornographers.[85] In addition, most of the problems in the country concerning pornography could be addressed if prosecutors would decide to bring charges only against the production and distribution of *visual images* (photos and videos) and not try to prosecute publications that contain only words, where standards are more blurry and some literary merit is easier to claim.

Therefore the ongoing problem with pornography in the United States is not that laws are inadequate but that prosecutors are not sufficiently willing to bring charges against those who produce and distribute pornography.

Former federal prosecutor Alan Sears claims that "obscenity laws, though far from perfect, are more definite than many other criminal laws successfully and regularly used in the criminal justice system."[86] He notes that the Attorney General's Commission on Pornography, for which he served as director, provided a useful definition of pornography as "sexually explicit material designed primarily for arousal."[87]

Sears also says,

> Pornography includes several classes of material: obscenity, material harmful to minors, child pornography, indecency, and lawful but nonetheless pornographic depictions....
>
> Depending on the type of material, its offensiveness ranges from the "merely immoral"—which depicts women and other persons as a subspecies of humans to be used, to be abused and to amuse—to what I have always called "crime scene photographs," actual depictions of unlawful sexual behavior for profit or exploitation.
>
> I call those who produce material that is unlawful part of a "criminal enterprise," not an "industry."
>
> So, pornography is shamefully large in its scope and, depending on how broadly it is defined, it is a multibillion-dollar enterprise. As large and pervasive as it may be, however, it is not too large to be reigned in and dramatically limited in any community with the will to do so.[88]

Under the administrations of two Republicans, President Ronald Reagan (1981–89) and President George H. W. Bush (1989–93), federal prosecutors were highly successful in prosecuting and winning convictions against numerous pornographers in the United States. Under the leadership of Patrick Trueman, chief of the Child Exploitation and Obscenity Section (CEOS) in the Department of Justice's Criminal Division, there were

85. See *United States v. Kilbride*, No. 07–10528, and *United States v. Schaeffer*, No. 07–10534, United States Court of Appeals for the 9th Circuit (2008).

86. Alan E. Sears, "The Legal Case for Restricting Pornography," in *Pornography: Research Advances and Policy Consid-*erations, ed. Dolf Zillman and Jennings Bryant (Hillsdale, NJ: Lawrence Erlbaum Associates, 1989), 327.

87. Interview with Sears "Pornography: the Degrading Behemoth."

88. Ibid.

multiple prosecutions, and the result was "50 individual or corporate convictions of sending obscene advertisements through the mails, and a 'Los Angeles project' that … led to the conviction of 20 out of 50 producers and suppliers of obscene materials targeted in the L.A. area."[89] They also obtained a conviction of Reuben Sturman, reputedly the nation's largest distributor of pornographic material, in 1992.[90]

But once President Clinton took office, Trueman reported, the Democratic administration "all but halted obscenity prosecutions," saying that it would focus instead on child pornography[91] (which effectively meant ignoring adult obscenity prosecution). When George W. Bush became President in 2001, veteran prosecutors saw some return to an emphasis on prosecuting pornographers under Attorney Generals John Ashcroft and Albert Gonzales, but it was not as great as under Reagan's Justice Department or that of George H. W. Bush. An *ABA Journal* article on this topic concludes: "… the real reason Internet obscenity has not been tackled stems from the fact that law enforcement seems not to have the time, resources or inclination to pursue it."[92]

J. THE IMPORTANCE OF LAWS CONCERNING MARRIAGE

It is hard to overstate the importance of laws concerning marriage, as discussed in this chapter. The future of the nation's children depends in large measure on how we define marriage and whether we continue to encourage and protect it. The future lives of millions of men and women in society will be affected by the way in which we define marriage. It is the foundational institution in our society, and it affects everything else.

Other reading

Davis, *Evangelical Ethics,* 113–36; James Dobson, *Marriage Under Fire* (Sisters, OR: Multnomah, 2004); Feinberg and Feinberg, *Ethics for a Brave New World,* 185–206; Daniel R. Heimbach, *True Sexual Morality* (Wheaton, IL: Crossway, 2004); Roger Magnuson, *Are Gay Rights Right?* (Portland, OR: Multnomah, 1990); Rae, *Moral Choices,* 270–301; Jeffrey Satinover, *Homosexuality and the Politics of Truth* (Grand Rapids: Baker, 1996); Thomas Schmidt, *Straight and Narrow? Compassion and Clarity in the Homosexuality Debate* (Downers Grove, IL: InterVarsity Press, 1995); Alan Sears and Craig Osten, *The Homosexual Agenda: Exposing the Principal Threat to Religious Freedom Today,* rev. ed. (Nashville: Broadman & Holman, 2003); Linda J. Waite and Maggie Gallagher, *The Case for Marriage: Why Married People Are Happier, Healthier, and Better Off Financially* (New York: Doubleday, 2000).

89. Jason Krause, "The End of the Net Porn Wars," *ABA Journal* (Feb. 2008). www.abajournal.com/magazine/article/the_end_of_the_net_porn_wars, Feb. 7, 2010.

90. Ibid.
91. Ibid.
92. Ibid.

Chapter 8

THE FAMILY

Should parents or the government have the primary responsibility for training children?

A. GOVERNMENTS SHOULD ENCOURAGE MARRIED COUPLES TO BEAR AND RAISE CHILDREN

From beginning to end, the Bible has a very positive view of bearing and raising children. In fact, the very first recorded command to human beings was the command to bear children:

> So God created man in his own image, in the image of God he created him; male and female he created them. And God blessed them. And God said to them, *"Be fruitful and multiply and fill the earth* and subdue it and have dominion over the fish of the sea and over the birds of the heavens and over every living thing that moves on the earth" (Gen. 1:27–28).

God was pleased with the man and woman whom he had made. He took delight in them (see Gen. 1:31) and indicated that they were the most wonderful part of his creation, for they alone were said to be "in the image of God." (This means that they were more like God than any other creature, and they represented him on earth.) Therefore we can understand why God wanted to have many more men and women on the earth, for they would also be human beings who would be "in his image" and would represent him and reflect his excellence. Because human beings are such wonderful creations, more human beings would bring more glory to their excellent Creator! This explains why God commanded Adam and Eve to "fill the earth" with

God-glorifying human beings, with generation after generation of God's image-bearers spreading over the whole earth.

God's desire for his people to bear more children is seen in several other passages, such as the following:

> Behold, children are a heritage from the LORD, the fruit of the womb a reward (Ps. 127:3).

> Did he not make them one, with a portion of the Spirit in their union? *And what was the one God seeking? Godly offspring.* So guard yourselves in your spirit, and let none of you be faithless to the wife of your youth (Mal. 2:15).

> So I would have younger widows marry, *bear children*, manage their households, and give the adversary no occasion for slander (1 Tim. 5:14; cf. Deut. 28:4; Hosea 1:10).

It is not surprising that the Bible views children in such a positive way. Unless each generation of a society bears and raises at least as many children as themselves, the entire population will dwindle and eventually the society itself will weaken and perhaps go out of existence.

Moreover, people all grow old eventually and become too weak to do productive work and support themselves. Unless there is a new generation of younger workers coming along, the society will become top-heavy with elderly people unable to work. Eventually fewer and fewer young people will be supporting more and more older, retired people, and a society's economy will spiral downward.

This has already happened in Europe. In 2003, researchers found that in the year 2000, the number of children in Europe had declined to the point that assured mathematically that there would be fewer parents than the previous generation. Brian O'Neill, a researcher at the International Institute for Applied Systems Analysis, said,

> The implications of negative momentum are small right now, but they are going to get bigger quickly. If you add another 10 years of low fertility, that decline (by 2100) would be 25 to 40 million. If we have two decades of low fertility, then it would be another 25 to 40 million.[1]

In America, the crisis will hit with Social Security and Medicare. According to David C. John, a research fellow at the Heritage Foundation,

> As millions of baby boomers approach retirement, the program's annual cash surplus will shrink and then disappear. Then, Social Security will not be able to pay full benefits from its payroll and other tax revenues. It will need to consume ever-growing amounts of general revenue dollars to meet its obligations—money that now pays for everything from environmental programs

---

1. Brian O'Neill, researcher at the International Institute for Applied Systems Analysis in Austria: quoted in Bootie Cosgrove-Mather, "European Birth Rate Declines," Associated Press (March 27, 2003). www.cbsnews.com/stories/2003/03/27/world/main546441.sthml.

to highway construction to defense. Eventually, either benefits will have to be slashed or the rest of the government will have to shrink to accommodate Social Security....

The reason that Social Security's deficits are inevitable is fairly simple. Demographics are more predictable than most events. Millions of baby boomers will begin to retire in 2008, when those born in 1946 reach Social Security's early retirement age of 62. From then until 2025, every year will see another crop of baby boomers reach the 62-year-old threshold. Because the baby boomers have not produced enough children to replace themselves, the number of taxpayer workers will shrink....

The future is coming with steady speed. Social Security's annual cash surpluses will begin to fall in 2008.... Over roughly the next ten years, those Social Security surpluses ... will continue to shrink and then disappear completely. Without those surpluses to reduce the size of the federal deficit, Congress will have to raise taxes to bring in billions of dollars of new revenues, cut programs, or let annual deficits climb.... Together, Social Security and Medicare will consume an estimate 60 percent of income taxes collected by 2040.[2]

Every society also needs children to pass on its cultural values and its moral and behavioral standards to succeeding generations. To the extent that a society stops bearing children, to that extent it fails to pass on its distinctive values to those who will live in the future.

But are there already too many people on the earth? There are certainly not too many God-glorifying people, which is what God expects the children of Christian believers to become. And there really are not too many people in general, as recent statistical studies indicate (see pp. 333–42 below).

B. PARENTS, NOT THE GOVERNMENT, SHOULD HAVE THE PRIMARY RESPONSIBILITY FOR TRAINING THEIR CHILDREN

It is remarkable how often the Bible places the responsibility for training children on their parents, not on "society" as a whole and not on the civil government. For example, Moses commanded the people of Israel that they should teach their children, and the language of the verse assumes the setting of a household or family:

"Hear, O Israel: The LORD our God, the LORD is one. You shall love the LORD your God with all your heart and with all your soul and with all your might. And these words that I command you today shall be on your heart. *You shall teach them diligently to your children*, and shall talk of them when you sit in your house, and when you walk by the way, and when you lie down, and when you rise" (Deut. 6:4–7).

---

2. David C. John, "Social Security's Inevitable Future," *Heritage Foundation Web Memo #696* (March 21, 2005). www.heritage.org/Research/SocialSecurity/wm696.cfm.

The commands in Proverbs also repeatedly assume that fathers and mothers are training their children:

> Hear, my son, your *father's* instruction, and forsake not your *mother's* teaching (Prov. 1:8).

> Hear, O sons, a *father's* instruction, and be attentive, that you may gain insight (4:1).

> My son, keep your *father's* commandment, and forsake not your *mother's* teaching (6:20).

> A wise son makes a glad *father*, but a foolish son is a sorrow to his *mother* (10:1).

> A wise son hears his *father's* instruction, but a scoffer does not listen to rebuke (13:1).

> A wise son makes a glad *father*, but a foolish man despises his *mother* (15:20).

> Listen to your *father* who gave you life, and do not despise your *mother* when she is old (23:22).

> The words of King Lemuel. An oracle that his *mother* taught him (31:1).

When we turn to the New Testament, instruction of children is also a responsibility given to parents:

> *Children, obey your parents in the Lord*, for this is right. "Honor your father and mother" (this is the first commandment with a promise), "that it may go well with you and that you may live long in the land." *Fathers*, do not provoke your children to anger, but bring them up in the discipline and instruction of the Lord (Eph. 6:1–4).

> *Children, obey your parents* in everything, for this pleases the Lord. *Fathers*, do not provoke your children, lest they become discouraged (Col. 3:20–21).

What is striking about these passages is the complete absence of *any indication* that *government* has the responsibility for training children *or for deciding what children should be taught*. The responsibility for teaching and training children, according to the Bible, falls entirely on their parents. This has significant implications for governmental policy regarding families and children.

First, this consistent pattern implies that *parents, not the government, should have the freedom to decide how best to educate their children*. This is the complete opposite of the policies of communist countries, who take children from their parents at a young age and seek to indoctrinate them with communist propaganda that in many cases is contrary to the convictions of the parents, particularly Christian parents. And it is completely opposite to the policy of the government of Germany today, which will actually take children from their parents by force in order to compel them to attend state-run schools, even when the parents object to the immoral and anti-Christian values taught in those schools.

In September 2006 the European Court of Human Rights outlawed homeschooling in Germany, and homeschooling families have been threatened with state seizure of their children and imprisonment. The Court of Human Rights ruled that Germany had not violated the human rights of parents when the government forbade them from educating their children at home because of religious reasons.[3]

Attorney Benjamin Bull of the Alliance Defense Fund, which provided funding in the legal effort to defend the rights of homeschool families in Germany, said: "The decision by the European Court of Human Rights opens the door to continued prosecution and should highlight to Americans the extreme dangers of allowing international law to be authoritative in our own court systems."[4]

In June 2008 two parents, Juergen and Rosemarie Dudek, were sentenced to three months in prison for homeschooling their children. Wolfgang Drautz, general counsel for the Federal Republic of Germany, said the government "has a legitimate interest in countering the rise of parallel societies that are based on religion."[5]

In May 2009, Alliance Defense Fund attorneys appealed to the European Court of Human Rights the conviction of two parents who chose to educate their child at home on sexuality rather than have her participate in a four-day "sexual education" course that taught values that conflicted with the family's Christian faith. The couple were fined for exercising their parental rights.[6]

The threat has now reached American shores. In July 2009 a ten-year-old homeschooled student in New Hampshire was ordered by a judge to attend public school because the girl "appeared to reflect her mother's rigidity on questions of faith" and the girl's best interests "would be best served in a public school setting" and by learning "different points of view at a time when she must begin to critically evaluate multiple systems of belief ... in order to select, as a young adult, which of those systems will best suit her own needs."[7] The judge issued this order even though the "marital master" who evaluated the young lady said she was "well-liked, social, and interactive with her peers, academically promising, [and] has more than kept up with the academic requirements of the ... public school system."[8]

But if the Bible teaches that it is the responsibility of parents and not of government to train children, then should Christians give *any* support to the idea of government-supported public schools? I think such schools can be supported by reasoning that the public schools are simply *helping* the parents fulfill their task of training their children. But parents should never begin to think that the public school system is *replacing* the parents as the party *primarily responsible* for training children. If we understand public

3. *Konrad v. Germany,* European Court of Human Rights (Sept. 18, 2006). www.telladf.org/UserDocs/KonradDecision.pdf.

4. "ADF: Homeschooling Outlawed in Germany: Americans Should Be on Guard," *ADF Press Release* (Sept. 27, 2006). www.telladf.org/news/pressrelease.aspx?cid=3864.

5. Bob Unruh, "Parents Sent to Jail for Homeschooling," *WorldNetDaily.com* (June 18, 2008). www.worldnetdaily.com/index.php?pageId=67413.

6. "ADF attorneys file second appeal involving German 'sex education' program," *ADF Press Release* (May 19, 2009). www.telladf.org/news/pressrelease.aspx?cid=4954.

7. *In the Matter of Kurowski and Kurowski,* court order issued by Judge Lucinda V. Sandler, Family Division of the Judicial Court for Belknap County, Laconia, New Hampshire (July 14, 2009). www.telladf.org/UserDocs/KurowskiOrder.pdf.

8. Ibid.

schools to be *helping parents* in their task, then the schools will be subject to and responsive to the concerns of the majority of parents in any district (rather than simply being run by educational "experts" who regularly override the desires and convictions of parents regarding their children's education).

C. A SCHOOL VOUCHER SYSTEM SHOULD BE ADOPTED BY EVERY SCHOOL DISTRICT

In the United States today I think the most beneficial change to our schooling system would be a system of school vouchers provided by the local government to pay for the education of children in each family. Parents could use these vouchers to pay for the cost of any public or private school they would choose for their children (including church-related schools).

This policy would have a number of benefits:

(1) It would restore much more parental influence in the training of children, a policy that would be consistent with the biblical teaching that parents have the primary responsibility for training their children.

(2) It would establish healthy competition in the educational system, with the result that the schools that give children the best training would gradually gain more and more students, and under-performing schools would either have to improve or they would have to close because they had no students. This would be far superior to the current government-run monopoly on the use of tax money for schools—a system that, on average, takes more and more money and produces fewer and fewer good results (when compared with other nations) year after year. In a 2001 study, Washington, DC, for instance, had the third highest per-capita expenditure per student, yet was last in achievement, and Delaware had the eighth-highest spending but landed in the bottom third with regard to results.[9]

Jay Greene, the author of *Education Myths*, said, "If money were the solution, the problem would already be solved.... We've doubled the per pupil spending, adjusting for inflation, over the last 30 years, and yet the schools aren't better."[10]

The results of this spending? In a 2006 study of educational achievement, the United States ranked twenty-first out of thirty countries in science, and twenty-fifth out of thirty in math.[11] In a recent survey of Oklahoma public school students, only one in four could identify George Washington as the first President of the United States.[12]

Meanwhile, in a September 2009 report on the difference between charter school students in New York City Public Schools compared with regular public school students,

9. Kirk A. Johnson, "Why More Money Will Not Solve America's Education Crisis," *Heritage Foundation Backgrounder #1448* (June 11, 2001). www.heritage.org/Research/Education/BG1448.cfm.

10. Jay Greene: quoted in John Stossel, "Stupid in America," *ABC News 20/20* (Jan. 13, 2006). http://abcnews.go.com/2020/print?id=2383857.

11. The Programme for International Student Assessment (PISA). www.pisa.oecd.org/dataoecd/15/13/39725224.pdf. Also see http://international-education.suite101.com/article.cfm/us_students_left_behind.

12. "75 Percent of Oklahoma High School Students Can't Name the First President of the U.S," *News9.com* (Sept. 16, 2009). www.news9.com/global/story.asp?s=11141949.

researchers found that by the third grade, the average charter school student was 5.3 points ahead on state English exams, compared with their peers in public schools, and 5.8 points ahead in math.[13]

(3) It would allow parents to send children to schools that supported their own moral and behavioral values.

(4) Children would be better educated. After the city of Milwaukee launched its school voucher program over the protests of the National Education Association (NEA), Caroline Hoxby of Harvard University performed a survey of the results. Comparing schools where at least 66% of students were eligible for vouchers with schools where fewer students were eligible, she found that in just one year schools with the most students eligible for vouchers made gains greater than those of other Milwaukee public schools. The schools with the voucher-eligible students went up 3 percentile points in math, 3 points in language, 5 points in science, and 3 points in social studies.[14]

According to Greg Forster, a research fellow at the Friedman Foundation for Educational Choice, every empirical study conducted in Milwaukee, Florida, Ohio, Texas, Maine, and Vermont showed that where vouchers were available, these programs improved public schools.[15]

The reason that the NEA (the largest teachers union) so vehemently opposes even small, localized experiments in using vouchers is that it knows that privately run schools *will do a much better job of educating children* if only they can compete on an equal basis for the tax dollars that support the public schools.[16] (See also pp. 540 –47 below.)

A common objection to the use of school vouchers is that parents will use them to send children to church-related schools and thus the government will be supporting training in a certain religion.

But this objection is not persuasive: (a) It is not the *government* that is supporting such church-related schools, but the *parents* of the children, because they are making the choice of where to send them. This principle has been upheld in a number of court decisions. In 2002 the US Supreme Court, in *Zelman v. Simmons-Harris,* decided that a limited school voucher program in Cleveland, Ohio, for children in woefully underperforming schools, was allowed under the US Constitution. The voucher program in Cleveland was only available to parents whose children were trapped in failing schools. Only three of the twenty-seven inner-city schools met minimal academic standards. Parents were allowed to take the $2,250-a-year voucher and place their children in the school of their choice, including faith-based schools.

The court ruled that the program was not in violation of the Establishment Clause of the First Amendment to the US Constitution. The program passed a five-part test to

13. Caroline M. Hoxby, Sonali Murarka, and Jenny Kang, "How New York City's Charter Schools Affect Achivement, August 2009 Report." Second report in series (Cambridge, MA: New York City Charter Schools Evaluation Project, September 2009). www.nber.org/~schools/charterschoolseval/how_NYC_charter_schools_affect_achievement_sept2009.pdf.

14. Caroline M.Hoxby, "Rising Tide," *Education Next,* Winter 2001: cited in Greg Forster, Ph.D., "A Win-Win Solution: The Empirical Evidence on How Vouchers Affect Public Schools," *School Choice Issues In Depth* (Jan. 2009), 16. www.friedman-foundation.org/downloadFile.do?id=357

15. Forster, "A Win-Win Solution," 16–21.

16. Ibid.

determine its constitutionality. The test, called the Private Choice Test, asked the program to meet the following criteria:

1. The program must have a valid secular purpose,
2. Aid must go to parents and not the schools,
3. A broad class of beneficiaries must be covered,
4. The program must be neutral with respect to religion, and
5. There must be adequate nonreligious options.

The court, in a 5-to-4 decision written by Chief Justice William Rehnquist, decided that the program met all these criteria.[17] As long as other voucher programs meet this criteria, the "freedom of religion" objection to school vouchers is effectively removed.

To use an analogy, if I get a tax-refund check from the government and then decide to give the money to my church, the government is not supporting my church. It is *my money*, and I am using it to support my church. Similarly, if the government gives a voucher to parents with the restriction it must be used for the education of children, then parents should have complete freedom to purchase education at any kind of school, so long as it meets certain requirements of academic quality.

(b) Sometimes people think this objection is based on the First Amendment to the Constitution, which guarantees religious freedom. But this objection misunderstands the First Amendment. The First Amendment was only intended to prohibit *the governmental establishment of one certain church* or religion as the official state church. It was never intended to prevent all government support for everything that is done by a church. (See discussion above in chapter 1, pp. 29–36.) In addition, the vouchers are not restricted to be used at only one particular denominational school or religiously oriented school, but can be used at any kind of school that the parents choose.

(c) The goal of civil government with regard to education should be to produce educated citizens for the next generation. If that is being done through a voucher system, then the government's goal is being accomplished. The goal of government should not be *to prevent children from obtaining education* in a school that also teaches religious values. It should be no part of the government's purpose to *prevent* children from receiving religious training.

The primary barrier to adopting a school voucher system is the massive political influence of the NEA and the support of this union by the Democratic Party. In 2007 a statewide voucher system was established in Utah, but the NEA mounted a massive political campaign, spent $3.2 million, and defeated the program in a state referendum.[18] If even one state could adopt such a system and the public could see its success for a few years, parents around the nation would demand a similar program.

One striking example of Democratic opposition at the national level to school vouchers was seen in 2009 in Washington, DC. This city voted 92.9% for President

17. *Zelman v. Simmons-Harris*, 536 U.S. 639 (2002).
18. "Utah Voters Defeat Measure to Create U.S. First State-

wide School Voucher Program," Associated Press (Nov. 7, 2007). www.foxnews.com/story/0,2933,308936,00.html.

Obama in the 2008 election,[19] and it is historically a Democratic stronghold. It also has unusually high poverty levels of 23%.[20] Yet the city established a very successful voucher program in a desperate attempt to improve the city's failing schools. However, the US Congress has governing authority over the District of Columbia, and when the new Democratic majority in both House and Senate took office in January 2009, they cut off future funding for this voucher program. The Senate vote was 58–39 to kill the voucher program in the Omnibus Appropriations Act.[21] Only two Democrats voted to keep the funding, while 36 Republicans and 1 independent voted to keep the voucher program alive.[22]

The Democratic mayor and other local political leaders vigorously protested these cuts, but Congress turned a blind eye. (Many Democratic members of Congress as well as President Obama choose to send their own children to private schools rather than the Washington public schools, but they would not allow this choice for poor parents in that same district.)

Where there is no voucher system, other plans can also significantly expand parental choice in education. For example, some states have established a system of tax credits for tuition payments to any public or private schools, a system that has an effect similar to that of vouchers.

Scholars Abigail and Stephan Thernstrom have devoted years of their lives to researching the state of education in the United States and especially the racial gaps in educational achievement. They report the glaring and tragic failure of American schools to educate children, especially black and Hispanic children:

> Another generation of black children is drifting through school without acquiring essential skills and knowledge. Hispanic children are not faring much better, and for neither group is there a comforting trend in the direction of progress....
>
> How do we actually know how much students are learning? The best evidence comes from the National Assessment of Educational Progress (NAEP).... The NAEP results consistently show a frightening gap between the basic academic skills of the average African-American or Latino student and those of the typical white or Asian American. By twelfth grade, on average, black students are four years behind those who are white or Asian. Hispanics don't do much better....
>
> Imagine that you are an employer considering two job applicants, one with a high school diploma, the other a dropout at the end of eighth grade.... an employer will seldom find the choice between the two candidates difficult.

19. See www.usatoday.com/news/politics/election2008/dc.htm.

20. District of Columbia: Poverty Rate by Race/Ethnicity, states (2006–2007), US (2007), StateHealthFacts.org. www.statehealthfacts.org/profileind.jsp?ind=14&cat=1&rgn=10.

21. Elizabeth Hillgrove, "Senate Kills GOP's D.C. Vouchers Bid," *Washington Times* (March 11, 2009). www.washington-times.com/news/2009/mar/11/senate-kills-gops-dc-vouchers-bid/.

22. The two Democratic senators were Robert Byrd of West Virginia and Mark Warner of Virginia. The independent was Joseph Lieberman of Connecticut. See Federally-Funded Private and Religious School Vouchers. http://action.aclu.org/site/VoteCenter?page=voteInfo&voteId=9110.

The employer hiring the typical black high school graduate (or the college that admits the average black student) is, in effect, choosing a youngster who has made it only through eighth grade. He or she will have a high school diploma, but not the skills that should come with it.... Blacks nearing the end of their high school education perform a little worse than white eighth-graders in both reading and U.S. history, and a lot worse in math and geography.... Hispanics do only a little better than African Americans.[23]

The Thernstroms illustrate this with a shocking graph of skill levels:[24]

Figure 8.1

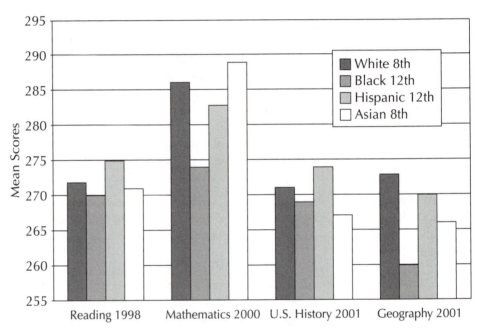

Sources: National Assessment for Educational Progress Data Tool

This is a national tragedy of immense proportions. Lack of educational skills perpetuates a permanent economic "underclass" in our society, for education is the primary determinant of earning capacity for life. But the responsibility for this tragedy lies squarely with the failed public school system and the NEA that uses its monopoly power over tax-supported schools to prevent real school choice.

Throwing more money at the same failed schools will not solve the problem, the Thernstroms point out, because the teachers unions have such a stranglehold on public

23. Abigail Thernstrom and Stephan Thernstrom, *No Excuses: Closing the Racial Gap in Learning* (New York: Simon & Schuster, 2003), 11–15.

24. Ibid., 13.

schools that poor teachers cannot be fired and the best teachers cannot be given enough incentives to excel or to stay in teaching as a career. The Thernstroms write,

> Big-city superintendents, as well as principals, operate in a straitjacket.... The enormous power of teachers unions stops almost all real change in its tracks.... It is no accident that the revolutionary schools we describe in Chapters 3 and 4 [where they detail several examples of high-performing schools in low-income areas] are outside the traditional public system.[25]

Later they continue the same theme:

> We have described some wonderful public schools where youngsters living in distressed communities thrive. But it is no accident that none of them is a traditional public school. They are charter schools.... The principals in these charter schools have real power—over their budgets, their discipline policies, and their staffing.... But no entire urban school district has been able to achieve results comparable to those we found in the best charter schools, and we doubt that any ever will without fundamental reform in the structure of public education....[26]
>
> The job of unions is to protect the interests of teachers. The job of schools is to educate the students. Many well-meaning reformers ... fail to understand the difference between the two objectives.... What's good for unions is not necessarily good for kids.... When there's a vacancy, the most senior applicant gets the position.... Quality is irrelevant.... Getting rid of an unwanted teacher, however, can be an expensive nightmare.... Tenured teachers who can't teach, can't control a class, and behave in manifestly unacceptable ways are in the system as long as they want to stay, with rare exceptions.[27]

As for a solution, the Thernstroms emphasize the importance of providing parents with *the ability to choose which schools their children attend*, which would introduce the necessary element of competition, leading to better quality schools. The Thernstroms write in their conclusion,

> Vouchers are a matter of basic equity. The term "middle class" is slippery, but here's one good definition: Middle-class parents are people who can choose where their children go to school by choosing where they live. Choice should not be a class-based privilege.... The racial gap is thus the most important civil rights issue of our time. If Americans care about racial equality ... they must demand more than the current reform movement is offering—standards, tests, some consequences for educational failure, and limited public school choice.[28]

What do the Thernstroms say is a real solution, one that will go beyond these current "reforms" that have had such limited success? These two experts, who know more than

---

25. Ibid., 7.
26. Ibid., 248–49.

27. Ibid., 259–61.
28. Ibid., 273–74.

perhaps anyone else in America about the shameful racial gap in education, say *the entire system must be reformed, with genuine educational choice* made available to lower-income parents, indeed to all parents. Their final conclusion is this:

> The nation's system of education must be fundamentally altered, with real educational choice as part of the package.[29]

I am convinced that care about racial reconciliation in our country, care for all our country's children, and care for the future of our country requires no less than such fundamental, total reform of our educational system.

D. DISCIPLINE OF CHILDREN AND SPANKING

The biblical passages cited above give strong support to the idea that parents have the primary responsibility for training their children. Other passages indicate that "discipline" will be a part of that process:

> Fathers, do not provoke your children to anger, but bring them up in the *discipline* and instruction of the Lord (Eph. 6:4).

> Besides this, we have had earthly fathers *who disciplined us* and we respected them. Shall we not much more be subject to the Father of spirits and live?... *For the moment all discipline seems painful* rather than pleasant, but later it yields the peaceful fruit of righteousness to those who have been trained by it (Heb. 12:9, 11).

In some European countries and elsewhere, laws now prohibit parents from spanking their children ("corporal punishment") as part of the disciplinary process. Australia, Sweden, Finland, Norway, Austria, Cyprus, Denmark, Latvia, Croatia, Bulgaria, Germany, Israel, Iceland, Romania, Ukraine, and Hungary have all outlawed corporal punishment.[30] (In Sweden, in spite of such a law, it is disturbing that assaults by adults against children between the ages of one and six had increased fourfold between 1984 and 1994.)[31] Similar laws have been considered in parts of the United States as well—Massachusetts[32] and California,[33] for example—but they have not been adopted.

One anti-spanking crusader named Jordan Riak proposed "no-spanking zones" that would stigmatize parents.[34] He wrote in 1997:

> Whether any child, on any pretext, in any circumstance, should be subjected to physical battery, and whether such treatment is beneficial to the child, should

---

29. Ibid., 274.

30. World Corporal Punishment Research, www.corpun.com/rules.htm.

31. "Kriminalistatistk vid SCB," 115 81 Stockholm, vol. 5 (1995): cited in John S. Lyons and Robert E. Lazelere, "Where Is Evidence That Non-Abusive Punishment Increases Aggression?" Presented at the XXVI International Congress of Pyschology (Aug. 18, 1996). http://faculty.biola.edu/paulp/sweden.html.

32. "Should Spanking Your Child Be Illegal?" *ABCNews.com* (Nov. 28, 2007). http://abcnews.go.com/GMA/story?id=3924024.

33. Nancy Vogel, "A Spanking Ban: Are We Going to Get It?" *Los Angeles Times* (Jan. 20, 2007). http://articles.latimes.com/2007/jan/20/local/me-spanking20.

34. Jordan Riak: quoted in Edward Wong, "No-Spanking Zone Sought in Oakland," *Los Angeles Times* (Jan. 24, 1999), A10.

have ceased long ago to be matters for serious debate. The fact is that the deliberate traumatization of a child by a caretaker is destructive to that child.... Some of our citizens cling to an anachronistic notion that children are chattels and that their owners have a right, or are even dutybound, to control their property by violent means and may assign that right to others, such as teachers. The Proverbs of King Solomon have been cited, on occasion as their authority.... My hunch is that the fundamentalists' fondness for Old Testament authority is driven by a need for self-exculpation over their mistreatment of children.[35]

The testimony of the Bible is clear, however, that effective discipline of children will at times include the infliction of some kind of physical pain, not to bring actual physical damage to the child's body, but to emphasize the significantly wrong or dangerous character of the behavior that led to the discipline. Such use of "the rod" (probably a wooden stick of some sort) to strike a child is viewed as the responsibility of a parent and an indication of the parent's love for a child (a love that strongly desires right behavior in the child). That is the point of the following verses:

> Whoever *spares the rod* [Hebrew *shebet*, here a rod or stick of wood] hates his son, but he who loves him is diligent to discipline him (Prov. 13:24).

> Folly is bound up in the heart of a child, but *the rod of discipline* drives it far from him (22:15).

This verse indicates that imposing physical punishment (in a wise and nonexcessive manner) is a help in overcoming the tendency to do wrong in every child's heart.

> Do not withhold discipline from a child; *if you strike him with a rod*, he will not die. If you strike him with the rod, you will save his soul from Sheol (Prov. 23:13–14).

> *The rod* and reproof give wisdom, but a child left to himself brings shame to his mother (29:15).

Related verses compare the discipline of earthly parents with the discipline of God himself and also show the benefit of such discipline in the life of a child:

> My son, do not despise the LORD's discipline or be weary of his reproof, for the LORD reproves him whom he loves, as a father the son in whom he delights (Prov. 3:11–12; see also Heb. 12:6).

> Discipline your son, for there is hope; do not set your heart on putting him to death (19:18).

> Discipline your son, and he will give you rest; he will give delight to your heart (29:17).

---

35. Jordan Riak, "Spanking and Hitting Are Perilous," *The Brown University Child and Adolescent Behavior Letter,* 13:9 (Sept. 1997), 1.

The laws already in place in the United States are sufficient to guard against genuine physical abuse of children and bring appropriate punishment where that occurs. But such laws should not be expanded to rule out the use of such physical discipline as spanking a child. A biblically based system of values understands that when spanking is administered wisely and with restraint, it is beneficial, not harmful, in the raising of children. Yet the Bible also cautions that parents should not be so demanding that they cause frustration and despair in their children: "Fathers, do not provoke your children, lest they become discouraged" (Col. 3:21).

From time to time the news media report various new scholarly studies claiming to "prove" that spanking does no good or is psychologically harmful to children. But these studies seldom if ever distinguish wise, nonabusive spanking that causes temporary pain but no physical harm from more violent beatings that bring serious bruising or other physical harm to children; they also fail to distinguish wise, restrained parental spanking from unjustified rage and actual physical abuse coming from drunken or pathologically abusive parents. Thus the studies are skewed and give distorted results.

Dr. Murray Straus of the University of New Hampshire is one of the most outspoken voices calling for the banishment of corporal punishment and has from time to time issued skewed and distorted studies to try to advance his agenda. Straus over the years has tried to link corporal punishment to lower IQs in children[36] and to antisocial behavior.[37]

In response to one of Straus's studies, even *Time* magazine, hardly an advocate for corporal punishment, wrote about the flawed methodology:

> The problem has to do with who was in the study. Straus and company culled their information from telephone interviews conducted by the U.S. Bureau of Labor Statistics beginning in 1979 with 807 mothers of children ages 6 to 9. They were then asked how many times they had spanked their children in the past week and what the kids' behavior was like—did they lie, cheat, act up in school? Then the bureau polled the same group two years later. Sure enough, the kids who had been spanked had become increasingly anti-social.
>
> But when you look a little closer at the findings, they start to seem a little murky. To begin with, observes Dr. Den Trumbull, a Montgomery, Alabama pediatrician ... the mothers ranged in age from 14 to 21. That is hardly a slice of American motherhood. Moreover, those who spanked did so on average twice a week. These factors, says Trumbull, plus the fact that some of the kids were as old as nine, "are markers of a dysfunctional family in my mind, and in the minds of most psychologists and pediatricians."
>
> Trumbull also observed that limiting the study to 6 to 9 year olds skewed the results; by then the kids can understand the consequences of their actions. For them frequent physical punishment is likely to be humiliating and traumatic—and might well lead to worse behavior down the line.

---

36. "Want Smarter Kids? Don't Spank Them," *Reuters* (Aug. 3, 1999), and "Children who are spanked have lower IQs, new research finds," www.physorg.com/pdf173077612.pdf.

37. Murray A. Straus, Ph.D.; David B. Sugarman, Ph.D.; Jean Giles-Sims, Ph.D., *Archives of Pediatric and Adolescent Medicine* 151 (Aug. 1997), 761–67.

Trouble is, while spanking is down, child abuse is up. It appears that well-meaning professionals have been using the wrong whipping boy—and Straus' study offers little reason to change that assessment.[38]

In 1993, a group of American pediatricians presented a review of all articles on corporal punishment to the American Academy of Pediatrics. Their results found that of the 132 studies that supposedly documented negative effects of corporal punishment on children, only 24 had any empirical data. All the others were either editorials, commentaries, opinions, or reviews. And of the 24 valid studies, 23 had ambiguous wording and broad definitions that skewed the results. They found that physical punishment was defined to include anything from mild spanking to beating a child with a hair brush or electrical cord to pouring boiling water on the child. They concluded that the studies failed to "entirely answer the real scientific issue—does occasional spanking aid or harm the development of a child's ability to learn?"[39]

Christians should be suspicious of supposedly conclusive "expert studies" that result in telling parents that they should not do exactly what the Bible tells them to do.

Of course, opponents of spanking can always bring up extreme examples of abuse and of harsh distortion of biblical standards. Christians shouldn't advocate such actions either, but should instead oppose them. It must be kept in mind, however, that the *abuse* of something (such as spanking of children) does not prove that *the action itself* is wrong. Anything good can be abused or used wrongfully.

Gene Edward Veith, provost at Patrick Henry College and former executive director of the Cranach Institute at Concordia Theological Seminary, wrote in *World* magazine that *not* spanking children is actually a form of child abuse:

> Not only the ACLU but also many educators, child psychologists, and even parents subscribe to the "expressive" theory of mental health. According to this model, human beings, deep down, are basically good. They simply need to express their feelings they have inside. Obstacles to this expression—such as "society rules," "oppressive" authority figures, and "judgmental" belief systems—cause repression and thus mental unhappiness and twisted behavior. Under this worldview, any attempt to control or punish or suppress the feelings of a child is construed as cruel. And disciplining a child becomes next to impossible.... For all the attempts to discipline children through "positive reinforcement" and such non-painful methods as "time outs" and guilt trips, young people are learning that since adults will not exert force against them, they can pretty much ignore those in authority.... Allowing children to grow up without discipline—however kindly it appears on the surface—is child abuse, an expression of our culture's hatred for children.[40]

---

38. Michael D. Lemonick, "Spare the Rod? Maybe," *Time* (Aug. 25, 1997).

39. Dr. David Larson, "Is Mild Spanking Abusive or Helpful for Young Children?" Physicians Research Forum Research Summary (1993).

40. Gene Edward Veith, "Hating Our Children," *World* (June 12, 1999). www.worldmag.com/articles/2936.

We should not be surprised that many non-Christians will seek to argue against spanking. Many of them do not think that there is a tendency toward evil in human hearts, including the hearts of children. But this is contrary to a Christian worldview, which holds that there is a tendency to evil (as well as a competing tendency to do good, by common grace) in every child's heart (see chap. 4, pp. 119–22). Therefore a non-Christian worldview is less likely to think that children should be disciplined for the wrong that they do. Moreover, many people's non-Christian worldview does not believe that superior physical force should be necessary to restrain evil, but a Christian view understands that some of the evil in people's hearts is so irrational that it cannot be restrained by reasoning but only by force (see above, pp. 121–22). When applied to the discipline of children, the Christian worldview understands that there is sometimes a need for a spanking and that this quickly overcomes willful or irrational wrongdoing in a way that hours of pleading and reasoning will not accomplish, and it helps build a more righteous character in the child.

Another deeper reason underlying the opposition to physical punishment of children may be, in at least some cases, opposition to the very idea of *parental authority* over children (because of a dislike of all authority) or opposition to the idea that parents can know better than children what is right and wrong (because of a belief that nobody can know right or wrong for anyone else). In a number of cases this opposition to all spanking may be strengthened by a deep spiritual influence (an evil influence) that seeks to undermine God's plan for the family and for the restraint of evil in children's lives.

Chapter 9

ECONOMICS

What should be the role of government regarding a nation's economic system?

This is a large question, and it involves many specific economic issues. This chapter will treat the following subtopics:

Private property

Economic development

Money supply

Free markets and regulation

The rich and the poor

Government and business

Taxes

Social Security

Health care

The cure for recessions

A. PRIVATE PROPERTY

According to the teachings of the Bible, government should both document and protect the ownership of private property in a nation.

The Bible regularly assumes and reinforces a system in which *property belongs to individuals*, not to the government or to society as a whole.

We see this implied in the Ten Commandments, for example, because the eighth commandment, "You shall not steal" (Exod. 20:15), assumes that human beings will own property that belongs to them individually and not to other people. I should not steal my neighbor's ox or donkey because *it belongs to my neighbor*, not to me and not to anyone else.

The tenth commandment makes this more explicit when it prohibits not just stealing but also *desiring* to steal what belongs to my neighbor:

> "You shall not covet your neighbor's house; you shall not covet your neighbor's wife, or his male servant, or his female servant, or his ox, or his donkey, or anything that is your neighbor's" (Exod. 20:17).

The reason I should not "covet" my neighbor's house or anything else is that *these things belong to my neighbor*, not to me and not to the community or the nation.

This assumption of private ownership of property, found in this fundamental moral code of the Bible, puts the Bible in direct opposition to the communist system advocated by Karl Marx. Marx said:

> The theory of the Communists may be summed up in the single sentence: abolition of private property.[1]

One reason why communism is so incredibly dehumanizing is that when private property is abolished, government controls all economic activity. And when government controls all economic activity, it controls what you can buy, where you will live, and what job you will have (and therefore what job you are allowed to train for, and where you go to school), and how much you will earn. It essentially controls all of life, and human liberty is destroyed. Communism enslaves people and destroys human freedom of choice. The entire nation becomes one huge prison. For this reason, it seems to me that communism is the most dehumanizing economic system ever invented by man.

Other passages of Scripture also support the idea that property should belong to individuals, not to "society" or to the government (except for certain property required for proper government purposes, such as government offices, military bases, and streets and highways). The Bible contains many laws concerning punishments for stealing and appropriate restitution for damage of another person's farm animals or agricultural fields (for example, see Exod. 21:28–36; 22:1–15; Deut. 22:1–4; 23:24–25). Another commandment guaranteed that property boundaries would be protected: "You shall not move your neighbor's landmark, which the men of old have set, in the inheritance that you will hold in the land that the LORD your God is giving you to possess" (Deut. 19:14). To move the landmark was to move the boundaries of the land and thus to steal land that belonged to one's neighbor (compare Prov. 22:28; 23:10).

---

1. Karl Marx, *Communist Manifesto* (New York: International Publishers, 1948), 23.

Another guarantee of the ownership of private property was the fact that, even if property was sold to someone else, in the Year of Jubilee it had to return to the family that originally owned it:

> It shall be a Jubilee for you, when *each of you shall return to his property* and each of you shall return to his clan (Lev. 25:10).

This is why the land could not be sold forever: "The land shall not be sold in perpetuity, for the land is mine. For you are strangers and sojourners with me" (Lev. 25:23).

This last verse emphasizes the fact that private property is never viewed in the Bible as an *absolute* right, because all that people have is ultimately given to them by God, and people are viewed as God's "stewards" to manage what he has entrusted to their care.

> The earth is the Lord's and the fullness thereof, the world and those who dwell therein (Ps. 24:1; compare Ps. 50:10–12; Hag. 2:8).

Yet the fact remains that, under the overall sovereign lordship of God himself, property is regularly said to belong *to individuals*, not to the government and not to "society" or the nation as a whole.

When Samuel warned the people about the evils that would be imposed upon them by a king, he emphasized the fact that the monarch, with so much government power, would "take" and "take" and "take" from the people and confiscate things for his own use:

> So Samuel told all the words of the Lord to the people who were asking for a king from him. He said, "These will be the ways of the king who will reign over you: he will *take* your sons and appoint them to his chariots and to be his horsemen and to run before his chariots. And he will appoint for himself commanders of thousands and commanders of fifties, and some to plow his ground and to reap his harvest, and to make his implements of war and the equipment of his chariots. He will *take* your daughters to be perfumers and cooks and bakers. He will *take* the best of your fields and vineyards and olive orchards and give them to his servants. He will *take* the tenth of your grain and of your vineyards and give it to his officers and to his servants. He will *take* your male servants and female servants and the best of your young men and your donkeys, and put them to his work. He will *take* the tenth of your flocks, *and you shall be his slaves.* And in that day you will cry out because of your king, whom you have chosen for yourselves, but the Lord will not answer you in that day" (1 Sam. 8:10–18).

This prediction was tragically fulfilled in the story of the theft of the vineyard of Naboth the Jezreelite by Ahab the wicked king and Jezebel, his even more wicked queen (see 1 Kings 21:1–29). The regular tendency of human governments is to seek to take control of more and more of the property of a nation that God intends to be owned and controlled by private individuals.

One of the primary reasons why God establishes a system of ownership of property among human beings is our creation "in the image of God" (see Gen. 1:27). God placed human beings on the earth as his representatives, and he wants us to be like him and to imitate his character in many ways: "Therefore be imitators of God, as beloved children" (Eph. 5:1). When we own possessions, he gives us many opportunities to imitate God's attributes and thus reflect something of his excellence (his "glory") on the earth.[2]

For example, just as God is sovereign over the whole universe, so he gives us opportunity to be sovereign over a small portion of land, or a car, or clothing and books, and so forth. In our stewardship of these possessions we have opportunities to imitate God's wisdom, his creativity, his love for other people, his justice and fairness, his mercy, his knowledge, and many other attributes. Ownership of possessions also provides many opportunities to test what is in our hearts and gives us opportunities to give thanks to God for what he has provided to us (see Col. 3:15; 1 Tim. 6:17).

Unfortunately, it is not only communist countries that make it impossible for individual people to own private property. In many other supposedly "capitalist" countries there is no effective free market system regarding ownership of private property either, because nearly all property is controlled by a few wealthy individuals, and they have enough influence that government laws are set up to prevent ordinary people from owning property themselves. Therefore most of the people cannot legally own property and as a result are trapped in poverty.

The Peruvian economist Hernando de Soto attempted, as an experiment, to register a small business in Peru, using some graduate students as a research team. They tried to open a small garment workshop (with one worker) on the outskirts of Lima, the capital. They worked at the registration process for six hours a day, and it took them 289 days! The cost was the equivalent of $1,231 US dollars, or thirty-one times the monthly minimum wage (approximately three years' salary for an ordinary person in Peru). De Soto then explained what happened when they tried to get permission to build a house:

> To obtain legal authorization to build a house on state-owned land took six years and eleven months requiring 207 administrative steps in 52 government offices.... To obtain a legal title for that piece of land took 728 steps.[3]

De Soto and his team document similar roadblocks to ownership of property and small businesses in other countries such as Egypt, the Philippines, and Haiti. They conclude that *legal ownership of property or a business is effectively impossible for the vast majority of the population in many Third World countries.* Thus citizens are trapped in poverty every bit as much as they would be if they were living in a communist society.

If people can never *own* property or *own* a business, they can never *build* a business and become even moderately well-off; they can never acquire rental property as a source of additional income; they can never take a second mortgage on a house as a means of starting a business; and they will find it nearly impossible to obtain anything more than a very tiny amount of credit to invest in building a business (because they have no permanent legal address).

---

2. See a further discussion of this idea in Wayne Grudem, *Business for the Glory of God: The Bible's Teaching on the Moral Goodness of Business* (Wheaton, IL: Crossway, 2003).

3. Hernando de Soto, *The Mystery of Capital: Why Capitalism Triumphs in the West and Fails Everywhere Else* (New York: Basic Books, 2000), 19–20.

This is why de Soto has argued—I think persuasively—that one of the most important factors for economic development of a nation is a system where ownership of private property is *easily documented* and *publicly known*.

The issue of private ownership of property also has practical application to the United States today, because threats to private ownership of property are increasing at the highest level of government. In the early months of 2009 (the opening months of the Obama administration), the federal government took unprecedented steps to acquire a near-controlling interest in some of the nation's largest banks, including Citigroup and Bank of America.[4] It forced Chrysler Corporation into accepting an agreement by which a large share would be bought by Fiat and a controlling interest in the company would be held by the auto-workers union, the United Auto Workers (UAW).[5] It effectively acquired a controlling interest in General Motors as well, so that one day President Obama could announce that he thought that the president of General Motors, Rick Wagoner, needed to resign, and immediately the company's president was gone.[6] It was previously unheard-of in America—and thought to be impossible—for the US President to be able to "fire" the president of one of America's largest corporations. But now government control of the nation's property has extended even to this action.

In addition, the Democratic majority in Congress in early 2010 passed legislation that gives the federal government significant control of the nation's health care system, which comprises approximately 17.6% of the nation's gross domestic product (GDP).[7] The bill calls for large segments of the American economy to be taken over by the federal government and essentially become *owned* by the government rather than by shareholders or private individuals.

In another area, in 2005, the US Supreme Court decided that government could use the power of eminent domain to transfer *private* land to another *private* owner.[8] (See discussion in chap. 5, pp. 137–39, regarding the case *Kelo v. City of New London.*)

Yet another source of threats to private ownership of property comes in the increasingly burdensome weight of government regulations on how people can use their property. Homeowners in sections of California that are prone to forest fires have been prohibited by environmental regulations from cutting down the trees that grow close to their homes, sometimes resulting in fires that needlessly destroy their homes.

For example, homeowners near Santa Cruz, California (about ninety miles south of San Francisco) have faced so many environmental regulations that it has become cost prohibitive for them to do the things necessary to protect them. One woman who had

4. Mike Allen and Craig Gordon, "Treas. and the Citi: Deal Announced," *Politico.com* (Feb. 27, 2009), www.politico.com/news/stories/0209/19401.html; and Binyamin Appelbaum and David Cho, "White House Banking on Nationalization," *Washington Post* (Feb. 24, 2009), www.cbsnews.com/stories/2009/02/24/politics/washingtonpost/main4823573.shtml?source=RSSattr=Politics_4823573.

5. "UAW, Chrysler, and Fiat Reach Concession Deal," *ABC-News.com* (August 26, 2009). http://abcnews.go.com/Business/wireStory?id=7435524.

6. Dan Strumpf, "GM CEO Wagoner Forced Out," Associated Press (March 30, 2009). www.myfoxdc.com/dpp/news/dpg_GM_Rick_Wagoner_Out_fc_200903302343214.

7. A. Siska et al., "Health Spending Projections Through 2018: Recession Effects Add Uncertainty to the Outlook," *Health Affairs* 28, no. 2 (March/April 2009), w346-w357: cited in "Health Care Costs: Costs," National Coalition on Health Care (July 2009), www.nchc.org/documents/Fact%20Sheets/Fact%20Sheet%20-%20Cost%208-10-09.pdf.

8. *Kelo et al. v. City of New London et al.*, 545 U.S. 469 (2005).

intended to clear some fire-prone eucalyptus from her six-acre property found out that she had to pay a county planner between $1,300 and $1,500 to survey her property before altering the landscape, without any certainty that she would get permission to cut the trees down.

One neighbor said, "You will go through this misery of trying to get a plan approved. If you're one of these citizens who wants to stay on the correct side of the law, you could really be off to the races with your checkbook."

The homeowner decided to forego removing the trees, and her 2,800-square-foot home eventually burned down.

These were *her* trees on *her* property, and she could not cut them down!

The county planning department was sympathetic to her plight, but said they were forced to enforce state and federal environmental laws. The planning director, Tom Burns, said, "There's got to be a balance between environmental protections and allowing people to protect their houses."[9]

In 2007, columnist Michelle Malkin reported on how environmental lawsuits kept the government from being able to proceed with procedures to stop wildfires:

> The government accounting office (GAO) examined 762 U.S. Forest Service (USFS) proposals to thin forests and prevent fires during the past two years. According to the study, slightly more than half the proposals were not subject to third-party appeal. Of those proposals subject to appeal, third parties challenged 59 percent. Appeals were filed most often by anti-logging groups, including the Sierra Club, Alliance for Wild Rockies, and Forest Conservation Council. According to the GAO, 84 interest groups filed more than 400 appeals of Forest Service proposals. The appeals delayed efforts to treat 900,000 acres of forests and cost the federal government millions of dollars to address.[10]

Dana Joel Gattuso, writing in *National Policy Analysis*, concurs:

> Appeals and lawsuits, along with regulations under the National Environmental Policy Act (NEPA) requiring the Forest Service to perform extensive environmental impact analyses before undertaking fuel reduction projects, all divert time, effort and dollars away from fire prevention. NEPA, for example, requires the Forest Service to consider between six and nine alternatives for each treatment plan proposed, each costing approximately $2 million. These costs, along with the expense of appeals and lawsuits, typically consume 30 to 45 percent of the agency's budget earmarked for fire prevention.[11]

9. Kurtis Alexander, "Environmental Regulations Blamed for Compromising Fire Safety of Homeowners," *Santa Cruz Sentinel* (June 30, 2008). www.santacruzsentinel.com/fire/ci_9744744.

10. Michelle Malkin, "Wildfires and Environmental Obstructionism," *MichelleMalkin,com* (Oct. 23, 2007). http://michellemalkin.com/2007/10/23/wildfires-and-environmental-obstructionism/.

11. Dana Joel Gattuso, "Signs of New Growth in Forest Debate?" *National Policy Analysis* (Oct. 2003), www.national-center.org/NPA491.html. Gattuso cites Molly Villamana, "Forests," *Environment and Energy Daily* (July 25, 2003), and David Rogers, "Timber Rivals Rally in Name of Wildfires," *Wall Street Journal* (Aug. 11, 2003).

After one destructive forest fire, Forest Ranger Kate Klein said, "If we had done all the thinning we wanted to over the years, we could have kept this fire from exploding, and we could have saved the towns it burned through."[12]

In still other situations, developers acquire land to build residential or commercial buildings and then find that oppressive environmental regulations and lawsuits keep them from developing the land for many years and greatly increase their building costs. But this is their own land!

Michael H. Schill, dean of the UCLA Law School, wrote:

> Government rules requiring developers and/or public entities to undertake environmental impact analyses ... are likely to generate higher costs and lead to a diminished supply of housing for two reasons. First, the review itself and the possible resulting environmental impact statement could be very costly. Second, potential lawsuits from neighbors or environmental activists challenging the review could be even more problematic. In addition to assuming the costs of defending the case, the developer would have to factor into the project the costs of delay and settlement. In some instances, this uncertainty actually may deter builders from undertaking projects, thereby reducing the overall supply of housing and increasing price.[13]

In the Pacific Northwest the entire logging industry has been destroyed by environmental regulations regarding logging and species such as the spotted owl, and such regulations prevent owners from cutting down trees and taking lumber *from their own land!* In 1992 the National Center for Public Policy Research reported:

> Recovery efforts for the Pacific Northwest Spotted Owl will cost an estimated 50,000–100,000 timber industry jobs. In 1990, the Northwest's Spotted Owl was listed as a "threatened species" under the Endangered Species Act even though it is virtually indistinguishable from the California Spotted Owl—an owl in abundant supply. Since 1990, 100 wood products mills, employing some 8,000 workers, have been closed in the Pacific Northwest.[14]

Dick Hammer, vice president of A.L.R.T. Corporation, a timber, logging, road, and trucking company in Washington state, said, "It doesn't cause me any pain to cut down a tree because I know when I cut down a tree I am going to plant a number of trees to take its place."[15] But despite the fact that logging companies replace the trees they cut down, environmental regulations have put many of these companies out of business.

---

12. Kate Klein: quoted in Paul Trachtman, "Fire Fight," *Smithsonian* (Aug. 2003), 46.

13. Michael H. Schill, "Regulations and Housing Development: What We Know," *Cityscape: A Journal of Policy Development and Research* 8:1 (2005), 10. www.huduser.org/periodicals/cityscpe/vol8num1/ch1.pdf.

14. "It's Not Easy Being Green: Excessive Environmental Regulations Hurt Working Class Americans," *Talking Points on the Economy: Follies of Regulation #2*, National Center for Public Policy Research (Feb. 26, 1992). www.nationalcenter.org/TPRegulations.html.

15. Dick Hammer: Quoted in Richard Quest, "Environment Meets Politics Amid Firs," *CNN.com* (Aug. 13, 2004). http://edition.cnn.com/2004/ALLPOLITICS/08/13/quest.trees/.

Of course, I agree that we need some regulations to protect the environment from harmful and destructive uses. (One has only to travel to large cities in Third World countries to experience the human health costs of unrestrained pollution, for example.) The restrictions I am objecting to are not done for the benefit of human beings, however, but primarily to prevent *even the wise use of natural resources*. An attitude that disregards the importance of private property rights and sees all property as ultimately belonging to the state will demand excessive environmental regulations that ignore the substantial costs in terms of loss of personal freedom and the right to use one's own property for one's own benefit.

Another erosion of the right to private property came under President Clinton when he, by executive order, classified millions of acres of private property in the western United States as protected land that could not be bought or sold or developed. Under Executive Order 13061, then-President Clinton designated fourteen rivers—with the authorization to subsequently add ten rivers per year—as federal property—regardless of whether they ran through private property.[16] The same thing has already begun to happen under President Obama, with millions of additional acres of land being confiscated by Congress and effectively removed from private use forever.[17]

In all of these ways and many others, the federal government today is behaving in much the same way that Samuel warned that the king in Israel would behave when he acquired too much power: "He will *take*.... He will *take*.... He will *take*.... He will *take*" (see 1 Sam. 8:10–18; quoted above, p. 263).

Whenever government takes over private companies and private property in this way, more personal freedom is lost. The people who work in the company or live on the land increasingly become servants of the government, subject to the government's dictates and controls. Their freedom to do *as they think best* with their companies or their property is taken away.

If this happens to the health care system in the United States, for example, then private doctors, nurses, pharmacies, hospitals, medical labs, medical employees, and medical supply companies will essentially become employees of the federal government. In effect, they will become its servants, and a huge amount of human freedom will be lost.

The fundamental issue at stake in the battle for ownership of private property in a nation is the issue of human liberty—liberty to be free to choose how to obey God or disobey him in our roles as stewards of what he has entrusted to us. When the government takes over more and more of people's property, such liberty is increasingly forfeited.

B. ECONOMIC DEVELOPMENT

Government should promote healthy economic development in a nation.

Is it any part of a government's responsibility to seek to promote conditions that will lead to economic growth and development in a nation? Should governments seek to

---

16. Executive Order 13061. http://clinton6.nara.gov/1997/09/1997–09–11-executive-order–13061-on-american-heritage-rivers.html.

17. "Congress votes to expand wilderness in 9 states," Associated Press (March 26, 2009). www.usatoday.com/news/washington/legislative/house/2009–03–25-wilderness_N.htm?csp=34.

increase the standard of living and the annual per capita income in a nation? Or is that kind of thing just promoting a wrongful type of "materialism"?

I believe that government *should* promote economic growth in a nation. This is because one of the primary responsibilities of government is to act as God's servant to "do good" for the citizens of a nation (see Rom. 13:4) or, in the words of the US Constitution, to "promote the general welfare" of a nation (see discussion in chap. 3, pp. 80, 86–87).

Sometimes people assume that "Christians should not promote economic growth because that is materialism, and materialism is evil." But I disagree. I do not believe that economic growth *in itself* is morally evil or simply the result of wrongful "materialism." Nor do I believe that economic growth is something that is morally "neutral." Rather, I believe that economic growth is, in itself, morally good and part of what God intended in putting human beings on the earth. It is right that government should promote it.

One of God's original purposes for human beings was to make the earth productive:

> And God blessed them. And God said to them, "Be fruitful and multiply and fill the earth and *subdue it* and *have dominion* over the fish of the sea and over the birds of the heavens and over every living thing that moves on the earth" (Gen. 1:28).

The word translated "subdue" is the Hebrew term *kābash*, meaning "to subdue, dominate, bring into servitude or bondage." This same term is used of "subduing" the land of Canaan so it would serve and provide for the people of Israel (Num. 32:22, 29; Josh. 18:1) and of David "subduing" the nations that he conquered so that they would bring tribute to him (2 Sam. 8:11). This expression in God's original command to Adam and Eve implies that he wanted them to investigate, understand, use, and enjoy the resources of the earth. They were to do this as God's image-bearers and with thanksgiving to God.

This implies that *developing and producing more and better goods from the earth* is not simply a result of sin or greed or wrongful "materialism," but something that God planned for human beings to do from the beginning. It is an essential part of how he created us to function.

Throughout the rest of the Bible, one of God's blessings is the blessing of increased productivity from the earth, and one of his curses on people who sin is that he will hinder their productivity, make their work painfully laborious, and ultimately send famine on them when a desolate earth will not bear its fruit: "Cursed is the ground because of you; in *pain* you shall eat of it all the days of your life; *thorns and thistles* it shall bring forth for you.... By *the sweat of your face* you shall eat bread, till you return to the ground" (Gen. 3:17–19; see discussion in chap. 4, p. 122, and the curses promised in Deut. 28:15–68).

By contrast, God often promised to give material abundance as a blessing to those who trust and obey him:

> For the LORD your God is bringing you into a good land, a land of brooks of water ... a land of wheat and barley ... a land of olive trees and honey, a land in which *you will eat bread without scarcity,* in which *you will lack nothing....* And

you shall eat and be full, and you shall bless the LORD your God for the good land he has given you (Deut. 8:7–10; see also 11:10–17; 28:1–14).

In fact, some places in the prophets foretell a future time of even greater productivity with much material blessing (see Isa. 35:1–2; Joel 3:18). Greater productivity will accompany times of greater blessing from God.

Another indication that *material productivity is good* is found in the New Testament reminders to help the poor. These imply that poverty is not something desirable but something that we need to work to overcome (see Gal. 2:10; 1 John 3:17).

Jesus himself practiced his trade as a carpenter (see Mark 6:3) and Paul did the same as a tent maker (see Acts 18:3; 2 Thess. 3:7–8), thus showing that an occupation of producing and selling goods from the earth is not in itself "greedy" or "materialistic," but something that is right and pleasing in the sight of God.

The New Testament also looks forward to a time when the earth will be renewed and will regain an amazing productivity and the rich fruitfulness that it had in the garden of Eden before God placed a curse on the earth. Paul writes that "the creation itself will be set free from its bondage to decay and obtain the freedom of the glory of the children of God" (Rom. 8:21). Also, the book of Revelation contains pictures of the age to come that portray it as a time of immense material abundance beyond anything we can imagine (see Rev. 21:10–26).

To summarize: One of God's purposes for human beings from Genesis to Revelation has been that we should *produce useful things from the earth*—things that we *enjoy* and for which we therefore give thanks to God. Therefore material things are not in themselves "unspiritual," but are gifts from God. We can and should use them with a clear conscience and with thanksgiving to God for the things he has provided to us. "For everything created by God is good, and nothing is to be rejected if it is received with thanksgiving" (1 Tim. 4:4; cf. 6:17).

Of course, there are temptations that accompany the production and ownership of material goods (such as pride, envy, selfishness, lack of love for one's neighbor, and laziness from having excessive possessions). The greatest temptation is setting our hearts on material things rather than the God who gives them: "You cannot serve God and money" (Matt. 6:24). But these *temptations to sin* must not cause us to think that material goods are evil in themselves, and surely it is not evil but *good* for a nation to continually *increase* its production of goods and services, for this is what God intended human beings to do on the earth, and that is the only long-term solution to poverty in a nation.

It is not surprising, therefore, that God has created us with a strong internal desire to create, develop, and produce things from the earth, whether this happens in gardening or cooking or carpentry or car repairs or many other crafts and hobbies as well as in producing many manufactured products.

When the wealth of a nation increases, it becomes easier for people to fulfill many of God's other commands, such as raising children, spreading the Gospel at home and abroad, caring for those in need, building up the church, even meeting together as a church in a suitable building. Even though the Bible says that God has "chosen those who are poor in the world to be rich in faith" (James 2:5), it never encourages people to *seek* to be poor or to make others poor, but just the opposite: we should help and care for those who are poor (see Gal. 2:10; 1 John 3:17), and seek to help them come out of poverty.

Therefore there are many reasons why it is morally *right* for governments to seek to increase the economic productivity of a nation. It helps people fulfill one of the purposes for which God put us on the earth; it enables people more effectively to obey many other commands of Scripture; it enables people to fulfill the desire to be productive that God has put in their hearts; it enables people to work and support themselves and so obey New Testament commands (see 2 Thess. 3:6–12); it enables many people to overcome poverty for themselves; and it provides many opportunities for giving thanks to God.

C. THE MONEY SUPPLY

Government should establish and maintain an effective money supply for a nation.

The Bible never says that money is evil, but rather it says that "*the love of money* is the root of all kinds of evils" (1 Tim. 6:10).

Money in fact is *good in itself* because it enables people to buy the goods they need and sell the goods they produce on the basis of a standard item (money, such as an American dollar or a British pound or a Euro) on which everybody agrees about the value. If we didn't have money, we would have to barter with one another, exchanging eggs or bags of apples or other such things, and most modern business transactions would effectively become impossible. (How many eggs would you trade for a new car?)

But since very few people now are able to produce everything they need for themselves (only subsistence farmers in primitive societies do that), *we need money to buy and sell* and thus enjoy the benefits of things that other people produce. This is a wonderful process because it forces us into personal interactions with others in which friendship and a level of trust can be developed, and honesty and integrity can be demonstrated.

Thus, money is a *measure of value*, and money itself *carries value* until we use it to purchase something else of value.[18]

But who can provide people with the money they need to buy and sell things? The best solution is that the government of each nation should have a currency that is known and accepted and that has a standard value across the nation (such as a dollar in the United States, a peso in Mexico, or a pound in the United Kingdom).

Yet, in order for the system to work, *the value of a currency must remain stable over time*. To take an extreme example, imagine this: Let's say that a painter agrees to paint a room in my house for $200. One week later, he comes and paints the room, and I pay him $200. Everything works just fine if the value of $200 has remained the same. But in some countries, inflation changes the value of money and effectively changes the rules in the middle of the game.

---

18. See further discussion of the moral goodness of money in Grudem, *Business for the Glory of God,* 47–50.

For example, suppose that when I agreed to pay him $200 for painting my room, a loaf of bread cost $4 and a gallon of gas to drive the painter's truck cost $2. His monthly rent was $800. Knowing all this, he agreed to paint my room for $200. But after he made the agreement, suppose that unrestrained inflation set in, and the price of a loaf of bread went to $40 and then to $400! A gallon of gas all of a sudden would cost $200, and his rent would cost $80,000 per month!

Some examples of terrible hyperinflation include:

Hungary—July 1946: 207% daily inflation rate. Prices would double within 15 hours.

Zimbabwe—November 2008: 98% daily inflation rate. Prices would double within 24.7 hours.

Yugoslavia—January 1994: 64.6% daily inflation rate. Prices would double within 1.4 days.

Germany—October 1923: 20.9% daily inflation rate. Prices would double within 3.7 days.

Greece—October 1944: 17.9% daily inflation rate. Prices would double within 4.3 days.

China—May 1949: 11% daily inflation rate. Prices would double within 6.7 days.[19]

When inflation like this occurs, then I might still pay the painter the $200 that I agreed on, but instead of buying fifty loaves of bread, it won't even buy him one loaf of bread! The government allowed the rules to change in the middle of the game, and all of a sudden *everybody is robbed* of the value of the money they have worked for. No one will want to make contracts anymore because no one will know what a dollar will be worth in a week or two or a month. The entire economic system will break down, and people will be reduced to bartering with precious metals or jewelry or other such things. Inflation like this will absolutely destroy an economy and a nation.

If inflation occurs at 10 or 15% a year, people might not notice it quite so abruptly, but the sinister, destructive effects will still be felt. They are still being robbed of 15% of the value of their money and their contracts each year! Therefore it is necessary for good governments to maintain a relatively stable currency over time.[20] This can even be understood as an issue of fairness. (That is, will people who make future commitments be treated fairly in the value they have agreed on to buy or sell something?) It can also be seen as an issue of truthfulness in the economic system as a whole. (That is, can people depend on the fact that "one dollar" in an agreement will truthfully reflect the value that they reasonably expected "one dollar" to have in the future?)

---

19. Steve H. Hanke and Alex K. F. Kwok, "On the Measurement of Zimbabwe's Hyperinflation." *Cato Journal* 29:2 (Spring/Summer 2009). www.cato.org/pubs/journal/cj29n2/cj29n2–8.pdf.

20. I say "relatively stable" because many economists would say that a moderate rate of inflation (such as 2 or 3% per year) is characteristic of a healthy, growing economy where productivity is increasing by about that much each year. But my concern here is inflation substantially in excess of that amount.

To put it another way, the *value of a currency* is the *standard* by which business trans-actions are evaluated, something like the "weights and measures" that a merchant would use in a transaction. But if the value of a currency is constantly fluctuating, there is no dependable standard by which people can evaluate what they are buying and selling. Therefore this verse in Proverbs is appropriate:

> Unequal weights and unequal measures are both alike an abomination to the
> Lord (Prov. 20:10).

To conclude: Government should establish and maintain an effective money supply for a nation, and that means one in which the value of the currency is relatively stable over time.

What causes excessive inflation? An excessive increase in the money supply in a nation. (In the United States this would be an increase in the total number of dollars in the economy.) To illustrate this, imagine some people playing the board game *Monopoly*. Let's say that most of the property has been sold and several players are bidding for the property "Atlantic Avenue," trying to get the player who has it to sell it. Tom looks at the cash he has and offers $1,200, Dick offers $1,250, and Harry offers $1,100 now and $200 more after he passes "Go." But now imagine that some outside authority (like a parent) comes along and suddenly doubles the amount of money each player has! All at once the bids go up: Tom might offer $2,400, and Dick $2,500, and Harry $2,200 plus $200 for the next two times he passes "Go"! The money supply in their "country" doubled, and Atlantic Avenue was still for sale, so all of a sudden the offered price doubled!

Inflation happened because the money supply increased excessively. This process gave rise to Nobel Prize-winning economist Milton Friedman's classic dictum, "Infla-tion is always and everywhere a monetary phenomenon."[21]

For this reason, the monetary policies of the Federal Reserve Board under the first few months of the Obama administration in 2009 were troubling. They decided to pump reserves into the financial system by purchasing $1.2 trillion in assets, including $750 billion in mortgage-backed securities from companies like Fannie Mae and Freddie Mac.[22] Banks then had huge amounts of additional money in their reserves. While such bank reserves are *not yet* part of the money supply, narrowly defined,[23] they are counted as part of what is called "the monetary base" and can be turned into new money added to the economy through future bank lending. The current level of the money supply was $8.5 trillion in January 2010,[24] so this increase in bank reserves is ready to become a 14% or more jump in the money supply when the economy starts to recover and banks are able to use these funds to increase their lending.[25] This is why Ben Bernanke, the Federal Reserve chairman, recently had to explain to Congress his "exit strategy":

---

21. Milton Friedman. *Money Mischief: Episodes in Monetary History* (Boston: Houghton-Mifflin/Mariner Books), 104.

22. Neil Irwin, "Fed to Pump $1.2 Trillion into Markets," *Washington Post* (March 19, 2009). www.washingtonpost.com/wp-dyn/content/article/2009/03/18/AR2009031802283.html?hpid=topnews.

23. The Federal Reserve defines the money supply as "M2," which includes currency, bank deposits, and money mar-ket mutual funds. See footnote 2 in www.federalreserve.gov/releases/h6/current/h6.htm.

24. Federal Reserve H6 release, www.federalreserve.gov/releases/h6/current/h6.htm.

25. The increase in the money supply would be more than 14% if the money multiplier comes into play, which is when banks lend out the same dollar more than once, knowing that these dollars will generally not all be used at the same time.

In due course, however, as the expansion matures the Federal Reserve will need to begin to tighten monetary conditions to prevent the development of inflationary pressures.... Although at present the U.S. economy continues to require the support of highly accommodative monetary policies, at some point the Federal Reserve will need to tighten financial conditions by raising short-term interest rates and reducing the quantity of bank reserves outstanding.[26]

But will the Federal Reserve do this and put the brakes on economic growth when it begins to heat up? With such record-setting government expenditures made in 2009 and projected for 2010 and later, the temptation will be simply to finance this government spending by pumping more and more dollars into the system, leading to increased inflation and thereby robbing everyone in society of the value of their dollars and their contracts. And out-of-control government spending promotes this behavior.

Richard Rahn, a senior fellow at the Cato Institute and chairman of the Institute for Global Economic Growth, wrote:

What is particularly frightening is that neither political party has offered a serious plan to defuse the debt bomb. The Democrats are just piling up more debt as if there were no limit, and the Republicans, to date, are only proposing measures to reduce the increase, rather than reverse it. When the debt bomb explodes—within the next one to three years—expect to see record high interest rates and/or inflation, coupled with the collapse of many "entitlements." It will be like the neutron bomb, the buildings will be left standing, but the people will not.[27]

Such irresponsible spending is morally wrong because it is theft—it is robbing our children and grandchildren for generations to come. A biblical view of government would demand that politicians take responsibility for this problem today, no matter who created it. "The wicked borrows but does not pay back" (Ps. 37:21). Voters need to demand that nations, like families, must live within their means.

D. FREE MARKETS AND REGULATION

All modern societies have come to agree that we need some government regulations to prevent fraud and injustice in business transactions. It is necessary, for example, for government to enforce contracts (so that people have to keep the agreements they make). And it is necessary for governments to impose some health and safety standards on the sale of medicines and foods or other products such as bicycles and cars. It is necessary for government to enforce health and cleanliness regulations on public restaurants. And some government regulation is necessary for weights and measures, so that the gasoline pump really does put one gallon of gasoline in my car when one gallon registers on the

26. Testimony of Chairman Ben S. Bernanke before the Committee on Financial Services, US House of Representatives, Washington, DC (Feb. 10, 2010). www.federalreserve.gov/news-events/testimony/bernanke20100210a.htm.

27. Richard W. Rahn, "The Growing Debt Bomb," Cato Institute (Sept. 22, 2009). www.cato.org/pub_display.php?pub_id=10563.

dial, and so that a gallon of milk really does contain one gallon of milk. Such regulations and others like them are necessary because it would simply be impractical, if not impossible, for individuals to attempt to check all such things for themselves before buying an item. (Therefore I differ with "libertarian" views of government that make human freedom of choice their ultimate standard of good rather obedience to God's moral principles in the Bible, and fail adequately to recognize that governments should do "good" for people [Rom. 13:4], not merely protect their freedom.)

For similar reasons, most people in modern societies would also agree that it works well for government to provide certain other goods that nearly everyone uses, such as roads, traffic regulation, supporting an army and police force and a fire department, and perhaps a postal service.

But beyond that point there is a large difference of opinion. Some people favor a "free market" approach to the rest of the economy, while others think a "socialist" system is preferable (where the government owns and controls most of the businesses and factories, what economists call the "means of production"). Still others have argued that a "communist" system is better (where the government owns and controls not only the means of production but also all property, so that there is no private ownership of property even for homes or apartment buildings or farms, but all is owned by the government).

In 2009 this question came up in many areas: Should the federal government own the US banking system and control every detail of it? Should the federal government run the nation's entire health care system? Should it run automakers General Motors and Chrysler, as it apparently began to do in April and May 2009? Should it begin to set wage levels for everyone in the banking and financial service industries, as the Obama administration seemed to suggest in mid-May of 2009?[28]

Several factors support the idea that the *free market* is almost always a better way of solving an economic problem than government ownership or control.

(1) The Bible's teaching on the role of government gives support to the idea of a free market rather than socialism or communism. This is because nothing in the Bible's teachings on the role of government would give the government warrant to take over ownership or control of private businesses, which would have included farms and traders and small shops in the ancient world. (See discussion of government in chap. 3, pp. 77–82, 86–87.) The government is to punish evil and reward those who do good and enforce order in society. It is not to own the property or businesses of a nation.

(2) The Bible gives repeated warnings against a ruler who would use his power to "take" what rightfully belongs to the people, including their fields and vineyards, for example (see discussion above, pp. 86–87). These are the ancient parallels to modern factories and companies.

(3) The Bible's teaching about private property indicates that property rightfully belongs to individual people, not to the government (and businesses are one form of property). (See discussion of private property above, pp. 261–68.)

28. "U.S. Eyes Bank Pay Overhaul," *Wall Street Journal* (May 13, 2009), 81.

(4) The Bible's emphasis on the value of human liberty (see above, pp. 91–95) also argues for a free market system rather than a socialist or communist system. A free market allows *individuals* to choose where they work, what they buy, how they run a business, and how they spend their money. But a government-controlled economy makes these decisions for people rather than allowing people freedom to make them for themselves.

(5) History demonstrates time and again that the free market brings better results than a government-controlled economy or government control of any section of the economy.

Here is what I mean by a free market:

> A wonderful, God-given process in human societies through which the goods and services that are *produced* by the society (supply) continually adjust to exactly match the goods and services that are *wanted* by the society (demand) at each period of time, and through which the society assigns a measurable value to each good and service at each period of time, entirely through the free choices of every individual person in the society rather than through government control. (But this process needs some government regulation to prevent wrongdoing such as theft, fraud, and breaking of contracts.)

The better results of a free market are seen in several ways:

(a) A free market is better than government control at producing goods and services. The economic "goods" that the free market produces are of better quality, at a lower price, and are the goods that people *actually want* rather than the goods that some government agency tells them they *should* want. This can be seen by numerous examples in recent history.

In 1985–86 I spent an academic year doing research and writing in England, and near the end of that time our family traveled to several countries in Europe. We made a point of crossing from West Berlin to East Berlin because I wanted my children (who were twelve, nine, and six) to see the difference between a free market economy and a state-controlled communist economy. West Berlin was prosperous, energetic, bright, modern, and teeming with all sorts of evidence of economic prosperity everywhere you looked. But as soon as we crossed the Berlin Wall (which was still there at that time) we entered into a gloomy world of brown and gray buildings, empty streets, and colorless shops with little to offer the East German people. It looked as if the life had been drained out of the city. The people were trapped in poverty. That was why they had to build the Berlin Wall—to keep people from leaving East Berlin.

What was the difference? The only difference was the economic system. Both halves of the city were filled with German people from the same ethnic and cultural and linguistic background. But one half had fallen under communist control at the end of World War II, and the other half had remained free.

We saw the same contrast a year later when we took a bus from Helsinki, Finland, to Leningrad (now St. Petersburg), Russia. The bus ride took only four hours (and part of that was spent at the border crossing), because the two cities are in the same geographic region of the world. The markets in Helsinki were brimming with an abundance of beautiful fruits and vegetables and meats produced by a free market economy. In Leningrad we wandered through the stores and saw rows of the same style of drab brown winter coat that no one wanted but had been produced in excess. We watched as women lifted up one milk bottle after another, hoping to find one that had not gone sour. We saw nearly empty shelves with a few cans of canned vegetables produced by a government cooperative with no competition from other brands, no incentive to produce quality goods, and no incentive to produce what people really wanted to buy. People's faces appeared to be drained of hope or any joy in life. Helsinki and Leningrad had the same climate, and both had access to the shipping lanes in the Baltic Sea, but one city was wealthy and the other was poor. Why? Because government control destroys economic productivity.

(b) A free market allows people freedom to work at the jobs they choose (rather than being assigned to a job by the government) and encourages people to get better training for the jobs they seek and to perform better when they know they will be rewarded for better quality work. All of this provides much greater job satisfaction.

(c) A free market gives an employer the benefit of being free *to hire* the employees that he or she thinks are best-suited for the job, and *not* to hire (or else to fire) those whose work is not providing adequate value to the company. This process improves the economic productivity of individual businesses and the nation as a whole.

(d) A free market offers the great benefit of consumer satisfaction by producing the goods and services that people actually want.

(e) A free market—unlike any government agency, no matter how large—is able to have enough information to predict accurately the economic wants of millions of people at any day in the future and then to plan effectively to meet those wants. The free market does this by itself, without anybody overseeing it, because decisions are made according to the "feet on the ground" instincts and experience of many thousands of people, each using the accumulated wisdom gained by trial and error over many years to decide how many eggs or gallons of milk will be purchased at each corner grocery store for each day of the year. If stores buy too much, they waste money and the product spoils. If they buy too little, they lose potential sales and waste their investment in empty shelf space, and they find that customers won't return to a store that does not have what they came for. But—with no direction from any government planning committee—somehow it all works! In a free market economy, the successful corner stores know how to order the right amount.

Day and night, year after year, dozens of delivery trucks come and go, supplying each convenience store, restaurant, gas station, and department store with *just enough* of each product to meet consumer demand in that neighborhood for that day. It happens tens of thousands of times every day in every city in a free market society. But how does it happen? *Nobody* tells all these suppliers and shop owners how much they should order or deliver. If we could observe this process for just one local convenience store from the air, it would seem nearly miraculous. No person or government agency or planning board directs all this activity, yet it all gets done!

Another example of the amazing working of the free market system can be seen even in a manufactured product as simple as a lead pencil. Consider the thousands of individual decisions that had to be made (in logging companies, rubber factories, paint companies, graphite factories, trucking firms, and so forth) in order to produce this pencil, and yet it happened with no central planning agency and no government control ordering it to be produced. Yet I can walk into any grocery store in the United States and buy a yellow pencil with a rubber eraser at the end, and I think nothing of it. The free market has anticipated my needs and provided for those needs (and thousands of other needs), all without any central direction. It "just happened" because the individuals who produce, supply, and sell these pencils have found that it is in their self-interest to estimate accurately and then provide for the economic wants of each segment of the population at each time of the year—and those who do it best are in the companies that best survive and thrive economically. They seek their own self-interests, but in a free market that is achieved by best providing for the interests of others.

(6) Application to current controversies:

As indicated above, several principles of the Bible as well as the superior results indicate that the free market is a much better solution than government control for many controversial areas of policy today. A government-controlled automobile industry would produce more and more cars that few people want to buy and would fail to produce other cars that consumers really want. (This will be evident when the government has to add large cash "rebates" or tax benefits to people who buy the government-mandated small, high-mileage cars or poorly made cars—essentially paying people a lot of money to buy a car they would not otherwise choose.) Such a policy of government-run companies failing to be sensitive to consumer demand will also shift people toward buying the cars they actually want from foreign companies, even if they have to pay more. The government will then respond by slapping huge tariffs on foreign cars, again denying consumer choice and attempting to force people either to spend much more or to buy cars they don't want.

Similarly, a government-controlled health care system would fail to provide enough of the services that people want, leading to the rationing of health care by which some government agencies would determine which kinds of patients are eligible to receive various kinds of care, and leading also to long waits for certain services (as is seen in the government-run health care systems of Canada or England, for example).

Governmental distortions of the free market mean that market prices are no longer a good signal of consumer demands or producer supplies. Therefore supply and demand will not match, and the market will not naturally "clear." Overproduction and waste of some things and underproduction and rationing of other things necessarily result. Both waste and rationing are very costly to an economy. Waste costs the public more tax dollars and the freedom to spend those dollars, since they have to pay for the government-caused waste. Rationing costs the public more time and personal freedom, as people have to wait on a list rather than be able to purchase the things they want or need.

E. THE RICH AND THE POOR

1. Government and the rich

Today I often hear comments in the media—or in conversation with people—that simply *assume* that rich people have somehow gotten their wealth unjustly, so it is right for government to take some of their wealth from them. This is seen in remarks such as, "It is time for folks like me who make more than $250,000 to pay our fair share"[29]—a comment by Barack Obama during the 2008 campaign that simply *assumes* (without argument) that whatever "fair" is, it must somehow be *more taxes* than what rich people are currently paying! Or people might say things like, "They can afford it," or "It won't hurt them."

But the Bible does not reflect this kind of thinking, nor is there any suggestion that governments have the right to take money from wealthy people *simply because they are wealthy*.

The emphasis in the Bible is on treating both rich and poor *fairly and justly*. If they have done wrong, they should be penalized, but if they have not done wrong, they should not be punished.

In some places the Bible warns against treating the poor unjustly: "You shall not pervert the justice *due to your poor* in his lawsuit" (Exod. 23:6). But at other times it warns against favoring the poor (and thus presumably having a bias against those who are rich): "Nor shall you be partial *to a poor man* in his lawsuit" (Exod. 23:3).

The question is not whether someone is rich or poor, but whether someone has done good or evil. It is wrong to punish those who have not done evil:

> To impose a fine on *a righteous man* is not good, nor to strike the noble for their uprightness (Prov. 17:26).

This is consistent with what the Bible teaches about the proper role of government: "to punish those who do evil and to praise those who do good" (1 Peter 2:14).

Of course, there are some wealthy people in the world who do evil. There are also middle-class people who do evil, and there are poor people who do evil. Wealth or poverty do not by themselves accurately indicate the morality of a person's conduct in society.

Those who break the law should be punished by the government, whether they are rich or poor or somewhere in between. But it is unfair—and contrary to the teaching of Scripture—to stereotype all rich people as "evil" or "probably evil," or to assume that they have somehow exploited other people and made their money in unjust ways.

Rather than thinking about "the rich" as a vague category to be viewed with suspicion, it might help to think of *specific wealthy people* and ask whether we think they have done something evil to get their money. (Perhaps readers now can actually think of someone who is wealthy in their own church or community, as a concrete example.) As I write this, I am thinking of three or four people whom I have known in Christian circles and are "wealthy." Yet, in every case they seem to spend most of their time doing good for other people, and they are men of high integrity who would not consciously or willfully do anything wrong.

In March 2009, *Forbes* magazine published a list of all 793 billionaires in the world, including photos and a bit more information about the top twenty. Do we really want to think of these people as evil? Here are some of their names, with a number indicating where they rank among the wealthiest people in the world: (1) Bill Gates, Microsoft

---

29. William McGurn, "For Obama, Taxes Are about Fairness," *Wall Street Journal* (Aug. 19, 2008). http://online.wsj.com/article/SB121910117767951201.html?mod=todays_columnists.

Corporation; (2) Warren Buffet, Berkshire Hathaway (including many companies such as GEICO Insurance); (4) Larry Ellison, Oracle Corporation (producer of software for managing databases for business); (5) Ingvar Kamprad, Sweden, Ikea Stores (discount furniture); (6) Karl Albrecht, Germany, Aldi Supermarkets (discount food stores); (9) Theo Albrecht, Germany, Trader Joe's (grocery store chain); (11) Jim Walton, Wal-Mart; (12) S. Robson Walton, Wal-Mart; (13) Alice Walton, Wal-Mart; (14) Christy Walton, Wal-Mart.[30]

As I looked at this list, I realized that I have helped make many of these people rich! I have bought many Microsoft computer programs. I have bought automobile insurance for many years from GEICO. My wife and I shop at Trader Joe's from time-to-time. And we shop at Wal-Mart.

Do I think that these people have gotten rich by "exploiting" other people or violating the law in some way? No. I think they have become wealthy by providing products and services that people want at a good price and with reliable quality. They have competed in the free market, and consumers have wanted more and more of their products, and they have become wealthy.

So what do I think of Bill Gates, who in 2008 had $58 billion in net worth? I think that consumers around the world have decided that Microsoft's products are worth $58 billion more than it cost Gates to produce them, so he ended up with that much wealth. By "voting" with their dollars, consumers have said that Bill Gates *added $58 billion of value to the world* with his software.

Or what do I think of the four members of the Walton family who together have a net worth of $70.6 billion? I think that shows that 200 million customers in 7,200 Wal-Mart stores have collectively "voted" freely to say that the Wal-Mart family has *provided them with value that is $70 billion greater than what it cost the Waltons* to purchase these goods to sell. Without any compulsion from anyone, but in a free market system, the Waltons have "added value" to the world in the amount of more than $70 billion, and this is in addition to all the 1.1 million jobs that Wal-Mart provides.[31] Wal-Mart has also supported millions of other employees of the companies who *made* the products that are sold at Wal-Mart. Have the Waltons done "evil" by finding quality goods and selling them at lower prices than others were doing? It seems to me that they have done something *good* for society, and everyone who shops at Wal-Mart is "voting with dollars" in agreement with that evaluation. (Some people object that Wal-Mart drives smaller stores out of business, but those who make this objection fail to take account of the benefit to *the whole society* that comes when *everybody* can buy goods for less money and therefore have more of their own money left over. *Every* consumer benefits from this, because of the downward pressure on prices. If people want to shop at smaller, more expensive stores that provide more personal service, they are free to do so—and sometimes I do that!—but they should not try to force everyone to spend their money that way.)

What should we think about the rich, and how should it affect our ideas about the role of government? My conclusion is that most rich people today got their money fairly

---

30. "The World's Billionaires," *Forbes* (March 11, 2009). www. forbes.com/2009/03/11/worlds-richest-people-billionaires–2009-billionaires_land.html.

31. Lorrie Grant, "Retail Giant Wal-Mart Faces Challenges on Many Fronts," *USA Today* (Nov. 10, 2003). www.usatoday.com/money/industries/retail/2003–11–10-walmart_x.htm.

and honestly, and government has no inherent right to take it from them *unless it can be shown that they got it through criminal activity of some sort*. We should not immediately assume that "the rich" are evil.

What about the attitude that says that money should be taken from the rich because "they can afford it" or because "it won't hurt them"? The teaching of the Bible is this: "You shall not steal" (Exod. 20:15). It is not right to steal from the poor, nor is it right to steal from the rich. If I were ever to visit the home of Bill Gates and see a few dollar bills lying out in some room, *it would still be wrong* in the sight of God to steal even one dollar from the $58 billion that Gates owns. It does not matter one bit whether I might think "he can afford it" or "it won't hurt him," because the dollar *belongs to him*, not to me. It is his property. It would be morally wrong to take the dollar, because God says, "You shall not steal."

2. Government and economic equality

Should it be the rule of government to "take from the rich and give to the poor"? Should government try to equalize the amount of income or possessions that people have, or at least take actions that move in the direction of equality?

Before answering that question directly, I need to make clear that I think there is some need for government-supported welfare programs *to help cases of urgent need* (for example, to provide a "safety net" to keep people from going hungry or without clothing or shelter).

I also think it is appropriate for government to provide enough funding so that everyone is able *to gain enough skills and education to earn a living*. So with regard to some basic necessities of life (food, clothing, shelter, and some education) I think it is right for government to "take from everybody else and give to the poor." Such assistance can be provided from general tax revenues.

Those convictions are based on the purpose of government *to promote the general well-being of the society,* or as the US Constitution says in its preface, "to promote the general welfare." That includes enabling every citizen to live adequately in the society. It is not based on any vague instinct that it would be "more just" to reduce the differences between rich and poor.

But apart from those basic requirements for government, I cannot find any justification in Scripture for thinking that government, as a matter of policy, should attempt to take from the rich and give to the poor. I do not think that government has the responsibility or the right to attempt to equalize the differences between rich and poor in a society. When it attempts to do so, significant harm is done to the economy and to the society.

In a free society, with no government confiscation of wealth, the amount of money that people earn will vary widely. This is because people have different abilities, different interests, and different levels of economic ambition. Only a very few people are able to become skilled surgeons or highly paid professional athletes or write best-selling novels or invent some amazing new computer software or start a small business and lead it to become highly profitable. Therefore, *if people are free from government intervention*, some will become very wealthy, others will have a comfortable level of income, and some will remain relatively poor. If the economic system is relatively free, and if people are allowed to be paid fairly for the different kinds of work they do, this is simply going to happen.

And even if, through some kind of social experiment, everyone in some city were given $100,000 cash to start with, after a few weeks some would have spent it all, some would have saved most of it, and some would have invested it in activities that would produce more income. After a few months there would be significant inequalities all over again. This is inevitable as long as people are allowed to be free.

If such an experiment continued, how could any government force people to have equal amounts of possessions? Only by continually redistributing money over and over again each year, taking from those who have been most frugal and most productive, and giving to those who have been least productive or who have simply wasted their money. In other words, equality of possessions could not be maintained apart from *penalizing good habits* (hard work, productivity, frugality) and *rewarding bad habits* (profligate spending, wastefulness, frittering time on unproductive activities). The longer such "redistribution of wealth" continued in this hypothetical city, the more the productive people would just decide to give up (for they cannot enjoy the fruits of their labor) and the society would spiral downward into poverty and despair.

It works in the same way, but to a lesser degree, when government attempts to equalize differences in *income* levels (rather than total possessions). Governments can use their power to *impose* income equality on a population, but wherever this happens, it is brought about through severe restrictions on human freedom, and the result is to trap most of the nation in the "equality" of poverty.

Another result of attempting to impose economic equality on a nation is that, if people are made equal in their *economic possessions*, they will inevitably be unequal in terms of *political power* and government-allocated *privilege*. This has been seen historically in communist countries such as the former Soviet Union, where high-ranking political officials had access to limousines, fancier homes, and opportunities for vacations on the Baltic Sea that were not available to anyone else. They could also buy desirable Western goods through private channels to which only they had access. If *economic inequality* is removed, it is simply replaced by any *inequality in privilege* and vast benefits that come from high political power.

The conclusion is that it should not be the role of government to attempt to equalize income or possessions among people in a society.

3. Government and poverty

Several verses in the Bible command people to help the poor. For example:

> At present, however, I am going to Jerusalem *bringing aid to the saints*. For Macedonia and Achaia have been pleased to make some contribution for the poor among the saints at Jerusalem (Rom. 15:25–26; see also 2 Cor. 8–9).

> Only, they asked us *to remember the poor*, the very thing I was eager to do (Gal. 2:10).

But if anyone has the world's goods and sees *his brother in need*, yet closes his heart against him, how does God's love abide in him? (1 John 3:17).

Therefore it is right for Christians to do what they can to help those who are poor. Yet I am surprised to discover that few people seem to realize that these verses say *nothing* about civil government overcoming individual citizens' poverty! In fact, I do not think there is any passage in Scripture that justifies the idea that *government* has the right to *compel* rich people to help the poor or to "take from the rich and give to the poor," apart from using general tax revenue (from all taxpayers) to provide for very basic needs (see discussion above, p. 281).

But we must remember that such government handouts of money are *never* going to solve the problem of poverty. These handouts simply have to be repeated month after month and year after year, and the recipients are still poor. The only long-term solution to poverty comes when people have enough skills and discipline to get *economically productive jobs* and keep them.

The government itself cannot provide people with economically productive jobs (except for some government-funded jobs such as police and fire protection, the military, highway maintenance, and teachers in the educational system). By far the largest number of *economically productive jobs*—jobs that actually contribute something new of value to a society—are found in the private sector, in the business world. Someone working for a bakery bakes new loaves of bread each day and creates that amount of new wealth in the society. Someone working in an automobile factory creates new automobiles and thus adds economic wealth to the society. In the service industries, a plumber repairs a leaky faucet and thereby adds the value of one working faucet to the society. A landscaper trims trees and bushes and adds the aesthetic value of beautiful trees and bushes to the society. In this way, *every successful business gives people economically productive jobs* for which they are paid, and in that way it contributes value to the society. The poor person working at such a job is paid according to that added value, and thus begins to climb out of poverty.

This is what should happen, for God intends people to be economically productive. He put Adam in the garden of Eden "to work it and keep it" (Gen. 2:15) before there was any sin or evil in the world, which shows that the need to work in a productive way is an essential part of how God created us as human beings. Therefore Paul could command the church in Thessalonica to "work with your hands, as we instructed you, so that you may live properly before outsiders and be dependent on no one" (1 Thess. 4:11–12). He also said, "If anyone is not willing to work, let him not eat" (2 Thess. 3:10). God actually created us with a need for food to survive, at least in part because this provides an incentive to regular work: "A worker's appetite works for him; his mouth urges him on" (Prov. 16:26).

Therefore, for those who desire to help the poor and overcome the problem of poverty, their *primary goal* should *not* be to increase and prolong government handouts of money to those who are poor, but to provide incentives and appropriate conditions for privately owned businesses to grow and thrive and thus provide the jobs that will be the only long-term solution to poverty and the only way for the poor to gain the dignity and self-respect that comes from supporting themselves.

It is important, therefore, that government not hinder the development and profitability of businesses, but rather encourage them. Such encouragement would include a free market with a functioning price system that will guide the allocation of resources, a stable system of money, and a government that effectively punishes crime, enforces contracts, enforces patent laws and copyrights, and documents and protects private ownership of property. It would also include a fair court system that is not partial to the rich or poor, or to the powerful or the weak. Relatively low levels of taxation, an effective educational system, and a trustworthy banking system, are also needed. When such factors are implemented by governments, then businesses can grow and thrive and provide the jobs that alone will lift people permanently out of poverty.

F. GOVERNMENT AND BUSINESS

As explained above, businesses should be encouraged and not penalized by government. This is because private businesses are the primary creator of wealth and productive jobs in a society. Businesses continue producing goods year after year and continue providing jobs and paying wages year after year.

Because businesses need to compete with one another to produce better goods at lower prices, the competitive free market *continually rewards those who improve their productivity and the quality of their products, while keeping their prices low.* Thus, economically beneficial activity is encouraged and rewarded in a free market economy.

Unfortunately, too many Christians in contemporary society are suspicious of economic competition. They think it is somehow "unspiritual" or "unchristian." I do not agree with that at all. Competition is simply a system that encourages people to strive for excellence in their work. Even people who say they dislike competition still encourage it by shopping for less expensive places to buy the same product or through buying the healthier strawberries and tomatoes at a farmer's market. In doing this, they are encouraging the more efficient, more effective farmer who produces a higher quality of product. People who read *Consumer Reports* to find the best brand of computer or washing machine or bicycle are also encouraging competition, because they are looking for a higher quality product that is a "best buy," that is, one produced at a more economical price. Therefore even those who say they dislike competition continually support it by their shopping habits! If Christians are going to be good stewards of their money, they have to act in ways that support healthy economic competition.

But the competition of the free market that continually improves products and prices is far different from what government does. Whatever government does, it is the only government in power at that time, and therefore it has a monopoly, both on the ability to collect taxes and on the ability to require people to buy its goods. (The US Postal Service is a government monopoly, for example, for the delivery of first class mail.)

Because government does not have to compete for customers, government in general is a poor creator of wealth in an economy. In fact, it is difficult to think of any goods or services that a government might produce that could not be produced better by private companies.[32]

G. TAXES

1. Does government have the right to collect taxes?

Taxes were a controversy even in Jesus' day. Some of Jesus' enemies came and asked him, "Is it lawful to pay taxes to Caesar, or not?" (Matt. 22:17). But Jesus, taking a denarius (a common coin) and noting that Caesar's likeness was on it, said, "Therefore *render to Caesar the things that are Caesar's*, and to God the things that are God's" (Matt. 22:21). Jesus thus endorsed the legitimacy of paying taxes to a civil government, for the coin that he held had Caesar's inscription and that coin was used for paying the tax (see v. 19).

Paul also told the Christians in Rome that the civil authority "is the servant of God" and then said,

> For the same reason you *also pay taxes*, for the authorities are ministers of God, attending to this very thing. *Pay to all what is owed to them: taxes to whom taxes are owed*, revenue to whom revenue is owed, respect to whom respect is owed, honor to whom honor is owed (Rom. 13:6–7).

Therefore it is right to pay taxes to the civil government, and it is right for government to collect taxes to carry out its responsibilities (including the provision of basic needs to those who are poor).

But as I explained above, it does not seem to me that the Bible gives any support for the idea that governments should use taxes simply to redistribute income from the "rich" to the "poor." The Bible's teachings about the purpose of civil government, about private property, and about economic productivity do not support this idea. Such redistribution of income (which is different from basic support of the very poor) is not part of punishing evil and rewarding good, and it is not part of impartially enforcing justice; rather, it is carrying out an additional social agenda that the Bible does not support.

2. Should tax rates be high or low in an economy?

Taxes are a powerful tool that can either help or hinder economic growth. They also have enormous effect on individual lives, and tax rates can either significantly hinder or significantly help individual liberty within a nation.

This is seen if we take the two extremes that are possible. If the tax rate is 0%, then the government has no money to support its functions, and it cannot carry out its responsibilities. On the other hand, if the tax rate is 100%, then government controls all economic life, and no one has freedom to invest or build or create anything, or even to give to others. So the proper solution is somewhere in between.

---

32. I realize of course that some services and products needed by the entire society are best provided by government, such as the judicial system, the enforcement of laws, police departments, national defense, and roads and highways. These are not ordinary consumer goods.

But every increase in taxes takes away that much more human freedom. If my taxes increase by $100, then I have $100 less to buy some new shoes or clothing, to take my wife to a movie or restaurant, to give to some missions program at my church, to buy books for additional research, to send as a gift to my children, or to do any of a thousand other things. My *freedom* to decide what to do with that $100 has been taken from me when the government collects another $100 in tax.

So it is every time that taxes increase: A little more freedom—another small portion of everyone's life—has been taken away by the government.

Now let's say that the government taxes me $100 and then *gives me back some kind* of benefit. Perhaps it subsidizes a public transit system so that I get a cheaper ride on the train. Or perhaps it decides to give additional welfare payments to those beneath the poverty line, so that I get the benefit of knowing that my society is helping a poor person. Or perhaps the government uses the money to build a new bridge on a new highway somewhere in Missouri; then (if I ever travel to Missouri) I get the benefit of being able to drive on that new bridge. But in all these cases *the choice of what to do with that $100 has been taken away from me,* and the choice has been made for me by the government. I have lost that much freedom.

In addition, governments all over the world are notorious for waste and inefficiency. Even if a government promises to give $100 in benefits for the $100 in increased taxes, I know that a good share of that $100—maybe $50 or so!—will go to pay numerous government employees who don't have to compete in the free market, so the society will never get back the same amount of value that it would have received if people had been free to spend the $100 for themselves and to watch carefully how it was spent.

3. The benefit of lower taxes

Several economic studies have demonstrated that when a government lowers its tax rates, it actually ends up collecting more money! How can this be? It is because the lower tax rates bring economic benefits in the following way:

(1) When tax rates are lowered, this encourages businesses to invest and grow.
(2) This provides more jobs and lower prices, both of which are beneficial for the economy, and both of which encourage overall economic growth.
(3) As the economy grows, businesses and individuals earn higher incomes.
(4) These higher incomes are taxed at the lower tax rate, but *more* tax money still flows into the government coffers because people are paying taxes on so much more income.

For example, if in 2009 Mr. Smith earned $80,000 and paid 25% in taxes, he would pay $20,000 in taxes. But if the tax rate drops to 20%, it provides an incentive for businesses to invest and grow, and people also work harder, knowing they can keep more of their money. Then perhaps in 2010 Mr. Smith's income will be $110,000. At the new tax rate of 20%, he ends up paying $22,000 in taxes. The government has lowered the tax rate, helped the economy, and collected more money in taxes! (And Mr. Smith has $88,000 left for himself instead of $60,000.) Everyone is better off.

In addition, there is a great benefit to society because lower taxes have increased people's personal freedom to do what they want with more of their own money.

Of course, there is a lower limit to how far tax rates can drop and still result in a total increase in taxes paid to government. Beyond a certain point, lowering taxes cannot stimulate enough economic growth to make up for the smaller percentage of income that is collected. (At a tax rate of 0%, the government would collect zero dollars.) The graph of how this works is called the "Laffer Curve," after Arthur Laffer, the economist who first explained this concept to President Ronald Reagan and persuaded him that he could cut tax *rates* and help the economy and still collect more actual tax dollars. The idea is not very controversial, because at a 100% tax rate nobody will want to work (all their pay would be taken away) and so the government would also collect zero dollars. At some point in between is the best rate for governments to maximize the tax money they collect.

Arguments occur over just where that maximum point lies. Let's look at an example of the Laffer Curve. ("Tax Revenue" refers to the total amount of money that the government collects in taxes, and "Tax Rate" refers to the percentage of people's income that they have to pay to the government in taxes.)[33]

Figure 9.1

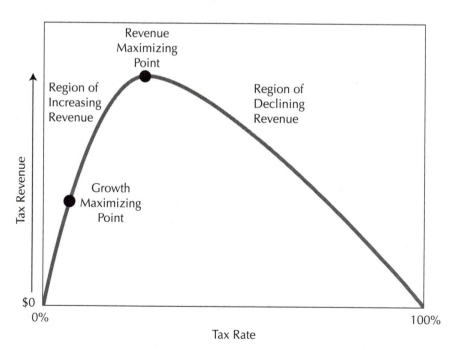

---

33. This graph is taken from Daniel J. Mitchell, "The Correct Way to Measure the Revenue Impact of Changes in Tax Rates," Heritage Foundation (May 3, 2002). www.heritage.org/ Research/Taxes/BG1544.cfm (accessed Feb. 12, 2010). Reprinted by permission of The Heritage Foundation.

It should also be remembered that the "Revenue Maximizing Point" might be best for the government's treasury but not best for the country. A lower tax rate might lead to more economic growth (as illustrated on this graph by the "Growth Maximizing Point").

This phenomenon of lower tax rates leading to a growing economy and therefore higher tax revenue for the government has actually happened more than once in recent US history. It happened with the Reagan tax cuts of 1981. In 1980, the year before the tax cuts, federal revenue was $956 billion (measured in 1996 dollars). By 1985, even with a much lower tax rate, the federal government took in more than $1 trillion in revenue. At the end of Reagan's term in 1988, government revenue was $1.1 trillion.[34]

Then it happened again with the Bush tax cuts of 2001 and 2003, which brought a huge boost to the economy. Author Stephen Moore wrote in the *Wall Street Journal*:

> Federal tax revenues surged in the first eight months of this fiscal year by $187 billion. This represents a 15.4% rise in federal tax receipts over 2004. Individual and corporate income tax receipts have exploded like a cap let off a geyser, up 30% in the two years since the tax cut. Once again, tax rate cuts have created a virtuous chain reaction of higher economic growth, more jobs, higher corporate profits, and finally more tax receipts.[35]

Therefore, when Christians are thinking whether they should favor higher or lower taxes in a state or nation, the question is whether, on the one hand, they want to *increase human freedom* and *also raise more money for government needs* and *also help the economy*, or on the other hand, they think that taking more money from the "wealthy" is *more important than all of these other three goals*.

When political leaders are asked about such choices, their answers can sometimes reveal their underlying economic beliefs. For example, when presidential candidate Obama was asked a question like this during one of the 2008 debates, he affirmed his conviction that his idea of "fairness" would still be a reason to raise taxes, even if it meant collecting *less* tax revenue for the government. In the April 17, 2008, presidential debate, ABC News' Charles Gibson cited the fact that when the capital gains tax rate dropped from 28 to 20% and then to 15%, "revenues from the taxes increased," but "in the 1980s, when the tax was increased to 28%, the revenues went down." So Gibson asked candidate Obama, "So why raise it at all, especially given the fact that 100 million people in this country own stock and would be affected?" Obama replied, "Well, Charlie, what I've said is that I would look at raising the capital gains tax for purposes of fairness."[36]

That conviction reflects the mentality of many in the Democratic Party today—as well as quite a few others in society who don't normally consider themselves Democrats.

---

34. Andrew Olivastro, "Tax Cuts Increase Federal Revenues," *Heritage Foundation Web Memo* #182 (Dec. 31, 2002). www.heritage.org/Research/Taxes/wm182.cfm?renderforprint=1.

35. Stephen Moore, "Real Tax Cuts Have Curves," *Wall Street Journal* (June 19, 2005). www.opinionjournal.com/extra/?id=110006842.

36. Charles Gibson and President Obama: quoted in Gerald Prante, "Obama and Gibson Capital Gains Tax Exchange," *The Tax Foundation* (April 17, 2008). www.taxfoundation.org/blog/show/23137.html.

It seems that envy of the rich, or animosity toward the rich, is such a deeply engrained characteristic in many people's minds that they are not willing to let the rich keep more of their money *even if* this would mean collecting more government money in taxes *and* helping the economy *and* increasing personal freedom in society as a whole. The most important thing is thought to be taking more money from the "wealthy," who presumably are thought to have gotten their money unjustly or are thought not to deserve the money that they have earned.

4. Taxes on corporations

Another misconception that people have today is the assumption that *imposing high taxes on corporations* is just another way of taking money from the rich that really doesn't affect ordinary people much at all. But this is an incorrect assumption. Higher taxes on corporations are just passed on to consumers in the form of higher prices, so *the entire society* actually pays this tax as a hidden part of the higher cost of the goods that the corporation produces. For example, if the corporate tax rate goes up 5%, then all the grocery stores in Arizona have to pay the government 5% more of their income. What will the stores do? Will they just say, "Well, our costs have just gone up by 5% of our income! But that doesn't matter to us. We will keep all our prices just the same!" Of course they will not do that. If their costs go up, their prices have to go up or they will begin to lose money and eventually go out of business. So they raise the prices of groceries, and the whole society pays this "invisible" tax.

This false idea that high taxes on corporations don't hurt ordinary people is the mistake that has allowed our corporate tax rate in the United States to climb to an astounding 39.3% (average combined federal and state taxes on corporations).[37] This is the second highest corporate tax rate *in the world* (only Japan is slightly higher), and in some states (California, Iowa, New Jersey, and Pennsylvania) the combined corporate tax rate is the highest in the world.[38] The *Wall Street Journal* notes that "over the past eighteen months, nine of the thirty most developed nations ... from Israel to Germany to Turkey—have cut their corporate tax rates. Nations are slashing rates to attract capital and jobs from the United States, and the tragedy is that our politicians keep making it easy for them"[39] In fact, the average European nation now has corporate tax rates *ten percentage points less* than the United States.[40]

Nevertheless, Democratic politicians continue their campaign of demonizing big corporations. For example, US Sen. Byron Durgan of North Dakota announced a new report showing that 28% of large corporations paid no income tax in 2005. "It's time for big corporations to pay their fair share," Durgan roared, according to the *Wall Street Journal*.[41] But on further investigation the *Journal* discovered what Senator

37. Scott A. Hodge, "U.S. Leads the World in High Corporate Taxes," *The Tax Foundation Fiscal Facts* (March 18, 2008). www.taxfoundation.org/publications/show/22917.html.
38. "America the Uncompetitive," *Wall Street Journal* (Aug. 15, 2008), 814. http://online.wsj.com/article/ SB121875570585042551.html?mod=opinion_main_review_and_outlooks.
39. Ibid.
40. Ibid.
41. Ibid.

Durgan conveniently failed to mention: among those large corporations that paid no taxes, the vast majority of them (85%) also made no profits that year.[42] No wonder they paid no taxes!

To restore competitiveness in the world economy, encourage business investment, and truly stimulate the economy, and bring about lower prices for goods produced in the United States, we should lower the corporate tax rate so that it is no higher than 20% (combined federal and state tax). This would attract much more foreign investment to the United States as well as encourage our own corporations to invest more here rather than abroad. Where would government get the money to make up for the "lost" taxes from the lower tax rate? A growing economy would soon provide even more *tax revenues* than before, both through corporate taxes and through higher collections of income taxes as people who work for these corporations earn more income.

5. Capital gains tax

The capital gains tax is a tax paid on the increase in the value of an asset that is held over a period of time. If I buy an apartment building for $800,000 and sell it two years later for $900,000, I have $100,000 in capital gains and have to pay a tax on that amount. In the United States, the most important capital gains tax rate is on long-term capital gains, which applies to assets that someone holds for more than a year. In 2003, with President Bush's tax cuts, the capital gains tax was reduced to 15%.[43] (Many Republicans wanted to abolish it completely.) However, this reduction is set to expire in 2010, after which the rate will revert to 20%.[44] What would be the outcome of the increase in that tax? The Heritage Foundation put out this sobering prediction:

- Increasing capital gains and dividend tax rates would reduce the capital stock by $12 billion (in constant 2000 dollars) by 2012.
- Potential employment would drop by 270,000 in 2011 and 413,000 in 2012.
- Personal incomes would decline by $1,675 (in 2000 dollars) for a family of four in 2012.
- The broadest measure of economic activity, GDP after inflation, would decline steadily over the forecast period of 2011 through 2018.
- In 2011, GDP would be $44 billion below where it would be if the tax cuts were made permanent. That figure would rise to $50 billion in 2012.
- Annual GDP after inflation losses would average $37 billion below baseline over that seven-year period.[45]

It is important to remember that this is a tax on the *increased value* of something purchased *as an investment* (for example, a rental property or an apartment building). Given that the owner already pays taxes on the income that is produced each year from that investment, should he also pay taxes on the increase in value on that property?

42. Ibid.
43. Moore, "Real Tax Cuts Have Real Curves."
44. William W. Beach, Rea S. Hederman Jr., and Guinevere Nell, "Economic Effects of Increasing the Tax Rates on Capi-

tal Gains and Dividends," *Heritage Foundation Web Memo #1891* (April 15, 2008). www.heritage.org/Research/Taxes/wm1891.cfm.
45. Ibid.

A strong argument can be made that the capital gains tax should be completely abolished, to encourage investment in the economy. At any rate, it is economically beneficial to the nation to have this rate be very low, since that encourages more investment, which helps an economy to grow. (This is based on the principle, "If you penalize something you get less of it, and if you reward something you get more of it.")

6. Income tax rates

The tax laws of the United States are set up so that the income tax rate a person pays increases according to the amount of income that person earns in a calendar year. To get an idea of such rates, here are the 2009 rates for income for a single person and for a married couple filing their tax return jointly in the United States:

Figure 9.2

Marginal Tax rate	Single	Married Filing Jointly
10%	$0 - $8,350	$0 - $16,700
15%	$8,351 - $33,950	$16,701 - $67,900
25%	$33,951 - $82,250	$67,901 - $137,050
28%	$82,251 - $171,950	$137,051 - $208,850
33%	$171,951 - $372,950	$208,851 - $372,950
35%	$372,951 +	$372,951 +

"Marginal tax rate" means the rate of tax *for each additional dollar* that is earned within a person's highest tax bracket. For example, if a married couple earned $46,700, they would pay 10% tax on the first $16,700, and then they would pay 15% tax on the remaining $30,000 of income. (They would not pay 15% on the entire $46,700.) Their *marginal tax rate* is 15%. The marginal tax rate is the rate that most affects people's economic behavior (because people use it to calculate how much they will be able to keep from any additional work they might do).

However, other factors go into calculating the amount on which tax is paid. For example, in 2009 there was a *personal exemption* of $3,650 per person, or $7,300 per couple. In addition, taxpayers were allowed a *standard deduction* from their income, which was $11,340 for a married couple filing jointly in 2009. This is a total of $18,640 of income that is not subject to income tax. Therefore, if a couple earned $28,640, they would pay no income tax on the first $18,640 and would pay 10% on the remaining $10,000 (that is, they would pay $1,000 in tax).

Single taxpayers are allowed a deduction of $5,700 and a personal exemption of $3,650, which means the first $9,350 of income is exempt from income tax for a single person. The term economists use to describe an income tax system where the rates increase at higher levels of income is "progressive." The US tax system is "progressive" in the sense that income tax rates "progress" to higher levels as one's income increases.

Now the question is, is such a system of tax rates *fair*?

In the Old Testament, all the people of Israel were required to pay a "tithe," by which they were to give 10% of their income to the Lord:

> You shall tithe all the yield of your seed that comes from the field year by year. And before the LORD your God, in the place that he will choose, to make his name dwell there, you shall eat the tithe of your grain, of your wine, and of your oil, and the firstborn of your herd and flock, that you may learn to fear the LORD your God always (Deut. 14:22–23).

> Every tithe of the land, whether of the seed of the land or of the fruit of the trees, is the LORD's; it is holy to the LORD.... And every tithe of herds and flocks, every tenth animal of all that passes under the herdsman's staff, shall be holy to the LORD (Lev. 27:30–32).

A "tithe" was exactly 10%. This system, therefore, was a like a "flat tax" because everyone paid the same percentage. There was no increase in the amount that had to be given by the wealthy and no decrease for those who were poor.

In such a system the wealthy would still pay much more than the poor in absolute terms. To use modern American equivalents, a farmer whose one-year crops were worth $30,000 would pay $3,000 for his tithe, while the farmer whose crops were worth $300,000 would pay $30,000 for his tithe. The wealthy man would pay ten times as much as the poor man.

The people of Israel also had a census tax that was imposed on every person in the amount of half a shekel:

> Each one who is numbered in the census shall give this: *half a shekel* according to the shekel of the sanctuary (the shekel is twenty gerahs), half a shekel as an offering to the LORD. Everyone who is numbered in the census, from twenty years old and upward, shall give the LORD's offering. *The rich shall not give more, and the poor shall not give less, than the half shekel,* when you give the LORD's offering to make atonement for your lives (Exod. 30:13–15).

Each person had to pay exactly the same amount in this case, which economists would call a "head tax," because the exact same amount was collected from each person (each "head") in a nation.

From this material on taxes and tithes, I can see no justification in the Bible for a "progressive" tax rate. Many societies and nations have adopted a progressive tax rate, but the justification for it will have to come from somewhere other than the explicit patterns of taxes and tithes found in the Bible.

7. But isn't it "fair" for the rich to pay a higher percentage?

This brings us back to the question about what is "fair" with regard to taxes. On what basis can we decide what is fair? People may have subjective preferences or emotional preferences for one rate or other being "fair," but those preferences will often be influenced strongly by self-interest rather than by some objective standard of fairness. Just using round numbers for convenience, imagine a case with Taxpayer A and Taxpayer B:

> Taxpayer A has $50,000 in taxable income.
> Taxpayer B has $500,000 in taxable income.

If we assume a tax rate of 20%, they pay the following taxes;

> Taxpayer A pays 20% of $50,000, equaling $10,000.
> Taxpayer B pays 20% of $500,000, equaling $100,000.

Would that be *fair*? If we ask Taxpayer A, he would probably say that what is truly "fair" is for him to pay $0 and for Taxpayer B, who is wealthy, to pay not $100,000, but $110,000!

But if we ask Taxpayer B, he might say that he is paying *far more* than his fair share even with a "flat tax" of 20%. He might say, "Why should I pay $100,000 to receive the same benefits as Taxpayer A when he only pays $10,000? We both get the same fire and police protection, we both use the same highways, we both benefit from the same military protection of our country, we both breathe the same air that is maintained by pollution-control standards enforced by the government, and so forth. We receive *exactly the same benefits* from the government, but I pay *ten times as much as taxpayer A* for these benefits! How can that be *fair* for one person to pay ten times more than someone else for the same things?"

Then a third person, Taxpayer C, might think Taxpayer B should pay *even more* than $110,000 because, even if he pays more, he still has more money left to live on. If they both pay 20% of their income, then Taxpayer A, after paying $10,000 in tax, only has $40,000 left to live on, yet Taxpayer B, after paying $100,000 in tax, still has $400,000 left to live on.

But there is a questionable assumption underlying that argument. The assumption is that Taxpayer B for some reason *does not deserve* to have $400,000 left to live on. In fact, he only *deserves* to have $300,000 left to live on. And we could go further and say that he doesn't even deserve $300,000 to live on. He should pay the tax for twenty more taxpayers in the same situation as Taxpayer A. He should pay another $100,000 in tax so that he has only $200,000 left to live on! And so on.

It is very easy for people in Taxpayer A's position or Taxpayer C's position to assume that they have some kind of superior moral judgment that is able to decide how much Taxpayer B "really deserves" to live on.

But the question then must be asked, how do we decide what someone *deserves*? Do we really believe everybody somehow *deserves* the same amount of money to live on in the end? Of course, that would be a communist totalitarianism of the worst kind, placing everybody in the nation at the same income level and destroying incentives for work and excellence and productivity.

There is a far better solution to the question of what each person "deserves." The solution is this: Each person deserves *what he has legally earned* in each year. "The laborer deserves his wages" (Luke 10:7). Even in the calculation of heavenly reward from God, Paul says, "He who plants and he who waters are one, and each will receive his wages according to his labor" (1 Cor. 3:8). In Jesus' parable of the ten servants who each received one mina to use in "business" (Luke 19:13), the servant who said, "Your mina has made ten minas more," was commended by the master and given great reward. The master said,

> "Well done, good servant! Because you have been faithful in a very little, you shall have authority over ten cities" (Luke 19:17).

In this parable, the master (who stands for Jesus) rewards the servants according to what they had done with what they had been given. What they "deserved" was what they had earned, even though it varied greatly from servant to servant (see also the parable of the talents in Matt. 25:14–30).

So it seems to me that the answer to the question, "What does each person deserve?" is, "Each person deserves what he has legally and fairly earned."

Then how much tax should each person pay? Again, the principle of a 10% tithe in the Bible would give some support to the idea of a "flat tax" by which each person pays a certain percentage of what he earns, whether 15 or 18 or 20% or whatever the society decides is the best rate of taxation to support the functions of the government.

It is very important to note that the "fair" or appropriate rate of taxation *does not depend on how much each person has left after paying taxes*. It is of no concern to the government how much Taxpayer B has left after he pays his taxes, because that money does not belong to the government or to society; it belongs to Taxpayer B.

This idea is based on the biblical teaching about private property, which we discussed above (see pp. 261–68). The reason God commands people, "You shall not steal" (Exod. 20:15), is that a person's property belongs to that person, not to the government or to society or to that person's neighbor. Therefore, if Taxpayer B has $500,000 in taxable income and pays $100,000, then the remaining $400,000 belongs to Taxpayer B. He deserves it because he has earned it fairly and legally, and so it is his.

Now someone might object that "nobody in society should be able to earn $500,000. That is just too much for any one person."

But the reason Taxpayer B has earned $500,000 is that the society as a whole, through individual decisions about how to spend their money, has "voted" with their dollars how much it wants to give Taxpayer B. If he is an executive at Wal-Mart, then people who shop at Wal-Mart have freely decided to shop at Wal-Mart enough to hire him at that rate. If he is a professional athlete, then people who watch sports on TV have freely voted with their viewing habits to watch his team enough that they can pay him that amount. If he is a Hollywood movie star, then people who watch his movies have freely chosen for him to be paid that much. Salaries are determined *according to the varying market demand* for certain skills and abilities. If we don't like it, the way to change it is to change the viewing habits and spending habits of the society. Society gets what it decides to pay for.

8. It is good for society if everyone who earns income pays some taxes, and it is destructive to society if most people who earn income pay little or no taxes

If everyone who earns income in a society pays at least some amount of tax, then the government is accountable to the broadest possible base of society for how it spends money. If the government raises taxes unnecessarily, or if it wastes taxpayers' money, then every wage-earner is thinking, "*They are wasting my money!*" Then it is likely that those elected representatives will be voted out of office at the next election.

Of course, I agree that some provision should be made so that people who earn a very small amount of income will pay only a small amount of tax. Even in the law code of ancient Israel, where a sacrifice of a lamb was required after the birth of a child (see Lev. 12:6), there was a provision for people who could not afford this:

> And if she cannot afford a lamb, then she shall take two turtledoves or two pigeons, one for a burnt offering and the other for a sin offering ... (Lev. 12:8).

But even people who earn very little should be required to pay *some tax* (even if very small), so that there will be a sense of responsibility to pay for the services of the government and a sense of accountability on the part of the government for how these taxes are used.

However, in the United States in 2009, after endless tinkering with the tax code, the government has now put us in a position where nearly half (47%) of the adult citizens *pay no federal income taxes at all*—71 million people![46] This is because people can earn quite a bit of money and still claim deductions for retirement accounts, education accounts, interest paid on a home mortgage, child and dependent care, charitable giving, care for the elderly and disabled, health savings accounts, and several other things.

But this means that *nearly half of the voters in the United States* do not really care whether the government doubles or triples the tax rate, because they don't see taxes really affecting their pocketbook. When a politician such as President Obama promises *trillions* of dollars in new government spending, half of the population doesn't think it matters at all, because they don't think it will cost them a dime. In this way the government is cut loose from accountability to the voters, and it can decide to tax and spend the nation into oblivion, with little fear that the majority of the population will care at all—until it is too late. The US national debt accumulated by massively increased spending will take a dreadful toll on the future economic health of the nation. By June 1 of 2009 alone, the spending that President Obama committed and that was approved by Congress increased the national debt over the next decade by more than $4 trillion compared with what it was on January 20, 2009, when Obama was inaugurated.[47] That is a future tax obligation of $38,943 for every one of the 307,000,000 people (every man, woman, and child) now living in the United States.[48] To put it another way, President

---

46. Jeanne Sahadi, "47% Will Pay No Federal Income Tax," *CNN.com* (Sept. 30, 1999). http://money.cnn.com/2009/09/30/pf/taxes/who_pays_taxes/index.htm?postversion=2009093012.

47. Rahn, "The Growing Debt Bomb."

48. See www.usdebtclock.org/index.html.

Obama's huge spending increases have resulted in an *increased* obligation of $110,023 for every person who is now paying income taxes in the United States.[49]

There was no outcry because the near-majority of the population, who now pay no income taxes at all, simply thought, "So what? It won't hurt me!" And the mainstream press, which overwhelmingly supported President Obama, was passive.

9. Who is paying most of the taxes in the United States today?

Another way to look at the present skewing of the tax burden in the United States is to ask who pays most of the taxes today. The truth is, the top 50% of wage earners paid 97% of all the taxes in 2006, and the bottom half of those who earned income paid less than 3%. The top 1% of wage earners paid 40% of the income taxes in 2006. (They earned 22% of the income reported.)[50] Although the government also collects money from corporate income taxes, estate taxes, and other sources, the *2009 Economic Report of the President* estimated that in 2008 income taxes accounted for 70.6% of federal revenues (excluding Social Security and Medicare). But this means that just 1% of the population is paying for 28% of the expenses of the federal government.

This shows a significant change over the previous fifteen years. In 1990, the richest 1% in the United States paid not 40%, but 25% of income tax revenue. By the year 2000, they were paying 37% of these taxes,[51] and then in 2006 they paid 40% of the taxes (see above).

Is such a system truly *fair*? On the principle that money does not belong to government or society but to individuals who earn it, and on the principle that it is healthy when everyone pays something in taxes, such a system does not at all seem to be *fair*. It is steeply "progressive" and had become more "progressive" over those fifteen years.

But now that people who pay almost no taxes have become a majority of the voters in the United States, the stage is set for this situation to continue in the same direction, so that a greater and greater share of the total tax burden will be borne by a smaller and smaller percentage of the population. I can see no justification for such a system in the pages of the Bible.

10. The economy as a whole, all the people in the nation, and the government all gain benefits from lower taxes on the rich

At first it seems hard to understand how it could bring a benefit to the economy as a whole to *lower* the current US tax rates for those who are wealthy. What good could that do for everyone else or for the economy? And what good could that do for the government?

But here is a situation where the study of economics provides greater insight that helps us understand what happens. This can be explained in a way that someone who is not an economist can understand quite easily.

---

49. Ibid.
50. "Their Fair Share," *Wall Street Journal* (July 21, 2008), A12.
51. "Fact Sheet: Who Pays the Most Individual Income Taxes?" U.S. Department of Treasury Fact Sheet (April 1, 2004). www.ustreas.gov/press/releases/js1287.htm.

For example, consider Taxpayer D who has a *taxable* income of $250,000, which puts him in the top 2% of American taxpayers.[52] Using round numbers for simplicity, let's assume that at the current tax rates he pays a total of $62,500 in taxes (or 25% of his taxable income). After taxes, he has $187,500 left for himself.

Now what would be the effect on the economy if his tax rate were *reduced* from 25 to 20% of his income? His tax would drop to 20% of $250,000, or $50,000. Instead of having $187,500 left over after taxes, he would have $200,000 left over. What will he do with the extra $12,500 that the government does not take away from him in taxes?

(1) The first result is that no matter what he does with the extra money, it will quickly begin to help others as well as himself. He has only three choices of what to do with it: he can (a) save it, (b) spend it, or (c) give it away.

(a) If he *saves* his $12,500, he could put it in the bank and earn interest, and the bank will then quickly loan out most of the $12,500 to someone else who wants to buy a house or start a business. So the $12,500 that the wealthy Taxpayer D puts in the bank will quickly begin doing good for other people too. But instead of putting it in the bank, it is likely that he will look for a place to invest it so it will earn him *more* money than just a savings account in a bank. In fact, wealthy people like Taxpayer D look for the *highest rate of return* on their money, within the range of risk that they are willing to tolerate. Some people like Taxpayer D will invest it in a new business, while others will invest it in expanding their business, both of which create new jobs and new productivity in the economy. Or Taxpayer D may buy stocks with it, which is simply a way of investing it in someone else's company so that that company can expand and produce more and provide more jobs. The important point is that what Taxpayer D "saves" does not sit idle in a cookie jar in the kitchen pantry, but is put to use in ways that bring economic benefit.

(b) If Taxpayer D *spends* some of this $12,500, it will also bring economic benefit in the private sector. If he goes out to eat at a restaurant, it brings benefit to the waiters, the cooks, the food suppliers, the truckers who brought the food, and the farmers who produced the food. If he uses it to buy a new car, it brings benefit to the car dealer, the sales force, the window washers who keep the windows clean, the gas station attendants where he buys gas for his car, the auto workers who produced the car, the vendors who supply the auto factory, and so forth.

All of these results that come from saving or spending are *far more helpful to the economy* than turning the $12,500 over to some government agency that will waste much of it and use it to pay government workers to file endless forms in triplicate in a cavernous building in Washington, DC. (I am not saying that government workers contribute no value to society, for certainly many government functions are necessary and beneficial, but because government is not accountable to the competitive forces of the free market, it will never use money as productively or efficiently as the private sector will.)

(c) The third option for Taxpayer D is that he could *give away* his $12,500. If he gives it to people who need it for daily necessities, that helps society and also helps the

---

52. See www.factcheck.org/askfactcheck/what_percentage_
of_the_us_population_makes.html.

economy because these people will spend it at the grocery store or buy clothing or shoes and so forth. No matter where he gives the money, if he does not give it to government but to a private charity, they will in turn spend the money in the private sector and more economic benefit will result. All three of these results seem to me to bring more benefit to the economy than giving the money to the government.

(2) There are still further benefits that come from lowering Taxpayer D's tax rate. With a lower rate he now has a greater incentive to work and be more productive next year, because he knows he will be able to keep more of his hard-earned money. Lower taxes *increase the incentives to work and be productive*, and when they increase incentives among the most economically productive members of society—those with the highest earnings—they bring the added benefit of more productivity that comes from the skilled work of Taxpayer D.

(3) There is still more benefit to the economy. As Taxpayer D invests more (because he has more money to invest) and works more (because of a higher incentive to work), he is going to *earn* more money next year as well. In fact, when the *permanent* tax rates in the United States have been reduced (so that people can plan for lower taxes next year *and the years following* as well), the result has been an amazing increase in personal income in the country.

For example, let's say that after two years, Taxpayer D's taxable income has grown from $250,000 to $320,000. Now, at this 20% tax rate he pays $64,000 in taxes—which is $1,500 more than he was paying at the higher 25% rate! The government has suddenly collected *more* money from Taxpayer D than it did before. And yet he is better off as well, because even after paying $64,000, he still has $256,000 left for himself. And it is not only Taxpayer D who has decided to earn more, but the entire population in general has decided to invest more and work more because they can keep a higher percentage of their income. So the entire economy is growing. And the amount of taxes collected by the *government is also growing at this lower tax rate*!

The results we saw with Taxpayer D do not happen only with rich people whose tax rates are reduced. The same results also happen to some degree for lower-income taxpayers, except that they will tend to spend more and save and invest less, and it is the savings and investment that have the largest positive influence on growing an economy.

This is not wishful thinking, but is what actually happened, both with the Reagan tax cuts in 1981 and with the Bush tax cuts in 2001 and 2003.

According to William Niskanen and Stephen Moore of the Cato Institute, the Reagan tax cuts had these results:

1. Real economic growth averaging 3.2% versus 2.8% during the Ford-Carter years, and 2.1% during the Bush I-Clinton years.
2. Real median family income growing by $4,000 during the Reagan period, compared to no growth during the pre-Reagan years, and a loss of approximately $1,500 in the post-Reagan years.
3. Interest rates, inflation, and unemployment falling faster under Reagan than they did immediately before or after his presidency.[53]

53. William A. Niskanen and Stephen Moore, "Supply-Side Economics and the Truth about the Reagan Economic Record," *CATO Policy Analysis* (Oct. 22, 1996). www.cato.org/pub_display.php?pub_id=1120&full=1.

Niskanen and Moore reported that family incomes plummeted 9% under Jimmy Carter, but rose 11 percent under Ronald Reagan.[54]

With regard to the Bush tax cuts, the National Center for Policy Analysis reported:

1. In the third quarter of 2003, the gross national product (GNP) grew at a 7.2 percent annual rate. The real annual GDP growth rate increased from 0.3% in 2001 to 2.5 in 2002.
2. 2003 and 2004 economic growth levels resulted in $300 billion of greater than expected growth, or roughly $2,500 per household.
3. 1.4 million jobs were added in the nine months after August 2003.[55]

Finally, according to one analysis, instead of costing the government $27 billion in revenues, the tax cuts actually *earned* the government *$26 billion* extra. Donald Luskin, the chief investment officer of Trend Macrolytics, an independent economics and investment research firm, explains how this occurred:

The 2003 tax cut on capital gains has entirely paid for itself. *More* than paid for itself. *Way* more. To appreciate the story, we have to go back in time to January 2003, before the tax cut was enacted. Table 3–5 on page 60 in CBO's *Budget and Economic Outlook* published in 2003 estimated that capital-gains tax liabilities would be $60 billion in 2004 and $65 billion in 2005, for a two-year total of $125 billion.

Now, let's move forward a year, to January 2004, after the capital gains tax cut had been enacted. Table 4–4 on page 82 in CBO's *Budget and Economic Outlook* of that year shows that the estimates for capital gains tax liabilities had been lowered to $46 billion in 2004 and $52 billion in 2005, for a two-year total of $98 billion. Compare the original $125 billion total to the new $98 billion total, and we can infer that CBO was forecasting that the tax cut cost the government $27 billion in revenues.

Those are the estimates. Now's let see how things really turned out. Take a look at Table 4–4 on page 92 of the *Budget and Economic Outlook* released this week. You'll see that actual liabilities from capital gains taxes were $71 billion in 2004, and $80 billion in 2005, for a two-year total of $151 billion. So let's do the math one more time: Subtract the originally estimated two-year liability of $125 billion, and you get a $26 billion upside surprise for the government. Yes, instead of costing the government $27 billion in revenues, the tax cuts actually earned the government $26 billion extra.[56]

(4) There is yet another benefit from lower taxes, one of gigantic significance. When taxpayers are allowed to keep more of their own money, there is an increase in the

---

54. Ibid.

55. "Are the Bush Tax Cuts Working?" http://taxesandgrowth. ncpa.org/news/are-the-bush-tax-cuts-working.

56. See Donald Luskin, "The 2003 Tax Cut on Capital Gains Entirely Paid for Itself, I'm Not Just Saying It—CBO Is," *National Review Online* (Jan. 27, 2006), www.nationalreview.com/nrof_luskin/luskin200601270946.asp; and "Are the

Bush Tax Cuts Working?" *National Center for Policy Analysis*, http://taxesandgrowth.ncpa.org/news/are-the-bush-tax-cuts-working: citing Congressional Budget Office, "The Budget and Economic Outlook: Fiscal Years 2007 to 2016," Congressional Budget Office (Jan. 2006). Table 4–4, p. 92. www.cbo.gov/ftpdocs/70xx/doc7027/01–26-BudgetOutlook.pdf.

amount of *personal liberty* in the society. This is because *individuals*, not the government, are deciding how that amount of money will be spent. Even a low-income taxpayer who keeps $120 more of his own money now has the freedom to decide if he wants to spend that $120 on buying healthier food at the grocery store, buying a new program for his computer, taking his family to a baseball game, giving it to some missionaries, or doing any of thousands of other things. The decision is wholly up to him because the money is still his and the government is no longer taking it and deciding for him how it should be spent. So it is with *every* taxpayer who is able to keep more of his own money.

To summarize, the benefits of lowering the permanent tax rates in a nation, and especially the benefits of lowering the tax rates on the wealthier members of society, are these:

(1) It means that each taxpayer is able to keep more of his own money, which not only helps him but also, because the money is quickly put to work, helps others in the economy, and the economy grows.
(2) It gives more incentive for people to work and to be productive, and this also means that the economy will grow.
(3) The government will soon collect more money in taxes.
(4) There will be a significant increase in personal liberty in the nation.

Once we understand this, and understand the tremendous benefits that came to the nation from the Bush tax cuts of 2001–3, we would hope that there would be a unanimous vote in Congress to extend these tax cuts beyond the date when they are set to expire at the end of 2010. But President Obama and the Democratic Party are adamantly opposed to extending these tax cuts. The only thing they can say about them is that they bring too much benefit to "the rich."

The truth is that the tax cuts bring benefit to every taxpayer, including rich taxpayers. But if these tax cuts are not extended, then the tax rates in the United States will go back to their harmful, pre–2003 levels. The Heritage Foundation reports that when the tax cuts expire in 2010:

• Tax rates will rise substantially in each tax bracket, some by 450 basis points [= 4.5%];
• Low-income taxpayers will see the 10-percent tax bracket disappear, and they will have to pay taxes at the 15-percent rate;
• Married taxpayers will see the marriage penalty return;
• Taxpayers with children will lose 50% of their child tax credits;
• Taxes on dividends will increase beginning on January 1, 2009;
• Taxes on capital gains will increase, also beginning on January 1, 2009; and
• Federal death taxes will come back to life in 2011, after fading down to nothing in 2010.[57]

The result of this is going to be the opposite of what we saw above when taxes were cut. These tax increases will harm the economy (by giving more of people's income to government), will take away the incentive of people to work and be more productive,

---

57. William W. Beach and Rea S. Hederman Jr., "Make The Bush Tax Cuts Permanent," *Heritage Foundation Web Memo #956* (Jan. 5, 2006). www.heritage.org/Research/Taxes/wm956.cfm.

will cause the economy to contract and therefore government will collect less money in taxes, and these tax increases will decrease personal liberty by taking away people's freedom to decide what to do with their own money.

So the question is a simple one: What do we want to do? Do we want to (a) help the economy, help people at every income level from poor to rich, help society, increase government tax revenue, and increase liberty, or do we want to (b) take a higher percentage of money from the rich, harm the economy, harm everybody in society from poor to rich, harm society, decrease taxes received by the government, and decrease liberty? Astoundingly, the Democratic Party is unanimously in favor of option (b).

Does the teaching of the Bible give us any guidance on these options? As we have indicated in previous sections, the biblical teachings (a) that property belongs to individuals, not to society and not to the government, (b) that governments should not take excessive amounts of money for itself, (c) that government should seek to bring economic benefit and economic growth to a society, and (d) that government should protect and safeguard individual liberty, all argue in favor of lower tax rates than we now have, especially on those who are in the higher categories of income earners in the society.

11. But are the rich getting richer and the poor getting poorer?

One argument commonly heard in support of higher taxes on the rich is that "the rich are getting richer and the poor are getting poorer." Therefore, it is said, we should tax the rich more to make life more "just" (which these people take to mean "more equal in wealth").

There are several mistakes with this argument. First, it is factually wrong. The poor are not "getting poorer" in the United States nor in any developed country.

Figure 9.3

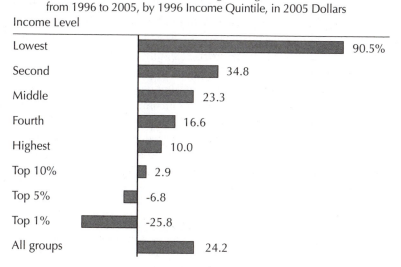

U.S. INCOME MOBILITY: Percentage change in Median Income from 1996 to 2005, by 1996 Income Quintile, in 2005 Dollars

Income Level

Income Level	Percentage change
Lowest	90.5%
Second	34.8
Middle	23.3
Fourth	16.6
Highest	10.0
Top 10%	2.9
Top 5%	-6.8
Top 1%	-25.8
All groups	24.2

Source: US Treasury Dept., 2007

This chart taken from data published by the US Treasury Department shows that from 1996 to 2005 the greatest percentage of economic growth has occurred with those who were at the lowest end of the income scale in 1996. In fact, nearly 58% of the tax filers in the poorest income group in 1996 had moved into a higher income category ten years later. Nearly 25% moved into the middle- or upper-middle-class income groups. The report said that the only group that saw their median income *decline* over that period was people who were in the top 1% of taxpayers in 1996—because quite a few people have very high income only for a few years and then it suddenly declines.[58] As the US economy grows, yes, many of the rich are getting richer. (Bill Gates was worth $58 billion in 2008,[59] but the world's richest man in the late 1960s was Bunker Hunt, whose net worth was estimated to be between $8 and $16 billion.[60]) But *the poor are also getting richer*, because as the economy grows, people *at every level of income* generally benefit.

It is a mathematical fact that when the economy grows by 10%, if everybody in the economy gains 10%, the rich will gain more in total dollars. To use round numbers, if Bill Gates would increase his net worth by 10% from $60 billion to $66 billion, he is $6 billion richer. But if a poor person whose net worth is $40,000 also increases 10% to $44,000, he is only $4,000 richer. Bill Gates has gained wealth at a faster pace, and he is now $5,999,996,000 farther "ahead" of the poor person. *That is inevitable if an economy grows and everyone benefits.*

It is simple mathematics that a 10% gain on a large amount is more than a 10% gain on a small amount. That will be true forever, and therefore as long as economies continue to grow, the rich will continue to get richer and the poor will continue to get richer, but at a slower rate. *The important point is that everybody is better off.*

The only way to prevent this is for government to confiscate $5,999,996,000 of the extra money Bill Gates makes, so that both he and the poor person each gain $4,000. But if that happens, then Bill Gates will decide to work less (why work when the government takes more than 99% of what you earn?) and thus will produce less and help the economy less. The rich person also might just decide to move to another country where government lets him keep more of what he earns (as many highly skilled, wealthy people have done in other countries when tax rates increase significantly).

In other words, government, by massive use of its tax power, can *force* everyone to live in *equality of poverty* (as in communist nations), but it is impossible to force everyone to live in equality of riches, or to live in equality of income in a healthy, growing economy.

There is another reason why we should not think that "the rich are getting richer and the poor are getting poorer." Many people who are poor one year actually start becoming wealthier the next year. If we divide the US population into five groups, with 20% of the people in each (5 quintiles) and study what happened to each group from 1975 to 1991 (a period of 16 years), 98% of those in the lowest income group had moved to

58. "Movin' On Up," *Wall Street Journal* (Nov. 13, 2007). www.opinionjournal.com/editorial/feature.html?id=110010855.

59. See www.forbes.com/lists/2008/10/billionaires08_William-Gates-III_BH69.html.

60. Doug J. Swanson, "Once World's Richest Man, Bunker Hunt Has 'No Regrets,' 29 Years After Silver Collapse," *Dallas Morning News* (March 22, 2009). www.dallasnews.com/sharedcontent/dws/dn/latestnews/stories/032209dnprobunkerhunt.3d93ff8.html.

a higher group! In the next-lowest income group, 78% had moved to a higher income group, while 58% of those in the third group had moved to a higher group. On the other hand, 31% of those in the top income group had moved to a lower group, as had 24% of those in the second-highest group. The following graph shows these changes:[61]

Figure 9.4

INCOME MOBILITY 1975–91

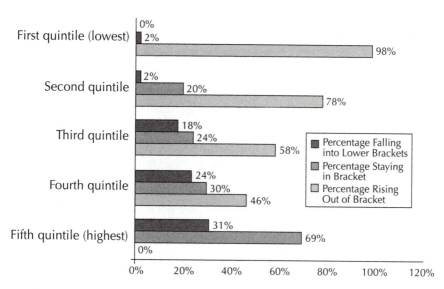

Such patterns have also been seen in more recent studies. A study on income mobility for 1996–2005 found that for those in the lowest income brackets, median pre-tax income rose 77.2% for 1996–2005, compared with 67.8% for the previous period.[62] Another study done by the Department of the Treasury found that roughly half of the taxpayers who began in the bottom quintile in 1996 had moved to a higher tax bracket by 2005. The study also found that among those with the very highest incomes in 1996—the top 1/100 of 1%—only 25% remained in this group in 2005. In addition, their median real income dropped during this period as well.[63]

In other words, various measures show that there is tremendous income mobility over time in the United States.

One example of such movement would be a poor medical school student who suddenly graduates and moves at once from "low income" status to "moderate/high income" status in one year and soon after that to "high income" status. A similar thing happens, in general, to poor college students once they begin climbing their career path. And it happens

61. "Income mobility 1975–91," in Stephen Moore and Julian Simon, *It's Getting Better All the Time: Greatest Trends of the Last 100 Years* (Washington, DC: Cato Institute, 2000), 79.

62. "Income Mobility in the United States: New Evidence from Income Tax Data," *National Tax Journal* LXII:2 (June 2009), 315.

63. "Income Mobility in the United States: 1996–2005," US Department of the Treasury (Nov. 13, 2007), 2.

to poor immigrant families who are just learning the language and looking for business opportunities at which they will soon begin to succeed.[64] This shift from "low income" to "high income" also happens to "low income" entrepreneurs who take no salary and live off savings for two or three years while starting a business; they show up as "the poor" in national income distribution charts (they have $0 income), but when the business does well, they will quickly join the ranks of middle- or upper-middle-income earners. So when people talk about "the poor" and "the rich" over time, we must remember that *there are different people in the groups over time.*

Finally, as I argued in the previous section, taxing the rich less will help the economy and help everybody, but the implication of this is that taxing the rich more will hurt the economy and hurt everyone as well.

12. The death tax (estate tax)

Currently in the United States there is a very high estate tax (often called the "death tax") on the value of a person's estate above a certain amount. This is a tax that has to be paid by a person's estate after the person dies.

Should a person's property be subject to a tax when he or she dies? At present, any value of an estate above a certain "exclusion amount" is taxed at a fairly significant rate before any of it can be given to the deceased person's heirs.

The actual tax has been changing in recent years, but here is a table of the rates from 2001 to 2011 (unless Congress passes a law that changes the 2011 rate):

Figure 9.5

Year	Exclusion Amount	Max / Top Tax Rate
2001	$675,000	55%
2002	$1.0 million	50%
2003	$1.0 million	49%
2004	$1.5 million	48%
2005	$1.5 million	47%
2006	$2.0 million	46%
2007	$2.0 million	45%
2008	$2.0 million	45%
2009	$3.5 million	45%
2010	Repealed	0%
2011	$1.0 million	55%

64. For numerous examples see Thomas J. Stanley, Ph.D., and William D. Danko, Ph.D., *The Millionaire Next Door* (New York: Pocket Books, 1998).

As this table shows, according to important changes passed in the Bush tax cuts of 2001 and 2003, the amount of an estate that was excluded from the taxable value has been increasing regularly since 2003, and the tax rate on the size of the estate over that amount has been decreasing. But *unless Congress passes another law*, in 2011 the estate tax will go back to a higher rate than it has been since 2001.

For example, if Taxpayer E dies in 2011 and owns a house worth $600,000 and a hardware store that he has built as a small business worth $1 million, and if he also has $400,000 in savings, then his estate is worth $2 million. One million would be excluded, but the estate would have to pay 55% on the other $1 million, or $550,000 in taxes.

Suppose Taxpayer E has four children, and he wishes to leave an inheritance to them in four equal amounts. If there were no estate tax, he would split his $2 million four ways and leave them $500,000 each. But with the 2011 rates that are scheduled to take effect with the estate tax, his children would first have to pay $550,000 in tax out of the estate. The $400,000 in savings does not provide enough cash in the estate to pay this tax, so they will have to sell the house at once or sell the business at once, just to raise enough cash to pay the tax. In many such situations a family business or a family farm just has to be sold.

Now the question is this: Is it right for the government to take $550,000 from the estate of Taxpayer E before he can give it to his children?

The first question is, *whose money is this $2 million?* Does it belong to Taxpayer E so that he should be free to do what he wants with it (assuming he has earned it legally)? Or does it belong to society or to the government? As indicated above, the principles of the Bible indicate that private property belongs to individuals, not to society and not to the government. Therefore the $2 million belongs to Taxpayer E. Why should the government have any right to take away money that he has honestly earned?

In addition, when Taxpayer E acquired this wealth through productive work and saving, he *already paid* income tax on that amount as he was earning it. Why should his estate be taxed *again* on that same money?

Economists have argued that the estate tax is a strong disincentive to entrepreneurship, that is, to investing in a business that one owns. If the business grows and the government is simply going to take away 55 cents on every additional dollar that the business is worth when the owner dies, then why should the owner work very hard at trying to build the business? Over half of his work is going to go to the government anyway, rather than any family members or charity to which he wishes to give the money.

Who benefits? Large corporations often buy small businesses that have to be sold because of this estate tax, as was shown in a study by economists Antony Davies and Pavel Yakovel of Duquesne University, as reported in the *Wall Street Journal*:

> The estate tax "impacts small firms disproportionately versus large firms"
> by encouraging well-capitalized companies to gobble up smaller ones at the

---

65. "The Tax That Won't Die," *Wall Street Journal* (Dec. 11, 2009), A20.

owner's death. The study shows the result is to "promote the concentration of wealth by preventing small businesses from being passed on to heirs."[65]

Economists Patrick Fleenor and J. D. Foster of the Tax Foundation wrote about the disincentive effect of the estate tax:

> Because the estate tax is a tax on wealth that has been accumulated over an individual's lifetime, it is often assumed to have little or no effect on that person 's economic decision making. This is a specious notion. An individual's decision to work and save is part of a life-long, forward-looking process. High effective estate tax rates, such as those currently in effect, cause people to reduce productive effort and lower the size of their targeted estates.[66]

Fleenor and Foster ran several simulations of how the estate tax (at the minimum rate of 17% for estates under $10,000 to the maximum rate of 55% for estates over $3 million, to which it will return in 2011) negatively impacts entrepreneurs and, as a result, economic growth. They wrote:

> The various simulations conducted using this model showed that the estate tax has roughly the same effect on entrepreneurial incentives as a doubling of income tax rates. In other words, income tax rates would need to be nearly twice their current levels, or roughly 70 percent, to produce the same disincentive effects as the current estate tax.
>
> Furthermore, given the progressivity of the estate tax, the increase in income tax rates is greater as the size of the estate increases. Given the fact that the estate tax raises only about 1 percent of federal revenue, it is clear that the disincentive effects of the tax are well out of proportion to the revenues associated with the estate tax.[67]

Fleenor and Foster concluded:

> Because many business endeavors require the accumulation of large amounts of business assets, high effective estate tax rates have a particularly deleterious effect on entrepreneurship.... The estate tax is a heavy burden to place on the nation's most productive citizens.[68]

13. The "fair tax"

Several proposals have been made to simplify the horribly complicated tax system in the United States. One such proposal is called the "fair tax," which would be a national sales tax (or "consumption tax") on retail sales. One current proposal would be to enact such a "fair tax" and simultaneously abolish personal income taxes, corporate income taxes, capital gains taxes, Social Security and Medicare taxes, other payroll taxes, gift

---

66. Patrick Fleenor and J. D. Foster, "An Analysis of the Disincentive Effects of the Estate Tax on Entreprenurship," *Tax Foundation Background Paper #9*, Tax Foundation, Washington, DC (June 1, 1994), 17. www.taxfoundation.org/files/bp9.pdf.

67. Ibid., 2.

68. Ibid., 17.

taxes, and estate taxes. I have to admit that the first time anyone looks at that list, a proposal to abolish all those taxes has some initial appeal.

But would it really be a good idea? Such a national sales tax, as proposed, faces some serious objections. First, while it is sometimes promoted as a 23% tax, the way it is defined shows that it is different from current sales taxes, because the 23% in this proposal is calculated *on the basis of the entire amount paid including the tax.* For example, if someone bought an item for $77.00, this "fair tax" on top of that would be $23.00, making a total expenditure of $100.00. But $23.00 added onto a $77.00 item *is really a 30% tax, as people ordinarily calculate sales tax today* (because 23/77 = .299). So the first question that has to be asked is whether people really want a 30% national sales tax, and the first objection is (1) the huge size of the sales tax.

Another objection is (2) tax creep from adding a new kind of tax. That is, because of the never-ending governmental desire for power, once there is a national sales tax, Congress will find it easy to let these other taxes creep back in as well—on top of the 30% sales tax—so soon there would be a 1% national income tax, then 2%, then up and up it would go. And a corporate income tax would probably also come back in. Soon this new kind of tax would be just another tax among many.

Of course, one way to prevent such a reimposition of income taxes would be to repeal the 16th Amendment to the Constitution, which empowers the government to "collect taxes on incomes." But it is exceptionally difficult to pass a constitutional amendment, and it is doubtful that this would ever happen. Such a proposal is basing an argument on wishful thinking, not on reality.

Another objection is that (3) it would place a much greater tax burden on poor people than the current tax system, because everything they buy would be taxed, whereas many of them now pay no tax. (It would burden them more than other people even if a substantial tax rebate were given to the poorest segments of society, at least for people who were just above the "rebate line.")

Still another objection is that (4) charitable organizations might not support the loss of tax benefits that come in the present system for charitable contributions. (That is, if there is no income tax, then of course there would be no deductions from income taxes for charitable contributions.) Another objection is that (5) a huge "black market" would swallow up large segments of the economy because people would simply make transactions in cash and keep no records, thus avoiding a 30% sales tax, which is a huge incentive for tax avoidance on transactions that are almost impossible to trace! Therefore (6) the revenue generated by such a tax might be far less than what is projected, and (7) the increase in tax evasion through cash transactions would have a corrosive effect on society in terms of obedience to law.

Proponents of the "fair tax" have responses to these objections, and I do not deny that the idea has some initial attractiveness. But it seems to me that some of these objections are extremely persuasive, so I cannot support this "fair tax" proposal. It seems to be unrealistic.

But I admit that my evaluation here is based much more on a set of practical concerns rather than on any clear principles from the Bible. (Note also some biblical considerations in favor of a "flat tax" in sections 6 and 7 above [pp. 292–94], a proposal that seems to me to have much more to commend it than the "fair tax" proposal.)

14. The Bible's teaching on inheritance

In ancient Israel, giving property and possessions to children through inheritance was a normal practice:

> A good man leaves an inheritance to his children's children (Prov. 13:22).

> House and wealth are inherited from fathers, but a prudent wife is from the LORD (Prov. 19:14).

It is interesting that the Lord gave to Moses specific directions regarding inheritance:

> And you shall speak to the people of Israel, saying, "If a man dies and has no son, then you shall transfer his inheritance to his daughter. And if he has no daughter, then you shall give his inheritance to his brothers. And if he has no brothers, then you shall give his inheritance to his father's brothers. And if his father has no brothers, then you shall give his inheritance to the nearest kinsman of his clan, and he shall possess it. And it shall be for the people of Israel a statute and rule, as the LORD commanded Moses" (Num. 27:8–11).

Notice that *in no case is any percentage of this inheritance taken by the government* in any kind of "estate tax." It is left to the deceased persons' descendants, and if he has no descendants, it is left to others who are the next of kin.

In fact, the prophet Ezekiel reported God's words prohibiting a ruler from taking away the "inheritance" of people that they would then be unable to pass it down to their heirs:

> *The prince shall not take any of the inheritance of the people,* thrusting them out of their property. He shall give his sons their inheritance out of his own property, so that none of my people shall be scattered from his property (Ezek. 46:18).

One argument in favor of the estate tax is that it prevents "excessive" amounts of wealth from accumulating in the hands of a few families. But who is to decide what is "excessive"? Are we to assume that wealthy people are more likely to misuse their money or use it in socially harmful and destructive ways? If they use it in illegal ways, they will be punished by the government. But if they do not use it in illegal ways, why should it be taken away from them?

The other side of this argument is that an estate tax simply accumulates more and more power for the government. A good argument could be made that a more powerful, increasingly wealthy government is *more* harmful to a nation than a lot of wealthy families, many of whom often do much good for the nation through wise investments and business and through immense charitable donations (neither of which are normally done by government agencies).

So the questions about an estate tax ultimately boil down to the matter of who ultimately owns the property of a nation: individuals or the government? The Bible clearly takes the side of individual ownership of property.

My conclusion is that the estate tax should be permanently repealed.

H. THE SOCIAL SECURITY SYSTEM

1. Overview of Social Security

The term "Social Security" in the United States is used as the common term to refer to the entire federal program officially called the Old-Age, Survivors, and Disability Insurance program (abbreviated OASDI). The taxes to support Social Security are called FICA taxes because they are collected under the Federal Insurance Contribution Act. Currently, employees pay 6.2% of their income in Social Security tax and 1.45% in Medicare tax, for a total of 7.65% of income. Employers have to pay an equal amount, making the total contribution equivalent to 15.3% of an employee's income collected as FICA tax. Self-employed people pay the entire 15.3% themselves. No FICA tax is collected on earnings over $102,000 in a year.

The first Social Security act was signed by President Franklin D. Roosevelt on August 14, 1935. Prior to that time, the United States had no governmental provision to care for those who had retired with no ongoing income, or those who were disabled and could no longer work, or those who were unemployed. The idea was that people would pay into the Social Security fund during their working life and then collect monthly benefits after they retired, until they died.

The system collected only a very small percentage of income at the beginning (equivalent to 2%), half from the employee and half from the employer, and the system worked very well at first. That figure has now risen to 12.4% of income.[69] That growth came because Congress began giving away more and more money. They were able to do this at first because many people were paying into the system and very few people had retired (approximately 6% of the population in 1930 was sixty-five and over).[70] So in the late 1930s and through the 1940s and 1950s, the program had a surplus of funds and Congress repeatedly increased the benefits, which was a popular action and tended to gain them votes.

But eventually many millions of people retired at age sixty-five, and then they continued to collect benefits for twenty or even thirty or more years beyond that time. According to US Census Bureau projections, a substantial increase in the number of older people will occur during the 2010 to 2030 period, after the first Baby Boomers turn sixty-five in 2011. The older population in 2030 is projected to be twice as large as in 2000, growing from 35 million to 72 million. [71] This worker-beneficiary ratio is projected

69. "Legislative History: Social Security Act of 1935," United States Social Security Administration, www.ssa.gov/history/35act.html; and "The 2008 Annual Report of the Board of Trustees of the Federal Old-Age and Survivors Insurance and Disability Insurance Trust Funds" (March 28, 2008). www.ssa. gov/OACT/TR/TR08/tr08.pdf.

70. See "65+ in the United States," United States Census Bureau (Dec. 2005), 9. www.census.gov/prod/2006pubs/p23–209.pdf.

71. Ibid., 1.

to continue to fall to 2.2 workers to beneficiary by 2030 as well.[72] In 1945, the ratio was 41.9 to 1.[73] In addition, medical care benefits were added in 1965 under the Medicare and Medicaid programs. Now Social Security and Medicare *are the largest expenditures in the federal budget.*[74] In the 2010 fiscal year, Social Security payments will constitute 18.6% of the federal budget, and Medicare/Medicaid will constitute an additional 19.6%, for a total of 38.2% of government expenditures. This is a program of immense size, equal to 10% of the gross domestic product (GDP) of the United States (that is, the total economic value of all goods and services produced in the United States in a year).[75] The other large component of the federal budget is defense, which accounts for 19% of the budget.[76] By 2050, spending on Social Security, Medicare, and Medicaid is projected to be 16% of GDP (not 16% of all government spending, but 16% of all the economic wealth produced in the entire nation in one year!), more than twice as much as spending on all other government programs.[77] And all this to make payments to people who are retired and still consuming, but are not necessarily contributing any economically productive benefits to the economy.

2. Concerns about insolvency

The largest concern today about Social Security is that it is quickly running out of money.

Current projections are that by the year 2016 the Social Security Trust Fund will be paying out more than it is taking in. At that point, the federal government, which is required by law to pay back with interest the loans that it takes from the Social Security Trust Fund, will owe $3.5 trillion to the Social Security program, or $10,400 for every man, woman, and child in America.[78] By 2041, it is projected that the trust fund will be exhausted. The Social Security Administration estimates that payroll taxes would have to increase by 28% to cover the projected deficit in 2041.[79] Because people are living longer and collecting so much in benefits, Social Security by 2080 will swamp the federal budget and require 20% of the gross domestic product simply to keep the payments going.[80] To solve this problem, many conservative political leaders have argued that Social Security should be gradually "privatized." This would mean that employees could decide that a small percentage of their Social Security tax, instead of going into government coffers, could be put in *private investments,* which the federal government would require them to do, but which they would individually own. The argument is that private investments would gain a much higher rate of return than giving the money to the government.

72. Ibid., 97: citing www.ssa.gov/OACT/TR/TR03/IV_Lrest. html.

73. "The 2008 Annual Report of the Board of Trustees of the Federal Old-Age and Survivors Insurance and Disability Insurance Trust Funds," op. cit. See also the 2009 report, 2. www.ssa. gov/OACT/TR/2009/tr09.pdf.

74. "Mid-Session Review Budget of the U.S. Government: Fiscal Year 2008," Office of Management and Budget, 4. www. whitehouse.gov/omb/budget/fy2008/pdf/08msr.pdf.

75. Ibid., 6.

76. Ibid., 4.

77. Ibid., 6.

78. "The 2008 Annual Report of the Board of Trustees of the Federal Old-Age and Survivors Insurance and Disability Insurance Trust Funds," op. cit.

79. Ibid.

80. "Mid-Session Review Budget of the U.S. Government: Fiscal Year 2008," op.cit., 6.

In fact, social security programs have successfully been privatized in other countries. Chile is a notable example. In 1981 the Chilean government instituted a social security personal ownership program. The contribution rate, including fees and taxes, is 14.4%. Each participant had an individual account in which his contributions were deposited, and people were then given the choice of five government-approved investment funds for investing the monies. The average yield on the accounts from 1981 to 2002 was 10.7% above the rate of inflation, and the program is self-funded and carries no deficit.[81] It is not hard to imagine that any kind of private investment would give a better rate of return than giving to the government. In fact, current estimates for a fifty-year-old show that he will receive back a rate of return of 0.24% on what he has paid into Social Security over his lifetime.[82] If that same person had been able to invest his money in a Personal Retirement Account, he could conceivably receive $6,000 a month *more* than he will receive from Social Security once he retires. (That is, a private retirement investment would pay him, when he retires, about $8,400 per month rather than $2,300 per month *for the rest of his life!*)

3. Conclusions regarding Social Security

There appear to be at least six conclusions we can draw concerning the current Social Security system.

(1) The root cause of the problem with Social Security is that, for the most part, *it is wastefully paying healthy, potentially productive people not to work.* This simply drains the life and vitality out of any economy. The idea that healthy, productive people should retire at age sixty-five and contribute no further productive work to an economic system is found nowhere in the Bible. In fact, as long as people are able to do so, the Bible tells them that they should work:

> But we urge you, brothers ... to aspire to live quietly, and to mind your own affairs, and *to work with your hands*, as we instructed you, so that you may live properly before outsiders and be dependent on no one (1 Thess. 4:10–12).

> Now we command you, brothers, in the name of our Lord Jesus Christ, that you keep away from any brother who is *walking in idleness* and not in accord with the tradition that you received from us. For you yourselves know how you ought to imitate us, because *we were not idle when we were with you*, nor did we eat anyone's bread without paying for it, but with toil and labor we worked night and day, that we might not be a burden to any of you. It was not because we do not have that right, but to give you in ourselves an example to imitate. For even when we were with you, we would give you this command: *If anyone*

81. See Barbara Kritzer, "Social Security Privatization in Latin America," *United States Social Security Administration* 63:2 (Dec. 2000), www.socialsecurity.gov/policy/docs/ssb/v63n2/v63n2p17.pdf.; and "The Chilean Pension System: Fourth Edition," *Superintendencia de Administradoras de Fon-dos de Pensiones* (Superintendent of the Chile Pension Fund Administration), (May 2003). www.safp.cl/573/articles–3523_chapter6.pdf.

82. Rate of return can be calculated at http://site.heritage.org/research/features/socialsecurity/SSCalcWelcome.asp.

is not willing to work, let him not eat. For we hear that some among you walk in idleness, not busy at work, but busybodies. Now such persons we command and encourage in the Lord Jesus Christ *to do their work quietly and to earn their own living* (2 Thess. 3:6–12; see discussion above, pp. 123, 268–71, on the value of productive work).

There is nothing wrong with the original idea behind Social Security as it was founded in 1935. It is appropriate to have some system of support for people who are no longer *able* to work due to old age or disability or involuntary unemployment. But it is *completely foolish* for any society to pay billions of dollars a year for retirement and medical benefits for people who are perfectly healthy, skilled, and experienced and thus are perfectly able to do productive work and bring benefit to the economy for many years after age sixty-five. Therefore the entire system is now burdened by a flawed idea that is economically invalid and theologically unjustifiable. And it is now maintained by the government because the voting block of those who receive such benefits is so large that anyone who questions the idea is unlikely to be re-elected to office.

(2) The system is deceptive at its core. While it was originally set up as a means by which people could pay into a fund *that would accumulate savings for them,* so that they would have retirement funds when they were unable to work, it quickly shifted to a "pay as you go" system by which current workers are supporting not *their own future* retirement but *present* retirees.

I saw this in my own family, because for many years I was paying thousands of dollars in Social Security tax while my father was receiving Social Security payments. But because of retirement savings and investments, he had a higher annual income than I did! I failed to see why I, with a lower income, and while working at economically productive tasks that brought benefit to the economy, should be paying thousands of dollars that went to him, who had a higher income than I did. What is the sense of that? It certainly was not saving for my own future, because the system is projected to be insolvent before I am able to draw any benefits from it.

(3) Therefore the entire Social Security system contains massive wasteful transfers of money from hard-working people to non-working people, many of whom have no need for this money.

(4) I want to reaffirm that I believe that it is right that government provide *some* kind of guarantee of support for those who are genuinely no longer able to work due to old age, disability, or involuntary unemployment. And it would of course make sense to provide provisions for *partial* benefits to be paid to people who wanted to take semi-retirement and then ease gradually into full retirement.

(5) There would be many benefits to a gradual privatization of Social Security:

(a) It would bring the system back into financial solvency, so that it doesn't bankrupt the federal government.
(b) It would give individuals instead of the government control over their retirement funds, which would increase individual liberty and responsibility.

(c) It would decrease government power over the population of the United States, which would again increase individual liberty.

(6) Why, then, do politicians not change the system? The opposition to change has come primarily from Democrats who have retained enough power in Congress to block any reforms. And they have been supported by some Republicans who are fearful of losing re-election if they alienate the vote of the senior citizens in their district.

But we can wonder about the possibility of mixed motives here. Do the Democrats who support Social Security in its present form and refuse to privatize it have as their primary motive only the protection of people's future income in retirement? Or do they see it not as a scheme for the needy but *as a means of retaining government power* and government control over more and more of people's money and therefore people's lives—an idea that is often a primary (but unspoken) goal of those who continually seek to expand the power of government. As long as politicians continue to argue for maintaining or increasing benefits, it helps to guarantee that they will get a significant portion of senior citizens' votes, and thus they can retain their political power. But they are not seeking what is best for the nation or what is necessary to put our financial house in order.

I. HEALTH CARE

The basic health care question that has faced the United States several times in the recent past is whether or not it should be provided by and managed by the federal government or controlled by individuals and private health care providers.

The health care proposals that came from President Obama and Democrats in Congress in late 2009 were based on the philosophy that the federal government should ultimately control all medical care in the United States. These proposals resulted in the Patient Protection and Affordable Care Act, which was ultimately signed into law by President Obama on March 23, 2010.

One objection to such a plan is that government is never an efficient provider of economic goods, because it does not have to face the competitive incentives of the free market. Therefore other objections follow naturally. Federal government control of health care will inevitably mean a steep increase in costs, a decline in quality, a decline in freedom of choice, and a decline in the availability of certain kinds of medical care.

Most critics of the Democratic plans believed (I think rightly) that experience in other nations shows one thing clearly: If a nation's government controls health care, then *some rationing system will be necessary* to decide who gets treatments and who does not, and there will be widespread instances of denial of care (for a government simply cannot provide an infinite supply of care for everyone who asks for it). While the quality of medical care in the United States in 2009 was the best that was available in the entire world (which is why foreign people who can afford to do so often come to the United States for specialized medical care), critics fear that Obama's plan will lead to rapid decline in the quality of care.

Peter Ferrara, director of entitlement and budget policy for the Institute for Policy Innovation, writes:

> The combination of several elements of the Obama health plan would lead to government rationing of health care.... The first factor will be the low reimbursements to doctors and hospitals that would prevail under the Obama health plan. We see this already in Medicare, which pays doctors and hospitals 20 to 30 percent less than market rates for the care and services they provide under the program. Doctors are dropping out of the Medicare program or refusing to accept more patients.[83] The situation is even worse under Medicaid, which pays doctors and hospitals 30 to 40 percent less than Medicare does. In 2008, over 33 percent of physicians had closed their practices to Medicaid patients and 12 percent had closed their practices to Medicare patients.[84] This restricts access to health care for the poor and the elderly served by the programs, who must scramble for short and hurried appointments with available doctors or wait for emergency hospital care. The lower quality of care provided to Medicaid patients results in poorer health outcomes, including more and earlier deaths from heart disease and cancer compared to privately insured patients.[85]

Ferrara continues:

> This underpayment would have a powerful effect on investment in the health care industry. Investors are not going to finance acquisition of the latest, most advanced equipment and technologies if the government slashes compensation for the services such technologies provide. Investors won't finance new or expanded hospital facilities or clinics, or even the full maintenance of existing ones. This is how the long waiting lines for diagnostics, surgery, and other referrals begin to develop in countries with socialized health care. It is why hospitals and other medical facilities in those countries are often old and deteriorating.[86]

By contrast, Republicans proposed several alternative plans. They recognized the need to provide health care coverage for those who want it and are unable to obtain it, but argued that this is only a small percentage of the population. In 2009, it was estimated that 18.8 million people were truly financially unable to purchase health insurance, approximately 6.1% of the total population of the United States.[87] But if the problem is that 6% of the population needs a way to get health insurance, why have the

---

83. Peter Ferrara, "The Obama Health Plan: Rationing, Higher Taxes, and Lower Quality Care, *The Heartland Institute*, no. 123 (Aug. 2009), 8–9: www.heartland.org/custom/semod_policybot/pdf/25813.pdf: citing The Physicians Foundation, "The Physicians' Perspective: Medical Practice in 2008," *Survey Key Findings* (Nov. 18, 2008), www.physiciansfoundations.org/news/news_show.htm?doc_id=728872.

84. Ibid.

85. Ferrara, op.cit., 9: citing Jeet Guram and John S. O'Shea, MD, "How Washington Pushes Americans into Low-Quality Health Care," *Heritage Foundation Backgrounder #2664* (April 24, 2009). www.heritage.org/Research/Healthcare/bg2664.cfm.

86. Ibid.

87. Ibid., 28.

government take over health care for the other 94%? This does not make sense (unless the real goal is more government control over people's lives). Some reforms that seem sensible to me include these:

(1) A *tax credit* for people to use to purchase health insurance on their own—which was one Republican proposal—would preserve the private health care system in the United States and also preserve freedom of individual choice. This would guarantee coverage for those who need it and would protect the free market and the quality of health care as well as freedom of choice. People would keep their own money to use for health care in the way that they think most wise.

(2) Individuals should be able to join together in voluntary groups in order to obtain the preferable insurance rates now available to people in larger companies.

(3) Congress should pass a law prohibiting individual states from forcing companies to cover high-risk people at the same rate as everyone else, thus increasing costs for everyone in the state. (Unfortunately, this expensive state practice just became national law under President Obama's plan.) In addition, the law should allow people to purchase health insurance from any company in any state, thus nullifying the terribly expensive costs of insurance that have been imposed by states such as New York, with their extensive requirements for the "Cadillac" plans that they mandate that insurance companies have to provide.

(4) Congress should pass medical malpractice reform (tort reform) that would bring immense savings in medicine by limiting the awards that can be given in lawsuits for medical malpractice. Such reform should also institute expert panels that would pre-qualify malpractice lawsuits so that frivolous, time-wasting lawsuits could be weeded out and prevented from clogging the system. With such tort reform, estimates from the Congressional Budget Office are that $5.4 billion could be saved each year out of the $35 billion that the nation spends on health care.[88] (See discussion in chap. 15, pp. 536–45.)

(5) Some provision should be made to care for those who truly cannot afford medical insurance. The solution that seems most helpful to me would be some kind of pooling of high-risk patients to be covered by funds in individual states as their legislatures decide, and also some kind of fund that would enable the truly poor to obtain a basic health insurance policy.

Unfortunately, none of these reforms were included in the 2010 health care reform plan that was passed by Democrats without any Republican support.

J. WHAT IS THE BEST CURE FOR RECESSIONS?

When President Obama took office in January 2009, the nation was facing a severe economic crisis. Many banks and other financial firms were facing insolvency because they had accumulated a large number of home loans that were made to people who had

---

88. According to the Congressional Budget Office in an October 9, 2009, letter to Senator Orrin Hatch, $54 billion would be saved over a ten-year period (or $5.4 billion per year) if caps were placed on non-economic damages at $250,000, a cap on punitive damages at $500,000, and the statute of limitations for filing lawsuits were shortened. www.cbo.gov/ftpdocs/106xx/doc10641/10–09-Tort_Reform.pdf.

no ability to repay them. The downturn in the real estate market meant that many homeowners owed more on their home than it could be sold for, and they found that they were unable to continue making payments on their mortgages. Large manufacturing companies such as General Motors and Chrysler were facing bankruptcy. Unemployment was 7.6% in January,[89] climbed to 9.8% by September 2009,[90] and eventually to over 10%. Such a widespread recession in the economy required some response, lest it continue spreading to more and more sectors of the economy and become a deeper and deeper recession.

What should the solution be in such a situation? There are two views. One view is that the government should spend a lot more money to "stimulate" the economy. That strategy is called the "Keynesian" view after British economist John Maynard Keynes (1883–1946), who advocated much new government spending to overcome recessions. The other strategy is called the "free market" view, because it emphasizes cutting taxes to let people keep more of their own money and then allowing the free market to overcome the recession. (This view was most famously advocated by economist Milton Friedman [1912–2006] and his colleagues at the University of Chicago.)

I will examine the 2008–9 situation in some detail, but the principles explained here are applicable much more broadly. (For causes of this crisis, see pp. 559–60.)

The option favored by President Obama was to begin a program of massive government spending. The spending programs that he favored and that the Democratic-controlled Congress passed were far beyond anything any government has ever spent in the history of the world.

According to Michael J. Boskin, a professor of economics at Stanford University and a senior fellow at the Hoover Institution, in the first year of the Obama administration the present and future debt commitments of the United States government increased *more than all previous presidents combined in the entire history of the United States.*[91] On Obama's inauguration day, the national debt was $10,626,877,048,913. On February 11, 2010, a little more than a year later, the national debt had climbed to $12,349,324,464,284, an increase of $1,722,447,415,371 (or $1.7 trillion).[92] Columnist Robert Samuelson of the *Washington Post* wrote for RealClearPolitics.com:

> From 2010 to 2019, Obama projects annual deficits totaling $7.1 trillion; that's atop the $1.8 trillion deficit for 2009. By 2019, the ratio of publicly held federal debt to gross domestic product (GDP, or the economy) would reach 70 percent, up from 41 percent in 2008. That would be the highest since 1950 (80 percent). The Congressional Budget Office, using less optimistic economic forecasts, raises these estimates. The 2010–19 deficits would total $9.3 trillion; the debt-to-GDP ratio in 2019 would be 82 percent.

89. US Bureau of Labor Statistics. http://data.bls.gov/PDQ/servlet/SurveyOutputServlet?series_id=LNS14000000&data_tool=XGtable.

90. US Bureau of Labor Statistics. www.bls.gov/eag/eag.us.htm.

91. Michael J. Boskin, "Obama's Radicalism Is Killing the Dow," *Wall Street Journal* (March 6, 2009). http://online.wsj.com/article/SB123629969453946717.html.

92. See www.theobamadebt.com/.

But wait: Even these totals may be understated. By various estimates, Obama's health plan might cost $1.2 trillion over a decade; Obama has budgeted only $635 billion. Next, the huge deficits occur despite a pronounced squeeze of defense spending. From 2008 to 2019, total federal spending would rise 75 percent, but defense spending would increase only 17 percent. Unless foreign threats recede, military spending and deficits might both grow.[93]

On January 28, 2010, Congress voted to raise the debt ceiling to $14.3 trillion, which translates to about $45,000 for every American.[94]

Where was all this money going to come from? No one gave any clear answers, but the fact is, there are not many choices for how the government can get money. If the money were simply borrowed from investors around the world who wanted to loan money to the United States Government through the purchase of Treasury bills, notes, and bonds, then it would have to be repaid by enormously increased tax burdens, extending to future generations.

What if America's creditors become concerned about our soaring deficits? They could demand higher interest rates and make the debt problem worse. Len Burman, Syracuse University professor and former director of the Tax Policy Center, wrote, "Taxes would rise to levels that would make a Scandinavian revolt. And the government would not be able to provide anything but the most basic public services. We would no longer be a great power (or even a mediocre one) and the social safety net would evaporate."[95] According to Burman, writing in 2005, even before President Obama's deficit explosion:

> I'm looking through the Congressional Budget Office's crystal ball into the future, and what I see is scarier than Oz's Wicked Witch. If federal spending follows its historical pattern of the last 40 years, by 2050, the government would spend almost one-third of our gross domestic product—not counting interest on the debt. (Government spending would explode mainly because the baby boomers will retire and health care costs will keep rising, which would swell the costs of the government's Medicare and Medicaid programs.) By comparison, in 2004, the federal government raised about 16% of GDP in taxes—half as much as we would need under this scenario.
>
> To balance the budget under the CBO's innocently named "Scenario 1," all taxes would have to double. The average income tax bill would increase by almost $7,000 at today's income levels. And that's only the start.
>
> Imagine losing twice as much of your paycheck to Social Security and Medicare taxes, and twice as much to the excise taxes on beer, gas and wine.

93. Robert Samuelson, "Obama's Dangerous Debt," *Real-ClearPolitics.com* (May 18, 2009). www.realclearpolitics.com/articles/2009/05/18/obamas_dangerous_debt_96539.html.

94. "Senate Lifts Debt Ceiling by $1.9 Trillion," Associated Press (Jan. 28, 2010). www.foxnews.com/politics/2010/01/28/senate-lifts-federal-debt-ceiling-trillion/.

95. Len Burman, "Catastrophic Budget Failure," *Washington Times* (July 14, 2009). http://www.washingtontimes.com/news/2009/jul/14/catastrophic-budget-failure.

And if, despite these taxes, you managed to die with your nest egg intact, your estate might face a super-sized estate tax.

To cover all of the additional spending with income taxes alone, they'd have to more than triple from today's levels. Tripling rates wouldn't work because the top rate would be more than 100%.

To raise that much, the government would have to slash deductions and credits. (No deductions for kids, pensions, mortgage interest, state taxes or charity—and no child credits.) Even then, rates would have to increase by at least 70%. The top income tax rate would soar to 59% (compared with 35% now). A family of four with an annual income of $75,000 would pay more than $16,000 in additional taxes.[96]

However, instead of borrowing money, there was another way to finance this massive debt of 2009. The federal government (through the Federal Reserve Board) could simply begin *printing more money*, pouring billions of new dollars into the economy. And that is also what the Obama administration and the Federal Reserve Board decided to do (see discussion above, pp. 273–74).[97] The actual mechanism was complex and involved some special financial procedures carried out by the Federal Reserve Board and the Treasury Department, but the net effect could be the same as if the United States Mint just began printing billions of dollars in additional money.

What is the problem with the government simply printing billions of dollars of additional money to pay its bills? The problem is that *these new dollars do not represent any increase in the economic wealth of a nation.* They do not represent any real goods and services that people can use. If a baker bakes a loaf of bread or an automobile factory produces a car, then there is *added wealth* in the nation—one more loaf of bread or one more car. If a teacher teaches a class or a popular singer performs a concert, that also adds wealth in the nation—the added value of the education people got in school or the entertainment they enjoyed. However, putting more dollar bills into banks doesn't contribute any value to the economy in the way that these things do. So what does it do?

When the money supply is expanded rapidly like this, it increases the probability of significant inflation in future years (see above the illustration of a *Monopoly* game, p. 273). This is because there is more money in the system but *the same amount of goods and services,* so the money will be used to bid prices up above what they otherwise would have been.

As for the Obama stimulus plan itself, much of it was designated not to genuinely "stimulate" the economy, but simply to promote social change of the sort favored by Democrats. For example, building a new bridge may temporarily provide jobs for construction workers, yet it is not economically as beneficial as starting a new private business, because

96. Leonard E. Burman, "If You Think Taxes are a Pain Now …," Tax Policy Center, Urban-Brookings Institute (April 15, 2005). www.taxpolicycenter.org/publications/url.cfm?ID=900801.

97. Irwin, "Fed to Pump $1.2 Trillion into Markets."

after the bridge is built, it doesn't employ anyone any longer. But a new business that is started continues to employ people and continues to produce economic benefit for the nation.

Was there any other solution to the economic crisis of 2009? An alternative proposal, one favored by many Republicans, was that *the government should have enacted huge tax cuts*.

For example, instead of increasing the national debt by having the government *spend* $800 billion in a "stimulus program," if the government had simply *cut taxes by $800 billion*, it would have left that much more money back in the hands of private individuals in the economy. What would they have done with it? People at the lower end of the economic spectrum probably would have spent most of it right away, but the benefit of that would be that these individuals, rather than the government, would be deciding where the money would be spent, and thus individual liberty would be advanced and there would be an increase in the competitive benefits that come from the free market economy. People at the higher end of the economic spectrum would probably have invested more of that money in expanding their businesses or in starting new businesses. As explained above, a *permanent* decrease in marginal tax rates is a huge incentive for entrepreneurship—the act of investing money and taking risk in order to build a business. And these businesses would then employ more people in more jobs, and the economy would begin to work its way out of the recession quite quickly. Rather than increasing unemployment to around 10% as the Obama "stimulus plan" did, this would rapidly provide many new jobs in the economy, and people would be working again.

In other words, if the government is going to go into debt one way or another, it is far better for it to go into debt by *cutting taxes* than by increasing government expenditures. That is because money retained by private individuals to use in the free market economy is always better in terms of economic growth, and better in terms of increasing individual liberty, than money given into the hands of the government that will use much of the money wastefully and use it to increase government control over everyone's life.

Chapter 10

THE ENVIRONMENT

What policies should governments adopt concerning the use and care of the environment?

A. BIBLICAL TEACHING

At this point I need to explain in more detail some of the main biblical principles concerning the creation that I only mentioned briefly in connection with a Christian worldview in chapter 4 (p.123).

1. The original creation was "very good"

When God first completed his work of creation, "God saw everything that he had made, and behold, *it was very good*" (Gen. 1:31). This was a world in which there was no disease and no "thorns and thistles" (see Gen. 3:18) to harm human beings. It was a world of great abundance and beauty, far beyond anything we can imagine today. Moreover, Adam and Eve were included in the pronouncement "very good," so they were perfectly free from sin. In addition, they were not subject to disease or aging or death (see Rom. 5:12; also Eccles. 7:29).

But even in this perfect world, God gave Adam and Eve work to do in caring for the garden: "The Lord God took the man and put him in the Garden of Eden *to work it and keep it*" (Gen. 2:15). God also set before Adam and Eve the entire created earth and told them to develop it and make it useful, with the implication that they would enjoy it and give thanks to him: "And God said to them, 'Be fruitful and multiply and fill the earth *and subdue it and have dominion* over the fish of the sea and over the birds of the heavens and over every living thing that moves on the earth'" (Gen. 1:28).

2. Because Adam and Eve sinned, God placed a curse on the entire natural world

The current state of the "natural world" is not the way God created it. After Adam and Eve sinned, one of the punishments that he imposed was to change the functioning of the natural world so that it was no longer an idyllic garden of Eden, but a much more dangerous and difficult place for human beings to live:

> And to Adam he said,
> "Because you have listened to the voice of your wife
> > and have eaten of the tree
> of which I commanded you,
> > 'You shall not eat of it,'
> cursed is the ground because of you;
> > in pain you shall eat of it all the days of your life;
> thorns and thistles it shall bring forth for you;
> > and you shall eat the plants of the field.
> By the sweat of your face
> > you shall eat bread,
> till you return to the ground,
> > for out of it you were taken;
> for you are dust,
> > and to dust you shall return" (Gen. 3:17–19)

At that point early in the history of mankind, God caused a tremendous change in the beautiful creation that he had made. He "cursed" the ground so that rather than being a place from which Adam could eat food in overwhelming abundance, raising crops would require "pain" (v. 17) and hard toil, for "by the sweat of your face you shall eat bread" (v. 19).

a. The earth would now contain "thorns and thistles" and many other dangerous and harmful things

God's words to Adam told him that now there would be danger and harm on the earth, for "thorns and thistles" (Gen. 3:18) would come forth. Here the expression "thorns and thistles" functions as a kind of poetic image, a specific, concrete example that represents a multitude of things—such as hurricanes, floods, droughts, earthquakes, poisonous plants, poisonous snakes and insects, and hostile wild animals—that make the earth a place in which its natural beauty and usefulness are constantly mixed with other elements that bring destruction, sickness, and even death. Nature is not now what it was created to be, but is "fallen."

This component of a Christian worldview has significant implications for how people view the environment today. The creation is *not now perfect,* as it someday will be. At present, nature still exists in a "fallen" state. Therefore *what we think of as "natural" today is not always good.* We must protect children from putting their hands on the hole of a cobra or an adder, and we must build floodwalls and levees to protect against hurricanes, for example. We heat our homes in winter and air-condition them in summer rather than living all the time in "natural" temperature. We irrigate fields to grow crops where "nature" did not decide to grow them. We put screens on windows or spray insect repellant to keep "natural" mosquitoes from biting us. *Fallen nature today is not the garden of Eden!* We improve on nature in thousands of ways, to make it a more suitable place to live.

The fact that nature is not perfect today has many other implications. It means that people with a Christian worldview may decide that it is morally right to use insecticides to kill malaria-bearing mosquitoes, for example. They may decide it is right to clear flammable dead branches in national parks so as to prevent huge forest fires, and to cut down dry trees next to homes so that the homes are not consumed in the next flash forest fire. It means that it can be morally right, and even pleasing to God, to breed seedless grapes (that are not "natural") and seedless oranges and watermelons, or to use biological research and selective breeding of plants to develop varieties of rice or corn that are resistant to insects and mold, even though all of these things are somehow "tampering with nature." They are tampering with *fallen* nature, making natural products better. *That is what God intends us to do.* Part of our God-given task of subduing the earth and having dominion over it (Gen. 1:28) is inventing various measures to overcome the way in which nature is sometimes harmful to man and sometimes less than fully helpful. (Even in the unfallen world God told Adam and Eve to "subdue" it, implying that God wanted them to *improve on* nature as it was originally created—that is, God created it to be investigated and explored and developed!)

Of course, people can make mistakes in their attempts to subdue the earth, and there can be harmful results. But evaluating whether those attempts are "helpful" or "harmful" is *merely a matter of assessing the resulting facts,* not something to be dismissed merely because they are "tampering with nature." Attempting to make such modifications to what is "natural" is, in general, morally right and part of what God wants human beings to do with the earth. It is not an area in which Christians should automatically assume that what is "natural" is probably or always better. It is merely a matter of evaluating the measurable results.

By contrast, some people today, especially among the more radical environmental movements, do not understand the "fallen" status of the natural world but think that what is "natural" is the ideal, and therefore they regularly oppose ordinary, beneficial human efforts to improve on the way things exist in the natural world. This tendency leads some people to oppose every new factory, dam, or residential development project—no matter how carefully constructed and how sensitive it is to protecting the surrounding environment—all because their highest good—their "god" in some sense—is the earth *in its untouched natural state.* Thus they oppose everything that "tampers" with the earth, everything that changes an animal habitat or a growth of trees. This is making nature to be God, and it is not consistent with a biblical worldview.

It is not wrong *in principle*, as many environmentalists think it is, for human beings to modify the world, from the macro scale (such as hydroelectric dams and river-taming projects) to the micro scale (genetically modified organisms). God created the earth to be occupied and developed by human beings made in his image. Isaiah says that God "formed the earth and made it (he established it; he did not create it empty, *he formed it to be inhabited!*)" (Isa. 45:18).

b. God did not destroy the earth, but he left much that is good in it

A biblical worldview also recognizes that God did not *completely destroy* the earth, nor did he make it *entirely evil and harmful* (not all plants are poisonous, for example). He simply changed it so that it is not perfect now. The earth that God created is still "good" in many ways. It is *amazingly resourceful* because of the great treasures that he has placed in it for us to discover, enhance, and enjoy.

God did not tell Adam and Eve that they would be *unable* to eat of the ground, but that their existence on it would be *painful*, and in the same verse in which he said, "thorns and thistles it shall bring forth for you," he added, "and *you shall eat* the plants of the field" (Gen. 3:18). This implies that there would still be much good for human beings to discover and use and enjoy in the earth.

In fact, many times in the Old Testament God promised abundant blessings on crops and livestock as a reward for the obedience of his people (see Deut. 28:1–14). With regard to various kinds of food, Paul could say, "*Everything created by God is good*, and nothing is to be rejected if it is received with thanksgiving, for it is made holy by the Word of God and prayer" (1 Tim. 4:4–5). Paul also said that God "richly provides us with everything to enjoy" (1 Tim. 6:17). This implies that human beings should feel free to use the earth's resources with joy and thanksgiving to God.

c. God promises a future time when the abundant prosperity of Eden will be restored to the earth

The Bible predicts a time after Christ's return when "the creation itself will be *set free* from its bondage to decay and obtain the freedom of the glory of the children of God" (Rom. 8:21). In that day,

> The wolf shall dwell with the lamb,
> and the leopard shall lie down with the young goat,
> and the calf and the lion and the fatted calf together;
> and a little child shall lead them....
> The nursing child shall play over the hole of the cobra,
> and the weaned child shall put his hand on the adder's den.
> They shall not hurt or destroy
> in all my holy mountain;

for the earth shall be full of the knowledge if the Lord
as the waters cover the sea (Isa. 11:6–9).

Therefore the prophet Amos could say that in this future time, crops will spring up and grow suddenly, just as soon as they are planted, and agricultural land will need no time to lie fallow and recover its productive abilities, because,

"Behold the days are coming," declares the Lord,
"when the plowman shall overtake the reaper
and the treader of grapes him who sows the seed;
the mountains shall drip sweet wine,
and all the hills shall flow with it" (Amos 9:13).

Other Old Testament prophetic passages also predict this future time of a wonderful renewal of nature, so that "the desert shall rejoice and blossom like the crocus" (Isa. 35:1), and God will make the "desert" of Zion "like the garden of the Lord" (Isa. 51:3; cf. 55:13). In New Testament times Peter echoed this in preaching that one day would come "the time for restoring all things" (Acts 3:21).

I also believe that such restoration of the earth need not completely wait until Christ's return and God's miraculous renewing of the earth, but that the redeeming work of Christ provides the basis for us even now *to work incrementally toward the direction that God shows us to be his future good intention for the earth*. Theologian and economist Cal Beisner puts it this way:

The effects of the atoning death, victorious resurrection, and triumphant ascension of Christ, then, sweep over all of creation, including man, animals, plants, and even the ground itself. They include the restoration of the image of God in the redeemed and through them—and by common grace even through many who are not redeemed—the restoration of knowledge, holiness, and creativity in working out the cultural mandate, including human multiplication, subduing and ruling the earth, transforming the wilderness by cultivation into a garden, and guarding that garden against harm.[1]

3. God now wants human beings to develop the earth's resources and to use them wisely and joyfully

As stated earlier, at the very beginning of human history, immediately after God created Adam and Eve, he told them to

"Be fruitful and multiply and fill the earth *and subdue it and have dominion* ... over every living thing that moves on the earth" (Gen. 1:28).

He also told them how they were to care specifically for the garden of Eden—primarily "to work it and keep it" (2:15).

---

1. E. Calvin Beisner, *Where Garden Meets Wilderness* (Grand Rapids: Acton Institute and Eerdmans, 1997), 107.

This responsibility to "subdue" the earth and "have dominion" over it implies that God expected Adam and Eve and their descendants to explore and develop the earth's resources in such a way that they would bring benefit to themselves and other human beings. (The Hebrew word *kābāsh* means "to subdue, dominate, bring into servitude or bondage" and is used later, for example, of subduing the land of Canaan so that it would serve and provide for the people of Israel; cf. Num. 32:22, 29; Josh. 18:1.)

a. Subduing the earth after the fall

The responsibility to develop the earth and enjoy its resources continued after Adam and Eve's sin, for even then God told them, "You shall eat the plants of the field" (Gen. 3:18).

David also says in Psalm 8,

> What is man that you are mindful of him...?
> *You have given him dominion* over the works of your hands;
>   you have put all things under his feet,
> all sheep and oxen,
>   and also the beasts of the field,
> the birds of the heavens, and the fish of the sea,
>   whatever passes along the paths of the seas (Ps. 8:4–8).

Another evidence that our responsibility to "subdue" the earth continues after the fall is the very necessity of cultivating the earth in order to grow food to eat. We have to "subdue" the earth to some extent or we will all starve!

Moreover, the fact that after the flood God explicitly told Noah, "Every moving thing that lives shall be food for you" (Gen. 9:3), confirms the fact that responsibility to exercise dominion over the natural creation, including the animal kingdom, is still given by God to human beings. In the New Testament, Paul implies that eating meat is morally right and no one should pass judgment on another person because of this (see Rom. 14:2–3; 1 Cor. 8:7–13; 1 Tim. 4:4; also Mark 7:19, where it says that Jesus "declared all foods clean").

Jesus also taught that *human beings are much more valuable in God's sight than animals*, and this tends to confirm our continuing responsibility to "have dominion" over the animal kingdom and to seek to make animals useful for us, since they are God's good provision for the human race. Jesus said, "Of how much *more value* is a man than a sheep!" (Matt. 12:12). He also said, "Look at the birds of the air.... Are you not of *more value* than they?" (Matt. 6:26). And again he said, "You are of *more value* than many sparrows" (Matt. 10:31).

However, these commands to subdue the earth and have dominion over it *do not mean that we should use the earth in a wasteful or destructive way* or intentionally treat animals with cruelty. Rather, "whoever is righteous has regard for the life of his beast" (Prov. 12:10), and God told the people of Israel to take care to protect fruit trees during a time of war (see Deut. 20:19–20). In addition, the command, "You shall love your neighbor as yourself" (Matt. 22:39), implies a responsibility to think of the needs of other human beings, even those who will come in future generations. Therefore we should not use the earth in such a way that we destroy its resources or make them unable to be used for future generations. *We should use the resources of the earth wisely, as good stewards*, not wastefully or abusively.

b. Contrasting a biblical view of the earth and a radical environmentalist view

This biblical principle about the moral goodness of developing and enjoying the earth's resources stands in contrast to the views of radical environmentalists, many of whom hold to "untouched nature" as their ideal and therefore object to activities like the use of animals (such as guinea pigs or chimpanzees) in medical research. Environmentalists will attempt to block many new building projects through the use of lawsuits claiming that some species of turtle or other small creature like the pygmy owl will be damaged.[2]

For instance, farmers in California's San Joaquin Valley have had the water they use for growing crops diverted to the Pacific Ocean to save a three-inch fish called the delta smelt.[3] As a result, unemployment rates have hit 40% in the region, which provides much of the produce for the rest of the nation and the world. Thus this environmentalist action has caused food shortages and higher prices, again harming the poor most of all. *The Wall Street Journal* wrote:

> California has a new endangered species on its hands in the San Joaquin Valley—farmers. Thanks to environmental regulations designed to protect the likes of the three-inch long delta smelt, one of America's premier agricultural regions is suffering in a drought made worse by federal regulations.... The state's water emergency is unfolding thanks to the latest mishandling of the Endangered Species Act. Last December, the U.S. Fish and Wildlife Service issued what is known as a "biological opinion" imposing water reductions on the San Joaquin Valley and environs to safeguard the federally protected hypomesus transpacificus, a.k.a., the delta smelt. As a result, tens of billions of gallons of water from mountains east and north of Sacramento have been channeled away from farmers and into the ocean, leaving hundreds of thousands of acres of arable land fallow or scorched.... The result has already been devastating for the state's farm economy. In the inland areas affected by the court-ordered water restrictions, the jobless rate has hit 14.3%, with some farming towns like Mendota seeing unemployment numbers near 40%. Statewide, the rate reached 11.6% in July, higher than it has been in 30 years. In August, 50 mayors from the San Joaquin Valley signed a letter asking President Obama to observe the impact of the draconian water rules firsthand.[4]

2. "Pygmy owl leaves a conservation legacy." *Arizona Star* (Aug. 5, 2005), www.azstarnet.com/sn/related/87256; and Leslie Carlson and Pete Thomas, "Back off, Bambi," *Los Angeles Times* (June 15, 2004), http://articles.latimes.com/2004/jun/15/news/os-deer15.

3. Peter Fimrite, "U.S. Issues Rules to Protect Delta Smelt," *San Francisco Chronicle* (Dec. 16, 2008). www.sfgate.com/cgi-bin/article.cgi?f=/c/a/2008/12/15/MNDD14OIOF.DTL.

4. "California's Man-Made Drought," *Wall Street Journal* (Sept. 2, 2009), A14. http://online.wsj.com/article/SB10001424052970204731804574384731898375624.html.

Secular environmentalists object to the killing of deer or geese in residential neighborhoods, even when these animals are so numerous they have become a significant public nuisance and even a danger to health (as with the prevalence of ticks that spread Lyme disease).[5] They will object to the killing of mosquitoes with pesticides even when the mosquitoes spread West Nile Virus and (in Africa) spread malaria that kills millions of people.[6] It seems to me a correct application of Matthew 10:31 to think that Jesus would have said, "People are of *more value* than many millions of mosquitoes."

Another tendency of secular culture is to view much use of the earth's resources with *fear*—fear that human beings will damage some part of "untouched nature," which seems to be the environmentalists' ideal. Such fear will lead people to oppose hydroelectric dams (they harm fish),[7] windmills (they harm birds),[8] oil and natural gas development (oil rigs ruin the appearance of nature, and there might be a spill),[9] any burning of coal or oil or gas (they might harm the climate),[10] and any use of nuclear energy (it might lead to an accident).[11]

They are always emphasizing the dangers (whether real or imagined) and never realistically evaluate an *insignificant risk* of danger in comparison to a *certain promise* of great benefit. Some of them give the impression that they think the major problem with the whole earth is the presence of human beings!

Radical environmentalist Paul Watson of the Sea Shepherd Institute wrote:

> Today, escalating human populations have vastly exceeded global carrying capacity and now produce massive quantities of solid, liquid, and gaseous waste. Biological diversity is being threatened by over-exploitation, toxic pollution, agricultural mono-culture, invasive species, competition, habitat destruction, urban sprawl, oceanic acidification, ozone depletion, global warming, and climate change. It's a runaway train of ecological calamities. It's a train that carries all the earth's species as unwilling passengers with humans as the manically insane engineers unwilling to use the brake pedal.[12]

Watson also called human beings the "AIDS of the Earth" and declared that human beings must reduce the world's population to less than one billion people (from its current 6.8 billion!), dwell in communities no larger than "20,000 people and separated from other communities by wilderness areas," and recognize themselves as "earthlings" dwelling in a primitive state with other species. Watson wrote, "Curing a body of cancer requires radical and invasive therapy, and therefore, curing the biosphere of the human virus will also require a radical and invasive approach."[13]

---

5. See www.eradicatelymedisease.org/environment.html.

6. Michael Doyle, "Environmentalists challenge pesticide rule," *McClatchy Newspapers* (Nov. 29, 2006).

7. "How Dams Harm Rivers," www.imhooked.com/for/damsharm.html; and Erik Robinson, "Latest dam plan already under fire from groups," *The Columbian* (May 6, 2008), www.wildsalmon.org/library/lib-detail.cfm?docID=772.

8. John Ritter, "Wind Turbines Take Toll on Birds of Prey," *USA Today* (Jan. 4, 2005).

9. "Congress Lifts Offshore Drilling Moratorium," World Wildlife Fund News. http://wwf.worldwildlife.org/site/PageServer?pagename=can_results_offshore_drilling.

10. See www.energyjustice.net/coal/.

11. "Nuclear Energy = Dangerous Energy." www.greenpeace.org/seasia/en/news/nukes-endanger-indonesia.

12. Paul Watson, "The Beginning of the End for Planet Earth?" Sea Shepherd Conservation Society (May 4, 2007). www.seashepherd.org/news-and-media/editorial–070504–1.html#.

13. Ibid.

Speaking about the environment in Great Britain, John Guillebaud, co-chairman of Optimum Population Trust and emeritus professor of family planning at University College in London, told the *Sunday Times* that parents ought to consider the environment first when they plan to have a child. He said, "The greatest thing anyone in Britain could do to help the future of the planet would be to have one less child."[14]

A report by that trust entitled *A Population-Based Climate Strategy* said, "Population limitation should therefore be seen as the most cost-effective carbon offsetting strategy available to individuals and nations."[15]

By contrast, God's perspective in the Bible is that the creation of human beings in his image and placing them on the earth to rule over it as his representatives is the crowning achievement of God in his entire work of creation.

A Christian worldview would consider it morally right—and pleasing to God, and no cause for irrational fear—when human beings wisely exercise widespread and effective dominion over the earth and its creatures. This worldview will present no moral objection to eating meat from animals or to wearing leather or fur made from animal skins. (God himself clothed Adam and Eve with animal skins [Gen. 3:21], setting a precedent for the beneficial use of animals for human beings.) Such a Christian worldview would also think it morally right—even morally imperative—to use animals (in a reasonably compassionate way) for medical research that can lead to solutions to human diseases.

Another implication of this component of a Christian worldview is that *we should view the development and production of goods from the earth as something morally good*, not merely an evil kind of "materialism." God placed in the earth resources that would enable man to develop much more than food and clothing. There are resources that enable the construction of beautiful homes, automobiles, airplanes, computers, and millions of other consumer goods. While these things can be misused, and while people's hearts can have wrongful attitudes about them (such as pride, jealousy, and coveting), *the things in themselves* should be viewed as *morally good* because they are part of God's intention in placing us on the earth to subdue it and have dominion over it.

Therefore the creation of large amounts of wealth in some of the world's more economically developed nations should not be seen as something that is morally evil in itself, but rather something that is fundamentally good. It is part of what God intended when he told Adam and Eve to subdue the earth and have dominion over it. This means that wealthy nations and wealthy individuals should not automatically be considered "evil" or even "unspiritual." Rather, we should do what we can to help other nations achieve similar levels of wealth for themselves—as is happening every year in more and more countries around the world. If subduing the earth and making it useful for mankind is a good activity, then it is right to *encourage* many different kinds of development of the earth's resources and many different kinds of production of material goods from the earth.

14. John Guillebaud, "Having Large Families Is an Eco-Crime," *Sunday Times* (May 6, 2007). http://www.washington-times.com/news/2009/jul/14/catastrophic-budget-failure.

15. Peter J. Smith and Steve Jalsevac, "Environmentalist Extremists Call Humanity 'Virus' a 'Cancer'; Large Families Guilty of 'Eco-Crime,'" *LifeSiteNews.com* (May 8, 2007). www.lifesitenews.com/ldn/2007/may/07050812.html.

God's command to subdue the earth and have dominion over it also implies that *it was not his intention for all human beings to live in abject poverty or live as subsistence farmers barely surviving from crop to crop.* Rather, his intention was that all people should enjoy the abundance of the earth's resources with thanksgiving to him. This implies that it is *morally right* for us to seek to overcome poverty wherever it is found. It is also *morally right* for us to help the world's poor to have the ability to develop and enjoy the earth's good resources in abundance.

4. God created an abundant and resourceful earth

Did God create an earth that would run out of essential resources because of human development? That is not the picture given in the Bible. God created an earth that he pronounced to be "very good" (Gen. 1:31). Although he cursed the earth after the sin of Adam and Eve, he also promised a future time when *this same earth* would be renewed and bring forth abundant prosperity (see above, pp. 323–24). That renewed earth will have the same resources (it is not a new creation),[16] but it will have the dangers and harmfulness and painfulness to man removed. It will once more become abundantly productive like the original garden of Eden.

Therefore the Bible's picture of the earth *in general* is that it has abundant resources that God has put there to bring great benefit to us as human beings made in his image. There is no hint that mankind will ever exhaust the earth's resources by developing them and using them wisely.

Does current information about the earth confirm this idea that it has abundant resources? That is the question of the next section.

B. THE CURRENT STATE OF THE EARTH'S RESOURCES

Many questions about applying biblical teachings to environmental questions have to do with *correctly evaluating the facts* about the current situation of the earth. What is the current status of the earth's resources, and what can we learn from long-term trend lines on various resources?

1. Are we destroying the earth?

People often fear that we are about to run out of land for food or run out of clean water or some other essential resource. That in turn leads them to live with a faint cloud of continual guilt whenever they drive a car or water their lawn or use paper cups and paper plates, and to live with a vague fear that in a few decades the earth's resources might be exhausted and unable to sustain human life.

In this section I present data indicating that *there is no good reason to think we will ever run out of any essential natural resource.* God has created for us an earth that has incredible

---

16. See Wayne Grudem, *Systematic Theology* (Grand Rapids: Zondervan: 1994), 1160–61.

abundance, and whenever it seems that some resource is becoming scarce, he has given us the wisdom to invent useful substitutes. I look at data regarding the following factors:

a. World population
b. Land for growing food
c. Water
d. Clean air
e. Waste disposal
f. Global forests
g. Species loss
h. Herbicides and pesticides
i. Life expectancy

2. The importance of using information from long-term, worldwide trends rather than short-term, local stories of disasters

In many conversations I have found that people's "vague impressions" about what is happening to the earth are almost always wrong. People have developed their opinions, not from actual data showing the true state of the earth as a whole and showing long-term trends, but from a barrage of media reports about specific local incidents where something has gone wrong—a certain oil spill, or a crop failure and famine in some country, or the cutting down of trees and loss of forest area in some country, or a polar bear jumping off a piece of melting ice somewhere in the Arctic, and so forth.

But we should always keep in mind that newspapers need readers and television programs need viewers, and fear is one of the great ways of increasing an audience. Therefore the media have a natural bias toward reporting alarming events—whether an airplane crash or a serial killer or a water or food shortage in some place or another. But such individual events almost always have specific local causes that may not exist elsewhere.

Another factor contributing to people's general impressions of resource scarcity is the existence of a number of special interest organizations that raise more money and keep themselves employed only by putting out press releases declaring that worldwide environmental disaster is just around the corner. Bjorn Lomborg, a Danish environmentalist and economic statistician, cites numerous examples of astoundingly blatant dishonesty in the use of data in publications by environmentalist organizations such as the Worldwatch Institute or the World Wide Fund for Nature or Greenpeace.[17]

For example, Lomborg writes that Lester Brown and the Worldwatch Institute make statements such as "The key environmental indicators are increasingly negative. Forests are shrinking, water tables are falling, soils are eroding, wetlands are disappearing, fisheries are collapsing, range-lands are deteriorating, rivers are running dry, temperatures are rising, coral reefs are dying, and plant and animal species are disappearing." Lomborg adds, "Powerful reading—stated entirely without references."[18]

---

17. See Bjorn Lomborg, *The Skeptical Environmentalist: Measuring the Real State of the World* (Cambridge: Cambridge University Press, 2001), 8–31.

18. Ibid., 16.

Lomborg goes on to refute these claims. He says that reports from the Food and Agricultural Organization (FAO) of the United Nations show that global forest cover has increased from 30.04% of the global land area in 1950 to 30.89% in 1994.[19] With regard to water shortages, Lomborg writes:

> One of the most widely used college books on the environment, *Living in the Environment*, claims that "according to a 1995 World Bank study, 30 countries containing 40 percent of the world's population (2.3 billion people) now experience chronic water shortages that threaten their agriculture and industry and the health of their people." This World Bank study is referred to in many different environment texts with slightly differing figures. Unfortunately, none mentions a source.
>
> With a good deal of help from the World Bank, I succeeded in locating the famous document. It turns out that the myth had its origin in a hastily drawn up press release. The headline on the press release was "The world is facing a water crisis: 40 percent of the world's population suffers from chronic water shortage." If you read on, however, it suddenly becomes clear that the vast majority of the 40 percent are not people who use too much water but those who have no access to water or sanitation facilities—the exact opposite point. If one also reads the memo to which the press release relates, it shows that the global water crisis which Lester Brown and others are worried about affects not 40 percent but about 4 percent of the world's population. And, yes, it wasn't 30, but 80 countries the World Bank was referring to.[20]

Therefore it is important for us to find some reliable data that accurately show the long-term trends in the earth's resources. What is the overall result of human development on the world environment that we live in? Is the presence of mankind actually destroying the earth? Taken as a whole, is human development of the earth's resources a helpful or harmful thing?

These questions are especially important in light of the biblical teachings that I discussed earlier (see pp. 320–29), especially the teaching that the earth God created was "very good" (Gen. 1:31) and the teaching that God told Adam and Eve that they were to "be fruitful and multiply and *fill the earth* and *subdue* it and *have dominion* over the fish of the sea and over the birds of the heavens and over every living thing that moves" (v. 28).

If God created an earth for man to subdue and develop, then it is reasonable to think that he created (a) an earth with abundant resources able to be developed, and (b) an earth that would *benefit* from man's developing it, not one that would *be destroyed* through such development. In addition, if God wanted human beings to "fill the earth," then it seems reasonable to expect that the spread of human population over the earth could be done without necessarily harming or destroying it.

The "curse" that God put on the earth in Genesis 3:17–18 would make development of the earth's resources more difficult and more painful, but it would not change the

---

19. Ibid.   20. Ibid., 20.

basic character of such development or turn it into something harmful rather than helpful. Instead, subduing the earth would be even more necessary in a land filled with "thorns and thistles" that had to be removed before the land was a suitable and enjoyable place for human beings.

Our overall viewpoint on these matters affects our basic expectations. Do we basically expect that development of the earth's resources will be *helpful* or *harmful* to the earth? Do we expect that obedience to God's commands will bring benefits to ourselves and to the earth or bring harm to both? Do we tend to assume that God made an earth that is about to run out of all sorts of resources necessary for human survival, or do we think that he made an incredibly abundant earth with incredibly rich and diverse resources that would be useful for human life and enjoyment?

If it is God's purpose for us to develop and enjoy the earth's resources with thanksgiving to him, then we would also expect it would be Satan's purpose to oppose and hinder such developmental activity at every point and in every way possible.

In the following section I will refer to *long-term trends* that show remarkable human progress in making the earth useful for mankind and doing so in a sustainable way. As the teachings of Genesis would suggest, modern evidence confirms that *God created an incredibly abundant and resourceful earth,* and he also created human beings with the wisdom and skill to develop and use those resources for God's glory and with thanksgiving to him.

3. Long-term trends show that human beings will be able to live on the earth, enjoying ever-increasing prosperity, and never exhausting its resources

Many of the statistics I cite below come from one of the most influential books of the past decade, *The Skeptical Environmentalist* by Bjorn Lomborg. The advantage of Lomborg's book is that as a professor of statistics he is an expert in the fair and accurate use of statistics and bases his arguments on official, publicly available information from sources such as United Nations agencies and the World Bank.[21] And he quotes long-term trends, not just an isolated bit of data from a two- or three-year period.

Because Lomborg's book mounted a massive challenge to widely accepted environmentalist views, it was severely criticized by a number of writers and organizations. But Lomborg has responded in an articulate and sensible way to the most serious of these criticisms, and anyone can read the exchanges on the Internet. From what I have read of the controversy, it appears clear to me that Lomborg has gotten the best of the arguments and that his critics are careless and emotional in their claims, but not very persuasive. It is not surprising that *Time* magazine named Lomborg one of the world's 100 most influential people in 2004[22] and *Foreign Policy* magazine named him one of the top 100 public intellectuals in 2008.[23] Also in 2008, *Esquire* magazine named him one of the 75 most influential people of the twenty-first century.[24]

21. Ibid., 31.

22. "Bjorn Lomborg," *Time* (April 26, 2004). www.time.com/time/magazine/article/0,9171,994022,00.html?iid=chix-sphere.

23. "The Top 100 Public Intellectuals: Bios," *Foreign Policy* (April 2008). www.foreignpolicy.com/story/cms.php?story_id=4293.

24. "The Heretic's New Book," *Esquire* (Sept. 24, 2007). www.esquire.com/features/esquire–100/globalwarming1007.

a. World population

The world population has grown from 750 million people in 1750 to 6.8 billion people today.[25] As the chart below shows, the rapid increase in growth began in the twentieth century but is already slowing down and is predicted to end at a world population of about 11 billion around the year 2200.[26] Other, more recent projections show world population stabilizing at even lower levels (such as 8–9 billion) and then declining, as the population already is doing in Western Europe.[27]

Figure 10.1

WORLD POPULATION 1750-2200

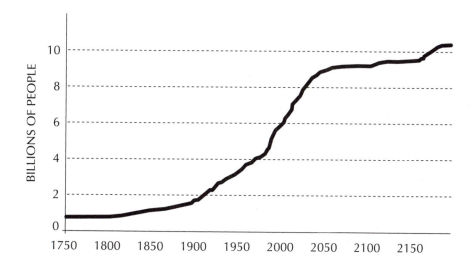

Source: The World at Six Billion, United Nations Population Division (October 1999), 5. www.un.org/esa/population/publications/sixbillion/sixbilpart1.pdf.

The reason world population grew so quickly is that modern development gave people better access to food, water, medical care, and sanitation, so on average they lived much longer. But the reason the world population will stabilize is that as nations increase in wealth, their birth rate declines, as is evident in the smaller birthrates in Europe today, for instance.[28] But will we run out of space on the earth? No, there is much more available

---

25. World Population Clock. www.worldometers.info/population/.

26. "World Population Would Stabilize at Nearly 11 Billion by Year 2200." www.un.org/News/Press/docs/1998/19980202. POP656.html.

27. Chart from Bjorn Lomborg, *The Skeptical Environmentalist*, 46, fig. 11.

28. Mark Henderson, "Europe Shrinking as Birthrates Decline," *London Times Online* (March 28, 2003). www.timesonline.co.uk/tol/news/world/article1123982.ece.

space for people to live. Some of the most densely populated countries in the world are in Europe, as shown on the following chart:

Figure 10.2

Country	Population/sq. mile
Netherlands	1,023
Belgium	880
United Kingdom	693
Germany	598
Italy	500
Switzerland	470

These figures are much higher than the United States, which has a population density of 79.6 persons per square mile.[29] But as anyone who has visited the Netherlands, Belgium, Germany, or the United Kingdom can attest, these countries have vast areas of uncrowded farmland and open spaces.

These can be seen in comparison with the following countries, which are commonly thought to have high population densities:[30]

Figure 10.3

Country	Population/sq. mile
Japan	873
India	851
China	353

To get an idea of what these densities mean, we can compare them with a few states in the United States as well:[31]

---

29. US Census Bureau, Census 2000 Redistricting Data (PL 94–171) Summary File. Cartography: Population Division, US Census Bureau. www.census.gov/population/cen2000/atlas/censr01–103.pdf#page=3.

30. These figures are converted from kilometers to square miles. For population density estimates, see US Census Bureau, International Data Base. www.census.gov/ipc/www/idb/region.php.

31. US Census Bureau, Census 2000 Summary File 1. http://factfinder.census.gov/servlet/GCTTable?_bm=y&-ds_name=DEC_2000_SF1_U&-CONTEXT=gct&-mt_name=DEC_2000_SF1_U_GCTPH1_US9&-redoLog=false&-_caller=geoselect&-geo_id=&-format=US–9|US–9S&-_lang=en.

Figure 10.4

State	Population/sq. mile
New Jersey	1,134.4
Massachusetts	809.8
New York	401.9
Florida	296.4
Ohio	277.3
Pennsylvania	274.0
Illinois	223.4
North Carolina	165.2
Indiana	169.5
Michigan	175.0
Wisconsin	98.8

Certainly our more densely populated states have a number of large cities, but they also have vast amounts of land area in forests, parks, and agricultural use.

Nor does increasing population seem to change the total use of land in a nation by very much, mostly because people move into cities and much of the rural area of a country is left untouched. For example, between 1945 and 1992 the US population almost doubled (from about 140 million to about 256 million people; it is now over 307 million).[32] But as the following chart indicates, a doubling of US population resulted in almost no change in the amount of land used for crops, forests, or grasslands.[33]

Figure 10.5

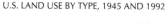

U.S. LAND USE BY TYPE, 1945 AND 1992

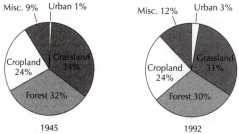

Misc. 9%   Urban 1%
Cropland 24%   Grassland 34%
Forest 32%
1945

Misc. 12%   Urban 3%
Cropland 24%   Grassland 31%
Forest 30%
1992

32. Population: 1900 to 2002. www.census.gov/statab/hist/ HS–01.pdf and www.census.gov/population/www/popclockus. html.

33. Stephen Moore and Julian Simon, *It's Getting Better All the Time: Greatest Trends of the Last 100 Years* (Washington, DC: CATO Institute, 2000), 203.

The urban area of the nation increased from 1% of the land to 3% of the land in 2002 and contains 79% of the population, but there is still an immense amount of land remaining.[34]

Does an increase in population mean that people are more crowded in their living space? No, because as nations increase in wealth, people tend to build larger houses and have more rooms per person rather than fewer rooms. This is seen in the following chart:

Figure 10.6

ROOMS PER PERSON

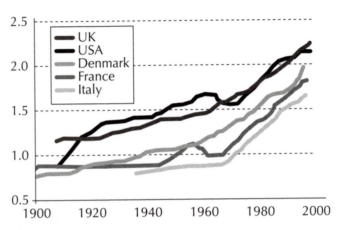

SOURCES: First European Quality of Life Survey: Social Dimensions of Housing, European Foundation for the Improvement of Living and Working Conditions, Table 2: Average number of rooms per person, by age and area, 23. http://www.eurofound. europa.eu/pubdocs/2005/94/en/1/ef0594en.pdf.
University of Liege, International Centre for Research and Information on the Public and Cooperative Economy, Housing Statistics in the European Union (2002), and U.S. Department of Energy, Energy Information Administration, Housing Characteristics 1993 (June 1995), 46-49, Table 3.4: cited in Robert Rector, "How Poor are America's Poor? Examining the 'Plague' of Poverty in America," Heritage Foundation Backgrounder, No. 2064 (August 27, 2007), 7, Table 3. http://s3.amazonaws.com/ thf_media/2007/pdf/bg2064.pdf.
Centre for Housing and Welfare, Housing in Denmark (September 2007) http://vbn. aau.dk/ws/fbspretrieve/13695523/Housing_130907.pdf.
Peter Flora, ed. *Growth to Limits: The Western European Welfare States Since World War II*, Vol. 2 (Berlin: Walter D. Gruyter and Co., 1986), 295, 302, 311, 324.
Stanley Lebergott, *The American Economy: Income, Wealth, and Want* (Princeton, N.J.: Princeton University Press, 1976), 94-95, 258.

In other words, world population is stabilizing, and there is an immense amount of room left on the earth in which everyone can live comfortably.

b. Land for growing food

But will we run out of land to grow enough food to feed the world's population? No, not at all. Out of the total ice-free land surface of the earth, about 24% of the land is "arable"[35]—that

---

34. Major Uses of Land in the United States 2002, Urban and Residential Land Use. www.ers.usda.gov/publications/EIB14/ eib14g.pdf.

35. Roger Revelle, "The World Supply of Agricultural Land," *The Resourceful Earth*, ed. Julian Simon and Herman Kahn (New York: Basil Blackwell, 1984), 184.

is, it could produce an acceptable level of food crops. That is about 3.2 billion hectares (7.9 billion acres) of land that could produce food. (The remaining land is in areas that are too cold or too dry, are too rocky or hard, or have soil that is too poor for crop use.) But this potential crop land is more than three times the area actually used for growing crops in any given year at the present time.[36] That is, we currently grow crops on *less than one-third of the earth's arable land*. How many people could the available land feed? Roger Revelle, former director of Harvard University's Center for Population Studies, estimated as far back as 1984 that even if this land produced less than half the average production of the "Corn Belt" in the United States, it could feed about 35 billion people "at an average intake of 2,350 kcal per day."[37] Another estimate was that the available land could readily feed about 18 billion people per year.[38] This is still nearly three times the current world population of about 6.8 billion, and it is much more than the best current estimates of world population stabilizing at about 11 billion people. We are not running out of land to grow crops.

In addition, *food production per acre* has increased remarkably in the last sixty years and will likely continue to increase in the future through better farming methods and greater use of modern technology. Our ability to grow more and more food—and better food—on more and more kinds of land should continue to increase, due to the amazing inventiveness that God has placed in the human mind.

Figure 10.7

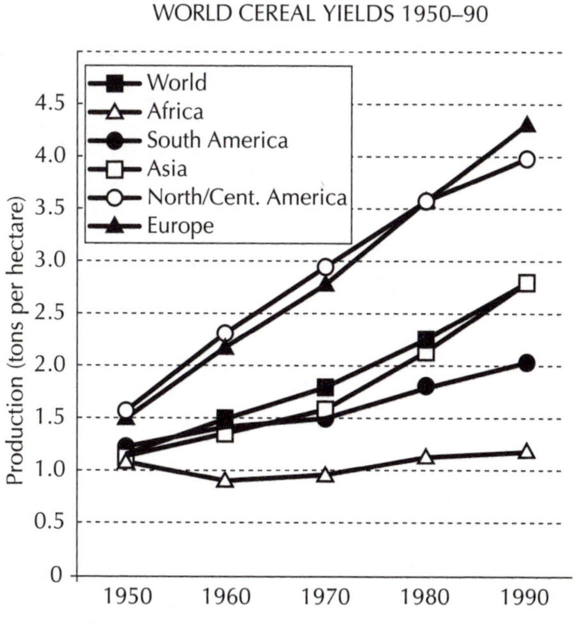

WORLD CEREAL YIELDS 1950–90

---

36. Ibid., 185.

37. Ibid., 186. A "kcal" is a kilogram calorie—that is, 1,000 grams of calories.

38. "Resources Unlimited," National Center for Policy Analysis" (Feb. 19, 1996). www.ncpa.org/sub/dpd/index.php?Article_ID=12935: citing Thomas Lambert, "Defusing the 'Population

As this chart[39] from the Food and Agriculture Organization of the United Nations shows, the amount of cereal grain grown per hectare in North America, Central America, and Europe more than doubled between 1950 and 1990 (the top two lines), and the amount grown per hectare in the world as a whole was showing a significantly increasing trend. (A "hectare" is a metric unit for measuring area and is equal to 2.47 acres.) These gains have come about through higher-yielding seeds, modern fertilizer, increased pest control, new plants that tolerate colder weather, and giving an earlier start to the growing season. [40]

Because of this increase in production of food crops, the last fifty years have seen a steady increase in the amount of food calories consumed per day per person in the world as a whole and in the developing world in particular, as the following chart indicates:[41]

Figure 10.8

DAILY CALORIES PER CAPITA 1964-2030

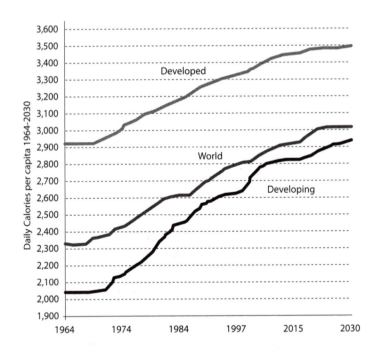

Daily intake of calories per capita in the industrial and developing counties and world. 1964-2030 (projected).
Source: Global and regional food consumption patterns and trends, Food and Agriculture Organization of the United Nations. www.fao.org/docrep/005/ac911e/ac911e05.htm.

Bomb' With Free Markets," Policy Study No. 129, Feb. 1996, Center for the Study of American Business, Washington University, St. Louis, Missouri.

39. Chart taken from *The State of Humanity*, ed. Julian Simon (Oxford and Cambridge, MA: Blackwell, 1995), 381.

40. See further discussion in Dennis Avery, "The World's Rising Food Productivity," in ibid., 376–91.

41. Future projections are also shown on this chart.

As this chart indicates, there has been a steady increase in available food and in the food actually consumed. Lomborg says, "Although there are now twice as many of us as there were in 1961, each of us has *more* to eat, in both developed and developing countries. Fewer people are starving. Food is far cheaper."[42] (Of course, the number of calories consumed has become *too great* for many people in developed countries, but that is another sort of problem!)

This does not mean that there are no remaining problems. Estimates are that the percentage of the population still starving in the world is around 12%. (The United Nations defines "starving" as not getting enough food to perform light physical activity.)[43] But the question is the long-term direction of the trend lines, and these are wonderfully encouraging. From 1970 to 2010 (estimate), a period of forty years, the percentage of the world's people who are starving has fallen from 35% to 12%.[44]

However, progress has not been uniform in all parts of the world. While most regions of the world have seen a rapid decline since 1970 in the proportion of people living in starving conditions, the progress in sub-Saharan Africa has not kept pace with the progress in the rest of the world, as the following chart indicates:

Figure 10.9

PROPORTION OF STARVING IN PERCENT–DEVELOPING WORLD BY REGION 1969-2015

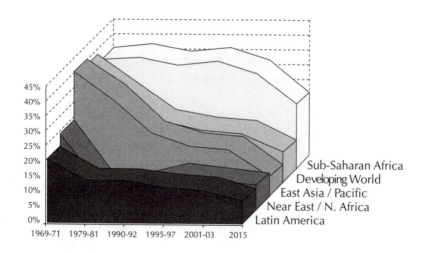

Sources: The State of Food and Agriculture, United Nations Food and Agriculture Organization (2006), 85, Table 16. www.fao.org/righttofood/kc/downloads/vl/docs/AH523.pdf. The State of Food Insecurity in the World, United Nations Food and Agriculture Organization (2006), 4. http://ftp.fao.org/docrep/fao/009/a0750e/a0750e00a.pdf.

42. Lomborg, op.cit., 60.
43. Ibid., 61.

44. Ibid.

c. Water

In a remarkable development over a thirty-year period, the percentage of people in developing countries with access to clean drinking water increased from 30% in 1970 to 80% in 2000![45] As mentioned above (p. 331), Lomborg also documents how a widely used college textbook on the environment quotes erroneous statistics on water shortages that it claims were from a World Bank study.[46]

Figure 10.10

PEOPLE WITH ACCESS TO DRINKING WATER AND SANITATION[47]

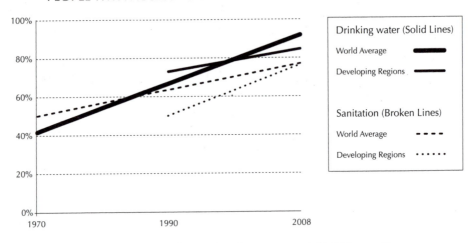

But are we using up the world's supply of water too quickly? Not at all.

There is a massive amount of water on the earth—71% of the earth's surface is covered by water. This is how the water is distributed:

Figure 10.11

TOTAL WATER ON EARTH

Water in the oceans	97.20%
Water in polar ice	2.15%
Remaining water, including all fresh water lakes, river, and ground water (water under the ground)	0.65%
Total	100.00% [48]

45. Lomborg, *Skeptical Environmentalist*, 21.

46. Ibid., 20.

47. Sources: "Progress on Sanitation and Drinking Water 2010 Update." World Health Organization, 2010. pp. 12-13. http://whqlibdoc.who.int/publications/2010/9789241563956 eng Part1b.pdf

"Access to Sanitation by Country, 1970 to 2004," *The World's Water 2008-2009*, pp. 221-230. http://www.worldwater.org/data20082009/table4.pdf.

48. Lomborg, *Skeptical Environmentalist*, 149–50.

Now, of that 0.65% of water that is potentially available for human use, some of it is in areas so remote that it is inaccessible to human beings for all practical purposes. But out of the remaining water that is accessible for human use, *we still use less than 17% of the annually renewable water on the earth.* That is not at all 17% of the fresh water on earth, but just 17% of the "readily accessible and renewable water" that is refreshed each year on the earth.[49] The current high-end predictions of how much will be used in 2025 are just 22% of the readily accessible, annually renewed water.[50] Who uses most of the water? In terms of global usage, here is the breakdown:

Figure 10.12

GLOBAL USAGE OF WATER

Agriculture	69.0%
Industry	29.0%
Households	8.0%
Total	100.00% [51]

Therefore, do we need to be concerned that we will use up the world's water in the future? I do not think so, for at least two reasons:

(1) There is an incredible amount of waste in the current usage of water in many countries, both through leakage and through inefficient agricultural usage.[52] But countries such as Israel have developed highly efficient water use, with both a drip irrigation system and effective water recycling.[53] If water prices were allowed to rise so that users were much more responsible in how they used water, much higher efficiencies could be achieved.[54] (2) Desalination of water is becoming more and more economically feasible. The price today for removing the salt from ocean water is about $.50/cubic meter, or less than one-fifth of a cent per gallon. This is actually less than the $.69/cubic meter that I currently pay at my home in Arizona! The average price of water today in the United States is $.74/cubic meter, while in the United Kingdom it is $2.37 and in Germany, $3.01/cubic meter.[55] Yet many of these costs reflect not only the raw production costs, but also delivery costs and no doubt other governmental fees. Actually, the city of Carlsbad in Southern California was to begin construction of a desalination plant in 2010, which will provide enough water for the daily use of 300,000 people.[56] Some countries today already derive a significant portion of their water supplies from salt water, such as Kuwait (over half of its total use), Saudi Arabia, and Libya. Worldwide, desalted water still makes up just 0.2% of all water use.[57] Therefore, when we take into account the stabilization of world population in the future, the increased efficiencies with which more developed countries use their water supply, the more than 80% of

49. Ibid., 150–51.
50. Ibid., 150.
51. Ibid., 154.
52. Ibid., 154–56.
53. Ibid.
54. Ibid.
55. *Wall Street Journal,* Asian edition (July 31–Aug. 2, 2009), 3.
56. Ibid. (July 10–12, 2009), 14–15.
57. Lomborg, *The Skeptical Environmentalist,* 153.

available and renewable fresh water supplies that are not being used today, and the virtually unlimited supply of water found in the oceans for a slightly higher price, we have no reason to expect that the earth will run out of water, *ever*. In providing the earth with water, God truly provided us with a wonderfully abundant resource.

So, are there local and regional areas where water supply is scarce and difficult to obtain? Yes, but those are local problems and deal with *access to water*, not with the total supply of water on the earth. In many cases, local water shortages are due either to lack of economic development of the nation as a whole (and therefore the lack of ability to transport, purify, deliver, and pay for water), or to local or national legal, economic, or political hindrances to water access.

For example, as I mentioned earlier, the state of California sits right next to the inexhaustible water resources of the Pacific Ocean, but local political opposition to constructing desalination plants has hindered Californians from tapping into this inexhaustible source of water to meet all their needs.

In addition, in 2009 there was a terrible and totally unnecessary *man-made drought* in central California. The San Joaquin Valley (including the cities of Fresno and Bakersfield) is one of the most productive agricultural areas of the entire world, but the water needed to flow from upstream rivers into that valley was diverted due to enforcement of environmentalist regulations. In December 2008, the US Fish and Wildlife Service issued a "biological opinion" that would protect a tiny three-inch fish called the delta smelt. As a result of this regulation, literally tens of billions of gallons of water have been diverted away and are flowing out into the ocean, leaving much of this agricultural land parched and dry and throwing thousands of farmers and agricultural workers out of work. Both Governor Arnold Schwarzenegger and President Barack Obama had the authority to take action to get the water flowing again, but both refused to do so, presumably because of their indebtedness to environmentalist forces.[58] The same Jesus who told his disciples, "You are of more value than many sparrows" (Matt. 10:31), would no doubt say to these needlessly drought-stricken Californian farmers, "You are of more value than many delta smelt!" And he would get the water running again, as would anyone who realizes that California's farmers and productive farmlands are much more valuable than an insignificant three-inch fish. (President Obama agreed to order the water restored in exchange for some congressmen's votes for the Obamacare health care plan in March 2010, so the water started flowing again to California farmers shortly thereafter.)[59]

d. Clean air

I remember as a child how unpleasant it was to walk on the sidewalk along any city street when a line of cars was waiting at the stoplight. The air pollution from the exhaust coming from the cars made the very act of breathing unpleasant and on some days would even make your eyes sting. But today if I walk on the same sidewalk beside a line of cars waiting at a stoplight, I can breathe freely and the automobile exhaust is almost undetectable. What happened?

58. "California's Man-Made Drought," *Wall Street Journal* (Sept. 2, 2009), A14.

59. Lance Williams, "Delta Democrat Denies Swapping Health Care Vote for Irrigation Water," *California Watch* (March 19, 2010). http://californiawatch.org/watchblog/delta-democrat-denies-swapping-health-care-vote-irrigation-water.

The change came about because the people of the United States (collectively, through their elected representatives) decided that it was worth the extra expense to require pollution controls on automobile engines. They did the same for trucks, factories, home furnaces, and many other sources of air pollution. As a result, the air became much cleaner.

This clean-up of the air is the pattern followed by all countries of the world as their economies grow and they become wealthier overall. They begin to spend the extra money that is required to control air pollution.

To take another example, the chart below shows the concentrations of sulfur dioxide (SO_2) and smoke in London over a 400-year period. Today these major pollutants are present in London's air in lower concentrations than they even have been since before 1585, long before the modern industrial period. Urban pollutants have also decreased 90% since 1930.[60, 61]

Figure 10.13

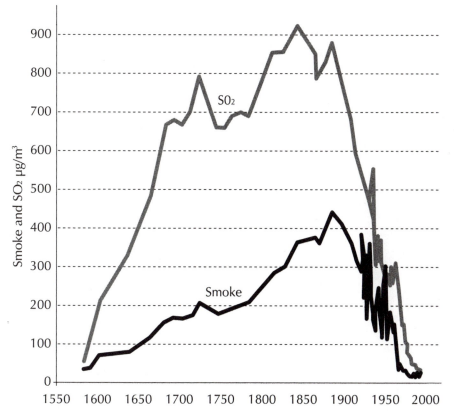

AVERAGE CONCENTRATIONS OF SULFUR DIOXIDE
AND SMOKE IN LONDON, 1585–1994/95

60. Derek M. Elsom, "Atmospheric Pollution Trends in the United Kingdom," in Simon, *The State of Humanity*, 476–90.

61. Chart from Lomborg, *The Skeptical Environmentalist*, 165, figure 86, by permission of Cambridge University Press.

Another remarkable graph shows that *economic development is the way that nations can overcome air pollution.* The graph below shows that extremely poor countries (the left side of the graph) have almost no particle pollution in their air. This is because they have almost no cars or trucks or factories to pollute the air. When nations begin to develop economically, they drive older cars and trucks that sputter along but pollute more, and they burn fuels in their homes and factories that increase air pollution until they get to about $3,000/person income per year (the peak of the chart in the center of the graph). But then people decide that the polluted air is so harmful to their quality of life that they begin to impose regulations and fees to decrease pollution. Finally, when nations develop to the point that they have a per capita income of $30,000/year or higher (the right side of the chart), their air has returned to the same quality of purity it has in undeveloped nations with essentially no cars or factories. The second graph shows the same progress with respect to sulphur dioxide (SO_2) pollution.

Figure 10.14

THE CONNECTION BETWEEN GDP PER CAPITA
AND PARTICLE POLLUTION IN 48 CITIES IN 31 COUNTRIES,
1972 AND 1986

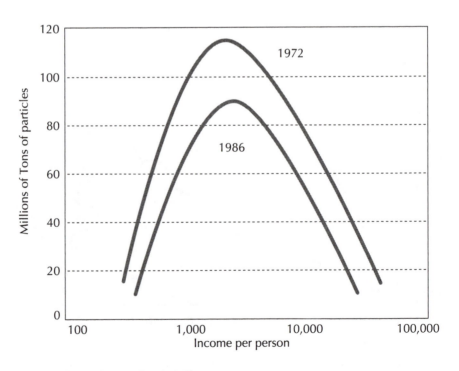

Source: See next chart (p. 345)

Figure 10.15

THE CONNECTION BETWEEN GDP PER CAPITA AND SO$_2$ POLLUTION IN 37
CITIES IN 31 COUNTRIES, 1972 AND 1986

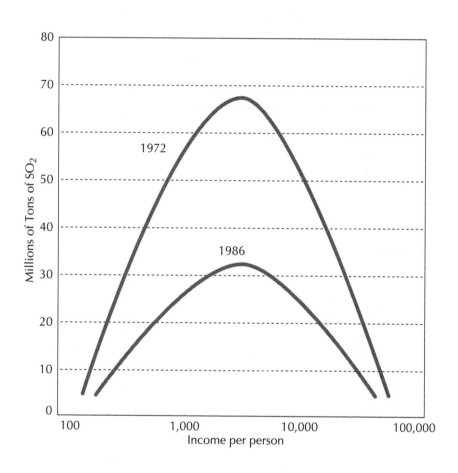

Source: World Development Report (1992), Development and the Environment,
World Bank (Oxford University Press, May 1992), 40-41.
www-wds.worldbank.org/external/default/WDSContentServer/WDSP/IB/2000/12/1
3/000178830_9810191106175/Rendered/PDF/multi_page.pdf.

What is more encouraging about these graphs is to notice the progress that was made
between 1972 and 1986. *The entire graph of pollution particles* is lower for every level of
economic development. Even the poorer countries were able to develop with less total
pollution, because of the use of cheaper and cleaner technology (including less-polluting
cars and trucks) that could be imported from more developed countries. (The chart also
shows that pollution reduction can occur at lower levels of income over time, as poorer
countries come to use technology developed in wealthier countries.)

As far as future trends in air pollution are concerned, Lomborg points to the example of the United States:

> In the US, the total number of car miles traveled has more than doubled over the past 30 years. The economy has likewise more than doubled, and the population has increased by more than a third. Nevertheless, over the same period emissions have decreased by a third and concentrations by much more. This is why it is reasonable to be optimistic about the challenge from air pollution.[62]

Speaking as a Christian, I am not at all surprised by these findings. It seems to me consistent with the teachings of the Bible, because if God put us on the earth to develop and use its resources *for our benefit*, and *with thanksgiving*, and *for his glory*, and if God is a good and wise creator, then it is completely reasonable to think that he would create in the earth the resources that we need and that there would be ways that we could discover to use these resources wisely. It is reasonable to think that he would make a way for us to use the good resources of the earth in a wonderful and enjoyable way while simultaneously improving human quality of life *and* protecting the environment. We have found that to be true not only with food supplies and water supplies, but also with the increasingly abundant supply of clean air on the earth.

e. Waste disposal

Will nations of the earth continue to produce more and more waste that will eventually overwhelm our cities and make life unpleasant if not actually dangerous? No, not when we look at reliable statistics on waste disposal.

Some of the waste that people generate is recycled or put into compost piles. Another portion of it is incinerated, in some cases in energy-producing incineration plants. Several European countries—especially France, Germany, Denmark, the United Kingdom, and Italy—make considerable use of modern incineration plants with extensive measures to minimize any air pollution or waste-disposal pollution from the resulting ashes. France alone has 225 incineration plants for energy production.[63] In addition, energy production from waste incineration seems to be the cheapest of all methods available, when measured per kilowatt-hour.[64]

The rest of the waste that people generate is put into landfills. Modern landfills in the United States are highly regulated by the Environmental Protection Agency and are considered very safe for the ground water in the area around them.[65]

But landfills are not simply "wasted space." I remember going to watch one of my sons run in a beautiful park with rolling hills when he was part of his high school cross-country team in Illinois. Only later did I find out that the park was built on the site

62. Lomborg, *The Skeptical Environmentalist*, 177.

63. Bernt Johnke, "Emissions from Waste Incineration," *Good Practice Guidance and Uncertainty Management in National Greenhouse Gas Inventories*, 456. www.ipcc-nggip.iges.or.jp/public/gp/bgp/5_3_Waste_Incineration.pdf.

64. The Cornwall Alliance for the Stewardship of Creation, *A Renewed Call to Truth, Prudence, and Protection of the Poor: An Evangelical Examination of the Theology, Science, and Economics of Global Warming* (Burke, VA: Cornwall Alliance, 2009), 66, Table 3, "Index of lifetime generation costs by generating type." Accessed online Feb. 15, 2010, at www.cornwallalliance.org/docs/a-renewed-call-to-truth-prudence-and-protection-of-the-poor.pdf.

65. Lomborg, *Skeptical Environmentalist*, 208.

of a landfill that had been carefully covered by soil. In fact, one of the largest landfills in the world, the Freshkills Landfill on Staten Island in New York City, is now closed so that it can be turned into landscaped public parkland about three times the size of Central Park. On the New York City Parks website, the New York Department of Parks and Recreation says:

> The transformation of what was formerly the world's largest landfill into a productive and beautiful cultural destination will make the park a symbol of renewal and an expression of how our society can restore balance to its land-scape. In addition to providing a wide range of recreational opportunities, including many uncommon in the city, the park's design, ecological restoration and cultural and educational programming will emphasize environmental sus-tainability and a renewed public concern for our human impact on the earth.[66]

How much space would be required to receive all the garbage being produced in the United States? Even with quite generous assumptions about the amount of waste produced per person and about the size of the growth of the American population, if all the waste generated in the United States for the next hundred years were placed in one landfill, it would fit within a square area less than 18 miles on each side and about 100 feet high (lower than the Fresh Kills Landfill in New York City). This single landfill would take up less than 0.009% of the land area of the United States.[67] And it could be made into another landscaped public park for people to use in centuries to come. Or if each state had to handle its own waste, it would have to find simply one site for a single square landfill of 2.5 miles on each side.[68] When it was full, of course, it too could be covered with soil and turned into a beautiful state park. (This assumes that it is filled with waste and dirt over each layer and compacted appropriately, according to modern environmental standards.)

In actual fact, thousands of local landfills much, much smaller in size will be used and will be entirely adequate to handle the waste that we generate. Dads like me will also watch their sons run cross-country meets on the rolling, wooded hills and never know that a landfill lies under the ground.

Another important factor is that with technological advances we continually dis-cover new uses for waste products and new ways to produce goods with less waste. So the amount of waste generated will probably be much less than these predictions. In any case, we will easily be able to handle that amount of waste. We will never run out of space to store our garbage.

Is recycling worthwhile, then? It does reduce the amount of waste that is put into landfills, but a sensible approach would ask, with respect to each kind of material being recycled, *is it worth the time and effort and expense it takes to do such recycling?* That is simply a *factual* analysis that needs to be carried out. For example, should we put resources into recycling paper, or should we simply burn it at incineration plants and

---

66. "Freshkills Park: Project Overview," New York City Department of Parks and Recreation. www.nycgovparks.org/sub_your_park/fresh_kills_park/html/fresh_kills_park.html.

67. Lomborg, *Skeptical Environmentalist*, 207.
68. Ibid.

produce energy with it? A quick trip to the local Staples store where I buy copy paper shows me that an ordinary package of twelve of the legal pads that I use costs $5.79, while a twelve-pack of the same size of legal pads on recycled paper costs $8.99! That is 55% higher! So the recycled paper costs *much more* than newly produced paper. Is there any good reason for me to spend 55% more for the paper I use? There is no need to do it to reduce the use of landfills, for which we have abundant space. Well, maybe I should use recycled paper so as not to cut down so many trees? That would only make sense if the world is going to run out of trees to make paper, which is simply not going to happen (see below).

Paper is a *renewable resource*, because trees can be planted and grown, just as oats and wheat and corn are grown. (Trees just take longer, but they are a renewable resource.) If the recycled paper costs more, it means that *the total amount of resources* used to produce recycled paper is *greater* than the resources used to produce new paper—for the price reflects, in general, the cost of production—and it probably reflects *less* than the cost of production for recycled paper because of government subsidies for recycling plants. Buying the recycled paper is simply wasting my $3.20, which I am not going to do. I buy legal pads made of ordinary paper.

f. Global forests

If we could never grow any more trees in the world, or if we were quickly depleting the amount of trees available for paper and wood production, then of course recycling would make a lot of sense. But is the world running out of trees? Once again, this is simply a question of analysis of *the facts that show worldwide trends.*

About one-third of the earth's land is covered by forests today, and *this number has remained relatively stable* since World War II, or for the last sixty years.[69] Four countries (Russia, Brazil, the United States, and Canada) together have more than 50% of the world's forests, and in the whole world about two to three times as much land is taken up by forests as by agricultural land used for crops.[70]

As for the United States, from its early history until about 1920 a significant amount of the forest cover was cleared, largely for agricultural use. But since 1920 (nearly a whole century), *the amount of forest land* has remained quite stable.[71]

When a natural forest area where trees are growing randomly is first cleared for wood or paper use, new trees are planted in neat rows so that much more total wood is grown in each land area. The result of this more efficient use of land has been that the *amount of wood* that is actually growing in the United States each year *is 3½ times what it was in 1920.*[72] The continuing trend is seen in the bar chart section below where the total number of cubic feet growing in the United States is shown to have increased significantly in the thirty-five years from 1952 to 1987. (Note that the regional trend lines use the left scale and the bar chart for the total nation uses the right scale.)[73]

69. Ibid., 117.
70. Ibid., 112.
71. Simon, *The State of Humanity*, 331.

72. Ibid., 331–32.
73. Chart from Simon, *State of Humanity*, 332, figure 33.2.

Figure 10.16

GROWING COMMERCIAL TIMBER IN THE USA, NET VOLUME

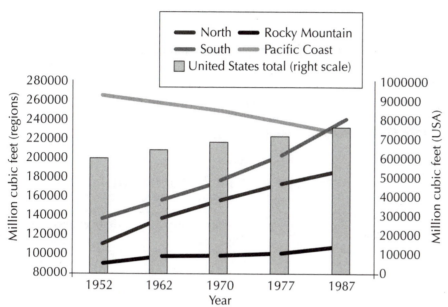

As far as the entire world is concerned, we have lost about 20% of the original forest cover on the earth since agriculture began,[74] but that percentage has now stabilized (see above). Developing countries tend to clear forests and put more land into agricultural use, but then that trend stabilizes as better agricultural methods are adopted and the food needs of the country are met. Another factor is that less developed societies tend to use wood for fuel in open fires, but with development, other sources of energy are used.

There is still a legitimate concern with loss of tropical rain forests in some countries. But earlier estimates of a loss of 2% or more of tropical rain forests have now been shown to be excessively high.[75] The rate of loss of tropical forests is now about 0.46% per year.[76]

By far the largest proportion of tropical rain forest in the world is in Brazil. The Amazon forest makes up about one-third of the world's tropical forest area. About 14% of the Amazon rain forest has been cut down since earliest human history, with 86% remaining.[77] The Brazilian government has recently imposed new restrictions on deforestation in the Amazon area. Ultimately this is a problem that can only be solved by the governments of each nation that has tropical forests, including Brazil. But the primary cause of loss of forest area is not wood used for paper, but over-use of wood

---

74. Ibid., 112.

75. Ibid., 114: citing William P. Cunningham and Barbara Woodworth Saigo, *Environmental Science: A Global Concern*

(Dubuque, IA: Wm. C. Brown Publishers, 1997), 297–98.

76. Ibid.

77. Ibid., 114–15.

fuel due to low income in less developed countries.[78] In any case, the world consumption of wood and paper can easily be satisfied without any significant deforestation throughout the world.

g. Species loss

Nobody knows how many species of plants and animals there are in the world, and estimates vary from 2 million to 80 million species. By far, the largest number of species is found among insects, followed by fungi, bacteria, and viruses.[79] Although the actual number of species extinctions is certainly higher than those that have been documented, the following table is useful in giving an approximate number of species and extinctions in the last five hundred years:[80]

Figure 10.17

NUMBER OF SPECIES AND DOCUMENTED EXTINCTIONS, 1600—PRESENT

Taxa	Approximate number of species	Total extinctions since 1600
Vertibrates	47,000	321
Mammals	4,500	110
Birds	9,500	103
Reptiles	6,300	21
Amphibians	4,200	5
Fish	24,000	82
Mollusks	100,000	235
Crustaceans	4,000	9
Insects	>1,000,000	98
Vascular Plants	250,000	396
Total	Approx. 1,600,000	1,033

Note that the number of insect species is somewhere over 1 million, and this is apparently the group that accounts for the high estimates of 10–80 million species on the earth. Moreover, this chart lists only the species that have been recorded and counted to date.

What is significant is that the total number of documented extinctions is only 1,033 out of 1.6 million species, or 0.06% total over the last five hundred years. The documented rate of species lost among mammals and birds is apparently about one

---

78. Ibid., 114.
79. Ibid., 250.
80. Chart from Lomborg, *Skeptical Environmentalist,* 250, table 6.

Lomborg says, "Because of the severe requirements for documenting extinctions, these figures certainly underestimate their true number."

per year.[81] That is far different from the claim of an influential book by Norman Myers, *The Sinking Ark* (1979), where he claimed that we lose about 40,000 every year. But the statement was an entirely unsubstantiated *guess* with no supporting data![82] Unfortunately, environmental advocate and former US Vice President Al Gore has continued to repeat this extraordinarily incorrect claim.[83] Also, Professor Paul Ehrlich, an influential Stanford biologist and environmentalist, claimed in 1981 that we were losing 250,000 species every year and that half the species on earth would be gone by the year 2000 and they would all be gone by 2010–25.[84] These are simply alarmist claims with no legitimate base within statistical reality. Lomborg's best estimate is that the rate of extinction will be about 0.7% per fifty years in the foreseeable future, but even that will probably decline as population growth slows down and the developing world becomes wealthy enough to spend more resources caring for the environment.[85]

Such a low rate of species loss may still be thought to be problematic because of the potential benefits that could come from such biodiversity, but put in the larger perspective of the course of decades or centuries, it is a problem that is certainly capable of a reasonable solution and not one that should be a cause of current panic.

In cases such as the delta smelt in California, mentioned above (p. 326, 342), Jesus' statements about the much greater value of human beings than animals need to be remembered (see Matt. 10:31; 12:12). There is no certainty that the delta smelt will becom extinct if the irrigation water is turned back on in the San Joaquin Valley, so even that species might not be lost. But even if the world loses one species of fish that exists only in this one part of California (out of 24,000 species of fish in the world, including 14 other species of smelt), that must be counted as a tiny cost (of no significant measurable economic value) compared with the great benefit of protecting the well-being and actual livelihood of thousands of California farmers and agricultural workers, and also of bringing benefit to the millions of people who eat the food produced in the San Joaquin Valley.

h. Herbicides and pesticides

One of the most significant causes of increased food production around the world has been the invention of modern herbicides (that kill harmful weeds) and pesticides (that kill harmful insects and bacteria). The benefits of herbicides and pesticides are that they improve crop yields and make fruit and vegetables cheaper. If pesticide use were restricted or even prohibited, it would perhaps double the proportion of income that a family in North America or Europe needs to spend on food. With less money to spend, people would eat fewer fruits and vegetables and would buy more primary starch and consume more fat. The effect on the poor would be the greatest, but this might lead to an increase of something like 26,000 additional cancer deaths per year in the United

---

81. Ibid., 252.
82. Ibid., 249, 252.
83. Ibid., 248.

84. Ibid., 249.
85. Ibid., 255–56.

States.[86] Therefore herbicides and pesticides create *great health benefits*, significantly *higher food production*, and *less required use of land*.

But are pesticides harmful? US government agencies such as the Food and Drug Administration (FDA) and Environmental Protection Agency (EPA) set limits in the use of pesticides based on the measurable amount that gets into the food and water that we consume. The limits are very strictly set. After extensive testing, there is a value established called the NOAEL (No Observed Adverse Effect Level). Then a level below this is a value called the ADI (Accepted Daily Intake). The set ADI limit is usually between 100 and 10,000 times lower than the NOAEL.[87]

One of the most respected studies of various causes of cancer in the United States, for example, concluded that they could find *no significant percentage of cancers caused by pesticides in the United States*. There are many causes of cancer (such as tobacco, diet, sun exposure, and infections), but pesticides do not even make the list. Lomborg concludes that the effect of pesticides on cancer in the United States is so low that "virtually no one dies of cancer caused by pesticides."[88] In another place, Lomborg summarizes a number of studies by saying, "Pesticides contribute astoundingly little to deaths caused by cancer."[89] He says that a "plausible estimate" for the added number of cancer deaths due to pesticide use in the United States is close to 20 deaths per year out of 560,000,[90] or one death out of every 28,000 people who die of cancer. When this is weighed against the immense benefits that come from pesticide use, and the great harm that would come to the world population and world diets if pesticide use were abolished, it appears that there should be no significant objection to their current level of wise and carefully restricted use.

Once again, this conclusion should not be surprising. If God wanted us to subdue the earth and develop its resources in useful ways, then it is reasonable to expect that he would give us the ability to discover means of overcoming the "thorns and thistles" that grow on the earth and also the pests that tend to destroy food crops. In addition, it must be recognized that many of the pesticides used are not synthetic chemical compounds but are derived from natural substances that already occur in one place or another in the plant world—substances that already allow some plants to fight off the pests that would attack them.[91]

i. Life expectancy

Is the earth becoming a safer or more dangerous place for human beings to live? One very important measure is overall life expectancy. When people have better health, when they are able to overcome diseases, when they are able to keep themselves safe from natural disasters, and when they have better nutrition, they will live longer. Therefore we would expect that people would have a longer life expectancy as they advance in developing the earth's resources and making them useful for human beings, as God intended them to do.

---

86. Ibid., 247–48.
87. Ibid., 226.
88. Ibid., 228–29.

89. Ibid., 245.
90. Ibid.
91. Ibid., 232–33.

This is in fact what we find has happened as nations have developed economically and human beings have discovered more ways to make the resources of the earth useful for themselves.

While records from earlier centuries are less detailed, enough information remains to gain a fairly good idea of overall life expectancy in a number of nations. England may be taken as typical of what happens as nations develop economically:[92]

Figure 10.18

LIFE EXPECTANCY IN ENGLAND AND WALES (1600–2000)

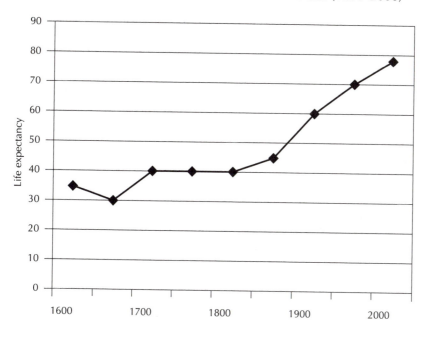

Note that life expectancy in the last 200 years has increased from about 38 years to about 78 years. This is an astounding increase. Other countries experienced similar growth so that the average life expectancy in developed countries is now 77 years.[93]

In less developed countries, the average life expectancy at the beginning of the twentieth century was under 30 years. By 1950 it had reached 41 years and in 1998 was at 65 years.[94] This is an astounding development, where life expectancy even in less developed countries has more than doubled in the last hundred years.[95] The predictions for future development are continually upward for all parts of the world, as is evident in the following chart:

92. Data taken from Matteo Cervellati and Uwe Sunde, "Human Capital Formation, Life Expectancy, and the Process of Economic Development," Discussion Paper 585, September 2002, p. 5.

93. Ibid., 50.
94. Ibid.
95. Ibid.

Figure 10.19

LIFE EXPECTANCY FOR INDUSTRIALIZED COUNTRIES, DEVELOPING
COUNTRIES, SUB-SAHARAN AFRICA, AND THE ENTIRE WORLD, 1950-2050

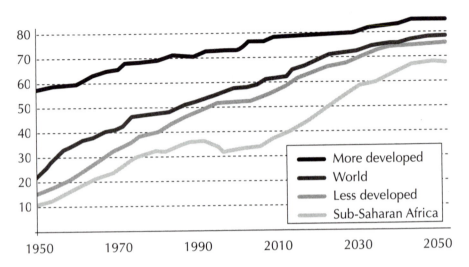

Sources: Monica Ferreira and Paul Kowal, "A Minimum Data Set on Ageing and Older
Persons in Sub-Saharan Africa: Process and Outcome," African Population Studies/
Etude de la Population Africaine, Vol. 21, No. 1 (2006), 19-36. www.who.int/health-
info/survey/ageing_mds_pub02.pdf and www.bioline.org.br/request?ep06002.
Social Indicators, United Nations Statistics Division, http://unstats.un.org/unsd/
demographic/products/socind/health.htm.
United Nations Population Division, "The World at Six Billion," Table 4 (1999).
www.un.org/esa/population/publications/sixbillion/sixbillion.htm.
Life Expectancy at Birth, 1950-2050, Figure 1, Congressional Budget Office, 3. www.
cbo.gov/ftpdocs/69xx/doc6952/12-12-Global.pdf.

These statistics are valuable in that they serve as an overall indicator of human progress in the ability to live productive lives on the earth, overcome dangers, and make the
resources of the earth beneficial for our overall health and well-being. The overall picture
that we get is a very encouraging one of continual growth and progress. We are making better use of the environment in which we live, and we are also taking better care of it each year.

God created an abundant and resourceful earth, and we are developing an ever-
greater ability to make wise use of the resources that he has placed in it for our benefit,
so that we would use these resources with thanksgiving and give glory to him.

C. ENERGY RESOURCES AND ENERGY USES

Sometimes people naively assume that we are quickly running out of energy sources,
but that is simply not true.

To get an overall picture of world energy production, we first need to understand
that energy is derived from several different sources. The following diagram shows the
distribution of energy sources used in a particular year for the entire world:

Figure 10.20
WORLD ENERGY PRODUCTION BY SOURCE 2006

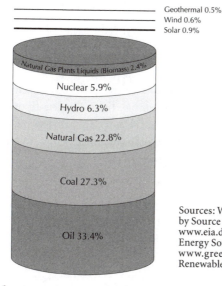

Geothermal 0.5%
Wind 0.6%
Solar 0.9%

Natural Gas Plants Liquids (Biomass) 2.4%

Nuclear 5.9%

Hydro 6.3%

Natural Gas 22.8%

Coal 27.3%

Oil 33.4%

Sources: World Primary Energy Production
by Source 1970-2006.
www.eia.doe.gov/aer/txt/ptb1101.html.
Energy Sources: Renewable Energy.
www.green3dhome.com/EnergySources/
RenewableSources.aspx.

1. Wind power

The amount of energy produced by wind power has increased somewhat since that 2006 diagram. In 2008, according to the Global Wind Energy Council, the total amount of world energy capacity from wind-power was 121 gigawatts, growing by 29% from 2007. (A gigawatt is one billion watts of electricity.)[96] However, wind-power "capacity" is not the best measure, because wind is unreliable, and actual energy produced may only be around 20% of "capacity." According to the US Department of Energy, wind power presently accounts for about 1.9% of America's electricity.[97] Wind power has some potential, but its contribution to world energy production will probably remain quite small, because it is not dependable in most areas of the world (wind does not blow all the time, and varies in intensity), and the energy is so diffuse that wind farms require huge land areas (or ocean areas) with hundreds of giant windmills that destroy the beauty of the landscape for miles around.

2. Hydroelectric power

While the United States currently gets 5.7% of its energy,[98] or 247,509,974 BTUs,[99] from hydroelectric dams on rivers, it is unlikely that its capacity is capable of much expansion

96. Global Wind 2008 Report. Global Wind Energy Council. www.gwec.net/fileadmin/documents/Global%20Wind%20 2008%20Report.pdf.

97. "Wind Powering America Update," U.S. Department of Energy (Aug. 20, 2009). www.windpoweringamerica.gov/filter_detail.asp?itemid=746.

98. BP Statistical Review—Full Report 2009. www.bp.com/ liveassets/bp_internet/globalbp/globalbp_uk_english/reports_ and_publications/statistical_energy_review_2008/STAGING/ local_assets/2009_downloads/hydro_table_of_hydroelectricity_consumption_2009.pdf.

99. Table 1.11, Electricity Net Generation from Renewable Energy by Energy Use Sector and Energy Source, 2003–2007. www. eia.doe.gov/cneaf/solar.renewables/page/trends/table1_11.pdf.

beyond that amount because most of the good locations where dams can be built already have dams built on them. The situation is similar in most developed countries, so it is unlikely that the 6.6% of the world's energy that is produced by hydroelectric plants will increase very much.

3. Oil

Because of new technology and further exploration, we are constantly discovering new reserves of oil and other energy sources. For example, the following figure shows a comparison of *known oil reserves* with annual production. Note that as oil usage has increased somewhat, the world's *known reserves* of oil have multiplied many times over. This is because people keep discovering new sources of oil.

Figure 10.21

KNOWN WORLD OIL RESERVES AND WORLD OIL
PRODUCTION – 1900-2008

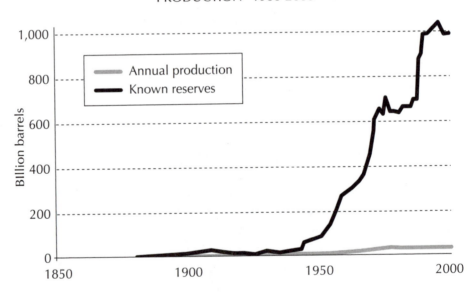

Sources: World Oil Production, U.S. Department of Energy.
www.eia.doe.gov/emeu/aer/txt/ptb1105.html.
World Annual Oil Production (1900-2008).
http://people.hofstra.edu/geotrans/eng/ch5en/appl5en/worldoilreservesevol.html.
CIA Worldfact Book 2009-1002.

Moreover, when the price of oil increases, oil in more difficult areas becomes economically more feasible to develop. If we factor in the oil available in tar sands and shale oil fields, the amount of oil remaining is equal to the total energy consumption of the entire world for more than five thousand years![100] But of course, we will also be using other energy sources as well, and technological developments in the next twenty-five to fifty years will likely shift our usage away from even the amount of world energy that it now produces. In other words, we will never run out of oil.

However, it seems to me wise for the United States to dramatically reduce its dependence on foreign oil, in two ways: (1) The nation should increase its use of alternative fuels where that is practical to do. But in many cases, oil-based gasoline and diesel fuel are going to remain the preferred fuel for years to come because of their high energy content and easy transportability—you can't burn coal in a car or plane engine, and electric batteries do not deliver enough energy for long enough to power most cars, all larger trucks, or airplanes. Oil is also still relatively cheap and abundant.

(2) The nation should develop more of its own supplies of oil, especially more of the offshore oil deposits off the coast of California and Florida (but far enough from land that they will not be seen, and with adequate safeguards to protect against spills and leaks). The United States should also develop even more urgently its abundant supplies in the Alaskan National Wildlife Refuge (ANWR), where there are no human inhabitants and where the United States could retrieve as much oil as it now imports from Saudi Arabia each year.[101] The Department of the Interior has estimated that ANWR would provide over 1.3 million barrels of oil a day.[102] (The United States currently imports more than 1 million barrels per day from Saudi Arabia.)[103] In addition, there are other large oil deposits in Western states like Colorado (which could provide more than 46,000 barrels of oil per day)[104] that could be profitably developed, for the good of the nation (by reducing the dependence on foreign oil and by bringing down oil prices due to increased availability of supplies).

In addition to that, we need to expand our oil-refining capacity, which has actually decreased over the last twenty-eight years, keeping the price of gas artificially high. Between 1981, when refineries operated at 69% of their capacity, and 2004, the number of refineries in the United States dropped from 324 to 153. Laurence Goldstein of the Petroleum Research Institute says, "There is no spare refining capacity in the US today."[105] We should also take steps to persuade the various states (such as Arizona) to adopt a uniform national standard for the types of gasoline that are sold, rather than paying the extra expense that comes when states pass their own special formulas for boutique mixtures of gas components that are allowed to be sold in each state—a big contributor to higher gas prices and periodic shortages.

100. Lomborg, *Skeptical Environmentalist*, 128.

101. "Drill Here. Drill Now. Drill ANWR." www.anwr.org/Latest-News/Drill-here.-Drill-now.-Drill-ANWR.php.

102. See www.doi.gov/news/anwrchart.pdf.

103. "Crude Oil and Total Petroleum Imports Top 15 Countries," Energy Information Administration (Oct. 29, 2009). www.eia.doe.gov/pub/oil_gas/petroleum/data_publications/company_level_imports/current/import.html.

104. Ibid.

105. "Lack of new refineries also factor in high gas prices," Alexander's Gas and Oil Connections, News and Trends: North America (June 14, 2004). www.gasandoil.com/goc/news/ntn42472.htm.

4. Coal

Coal is another widely used source of energy, and modern coal-burning power plants are much cleaner and more efficient than in previous years. The total coal resources available in the world will be sufficient for "well beyond the next 1,500 years."[106]

5. Natural gas

Natural gas is an excellent source of energy for home heating and is also widely used to generate electrical power. Some areas have used natural gas to power automobiles and buses, but the special refueling stations are only found in certain places. Its existence in a gas rather than a liquid state under normal temperatures makes it readily transportable by pipelines. But it has to be put under pressure to keep it in a liquid form, so it requires specially pressurized refueling pumps and thick, heavy, reinforced tanks in cars that use it. It burns very cleanly and is now less expensive than gasoline produced from oil.

6. Nuclear power

Nuclear power is also a wonderful source of energy. The energy produced by one gram (that is, 1/28th of an ounce) of uranium–235 is equivalent to the energy produced by almost three tons of coal![107] Nuclear power gives off almost no pollution, but the radioactive waste materials need to be stored safely. This has become a political controversy in the United States, but many nations have already solved this problem for themselves, and it should not be a problem in the United States either. Senator Pete Domenici of New Mexico points out that in France, to dispose of nuclear waste, "a single 150-liter glass canister contains the waste (fission products and actinides) from 360,000 families of four heating their homes with electricity for one year."[108] To give some comparison, 150 liters is about the size of a common 40-gallon steel drum (or the inner water tank that is inside all the insulation of an ordinary 40-gallon home water heater). This means that the yearly nuclear waste of *over a million people* could be stored in a container of this size. (This would require that the United States adopt a method of reprocessing nuclear fuel that is now used safely in France and other countries.)

According to the US Department of Energy Civilian Nuclear Waste Management, France stores its spent nuclear fuel for one year at its nuclear power plants in specially constructed storage pools. Following storage, spent nuclear fuel is then transported to the La Hague and Marcoule reprocessing plants and stored for two to three years. France has also reprocessed nuclear fuel for Germany, Belgium, Japan, and the Netherlands.[109] The fuel

106. Lomborg, *Skeptical Environmentalist*, 127: citing James R. Craig, David J. Vaughn, and Brian J. Skinner, *Resources of the Earth: Origin, Use, and Environmental Impact* (Upper Saddle River, NJ: Prentice Hall, 1996), 159.

107. Ibid., 129: citing Craig et al., *Resources of the Earth*, 164.

108. Pete Domenici, *A Brighter Tomorrow: Fulfilling the Promise of Nuclear Energy* (Lanham, MD: Rowman & Littlefield, 2004),

157. This book contains an abundance of information on the benefits of more nuclear energy, with detailed responses to objections.

109. "France's Radioactive Waste Program," U.S. Department of Energy Fact Sheet Office of Civilian Nuclear Radioactive Waste Management. www.ocrwm.doe.gov/factsheets/doeymp0411.shtml.

and radioactive waste is buried 400 to 1,000 meters below the ground. In Japan, the waste is buried 300 meters underground.[110] Some 76.8% of the electricity generated in France is from nuclear power.[111] Japan gets 25.6% of its electricity supply from nuclear power.[112]

There are currently 104 operating nuclear power plants in the United States (including the Palo Verde Nuclear Generating Station west of Phoenix, which is probably providing the electricity powering my computer as I type this sentence). They provide over 20% of the electricity generated for the United States.[113]

Several hundred more nuclear power plants had been planned up until about the mid–1970s, but because of endless legal and regulatory barriers, no new nuclear power plants have been built in the United States since 1975.

Why is this? Senator Domenici, who has devoted many years to learning about nuclear energy and is a past chairman of the Energy and Natural Resources Committee of the US Senate, attributes the failure of the United States to change these prohibitive barriers to two causes: (1) "many Americans have an irrational fear of anything 'nuclear,'" and (2) "the policy of deliberate misinformation that opponents of nuclear energy employ with shameless disregard of the truth."[114] Contrary to popular impressions, for example, the accident with a cooling system malfunction at the Three Mile Island Nuclear Generating Station in Pennsylvania on March 29, 1979, involved no human deaths and no injuries to plant workers or nearby residents.[115] The generator that had experienced the accident resumed operation in October 1985, after repairs and lengthy litigation.[116]

What about Chernobyl? It is true that in the former Soviet Union, the Chernobyl Nuclear Reactor in Ukraine was destroyed by a terrible accident April 26, 1986, but that was due to flagrantly poor quality construction and maintenance under the communist government, with a blatant disregard for safety that has never been allowed in the United States, France, the United Kingdom, Japan, or other countries with significant nuclear power production. According to the US Nuclear Regulatory Commission, "U.S. reactors have different plant designs, broader shutdown margins, robust containment structures, and operational controls to protect them against the combination of lapses that led to the accident at Chernobyl."[117]

I was pleased to learn that on February 16, 2010, President Obama pledged $8 billion in loan guarantees to build the first new nuclear reactors in the United States in nearly three decades.[118] I hope this initiative will lead to the construction of many new nuclear reactors.

110. The Federation of Electric Power Companies of Japan. www.japannuclear.com/nuclearpower/program/waste.html. See also Nuclear Waste Management Organization of Japan. www.numo.or.jp/en/faq/main1.html.

111. Nuclear Energy Agency. www.nea.fr/html/general/profiles/france.html.

112. Ibid. www.nea.fr/html/general/profiles/japan.html.

113. See www.nea.fr/html/general/profiles/usa.html.

114. Domenici, *A Brighter Tomorrow*, xii.

115. "Backgrounder on the Three Mile Island Accident," United States Nuclear Regulatory Commission (Aug. 2009). www.nrc.gov/reading-rm/doc-collections/fact-sheets/3mile-isle.html.

116. "Three Mile Island Unit 1 Outage Dates: February 17, 1979 to October 8, 1985." www.ucsusa.org/assets/documents/nuclear_power/three-mile-island–1.pdf.

117. "Background on the Chernobyl Nuclear Power Plant Accident," United States Nuclear Regulatory Commission (April 2009). www.nrc.gov/reading-rm/doc-collections/fact-sheets/chernobyl-bg.html.

118. Jim Tankersley and Michael Muskal, "Obama pledges $8 billion for new nuclear reactors," *Los Angeles Times* (Feb. 16, 2010). http://articles.latimes.com/2010/feb/16/nation/la-na-obama-nuclear17–2010feb17 (accessed Feb. 17, 2010).

With a special development called a fast-breeder reactor, there is now sufficient uranium for "up to 14,000 years" of energy production.[119] And then there is another method of producing nuclear energy—not from nuclear *fission*, but from nuclear *fusion*. The fuel for this is not uranium, but is taken from ordinary seawater, and therefore the supply is unlimited. However, this technology has not yet been successful to a level that would be commercially useful, and it is unknown when a technological breakthrough will occur. Even without nuclear fusion, however, plants based on nuclear *fission* could easily provide the energy needs of the entire United States for thousands of years to come, if they were not prevented from being built by opposition "based on irrational fear led by Hollywood-style fiction, the Green lobbies and the media. These fears are unjustified, and nuclear energy from its start in 1952 has proved to be the safest of all energy sources."[120]

7. Solar energy

Prices for both wind energy and solar energy have dropped considerably in recent years, but they are still not widely used, primarily because they are not yet economically competitive with coal, natural gas, oil, hydroelectric power, and nuclear energy. But recent developments with solar cells have made solar energy much more affordable, and its use will likely increase. Solar energy is unreliable in many areas that are frequently overcast, and of course it cannot be generated at night, which requires that the energy generated be stored in large batteries. Solar energy is by far the greatest source of energy available, however. The amount of solar energy falling on the earth *each year* is equal to about 7,000 times our present global energy consumption.[121]

8. Conclusion

In conclusion, there is an incredibly abundant amount of energy available for human use on the earth. Once again, this is not surprising. If God put us on the earth so that we would develop and use his resources wisely, then it is reasonable that he would provide us with multiple sources of energy that we could discover in order to perform the tasks he gives us to do.

Therefore it makes no sense for people to think that there is some virtue in always seeking to "reduce our energy use." *Energy is what replaces human physical work* (such as walking everywhere and carrying everything by hand rather than driving) and animal work (such as plowing fields or grinding grain with oxen), and energy is what makes economic development possible. When we *increase our use of these energy sources* that God has provided, by using a truck to carry goods hundreds of miles, or flying by airplane to a distant city, or driving quickly to a meeting thirty miles away, or using a tractor to plow a field, or turning on the dishwasher or washing machine, or living comfortably in a climate-controlled house in hot summers and cold winters—when we increase our energy use, we *decrease the time we have to spend* on travel or menial labor,

119. Lomborg, *Skeptical Environmentalist*, 129: citing Craig et al., *Resources of the Earth*, 181.

120. Domenici, *A Brighter Tomorrow*, 211.

121. Lomborg, *Skeptical Environmentalist*, 133.

we *increase the amount of work* we can get done (and thus increase human prosperity), we *increase human freedom* because we have more time left to devote to more creative and valuable tasks of our own choosing, and we make life more pleasant! Using all of these energy sources is a wonderful ability that God has provided the human race, and it sets us far above the animal kingdom as creatures truly made in the image of God. We should be *thankful* for the ability of the human race to use more and more of the energy resources that God has placed in the world for our benefit and enjoyment.

If people want to reduce their energy use *to save money* (turning off unused lights, for example), that of course is wise. But if reducing energy use means you will get less work done, or you just have to work longer in order to accomplish the same task (washing a large load of dishes by hand when you have a dishwasher), or if it means you will reduce your quality of life (shivering in a cold, dark room on winter nights to "save energy" when you could easily afford to heat and light your home), then I see no virtue in it. You are just wasting your time when God gives you the wonderful gift of abundant energy in the earth.

We should also realize that during the past hundred years the most significant resource of all has been *human ingenuity* in discovering and developing new sources of energy and discovering more efficient ways to carry out various tasks. It is certainly reasonable to expect that human ingenuity will continue to develop new sources of energy and better ways of using energy in the future so that, just as past predictions have vastly underestimated the amount of remaining energy on earth,[122] so it is likely that present predictions of the amount of energy remaining are themselves too pessimistic, and as further technological progress is made, we will realize that the amount of energy remaining in these sources will last even beyond the current predictions.

D. GLOBAL WARMING AND CARBON FUELS

Before we can decide what to do about the question of "gobal warming," it is necessary to understand some of the scientific factors related to the earth's temperature and carbon dioxide.[123]

1. The earth's atmosphere brings both warming and cooling influences on the earth

a. Warming effects from the atmosphere

We are able to live on the earth only because the earth's atmosphere retains some heat from the sun. If the earth had no atmosphere, its average surface temperature would be about 0° Fahrenheit—too cold to sustain most life. Yet, because there is an atmosphere surrounding the earth, average worldwide temperatures tend to hover around 59°F—but

---

122. Ibid., 118–36.

123. I wish to thank my friend Dr. E. Calvin Beisner, who (in my opinion) knows more than anyone else about issues related to Christian stewardship of the environment, for writing the initial draft of this entire section on global warming. However, I have rewritten several portions and added others, and the final responsibility for the content of this section is mine.

much colder near the poles, much warmer near the equator, and cooler at night and warmer in the daytime, cooler in winter and warmer in summer, and so forth. Over most of the earth, most of the time, the temperature is well-suited to human life and to plant and animal life of various kinds.

The way the atmosphere warms the earth is often called the "greenhouse effect"—that is, some of the atmosphere retains the heat energy that comes from the sun. Not all of the atmosphere does this, however. Nitrogen (which makes up 78% of the atmosphere) and oxygen (which makes up 21%) don't retain the sun's heat. That makes 99% of the atmosphere that does not retain heat or function as a "greenhouse gas."

In the remaining 1% of the atmosphere there are fourteen other elements or compounds. Most of these do not have a warming effect either, but the ones that do are called "greenhouse gases," and they constitute about 0.45% of the atmosphere—just under one-half of 1%. Water vapor makes up 89% of these greenhouse gases, or about 0.4% of the entire atmosphere (higher at the earth's surface, but diminishing with altitude). The other greenhouse gases are carbon dioxide (about 0.039% of the total atmosphere), methane (about 0.00018%), nitrous oxide (about 0.00003%), ozone (less than 0.000007%), and miscellaneous trace gases—all of these other greenhouse gases (apart from water) totaling under 0.05% of the atmosphere. The remaining 0.55% of the atmosphere consists of other elements or compounds that do not have a warming effect on the earth.

Water vapor, then, is the most important greenhouse gas. How important is water vapor? It is responsible for about 80% of the total warming effect of the entire atmosphere.

Another 15% of the warming effect of the entire atmosphere comes from clouds. (Clouds are not included in water vapor because they are actually made of water droplets.) But the effect of clouds is complex, because some clouds warm the earth and some cool the earth. The *low-altitude clouds* mostly *cool* the earth by reflecting the sun's heat back into space before it reaches the surface. (We notice this when a cloud passes in front of the sun on a hot day, and the shade from the cloud feels cooler to us than the direct sunlight.) By contrast, the *warming clouds* are mostly high-altitude cirrus clouds, because they retain more heat than they reflect back into space.

For convenience, most scientists just combine water vapor (80% of warming) and warming clouds (15%) to say that water causes about 95% of "greenhouse warming." The remaining approximately 5% of greenhouse warming comes from carbon dioxide (about 3.6%), methane (about 0.36%), nitrous oxide (about 0.95%), and miscellaneous gases including ozone (about 0.072%).[124]

---

124. Data on composition of the entire atmosphere are readily available in standard sources, but precise amounts vary slightly from source to source, the main variations being in percentage of carbon dioxide, which has risen over recent years, so it is lower in older sources, higher in newer ones. The percentages stated here reflect those in PhysicalGeography.net Fundamentals eBook, Chapter 7, "Introduction to the Atmosphere," Table 7a–1, online at www.physicalgeography.net/ fundamentals/7a.html, updated in the case of carbon dioxide from 360 to 385 ppmv. See also John Houghton, *Global Warming: The Complete Briefing*, 3d ed. (Cambridge: Cambridge University Press, 2004), 16. Greenhouse gas composition data are from Geocraft.com, "Global Warming: A closer look at the numbers," online at www.geocraft.com/WVFossils/greenhouse_data.html, Table 4a.

How exactly do these greenhouse gases warm the earth? Despite the metaphor, they don't work at all like a greenhouse, because in a greenhouse the glass walls and roof warm the interior by trapping warm air inside—the glass keeps the air that is warmed by incoming sunlight from rising and blowing away. But greenhouse gases don't keep warm air from rising and blowing away. Instead, they *absorb* heat energy and then *radiate* it outward.

Here is what happens: First, energy comes from the sun mostly in the form of light. When that light hits the surface of the earth, the earth absorbs light energy from the sun and then radiates it back in the form of *infrared energy*—what we call heat. (Imagine holding your hand above a rock that has been sitting out in the sun, and you can feel the heat energy radiating from the warm rock.) Now let's say that after holding your hand above the warm rock, your hand also becomes warm. Your hand has been absorbing heat energy from the warm rock, and now your hand is also radiating heat energy. If you put your hand to your cheek, you will feel the heat energy from your hand.

In a similar way, greenhouse gases *absorb* infrared energy (heat) and then, having absorbed it, radiate it outward. Some of it goes up into space, thus cooling the earth by moving the heat away, but some of it radiates heat back down to the earth's surface and warms the earth.

It is good for us that not all of the sun's energy stays at earth's surface, or we would cook. It is also good that not all of it bounces back into space, or we would freeze. As Christians, we can be thankful that by God's wise design, such infrared absorption by greenhouse gases ensures that the earth retains the right balance of incoming and outgoing energy.

b. Cooling effects from the atmosphere

I mentioned earlier that without the "greenhouse effect," earth's average surface temperature would be about 0°F and with it, it's about 59°F. But if the atmosphere didn't have any *balancing factors to modify the greenhouse effect*, there would be another problem: the total warming by the greenhouse gases in earth's atmosphere would keep average surface temperature at about 140°F—much too hot for most life.[125] So why is the average temperature only 59°F? Because, in addition to *warming influences*, the atmosphere also has some *cooling influences* that moderate the greenhouse effect. These fall in the general category of climate "feedbacks" (changes in the atmosphere that are caused by other changes in the atmosphere, which then lead to other changes).

These feedbacks, whose net effect is to bring cooling influences to the earth, include such things as evaporation, precipitation (rain, snow, dew, and sleet), convection (upward movement of warm air), and advection (sideways movement of air—that is, wind!). Together we call these "weather," and they include everything from gentle breezes to hurricanes, from the violent downdrafts of wind shear to the massive, twisting updrafts of tornados, and much more.

---

125. Earth's temperatures with no greenhouse effect, with greenhouse effect but no feedbacks, and with feedbacks are from S. Manabe and R. F. Strickler, "Thermal equilibrium of the atmosphere with a convective adjustment," *Journal of the Atmospheric Sciences* 21 (1964), 361–65.

There are other feedbacks too, such as changes in cloudiness (which can warm or cool the earth), expansion or contraction of ice (ice reflects solar energy away from earth and so cools it), expansion or contraction of forests and grasslands and deserts, and changes in how rapidly plants take up or give off water through their leaves.

Complete understanding of all these feedbacks is not crucial to the global warming debate. What *is* important is knowing whether, on balance, they *increase* or *decrease* the warming caused by greenhouse gases, and by how much. There is a very simple way to answer that question. With no greenhouse effect, average surface temperature would be about 0°F; with it but without feedbacks, it would be about 140°F; yet, with the greenhouse effect plus feedbacks, it is about 59°F. It seems evident, then, that on balance, these feedbacks decrease the greenhouse effect. By how much? Well, 59 is about 42% of 140, which implies that the feedbacks eliminate about 58% of "greenhouse warming."

c. Then what is the controversy about carbon dioxide?

The global warming controversy has focused mostly on carbon dioxide (CO_2). The people who warn about the dangers of global warming argue that human activities are causing the concentration of greenhouse gases—primarily carbon dioxide, secondarily methane, and to a much lesser extent ozone and chlorofluorocarbons—to increase, and that their increased concentration could warm the earth enough to cause significant, perhaps even catastrophic, harm to people and ecosystems.

The biggest culprit, according to this position, is carbon dioxide, which is responsible for about 3.6% of the total greenhouse effect.

What is carbon dioxide? It is a colorless and nearly odorless gas. It is used to produce the bubbles (carbonation) in carbonated beverages. In a frozen form, it is known as dry ice. When an organic material such as wood burns in a fire, it releases carbon dioxide. Carbon dioxide is also released when coal or gasoline or natural gas (methane) burns. Therefore much energy production releases carbon dioxide into the atmosphere.

In our bodies, carbon dioxide plays an important role in regulating our blood flow and rate of breathing. When we breathe, we inhale oxygen and exhale carbon dioxide in every breath. In fact, all insects, animals, and people emit carbon dioxide when they exhale. In addition, oceans, volcanoes, and other natural sources emit it too. Carbon dioxide is part of the natural way God has made the world to function.

Carbon dioxide is also crucial for plants, because they need it for photosynthesis, a process that uses light energy to produce various compounds necessary for a plant to live and grow. During photosynthesis, plants absorb carbon dioxide and release oxygen. Thus, in a wonderful cycle of nature that has been designed by God, animals and people continually use up oxygen and release carbon dioxide for plants to use, and then plants use up that carbon dioxide and release oxygen for people and animals to use. *Carbon dioxide is thus essential to all the major life systems on the earth.* We should not think of carbon dioxide as a pollutant, but as an essential part of God's wise arrangement of life on earth.

Many atmospheric scientists believe the concentration of carbon dioxide in the atmosphere has risen from about 270 to about 385 parts per million by volume (ppmv), or from about 0.027% to 0.039%, since preindustrial times (before about 1750).[126] Where did this increase in carbon dioxide come from? Primarily, so goes the theory, from burning carbon-based ("fossil") fuels: coal, oil, and natural gas. (However, there are some reasons to question whether atmospheric carbon dioxide has increased that much, and whether burning fossil fuels caused all or most of the increase.)

What is the effect of increasing carbon dioxide from 270 to 385 parts per million? We can compare that with some estimates of what the temperature effect would be from actually *doubling* carbon dioxide concentration from preindustrial times (from 270 to 540 ppmv). This, according to different estimates, would have a net result of raising earth's average surface temperature, *before feedbacks*, by about 1.8° to 2.16°F.[127] And, frankly, that is a relatively small increase in average temperature that does not scare anybody.

What causes some people to fear much greater warming is the belief that climate feedbacks *magnify* this warming. So that belief is built into the computer models that predict the weather for many decades into the future. All of the computer models used by the United Nation's Intergovernmental Panel on Climate Change (IPCC) assume that climate feedbacks magnify the warming that comes from greenhouse gases.

It is important to understand here that the fears of future global warming rest on *predictions of future weather produced by computer "models"* that give different weights to different factors. The computer programs are not infallible, but will predict whatever is required by the data and formulas fed to them; different data and different formulas, based on different assumptions, will give different predictions.

Therefore the fears of future global warming rest on *hypotheses* represented by computer models, *not on empirical observations* of the real world. These models, *by assuming various feedbacks that add to the greenhouse effect*, predict that warming from *doubled* carbon dioxide since preindustrial time would result in an increase of 3.5°F to a mid-range estimate of 5.4°F to a high estimate of about 7°F.

Then some *other* computer formulas (other models) have used the *upper range* of this first set of predictions and have gone on to predict serious harm from such warming. (But remember: model results are not *evidence*; they are merely *hypotheses*. Only empirical observations are evidence.)

Other scientists, however, have raised significant objections to this entire process of making predictions. They point out that climate feedbacks are climate feedbacks, and there is no reason to think the feedbacks will act differently on man-made "greenhouse gases" than on natural ones. Since the feedbacks currently eliminate about 58% of the warming effect of natural greenhouse gases, it stands to reason that they will do the same to the warming effect of man-made ones.

126. Roy W. Spencer et al., "The Science of Global Warming," in *A Renewed Call to Truth, Prudence, and Protection of the Poor: An Evangelical Examination of the Theology, Science, and Economics of Global Warming* (Burke, VA: Cornwall Alliance for the Stewardship of Creation, 2009). www.cornwallalliance.org/docs/a-renewed-call-to-truth-prudence-and-protection-of-the-poor.pdf, 27.

127. The low figure (1.8°F) is from Spencer et al., "Science of Global Warming," 27. The high figure (2.16°F) is from Martin L. Weitzman, "On Modeling and Interpreting the Economics of Catastrophic Climate Change," *Review of Economics and Statistics* 91 (Feb. 2009), 1–19, abstract online at http://ideas.repec.org/a/tpr/restat/v91y2009i1p1-19.html; pre-publication full text online at www.economics.harvard.edu/faculty/weitzman/files/modeling.pdf.

These scientists say that the proponents of global warming *have the feedbacks backward in their computer formulas*. Appealing to what we already know *by observing the real world*, they say that although some feedbacks may be positive and tend to warm the earth, *the combined feedback effect* must be negative—very strongly negative—and therefore the feedbacks will tend to have an overall cooling effect on additional manmade greenhouse gases.

The result? I mentioned above that *if we did not factor in climate feedbacks*, doubling the amount of carbon dioxide from preindustrial times, so that it would increase from 270 to 540 parts per million by volume (ppmv), would have a net result of raising earth's average surface temperature, *before feedbacks*, by about 1.8° to 2.16°F. But if we expect climate feedbacks to *subtract* from warming, we can expect they will lower the warming effects by about 58% to between 0.76°F to 0.9°F—in other words, actually *doubling* the amount of carbon dioxide from preindustrial times would lead to a total "global warming" of less than 1°F.[128]

An increase in average world temperature of less than 1°F is not dangerous. In fact, in general such slight warming would be beneficial, especially to agriculture. This is because most of the warming would occur in higher latitudes (near the poles), in the winter, and at night, not in already hot places at hot times. The result would be *longer growing seasons in cooler climates, less crop damage* from frost, and *fewer deadly cold snaps* (which tend to kill about ten times as many people per day as heat waves). Longer growing seasons would make food more abundant and therefore more affordable, a great benefit to the world's poor.[129]

This way of arguing for low climate sensitivity to increases in greenhouse gases—from the big picture of what we know about the effect of overall feedbacks on "greenhouse warming"—isn't the only way to reach this conclusion. More narrowly focused studies have reached it also. For example, Richard Lindzen and Yong-Sang Choi conclude their analysis from the Earth Radiation Budget Experiment by saying that "ERBE data appear to demonstrate a climate sensitivity of about 0.5°C [0.9°F]."[130] So this study also shows less warming than 1°F.

128. Spencer et al., "Science of Global Warming," 26–27, figures recalculated using Weitzman's higher (2.16°F) estimate of warming from doubled carbon dioxide. If Spencer's lower estimate (1.8°F) for warming from doubled carbon dioxide is correct, the IPCC's estimates require much greater added increments—94 percent, 200 percent, or 289 percent—and the net warming after feedbacks is about 0.76°F instead of 0.9°F.

129. William Nordhaus, *A Question of Balance: Weighing the Options on Global Warming Policies* (New Haven: Yale University Press, 2008); Bjørn Lomborg, *Cool It: The Skeptical Environmentalist's Guide to Global Warming* (New York: Alfred A. Knopf, 2007); Robert Mendelsohn, *Climate Change and Agriculture: An Economic Analysis of Global Impacts, Adaptation and Distributional Effects*, New Horizons in Environmental Economics (Northampton, MA: Edward Elgar, 2009).

130. Richard S. Lindzen and Yong-Sang Choi, in "On the determination of climate feedbacks from ERBE [Earth Radiation Budget Experiment] Data," *Geophysical Research Letters* 36

(Aug. 26, 2009), www.drroyspencer.com/Lindzen-and-Choi-GRL–2009.pdf, 5). Stephen E. Schwartz, in "Heat Capacity, Time Constant, and Sensitivity of Earth's Climate System," *Journal of Geophysical Research* 112 (Nov. 2, 2007), (www.ecd.bnl.gov/steve/pubs/HeatCapacity.pdf, 17), concludes that climate sensitivity could range from 1.08° to 2.88°F (1.1 ± 0.5 K). Richard S. Lindzen, Ming-Dah Chou, and Arthur Y. Hou, in "Does the Earth Have an Adaptive Infrared Iris?" *Bulletin of the American Meteorological Society* 82:3 (March 2001), (www-eaps.mit.edu/faculty/lindzen/adinfriris.pdf), provide evidence that clouds respond to surface warming by allowing more heat to escape into space, thus acting as a strong negative feedback. Roy W. Spencer, William D. Braswell, John R. Christy, and Justin Hnilo, in "Cloud and radiation budget changes associated with tropical intraseasonal oscillations," *Geophysical Research Letters* 34 (Aug. 9, 2007), (www.drroyspencer.com/Spencer_07GRL. pdf), reached similar conclusions using different methods.

Therefore, should we believe these predictions of dangerous results that will come from increased temperatures? I don't think so, for three reasons: (1) Actual empirical data about the effects of climate feedbacks show that they do not multiply the warming effect of greenhouse gases as the global warming computer programs would have us believe (as explained above); (2) some principles from the Bible make me doubt these global warming predictions; and (3) some important facts from other scientific evidence make me doubt them as well. The material that follows will explain reasons 2 and 3.

2. The Bible's teaching about the earth

a. Did God design a fragile earth or a resilient one?

The predictions of global warming that have most prominently come from the U.N.'s IPCC require us to believe that the net climate feedback response to "greenhouse warming" is very strongly positive (or warming) and therefore that dangerous global warming is likely.

But should Christians believe that God has actually designed the earth to be this fragile in response to human activity? This would be analogous to believing that an architect designed a building so that if someone leaned against one wall, its structural feedbacks would so magnify the stress of that person's weight that the building would collapse! No one would consider such an architectural design "very good." Yet Genesis 1:31 tells us, "God saw everything that he had made, and behold, it was very good."

If the earth is the product of the infinitely wise and omniscient God and is sustained by his providence, is seems to me more reasonable to think that the fundamental mechanisms of the earth's climate system are robust, self-regulating, and self-correcting—that they are designed to operate somewhat like a thermostat, cooling the planet when it begins to warm, and warming it when it begins to cool.

Evidence that the earth has warmed and cooled cyclically throughout its history is consistent with this view. As Fred Singer and Dennis Avery put it in the prologue to their book *Unstoppable Global Warming—Every 1,500 Years*:

> The history of Earth's climate is a story of constant change. Through at least the last million years, a moderate 1,500-year warm-cold cycle has been superimposed over the longer, stronger Ice Ages and warm interglacials. In the North Atlantic, the temperature changes about 4°C [7.2°F] from peak to trough during these "Dansgaard-Oeschger cycles."[131]

b. God's promises to maintain stability in seasons and oceans

Some other biblical truths point in this same direction, reflecting details of God's protection of the earth's seasons and oceans. For example, after the great flood of Noah's

---

131. S. Fred Singer and Dennis T. Avery, *Unstoppable Global Warming—Every 1,500 Years*, 2d ed. (Lanham, MD: Rowman & Littlefield, 2008).

day, God promised, "While the earth remains, seedtime and harvest, cold and heat, summer and winter, day and night, shall not cease" (Gen. 8:22). This suggests God's commitment to sustain the various cycles on which human, animal, and plant life on earth depend, until the final judgment.

Also following the flood, God promised, "Never again shall there be a flood to destroy the earth" (Gen. 9:11; see also v. 15). While that by itself doesn't rule out the possibility of major sea level increase (probably the most feared effect predicted from global warming), it does indicate that God controls the sea level. Psalm 104:9 likewise says, regarding the waters of the seas, "*You set a boundary that they may not pass*, so that they might not again cover the earth." And in Jeremiah, God says,

> I placed the sand as the boundary for the sea, a perpetual barrier that it cannot pass; though the waves toss, they cannot prevail; though they roar, they cannot pass over it (Jer. 5:22).

c. People displease God when they fail to acknowledge his control of the weather

In the next verses after Jeremiah 5:22, God rebukes Israel for not acknowledging that he controls their weather:

> But this people has a stubborn and rebellious heart; they have turned aside and gone away. They do not say in their hearts, "Let us fear the LORD our God, who gives the rain in its season, the autumn rain and the spring rain, and keeps for us the weeks appointed for the harvest." Your iniquities have turned these away [that is, the rains and the harvest seasons], and your sins have kept good from you" (Jer. 5:23–25).

This passage sounds remarkably similar to the proponents of dangerous global warming today—they fear a fragile, out-of-control climate pattern that will destroy the earth, but "do not say in their hearts, 'Let us fear the LORD our God, who gives the rain in its season.'" This suggests that the underlying cause of fears of dangerous global warming might not be science, but rejection of belief in God.

In the New Testament, the apostle Paul speaks similarly of people who "suppress the truth" about God's existence and attributes (Rom. 1:18). These people "did not honor him as God or give thanks to him, but they became futile in their thinking, and their foolish hearts were darkened" (v. 21). Surely that includes people who did not honor God or give thanks to him for the brilliant order and structure of his creation, so, "claiming to be wise, they became fools" (v. 22) and "exchanged the truth about God for a lie and worshiped and served the creature rather than the Creator" (v. 25). Such a description could be applied to much of the environmentalist movement, for whom "Mother Earth" rather than the one true God is their highest object of devotion.

Many other passages of Scripture also affirm God's control over the earth's weather (see Lev. 26:18–20; Deut. 28:12, 23–24; 2 Sam. 21:1; 1 Kings 17–18; Job 37:9–13; Pss. 107:23–38; 148:8; Amos 4:7–8; Jonah 1:4–16; Matt. 8:26–27).

d. God did not design the earth so that we would destroy it by obeying his commands

God originally commanded Adam and Eve (and by implication all mankind):

> "Be fruitful and multiply and *fill the earth and subdue it* and have dominion over the fish of the sea and over the birds of the heavens and over every living thing that moves on the earth" (Gen. 1:28).

This command seems inconsistent with a belief in dangerous, man-made global warming. Do we think God set up the earth so that we would destroy it by obeying these commands to develop the earth's resources and use them for our benefit? Did he set up the earth so that when we burn wood to warm ourselves or cook food, or when we burn gasoline to drive to work or school or church, or when we use diesel fuel to transport food and clothing and household goods from farm or factory to market, or when we burn oil or coal or natural gas to produce electricity to cook with or to heat or cool our homes or to provide light—do we really think God set up the earth to work in such a way that *the more we do these morally right things*, the more we will *destroy the earth?*

I do not think God made the earth to work that way. Rather, I think that God put wood on the earth and coal and oil and natural gas in the earth so that we could have abundant, easily transportable sources of fuel for use in various applications. Of course, all of these things can be used foolishly and dangerously—instead of building a safe fire to cook food, someone can carelessly start a forest fire. And coal-burning plants and factories can spew out soot and chemicals and pollute the air. I am not advocating reckless, dangerous use of these fuels.

But that is not all that global warming alarmists are complaining about. They are also warning against *clean and safe use of all these fuels*. They are saying that there is *no* safe use of these fossil fuels, because even if they are burned with 100% pollution-free flames, *they will still necessarily emit carbon dioxide* because that is an unavoidable by-product of combustion. They object not to the *abuse* of fossil fuels to pollute or destroy the environment but to their very *use*. They want to take away from human beings the best, most convenient, and cheapest energy sources we have.

Do we really think God has created the earth so that it would be destroyed by such morally right human activities, done in obedience to him? Do we really think God created the earth so that its climate system would careen off into catastrophe if carbon dioxide rose from 0.027% to 0.054% of the atmosphere (that is, from 27 to 54 *thousandths of one percent* of the atmosphere)? That is what global warming alarmists imply. Or do we think, by contrast, that God has set up an earth that is immensely resilient and will be able to adapt and be useful for human life under a wide variety of conditions?

My own view is that God has placed in the earth and its atmosphere a number of self-regulating, self-correcting mechanisms by which it can manage its own temperature. One example of this is the "global iris" effect of clouds over the oceans.[132] When the

---

132. Lindzen et al., "Does the Earth Have an Adaptive Infrared Iris?"

surface becomes warmer, high-level clouds diminish, permitting more heat to escape into space. When the surface cools, high-level clouds increase, retaining more heat. This and other studies showing that clouds regulate earth's temperature should, as Christian environmental theologian E. Calvin Beisner puts it, lead

> Christians to praise God for the way in which the Earth, like the human body, is "fearfully and wonderfully made." In some senses this planet, like the eye, may be fragile. But it may also, by God's wise design, be more resilient than many fearful environmentalists may imagine.[133]

This high-level cloud variation certainly looks like a self-correcting mechanism that God built into the earth's system to keep temperatures relatively stable. Who knows whether there are other systems like this that we have not yet discovered, where a heating factor triggers a balancing cooling factor and vice-versa? It would not be surprising, since the earth's long-term temperature averages tend to go back and forth between warming trends followed by cooling trends followed by warming trends.

e. Global warming alarmists remove our motivation to thank God for his wonderful gifts of cheap, abundant energy resources

The Bible praises God for his creation of the earth:

> And God saw everything that he had made, and behold, *it was very good* (Gen. 1:31).

> The earth is the LORD's and the fullness thereof, the world and those who dwell therein (Ps. 24:1).

> … *everything created by God is good*, and nothing is to be rejected if it is received with thanksgiving (1 Tim. 4:4).

These passages and others tell us that we should give thanks and praise to God for the excellence of the earth that he created. He wants us to develop and use the earth's resources because "he formed it to be inhabited!" (Isa. 45:18). We should use the resources he placed in the earth with thanksgiving to him.

Those who warn that we face dangerous global warming tell us we should feel guilty about using wood, coal, oil, and natural gas to produce energy. Rather than using God's good gifts with thanksgiving, they load us with guilt for using God's good gifts. Therefore they rob people of the motivation to thank God for the wonderful things he has given.

3. What does the scientific evidence say about global warming?

One response to the arguments above is to say that "scientists agree" that human emissions of greenhouse gases are causing global warming that could do great harm. For

---

133. E. Calvin Beisner, *What Is the Most Important Environmental Task Facing American Christians Today?* Mt. Nebo Papers, No. 1 (Washington, DC: Institute for Religion and Democracy, 2008), 23, in sidebar "Climate Science and Doxology." www.theird.org/Document.Doc?id=25.

example, that is the message trumpeted endlessly by Al Gore, whose video documentary *An Inconvenient Truth* has been shown in thousands of schools and even won an Oscar, and who with the IPCC received the Nobel Peace Prize for warning the world of impending climate disaster.

But is the scientific consensus really that clear? No, it certainly is not. Every attempt to prove the existence of such a scientific consensus has failed.

a. Scientific opinion is strongly divided about global warming

First, it is now beginning to seem that more scientists *reject* than embrace the idea of dangerous man-made global warming—possibly many times more. In one list compiled by a US Senate panel, *more than 700 scientists* have published their rejections of the whole or significant parts of the global warming hypothesis.[134]

On another list, *more than 31,000 degreed scientists*, including over 9,000 with PhDs, have signed the "Global Warming Petition" saying:

> There is *no convincing scientific evidence* that human release of carbon dioxide, methane, or other greenhouse gases is causing or will, in the foreseeable future, cause catastrophic heating of the Earth's atmosphere and disruption of the Earth's climate. Moreover, there is substantial scientific evidence that increases in atmospheric carbon dioxide produce many beneficial effects upon the natural plant and animal environments of the Earth.[135]

Another important resource in this regard is Lawrence Solomon's book *The Deniers: The World-Renowned Scientists Who Stood Up against Global Warming Hysteria, Political Persecution, and Fraud.*[136] He shows that those who reject the global warming alarms include many of the world's top experts in their fields.

Second, the published scientific literature is divided about this issue. A 2003 review, by history professor Naomi Oreskes, of scientific abstracts that purported to demonstrate scientific agreement about global warming was shown to have been badly flawed, and a re-examination of the same database found no such consensus.[137] Then a study of the same database covering up to 2007 actually showed a significant shift away from what had earlier (and mistakenly) been claimed as the consensus. As Klaus-Martin Schulte put it in the last of those studies,

---

134. U.S. Senate Minority Report: Over 700 International Scientists Dissent over Man-Made Global Warming Claims (Dec. 11, 2008). http://epw.senate.gov/public/index.cfm?FuseAction=Minority.Blogs&ContentRecord_id=2674E64F–802A–23AD–490B–BD9FAF4DCDB7.

135. Oregon Institute of Science and Medicine, "Global Warming Petition Project," emphasis added, http://petitionproject.org/. The site includes complete lists of signers and, at http://petitionproject.org/qualifications_of_signers.php, summarizes the numbers from various specialties relevant to the debate.

136. Lawrence Solomon, *The Deniers: The World-Renowned Scientists Who Stood Up against Global Warming Hysteria,*

Political Persecution, and Fraud (Minneapolis: Richard Vigilante Books, 2008), 207–8.

137. Naomi Oreskes, "The scientific consensus on climate change," *Science* 306:5702 (Dec. 3, 2004), 1686; www.sciencemag.org/cgi/content/full/306/5702/1686. This was refuted by Benny J. Peiser's Letter to *Science* (Jan. 4, 2005), submission ID: 56001; www.staff.livjm.ac.uk/spsbpeis/Scienceletter.htm. The surveys were reported in Dennis Bray and Hans von Storch, *The Perspectives of Climate Scientists on Global Climate Change* (Geesthacht, Germany: GKSS–Forschungszentrum Geesthacht, 2007); http://dvsun3.gkss.de/BERICHTE/GKSS_Berichte_2007/GKSS_2007_11.pdf.

Though Oreskes said that 75% of the papers in her sample endorsed the consensus, fewer than half now endorse it. Only 6% do so explicitly. Only one paper refers to "catastrophic" climate change, but without offering evidence. There appears to be little evidence in the learned journals to justify the climate-change alarm that now harms patients.[138]

Third, as Thomas Kuhn so famously pointed out in *The Structure of Scientific Revolutions*, great advances in science, often involving major paradigm shifts, occur when small minorities patiently—and often in the face of withering opposition—point out anomalies in the data and inadequacies in the reigning explanatory paradigms until their number and weight become so large as to require a wholesale paradigm shift, and what once was a minority view becomes a new majority view. Something like this process seems to be happening now to gradually change the media-driven claims of "consensus" about man-made global warming.

b. The earth's temperature has fallen or remained steady for the past fifteen years, a result not predicted by global warming computer models

The normal process in scientific investigation is to propose a hypothesis and then test it by seeing if the actual empirical data confirm or falsify it. What has happened with respect to global warming? The hypothesis was that recent increases in atmospheric carbon dioxide would lead to increasing global temperatures. But the actual facts have not shown that hypothesis to be true.

For one thing, there has been no "statistically significant" increase in average global temperatures in the last fifteen years, even according to a BBC News interview on February 13, 2010, with Dr. Phil Jones, long-time director of the Climatic Research Unit at the University of East Anglia (until he stepped down in December under investigation for scientific misconduct). Jones has been the provider of much of the most important data on which the U.N. IPCC and many governments have based fears of global warming. He reported a positive warming trend of 0.12°Centigrade per decade (0.216°F per decade, or an average of 0.02°F per year, too small to be statistically significant) from 1995 to 2009, but also said that there was a negative (cooling) trend of–0.12°C per decade if you calculate from January 2002 to 2009![139] How can this be? Such stability or even cooling in the presence of *increased* carbon dioxide is not the predicted result from the global warming computer models. (In the midst of the fallout from the "Climategate" data-rigging scandal in early 2010 [see pp. 375–76 below], England was covered in more snow than it has known for many years, and so was Washington, DC, which could lead one to wonder if the frigid temperatures might be an indication of an ironic divine exclamation mark over the scandal!)

In that same interview, when asked about the statement, "the debate on climate change is over," Jones amazingly replied,

---

138. Klaus-Martin Schulte, "Scientific Consensus on Climate Change?" *Energy and Environment* 19, no. 2 (July 2009), 281–86. http://scienceandpublicpolicy.org/images/stories/papers/reprint/schulte_two_colmun_fomat.pdf.

139. BBC interview with Professor Phil Jones, at http://news.bbc.co.uk/2/hi/science/nature/8511670.stm (accessed Feb. 25, 2010).

I don't believe the vast majority of climate scientists think this. This is not my view. There is still much that needs to be undertaken to reduce uncertainties, not just for the future, but for the instrumental (and especially the palaeoclimatic) past as well.[140]

In addition, earlier changes in average global temperatures have not coincided with changes in atmospheric concentrations of carbon dioxide. Here is a graph showing changes in global temperatures for the last 160 years:[141]

Figure 10.22

GLOBAL AVERAGE TEMPERATURES 1850–2009

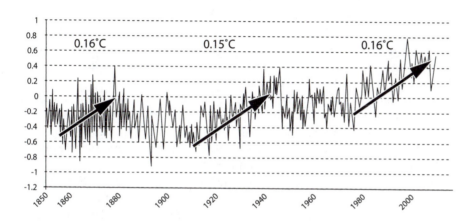

Source: http://joannenova.com.au/2010/03/the-bom-csiro-report-its-what-they-dont-say-that-matters/. Reprinted by permission.

Note that the increase in temperature from 1910 to 1940 was *prior to* most of the world's increasing production of carbon dioxide (after World War II). Then there was a cooling period from about 1945 to 1975, then a warming period from 1975 to 2000, then a cooling period from 2000 to the present. (And all of these changes are relatively small—the graph is measuring just tenths of a degree Centigrade).

---

140. Ibid.

141. Chart taken from http://joannenova.com.au/2010/03/
the-bom-csiro-report-its-what-they-dont-say-that-matters/

In addition, especially in light of the Climategate scandal, there is some doubt even about the reliability of these temperature measurements, especially whether they adjusted adequately for the "urban heat island" effect—that is, a temperature-monitoring station placed in an uninhabited area that was far from a city thirty years ago might now be surrounded by homes and office buildings and asphalt parking lots, all of which retain heat long after the sun goes down, so the thermometer will have higher average temperatures, but that has nothing to do with carbon dioxide concentrations or trends in overall global temperatures. The weather station might even now be located next to an air-conditioning unit or an exhaust fan![142]

Finally, other factors seem better able to explain the changes that have been observed in global temperatures, especially changes in ocean currents and solar activity.[143]

c. Should the UN's Intergovernmental Panel on Climate Change (IPCC) be trusted to have the last word?

Many people refer to the IPCC as the world's most authoritative body on global warming and describe its pronouncements as those of "thousands of climate scientists." The IPCC certainly warns of dangerous global warming. But we need to understand just what the IPCC has said, and what kind of organization it is.

The "Summary for Policymakers" that the IPCC publishes does not always accurately represent the detailed science in its Assessment Reports (which have been issued in 1992, 1995, 2001, and 2007). Instead, the Summary for Policymakers generally exaggerates the actual scientific conclusions. But because few journalists or politicians ever read the actual science, they tend to be unaware of this problem.[144]

In addition, we should not assume that the IPCC is an *objective* body of *objective* scientists not serving particular political agendas. On the contrary, the IPCC is *highly politicized*. Its charter called for it to study *human* influence on global temperature; consequently, it largely ignores *natural* influences. (And hundreds of staff workers now know that their jobs depend on continuing to find and publish evidence supporting the theory of dangerous man-made global warming, which gives a built-in bias factor in their data.) The crucial chapter 9 of its 2007 Assessment Report, which assesses likely temperature change from human "greenhouse gas" emissions and on which all the rest depends, relies heavily on the work of a small group of scientists prone to "group think" for lack of adequate interaction with others. Structural flaws seriously reduce the IPCC's credibility.[145]

---

142. See examples and information at www.surfacestations.org.

143. See p. 31 of the Cornwall Alliance's statement on scientific analysis of climate: www.cornwallalliance.org/docs/a-renewed-call-to-truth-prudence-and-protection-of-the-poor.pdf.

144. Mark W. Henderson, "A Closer Look at the IPCC," Center for Vision and Values, Grove City College (May 22, 2009). www.visandvals.org/A_Closer_Look_at_the_IPCC.php.

145. David Henderson, "Governments and Climate Change Issues: A Flawed Consensus" (prior version online at www.

heartland.org/custom/semod_policybot/pdf/19306.pdf), and Ross McKitrick, "Response to David Henderson's 'Governments and Climate Change Issues'" (http://ross.mckitrick. googlepages.com/McKitrick.final.pdf), both in *American Education Bulletin* XLVIII:5 (May 2008); John McLean, *Prejudiced Authors, Prejudiced Findings: Did the UN bias its attribution of "global warming" to humankind?* (Washington, DC: Science & Public Policy Institute, 2008), http://scienceandpublicpolicy. org/images/stories/papers/originals/McLean_IPCC_bias.pdf.

Finally, the IPCC's authority was deeply undermined by a large number of scandals that surfaced in late 2009 and early 2010. These include particularly "Climategate" and discoveries that the IPCC based some of its most frightening predictions on unscientific sources—such as press releases from environmental advocacy groups—while the actual scientific data refuted them.[146]

The term "Climategate" refers to the November 2009 leak, from the Climatic Research Unit at the University of East Anglia in England, of thousands of emails, computer codes, and other documents. These documents revealed that a core group of climate scientists at a wide range of agencies—the CRU, NASA's Goddard Institute for Space Studies, the National Oceanic and Atmospheric Administration, the National Center for Atmospheric Research, the National Climatic Data Center, the UK Meteorological Office, and elsewhere—on which the IPCC and national governments relied for data basic to global warming projections, had committed some serious scientific misconduct. Among the misdeeds were these:

- Fabricating, cherry-picking, suppressing, withholding, and destroying data related to historic and present temperatures;
- Failing to keep proper research archives;
- Using computer programs intentionally designed to exaggerate recent warming and minimize earlier climate variability (both warming and cooling) to create the appearance that recent warming was unprecedented when it was not;
- Refusing to share data and source code with other scholars on request, as required both by standard scientific practice and, in some cases, by the written standards of journals in which their work was published;
- Intimidating dissenting scientists to deter them from publishing research contrary to belief in dangerous man-made global warming;
- Corrupting the peer review process to prevent publication of dissenting research;
- Attempting to have journal editors who published dissenting research removed from their jobs;
- Boycotting journals that published dissenting papers; and
- Violating the law by refusing to turn over information subject to Freedom of Information laws in both the United States and the United Kingdom.

This is simply not the way researchers act when they are confident that the actual facts are overwhelmingly on their side. The misconduct was so serious and systemic that *it simply undercuts the credibility of all historic and contemporary temperature data* published in the IPCC's Scientific Assessment Reports.[147] But these sets of data were the

146. Mark Landsbaum, "What to say to a global warming alarmist" (Feb. 12, 2010), (www.ocregister.com/articles/−234092—.html), provides a helpful list and summary of such IPCC errors.

147. The three most thorough analyses of "Climategate" at the time of this writing are John P. Costella, *Climategate Analysis*, SPPI Reprint Series (Jan. 20, 2010) from the Washington: Science & Public Policy Institute (2010), (http://scienceandpub-licpolicy.org/images/stories/papers/reprint/climategate_analysis.pdf); Steven Mosher and Thomas Fuller, *Climategate: The CRUtape Letters* (Charleston, SC: CreateSpace/Amazon.com, 2010); Brian Sussman, *Climategate: A Meteorologist Exposes the Global Warming Scam* (Torrance, CA: WND Books, 2010); and A. W. Montford, *The Hockey Stick Illusion: Climategate and the Corruption of Science* (London: Stacey International, 2010).

basis for the claims of the global warming alarmists! In short, the IPCC's authority on global warming is poor. It is doubtful that it will be able to regain the credibility it previously had in the scientific world. It was using distorted, incorrect data.

The top climate-change official at the United Nations, Yvo do Boer, announced his resignation February 19, 2010. The *Washington Times* reported, "The bureaucrat's departure is no surprise because his pseudo-scientific global warming religion was proved to be a hoax on his watch."[148] In the same article, the *Times* also reported the following remarkable disclosure:

> Joseph D'Aleo, the first director of meteorology and co-founder of the Weather Channel, and Anthony Watts, a meteorologist and founder of SurfaceStations. org, are well-known and well-respected scientists. On Jan. 29, they released a startling study showing that starting in 1990, the National Oceanic and Atmospheric Administration (NOAA) began systematically eliminating climate-measuring stations in cooler locations around the world. Eliminating stations that tended to record cooler temperatures drove up the average measured temperature. The stations eliminated were in higher latitudes and altitudes, inland areas away from the sea and more rural locations. The drop in the number of weather stations was dramatic, declining from more than 6,000 stations to fewer than 1,500.[149]

Lawrence Solomon, in *The Deniers*, had already written that the Climategate scandal made the historical temperature data suspect and that carbon dioxide's "contribution to global warming remains approximately nil."[150] The broader implications of Climategate and related data-manipulation scandals were still unfolding at the time of this writing.

d. Are glaciers melting and sea levels rising?

For years now, the public has been bombarded with messages that man-made global warming is causing disastrous consequences, such as melting glaciers, endangered polar bears, and rising sea levels. What should we think of these claims?

First, even if we did see glaciers melting and sea levels rising, these might well be due to other factors such as variations in sun activity, variations in ocean currents, and ordinary long-term weather cycles and not due to changes in carbon dioxide levels (as explained above).

Second, none of the claimed disasters is well supported by evidence. Here are some examples:

(1) *Glaciers and ice caps:* Glaciers have been shrinking slowly ever since the end of the last Ice Age (perhaps around 18,000 years ago)—during more than 99% of which time people have not emitted enough greenhouse gas for anybody to claim any effect on global average temperatures. So the mere fact of their shrinking is nothing new and nothing caused by human beings.

---

148. *Washington Times* (Feb. 18, 2010). www.washington-times.com/news/2010/feb/18/more-errors-in-temperature-data/?feat=home_editorials.

149. Ibid.

150. Lawrence Solomon, "The Ozone Hole Did It," *Financial Post* Comment (Jan. 9, 2010). http://network.nationalpost.com/np/blogs/fpcomment/archive/2010/01/09/the-ozone-hole-did-it.aspx.

But is there recent shrinkage evidence pointing to accelerated warming and thus, indirectly, evidence that *something* new is going on? No. The data are simply insufficient to establish accelerated shrinkage compared with their long-term rate since the Ice Age.[151]

As for ice caps in the Arctic and Antarctic, short-term observations do not prove much of anything. Ice melts in warmer seasons and freezes in cooler seasons every year, and there are warmer years and colder years, so a photo of melting Arctic ice does not prove a long-term trend. But if people want to use short-term observations, the recent ones show that both Arctic and Antarctic ice has been *expanding*:

> In October 2008, it was reported that Arctic ice was actually increasing at a rapid rate. According to the International Climate and Environmental Change Assessment Project (ICECAP), an organization of respected climatology academics, the Arctic ice had increased at a rate of 31.3% or from 5,663,125 square kilometers in 2007 to 7,436,406 square kilometers just a year later.[152] They also reported in 2008 that Antarctica had set a record for the maximum amount of ice since monitoring began in 1979.[153]

(2) *Sea levels.* Al Gore, in his book *Earth in the Balance*, dramatically claimed, "Many residents of low-lying Pacific Island nations have already had to evacuate their homes because of rising seas"—a claim illustrated by a photo of Tuvalu (an island nation of 12,000 people between Hawaii and Australia).[154]

But as Marlo Lewis pointed out in his 154-page, devastating critique of Gore's book, "Tide gauge records show that sea levels at Tuvalu *fell* during the latter half of the twentieth century. Altimetry data from the Topex-Poseiden satellite show that Tuvalu sea levels fell even during the 1990s...."[155] Indeed, no one has had to evacuate any Pacific island nations because of rising sea level. Gore's claim was just misleading.

In the film *An Inconvenient Truth* Gore claimed that melting ice from West Antarctica and Greenland would cause a twenty-foot increase in sea level worldwide. Although he did not specify *when* this would happen, the context makes it clear that he intends the prediction to prompt action *now* to protect our children or perhaps our grandchildren. Clearly, he had the remainder of this century in mind.

Yet the IPCC, even with its questionable assumption of high warming from rising greenhouse gases, estimated instead that melt from those two locations would add only about *2.5 inches* to sea level over the next hundred years.[156] In fact, sea level, which has

151. Idso and Singer, *Climate Change Reconsidered*, 135–52.

152. Joseph D'Aleo, "Arctic Ice Increasing Rapidly" (Oct. 14, 2008). http://icecap.us/index.php/go/joes-blog/arctic_ice_increasing_rapidly/. (It should be noted that 2007 was an especially low year for Arctic ice, so it is not surprising that the following year would show a significant increase.)

153. Joseph D'Aleo, "Latest Antarctic Ice Extent" (Jan. 14, 2008). http://icecap.us/index.php/go/joes-blog/latest_antarctic_sea_ice_extent2/.

154. Al Gore, *Earth in the Balance* (Emmaus, PA: Rodale Books, 2006), 186.

155. Marlo Lewis Jr., *Al Gore's Science Fiction: A Skeptic's Guide to An Inconvenient Truth,* Congressional Briefing Paper (Washington, DC: Competitive Enterprise Institute, n.d.), 88, online at http://cei.org/pdf/5820.pdf. See also Cliff Ollier, "Sea Level in the Southwest Pacific is Stable," *New Concepts in Global Tectonics Newsletter* 51 (June 2009), http://nzclimatescience.net/images/PDFs/paperncgtsealevl.pdf.

156. Christopher Monckton, *35 Inconvenient Truths: The Errors of Al Gore's Movie* (Washington, DC: Science and Public Policy Institute, 2007), 4. http://scienceandpublicpolicy.org/images/stories/press_releases/monckton-response-to-gore-errors.pdf.

been slowly rising ever since the end of the last Ice Age, rose only about 6.3 inches in the entire twentieth century—and the *rate* of increase *declined* in the latter half of the century.[157]

Gore's movie was judged by a British court to have so many and such serious errors that it could no longer be shown in British government schools without an accompanying list and refutation of its errors. Otherwise, said the judge, it would violate an Act of Parliament prohibiting political indoctrination of children.[158]

e. What about severe weather and other claims about damage from global warming?

Has there been more frequent or more intense *severe weather* caused by a warming earth? No.[159] The most common claim—that hurricane frequency and strength rose with recent global warming—has been not only refuted empirically but also abandoned by the scientist who most strongly promoted it.[160] An attempt by climatologist Michael Mann (author of the discredited "hockey stick" graph that eliminated the Medieval Warm Period and Little Ice Age to make twentieth-century warming appear extraordinary) to show an increase in hurricanes in recent years brought a devastating rebuttal by Chris Landsea, one of the world's leading hurricane experts.[161]

What about *droughts and floods*? Are they growing more frequent and intense? Even if they were, that alone would not prove that this is caused by increases in carbon dioxide. But in fact, droughts and floods are not increasing in frequency or intensity.[162]

4. The benefits that come from increased carbon dioxide in the atmosphere

We should also not ignore a completely different aspect of the discussion. Carbon dioxide's effect on *global average temperature* is most likely insignificant and benign, as I argued above. But its effect on *plant life*—and therefore on all other life, which depends on plant life—is large and *overwhelmingly beneficial*.

157. S. J. Holgate, "On the decadal rates of sea level change during the twentieth century," *Geophysical Research Letters* 34 (2007): cited in Craig Idso and S. Fred Singer, *Climate Change Reconsidered: 2009 Report of the Nongovernmental International Panel on Climate Change* (NIPCC) (Chicago: Heartland Institute, 2009), 186–87, www.heartland.org/publications/NIPCC%20report/PDFs/NIPCC%20Final.pdf.

158. Monckton, *35 Inconvenient Truths*, 3. See also William Lee Adams, "British Court: Gore Film 'Political,'" *Time* (Oct. 12, 2007). www.time.com/time/world/article/0,8599,1670882,00.html.

159. Idso and Singer, *Climate Change Reconsidered*, 281–360; Randall S. Cerveny, "Severe Weather, Natural Disasters, and Global Change," in *Shattered Consensus: The True State of Global Warming*, ed. Patrick J. Michaels (Lanham, MD: Rowman & Littlefield, 2005), 106–20; Patrick J. Michaels, *Meltdown: The Predictable Distortion of Global Warming By Scientists, Politicians,* *and the Media* (Washington, DC: Cato Institute, 2004), 111–61.

160. National Oceanic and Atmospheric Adminstration, "NOAA Attributes Recent Increase in Hurricane Activity to Naturally Occurring Multi-Decadal Climate Variability" (Nov. 29, 2005), www.magazine.noaa.gov/stories/mag184.htm; Eric Berger, "Hurricane expert reconsiders global warming's impact," *Houston Chronicle* (April 12, 2008), www.chron.com/disp/story.mpl/tech/news/5693436.html; Kerry Emanuel, Ragoth Sundararajan, and John Williams, "Hurricanes and Global Warming: Results from Downscaling IPCC AR4 Simulations," *Bulletin of the American Meteorological Society* 89:3 (March 2008), 347–67, http://ams.allenpress.com/archive/1520-0477/89/3/pdf/i1520-0477-89-3-347.pdf.

161. Chris Landsea, untitled letter in response to Michael Mann and co-authors. http://icecap.us/images/uploads/LetterMann.pdf.

162. Idso and Singer, *Climate Change Reconsidered*, 281–309.

Hundreds and hundreds of peer-reviewed scientific studies have demonstrated that increased atmospheric carbon dioxide leads to enhanced plant growth. Indeed, on average, doubled carbon dioxide increases plant growth efficiency by about 35%. With enhanced carbon dioxide, plants grow better, whether subjected to higher or lower temperatures and to drier or wetter soil. Consequently, their geographical range expands, and so does that of the various animals that depend on them. The plants also resist diseases and pests better.[163]

Earth's atmospheric carbon dioxide level is now very low compared with many past geologic periods—periods during which its plant and animal life thrived. The IPCC and other global warming alarmists tend to hide this fact by referring to carbon dioxide's increase only since preindustrial times. As mentioned before, we can see the great variation by comparing earlier periods with our current concentration of 385 parts per million by volume (ppmv). Many scientists believe the concentration was 270 ppmv in preindustrial times.[164]

But what about much earlier periods? One study says that early in the Paleozoic era (540-to-250 million years ago [mya], according to time scales used in modern geological studies), carbon dioxide climbed from about 5,000 to 7,000 ppmv and then fell back again, then fell in fits and starts to about 3,000 ppmv late in the Silurian period (440–415 mya), rose to about 4,000 in the first half of the Devonian period (415–360 mya), fell to around 400 in the Carboniferous (360–300 mya) and Permian (300–250 mya) periods, rose again to about 2,000 in the Triassic period (251–200 mya), fell stepwise to about 1,300 by the middle of the Jurassic period (240–145 mya), rose for a while in that period to about 2,800, and then began a long decline through the Cretaceous (145–65 mya) and Tertiary (65–3 mya) periods, reaching around 200 to 300 in the Quaternary period (3 mya to present).

Did these changes in carbon dioxide result in massive temperature changes? Contrary to the view that carbon dioxide drives temperature, throughout geologic history there has been no clear correlation between the two. Sometimes they rose together, sometimes they fell, and sometimes they went in opposite directions.[165]

What is clear is that the periods of higher carbon dioxide have also been periods of *much more prolific plant growth*. As Ian Plimer puts it,

> The CO_2 content of air has hardly ever been as low as today and ecosystems suffer because of this. Early in the Earth's history, the CO_2 content of air was tens to hundreds of times higher than today and, over time, this CO_2 has been stored as carbon compounds in rocks, oil, gas, coal and carbonate rocks.[166]

163. The Center for the Study of Carbon Dioxide and Global Change (www.co2science.org) maintains an enormous and growing database of published scientific studies on the subject. A review of the findings is in Idso and Singer, *Climate Change Reconsidered*, 361–578.

164. Roy W. Spencer et al., "The Science of Global Warming," in *A Renewed Call to Truth, Prudence, and Protection of the Poor: An Evangelical Examination of the Theology, Science, and Economics of Global Warming* (Burke, VA: Cornwall Alliance for the Stewardship of Creation, 2009), 27. www.cornwallalliance. org/docs/a-renewed-call-to-truth-prudence-and-protection-of-the-poor.pdf.

165. Robert A. Berner and Zavareth Kothavala, "Geocarb III: A revised model of atmospheric CO2 over Phanerozoic Time," *American Journal of Science* 301 (Feb. 2001), 182–204: summarized in Ian Wishart, *Air Con: The Seriously Inconvenient Truth About Global Warming* (North Shore, NZ: Howling at the Moon Publishing, 2009), 33–36.

166. Ian Plimer, *Heaven and Earth: Global Warming the Missing Science* (Lanham, MD: Taylor Trade Publishing, 2009), 411.

The release of carbon dioxide now, by our burning of fossil fuels, is restoring some of it to the atmosphere and greatly benefiting life on earth. It appears to be causing deserts to green, and it has contributed significantly to increasing crop yields since 1950, making food more abundant and less expensive and therefore reducing the percentage of the human population experiencing hunger and starvation.

Sherwood Idso, one of the world's foremost researchers on the subject, says, "We appear to be experiencing the initial stages of what could truly be called a *rebirth of the biosphere*, the beginnings of a biological rejuvenation that is without precedent in all of human history."[167]

For this reason, intentionally forcing people to reduce carbon dioxide emissions would actually do enormous harm, not only to human economies but also to the whole biosphere.

5. The unacceptable loss of human freedom that would come with government control of energy use

A neglected factor in this discussion is how much we think that governments should control our lives. The controversy over global warming is to a very large degree a controversy over human liberty versus government control. The liberal politicians who continually seek more government control do so because they think that enlightened governing officials can run people's lives better than they can run them themselves. Such people will eagerly flock in large groups to the global warming crusade, because it appears to be a wonderful mechanism by which government can control more people's lives.

Regulating people's use of energy is an incredibly effective way of increasing the control of central governments over our entire lives. If the government can dictate how far you drive your car, how much you heat or cool your home, how much you will use electric lights or computers or a TV, how much energy your factory can use, and how much jet fuel you can have to fly an airplane, then it can control most of the society.

Václav Klaus, president of the Czech Republic, said that in his opinion the alarm about global warming and the campaign to reduce carbon dioxide provide the greatest threat to human liberty that has come to the earth since communism. He wrote in the *Financial Times* that "global warming hysteria has become a prime example of the truth versus propaganda problem." He continued:

> As someone who lived under communism for most of his life, I feel obliged to
> say that I see the biggest threat to freedom, democracy, the market economy

---

167. Sherwood B. Idso, *CO$_2$ and the Biosphere: The Incredible Legacy of the Industrial Revolution* (St. Paul: University of Minnesota Department of Soil, Water and Climate, 1995). The Center for the Study of Carbon Dioxide and Global Change offers two excellent video documentaries on the benefits of increased carbon dioxide: *The Greening of Planet Earth* and *The Greening of Planet Earth Continues* (www.co2science.org).

and prosperity now in ambitious environmentalism, not in communism. This ideology wants to replace the free and spontaneous evolution of mankind by a sort of central (now global) planning.

The environmentalists ask for immediate political action because they do not believe in the long-term positive impact of economic growth and ignore both the technological progress that future generations will undoubtedly enjoy, and the proven fact that the higher the wealth of society, the higher is the quality of the environment. They are Malthusian pessimists.[168]

This is significant because Klaus lived through many years of communism in the former Czechoslovakia. He is also a trained economist.

6. The unacceptable costs of reducing our use of carbon fuels

Global warming alarmists want the world to drastically reduce the use of fossil fuels to cut carbon dioxide emissions. But the best economic analyses show that trying to reduce fossil fuel use would cause far more harm than good.[169] Why? Because abundant, affordable energy is crucial to economic production, especially to societies that seek to climb out of abject poverty. It is important to remember that *when we use energy sources, we reduce the need for human work:* plowing a field with a tractor rather than walking behind a horse, driving a car rather than walking huge distances, driving a truck rather than pushing a cart, and so forth. *Energy use makes possible all human economic progress* and frees us to use our time in higher levels of intellectual endeavor or interpersonal human relationships or even various Christian ministries. Energy use gives us freedom that we can use as we choose—for good or for ill.

Where can we obtain energy? Fossil fuels are (along with nuclear energy) the most abundant and affordable sources of energy available. Forcing people to replace carbon fuels would require them to switch to alternative energy sources, and solar, wind, and biofuels—the sources frequently mentioned—tend to cost from two to eight times as much as fossil fuels for generating electricity.[170] Such a switch would mean *drastically increasing the price of energy* and thus slowing economic development, trapping the world's poor in their poverty, and perpetuating the high rates of disease and premature death that stem from their poverty.

Human beings already live in climates from the freezing Arctic to the searing Sahara. Temperature is not a significant challenge. The wealthier people are, the better

168. Václav Klaus, "Freedom, Not Climate, At Risk," *Financial Times.com*. (June 13, 2007). www.ft.com/cms/s/2/9deb730a–19ca–11dc–99c5–000b5df10621.html.

169. Nordhaus, *A Question of Balance*; Lomborg, *Cool It*; Bjørn Lomborg, ed., *Global Crises, Global Solutions* (Cambridge: Cambridge University Press, 2004); *Solutions for the World's Biggest Problems: Costs and Benefits* (Cambridge: Cambridge University Press, 2007); and *How to Spend $50 Billion to Make the World a Better Place* (Cambridge: Cambridge University Press, 2006).

170. Cornelis van Kooten, "The Economics of Global Warming Policy," in Spencer et al., *A Renewed Call to Truth, Prudence, and Protection of the Poor*. www.cornwallalliance.org/docs/a-renewed-call-to-truth-prudence-and-protection-of-the-poor.pdf, 66.

they can cope with heat and cold, droughts and floods, storms, diseases, and other challenges. Forced reductions in fossil fuel use would cause economic harm to every person in the world (as prices for everything would rise), but especially immense harm to the world's poor.

Bjorn Lomborg, a respected Danish environmentalist and professor of statistics, convened a series of meetings under the title Copenhagen Consensus, beginning in 2004. The participants assumed (for the purpose of their discussions) that man-made global warming is occurring and then asked what the best human response to that would be. They concluded that "for some of the world's poorest countries, which will be adversely affected by climate change, problems like HIV/AIDS, hunger, and malaria are more pressing and can be solved with more efficacy."

Consequently, after carefully comparing the severity of many challenges and the cost-benefit ratios of proposed solutions, they agreed that top priority should go to fighting communicable diseases, relieving malnutrition and hunger, and eliminating trade subsidies and barriers—all of which have benefits far outweighing their costs, while proposals to fight climate change were the *worst* use of funds, with their costs far outweighing their benefits.[171]

Christians who are concerned about alleviating poverty in the world cannot ignore the tremendous economic harm that would come from forcing reductions in carbon-based energy sources. The policies promoted to fight global warming would harm the poor more than the warming itself, even if it were real.

I joined with the twenty-nine evangelical scholars who authored and endorsed the statement *A Renewed Call to Truth, Prudence, and Protection of the Poor: An Evangelical Examination of the Theology, Science, and Economics of Global Warming*[172] in concluding that

> Policies requiring drastic reductions in carbon dioxide emissions are unrealistic and threaten human well-being, especially in developing countries, where, by curtailing use of the most abundant, reliable, and affordable energy sources, they would prolong abject poverty and the miseries of toil, disease, and premature death that accompany it....
>
> The most scientifically, economically, and ethically defensible policy response to alleged dangerous anthropogenic global warming is to promote economic development, especially for the world's poor, through policies that ensure abundant and affordable energy, on the one hand, and reduce specific risks from which the poor suffer regardless of climate change (e.g., under-nutrition and malnutrition; waterborne, pest-borne, and communicable diseases; depressed income because of tariffs, trade restrictions, and corrupt govern-

---

171. Lomborg, *How to Spend $50 Billion to Make the World a Better Place.*

172. See www.cornwallalliance.org/docs/a-renewed-call-to-truth-prudence-and-protection-of-the-poor.pdf, 68. See also the conclusions of Nobel Prize-winning economists of the Copenhagen Consensus Center, http://copenhagenconsensus.com/CCC%20Home%20Page.aspx.

ments; high rates of accidental injury and death because of poor transport and industry infrastructure), on the other hand.

7. Conclusion

In conclusion, the warnings about dangerous man-made global warming are based on poor scientific evidence and poor scientific method, are not proven by previous empirical data, conflict with the Bible's teachings about the nature of the earth and man's purpose on the earth, and propose solutions that would cripple the world's economies and bring immense harm to the poor. These solutions would also bring unacceptable losses of human freedom and immense increases in government power.

While carbon dioxide does not contribute in any significant measure to dangerous levels of global warming, increasing its amount in the atmosphere would bring important agricultural benefits in terms of increased plant growth. Slight increases in global temperature would on the whole bring important agricultural benefits as well, especially in terms of longer growing seasons in cool climates.

In light of these factors, governments should not adopt any policies to regulate the amount of carbon fuel used or to diminish the amount of carbon dioxide in the atmosphere.

E. CAFE STANDARDS FOR AUTOMOBILE MILEAGE

Congress first enacted fuel economy standards for US vehicles in 1975 (after the shock of the Arab oil embargo in 1973).[173] These standards were designed to force Americans to use less oil by manufacturing more fuel-efficient cars. They are called Corporate Average Fuel Economy (CAFE) standards, and they specify the *average* miles-per-gallon performance required for the cars and trucks produced by each manufacturer in each year.

For 1978, passenger cars had to average 18 miles per gallon (MPG). For 1979, it went up to 19 MPG, and light trucks had to average 17.2 MPG. The CAFE standards gradually increased after that and leveled off at 27.5 MPG for passenger cars in 1990. For the category of light trucks (which includes minivans and sport utility vehicles—SUVs), the standard was 20 MPG in 1990 and has increased to 23.1 MPG for 2009.[174]

How did manufacturers reach these averages? Some improvements were made in engine technology to squeeze more miles out of each gallon, but there is only so much energy in each ounce of gas, so there is a limit to how much improvement can come that way. Moreover, these improvements become increasingly expensive, driving up the price of the vehicle. Therefore the only practical way to meet these standards has been to make a lot of *smaller, lighter cars* that take less energy to power. (You can drive a go-cart a long

---

173. National Highway Traffic Safety Administration. "CAFE Overview, Frequently Asked Questions." www.nhtsa.dot.gov/CARS/rules/CAFE/overview.htm.

174. Ibid.

distance on a gallon of gas!) There are some lightweight composite materials that would increase crash strength in cars, but they are more expensive[175] and would just lead to significantly higher car prices.

This means that most Americans are now driving smaller, lighter cars than they did thirty years ago. This is not because drivers *chose* to ride in smaller, more cramped quarters, or *chose* to drive cars that provide them very little protection in an accident. It is because government standards have driven larger cars (like the family station wagon) off the market; making such cars would drive up the manufacturer's CAFE totals too high, and for that they would face huge government fines.

Therefore manufacturers can only make a very few larger cars to factor into their averages, and they then price them so high that only wealthy customers can afford them. Tom Libby, Senior Director of Industry Analysis for the J.D. Power Information Network, said, "Mercedes Benz, for instance, will have to adjust their powertrains and model mix.... It will be difficult for them." Michael Omotoso, also of J.D. Power, added, "Even though they can achieve the standards, they say it may cost $4,000 to $6,000 more per vehicle. So manufacturers can either pass the entire cost onto the consumer, or they will have to eat some of the costs, and thus lower their profits or lose money on every vehicle they sell."[176]

When allowed to choose between cars of similar price, most customers will choose larger cars for safety and comfort. (There are many small cars with very high fuel efficiency on the market, but they have not been bestsellers.) Yet this choice of larger cars is being systematically denied to them by government.

What are the costs of the CAFE standards? Smaller cars are demonstrably more dangerous. The death rate in accidents in multivehicle crashes is *twice as high* in minis as in large cars; in single-vehicle crashes involving *only* a small car, "passengers in minis suffered *three times as many deaths* as in large cars."[177] Already in 2002, a National Research Council study found that the 27.5 MPH CAFE standards "contributed to about 2,000 deaths per year through their restrictions on car size and weight."[178] That is 2,000 more Americans dead each year (and many thousands more seriously injured) simply because of CAFE requirements imposed by Congress.

It was troubling, therefore, that on May 19, 2009, President Obama announced an agreement with the Detroit automakers (including General Motors and Chrysler, which the federal government now in effect controls) to institute a huge increase of CAFE standards from 27.5 MPG in 2010 to 35.5 MPG by 2016. Passenger cars would have to average 39 MPG.[179] SUVs and minivans will also have to be factored into the overall formula, and this will require even smaller and lighter cars as well as switching to the

175. Statement by Jeffrey Runge, former head of the National Highway Traffic Safety Administration (NHTSA), in *USA Today* (May 20, 2009), 2B.

176. Don Hammonds, "New Fuel Standards Advancing Lighter Cars, Hybrids," *ScrippsNews.com* (May 27, 2008). www.scrippsnews.com/node/33526.

177. "Small Cars Are Dangerous Cars," *Wall Street Journal* (April 17, 2009), A11, citing studies by the Insurance Institute for Highway Safety.

178. Ibid.

179. Steven Mufson, "Vehicle Emission Rules to Tighten," *Washington Post* (May 19, 2009). www.washingtonpost.com/wp-dyn/content/article/2009/05/18/AR2009051801848.html.

more-expensive hybrid or all-electric cars. The cost will be paid by the American people in terms of significantly higher prices for cars overall (which makes this a sort of "hidden tax" on everyone who drives). The cost will also be paid through even less safe cars, with even more injuries and more deaths. There is also a significant loss in consumer freedom because, when given a chance, Americans in general prefer to drive larger, safer, more comfortable cars. But those cars will simply be unavailable or unaffordable for most middle-class drivers.

Alan Reynolds of the Cato Institute wrote about how these standards negatively impact auto manufacturers, focusing on General Motors. He said:

> The actual Corporate Average Fuel Economy (CAFE) results will depend on the mixture of fuel-thrifty and fuel-thirsty vehicles consumers choose to buy from each manufacturer—not on what producers hope to sell. That means only those companies most successful in selling the smallest cars with the smallest engines will, in the future, be allowed to sell the more profitable larger pickups and SUVs and more powerful luxury and sports cars....
>
> General Motors is likely to become profitable only if it is allowed to specialize in what it does best—namely, midsize and large sedans, sports cars, pickup trucks and SUVs. The company can't possibly afford to scrap billions of dollars of equipment used to produce its best vehicles simply to please politicians who would rather see GM start from scratch, wasting more taxpayer money on "retooling" to produce unwanted and unprofitable subcompacts and electric cars. The average mileage of GM's future cars won't matter if nobody buys them.
>
> Politicians are addicted to CAFE standards because they create an illusion of doing something sometime in the future without voters experiencing the slightest inconvenience in the present. Tighter future CAFE rules will have no effect at all on the type of vehicles we choose to buy. Their only effect will be to compel us to buy larger and more powerful vehicles from foreign manufacturers. Americans will still buy Jaguars, but from an Indian firm, Tata, rather than Ford. They'll buy Hummers, but from a Chinese firm, Tengzhong, rather than GM. The whole game is a charade; symbolism without substance....
>
> The bottom line is that CAFE standards are totally unenforceable and ineffective. Regardless of how much damage the rules do to GM and Chrysler, Americans can and will continue to buy big and fast vehicles from German, Japanese, Korean, Chinese and Indian car companies. CAFE standards might just be another foolhardy regulatory nuisance—were it not for the fact that they could easily prove fatally dangerous for any auto maker overly dependent on the uniquely overregulated U.S. market.[180]

---

180. Alan Reynolds, "Fuel Standards Are Killing GM," *Wall Street Journal* (July 2, 2009). www.cato.org/pub_display.php?pub_id=10326. I think Reynolds's conclusions are overstated, but what he says rightly warns of harm to the American auto industry and to customers.

What is the reason for the CAFE standards? The primary reason is a desire to reduce "greenhouse gas emissions" from automobiles, as the Obama administration explained in announcing its plan May 19, 2009.[181] But if (as I argue in the previous section) using carbon fuels has almost no measurable effect on the earth's climate, then these CAFE standards are just forcing Americans to drive smaller, less comfortable, more dangerous cars for no good purpose.

It is also another example of growing government control of more and more of our lives, including the size of cars we are allowed to drive.

F. CAP AND TRADE

"Cap and trade" as currently proposed is a system that would allow the government to control energy use. The government would set a limit (a "cap") on the carbon emissions that each company produces and allocate (or probably sell!) each company enough "credits" to allow just that amount of emissions. Then the government would *gradually lower the cap over time*, thus forcing companies to reduce overall carbon emissions by *reducing overall energy use*. In this way, "cap and trade" would allow the government to tightly regulate energy use—something that has never been done before in America. The reason to do this is said to be the need to prevent global warming.

The "trade" part would kick in if some companies decided to use less energy, such as by shutting down some factories or taking some of their trucks or airplanes out of commission. Then they could sell (or "trade") their energy credits to other firms that want to keep their factories and trucks running with the new, reduced energy limits. (Some limited energy savings might also be made through greater efficiency, but presumably market forces have already driven companies to be as energy efficient as would be economically beneficial to them.) Therefore the entire system would *penalize* productive companies (that want to grow and produce more) and *reward* unproductive companies (that decide to shut down their factories and sell their credits!). The overall effect of cap and trade would thus be to hinder the economic productivity of a nation by restricting energy use, and thus it would drive up prices. Based entirely on the unproved theory of global warming, the cap and trade system would damage any economy, perhaps in very significant ways.

---

181. Statement by Jeffrey Runge, *USA Today,* op. cit.

Chapter 11

NATIONAL DEFENSE

Should governments use military power to defend themselves against other nations? If so, when and how should such forces be used in war? What moral restrictions should nations place on the actions of their military forces in wartime?

After those general considerations, specific political issues also must be answered:

How should nations respond to the threat of worldwide terrorism?

What should be done about the wars in Iraq and Afghanistan?

Should the United States have nuclear weapons, and if so, how many?

Should the United States develop a more extensive missile defense system?

What should be the role of the CIA, and what limits should be placed on its activity?

What should the nation's policy be regarding torture of enemy forces in its custody?

Should homosexuals be allowed to serve in the military?

Should women serve in combat situations?

A. BIBLICAL TEACHING

1. Governments are responsible to defend their nations from attacks by other nations

As we saw in chapter 3 above (see pp. 77–82), one of the most basic responsibilities of government is to punish those who do evil. When a government does this, it defends the weak and defenseless and deters further wrongdoing. The apostle Peter says the civil government is intended "to punish those who do evil and to praise those who do good" (1 Peter 2:14). Paul says that the government is authorized by God to "bear the sword" (Rom. 13:4) against evildoers so that it can be "a terror" to bad conduct (v. 3), and it also "carries out God's wrath on the wrongdoer" (v. 4). According to Paul, when the ruler uses superior force—even deadly force—against evil, he is "God's servant for your good" (v. 4).

Now, if a government is commanded by God to protect its citizens from the robber or thief who comes from *within* a country, then certainly it also has an obligation to protect its citizens against thousands of murderers or thieves who come as an army from somewhere *outside of* the nation. Therefore a nation has a *moral obligation to defend itself* against foreign attackers who would come to kill and conquer and subjugate the people in a nation.

Further evidence for this is seen in Old Testament narratives where the nation of Israel repeatedly had to defend itself against attacks by nations such as the Philistines, the Assyrians, and the Babylonians. When God blessed Israel, they defeated their enemies who were attacking them (see Judg. 2:16–18; 1 Sam. 17; 2 Sam. 5:17–25; and numerous other examples in the Old Testament narratives). But when the people disobeyed God and turned from him, he allowed other nations to defeat them as a manifestation of his judgment against them:

> They abandoned the LORD and served the Baals and the Ashtaroth. So the anger of the LORD was kindled against Israel, and he gave them over to plunderers, who plundered them. And he sold them into the hand of their surrounding enemies, so that *they could no longer withstand their enemies.* Whenever they marched out, the hand of the LORD was against them for harm, as the LORD had warned, and as the LORD had sworn to them. And they were in terrible distress (Judg. 2:13–15).

This was a fulfillment of what God had promised through Moses in Deuteronomy 28. If the people were obedient to God, he promised, "The LORD will cause your enemies who rise against you to be defeated before you. They shall come out against you one way and flee before you seven ways" (v. 7). But if they disobeyed, "The LORD will cause you to be defeated before your enemies. You shall go out one way against them and flee seven ways before them" (v. 25).

These promises were fulfilled multiple times in the history of Israel. They demonstrate that it is a good thing in God's sight—a special blessing—when a government has enough military power to defeat the enemies who would bring armies to attack it (that is, it is a good thing as long as a government has not become so corrupt and evil that God would be pleased to see it conquered).

Sometimes people wonder how it can be consistent for the Ten Commandments to say, "You shall not murder" (Exod. 20:13), and then also command that soldiers and armies go forth to kill the soldiers in an attacking army. Doesn't this mean that soldiers who kill in combat are violating one of the Ten Commandments? No, it does not, because that is not what that verse means.

The Hebrew word translated "murder" in Exodus 20:13 is *rātsakh*, a word used forty-nine times in the Old Testament. It is *never* used to refer to killing in war (other Hebrew words are used for this). Rather, the word refers to what we would call "murder" in English today (the unlawful killing of another human being) and also "causing human death through carelessness or negligence" (as the ESV marginal note says at this verse). The command is not speaking about killing in war, and the original Hebrew readers would not have understood it to apply to soldiers who kill in combat.

In fact, at various times in the Old Testament, God himself commanded the people of Israel to go to war (see Deut. 20:1), and it would be contradictory for him to command something and forbid it at the same time. In the New Testament, soldiers are not condemned for being soldiers in the Roman army, but John the Baptist tells them, "Be content with your wages" (Luke 3:14), and Cornelius, a Roman centurion in charge of one hundred soldiers, came to faith and was baptized as a believer in Jesus with no indication that there was anything morally wrong about the occupation of being a soldier (see Acts 10:1, 44–48; see also Luke 14:31). (See also the discussion on taking a life in capital punishment on pp. 186–97 above.)

B. HOW CAN WE KNOW IF A WAR IS A "JUST WAR"?

Of course, there are wrong wars such as wars merely for conquest and plunder. How can we tell if a war is right or wrong? During centuries of ethical discussions regarding the question of war, one common viewpoint that developed, with much input from Christian scholars, is the "just war" tradition. That viewpoint argues that a war is morally right (or "just") when it meets certain criteria. It also argues that there are certain moral restrictions on the way that war can be conducted.

It seems to me that this "just war" tradition, in general, is consistent with biblical teachings about the need for nations to defend themselves against their enemies. Here is a useful recent summary of the criteria for a just war, together with biblical references that support these criteria. I think that these criteria, in general, are consistent with these biblical teachings:

> Over time, the just war ethic has developed a common set of criteria that can be used to decide if going to war in a specific situation is right. These include the following: (1) *just cause* (is the reason for going to war a morally right cause, such as defense of a nation? cf. Rev. 19:11); (2) *competent authority* (has the war been declared not simply by a renegade band within a nation but by a

recognized, competent authority within the nation? cf. Rom. 13:1); (3) *comparative justice* (it should be clear that the actions of the enemy are morally wrong, and the motives and actions of one's own nation in going to war are, in comparison, morally right; cf. Rom. 13:3); (4) *right intention* (is the purpose of going to war to protect justice and righteousness rather than simply to rob and pillage and destroy another nation? cf. Prov. 21:2); (5) *last resort* (have all other reasonable means of resolving the conflict been exhausted? cf. Matt. 5:9; Rom. 12:18); (6) *probability of success* (is there a reasonable expectation that the war can be won? cf. Luke 14:31); (7) *proportionality of projected results* (will the good results that come from a victory in a war be significantly greater than the harm and loss that will inevitably come with pursuing the war? cf. Rom. 12:21 with 13:4); and (8) *right spirit* (is the war undertaken with great reluctance and sorrow at the harm that will come rather than simply with a "delight in war," as in Ps. 68:30?).

In addition to these criteria for deciding whether a specific war is "just," advocates of just war theory have also developed some moral restrictions on how a just war should be fought. These include the following: (1) *proportionality in the use of force* (no greater destruction should be caused than is needed to win the war; cf. Deut. 20:10–12); (2) *discrimination between combatants and noncombatants* (insofar as it is feasible in the successful pursuit of a war, is adequate care being taken to prevent harm to noncombatants? cf. Deut. 20:13–14, 19–20); (3) *avoidance of evil means* (will captured or defeated enemies be treated with justice and compassion, and are one's own soldiers being treated justly in captivity? cf. Ps. 34:14); and (4) *good faith* (is there a genuine desire for restoration of peace and eventually living in harmony with the attacking nation? cf. Matt. 5:43–44; Rom. 12:18).[1]

C. PACIFISM

Although the just war view has been the one most commonly held throughout the history of the church, a minority view has been that of military pacifism. The pacifist view holds that it is always wrong for *Christians* to use military force against others and thus it is wrong for Christians to participate in military combat, even to defend their own nation. A similar pacifist view holds that it is wrong for *anyone* to participate in military combat and that such "violence" is always morally wrong.

I have responded in some detail (in chap. 1 above, pp. 36–44) to several of the arguments for pacifism, because they are often related to the "all government is demonic" view advocated by Greg Boyd. Another recent advocate of pacifism is Jim Wallis, in his book *God's Politics*.[2] Similar arguments are also found in Shane Claiborne and Chris

---

1. "War," in *ESV Study Bible*, p. 2555.
2. Jim Wallis, *God's Politics: Why the Right Gets It Wrong and* the Left Doesn't Get It (San Francisco: HarperSanFrancisco, 2005), especially 87–205.

Haw's *Jesus for President*, which advocates a pacifist perspective.[3] What follows here is a shorter analysis of the key pacifist arguments as they apply to war.

The arguments commonly used to support pacifism are that (1) Jesus commanded us to turn the other cheek (in Matt. 5:39), (2) Jesus commanded us to love our neighbors as ourselves (Matt. 22:39), (3) engaging in military combat involves failure to trust God, and (4) the use of violence always begets further violence, and pacifism should be adopted to stop that vicious cycle.

In response, I would argue that (1) the pacifist viewpoint wrongly uses Jesus' teaching about individual conduct in turning the other cheek (Matt. 5:39) to apply to civil government (see discussion above, pp. 42, 82 ,201–2), but the explicit teaching on civil governments in Romans is that it should "bear the sword" to oppose evildoers and execute God's wrath on the wrongdoer (Rom. 13:4). In addition, in Luke 22:36 Jesus actually commanded his followers to carry a sword (which was used for self-defense and protection from robbers; see discussion above, pp. 201–3).

(2) If we truly love our neighbors (as Jesus commanded in Matt. 22:39), then we will be willing even to go to war to protect them from evil aggressors who are attacking the nation. While the pacifist might ask, "How can you love your neighbor or even love your enemy and then kill him in war," the answer has to be that God commanded *both* love for one's neighbor and going to war, for the command "You shall love your neighbor as yourself" is found in Leviticus 19:18 in the Old Testament, and Jesus quotes it from there. Therefore it must be consistent for God to command *both* things and the one command should not be used to nullify the other. One example of this is found in the tragic story of David sending out his army to defeat Absalom, his son, in 2 Samuel 18:1–33. David had great love for his son Absalom and yet he was responsible to protect the office of king that God had entrusted to him. Therefore, with sorrow, and while still loving Absalom, David sent the army out against him.

(3) Christians have no right to tell others to "trust in God" for things that are different from what the Bible teaches, and Romans 13:1–4 teaches that God authorizes governments to use deadly force if necessary to oppose evil. Therefore, at this point the pacifist argument is telling people to disobey what Romans 13 says about government and then to trust God to protect them anyway. This would be like telling people they should not work to earn a living, but should "trust God" to provide their food anyway! A better approach is to *obey* what God says in Romans 13:1–4 about the use of government power to restrain evil and then *trust God* to work through that government power to restrain evil, which is how he intends governments to function.

This is the problem I have with Jim Wallis when he criticizes the American reliance on military power to protect the nation from terrorists as "a foreign policy *based primarily*

---

3. Shane Claiborne and Chris Haw, *Jesus for President: Politics for Ordinary Radicals* (Grand Rapids: Zondervan, 2008), especially 199–224 and 338–47 but also at various other places in the book, most of which is structured as a loosely connected set of narratives rather than an organized, sequential, logical argument. Claiborne and Haw also list at least two widely used pacifist books in their recommended bibliography: Greg Boyd, *The Myth of a Christian Nation* (Grand Rapids: Zondervan, 2007), and John Howard Yoder, *The Politics of Jesus* (Grand Rapids: Eerdmans, 1994).

on fear."[4] And then he also attributes another wrong motive to Americans when he puts military responses to terrorist attacks in the category of "anger and vengeance" that leads a nation to "indiscriminately retaliate in ways that bring on even more loss of innocent life."[5] Wallis sees military action against terrorism as based on "fear" and "vengeance."

By contrast, Romans 13 teaches that military action used to defend a nation is not a wrongful or sinful activity, *nor is a desire to depend on military action (under God's guidance) a wrongful attitude to have,* because God has *authorized* nations to use such military power. What pacifists like Wallis fail to realize is that it is completely possible—as millions of Christians who have served in military forces have demonstrated—to *trust in God* that he will enable them to use the military power he has put in their hands to successfully defend their country. The solution is not pacifism, but *trust in God* to give success *while obeying him* by using the military defense that he has appointed.

This is also why pacifists such as Wallis are actually unbiblical when they say that nations like the United States should not act alone and use "unilateral action" to defend themselves, but should rather depend on a "world court to weigh facts and make judgments, with effective multi-national law enforcement."[6] Elsewhere Wallis wants us to depend on a much more powerful "international law" and "global police forces."[7] Wallis says that only such a world court with effective power "will be able to protect us."[8]

There are several objections to Wallis's argument:

(a) It is mere wishful thinking. Such an effective worldwide government over the entire earth has never occurred in the entire history of the human race. (Even the Roman Empire at its largest extent did not reach to China or India or sub-Saharan Africa or North and South America.) It is foolishness to depend on something that has never existed to save us from a terrorist threat that we are facing at this very minute.

(b) If such a powerful world government ever did exist, it would likely be dominated by the votes of numerous small nations who are largely anti-American because their governments are communist or totalitarian or devoted to expanding the Muslim religion and therefore opposed to the United States. In this way it would be like the present make-up of the United Nations with its frequent anti-American votes.

(c) Depending on such a world government to keep peace in the world would require nations to give up their individual sovereignty and would require the United States to give up a significant measure of its individual sovereignty. This would open the door to reducing the United States to a condition of servitude and domination by nations or leaders that seek its demise.

Far better than the pacifist position of trusting in a world court and world police force is trusting in the Lord to use the means he has designated, which is the use of each nation's own military power, as I have argued above from Romans 13 and other passages.

(4) It is simply untrue to say, as pacifists do, that "violence always begets more violence." The deadly force used by local police in restraining or killing a murderer brings

---

4. Wallis, *God's Politics*, 88, emphasis added.

5. Ibid., 92; see also 94.

6. Ibid., 106.

7. Ibid., 164.

8. Ibid., 106.

that murderer's violence to an end. It is the same situation when armies are used to defend nations against aggressors. In fact, the use of military power stopped Adolf Hitler from taking over all of Europe and ultimately all the world in World War II. It stopped the North Koreans from taking over South Korea in the Korean War. In the American Civil War, it stopped the Confederate armies from establishing a separate nation in which slavery would be preserved and protected.

The pacifist slogan "violence always begets more violence" is misleading, because it uses the same word, "violence," to refer to two very different things—the morally *good* use of deadly force to stop evildoers and the morally *wrong* use of force to carry out attacks on innocent people. A better slogan is, "Just governments should use superior force to stop criminal violence against innocent people." Or even shorter, "Superior force stops criminal violence."

This is the shortcoming of the pacifist position of Wallis, who says that the solution to international terrorism is "the mobilization of the most extensive international and diplomatic pressure the world has ever seen against the Bin Ladens of the world and their networks of terror."[9] Consistent with that position, Wallis argues that rather than going to war against Iraq,

> The international community could have united in an effective strategy to isolate, contain, disarm and ultimately undermine and remove the brutal and dangerous regime of Saddam Hussein.

Wallis adds, "The Iraqi people themselves could have been supported internationally to create civil resistance within their own country to achieve [regime change]."[10]

But Wallis's pacifist solution here is very much like the wishful thinking of Greg Boyd that I discussed in chapter 1 (see pp. 42–43). He is simply saying that we "could have" overthrown Saddam and protected ourselves from international terrorists without military action against them by the United States. The phrase "could have" in pacifist arguments can justify almost any wishful thinking. We "could have" waited for some future day when a supposed international police force would come on the scene. And we "could have" waited for the day when the Iraqi people would rise up and overthrow a brutal dictator who controlled one of the most powerful armies in the world. But in fact, these things did not happen, although alternative solutions had been tried for many years. In actual fact, it was only the superior force of the United States military that overthrew Saddam. It was only the superior power of the United States military that defeated terrorists in Afghanistan. It was only the superior power of the United States military that protected us for many years following 9/11.

This kind of "history could have been different" argument is common in pacifist literature. Instead of acknowledging that military power is necessary to achieve a triumph over evil forces, it claims, "If the events of history had turned out differently, they would support my case." But that is simply saying, "If the facts were different, they would support my case." That is not a persuasive argument. It is merely wishful thinking.

---

9. Ibid., 163.

10. Ibid.

The logic of pacifism leads ultimately to a total surrender to the most evil of governments, who will stop at nothing to use their power to oppress others. (See further discussion above, in chap. 1, pp. 41–44.) For all of these reasons, the pacifism of Jim Wallis and others is not a persuasive position for Christians to adopt.

D. DEFENSE POLICY IN THE UNITED STATES

If governments have a moral responsibility to defend their nations from attacks, then the first point of application to the United States is that it should have enough military power to be able to defeat any other nation or combination of nations that has the potential to attack it.

Someone might object that having so much military power is dangerous. In fact, someone holding a pacifist position might claim that *military weaponry itself* increases tension and instability in the world and therefore makes war more likely. But this claim comes from an underlying assumption that the ultimate cause of evil is not in the hearts of human beings but is in some influence (such as powerful weapons) *outside of* human beings.

To the contrary, as we saw in chapter 4, a Christian worldview understands that there is both good and evil in every human heart and also that in some people the tendency toward evil becomes so powerful that those people cannot be reached by reason or negotiation or compromise, but can only be restrained by the superior power of a just government. Therefore God gives civil governments the power of the sword (Rom. 13:4) to restrain such unreasoning commitments to evil. Military weapons for governments are God-ordained and are not themselves the cause of evil.

However, we must be clear that no nation has the right ever to use military power simply to conquer other nations or impose their ideas of social good on another nation.

1. Twentieth-century attacks by nations committed to evil aggression

At various times in history some nations have been ruled by despots who exercised tremendous evil over their own people and also pursued evil acts of aggression against other nations. Hitler was one example in his rule over Germany before and during World War II. Joseph Stalin was another example in his rule over the Soviet Union and his conquering of the nations of Eastern Europe. The leaders of Japan were yet another example before and during World War II, in which they carried out militarized aggression and horrible brutality against Manchuria and much of China. In December 1937, the Japanese Imperial Army marched into China's capital city of Nanking and proceeded to murder 300,000 out of 600,000 civilians and soldiers in the city. The six weeks of carnage would become known as the Rape of Nanking as Japanese soldiers buried Chinese citizens alive or would hack them apart with swords, among other horrible atrocities.[11]

---

11. "1937 Nanking Massacre." www.nanking-massacre.com/
RAPE_OF_NANKING_OR_NANJING_MASSACRE_1937.
html.

2. Current threats of possible attack against the United States or its allies

At the present time (in early 2010, as I am writing) there are still evil rulers who would use military force to invade and conquer another nation if they thought they could succeed. Countries need to have a strong enough military force to defend against them. Such evil rulers include the leaders of *North Korea* and *Iran*. While these countries are not likely to attack the United States directly, they might launch a missile strike or a terrorist bomb against US territory or US military bases overseas, and it is very possible that they would attack other countries near them (such as Israel or South Korea, both US allies).

What about *Russia*? From 1945 until 1991—the period of the Cold War—the United States' primary potential enemy was the Soviet Union. The current government of Russia, the successor to the Soviet Union, is not a genuine democracy but essentially a dictatorship run by a small group of Communist Party officials who have continued to tighten their grip on power under Vladimir Putin. Russia sometimes acts as an ally now, but it is unreliable and could again become a threat to the United States as well as to many countries in Eastern Europe.

In Latin America, both *Venezuela* (under Hugo Chavez) and *Cuba* (under Fidel Castro) are military dictatorships that have destabilized several countries in Central and South America. Chavez has engaged in ongoing military threats against Colombia through the placement of troops on their border,[12] and he has convinced Ecuador to go along and place troops there as well.[13] In addition, Cuba has a long history of supporting anti-democratic thugs within Nicaragua, the Dominican Republic, Bolivia, and El Salvador, attempting to weaken their governments.[14] The more this Castro-Chavez influence grows and overthrows governments in Latin America, the more the United States will have to deal with hostile neighboring countries on its doorstep.

China now has good relationships with the United States, especially because of trade. We should hope that those relationships continue, but China's government is totalitarian and autocratic, not democratic. The government in China is controlled by nine members of the Politburo Standing Committee. This means that the future direction of China is unknown. China has been establishing bases of influence in Asia,[15] Latin America,[16] and Africa[17] that could become centers to project its military power. With regard to Asia, the late Congressman Henry Hyde said, "I fear that a future American

---

12. "Hugo Chavez Warns of War in South America," *London Telegraph* (Aug. 11, 2009). www.telegraph.co.uk/news/world-news/southamerica/colombia/6007459/Hugo-Chavez-warns-of-war-in-South-America.html.

13. "Ecuador Follows Chavez in Deploying Troops to Columbian Border," Associated Press (March 3, 2008). www.foxnews.com/story/0,2933,334409,00.html.

14. Eileen Scully, "The Castro Doctrine Makes Gains," *Heritage Foundation Backgrounder #289* (Sept. 12, 1983), (www.heritage.org/Research/LatinAmerica/bg289.cfm), and Clifford Krauss, "The Last Stalinist," *New York Times* (Feb. 10, 1991), (www.nytimes.com/1991/02/10/books/the-last-stalinist.html).

15. Testimony of Lisa Curtis before the U.S.-China Economic and Security Review Commission" (March 18, 2008). www.heritage.org/Research/AsiaandthePacific/tst032008.cfm.

16. Peter Brookes, "China's Influence in the Western Hemisphere," *Heritage Foundation Lecture #873* (April 19, 2005). Remarks were delivered at a hearing of the Subcommittee on the Western Hemisphere of the House Committee on International Relations.

17. Peter Brookes and Ji Hye Shin, "China's Influence in Africa: Implications for the United States," *Heritage Foundation Backgrounder #1916* (Feb. 22, 2006). www.heritage.org/Research/AsiaandthePacific/bg1916.cfm.

generation may awaken from its Pacific slumber to find our influence removed entirely from the Asian mainland."[18] Regarding Africa, Peter Brookes of the Heritage Foundation wrote, "The most pernicious effect of the renewed Chinese interest in Africa is that China is legitimizing and encouraging Africa's most repressive regimes, thereby increasing the likelihood of weak and failed states."[19]

China has an increasingly powerful navy with 255,000 men, 58 active submarines, 77 principal surface combatants, 387 coastal warfare vessels, and approximately 500 amphibious warfare vessels,[20] along with a total amount of armed forces of 2.3 million personnel[21] and a space system that demonstrated its ability in January 2007 to shoot US communications satellites out of the sky.[22] Chinese hackers with remarkable skills continue to launch periodic attacks against the highest levels of US military information networks. In a 2008 report to Congress, it was stated that "China even now is planting viruses in US computer systems that they will activate" in the event of a military conflict with the United States.[23] In 2008, China announced a 14.9% rise in military spending, to 480.68 billion yuan ($70.36 billion).[24] In January 2007, John D. Negroponte, the Director of National Intelligence, reported, "The Chinese are developing more capable long-range conventional strike systems and short- and medium-range ballistic missiles with terminally guided maneuverable warheads able to attack US carriers and airbases."[25] Although we hope it would never happen, it is possible that China could become an extremely powerful aggressor nation in the future.

Islamic terrorist threats stemming from groups within various Muslim countries continue to pose the most prominent military challenge today and constitute the most imminent current threat to the security of the United States.

3. Defense alliances and responsibilities to help protect other countries

Another factor makes the responsibility of the United States more complicated. In 2009, the United States was the most powerful military force in the world, far surpassing every other nation in its military power, with 1,454,515 people on active duty,[26] and an additional 848,000 in reserve.[27] The US defense budget was $515.4 billion, the largest in

18. Tyler Marshall, "China Poised to Dominate Influence in Asia," *Boston Globe* (Aug. 13, 2006). www.boston.com/news/world/asia/articles/2006/08/13/china_poised_to_dominate_influence_in_asia/.

19. Brookes and Shin, "China's Influence in Africa."

20. "Chinese Naval Forces." www.sinodefence.com/navy/default.asp.

21. "China's Navy 2007," Office of Naval Intelligence. www.fas.org/irp/agency/oni/chinanavy2007.pdf.

22. "China Confirms Satellite Downed," *BBCNews.com* (Jan. 23, 2007). http://news.bbc.co.uk/2/hi/asia-pacific/6289519.stm.

23. Eric McVadon: as quoted in Dave Ahearn, "U.S. Can't Use Trade Imbalance to Avert China Invasion of Taiwan," *Defense Today* (Aug. 2, 2005), 1–2: cited in "China Naval Modernization: Implications for U.S. Navy Capabilities—Background and

Issues for Congress," CRS Report for Congress (Feb. 4, 2008). http://assets.opencrs.com/rpts/RL33153_20080204.pdf.

24. Henry Sanderson, "China's Navy to Build New Ships, Planes," Associated Press (April 16, 2009). www.boston.com/news/world/asia/articles/2009/04/16/chinas_navy_to_build_new_ships_planes/?rss_id=Boston.com+—+World+news.

25. John D. Negroponte, Annual Threat Assessment of the Director of National Intelligence (Jan. 11, 2007), 10.

26. Department of Defense Active Military Personnel by Rank/Grade (Feb. 28, 2009). http://siadapp.dmdc.osd.mil/personnel/MILITARY/rg0902.pdf.

27. Bryan Bender, "Gates calls for buildup in troops," *Boston Globe* (Jan. 12, 2007). www.boston.com/news/nation/washington/articles/2007/01/12/gates_calls_for_buildup_in_troops/.

the world.[28] As of November 2009, the US Navy had 328,798 active personnel, 109,158 reservists, 286 deployable battleships, and 3,700 aircraft.[29] As of September 2008, the US Air Force had 327,452 personnel on active duty, 115,299 in the Selected and Individual Ready Reserves, 106,700 in the Air National Guard, and 5,603 active aircraft.[30]

Because of the great military power of the United States, we also carry a great deal of responsibility for maintaining world peace in several ways. Many other nations look to us and depend on us to help defend their freedom. For example, membership in the NATO Alliance (North Atlantic Treaty Organization), of which the United States is a member, involves a pledge that other members will come to the aid of any NATO member that is attacked by another country. (The treaty was first signed on April 4, 1949.)

But such a sense of responsibility to join in the defense of allies is not new to US history. The Monroe Doctrine was a policy first stated by President James Monroe on December 22, 1823. It affirmed that if any European nation attacked or attempted to colonize any nation in North or South America, the United States would intervene to oppose such action. Although there is dispute today over how extensively the Monroe Doctrine should be applied, it has been invoked on numerous occasions by US presidents.

In addition, the United States has entered into mutual defense treaties or agreements with other friendly nations, such as Taiwan and Israel.

Are such defense agreements appropriate? As long as nations voluntarily enter into such agreements and believe that both countries benefit from them, I see no reason in principle to say that they are wrong. The United States has decided in the past that it is in the best interest of the nation and that it contributes to the protection of world peace for it to enter into such agreements, because they provide a significant deterrence against other countries beginning to take over various parts of the world. The countries with which we have such agreements are valuable to the United States in many ways, through mutual trade, tourism, cultural and educational exchange, and the preservation of stability in different regions of the world.

Another reason why the United States is right to commit itself to defending the independence and freedom of democratic nations is that its foundational document, the Declaration of Independence, asserts that *we as a nation* hold certain truths to be "self evident" and that among those truths are the following:

> That all men are created equal, that they are endowed by their Creator with certain unalienable rights, that among these are life, liberty, and the pursuit of happiness—that to secure these rights, governments are instituted among men, deriving their just powers from the consent of the governed.[31]

28. Department of Defense Budget 2009. www.gpoaccess. gov/usbudget/fy09/pdf/budget/defense.pdf.

29. See www.navy.mil/navydata/navy_legacy_hr.asp?id=146.

30. "2009 Air Force Almanac," *Air Force Magazine* (May 2009), 48–49. www.airforce-magazine.com/MagazineArchive/

Magazine%20Documents/2009/May%202009/0509facts_fig. pdf.

31. Transcript of the Declaration of Independence. www. archives.gov/exhibits/charters/declaration_transcript.html.

This means that *as a nation* the United States has formally declared from the beginning that God (the "Creator") has granted to every individual on earth certain basic rights, including both "life" and "liberty." This implies that it is in our best interest and also *consistent with our foundational convictions as a nation* to promote the protection of life and human freedom in various nations around the world. Therefore such alliances for the purpose of defending other countries are based on convictions that are at the basis of our very existence as a nation.

For these reasons, I disagree with the "noninterventionist" viewpoint of Congressman Ron Paul. In his book *The Revolution: A Manifesto*, Ron Paul quotes from some of America's Founding Fathers, including Thomas Jefferson and George Washington, to argue that we should not use military force to intervene in other nations. Therefore, for example, Ron Paul opposed the Iraq War.[32] Paul says, "In time it will become apparent to all of us that foreign interventionism is of no benefit to American citizens, but instead is a threat to our liberties."[33]

Paul also says, "I oppose all foreign aid on principle," and that means that he is opposed even to any foreign aid to Israel.[34] He also opposes the stationing of US troops in places such as Korea, Japan, and Europe, saying, with regard to them, "How many years is enough?"[35] Paul's noninterventionism even led him to blame the United States for the attacks on 9/11, saying, "Have you ever read about the reasons they attacked us? They attack us because we've been over there. We've been bombing Iraq for 10 years."[36] I think that such blaming of the United States for the attacks of 9/11 shows how deeply flawed Ron Paul's understanding of foreign policy actually is.

I disagree with Ron Paul for three primary reasons. (a) It is significant that while he quotes some of the American Founding Fathers to defend noninterventionism, he cannot quote the US Constitution in support of this view, because it cannot be found there. While some of the Founding Fathers, including George Washington and Thomas Jefferson, may have *thought* that it would be wise for the United States to stay out of foreign disputes at a time when we were a new and tiny nation, they and the others who drafted the Constitution were wise enough not to set that opinion about the current situation in concrete as they wrote the Constitution. They no doubt realized that situations might change and that what was not appropriate for a young, relatively weak nation might be very different for a more mature, more powerful nation. Today we have grown more powerful and more influential in the world than Washington and Jefferson could ever have imagined.

(b) I see no reasons from the teachings of the Bible that would lead me to support Ron Paul's noninterventionism. In fact, at one point God, through the prophet Obadiah, rebuked the nation of Edom for its "noninterventionist" policy with regard to Israel:

On the day that you stood aloof,

---

32. See Ron Paul, *The Revolution: A Manifesto* (New York: Grand Central Publishing, 2008), 10–17, 19, 21–24.

33. Ibid., 17.

34. Ibid.

35. Ibid., 37.

36. "Ron Paul Gets Turn in Spotlight in South Carolina Debate," Reuters.com (May 16, 2007).

on the day that strangers carried off his wealth
 and foreigners entered his gates
  and cast lots for Jerusalem,
   you were like one of them (Obad. 11).

When the foreign invaders (the Babylonians) attacked Jerusalem, the neighboring country of Edom "stood aloof" and failed to give military support to help Jerusalem defend itself. God says that Edom was guilty of failing to intervene in that conflict and help their neighbor: "You were like one of them."

(c) It seems to me that the great power of the United States gives us an obligation to help weak nations who are attacked when we have made alliances with them and are able to help them. The NATO alliance was a major factor in preventing Soviet expansion of its power into Western Europe after 1949. The US alliance with Taiwan has been the major reason that China has not attacked it. Our alliance with and military presence in South Korea has been the primary deterrent that has kept the fanatical and militaristic regime in North Korea from overrunning its neighbor. And the US agreements to defend Israel, together with massive amounts of military aid, have been a significant factor in preventing Arab nations from destroying that country. If we had not driven Saddam Hussein out of Kuwait in the First Gulf War (1990–91), he would have controlled the Kuwaiti oil fields and very likely would have invaded and captured Saudi Arabia as well.

All of these relationships and others have extended the protections of democracy and the benefits of "certain unalienable rights" to millions of people in the world, and they have made the world more peaceful and more secure for the last two centuries. It is consistent with our foundational convictions as a nation, as embodied in the Declaration of Independence, that the United States should promote the protection of life and human freedoms in various nations around the world. For this reason also, I strongly disagree with the noninterventionist views of Congressman Paul.

Does Ron Paul really think that the world would be better off with the horrible communist government of North Korea controlling South Korea, with Communist China controlling Taiwan, and with Saddam Hussein controlling Saudi Arabia and Kuwait and exporting terrorism around the world? Does he think the world would be better off if the Soviets under Stalin had been allowed to overrun Western Europe, including Germany and France and other countries, after World War II? Does he think the world would be a better place if the US Navy did not protect the international shipping lanes of all the oceans of the world? I am convinced that these actions by the United States have made the world a much better and more peaceful place.

For all of these reasons, I cannot believe that Paul's noninterventionist policies would do anything but bring about a much less free, much less peaceful, and much more antagonistic and dangerous world.

4. The value to the world of a strong US military

If we do not accept a pacifist position that weapons are in themselves evil, then it is wise to realize that *superior military weaponry* in the hands of a nation that protects freedom for itself and other countries *is a good thing for the world*, not a harmful thing. The existence of superior military power in the hands of a peace-loving, freedom-supporting nation brings great benefits to the world.

Genuine peace in the world comes through the strength of the United States and other democratic, peace-loving nations. By contrast, US military weakness would simply invite war and provoke multiple attempts at conquest by aggressive nations led by evil rulers.

Unfortunately, the facts show that President Obama in 2009 began reducing the strength of US military forces, just as Democratic President Jimmy Carter did in the 1970s. Practically the only area of government spending that was cut in 2009 by President Obama was defense spending. The *Wall Street Journal* wrote:

> More ominously, Mr. Obama's budget has overall defense spending falling sharply starting in future years—to $614 billion in 2011, and staying more or less flat for a half decade. This means that relative both to the economy and especially to domestic priorities, defense spending is earmarked to decline. Some of this assumes less spending on Iraq, which is realistic, but it also has to take account of Mr. Obama's surge in Afghanistan. That war won't be cheap either.
>
> The danger is that Mr. Obama may be signaling a return to the defense mistakes of the 1990s. Bill Clinton slashed defense spending to 3% of GDP in 2000, from 4.8% in 1992. We learned on 9/11 that 3% isn't nearly enough to maintain our commitments and fight a war on terror—and President Bush spent his two terms getting back to more realistic outlays for a global superpower.[37]

One example among many such cuts is the most advanced jet fighter in the world, the F–22 "Raptor." In early 2009, in the midst of massive increases in federal government spending—far in excess of any increases promoted by any administration in American history—President Obama insisted on cutting funds for the F–22.[38] No aircraft in the world comes close to the fighting capabilities of this plane. It is so advanced that it can fight battles against multiple attacking aircraft and defeat them all simultaneously. Its advanced electronics allow it to "see" an approaching enemy aircraft over the horizon and destroy it before the enemy is even able to see the F–22 approaching.[39] W. Thomas Smith, a former US Marine rifle-squad leader and counterterrorism instructor, wrote in *Human Events*, "The F–22 was built for speed: Though her numbers are classified, she can outrun, outclimb, and outmaneuver any fighter aircraft a potential adversary might be able to put up against us."[40]

But following President Obama's insistence, the US Senate voted on July 21, 2009, to end production of the F–22 at 187 fighters, far less than the 250–380 that were originally

37. "Declining Defense," *Wall Street Journal* (March 2, 2009). http://online.wsj.com/article/SB123595811964905929.html.

38. "Senate Sides with Obama, Removes F–22 Money," Associated Press (July 21, 2009). www.sfgate.com/cgi-bin/article.cgi?f=/n/a/2009/07/21/national/w000457D19.DTL&tsp=1

39. "F–22: Unseen and Lethal," *Aviation Week* (Jan. 8, 2007). www.f22-raptor.com/media/documents/aviation_week_010807.pdf.

40. W. Thomas Smith, "We Need Both," *Human Events* (Oct. 29, 2009). www.humanevents.com/article.php?id=34173.

planned and needed.[41] The President signed the defense authorization bill killing the production of more F–22s, as he wished, on October 28, 2009.[42] In making such cuts, the President "rejected the notion that 'we have to waste billions of taxpayer dollars to keep this nation secure.'"[43] I think this was a tragic mistake.

E. ISLAMIC JIHADISM (INTERNATIONAL TERRORISM)

The greatest threat of attack against the United States today comes not from any specific nation, but from an international terrorist movement that is sometimes called Islamic Jihadism. This term actually refers to a number of loosely related Islamic terrorist groups such as al-Qaeda, Hamas (a Palestinian group), Hezbollah (based in Lebanon), the Muslim Brotherhood (in several countries, but with strong roots in Egypt), and various other smaller movements with similar convictions and goals.

In my judgment and in the judgment of many other analysts, such radical Islamic Jihadism constitutes the single greatest threat to American peace and security in the world today. Its cause is ultimately not poverty in certain Muslim nations (for many terrorist leaders come from wealthy backgrounds, such as Osama bin Laden). Nor is its cause any recent action by the United States (for there were numerous terrorist attacks on American interests even prior to the First Gulf War, and certainly prior to the Iraq War—see historical details below). Its cause is a profoundly evil religious belief that the use of any violent means, even the intentional murder of civilians, is justified in order to advance the goal of forcible Muslim domination of other nations and eventually of the entire world.

1. Origins and beliefs of al-Qaeda and similar organizations

The most extensive and authoritative history of Islamic terrorism in recent times is *The Looming Tower: Al-Qaeda and the Road to 9/11* by Lawrence Wright.[44] Wright says that the great majority of Muslims around the world would *not* hold to the beliefs of Islamic Jihadism. Wright points out that views common to today's terrorists have been a *minority* voice within Islam for centuries, beginning with *Abdul Wahhab* (1703–92), a Muslim teacher and revivalist who in 1744 came under the protection of Mohammed bin Saud, the founder of the first Saudi state.[45] Wahhab taught that his followers could kill and rape and steal from people who would not obey his teachings. He also taught that men should not trim their beards and that there was "no difference between religion and government."[46] People sometimes refer to modern followers of Wahhab's teachings as Wahhabi Muslims and to the viewpoint itself as Wahhabism (though Wahhab's followers do not prefer that name for themselves).

41. "Senate Sides with Obama, Removes F–22 Money," Associated Press.

42. "Obama Inks Defense Bill with Hate Crimes Provision," Associated Press (Oct. 28, 2009). www.washingtonpost.com/wp-dyn/content/article/2009/10/28/AR2009102803147.html?hpid=moreheadlines.

43. Roxana Tiron, "Obama Signs Defense Bill, Attacks Waste," *The Hill* (Oct. 28, 2009). http://thehill.com/homenews/administration/65183-obama-signs-defense-bill-attacks-waste.

44. Lawrence Wright, *The Looming Tower: Al-Qaeda and the Road to 9/11* (New York: Alfred Knopf, 2006). Reprinted by permission.

45. Ibid., 63.

46. Ibid.

In recent years the most influential writer persuading Muslims to use violence to purify and advance Islam was the Egyptian author *Sayyid Qutb* (1906–66), in his book *Milestones* (published in 1964). Before he left Egypt, Qutb (pronounced *kuh-tub*) was already one of that country's most popular writers, and when he came to America as a foreign student in 1948, he sailed in a first-class stateroom on a cruise ship.[47] Qutb studied in New York City, in Washington, DC, and especially at Colorado State College for education in Greeley, Colorado (in 1949). During his time in America, he became hardened in his opposition to what he saw as the evils of American society, with its commitment to modern ways of life and what he saw as frequent immorality.[48]

When he returned to Egypt, Qutb became increasingly troubled that the Egyptian government, under Gamal Nasser, was not sufficiently strict in enforcing Islamic law. He became vocal in his opposition to Nasser through editing a Muslim Brotherhood (or Muslim Brothers) magazine. After some members of the Muslim Brothers tried to assassinate Nasser in 1954, Qutb was put in prison, where he stayed until 1965.[49] He experienced much physical suffering in prison, but also wrote extensively. His book *Milestones* was smuggled out of the prison in Cairo and published in 1964.[50] Although Qutb was released for a few months at the end of 1964, he was soon arrested again, charged with conspiracy to overthrow the government, and sentenced to death. He was hanged August 29, 1966,[51] but his influence continues today.

Another influential leader in Islamic terrorism has been *Ayman al-Zawahiri* (1951–), also an Egyptian. Zawahiri was a brilliant student from a prominent Egyptian family who finished medical school and became a recognized surgeon.[52] He was influenced by Qutb's writings and became the leader of a group of Egyptians who were determined to overthrow the leadership of Egypt, including President Anwar Sadat.[53]

Zawahiri was closely involved with the group that successfully planned the assassination against Sadat that occurred on October 6, 1981. Zawahiri was arrested and imprisoned and was tortured severely in an Egyptian prison.[54] He then became the public spokesman for all three hundred defendants at the trial that began December 4, 1982,[55] and during his time in prison he became a hardened radical and recognized leader for Islamic militant beliefs. But he had not directly participated in the assassination, and he was released from prison in 1984, after which he traveled to Saudi Arabia and then to Afghanistan, where he would meet Osama bin Laden.[56]

Osama bin Laden (1957–) was born to an extremely wealthy family in Saudi Arabia. His father was Muhammad bin Laden, who owned a huge construction company that was responsible for building many of the highways as well as the largest mosques in the country,[57] including the Grand Mosque in Medina.[58] Bin Laden joined the Muslim

47. Ibid., 7.
48. Ibid., 16–23.
49. Ibid., 27–30.
50. Ibid., 29.
51. Ibid., 30–31.
52. Ibid., 32–34.

53. Ibid., 40–42, 48–49.
54. Ibid., 50–54.
55. Ibid., 54.
56. Ibid., 57–58, 60–61.
57. Ibid., 64–68.
58. Ibid., 66–71.

Brothers while he was in high school. He studied economics in the university in Jeddah, but spent more of his time involved in campus religious activities.[59]

Bin Laden eventually traveled to Afghanistan, where he became a leader of the forces that fought to drive out the Soviets. He then returned to Saudi Arabia and worked in the family business overseeing construction projects. His share of the company at that time was equal to about $7 million (US), plus he had a substantial annual income. But his deepest commitment was to advancing Islam through radical means, and he eventually returned to Afghanistan, where he connected with other leaders and radicals who shared his convictions, including Zawahiri.

Although the United States had helped him and his followers drive the Soviets out of Afghanistan, bin Laden eventually turned against the United States because of his commitment to radical Islam. Lawrence Wright explains it this way:

> Why did these men turn against America, a highly religious country that had so recently been their ally in Afghanistan? In large part, it was because they saw America as the locus of Christian power.... Viewed through the eyes of men who were spiritually anchored in the seventh century, Christianity was not just a rival, it was the archenemy. To them, the Crusades were a continual historical process that would never be resolved until the final victory of Islam.... Yet bin Laden and his Arab Afghans believed that, in Afghanistan, they had turned the tide and that Islam was again on the march.[60]

Wright goes on to explain how radically opposed to Western values this brand of Islam is:

> By returning the rule of Sharia [Islamic law governing all of life], radical Islam could draw the line against the encroaching West. Even the values that America advertised as being universally desirable—democracy, transparency, the rule of law, human rights, the separation of religion from governments—were discredited in the eyes of the jihadis because they were Western and therefore modern.

Wright also reports that Zawahiri, who partnered with bin Laden in Afghanistan, had become convinced of an extreme interpretation of Islam known as *takfir* ("excommunication"), which was applied to those who are thought to have abandoned true Islamic beliefs. Wright explains that this is an extreme view, but so influential that it led to the assassination of President Sadat in Egypt:

> *Takfir* is the mirror image of Islam, reversing its fundamental principles.... The Quran explicitly states that Muslims shall not kill anyone, except as punishment for murder.... How, then, could groups ... justify using violence against fellow Muslims in order to come to power? Sayyid Qutb had pointed the way by declaring that a leader that does not impose Sharia on the country must be an apostate. There is a well-known saying of the Prophet that the

---

59. Ibid., 78.
60. Ibid., 171.

blood of Muslims cannot be shed except in three instances: as punishment for murder, or for marital infidelity, or for turning away from Islam. The pious Anwar Sadat was the first modern victim of the reverse logic of *takfir*.[61]

Wright then explains how this doctrine was taken further and further by the new Islamic militants, because they

extended the death warrant to encompass, for instance, anyone who registered to vote. Democracy, in their view, was against Islam because it placed in the hands of people authority that properly belonged to God. Therefore, anyone who voted was an apostate, and his life was forfeit. So was anyone who disagreed with their joyless understanding of Islam.... [They] believed that they were entitled to kill practically anyone and everyone who stood in their way; indeed, they saw it as a divine duty.[62]

On August 11, 1988, a few months before the final withdrawal of Soviet forces from Afghanistan in 1989, bin Laden and other leaders of the Arab resistance had a decisive meeting in Peshawar and decided to form an organization called al-Qaeda (meaning "the base") that would be "the solid base ... for the hoped-for society" that would implement a strict Islamic rule in many nations.[63]

Wright goes on to describe how al-Qaeda's philosophy developed. It increasingly focused on carrying out terrorist attacks against civilians in strategic locations around the world: "al-Qaeda would concentrate not on fighting armies but on killing civilians."[64] Yet the main focus of al-Qaeda's attacks would be the United States because it stood in the way of establishing Islamic rule over more and more nations:

America was the only power capable of blocking the restoration of the ancient Islamic *caliphate* [government], and it would have to be confronted and defeated.[65]

To get a picture of what kind of life Islamic terrorists would impose upon a nation if they obtained power, we can look at the Taliban regime that was imposed in Afghanistan before the American military attack drove them out of power in November 2001. Here is a picture of life under the Taliban:

Work and schooling for women were halted at once, which destroyed the health-care system, the civil service, and effectively eliminated elementary education.... The Taliban ... forbade kite-flying and dog racing.... "Unclean things" were banned, an all-purpose category that included ... satellite dishes, cinematography, any equipment that produces the joy of music, pool tables, chess ... alcohol ... computer, VCR's, television ... nail polish ... sewing catalogues, pictures, Christmas cards.... The fashion dictators demanded that a man's beard be longer than the grip of his hand. Violators went to jail....

---

61. Ibid., 124.
62. Ibid., 125.
63. Ibid., 130–34.

64. Ibid., 175.
65. Ibid.

Should a woman leave her home without her veil, "Her home will be marked and her husband punished."[66]

From the perspective of the Bible, my response to such a view is as follows: Although militant Muslims frequently refer to the United States as "the great Satan," it seems evident that the movement truly motivated by Satan himself is such a movement that would justify killing anyone who disagrees with it. Jesus said that Satan "was a murderer from the beginning" (John 8:44), and such a movement that believes it right to violently suppress and murder all disagreement shows marks of having its deepest spiritual motivation, not in God, but in demonic forces that are opposed to God and his truth. The results of such a reign of strict Sharia law are an intolerable loss of human freedom, essentially reducing human beings to dehumanizing slavery ruled by the Islamic religious leaders. This is a work of Satan, not a work of God. Jesus said, "The thief comes only to steal and kill and destroy. I came that they may have life and have it abundantly" (John 10:10). He also proclaimed not slavery, but liberty: "The Spirit of the Lord is upon me, because he has anointed me to proclaim good news to the poor. He has sent me *to proclaim liberty to the captives* and the recovering of sight to the blind, to set at *liberty* those who are oppressed" (Luke 4:18).

I have devoted so much space to explaining the background of al-Qaeda because it is crucial to understand that the terrorist attacks directed against the United States and other countries *are not caused by people experiencing poverty or oppression in poor nations.* Qutb, Zawahiri, and bin Laden were all well-educated and well-to-do (bin Laden was a multi-millionaire). Wright points out that most young men who joined up with al-Qaeda in Afghanistan were "middle or upper class" and "were largely college-educated, with a strong bias toward the natural sciences and engineering."[67]

Even al-Qaeda's opposition to the presence of American troops in Saudi Arabia and to the US attack against Iraq in the First Gulf War[68] were essentially *religious* objections as well, since these were non-Muslim troops in Muslim countries, even if they were there to protect Saudi Arabia from Saddam Hussein's Iraq.

Therefore the explanation for al-Qaeda and similar Islamic terrorist movements can only be rightly understood as a deeply and profoundly *religious motivation*—a conviction that they must use murder and terrorism to advance the rule of Islamic law by force throughout the nations of the world. The movement has its modern origins in a campaign to institute more strict Islamic law in Egypt (Qutb, Zawahiri), in Saudi Arabia (bin Laden[69]), and then in other countries.

Radical Islamic opposition to Israel must also be understood in this light. Whereas Islam is the dominant religion in all the countries of the Middle East that surround Israel, the presence of Judaism as the dominant religion in Israel stands out as an intolerable exception, and therefore many Muslim leaders declare that Israel has no right to exist and that they will not rest until all the Jews are driven out of the land of Palestine or driven into the sea. Then pure Islamic rule can be established in Palestine as well.

---

66. Ibid., 230–31.
67. Ibid., 301.

68. Ibid., 234, 247, and 259–60.
69. Ibid., 246.

Islamic scholar Nihal Sahin Utku has written, "History has shown, as the Torah states, that the Palestinian land, the promised land of God, really belongs to the descendants of Abraham. However, not those who descended from Isaac, but those who descended from Ismail, one of whom was Prophet Muhammad."[70]

Elsewhere in his analysis Wright returns again and again to the religious domination goals as the true explanation of the convictions of al-Qaeda and related groups:

> On August 23, 1996, Osama bin Laden issued a "declaration of war" against America.[71] His first reason given was American support for Israel and the second was the presence of American troops in Muslim lands, particularly in Saudi Arabia (following the First Gulf War).[72]

In 1998 Zawahiri and bin Laden wrote a formal declaration with three reasons for terrorist attacks against the United States: (1) the continuing presence of American troops in Saudi Arabia even though the First Gulf War had ended (and even though they were there with the blessing of the Saudi government because of the continuing protection they provided against Saddam Hussein), (2) America's action against Iraq (in the First Gulf War), and (3) America's support of Israel. Therefore they issued a *fatwa* (authoritative religious opinion) signed by bin Laden, Zawahiri, and others with this chilling statement:

> The ruling to kill the Americans and their allies—civilian and military—is an individual duty for every Muslim who can do it in any country in which it is possible to do it.[73]

2. Explanations that primarily blame America for terrorism are mistaken and harmful

This historical analysis of the origins of Islamic terrorism shows why the primary explanations for terrorism that are given again and again in Jim Wallis's book *God's Politics* simply misunderstand the causes of terrorism. I realize that at one point Wallis rightly says that "the root of the terror attacks is not a yearning for economic justice for the poor and oppressed of the world," and "it is motivated rather by the ambition of a perverted religious fundamentalism for regional and global power; one that rejects the values of liberty, equality, democracy, and human rights."[74] But those brief comments are not at all central to his argument, nor are they emphasized at all. In his overall discussion of terrorism Wallis minimizes the underlying religious causes and points instead to what he sees as *American shortcomings* that provided great help for the terrorist cause.

For example, Wallis says, regarding his recommendation for Americans,

70. Nihal Sahin Utku, "Palestine: The Eternal Domain of the Prophet's Descendents," *LostProphet.info.* www.lastprophet.info/en/nihal-sahin-utku-phd/palestine-the-eternal-domain-of-the-prophet-s-descendents.html.

71. Wright, *The Looming Tower,* 234.
72. Ibid., 247.
73. Ibid., 259–60.
74. Wallis, *God's Politics,* 99.

An even more courageous national commitment would be to face honestly the grievances and injustices that breed rage and vengeance and are continually exploited by terrorists to recruit the angry and the desperate.... It is indeed impossible to comprehend adequately the terrorist acts of September 11 without a deeper understanding of the grievances and injustices felt by millions of people around the world.[75]

Wallis returns again and again in his book to what he thinks are shortcomings of the United States that have led to these "grievances and injustices" that have given support to the terrorist cause. He mentions US support for military dictators, the United States' failure to be "an honest broker for Middle East peace," "American and Western appetites for oil," and the fact that "the United States sits atop and is the leader of a global economy in which half of God's children still live on less than two dollars a day." Wallis says that "the United States will be blamed around the world for the structures of injustice that such a global economy daily enforces."[76] He says that "we have contributed to the grievances and injustices that breed terrorism."[77] Again and again Wallis returns to this "blame America" theme, saying that a serious agenda of "global poverty reduction" would be a good strategy for opposing terrorism.[78]

Then Wallis also says that our military attacks on terrorists lead to "recruiting even more terrorists, and fueling an unending cycle of violence."[79] This particular argument has the situation exactly backward, because it says that our successful military attacks actually help the terrorists. In other words, when we defeat the terrorists militarily, it helps them. Another way of putting this argument is to say that winning is actually losing! Wallis fails to recognize that the supply of terrorist recruits dries up as soon as it becomes evident that they will be defeated by superior military power at every point and that their cause is futile.

Wallis's argument here is just the opposite of the apostle Paul, who gives this explanation for the military power of civil government: "*But if you do wrong, be afraid*, for he does not *bear the sword* in vain. For he is the servant of God, an avenger who carries out God's wrath on the wrongdoer" (Rom. 13:4). The sword in the hand of good government is God's designated weapon to defeat evildoers.

It is important to recognize that Wallis's arguments when he heaps blame on America for terrorism are not carefully reasoned and well-documented proofs that supposed American wrongdoing has led to terrorist attacks. They are simply broad accusations thrown out as if they needed no proof or argument. But they lack any convincing substantiation.

What is the function of this kind of "blame America" argument for a pacifist position? *It allows a pacifist always to change the subject* from how to defend against evil terrorists to accusations against the United States for contributing to the terrorism that

---

75. Ibid., 96.
76. Ibid., 97.
77. Ibid., 101. Similar statements are found on pages 104, 105, and 106.

78. Ibid., 99.
79. Ibid., 101.

attacked it! Although the United States was attacked on 9/11, the entire force of Wallis's discussion is to turn the victim (the United States) into the culprit! He is saying that the victim was mostly responsible for the attacks against it.

By this kind of argument, the continuing existence of *any poverty anywhere in the world* provides Wallis with a basis for accusing the United States of wrongdoing. He can always bring up world poverty to argue how "evil" the United States is, using vague and unsubstantiated accusations. (He makes these accusations even though world poverty is not the fault of the US government or US citizens or American corporations and even though the people of the United States do more than any other nation to alleviate poverty throughout the world [see discussion in chap. 9].)

The harmful result of these repeated accusations from Jim Wallis is *to undermine any sense of moral right and wrong in the battle against terrorism.* In actual fact, the terrorists who attack innocent civilians in the United States are committing profound evil, and the military forces of the United States who defend against such terrorists are doing good, according to Romans 13 and 1 Peter 2. So there is a clear distinction between "good" and "evil" *with respect to the specific question of terrorist attacks and defense against them.* I am not saying that the United States is a perfect nation, or that it has no shortcomings, which it certainly does. I am saying that in the matter of the attacks by Islamic terrorists such as 9/11 and elsewhere (see the list in the next section), there was clearly a moral right and wrong. Terrorists who attack innocent civilians are wrong. Innocent civilians whom they attack and military actions that attempt to stop such attacks are morally good with respect to this particular issue. Wallis just muddies the waters and confuses this clear moral difference.

Wallis erodes the sense of moral rightness we should have as we defend our nation, saying over and over that we too are "evil." This is a profoundly mistaken argument and will cripple the ability of any nation to defend itself against evil.

3. Terrorist attacks carried out by al-Qaeda and its allies

Here is a brief list of terrorist attacks by al-Qaeda and related forces:[80]

February 26, 1993	First World Trade Center bomb
June 25, 1996	Bombing of Khobar Towers, a US military barracks in Saudi Arabia
August 7, 1998	Bombing of US embassy in Nairobi, Kenya
August 7, 1998	Bombing of US embassy in Dar es Salaam, Tanzania
October 12, 2000	Bombing of USS *Cole* in port in Yemen
September 11, 2001	Attack on the World Trade Center and the Pentagon

---

80. Wright, *The Looming Tower*, 177.

Therefore the attacks of 9/11 did not suddenly appear out of the blue, but were the culmination of a series of militant actions undertaken *with the goal of imposing radical Islam on the nations of the world*—attacks that had begun (long before the formation of al-Qaeda) in an assassination attempt against President Gamal Abdel Nasser in Alexandria, Egypt, on October 26, 1954, carried out by members of the Muslim Brothers, with whom Sayyid Qutb was already associated.[81] These attacks continued in the 1981 assassination of Anwar Sadat. They continue to be perpetuated in terrorist attacks in various countries of the world to this day.

4. Solutions to Islamic Jihadism

Defeating Islamic Jihadism will require several solutions.

a. Superior force

The hardened supporters of al-Qaeda have a deeply religious commitment to violent evil deeds. There should be no reasonable expectation that they can be turned from their commitment to violence *by any reasoning or bargaining or concessions or negotiation*, nor is there any persuasive historical evidence that negotiation will ever deter them from their single goal of imposing radical Islamic law on the nations of the earth.

The only method that has shown any success, or that shows any promise of success in stopping them, is *the use of superior force by military and police forces* within each nation, so that these hardened supporters can be captured or killed before they are able to carry out an attack. Lawrence Wright's book recounts in various places how Nasser and Sadat in Egypt and the Royal Family in Saudi Arabia attempted to appease the terrorist elements in their own countries with various concessions at various times, but without any success.[82]

The use of superior military and police power to defeat such evildoers is the proper role of government, because, as said earlier, God has appointed it to "bear the sword" (Rom. 13:4), to be a "terror" to those who would do evil (v. 3), and to act as "an avenger who carries out God's wrath on the wrongdoer" (v. 4). Therefore it is right for the United States and other countries who would oppose Islamic terrorism to use all their military and police might to capture and imprison or, if necessary, to kill hardened supporters of al-Qaeda and those with similar commitments. The United States in particular should use all of its military, electronic, economic, and diplomatic power to defeat followers of al-Qaeda wherever they are in the world.

But defeat of such terrorists poses a particular law-enforcement problem, because many of them are committed to giving their lives in what they think of as "martyrdom in the cause of God" in carrying out terrorist attacks.[83] This means that the older forms of criminal investigation that are aimed at capturing and punishing the wrongdoer *after*

---

81. Ibid., 27–28.
82. Ibid., 26, 31, 39, 48, 209–10.
83. Ibid., 302.

the attack will simply not work, because with a suicide bomber, the wrongdoer is already dead. Therefore they must be defeated before they can launch an attack.

b. What about wiretapping?

The technological expertise of American counter-terrorism specialists gave them two particularly effective weapons that were being used secretly and very successfully against terrorism. But they were both compromised by a combination of media leaks and the opposition of anti-war members of Congress.

One method was the secret tracing of inter-bank transfers of terrorist funds, many of which were going through large banks in Europe to which American and European anti-terrorist specialists had been given access. Therefore they were able to trace the destination of funds that were to be used to prepare for terrorist attacks. But such tracking of funds was recklessly exposed in an article in the *New York Times* on June 23, 2006.[84] Edward Turzanski of LaSalle University said, "I do know that the government official who told the *Times* reporter about this broke the law, ought to be prosecuted, and the *New York Times* ought to wake up and get it. They are harming our ability to prevent terror attacks. This isn't some sort of academic game. This is going to cost lives, and they are harming our abilities to connect the dots. And that's what the 9/11 commission was all upset about is our inability to connect dots."[85]

This reckless publication of a highly classified secret anti-terror program meant that terrorists largely stopped using these banks for transfers of funds and that this effective anti-terrorism tool was taken away from the US government. I consider this action by the *New York Times* so damaging to our national security interests that I think it was treasonous and should be prosecuted as such. But the liberal opposition to President Bush and to the War on Terror was so strong that the government did nothing in response to this publication of defense secrets.

The second effective technological tool was the ability of the US government to listen in on telephone conversations between terrorists even when they were *both* outside the United States. Because of some particular aspects of international telecommunications, many calls made around the world, even from one cell phone to another when both are outside the United States, still are transferred electronically through switching equipment in the United States. According to Wired.com, "International phone and internet traffic flows through the United States largely because of pricing models established more than 100 years ago in the International Telecommunication Union to handle international phone calls. Under those ITU tariffs, smaller and developing countries charge higher fees to accept calls than the US-based carriers do, which can make it cheaper to route phone calls through the United States than directly to a neighboring country."[86] Therefore US anti-terrorism forces were able to eavesdrop on many terrorist phone calls

---

84. James Risen and Eric Lichtblau, "Bank Data Sifted in Secret by U.S. to Block Terror," *New York Times* (June 23, 2006). www.nytimes.com/2006/06/23/washington/23intel.html.

85. "New York Times Outs Another Anti-Terror Program," *The Big Story with Jon Gibson, Fox News* (June 26, 2006). www.

foxnews.com/story/0,2933,201011,00.html.

86. Ryan Singel, "NSA's Lucky Break: How the U.S. Became Switchboard to the World," *Wired.com* (Oct. 10, 2007). www.wired.com/politics/security/news/2007/10/domestic_taps.

around the world and discover plots for terrorist attacks before the attacks were to occur. They were also able to locate and capture many terrorist leaders.

In addition to monitoring these calls entirely between foreign callers, the National Security Agency, which collects such telephone calls as well as email traffic, was monitoring communications from places such as the area of Afghanistan where Osama bin Laden was thought to have been hiding to various locations in the United States (which were then suspected to be indications of a possible al-Qaeda cell within the United States).

But when liberal opponents of the War on Terror discovered that this was happening, once again they betrayed the urgent defense interests of the United States and opposed what they called "warrantless wiretapping." Of course, if you are listening to a call between terrorists that lasts two minutes, there is no time to go to a local court and get the nearest judge to issue a warrant for that call because you will miss it. And with terrorists using disposable cell phones for a short time and then discarding them, the requirement for specific warrants in each case would make such listening to terrorist conversations impossible.

Opponents of this electronic anti-terror procedure have claimed that it violates the civil rights of Americans and also violates a law passed in 1978 called the Foreign Intelligence Surveillance Act (FISA) because it intercepts telephone communications without a warrant. So it was called "warrantless wiretapping." But the Bush administration steadfastly maintained that it was not violating any American law. Law professor John Yoo of the University of California, Berkeley, who was a Justice Department official in the Bush administration, notes the following:

> Every Federal Appeals Court to address the question has agreed that the President may gather electronic intelligence to protect against foreign threats. This includes the special FISA appeals court, which in a 2002 sealed case upholding the constitutionality of the Patriot Act held that "the President did have inherent authority to conduct warrantless searches to obtain foreign intelligence information." The court said ... that "FISA could not encroach on the President's constitutional power."[87]

Because of his support for former President Bush's attempt to keep the country safe, Yoo was labeled a "war criminal" by the "far left."[88]

The very existence of this top-secret program to monitor terrorist phone calls was also first revealed to the public by an article in the *New York Times* on December 16, 2005. Even the liberal *Times* had to admit that the program was successful:

> Several officials said the eavesdropping program had helped uncover a plot by Iyman Faris, an Ohio trucker and naturalized citizen who pleaded guilty in

87. John Yoo, "Why We Endorsed Warrantless Wire-Taps," *Wall Street Journal* (July 16, 2009), A13.

88. Glenn Greenwald, "John Yoo's War Crimes," *Salon.com* (April 2, 2008), (www.salon.com/opinion/greenwald/2008/04/02/yoo/index.html); and Maria L. La Ganga, "Scholar Calmly Takes Heat for His Memos on Torture," *Los Angeles Times* (May 16, 2005), http://articles.latimes.com/2005/may/16/local/me-yoo16.

2003 to supporting Al Qaeda by planning to bring down the Brooklyn Bridge with blowtorches. What appeared to be another Qaeda plot, involving fertilizer bomb attacks on British pubs and train stations, was exposed last year in part through the program, the officials said.[89]

The primary opposition to this program has been from the American Civil Liberties Union (ACLU), which has filed numerous lawsuits to stop it,[90] and from many Democratic members of Congress. After an incredibly long battle with Congress, President Bush was finally able to persuade enough members of Congress to pass a bill granting immunity to telecommunications companies that would help in this process; he signed the bill July 10, 2008. Without this law, the companies that owned the telecommunications equipment could have been driven out of business by having to defend themselves against lawsuits regarding this program. The ACLU immediately promised to challenge the law in court.[91]

My own viewpoint is that such a program is essential to national security and essential in the battle against the threat of terrorist attacks. Because it is limited to protecting against terrorist attacks, the small threat of invasion of the privacy of ordinary citizens is insignificant in comparison to the huge benefit of protection against deadly attacks. The program should be continued.

c. Holding nations accountable that harbor terrorists

Another step in defeating Islamic Jihadism was begun by President Bush when he declared on September 20, 2001—just after the attacks of 9/11—that the United States would hold accountable any nation that harbored terrorists or gave support to terrorists. The President said:

> We will starve terrorists of funding, turn them one against another, drive them from place to place, until there is no refuge or no rest. And we will pursue nations that provide aid or safe haven to terrorism. Every nation, in every region, now has a decision to make. Either you are with us, or you are with the terrorists. From this day forward, any nation that continues to harbor or support terrorism will be regarded by the United States as a hostile regime.[92]

This is an important step, because without at least passive tolerance by a national government, it is hard for terrorist training camps and cells to remain for long within any nation.

89. James Risen and Eric Lichtblau, "Bush Lets U.S. Spy on Callers Without Courts," *New York Times* (Dec. 16, 2005). www.nytimes.com/2005/12/16/politics/16program.html?ex=1292389200&en=e32072d786623ac1&ei=5090&partner=rssuserland&emc=rss.

90. For examples of how the ACLU has tried to stop the surveillance program, go to www.aclu.org/national-security/surveillance.

91. "Bush Signs Terror Surveillance Bill Granting Legal Immunity to Companies That Aided Eavesdropping," *Fox News* (July 10, 2008). www.foxnews.com/story/0,2933,379843,00.html.

92. George W. Bush, Address to a Joint Session of Congress Following 9/11 Attacks. www.americanrhetoric.com/speeches/gwbush911jointsessionspeech.htm.

The US government under the leadership of President Bush began to pursue aggressive policies to intercept and attack terrorists before they could attack us, and the result was an amazing success that no one would have believed possible shortly after 9/11. For the entire remaining seven years of the Bush administration, and so far in President Obama's administration (as I am writing in early 2010), no successful terrorist attack has been carried out inside the United States.

Journalist Ronald Kessler, an expert on anti-terrorism, writes, "Terrorists haven't attacked during the past seven years because of the work of the FBI, the CIA (Central Intelligence Agency), and our military, as well as the sweeping changes President Bush instigated in the intelligence community."[93] Kessler goes on to say, "When Bush proclaimed that any country harboring a terrorist would be considered terrorist, Arab countries began cooperating in the War on Terror, turning over thousands of terrorists and leads."[94] He adds, "Since 9/11, the FBI, the CIA, and the military have rolled up about 5,000 terrorists world-wide."[95]

d. Persuading people in Muslim nations to turn against terrorist groups

We can be thankful that the vast majority of Muslims throughout the world have not advocated or supported such terrorist activities. In fact, it was the resistance of the Muslim governments in Egypt to the imposition of strict Islamic law that made them the first targets of Islamic Jihadism. As journalist and former Army Green Beret Michael Yon explains again and again in his book *Moment of Truth in Iraq*,[96] the local populations in one region after another have turned decisively against al-Qaeda and told American and Iraqi forces where terrorists were hiding and where they had planted bombs. But this turn of events happened only after Americans did two things: They used military power to provide security and safety, and they used local contacts and charitable acts to build confidence and trust with the Iraqis who had been terrorized by violent al-Qaeda members.

To the extent that this happens in areas where al-Qaeda pockets are found in the world, the local forces opposing these terrorists will find and imprison or destroy them, and terrorism will be marginalized and given no place to thrive. But as Yon points out, it will require a strong, committed US military presence in Iraq and Afghanistan to provide the neighborhood security within which such other peace-making efforts can be successful.

Moreover, Christians must realize that as we hope to persuade Muslims to turn against terrorism and renounce the idea that Islam can be imposed by force on non-Muslim peoples, we are asking them to reject a conservative, more literal reading of the Quran (as promoted by terrorist factions), in which "peace" means not coexistence with other religions, but total surrender to Muslim rule over society. Therefore, when Muslims claim they hold to a "religion of peace," we should ask for clarification about what is meant by "peace."

---

93. Ronald Kessler, "The secret to why we have not been attacked," *Newsmax.com* (accessed Sept. 11, 2008).
94. Ibid.

95. Ibid.
96. Michael Yon, *Moment of Truth in Iraq* (Minneapolis: Richard Vigilante Books, 2008).

e. Moral reformation in American culture

One factor that gives Islamic radicals "intellectual ammunition" to vilify America is the very evident moral breakdown in American society, which they can criticize in order to argue that every nation badly needs the imposition of strict Islamic law. The radicals point to widespread moral decline in America characterized by alcoholism, addiction to drugs or gambling, pornography, widespread break-up of marriages, sexual immorality before and after marriage, undisciplined and disrespectful children in schools, the breakdown of parental authority, widespread shoplifting and employee theft, dishonesty in all areas of life, and more.

At this point Christians should realize that historically it has been *the proclamation by Christian pastors of the moral law of God* and of universal accountability before God that has brought positive moral transformation in many societies. Christians would do well to consider again at this point in history how they might persuasively teach the society at large about God's moral standards in the Bible.

f. Spiritual revival

The type of moral proclamation and transformation that I mentioned in the previous section can bring beneficial changes to the accepted moral standards in a society. But genuine transformation will not come about unless a substantial number of people in a society or nation also have their hearts transformed by the message of the Christian gospel that proclaims forgiveness of sins and the opportunity for new life through faith in Jesus Christ. This has application in two ways.

First, if there is a spiritual revival that brings many people to personal faith in Christ in the United States or other nations, it will bring about a more effective kind of moral transformation in society and thereby will begin to provide a better answer to the attempts by Islamic terrorists to claim the moral high ground in terms of personal morality and Islamic law.

Second, such a revival would also have the potential for reaching even the hardened hearts of al-Qaeda terrorists, if they would give consideration to it. If such a spiritual revival were to occur not only in the United States but also in nations with large Muslim populations, it would provide evidence that genuine Christianity is not represented by the kind of decadence that many Muslims see in popular American culture and especially in movies, but that genuine Christianity results in a transformation of the heart and shows itself in moral conduct and love for one's neighbor as manifested in the life and teachings of Jesus Christ.

F. WARS IN IRAQ AND AFGHANISTAN

According to the criteria for a just war mentioned above (see pp. 389–90), I believe that the wars in Iraq and Afghanistan were just wars.

(1) These wars were undertaken for a *just cause*, first, because the United States had already been attacked by Islamic terrorists on 9/11 and previously (see above, pp. 408–9), and second, because these wars were launched against hotbeds of Islamic

terrorism. Therefore their primary justification was *to defend the United States* against another similar terrorist attack that could come, not from one specific nation, but from a worldwide network of terrorists that was receiving support or at least safe harbor from various nations. The Taliban and the al-Qaeda forces were controlling Afghanistan and carrying out terrorist attacks from there. In the Middle East, Saddam Hussein was giving repeated support to terrorist activities, providing training grounds, paying $25,000 to the family of every terrorist who committed a suicide attack in Israel,[97] and developing or perhaps possessing weapons of mass destruction. With respect to Iraq, another *just cause* was that Saddam had never complied with the terms of surrender in the First Gulf War in 1993, because he was continuing to prevent site visits to verify that he had no nuclear weapons.

Although no weapons of mass destruction were found after the invasion of Iraq, the intelligence services of the United States and many other Western countries were convinced that he had chemical and biological weapons (he had used them previously against Kurds in the northern part of Iraq), and there was substantial evidence that he was attempting to acquire nuclear weapons as well. (Israel had destroyed Saddam's Osirak nuclear reactor as far back as June 7, 1981, in a surprise air attack, because Israel was convinced that Saddam was soon going to be able to develop nuclear weapons from it.) According to the British Broadcasting Corporation (BBC), "The Israeli Government explained its reasons for the attack in a statement saying, "The atomic bombs which that reactor was capable of producing, whether from enriched uranium or from plutonium, would be of the Hiroshima size. Thus a mortal danger to the people of Israel progressively arose.' "[98]

In addition, there is still reason to believe that these intelligence reports were accurate, because some apparently reliable sources have reported that Saddam transported large quantities of weapons of mass destruction to Syria just prior to the American invasion. In January 2004, *Agence France Presse* (the French news service) reported:

> An exiled Syrian dissident has reiterated claims that Iraqi biological and chemical weapons were smuggled into Syria just before the start of the United States-led attack on Iraq in March last year. "The Iraqi chemical and biological weapons were at first put in (Syrian) Presidential Guard depots, at its headquarters in Damascus," Nizzar Nayyouf told the French-based Internet news site Proche-Orient.info, which specialises in news from the Middle East. He said the operation took place "between February and March 2003, when Saddam Hussein realised that the Americans had decided to act" against Iraq. The operation took place under supervision of General Zoul-Himla Shalich, the head of the guard in Syria and considered close to Syrian President Bashar al-Assad, Nayyouf said, citing as his sources "superior officers who themselves took part in the operation."[99]

97. John Esterbrook, "Salaries for Suicide Bombers," *CBSNews.com* (April 3, 2002). www.cbsnews.com/stories/2002/04/03/world/main505316.shtml.

98. "1981: Israel Bombs Iraq Nuclear Reactor," *BBCNews.com* (June 7, 1981). http://news.bbc.co.uk/onthisday/hi/dates/stories/june/7/newsid_3014000/3014623.stm.

99. "Iraq Hid Weapons in Syria, Dissident Claims," *Agence France Presse* (Jan. 19, 2004). www.iol.co.za/index.php?click_id=3&art_id=qw1074472561910B262&set_id=1.

Then-Israeli Prime Minister Ariel Sharon also made this claim in December 2002, saying, "We have some information to that effect. We are now working to confirm the information."[100]

But an even broader justification for the war was the conviction of President Bush and others in the leadership of both parties that if a genuinely functioning free and democratic government could begin to succeed in Iraq, *it would provide a more effective long-term antidote to Islamic terrorism*, a movement that had attacked us several times, because *countries that are governed by open democratic processes do not launch wars of conquest against other nations.* This position was argued, I think persuasively, by Natan Sharansky in *The Case for Democracy.*[101] But Sharansky contends that in order to be a *genuine* democracy, a country must pass this "town square test": Can a citizen stand in the middle of the town square and openly criticize the government without fear of arrest, imprisonment, or physical harm?[102] Therefore, Sharansky says, the present government of Hamas in Gaza does not constitute a genuine democracy, for example, because it cannot pass that town square test. I would add, nor does the current government of Russia pass the town square test, nor does the government of China. These are not now genuine democracies.

But Iraq is a genuine, functioning democracy. It has held successful elections, first to elect delegates to a constitutional convention, then later to approve the constitution (Oct. 15, 2005), in an election in which 63% of eligible Iraqis voted, passing it with 78% of the vote.[103] Still later, another successful election was held to elect members of Parliament (Dec. 15, 2005),[104] and another successful parliamentary election was held on March 7, 2010. Afghanistan is also a functioning democracy.[105] These countries still have internal struggles and conflicts (as all countries do, and especially new democracies as they begin to function), but they are living proof that functioning democracies are able to work within predominantly Muslim nations.

Some people object that predominantly Muslim countries will never be able to function as democracies. But Turkey is 99.8% Muslim and has a democratically elected government,[106] and Pakistan is 95% Muslim and has a democratically elected government as well.[107] Indonesia is 86% Muslim (and 6% Protestant and 3% Roman Catholic) and is a functioning democracy.[108]

---

100. "Syria Denies It Received Iraqi Weapons," Associated Press (Dec. 25, 2002). www.usatoday.com/news/world/2002–12–25-syria-iraq_x.htm

101. Natan Sharansky, *The Case for Democracy: the Power of Freedom to Overcome Tyranny and Terror* (New York: Public Affairs, 2004).

102. Ibid., 40.

103. Kenneth Katzman, "Iraq: Elections, Government, and Constitution," *CRS Report for Congress* (Feb. 27, 2007). http://fpc.state.gov/documents/organization/81355.pdf.

104. Ibid.

105. Griff Witte, "A Sign of Democracy in Afghanistan,"

Washington Post (Dec. 20, 2005). www.boston.com/news/world/middleeast/articles/2005/12/20/a_sign_of_democracy_in_afghanistan/.

106. "Turkey," *The World Factbook*, Central Intelligence Agency (Oct. 28, 2009). www.cia.gov/library/publications/the-world-factbook/geos/tu.html.

107. "Pakistan," *The World Factbook*, Central Intelligence Agency (Oct. 28, 2009). https://www.cia.gov/library/publications/the-world-factbook/geos/pk.html.

108. "Indonesia," *The World Factbook*, Central Intelligence Agency (Feb. 7, 2010). https://www.cia.gov/library/publications/the-world-factbook/geos/id.html.

The hope of President Bush was that a successful, peaceful, economically grow-ing Iraq would be a persuasive, visible model that would challenge the people of other Islamic nations, because it would demonstrate that even the nation with the Middle East's worst Islamic dictatorship (under Saddam Hussein), once the oppressive govern-ment is overthrown, can begin to function with a non-oppressive, democratic govern-ment. This would provide impetus for the same process happening in other Muslim nations (such as Iran). In this way this model has the potential to change the course of history in the Middle East.

My own expectation is that this process holds the most hope of long-term defeat of Islamic terrorism. Functioning democracies in Muslim nations will eventually give Islamic terrorists no place to train and no place to hide.

Therefore the war in Iraq was a necessary, strategic, and highly significant step in defending the United States against radical Islamic terrorism. It was undertaken for a *just cause.*

(2) The Iraqi and Afghan wars were declared by a *competent authority* (the President, with Congress authorizing the expenditures).

(3) There was truly *comparative justice* on our side, because of the great evil propa-gated by the Taliban in Afghanistan and Saddam Hussein in Iraq.

(4) We had the *right intention*, to free both countries from oppressive dictatorships and simultaneously to remove the threat of terrorism against us that was coming from those countries.

(5) Both were wars of *last resort,* because other negotiations and diplomacy had gone on for years without any significant change in those countries.

(6) The United States had a great *probability of success.*

(7) The *proportionality of projected results* was massively in favor of these two wars because of the world-threatening nature of terrorism emanating from those countries and because of the great good that would come about if their governments were changed. As a matter of fact, the *actual* results have been that these two nations are now func-tioning democracies, and a total of nearly 60 million more people (nearly 29 million in Iraq[109] and more than 28 million[110] in Afghanistan) who were formerly under extremely oppressive regimes are now living in comparative freedom. This is an excellent result.

(8) The wars were carried out in a *right spirit*, with regret that war had to be under-taken, but with determination to bring it to a successful conclusion.

Therefore I strongly disagree with Jim Wallis when he writes in *God's Politics* that the Iraq War did not meet the criteria of a just war.[111] And it is seriously misleading when he says repeatedly that most churches from various denominations were opposed to the Iraq War (see pp. 109, 113, 134, and 155). Wallis gives almost no documentation for this claim, except at one point (p. 155) he does list some signers to a vague anti-war state-ment. What he does not mention is that the signers are mostly people who are already

109. "Iraq," *The World Factbook,* Central Intelligence Agency (Oct. 28, 2009). https://www.cia.gov/library/publications/the-world-factbook/geos/iz.html.

110. "Afghanistan," *The World Factbook,* Central Intelligence

Agency (Oct. 28, 2009). https://www.cia.gov/library/publica-tions/the-world-factbook/geos/af.html.

111. Wallis, *God's Politics,* 111, 113.

committed to his pacifist position or are from much more liberal rather than evangelical colleges and seminaries. In actual fact, very few evangelical churches ever considered or voted on any resolutions in support of the war or against it (and Wallis himself notes that Southern Baptists supported it).[112] Certainly Wallis is mistaken if he is implying that opposition to the Iraq War was a dominant "evangelical Protestant" viewpoint, which it certainly was not.

My present concern, however, is that President Obama might actually lose both Iraq and Afghanistan to terrorists once again through weakness and indecision. He is decreasing our military presence in Iraq and seems to be weakening our resolve to establish a strong and successful government there that can successfully oppose terrorist forces. He has insisted on an arbitrary timetable for withdrawal of American troops from Iraq,[113] and there were early indications that this may be destabilizing some regions and giving terrorists new hope that they might yet be able to defeat the forces of freedom that have brought such stability to the nation. Regarding Afghanistan, he delayed for thirteen weeks[114] a response to General Stanley McChrystal's request for 60,000 more troops in Afghanistan,[115] and he eventually agreed to send approximately half that number or 34,000.[116] But that might not be enough strength to defeat the terrorists and preserve the hard-won peace in Afghanistan.[117]

If the United States loses both the war in Iraq and the war in Afghanistan, so that these countries once again fall under terrorist domination, the destructive consequences for America and for the rest of the world would be far beyond anything that has happened up to this point. If that happens, the responsibility for such losses and such a renewed campaign of terror throughout many nations will belong solely to President Obama. I deeply hope that this does not happen.

G. NUCLEAR WEAPONS

1. History of nuclear weapons

The only two nuclear weapons ever used in war were exploded by the United States over Hiroshima and Nagasaki, Japan—on August 6 and 9, 1945, respectively. Both of these large cities had industrial and military significance for the Japanese war effort. Estimates ranging from 90,000 to 150,000 people were killed in Hiroshima (out of 340,000),

---

112. Ibid., 113.

113. Karen DeYoung, "Obama Sets Timetable for Iraq," *Washington Post* (Feb. 28, 2009). www.washingtonpost.com/wp-dyn/content/article/2009/02/27/AR2009022700566.html.

114. President Obama took from September 2 to November 24, 2009, to respond to the request. See Toby Harnden, "Barack Obama to Send 34,000 More Troops to Afghanistan," *Telegraph.co.uk* (Nov. 24, 2009). www.telegraph.co.uk/news/worldnews/northamerica/usa/6646411/Barack-Obama-to-send-34000-more-troops-to-Afghanistan.html?utm_source=Left+Foot+Forward+List&utm_campaign=f3bbdd60a7-Left_

Foot_Forward8_18_2009&utm_medium=email.

115. Peter Spiegel and Yochi Dreazen, "Top Troop Request Exceeds 60,000," *Wall Street Journal* (Oct. 9, 2009). http://online.wsj.com/article/SB125504448324674693.html?mod=WSJ_hpp_sections_news.

116. Harnden, "Barack Obama to Send 34,000 More Troops to Afghanistan."

117. Yochi Dreazan, "Afghan Troop Request Simmers," *Wall Street Journal* (Sept. 26, 2009). http://online.wsj.com/article/SB125391851405042437.html?mod=rss_Politics_And_Policy.

and about 80,000 people were killed in Nagasaki (out of 212,000).[118] (About half of those numbers were killed immediately, and half died afterward from burns, radiation, and other injuries.) In both cases, the bomb destroyed everything within a one-mile radius in all directions and caused fires as far as two miles from the bomb.

President Harry S. Truman's goal in authorizing the use of these bombs was to bring an end to World War II, and that was in fact the result. Six days after the second bomb, Japan announced its surrender to the Allied Powers. While dropping these bombs caused the loss of approximately 200,000 Japanese lives, a commonly repeated estimate (from analysts who understand the US and Japanese force strength at that time) is that if the war had gone on without these bombs, the result would have been the loss of at least 500,000 American lives and possibly hundreds of thousands of Japanese lives.[119]

In his 1955 autobiography, President Truman affirmed that the atomic bomb probably saved half a million US lives, not to mention many Japanese casualties. The Japanese had already shown in previous battles in the Pacific campaigns that they would not surrender. Still, leftist critics claim that the number of 500,000 possible casualties was a "myth." In an article in the *New England Journal of History* in 2007, Michael Kort, professor of General Studies at Boston University, answered those critics:

> Writing in *The Journal of Military History*, [military historian] D. M. Giangreco explained that in military hands these projections took three forms: Medical estimates, manpower estimates, and strategic estimates. He then demonstrated that there was substantial documentation for high-end casualty projections—which, to be sure, varied widely—from both military and civilian sources that reached upward of 500,000. Equally important, one estimate that reached Truman—from former president Herbert Hoover, who had high-level government contacts—led the president to convene an important meeting with the Joint Chiefs of Staff and top civilian advisors on June 18, 1945, to discuss the projected invasion of Japan. In short, as Giangreco stressed in a later article in the *Pacific Historical Review*, Truman both saw and was concerned about high-end casualty estimates prior to the scheduled invasion.[120]

Whatever the precise number would have been is impossible to know, but it is clear that the use of the atomic bombs saved countless numbers of lives.

Since 1945, several other nations have acquired nuclear weapons, but no other nuclear weapon has ever been used in war. What prevented their use, for example, during the entire period of the Cold War between the Soviet Union and the United States and its allies? What prevented the Soviets from launching nuclear attacks against the United States or Western Europe? It was primarily the fear of overwhelming retaliation by the United States, the United Kingdom, and France that would result in horrifying

118. C. Peter Chen, "Atomic Bombing of Hiroshima and Nagasaki," World War II Database. http://ww2db.com/battle_spec.php?battle_id=49.

119. Jing Oh, "Hiroshima and Nagasaki: The Decision to Drop the Bomb," University of Michigan. www.umich.edu/~historyj/pages_folder/articles/Hiroshima_and_Nagasaki.pdf.

120. Michael Kort, "The Histography of Hiroshima: The Rise and Fall of Revisionism," *New England Journal of History* 64:1 (Fall 2007), 31–48. http://theamericanpresident.us/images/truman_bomb.pdf.

destruction of the Soviet Union itself. In other words, it was *the possession of overwhelming numbers of nuclear weapons* by peace-loving nations that prevented their use by any aggressor nation. That system of deterrence has worked perfectly now for more than six decades (since 1945).

2. Which nations have nuclear weapons today?

According to the Pentagon, the United States now has a total of 5,113 operational nuclear weapons,[121] and current estimates are than Russia has 5,200.[122] The US total is what remains after the nation "has dismantled more than 13,000 nuclear weapons since 1988."[123] The reason for retaining such a large number is that in the event of a nuclear war, many weapons might be destroyed before they could be launched, others would fail, and others would not reach their targets. (The weapons depend on a three-part delivery system: bombers, missiles, and submarines.)

In addition to the United States and Russia (which now controls the nuclear arsenal of the former Soviet Union), the following nations also possess nuclear weapons: (3) United Kingdom, (4) France, (5) China, (6) India, (7) Pakistan, and (8) North Korea. In addition, (9) Israel is widely thought to possess nuclear weapons but has never publicly confirmed this.

Besides these nations, Iran is aggressively pursuing nuclear power, and al-Qaeda has tried to obtain nuclear weapons. Moreover, when Israel destroyed Saddam's Osirak nuclear reactor on June 7, 1981, it temporarily destroyed Iraq's ability to develop nuclear weapons.[124]

3. Can the world successfully abolish nuclear weapons?

Many people today believe that the danger from nuclear weapons comes from the *mere presence* of so many of them in the world. If people believe this, then it seems evident to them that reducing the number of nuclear weapons in the world would reduce the threat that any nation would ever launch a nuclear attack. Their goal, then, is complete nuclear disarmament around the world. Their hope is that the world will be able to get rid of all nuclear weapons once and for all. Democratic Senator Diane Feinstein of California has said that nuclear weapons are "not a deterrent, but a grave and gathering threat to humanity."[125]

Will worldwide nuclear disarmament ever be possible? The short answer is no.

The history of the world shows that once new weapons are developed, they never disappear from the earth. Crossbows were declared illegal by the Second Lateran Council

---

121. "U.S. Releases Details of Nuclear Weapons Inventory," Associated Press (May 3, 2010). Accessed at www.foxnews.com/politics/2010/05/03/release-details-nuclear-weapons-inventory/.

122. "To Russia with Love," editorial in *Wall Street Journal* (April 4–5, 2009), A10.

123. Jack David, "There's No Reason for a Nuclear Test Ban," *Wall Street Journal* (Feb. 21–22, 2009), A9.

124. "1981: Israel Bombs Iraq Nuclear Reactor," *BBCNews.com* (June 7, 1981).

125. Dianne Feinstein, "Let's Commit to a Nuclear-Free World," *Wall Street Journal* (Jan. 3–4, 2009), A9.

in 1139, but people kept using them anyway. After airplanes were invented, The Hague Convention banned aerial bombardment in 1899, but people continued to use planes to drop bombs.[126] The reason is that the earth will always have people whose hearts are evil and who will pursue the most destructive weapons they can obtain in order to carry out their evil purposes. "The heart is deceitful above all things, and desperately sick; who can understand it?" (Jer. 17:9).

Therefore, to hope that nuclear weapons can be abolished from the nations of the earth is merely wishful thinking, with no basis in reality. To say it is possible would be to say that it is possible to reverse the entire course of all of human history from the beginning of time with regard to the development of new weapons. Such an expectation should not qualify as a rational defense policy for a nation.

Just after President Obama proclaimed to the United Nations his goal of a world without nuclear weapons, the editorial board of the *Wall Street Journal* rightly observed:

> In the bitter decades of the Cold War, we learned the hard way that the only countries that abide by disarmament treaties are those that want to be disarmed.[127]

4. How can we effectively reduce the risk of using nuclear weapons?

If it is not possible to rid the world of nuclear weapons, then the most important question is, how can we prevent nations from using nuclear weapons? There are two answers to this question: (1) deterrence by the credible threat of a superior nuclear force, and (2) an anti-missile defense system that will prevent nuclear weapons from reaching their targets.

Since it is the responsibility of governments to protect the people over whom God has placed them in authority (see discussion of Rom. 13:1–4 above, pp. 79–81), it is now necessary, in a world with nuclear weapons, for nations to be able to defend themselves in these two ways or else be able to depend on more powerful peaceful nations to defend them against such attacks. That is why the United States, in particular, has a weighty responsibility to maintain a clearly superior nuclear force that can defeat any potential attacker, and it must speak and act in such a way that the potential attacker is convinced the United States will overwhelmingly retaliate if a nuclear weapon is launched against it. To fail to do this would be to fail to protect the citizens of this nation effectively.

In addition, there are more than thirty other allied nations who depend on the United States for their protection from nuclear attack.[128] If the United States were to fail to maintain a sufficiently strong nuclear response capability, it would also be failing these allies who depend on our protection—and would prompt them to decide they have to develop their own nuclear arsenal.

---

126. "To Russia with Love," *Wall Street Journal.*

127. "The Disarmament Illusion," *Wall Street Journal* (Sept. 26, 2009), A14.

128. "Atomic Bombshells," *Wall Street Journal* (Jan. 24–25, 2009), A10; Jack David, "No Reason," *Wall Street Journal* (Feb. 21–22, 2009), A9.

In addition, because of the persistent threat of the use of nuclear weapons by an aggressor nation (whether Russia or North Korea or Iran or perhaps even China), the United States has a clear responsibility to continue to develop and deploy an effective anti-missile defense system that would shoot down an attacking missile before it could reach its target.

In fact, the anti-missile defense system that the United States has now partially deployed in Alaska and California is a wonderful alternative to the horrible possibility of having to launch a nuclear attack in response to an attack against us. Instead of two nations blowing up each others' cities, anti-missile defense systems will shoot down the incoming missile from an attacker before it reaches its target, so that no nuclear weapons are exploded in the first place. (The nuclear payload would ordinarily not detonate in such cases.) All Christians who love peace and believe in the protection of human life should rejoice greatly that military technology has advanced to the place where such systems are actually quite effective, as they have shown in many tests. On January 26, 2002, it was reported that a ground-based interceptor missile fired from a Navy ship hit a dummy armed missile in space that had been fired over the Pacific.[129] In another test, conducted on September 1, 2006, a missile was fired from a silo at Vandenberg Air Force Base and shot down a missile launched from Kodiak Island in Alaska.[130] In a test of an airborne anti-missile system, on February 11, 2010,

> A flying Boeing 747 jumbo jet equipped with a massive laser gun shot down a Scud-like missile over the Pacific late Thursday night, marking what analysts said was a major milestone in the development of the nation's missile-defense system.... The laser shot a heated, basketball-size beam that traveled 670 million mph to incinerate a missile moving 4,000 mph, the Pentagon said.[131]

When President Reagan first proposed such anti-missile defense systems, he was ridiculed by the political left and the media in the United States, who called it a "Star Wars" system and predicted that "it will never work." But now such a system actually has been shown to work in tests time and again. Christians should eagerly and enthusiastically support such a defensive system.

These two means of defense against nuclear attacks (maintaining strong nuclear weapon capabilities and building a strong anti-missile defense system) have another advantage as well: When the United States has such great superiority to other nations in both areas, it discourages any potential enemies from trying to match our power or engage in an arms race with us.

By contrast, if the United States proceeds in a unilateral way to disarm itself further and further, it will simply encourage hostile nations into an immediate rush to begin to develop more nuclear weapons and delivery systems that they think might possibly be able to attain a victory over the United States if they were able to attack. Thus America's

---

129. "Missile Shield Test Dubbed A Hit." Associated Press (Jan. 26, 2002). www.cbsnews.com/stories/2002/01/26/national/main325718.shtml.

130. Robert Jablon, "Anti-Missile Test Succeeds," *Chicago Tri-bune* (Sept. 2, 2006). http://archives.chicagotribune.com/2006/sep/02/news/chi–0609020154sep02.

131. W. J. Hennigan, "Pentagon: Laser shoots down missile in test," *Arizona Republic* (Feb. 13, 2010), A8.

disarmament would lead to an *arms race* on the part of other nations. It would also lead many of the allies who depend on US protection to think that they themselves must acquire nuclear weapons for their own defense, which would lead to further proliferation of the weapons.

During 2009, however, it became increasingly clear that President Obama would pursue exactly the opposite strategy from what I have advocated here, for he took several steps to weaken the US nuclear weapons arsenal and opposed further anti-missile defenses. He sought a new treaty with Russia that would set a maximum of 1,000 nuclear warheads each for the United States and Russia[132] (down from our current total of 5,113 warheads). He sought to kill the Reliable Replacement Warhead program, which would modernize and update the nuclear arsenal for a long time to come and which is supported by both Defense Secretary Robert Gates and Chairman of the Joint Chiefs of Staff, Admiral Mike Mullen. Killing this program would leave our nuclear arsenal in its current state of "gradual physical deterioration."[133] He also asked the Senate to ratify the Comprehensive Test Ban Treaty (CTBT), which the Senate had rejected in 1999.[134] Such an action would unwisely commit the United States to never being able to test its nuclear weapons systems, which would leave them vulnerable to gradually becoming outmoded.

Even more harmful to world peace than these decisions was President Obama's decision on September 17, 2009, to abandon a missile defense agreement that President George W. Bush had negotiated with Poland and the Czech Republic to station anti-missile defense systems in these two important countries in Eastern Europe.[135] Abandoning this program betrayed the trust that the Poland and Czech governments had placed in us. This missile system would have protected Europe from Iranian or Russian attacks, and it would have provided significant protection for us against missiles launched from Russia or Iran toward the east coast of the United States, since it would have intercepted them early in their flight paths.

Russia was delighted with President Obama's decision—a decision that left Eastern Europe more vulnerable to future Soviet attempts to attack and regain control over it. One Polish newspaper proclaimed, "Betrayal! The U.S. sold us to Russia and stabbed us in the back." A respected newspaper in the Czech Republic said, "An ally we rely on has betrayed us, and exchanged us for its own, better relations with Russia, of which we are rightly afraid."[136] *The Wall Street Journal* on the next day wrote this:

> The reality is that the U.S. is working hard to create antagonists where it previously had friends.... Officials in Warsaw surely noticed that President Obama cancelled the missile system 70 years to the day that the Soviet Union invaded Poland.[137]

132. "To Russia with Love," *Wall Street Journal.*

133. Ibid.

134. Jack David, "No Reason," *Wall Street Journal* (Feb. 21–22, 2009), A9.

135. "Obama's Remarks on Strengthening Missile Defense in Europe," *Council on Foreign Relations* (Sept. 17, 2009). www.cfr.org/publication/20226/obamas_remarks_on_strengthen-ing_missile_defense_in_europe_september_2009.html.

136. Vanessa Gera, "Poles, Czechs: U.S. Missile Defense Shift a Betrayal," Associated Press (Sept. 18, 2009). www.washingtontimes.com/news/2009/sep/18/poles-czechs-us-missile-defense-shift-betrayal/print/.

137. "Obama's Missile Offense," *Wall Street Journal* (Sept. 18, 2009), A22.

The Obama administration also canceled the Kinetic Energy Interceptor project for basing anti-missile defenses in Germany and Turkey. It canceled this as part of the $1.4 billion in cuts to the Pentagon's missile defense budget in early 2009, while it was in the midst of increasing government spending in almost every other area, far in excess of spending done by any previous administration in history.[138] The administration was so opposed to such military spending that this was the only budget area subject to significant cuts. These were tragic decisions, immensely harmful to future national security.

H. THE CIA

The Central Intelligence Agency (CIA) is the primary organization that gathers and analyzes information about other countries, especially about potential enemies of the United States. In other words, the CIA coordinates America's spy network abroad.

Is this a good thing? It seems to me that a necessary part of defending a nation is seeking to know about potential enemies and possible attacks before they happen, so that the nation can be defended against them. Because of this function, the CIA has no doubt prevented immense harm to the United States and to its interests both at home and elsewhere.

In the Bible, spies were not unknown. Joshua sent spies into the Promised Land before the conquest of Canaan (Josh. 2:1), David sent out spies to learn the whereabouts of King Saul (1 Sam. 26:4), and David later sent Hushai the Archite to serve as an undercover agent when Absalom was about to capture Jerusalem (2 Sam. 15:32–37; 16:15–19; 17:5–22).

Americans should, in general, be thankful for the CIA and the valuable intelligence it provides for our government. But instead of appreciation, the CIA constantly faces hostility and criticism from much of the American media and Hollywood. Because of unrelenting criticism over the years, much of which cannot be effectively answered without revealing national secrets, a sort of anti-CIA attitude has grown up in the United States. One example is the recent series of three movies called "The Bourne Trilogy," starring Matt Damon as Jason Bourne. Although I have enjoyed several of Robert Ludlum's novels (from which the lead character was taken), and although these movies were great fun to watch and very well made, their plots were completely different from Ludlum's novels, and the main villain turns out to be not any evil terrorist but the CIA itself!

Such an anti-CIA mindset is both unfortunate for the country and highly inappropriate to the crucial work that is carried out by the agency. Although there are no doubt occasional breeches of good conduct and unwise decisions, for the most part the tens of thousands of people who work for the CIA do so at the cost of significant personal sacrifice and often in the face of great danger. Criticism of the CIA or its activities in general has a destructive effect on the nation because it undermines the morale of CIA

---

138. "Our Missile-Defense Race Against Iran," *Wall Street Journal* (Sept. 21, 2009), A19.

employees who often perform extremely dangerous tasks at great personal sacrifice, largely out of devotion to protecting the nation. It also creates an atmosphere in which it is more difficult for the agency to recruit employees and carry on its work.

Opposition to the CIA *as a general attitude of mind* or a general policy position runs contrary to the very ability of the nation to defend itself; it is therefore opposition to the United States itself.

Of course, it is necessary that Congress have some oversight of the activities of the CIA and related intelligence agencies, all of which are part of the executive branch and ultimately report to the President. But too often congressional oversight has led to damaging leaks of information (from anti-CIA congressmen or their staff members), leaks that have been destructive to the CIA's ability to protect national security and have actually hampered the CIA in fulfilling its tasks.

Christians who believe it is right, according to Romans 13 and 1 Peter 2, for nations to defend their citizens should be supportive of the CIA in general rather than being instinctively critical of activities about which they actually know very little.

I. COERCIVE INTERROGATION OF PRISONERS

What should the policy of a government be regarding what the press commonly calls the "torture" of captured prisoners? This question has been the focus of significant debate in the United States as a result of the terrorist attacks of 9/11 and the subsequent capture of al-Qaeda operatives who were thought to have information about plans for future attacks in the US and elsewhere.

The discussion has been made more difficult by lack of clarity in definition of terms, especially the word "torture." Some people think "torture" means extreme measures like cutting off a person's fingers or toes or gouging out an eye. Others think that merely shouting at a prisoner is torture, or waking him up from a sound sleep for more questioning under a bright light. In ordinary English today, "torture" can be used very broadly, as in, "Listening to that boring sermon for thirty minutes this morning was sheer *torture!*"

When a word has this many different meanings, it becomes difficult to use the word in a way that does not confuse at least some hearers. Ethicist Daniel Heimbach rightly criticized a statement on torture issued by the National Association of Evangelicals on March 11, 2007, by noting, "While it loudly renounces 'torture,' it nowhere—in 18 pages of posturing—defines what signers of the document claim so vehemently to reject."[139]

Therefore, in this section I will attempt to define explicitly what I am talking about, but I will try to avoid the word "torture" unless I specify clearly what is meant or when I am directly quoting others. The word's wide variety of meanings only confuses the discussion.

---

139. "Ethicist: NAE torture declaration 'irrational,'" *Baptist Press* online edition (March 15, 2007). www.sbcbaptistpress. org/BPnews.asp?ID=25190 (accessed Oct. 29, 2009).

Former presidential candidate Senator John McCain, who had himself endured severe torture that caused permanent physical harm as a prisoner in North Vietnam, insisted that the US policy should be "no torture, ever."[140] He said, "One of the things that kept us going when I was in prison in North Vietnam was that we knew that if the situation were reversed, we would not be doing to our captors what they were doing to us."[141] His amendment prohibiting any "cruel, inhuman, or degrading" treatment of prisoners passed the US Senate by a vote of 90–9 in 2005.[142]

But under questioning, McCain admitted he did not intend this prohibition to be absolute! When asked what to do if we captured a terrorist who had planted an atomic bomb that was set to go off in New York City, he responded, "You have to do what you have to do. But you take responsibility for it."[143] So the language of the amendment allowed *no exceptions,* but McCain himself admitted *there had to be exceptions.* This is inconsistent. Worse than that, even if a president authorizes extreme coercive measures and extracts the location of the bomb, and a bomb squad then diffuses it and saves thousands of lives, that same president and everyone who participated in the questioning of the terrorist would later be subject to prosecution and imprisonment for violating McCain's amendment. Given the power of pacifist and anti-violence lobbying groups in the United States, it is nearly certain that some prosecuting attorney could be persuaded that such prosecutions should go forward "so that it will be clear to the world that we will always take the high moral ground and never torture anyone, and those who do will be held accountable." Therefore Senator McCain's position is contradictory and would ultimately prove to be vindictive against those who are most responsible for protecting the nation from attack.

What, then, should the US policy be? My own conclusion is that we should have a standard policy, but with some carefully defined exceptions.

1. Standard policy

The standard policy of the United States regarding the treatment of prisoners of war should be one of humane treatment that exhibits compassion and care in accordance with the Geneva Conventions of 1949. These policies for the proper treatment of prisoners captured in wartime say in part:

> Protected persons are entitled, in all circumstances, to respect for their persons, their honour, their family rights, their religious convictions and practices, and their manners and customs. They shall at all times be humanely treated, and

---

140. John McCain: quoted in Charles Krauthammer, "The Truth about Torture," *Weekly Standard* (Dec. 5, 2005). http://weeklystandard.com/Content/Public/Articles/000/000/006/400rhqav.asp.

141. Marc Santora, "McCain Finds Sympathy on Torture Issue," *New York Times* (Nov. 16, 2007). www.nytimes.com/2007/11/16/us/politics/15cnd-.mccain.html?ex=1352869200&en=73fdf47bcf1916b9&ei=5088&partner=rssnyt&emc=rss

142. Charles Babington and Shailagh Murray, "Senate Supports Interrogation Limits," *Washington Post* (Oct. 6, 2005). www.washingtonpost.com/wp-dyn/content/article/2005/10/05/AR2005100502062.html.

143. Evan Thomas and Michael Hirsh, "The Debate Over Torture," *Newsweek* (Nov. 21, 2005). www.newsweek.com/id/51198.

shall be protected especially against all acts of violence or threats thereof and against insults and public curiosity. Women shall be especially protected against any attack on their honour, in particular against rape, enforced prostitution, or any form of indecent assault. Without prejudice to the provisions relating to their state of health, age and sex, all protected persons shall be treated with the same consideration by the Party to the conflict in whose power they are, without any adverse distinction based, in particular, on race, religion or political opinion. However, the Parties to the conflict may take such measures of control and security in regard to protected persons as may be necessary as a result of the war.[144]

Such humane treatment of prisoners of war is entirely consistent with the purpose of keeping such prisoners in confinement, for the purpose should not be *to punish them* (for they were breaking no law by merely serving in the army of their country) but simply *to prevent them from re-engaging in war against the United States* as long as that war is going on. Therefore their confinement should not include any measures whose primary purpose would be to cause them suffering or pain.

Abraham Lincoln concluded his Second Inaugural Address with this kind of spirit, which exemplifies well what the United States has so long stood for:

> With malice toward none; with charity for all; with firmness in the right, as God gives us to see the right, let us strive on to finish the work we are in; to bind up the nation's wounds; to care for him who shall have borne the battle, and for his widow, and his orphan—to do all which may achieve and cherish a just and lasting peace, among ourselves, and with all nations.[145]

Such a policy is consistent with Jesus' command, "Love your enemies" (Matt. 5:44). Such treatment of enemy soldiers also holds up for any foe and for all the world a standard of moral conduct that takes the "high road" and exemplifies what is so good about our nation. We will defend ourselves when attacked, as governments have an obligation before God to do, but we will not be vindictive against those who are defeated. (In a similar spirit, the United States helped to rebuild both Germany and Japan, its defeated enemies, after World War II.)

2. Exceptions

Should there be any exceptions to this policy?

When someone enters the United States to carry out a terrorist attack, that person forfeits the status of prisoner-of-war for two reasons: (1) he is deliberately attacking civilians, and (2) he is fighting out of uniform (since he is trying to disguise himself as

---

144. Convention (IV) relative to the Protection of Civilian Persons in Time of War, Part III: Status and Treatment of Protected Persons, Geneva (12 Aug. 1949). www.icrc.org/ihl.nsf/FULL/380?OpenDocument.

145. Abraham Lincoln Second Inaugural Address (March 4, 1865). www,bartleby.com/124/pres32.html.

an innocent civilian). Therefore, according to international law, *he is not entitled to the protections of the Geneva Conventions.*

How should the United States treat a captured terrorist, especially when it has strong reason to believe the terrorist has planned a future terrorist attack against it or has detailed knowledge about a future attack? Newspaper columnist Charles Krauthammer has called this the "ticking time bomb" problem.[146]

The moral and legal status of this terrorist is different because he is still *currently* engaged in the immoral and illegal process of concealing information that could save thousands of lives from terrible destruction—that is, he is *currently* complicit in mass murder on an unimaginable scale. The moral question in this case is whether the US government has a moral right to use less-than-humane treatment, including treatment that causes discomfort and even significant pain, *in order to attempt to compel the terrorist to do what is morally right*, namely, to disclose the location of the ticking bomb or the identities and locations of those planning to carry out the future evil attack.

In such cases I think the US government has a right—even a moral obligation—*within specified limits*, to use such compulsion. Not to do this would be to completely fail in the government's God-given responsibility to "rescue the weak and the needy" and to "deliver them from the hand of the wicked" (Ps. 82:4). It would also utterly fail in its responsibility to "bear the sword" as a "servant of God" to be a "terror" to evildoers and thus protect its citizens from attack (Rom. 13:3–4).

Someone might object that the *terrorist* thinks it is *morally wrong* to reveal his plans to murder thousands of civilians. He thinks he is morally right to carry out his terrorist attack! Who am I to say that his plans are morally wrong? Pastor-author Greg Boyd argues along these lines when he says to Americans:

> You probably passionately believe that our cause is just, and theirs is evil, but the terrorists passionately believe that their cause is just and ours is evil. Your passion for American justice is mirrored by their passion for Islamic justice.[147]

My response is that there is a clear moral difference. The Islamic terrorists' actions are clearly morally wrong, because (1) their war is contrary to the historic standards for a just war in that its purpose is to conquer other nations and impose Islamic law (see pp. 389–90 above), and (2) they are intentionally targeting innocent civilians, which is contrary to the Bible's standards for the conduct of war (see p. 390) and contrary to international law. In 2004 the Security Council of the United Nations said, "The Security Council reaffirms its strong condemnation of all acts of violence targeting civilians or other protected persons under international law."[148] Boyd has lost all sense of moral compass when he sees Islamic terrorist attacks and American defense against those attacks as morally equivalent. He is simply wrong.

---

146. Krauthammer, "The Truth about Torture," op. cit.
147. Boyd, *The Myth of a Christian Nation*, 25.
148. "In Presidential Statement, Security Council Reaf- firms Strong Condemnation of Violence Targeting Civilians in Armed Combat," United Nations Press Release SC/8267 (Dec. 14, 2004). www.un.org/News/Press/docs/2004/sc8267.doc.htm.

But what about taking the "high moral ground"? Critics of enhanced interrogation techniques argue that if we inflict pain to extract information, it will cause us harm in terms of world opinion—other nations will cease to respect us. But they fail to recognize that what our terrorist enemies respect is not timidity and weakness, but courage and superior strength. It is not pampering captured terrorists but rather the use of superior military force and intelligence that will defeat hardened al-Qaeda terrorists. The "high moral ground" must certainly exclude doing things that are always morally wrong (see the next section), but it also must surely include doing everything we can to defend our nation from attack. What our allies also respect *and depend on us for* is to use our strength to protect ourselves *and them* from terrorist attacks when we are able to do so.

3. Inherently evil actions should be prohibited in all circumstances, without exceptions

However, there still must clearly be limits to what a government should be allowed to do in *any* situation, no matter what ticking time bomb scenario arises. Even if *some* infliction of pain would be morally right (under circumstances and limits that I describe below), no agency of government should *ever* be allowed:

(1) To commit actions that are in themselves always immoral, such as raping a prisoner;
(2) To deny medical treatment;
(3) To carry out the sadistic humiliation of prisoners such as what occurred at Abu Ghraib prison in Iraq (which had nothing to do with intelligence gathering, and for which the military persons responsible were punished);[149]
(4) To attempt to force a prisoner to violate the religious convictions that he has *that pose no threat to the United States or its defense* (for example, it would be wrong to give a Muslim prisoner only pork to eat or only alcoholic beverages to drink, so as to force him to sin against his religion or starve to death);
(5) To carry out any actions that would "shock the conscience" of a US court, such as doing anything that would cause lasting physical damage to the prisoner. This would include cutting off fingers or toes, gouging out eyes, branding someone's face, or twisting and binding limbs so severely as to cause permanent disability of the type that Senator McCain has from his imprisonment in North Vietnam (he cannot raise his arms above his shoulders).

None of these actions serve any valid purpose in obtaining the needed information when it could be more readily obtained by inflicting bodily pain (within the moral limits described below) in a way that does no long-term damage.

---

149. Regarding the Abu Ghraib controversy, see, for example,
www.globalsecurity.org/intell/world/iraq/abu-ghurayb-prison.
htm (Jan. 5, 2006).

4. What kind of means of coercion?

What kind of infliction of pain do I mean in these exceptional cases? I can give two personal examples, both of which are quite minor but may clarify what I mean. When our children were young and would engage in actions of willful disobedience, my wife or I would sometimes use a quick "shoulder squeeze." This was squeezing the trapezius muscle that runs between the shoulder and the neck. It hurts! And it was an effective means of discipline with no physical damage.

When my sons were in high school, I paid the fees for them to take martial arts classes for self-defense (in this case, Tae Kwon Do). After a few weeks they wanted to demonstrate what they had learned about certain "pressure points" in the human body. So I volunteered, and I soon learned that by merely pressing their thumb firmly against a certain point in my back, for example, they could cause immense pain. I ended the demonstration!

These are minor examples, but skilled military interrogators would no doubt be able to inflict even more acute pain in various ways (and I suppose they would find my examples humorous and trivial—but I am just making the point that real pain can be inflicted without causing lasting physical damage).

I cannot see any biblical basis for prohibiting governments from using these and similar means of inflicting pain—even much more significant pain—on a terrorist in order to coerce him into revealing the location of a hidden time bomb that will soon go off. (Some of the stress positions and confinement used in the CIA's enhanced interrogation procedures would achieve this.) In Proverbs, the disciplining of children with "the rod" (which caused pain but not lasting damage) was required: "Whoever spares the rod hates his son, but he who loves him is diligent to discipline him" (Prov. 13:24; see also 22:15; 23:13–14; 29:15). So how can there be moral objection to *all* infliction of pain to attempt to compel a right action?

A related issue is the injection of Sodium Pentathol, commonly called "truth serum." It tends to reduce a person's inhibitions and make him more willing to talk with interrogators. It has also been widely used in previous years as an anesthetic for surgery. I see no moral objection to the use of this or similar drugs in exceptional cases to obtain valuable information about terrorist attacks.

What about "waterboarding"? This involves holding a prisoner down so that his head is lower than the rest of his body while he faces up. Then a cloth is put over his nose and mouth, and water is poured over the cloth, giving the prisoner a sensation of drowning. For a number of years this same process has been used on thousands of US troops in giving them Survival Evasion Resistance Escape (SERE) training to resist an enemy if captured, and this has been done "with the full knowledge of Congress."[150]

Waterboarding was the most controversial of the "enhanced interrogation methods" used in questioning of al-Qaeda terrorists under the Bush administration. According to Victoria Toensing, former chief counsel for the Senate Intelligence Committee, the

150. David B. Rivkin Jr. and Lee A. Casey, "The Memos Prove We Didn't Torture," *Wall Street Journal* (April 20, 2009), A15.

US Senate in September 2006 rejected, by a vote of 53–46, an amendment that would have made waterboarding illegal.[151] So the US Senate refused to prohibit it. However, President Obama completely prohibited it in an executive order on his second full day in office in January 2009.[152]

This procedure does not seem to me to be inherently morally wrong. It inflicts pain and a feeling of panic, and apparently it is very persuasive in getting a terrorist to reveal hidden information. When used within appropriate guidelines, it causes no permanent damage. (US interrogators were given specific limitations to prevent water from getting into the person's lungs and prevent any lasting physical damage.)

Daniel Heimbach, former deputy undersecretary of the Navy and now an ethics professor, formulates some "just war" criteria that would prescribe limits on the use of coercion in interrogation:

> [Charles] Krauthammer's appeal to the principles of proportionality (no more force than necessary), right intent (only to obtain necessary information and nothing more), last resort (only when no other means will work), competent authority (only with authorization from cabinet-level political authority), and no evil means (no sick sadomasochism) are certainly apropos.
>
> In fact, we should go beyond Krauthammer to also consider other just-war principles such as just cause (only to correct injustice), comparative justice (only if stakes on our side are more worthy than stakes on theirs), probability of success (only if good reason to believe the one interrogated actually knows important information), proportionality of projected results (only if information needed is worth more than what it costs to obtain), right spirit (only with regret), and good faith (never breaking promises).... after setting proper boundaries for moral use, we should without apology defend [the] obligation to exercise justified coercion within proper restraints.[153]

5. But does it work?

Critics of waterboarding and similar enhanced interrogation methods sometimes point to "expert" academic opinions arguing that "torture never works" and that the prisoner will make up all sorts of lies just to bring the pain to an end. But the facts of recent history show that argument to be incorrect.

Former CIA director Michael Hayden and former US Attorney General Michael Mukasey disclosed publicly on April 17, 2009, that the coercive interrogation techniques used on al-Qaeda operatives brought very significant results:

---

151. Victoria Toensing, "Critics Still Haven't Read the 'Torture' Memos," *Wall Street Journal* (May 19, 2009); Martin Kady II, "Mukasey, GOP Waffle on Waterboarding," *Politico.com* (Oct. 31, 2007), www.politico.com/news/stories/1007/6660.html.

152. Executive Order, Ensuring Lawful Interrogations (Jan. 22, 2009). www.whitehouse.gov/the_press_office/Ensuring_Lawful_Interrogations.

153. Daniel R. Heimbach, "Untitled Essay on Torture," n.p. http://evangelicaloutpost.com/archives/2005/12/daniel-r-heimbach.html. For Krauthammer's column, see www.weeklystandard.com/Content/Public/Articles/000/000/006/400rhqav.asp.

As a result of such coercive methods, terrorist Abu Zubaydah disclosed information that led to the capture of Ramzi bin al Shibh, another of the planners of Sept. 11, who in turn disclosed information which ... helped to lead to the capture of KSM [Khalid Sheikh Mohammed, mastermind of 9/11 attacks] and other senior terrorists, and the disruption of follow-on plots aimed at both Europe and the U.S.[154]

Far from being secret, details of these methods and their results were widely known in Congress, and there was no congressional action to prohibit them:

Details of these successes, and the methods used to obtain them, were disclosed repeatedly in more than 30 congressional briefings and hearings beginning in 2002.... Any protestation of ignorance of those details, particularly by members of those committees, is pretense. The techniques themselves were used selectively against only a small number of hard-core prisoners who successfully resisted other forms of interrogation, and then only with the explicit authorization of the director of the CIA.... as late as 2006 ... *fully half of the government's knowledge about the structure and activities of al Qaeda came from these interrogations.*[155]

William McSwain, a lawyer and former Marine who was deeply involved in Defense Department reviews of these techniques, wrote:

It is doubtful that any high-level al Qaeda operative would ever provide useful intelligence in response to traditional methods [of interrogation]. Yet KSM and Zubaydah provided critical information after being waterboarded—information that ... helped to prevent a "Second Wave" attack in Los Angeles.[156]

In other words, these enhanced interrogation techniques *worked remarkably well*. The claim that they "don't work" is disproven by recent US history. Hayden and Mukasey say that the idea that these measures never work is an "ignorant view."[157] These techniques prevented several attacks and saved thousands of American and European lives. Any residents of Los Angeles, for example, who are still alive today because there was no second wave of attacks should be thankful that the government used them. *Not to have used them would have been morally wrong,* because it would have meant *having the ability to stop the murder of thousands and thousands of people* and not doing it. What could be a greater moral wrong for any government than this?

But in 2009 Attorney General Eric Holder began to threaten prosecutions against some Justice Department lawyers in the recent Bush administration who wrote internal memos arguing that such methods, within clear limits, were legal. He said, "We are going to follow the evidence, follow the law, and take that where it leads. No one is above

154. Michael Hayden and Michael B. Mukasey, "The President Ties His Own Hands on Terror," *Wall Street Journal* (April 17, 2009), A13.

155. Ibid., emphasis added.

156. William M. McSwain, "Misconceptions About the Interrogation Memos," *Wall Street Journal* (April 27, 2009), A15.

157. Ibid.

the law."[158] *Prosecutions* for writing a legal memo? For carrying out what the Justice Department's Office of Legal Counsel told the CIA was legal? This is a vindictive attempt by the highest legal officer in the nation to use the courts to bring retribution against people for holding a different opinion on a widely debated political question. It is an attempt to criminalize political differences after you have won an election—something done by Third World despots but deeply unworthy of the United States of America. It can only poison the political atmosphere in the country still further.

Such threats will also breed institutional timidity in the CIA and the Department of Justice, and eventually we will suffer more horrible attacks. Even if a future president reauthorizes such enhanced interrogation techniques in exceptional cases, how will the CIA and the Justice Department know that some future administration won't release all the details of what was done and then attempt to send those involved to prison? The "safe" route now will be for government officials to pamper terrorists, opening the country both to their contempt and to their future attacks.

J. HOMOSEXUALS IN THE MILITARY

The US military policy has always been that known homosexuals should not serve in the armed forces. The current enforcement of that policy has been called by the press "Don't ask, don't tell" because military officials are not allowed to launch an investigation of someone in the absence of some evidence indicating homosexual conduct or intent.

The actual wording of the policy is this:

> Sexual orientation will not be a bar to service unless manifested by homosexual conduct. The military will discharge members who engage in homosexual conduct, which is defined as a homosexual act, a statement that the member is homosexual or bisexual, or a marriage or attempted marriage to someone of the same gender.[159]

The current policy says that anyone who "demonstrate(s) a propensity or intent to engage in homosexual acts" will be prohibited from serving in the military. The reason is that "it would create an unacceptable risk to the high standards of morale, good order and discipline, and unit cohesion that are the essence of military capability."[160]

For reasons explained in an earlier chapter on marriage, I am convinced that homosexual conduct is contrary to the moral standards of the Bible (see pp. 217–19). Therefore I believe that Christians who follow the moral authority of the Bible should uphold the continuation of this policy. In addition, military personnel have repeatedly stated that inclusion of homosexuals in the armed forces harms combat preparedness and effectiveness. In her testimony before Congress, Elaine Donnelly of the Center for Military Readiness said:

158. Terry Frieden, " 'No One Is Above the Law,' Holder Says of Torture Inquiry," *CNN* (April 22, 2009). www.cnn.com/2009/POLITICS/04/22/torture.prosecution/index.html.

159. "Gay Rights in the Military; The Pentagon's New Policy Guidelines on Homosexuals in the Military," *New York Times*

(July 20, 1993). www.nytimes.com/1993/07/20/us/gay-rights-military-pentagon-s-new-policy-guidelines-homosexuals-military.html?sec=&spon=&pagewanted=all.

160. Ibid.

Repealing the 1993 law would be tantamount to forcing female soldiers to cohabit with men in intimate quarters, on all military bases and ships at sea, on a 24/7 basis. Stated in gender-neutral terms, forced cohabitation in military conditions that offer little or no privacy would force *persons* to live with *persons* who might be sexually attracted to them.

Inappropriate passive/aggressive actions common in the homosexual community, short of physical touching and assault, will be permitted in all military communities, to include Army and Marine infantry battalions, Special Operations Forces, Navy SEALS, and cramped submarines that patrol the seas for months at a time.

The ensuing sexual tension will hurt discipline and morale, but commanders will not have the power to improve the situation. Individuals whose beliefs and feelings about sexuality are violated by the new policy will have no recourse. The only option will be to avoid or leave the service. Forced cohabitation with homosexuals in the military, 24/7, would be unfair, demoralizing, and harmful to the culture of the volunteer force, on which our national security depends.[161]

One thousand military officers sent a letter to President Obama asking him to maintain the Don't Ask, Don't Tell policy, stating that abolishing it "would undermine recruiting and retention, impact leadership at all levels, have adverse effects on the willingness of parents who lend their sons and daughters to military service, and eventually break the All-Volunteer Force."[162]

Among the signatories were General Carl E. Mundy Jr., a former commandant of the Marine Corps; Admiral Leighton W. Smith, a former commander of US Naval Forces Europe; General Charles A. Horner, who commanded US aerial forces during the 1990–91 Gulf War; and Admiral Jerome L. Johnson, a former vice chief of Naval Operations.

Unfortunately, President Obama, in his State of the Union Address on January 27, 2010, called for an end to the current policy so as to allow homosexuals to serve openly in the US military. He said, "This year, I will work with Congress and our military to finally repeal the law that denies gay Americans the right to serve the country they love because of who they are."[163] A few days later, on February 2, Chairman of the Joint Chiefs of Staff Admiral Michael Mullen said he favored including homosexuals in the military. He did add, "That there will be some disruption in the force I cannot deny." He also said, "That there will be legal, social and perhaps even infrastructure changes to be made certainly seem plausible."[164] This is despite the fact that when the troops were surveyed by the Military Officers Association of America, they said, by a 2–1 margin,

161. Testimony of Elaine Donnelly before the House Armed Services Personnel Subcommittee (July 23, 2008). http://armedservices.house.gov/pdfs/MilPers072308/Donnelly_Testimony072308.pdf.

162. David Crary, "Retired Military Officers: Keep Ban on Gays," Associated Press (March 31, 2009). www.guardian.co.uk/world/feedarticle/8431955.

163. President Barack Obama, State of the Union Address

(Jan. 27, 2010). www.whitehouse.gov/the-press-office/remarks-president-state-union-address.

164. Gregg Zoroya, "Mullen Says Repealing Gay Military Ban Is 'Right Thing to Do,'" *USA Today* (Feb. 2, 2010). www.usatoday.com/news/washington/2010–02–01-gay-ban-military_N.htm?csp=34&utm_source=feedburner&utm_medium=feed&utm_campaign=Feed%3A+usatoday-NewsTopStories+(News+-+Top+Stories).

that the armed forces should have an even stronger policy against homosexuals in military service.[165] The MOAA survey also found that 68% of respondents believe that repeal of the law would have a very negative effect (48%) or moderately negative effect (20%) on troop morale and military readiness.[166] I believe this is exactly the wrong policy to pursue. The final decision in this matter will be left to Congress.

K. WOMEN IN COMBAT

Historically the position of the United States has been that women should never be sent into combat. Women could serve in other capacities in the armed forces, but not in responsibilities where they were likely to engage in combat. In the last thirty years there has been pressure to change that policy, and we already have some women serving as fighter pilots in Afghanistan. The first female fighter pilots were employed in Kosovo in 1993, and the first woman who joined the Navy specifically to be a pilot did so in 1981.[167]

I believe that the historic position of the United States is correct and that it is wrong to send women into combat. The biblical argument for this position is expressed well in the *ESV Study Bible* article on "War":

Most nations throughout history, and most Christians in every age, have held that fighting in combat is a responsibility that should fall only to men, and that it is contrary to the very idea of womanhood, and shameful for a nation, to have women risk their lives as combatants in a war. The assumption that only men and not women will fight in battle is also a frequent pattern in the historical narratives and is affirmed by leaders and prophets in the OT (see Num. 1:2–3; Deut. 3:18–19; 20:7–8; 24:5; Josh. 1:14; 23:10; Judg. 4:8–10; 9:54; 1 Sam. 4:9; Neh. 4:13–14; Jer. 50:37; Nah. 3:13).[168]

165. Grace Vuoto, "Is Obama Administration Listening to the Troops?" *Washington Times* (July 30, 2009). www.cmrlink.org/CMRDocuments/WT070309.pdf.

166. Ibid.

167. "Women Fighter Pilots Flying Combat Missions over Afghanistan with Little or No Fanfare," Associated Press (Oct. 23, 2001). www.military.com/Content/MoreContent?file=FL_womenpilots_102301.

168. *ESV Study Bible*, "War," p. 2555.

Chapter 12

FOREIGN POLICY

How should the government of a nation relate to the other nations of the world?

What should be the goals of the foreign policy of a nation?

Is it right for the United States to try to promote freedom and democracy in other nations?

Should Israel be treated just the way we treat any other nation, or does Israel have some special status in the eyes of God?

What should be the policy of the United States regarding the immigration of people from other countries?

What should we do about illegal immigrants who are now in the United States?

A. BIBLICAL TEACHING

The biblical basis for foreign policy in a nation flows from our understanding of the purpose of government in general, as described in chapter 3 (see pp. 77–115), and the responsibility of government in particular to defend itself and its citizens against other nations, as discussed in chapter 11 (see pp. 388–89). The civil government is established by God to do "good" for its people, as God's "servant" (Rom. 13:4), and it should "praise those who do good" (1 Peter 2:14). It must also "punish those who do evil" (1 Peter 2:14), both to prevent wrongdoing and protect its citizens and also to act as God's "servant" who "carries out God's wrath on the wrongdoer" (Rom. 13:4).

Therefore the foreign policy of a nation must first of all work toward the goal of defending itself against attack or harm from other nations. As I argued in the previous chapter (pp. 396–99), it is appropriate for governments to form mutually beneficial alliances with other nations in order to further this purpose of defending themselves.

These considerations lead to several principles regarding foreign policy.

1. The foreign policy of a nation should serve to protect the sovereignty and independence of that nation and to protect and defend the interests of its citizens in their relationships with other countries

Protecting the sovereignty and independence of a nation serves the purpose of protecting it from conquest and oppressive domination by some other aggressive foreign country. As governments function to protect their own sovereignty, they also serve, in the wise providence of God, to protect the nations of the world from the horrible tyranny that would result from the dissolution of the sovereignty of individual nations and the establishment of one worldwide government. Such a government would have far too much power, which would lead to immense corruption in the government (since power nearly always corrupts; see p. 125 above); such corruption would then lead to a horrible kind of oppression from which there would be no place to flee.

2. Governments should seek to do good for other nations as they are able to do so

The command of Jesus, "You shall love your neighbor as yourself" (Matt. 22:39), gives warrant for thinking that nations should seek to do good for other nations insofar as they have opportunity to do so. A government's first obligation should be to defend and seek the good of its own citizens, but it can often bring positive influences to other nations without significantly hindering that primary goal.

Such positive influence can come through diplomatic negotiation. It can also come through cultural exchanges, educational exchanges, commercial relationships, and fair and honest media reporting about events in other nations. Another means is military alliances, as I discussed in chapter 11 (see pp. 396–99). In addition, nations can sometimes help other countries through foreign aid of various sorts, as discussed in the section below.

The United States carries out, I suppose, hundreds of unheralded activities that bring benefit to the world as a whole. One example is protecting the sea lanes of the world from piracy or from one nation's ships attacking the merchant or passenger ships of another nation. It is primarily the US Navy that keeps the sea lanes of the world free in this way, a fact that is seldom known. Thomas Keaney, acting director of the Strategic Studies at the Paul H. Nitzke School of Advanced International Studies at Johns Hopkins University, writes:

> Oceans and other waterways have long figured prominently in commercial
> activity, transportation routes and, ultimately, warfare. Even in an age of air,

space and cyberspace, the sea remains the prime mode of transportation of goods worldwide, and thus vital to the world's economies—access to oil supplies serves as the key example of this dependence.

For the United States, concerns for the security of international trade, energy supplies and even fishing rights have played a prominent part in its history and have led to two parallel interests advocated by U.S. policymakers through the years. The first is the promotion of freedom of the seas for commerce and international trade. The second is the impulse to build a powerful navy to protect those activities. Those interests continue today in a world of globalized trade networks, as the United States has extended itself to assure freedom of the seas for international trade on a worldwide basis. It is a mission of enormous responsibilities and consequences.

While the United States has committed itself to the defense of freedom of the seas worldwide, it is not alone in its desire for free transit—all countries engaged in intercontinental trade or who import oil share that goal. Few countries other than the United States have any capability to defend the freedom of the seas for that trade.[1]

The continuation of piracy off the coast of Somalia is an aberration due to the absence of any legitimate governmental authority in Somalia and the ambiguities of international law in the ocean next to Somalia because of that situation. According to France 24/7, the country's national news service, "Somalia's transitional government has very little real authority.... Experts and military personnel have been saying that policing the seas to stop pirates simply won't work as long as Somalia remains a lawless country. It's been without an effective government since the fall of Siad Barre [the former president of Somalia] 17 years ago."[2]

Another benefit the United States provides has been the maintenance of the Internet system for the benefit of the entire world. Until a few years ago, 70% of all Internet traffic sent between two locations passed through the United States. Recently, other governments have taken steps to maintain their own Internet systems.[3] In November 2005, scholars with the Heritage Foundation outlined the role the United States has played in maintaining the Internet and the reasons why other countries want to seize control or turn control over to the United Nations. They wrote:

> For decades, the Internet has developed with a minimum of government interference. The core governance of the medium has been performed by non-governmental entities and overseen by the U.S. government, which has exercised a light regulatory touch. It is no coincidence that the medium has prospered

1. Thomas Keaney, "Ruling the Waves: American Sea Power," Paul H. Nitzke School of Advanced International Studies at Johns Hopkins University, Washington DC (2008). www.sais-jhu.edu/pressroom/publications/saisphere/2008/keaney.htm.

2. "Somalia: A Failed State?" France 24/7 (Nov. 20, 2008).

www.france24.com/en/20081120-pirates-thrive-lawlessness-ethiopia-somalia.

3. John Markoff, "Internet Traffic Begins to Bypass the U.S.," New York Times (Aug. 30, 2008). www.nytimes.com/2008/08/30/business/30pipes.html?_r=3&oref=slogin&pagewanted=print.

from this benign neglect, growing from a research curiosity into a major force in the world economy and an invaluable venue for the exchange of information.

Most people appreciate this success as a convenience that makes their lives easier and their work more productive. However, the Internet represents something quite different to many foreign governments. Some, including members of the European Union, are frustrated by their inability to regulate or tax it as they desire. Others, such as China and Iran, see the Internet as a threat and are desperate to prevent their citizens from encountering ideas that might undermine their authority or communicating with foreigners. As a result, the United States is coming under increasing criticism that because the Internet is an international resource, no one country should control it.

The result of a UN-controlled and regulated Internet would be that non-democratic countries that oppose the right to free speech such as China and grasping, anti-market impulses like those of the European Union would have a greater voice in guiding the Internet in a direction away from "freedom, education, and innovation."[4]

A third benefit is that NASA's Earth Science Enterprise operates more than thirty earth-observation satellites, many in cooperation with other agencies and countries. These satellites provide images and data on many aspects of the earth's atmosphere, ocean, and land, including atmospheric temperature, moisture content, clouds, and precipitation.[5]

Still another benefit is the substantial role that the United States plays in the linking of telecommunication lines from various nations of the world. However, in 1992, President George H. W. Bush split the oversight and licensing jurisdiction of commercial satellites, allowing commercial communication satellites that do not incorporate advanced technologies to be exported as civil or commercial goods under the supervision of the Commerce Department.[6]

An additional benefit is allowing the United Nations headquarters to be in New York City and providing all the police and security protection required in the area surrounding the presence of representatives of so many nations. According to the US Mission to the United Nations,

> In accordance with its obligations under the United Nations Headquarters Agreement, the United States, as host country to the United Nations, is committed to assuring the safety and security of the United Nations Headquarters, the Permanent and Observer Missions accredited to the United Nations, and the members of the United Nations diplomatic community. This responsibility is one of the most important of our obligations, and is codified in United States

4. Brett D. Schaefer, John J. Tkacik Jr., and James L. Gattuso, "Keep the Internet Free of the United Nations," *Heritage Foundation WebMemo #904* (Nov. 2, 2005). www.heritage.org/Research/InternationalOrganizations/wm904.cfm.

5. George Abbey and Neal Lane, "United States Space Policy:

Challenges and Opportunities," American Academy of Arts and Sciences (2005), 4. www.amacad.org/publications/space-Policy.pdf.

6. Ibid., 8.

law under the Act for the Protection of Foreign Officials and Official Guests of the United States.[7]

(I realize that the United Nations does many things that are now contrary to the best interests of the United States and that hinder democracy and human rights around the world, so housing the UN is a mixed benefit!)

In addition, the United States gives massive amounts of both private and public aid to other nations and groups within other nations. According to a 2003 report by Lino J. Piedra, a member of the US Delegation to the United Nations Commission on Human Rights,

> In 2003, the United States was the origin of over seventy percent of all financial flows reaching developing countries from the G–7 developed world, through private investment, private philanthropy, public aid and private remittances. When net purchases of goods and services, private investment, private philanthropy, public aid and private remittances are all added together, the United States accounted for over $340 billion in financial flows to developing countries in 2003. Private remittances from the United States totaled almost $28 billion, while US aid accounted for almost one-third of all overseas development assistance from developed countries.[8]

3. The United States should seek to promote freedom and respect for human rights in other nations

Is it right for the United States to use noncoercive means such as diplomatic negotiations, cultural and educational exchanges, public relations strategies, media reporting, and foreign aid to attempt to promote greater human freedoms and human rights in other nations? To that question, it seems to me that the answer is certainly yes.

One objection should be addressed, however. Sometimes people object to trying to influence other countries, saying something like, "We should not impose our view of human rights and freedom on other nations." But this way of phrasing the matter is highly misleading. The word "impose" implies using military conquest to forcibly change the government of another nation. That is a "just war" question (see chap. 11, pp. 389–90), which is not the issue I am discussing here. I am talking about *influencing* another nation, not *imposing* anything.

The first reason I think we should try to *influence* nations positively for human freedom and human rights is that according to the moral standards found in the Bible, the promotion of human liberty within nations is a morally good thing (see chap. 3, pp. 91–95). Slavery and oppression are always viewed negatively in Scripture, while freedom is viewed positively (see Exod. 20:2; Lev. 25:10; Deut. 28:28–29, 33; Judg. 2:16–23; Isa. 61:1). Moreover, the Bible gives indirect but significant support to the

7. Security and Protective Services, United States Mission to the United Nations. http://usun.state.gov/about/host_aff/c32154.htm.

8. Statement by Lino J. Piedra, "Item 7: The Right to Development" (March 22, 2005). http://geneva.usmission.gov/humanrights/2005/0322Item7.htm.

idea that governments should be chosen by the people over whom they govern, and this implies the desirability of some kind of democracy (see the argument for this in chap. 3, pp. 105–9). Some kind of democracy gives greater accountability to rulers, helps prevent a misuse of power, and helps to guarantee that government will serve for the benefit of the people rather than for the benefit of the rulers, as Scripture says it should (Rom. 13:4; 1 Peter 2:13–14).

The Declaration of Independence, the document on which the existence of the Untied States is based, declares that we as a nation are committed to the idea that all human beings "are endowed by their Creator with certain unalienable rights," and that those rights include "life, liberty, and the pursuit of happiness." This means that the nation has declared as a founding belief the idea that human rights come ultimately from God ("their Creator"), that these rights can never be legitimately taken away (they are "unalienable rights"), and that one of those rights is the right to "liberty" or human freedom. Then the Declaration of Independence in the very next sentence says that governments are established among people "to secure these rights," and that governments that are set up should be "deriving their just powers from the consent of the governed," that is, by *some kind of democratic process* that elects or affirms governments in power.

In brief, the beginning of the Declaration of Independence declares that the United States as a nation is committed to the idea that God has given people the right to liberty and that governments are only valid *if they have the consent of the people* over whom they govern. This means that promotion of human freedom, human rights, and democratic government is consistent with the most foundational convictions of our nation.

A further reason why the United States should seek to increase human freedom and democracy in other nations is that this promotes the nation's self-interest. This is because *genuine democracies* are less likely than any other form of government to launch aggressive attacks against other countries, as was persuasively argued by Natan Sharansky in *The Case for Democracy*[9] (see the discussion of Sharansky and his idea of genuine democracies in chap. 3 above, p. 416). Thus, promoting human liberty and the rule of genuine democratic governments is a very effective way to promote world peace.

My conclusion, therefore, is that biblical moral standards, our Declaration of Independence, our own self-interest as a nation, and the promotion of world peace all argue that the United States should promote freedom and democracy wherever it is able to do so around the world. We should help our friends who similarly promote freedom and democracy. We should help to support forces within oppressive nations that are working for increased freedom and democracy. We should also oppose the enemies of freedom and democracy wherever we are able to do so.

For many years, one of the most effective means of doing this was through Voice of America, a radio network that transmitted radio broadcasts in dozens of languages that were heard by oppressed peoples in various nations of the world. But in the last two

9. Natan Sharansky, *The Case for Democracy: The Power of Freedom to Overcome Tyranny and Terror* (New York: Public Affairs, 2004).

decades or so, its budgets have been cut and the Voice of America has significantly curtailed its broadcasts. When we are increasing spending on everything else, why should we reduce our promotion of democracy and our explanations of what is good about America to counter its many critics? Have our government officials become hesitant about angering oppressive governments around the world?[10] According to Halle C. Dale of the Heritage Foundation, "Due to budget cuts and emphasis on the use of surrogate radio outlets, Voice of America does not send a single broadcast under its own name to the Middle East. And yet, an integral part of VOA's mission is to inform others about American society and US policy. In a world where anti-Americanism is rampant, that mission surely has not become obsolete."[11]

This is a tragic turn of events that gives one sign that the leadership of the United States has become confused about the fundamental values that are essential to the founding documents on which the very existence of our nation is based. Our leaders are confused about beliefs that are essential to our deepest values as a nation. Rather than being *embarrassed* about advocating freedom and democracy for all peoples of the earth, we should be *vastly expanding* the scope of the broadcasts both by radio and by Internet and through the use of any other media (such as documentary films, pamphlets, and books). We should be clearly and unashamedly promoting the values of freedom and genuine democracy to all nations of the world, especially to people living in countries hostile to these values, such as communist nations or nations with oppressive governments. We should be *unashamedly proclaiming* that a system of democracy that includes freedom of religion is far superior to any oppressive government that seeks to impose the Muslim faith and practices on entire populations.

In addition, if it is morally right and in our best interest to promote freedom and democracy, then we should do this through our use of all diplomatic channels (including the United Nations) and all of our foreign aid as well.

4. A mistaken policy of encouraging enemies and hindering friends

Unfortunately, President Obama's administration, rather than *helping* our friends who promote freedom and democracy and *opposing* our enemies who fight against freedom, began in various ways throughout 2009 to do exactly the opposite. They followed policies that seemed quite evidently to be *abandoning* our friends and *helping* our enemies. This can be seen with respect to several countries in different regions of the world.

In *Iran*, when President Ahmadinejad shamelessly stole the election on June 12, 2009, and courageous protestors took to the streets by the tens of thousands—no doubt hoping for support from the United States in the court of world opinion—President Obama remained indecisive and noncommittal. He merely said that he was "deeply troubled"

---

10. Kasie Hunt, "Voice of America Shifts Priorities," Associated Press (Feb. 23, 2007), www.foxnews.com/printer_friendly_wires/2007Feb23/0,4675,USVOACuts,00.html; "Former VOA Directors Appeal for Reversal of Plan to Reduce Network's Presence on the World's Radio Airwaves" (March 5, 2007), www.

publicdiplomacy.org/78.htm; Halle C. Dale, "Voices of America," *Heritage Foundation Commentary* (May 3, 2007), www.heritage.org/Press/Commentary/ed050307a.cfm.

11. Dale, "Voices of America."

but would "pursue a tough, direct dialogue between our two countries."[12] Yet he did nothing to voice immediate public support of the protestors, some of whom were killed. Jamie M. Fly, a former member of the National Security Council, wrote:

> By sanctioning the fraudulent re-election of [President] Ahmadinejad and overseeing the brutal crackdown underway in its aftermath, [Supreme Leader of Iran] Khamenei has revealed the true despotic nature of the regime he oversees. Additionally, Khamenei oversees Iran's support for Hezbollah, Shiite militias in Iraq, and the Taliban in Afghanistan, which has resulted in thousands of deaths, including those of many Americans. This man, now with the blood of his own people on his hands, is the person the Obama administration is attempting to curry favor with during this time of uncertainty in Iran."[13]

Thus President Obama abandoned the pro-democracy forces and allowed Ahmadinejad to retain power with no effective pressure from the United States. But Ahmadinejad is so deluded that he denies the Holocaust ever existed, saying, "They have created a myth today that they call the massacre of Jews and they consider it a principle above God, religions and the prophets,"[14] and he insists he is going to wipe Israel off the map.[15] So this opportunity to call for international sanctions against Iran's sham elections and its despotic regime was lost.

In *Latin America*, Fidel Castro's government in Cuba and Hugo Chavez's government in Venezuela are the two greatest threats to freedom and democracy in North and South America. Both Castro and Chavez are military dictators who send money and soldiers to other Latin American countries to attempt to destabilize their governments and bring them into the Cuba-Venezuela orbit of totalitarian states that incline toward socialism or communism (see chap. 11 above, p. 395).

As one expert on Latin America writes, "A Chavez-style takeover of institutions in Bolivia, Ecuador and Nicaragua has quashed political pluralism, free speech, and minority rights in those countries. There is now a heavy presence of Cuban state intelligence throughout the Venezuelan empire.... Argentina is also in his [Chavez's] sights."[16]

But President Obama simply took steps to endorse the continued legitimacy of these governments and gave no help for any democratic opposition within those countries. After he took office, he promised a "new beginning" with Cuba, lifting restrictions on travel, commerce, and mail to that nation.[17]

President Obama has failed again and again to give public support to democratic movements within oppressive countries. Daniel Henninger, deputy director of the *Wall Street Journal* editorial page, wrote:

---

12. Jamie M. Fly, "Obama's Iran Election Ineptitude Worsens Nuclear Threat," *U.S. News and World Report* (June 19, 2009). www.usnews.com/articles/opinion/2009/06/19/obamas-iran-election-ineptitude-worsens-nuclear-threat.html.

13. Ibid.

14. "Iranian Leader Denies Holocaust," *BBCNews.com* (Dec. 14, 2005). http://news.bbc.co.uk/2/hi/middle_east/4527142.stm.

15. Ibid.

16. Mary Anastasia O' Grady, "Anti-American Amigos," *Wall Street Journal* (Aug. 27, 2009), A9.

17. Jake Tapper and Emily Friedman, "Obama Deals with Cuba, Venezuela—as Chavez Gives Him Book Assailing U.S.," *ABCNews.com* (April 18, 2009). http://abcnews.go.com/Politics/story?id=7370989&page=1.

If the Obama team wanted to make a really significant break from past Bush policy, it would say it was not going to just talk with the world's worst strongmen but would give equal, public status to their democratic opposition groups. Instead, the baddest actors in the world get face time with Barack Obama, but their struggling opposition gets invisibility.

Iran's extraordinary and brave popular opposition, which broke out again this week at two universities, seems to have earned these pro-democracy Iranians nothing in the calculations of U.S. policy....

In July, Mr. Obama made a historic journey to Africa, giving a widely praised speech in Ghana in support of self-help and self-determination. In August, Secretary of State Hillary Clinton grandly visited seven African nations with a similar message. Three days ago in Guinea, government troops fired on a pro-democracy rally estimated at 50,000 in the capital of Conakry, killing more than 150 people. The State Department got out a written statement of condemnation. Why is it not possible for President Obama or Secretary of State Clinton, having encouraged these aspirations, to speak publicly in their defense, rather than let democratic movements rise, fall and die?

In trying to plumb why the U.S. won't promote or protect its own best idea, one starts with Mr. Obama's remarks at the "reset" visit in Moscow: "America cannot and should not seek to impose any system of government on any other country, nor would we presume to choose which party or individual should run a country."

Setting aside that no one is talking about the U.S. literally "imposing" a government in this day and age, what is one to make of a left-of-center American political leader taking such a diffident stance toward democratic movements? The people who live under the sway of the top dog in all the nations that have earned high-level Obama envoys are the world's poor, and one would expect the social-justice left to support them. That may no longer be true on the American or European left....

Our dictator chat partners are getting brazen about staging and then rigging elections. Iran's mullahs proved there will be no sustained push-back from the U.S. or Western Europe to a fraudulent election. Instead the great powers' energies go into pounding tiny Honduras, which tried to save itself from the Chávez- and Castro-admiring Manuel Zelaya.

What if the world's real democrats, after enough bullets and dungeon time, lose belief in the American democracy's support for them on this central idea? They may come to regard their betters in the U.S. and Europe as inhabiting a world less animated by democratic belief than democratic decadence.[18]

---

18. Daniel Henninger, "Obama, Dictators, and Democrats," *Wall Street Journal* (Oct. 1, 2009), A21. http://online.wsj.com/article/SB10001424052748704471504574444890430083018.html. Reprinted by permission of *The Wall Street*

With regard to *China*, President Obama has raised not even a whisper of protest against increasing harassment and imprisonment of leaders of the house church movement, a loose network of evangelical, Bible-believing churches that have remained independent of government registration and control, despite pleas from human rights groups to do so.[19] In fact, he refused to meet with the Dalai Lama when he visited Washington, DC, breaking a precedent set by former presidents.[20] Before a visit to China in February 2009, Secretary of State Hillary Rodham Clinton said advocacy for human rights could not "interfere with the global economic crisis, the global climate-change crisis and the security crisis."[21]

By contrast, President George W. Bush visibly and publicly expressed his support for the house-church movement when he was in China, thus giving significant support and encouragement to the Christians who were leading these meetings and seeking to gain greater freedom and protection from the Chinese government. In an interview with NBC's Bob Costas, President Bush said, "I went to church here, and I'm sure the cynics say, 'Well, you know, it was just a state-sponsored church,' ... and that's true. On the other hand, it gave me a chance to say to the Chinese people, 'Religion won't hurt you; you ought to welcome religious people.' And it gave me a chance to say to the government, 'Why don't you register the underground churches and give them a chance to flourish?'"[22]

What about other nations that are actually encouraging democracy? President Obama and the Democrats in Congress have made life hard for these friends. Congress has repeatedly refused—even before Obama took office—to ratify an excellent free-trade agreement that would help the nation of *Colombia*, which has courageously overcome much of its drug-trafficking problem under the leadership of strongly pro-American president Alvaro Uribe.[23] And so the United States has abandoned the poor farmers of Colombia, one of our closest allies, making it impossible for them to export agricultural products to us at a competitive price and essentially refusing to open our huge market to them. This refusal to ratify the agreement was due to the opposition of the US labor unions, strong supporters of Democratic candidates, who did not want more trade with Colombia even though there would be considerable economic benefit to both nations. The *Wall Street Journal* editorial board writes, "The U.S. failure to get this deal done is a long-running travesty," and points to the primary culprit as House Speaker Nancy Pelosi, who is giving in to pressure from labor union leaders.[24]

In *Honduras*, the term of President Manuel Zelaya was going to expire in January 2010. The constitution of Honduras limits presidents to one term. But Zelaya, with the encouragement and financial support of Hugo Chavez in Venezuela, decided to call for a referen-

19. Penny Starr, "Obama Should Address Human Rights Abuses during Trip to China, Group Says," *CNSNews.com* (Nov. 11, 2009). www.cnsnews.com/news/article/56958.

20. James Pomfret, "Obama's Meeting with Dalai Lama Delayed," *Washington Post* (Oct. 5, 2009). www.washingtonpost.com/wp-dyn/content/article/2009/10/04/AR2009100403262_pf.html.

21. Ibid.

22. "Bush Attends Church in China," *Baptist News Service* (Aug. 11, 2008). www.bpnews.net/bpnews.asp?id=28660&ref=BPNews-RSSFeed0811.

23. Henninger, "Obama, Dictators, and Democrats."

24. "Southern Discomfort," *Wall Street Journal* (June 27, 2009), A12.

dum to rewrite the constitution so that he could seek a second term. The Honduran courts then determined that to be an illegal activity, and when he persisted in attempting to hold this referendum—even flying in ballots that been printed in Venezuela—the Supreme Court in Honduras ordered him removed from office.[25]

The Honduras military forces then forcibly removed President Zelaya. Governmental power, including the office of president, was lawfully taken over by Roberto Micheletti, a man from Zelaya's own political party, who was selected by the Congress in a process that followed Honduran law.

Therefore it seemed as though Honduras had successfully resisted the attempts of Chavez to subvert its freedom and establish a Chavez-controlled president for years to come. This should have been wonderful news for freedom-loving people everywhere. This was also the conclusion of respected Roman Catholic Oscar Rodriguez Maradiaga, who was joined by all the Roman Catholic bishops in Honduras in stating that the removal of Zelaya was lawful according to Honduran law and that democratic processes were continuing to function. Miguel Estrada, a Honduran native who had been nominated to the US Court of Appeals by President Bush but was denied confirmation by Senate liberals because of his conservative views, reported that all of this was legal, writing:

> Something clearly has gone awry with the rule of law in Honduras—but it is not necessarily what you think. Begin with Zelaya's arrest. The Supreme Court of Honduras, as it turns out, had ordered the military to arrest Zelaya two days earlier. A second order (issued on the same day) authorized the military to enter Zelaya's home to execute the arrest. These orders were issued at the urgent request of the country's attorney general. They make for interesting reading.
>
> What you'll learn is that the Honduran Constitution may be amended in any way except three. No amendment can ever change (1) the country's borders, (2) the rules that limit a president to a single four-year term and (3) the requirement that presidential administrations must "succeed one another" in a "republican form of government."
>
> In addition, Article 239 specifically states that any president who so much as proposes the permissibility of re-election "shall cease forthwith" in his duties, and Article 4 provides that any "infraction" of the succession rules constitutes treason. The rules are so tight because these are terribly serious issues for Honduras, which lived under decades of military rule.
>
> Zelaya is the type of leader who could cause a country to wish for a Richard Nixon. Earlier this year, with only a few months left in his term, he ordered a referendum on whether a new constitutional convention should convene to write a wholly new constitution. Because the only conceivable motive for such a convention would be to amend the unamendable parts of the existing constitution, it was easy to conclude—as virtually everyone in Honduras did—that this

25. "The Wages Chavismo," *Wall Street Journal* (July 1, 2009), A12.

was nothing but a backdoor effort to change the rules governing presidential succession.[26]

But the Obama administration immediately responded exactly the wrong way, calling Zelaya's removal a "coup" and demanding that Honduras return him to the presidency. The President said:

It would be a terrible precedent if we start moving backwards into the era in which we are seeing military coups as a means of political transition rather than democratic elections. The region has made enormous progress over the last 20 years in establishing democratic traditions in Central America and Latin America. We don't want to go back to a dark past.[27]

Obama said this even though Zelaya was trying to subvert his country's constitution. The United States cut off $30 million in foreign aid to Honduras[28] and brought other forms of diplomatic pressure against the country. Hilary Clinton, as Secretary of State, continued to bring pressure against Honduras, issuing a statement that read, "The action taken against Honduran President Mel Zelaya violates the precepts of the Inter-American Democratic Charter, and thus should be condemned by all."[29]

Latin American expert Mary Anastasia O' Grady wrote, "In its actions toward Honduras, the Obama administration is demonstrating contempt for the fundamentals of democracy."[30] Adding to the international insult, the US State Department revoked the US visas of all fifteen justices of the Honduras Supreme Court because of their interpretation of their own constitution![31]

In other words, while President Obama refused to "meddle" in the affairs of Iran and give any kind of support to the *pro-democracy* demonstrators, he did decide to meddle in the affairs of tiny Honduras and give support to the *anti-democratic* forces attempting to bring the nation under essentially increasing dictatorial control. Thus, former president Zelaya was supported by Fidel Castro, Hugo Chavez, and Barack Obama. Obama sided with our enemies and opposed our friends.

Why has President Obama followed such policies? One possible explanation is that the most liberal elements of the Democratic party, from which he originates, are sympathetic toward socialism (government ownership of factories, companies, and other means of production) and therefore would like to see several socialist-leaning (Venezuela) or even communist (Cuba) governments succeed, but would not like to see free market-oriented countries like Colombia succeed.

26. Miguel A. Estrada, "In Honduras, 'Coup' Was Legal Reaction to Zelaya," *Atlanta Journal Constitution* (July 20, 2009). www.ajc.com/opinion/in-honduras-coup-was-95580.html.

27. Jake Tapper, "In Russia, President Obama Expresses His Support for Ousted President of Honduras," *ABCNews.com* (July 7, 2009). http://blogs.abcnews.com/political-punch/2009/07/in-russia-president-obama-explains-his-support-for-ousted-president-of-honduras.html.

28. Arhsad Mohammed and David Alexander, "U.S. Cuts More Than $30 Million in Aid to Honduras," *Reuters.com* (Sept. 3, 2009). www.reuters.com/article/honduras/idUS-TRE58251N20090903.

29. Statement by Secretary of State Hillary Rodham Clinton, "Situation in Honduras," U.S. Department of State (June 28, 2009). www.state.gov/secretary/rm/2009a/06/125452.htm.

30. Mary Anastasia O'Grady, "Hilary's Honduras Obsession," *Wall Street Journal* (Sept. 29, 2009), A17.

31. Ibid.

In spite of US opposition, Honduras appears to have resolved its own internal conflict. On October 29, 2009, the various sides to the conflict in Honduras signed an agreement that President Zelaya would be temporarily returned to office, but the November 29 elections would go forward, and a vote in Congress would decide the outcome of the leadership of the country if necessary. The Honduran Embassy reported that the result was a landslide victory for the National Party and its candidate, Porfirio Lobo. They took more than 55% of the vote, while the Liberal Party only took 40%. The National Party won 70 of the 128 seats in the Congress and also carried 200 out of 298 mayorships.[32]

A similar refusal to help a friend happened in 1999–2000, when Democratic President Bill Clinton—I think shamefully—refused to grant asylum to Elian Gonzalez, a young Cuban boy who was living with relatives in Florida. Elian's mother had drowned while trying to help him escape the Castro dictatorship, but Elian survived and did reach the United States. Attorney General Janet Reno sent in US agents to forcibly remove the young boy from his relatives and have him sent back to Cuba.[33] Why support dictators who are our enemies and refuse to help a child who nearly lost his life trying to escape to freedom?

B. THE UNITED NATIONS

Because the United Nations is now the only effective forum where representatives of all nations can meet and negotiate and debate, I think the United States has no choice but to stay actively involved with it. If the United States were to pull out, the United Nations' decisions and policies would become even more forcefully anti-democratic and anti-American.

But the fact remains that with a large block of Muslim nations, supported by a number of other dictatorial or autocratic nations such as North Korea, Cuba, Venezuela, and sometimes Russia and China as well as several anti-democratic African nations, the United Nations has become dominated by a significant majority of countries who are anti-American and even more strongly anti-Israel. So the United States must recognize that the United Nations, by majority vote of a number of smaller nations, has come to the point where it is hostile to freedom and to actions that are consistent with biblical standards of moral conduct in many areas of the world. Former State Department official Stefan Halper wrote back in 1996:

> The vastly expanded General Assembly was soon dominated by non-Western states whose elites seldom shared the political culture of the democratic West, much less any belief in market economics. The new majority felt free to exercise its power by passing resolutions favorable to the Third World and its member-states' various pet projects. Although the Third World was hardly homogeneous,

32. Honduras Election Analysis, The Embassy of Honduras (Dec. 9, 2009). http://hondurasemb.org/2009/12/09/honduras-election-analysis/.

33. "Federal Agents Seize Elian in Pre-Dawn Raid," *CNN.com* (April 22, 2000). http://archives.cnn.com/2000/US/04/22/cuba.boy.05/index.html.

operating on an identical agenda, a mutually convenient system of logrolling soon came into being. For example, Arab states would vote for black African resolutions against South African apartheid, provided that the black African countries in turn voted against Israel when called upon to do so. All factions frequently voted against the United States, although they were seldom as harsh with the Soviet Union—as President John F. Kennedy discovered when the non-aligned states refused to condemn the USSR for resuming aboveground nuclear tests in September 1961.[34]

The United Nations has also become incredibly corrupt in its use of funds. Halper reported:

> The salary and benefits packages of UN employees based in New York City are incredibly lucrative. Statistics compiled in 1995 revealed that the average annual salary for a midlevel accountant at the United Nations was $84,500. The salary for a comparable position in non-UN businesses and agencies was $41,964. A UN computer analyst could expect to receive $111,500 compared to $56,836 paid counterparts outside the UN bureaucracy. An assistant secretary general received $190,250; the mayor of New York City was paid $130,000. The raw figures do not convey the extent of the disparity, however, since the salaries of UN employees are free of all taxes. In addition to their bloated salaries, UN bureaucrats enjoy an array of costly perks, including monthly rent subsidies of up to $3,800 and annual education grants (also tax-free) of $12,675 per child. The UN pension program is so generous that entry-level staffers whose pay rises only as fast as inflation can retire in 30 years with $1.8 million.[35]

Halper added that the UN Children's Fund lost approximately $10 million because of mismanagement in Kenya. Nearly $4 million in cash was stolen outright at UN headquarters in Mogadishu, Somalia.[36]

When asked about the United Nations' waste of funds, *Fox News* correspondent Eric Shawn, author of the book *The UN Exposed: How the United Nations Sabotages America's Security and Fails the World*, replied:

> I titled one chapter of the book "$400,000 in a Desk Drawer" because a review of 58 audits released by the [Paul] Volcker investigation revealed billions frittered away, from the 400 grand stashed in a U.N. office in Iraq with "unrestricted access" that the staff would dip into for "loans," to overpaying Gulf War reparations to Kuwait by $2 billion. A recent internal U.N. investigation found what it called "a culture of impunity" when it comes to U.N. spending. It said peacekeepers spent $10.4 million leasing a helicopter that should have cost $1.6 million. $65 million was spent for fuel in the Sudan and Haiti that wasn't needed, $2.4 million for hangers in the Congo that were never used, and

34. Stefan Halper, "A Miasma of Corruption: The United Nations at 50," *Cato Institute Policy Analysis* 253 (April 30, 1996). www.cato.org/pubs/pas/pa–253.html.

35. Ibid.
36. Ibid.

on and on. In January, one U.N. study found overpayments in the Peacekeeping department amounted to more than $300 million.[37]

Therefore the United States should seek to minimize the influence of the United Nations wherever it is bringing harmful and destructive results throughout the world.

On the other hand, the United Nations does some good in educational and scientific areas and in matters of cultural exchange. In addition, it has sent peacekeeping forces to a number of hotspots in the world, and they have probably done some good. Former US diplomat James Dobbins cited the Sinai in the 1950s–1960s and again in the 1970s and Cyprus since 1964 as U.N. peacekeeping missions that were successful.[38]

There does not appear to be much hope for reforming the corruption in the United Nations or for bringing about fundamental change in its anti-American stance or its refusal to protest human rights abuses by some of the worst governments in the world. Former US Ambassador to the United Nations John Bolton said:

> … the quality of membership of the Human Rights Council is going to go a long way to determining its success. The Commission on Human Rights was widely discredited on many fronts, but the most visible sign of the Commission's decay was the inclusion, and in some cases the leadership, of such countries as Cuba, Zimbabwe, and Sudan. We cannot allow that to happen again.
>
> Additionally, the membership of the inaugural Council will be of particular procedural importance. Many of the processes that will permanently characterize the meeting and the actions of the Council will be decided by the first collection of nations to hold those seats.
>
> Members elected this week include Algeria, China, Cuba, Pakistan, Russia and Saudi Arabia. Heritage Foundation analyst Brett D. Schaefer [has concluded] …, "These countries were key players in undermining the effectiveness of the now-defunct Commission on Human Rights, and so it is very likely that they will play the same role on the Council, steering it away from confronting human rights abuses within their borders and in general."[39]

Therefore it would seem wise for the United States also to become more aggressive in building alternative associations of freedom-loving nations in the world—associations (or perhaps one association) that could provide a counterbalance to the negative influence of the United Nations in future years.

C. FOREIGN AID

Foreign aid is a specific area that the United States can use to promote its own interests and also do good for other nations.

---

37. Paul Weyrich, "United Nations: A Human Rights Farce," *RenewAmerica.com* (May 16, 2006). www.renewamerica.com/columns/weyrich/060516.

38. George Gedda, "Lebanon Peacekeeping Force Hard to Create," Associated Press (Aug. 23, 2006). www.foxnews.com/printer_friendly_wires/2006Aug23/0,4675,USUNPeacekeepers,00.html.

39. Weyrich, "United Nations: A Human Rights Farce."

1. Military aid

Military aid, whether through gifts or sales of weapons and airplanes and military training, should be used to help other nations defend themselves against attack and to maintain their freedom, in accordance with just war principles (see discussion in chap. 11, pp. 389–90).

2. Humanitarian aid

Humanitarian aid in the form of food, clothing, medical supplies, and funds should be sent to areas where there are *natural disasters* such as floods, hurricanes, or droughts. The United States gives large amounts of such aid—more than any nation in the world—both directly from the government (which is from tax dollars) and also through private organizations (see below, p. 440).

3. Economic development aid

Should the United States give financial aid also for *economic development* in poor nations? For years we have assumed that we should, and we and other nations have given *over $1 trillion* in foreign aid, especially to African countries.

But more recently a number of studies have sharply criticized the policy of giving foreign aid to poor nations for economic development or related purposes (as distinct from emergency relief in cases of disaster and as distinct from medical relief).[40] Several books have argued that such aid has been harmful rather than helpful to poor nations because the aid has always been channeled through corrupt governments and *has simply tended to entrench these corrupt governments more firmly in power,* since government officials are the ones who dispense the aid! In addition, this aid *creates a culture of dependency* in poor nations, and this in effect prevents them from becoming self-sustaining, economically healthy countries.[41] I think these critiques are largely correct.

4. Debt forgiveness

Some Christians propose that the United States and other wealthy countries should forgive the debts of extremely poor nations, arguing that they will never be able to repay

40. See especially Dambisa Moyo, *Dead Aid: Why Aid Is Not Working and How There Is a Better Way for Africa* (New York: Farrar, Straus and Giroux, 2009).

41. Ibid. (Moyo is a native of Zambia who holds a PhD in economics from Oxford and a masters degree from Harvard and who has worked both at Goldman Sachs and at the World Bank. She explains how *more than $1 trillion in aid* has been transferred from rich countries to Africa in the last fifty years, with harmful results). See also the earlier work by British economist and foreign aid expert P. T. Bauer, *Equality, the Third World and Economic Delusion* (Cambridge, MA: Harvard University Press, 1981); also, William Easterly, *The White Man's Burden: Why the White Man's Efforts to Aid the Rest Have Done So Much Ill and* *So Little Good* (New York: Penguin, 2006). (Easterly has worked for most of his life as an economist in Africa, Latin America, and Russia.) See also Easterly's earlier book, *The Elusive Quest for Growth: Economists' Adventures and Misadventures in the Tropics* (Cambridge, MA: MIT Press, 2001). These books from experts on Third World economic development provide strong refutations of the widely publicized book by Jeffrey Sachs, *The End of Poverty: Economic Possibilities for Our Time* (New York: Penguin, 2005). Sachs, who helps the United Nations allocate much aid to poor nations, recognizes that previous decades of aid have done little good. But he argues that if we would just give more aid, it would solve the problem—as if constant repetition of a failed solution makes for a wise plan!

them anyway. For example, Jim Wallis spends several pages in *God's Politics* extolling the virtues of a grassroots campaign among churches in the United States and the United Kingdom to cancel such debts. "Jubilee 2000 is now the Jubilee Network, and its supporters still call on the Word Bank and IMV to cancel 100 percent of the debt owed to them."[42] Wallis makes reference to the Jubilee Year in Leviticus 25:8–55, when debts were canceled after forty-nine years.

What Wallis does not discuss, however, is a crucial difference between today's debts and those in ancient Israel: *People made loans knowing the Jubilee rules in advance.* In ancient Israel, everyone was aware that debts would be canceled after forty-nine years, and financial arrangements were made taking that into account. For instance, in transactions concerning land, the law said, "If the years are many, you shall increase the price, and if the years are few, you shall reduce the price, for it is the number of the crops that he is selling to you" (Lev. 25:16).

But modern loans to poor nations were not made with the expectation that they would be canceled after forty-nine years or any other period of time. So it is not fair to the lenders when Christians suddenly demand that they live up to a "Jubilee" law that they were not aware of when they made the loan. It is changing the rules after the agreements have been made.

Therefore these campaigns for debt forgiveness must be understood clearly for what they are: *They are a plea to lenders that they should make voluntary charitable contributions toward the poor countries that have borrowed from them.*

In addition, the frequent moral flavor of these pleas places an implicit accusation of guilt against the lenders. The banks and governments that made loans to poor nations in good faith—probably thinking they were helping the poor nations by making these loans—*are suddenly viewed as wrongdoers* because they actually expect that the loans will be repaid!

Of course, if a country simply cannot repay a debt, then the lender (the World Bank or the International Monetary Fund) is forced to simply write it off as a bad debt. That is a business loss, and there should be accountability for those who make such loans that cannot be repaid. No public campaign is needed for declaring the loan a bad debt. But the borrowing nations do not want this, because this would make them unable to borrow in the future, a condition these nations are not willing to accept.

The campaign for "debt forgiveness" was something other than a campaign to decide that these loans were just bad debts. It was a plea for wealthy nations to somehow provide the equivalent funds to pay off these loans so they would not be classified as bad debts. It was really a campaign for more welfare payments to poor countries.

For instance, in 2005 the G8 Summit voted to cancel $40 million in debt owed to the International Monetary Fund, the World Bank, and the African Development Fund. According to the United Nations Environment Programme, the US was expected to pitch in up to $1.75 billion over ten years. The UN Programme reported, "This amount is its share of a pledge by rich nations to cover $16.7 billion in debt repayments the 18 countries would have made. The International Monetary Fund (IMF) will pay one of the

42. Wallis, *God's Politics.*

larger bills (some $6 billion). Under the deal, the IMF is supposed to cover those debts from its own 'existing resources.' "[43] But those resources come from member nations; they are not created out of thin air. (The largest share comes from the United States.)

The Jubilee 2000 movement was an international coalition of people from over forty countries that called for the cancellation of Third World debt by the year 2000. The University of Iowa Center for International Finance and Development reported on its efforts:

Jubilee 2000 staged demonstrations at the 1998 G–8 meeting in Birmingham, England.... The protestors caught the attention of Prime Minister Tony Blair, who met with the directors of Jubilee 2000 to discuss the issue of heavy debt in poor countries. Subsequently, the Prime Minister publicly expressed his personal support for, and dedication to, debt forgiveness. Other notable successes that resulted, at least in part, from Jubilee 2000 pressure included a promise from the United States during the G–7 (G–8 financial ministers, excluding Russia) meeting in Cologne, Germany, in 1999 to cancel 100% of the debt that qualifying countries owed the U.S. Jubilee also lobbied the U.S. Congress to make good on this promise. Congress responded to the growing pressure to address debt relief issues in 2000 by committing $769 million to bilateral and multilateral debt relief.[44]

But then the center went on to discuss some of the potential pitfalls of such debt relief:

... debt relief has been the subject of much criticism. Some critics view debt relief as counter-productive. For example, many object to the criteria used to determine which governments qualify for debt relief. Some fear that debt forgiveness perpetuates corrupt regimes in the same manner as illegitimate debt because it frees up government funds without any guarantee that the government will apply them to legitimate social or development programs. Another fear, referred to as the "moral hazard," is that countries relieved of their debts will engage in reckless over-borrowing with the expectation that, once their debts reach unsustainable levels, international creditors will forgive them again.[45]

The central difficulty with focusing so much attention on such debt forgiveness is this: *Will debt forgiveness really solve the problems that kept these poor nations in poverty in the first place?* What these poor nations need most of all is to develop productive, self-sustaining, growing economies. Forgiving debt or giving aid may meet some short-term need, but it does not change the governmental corruption, oppression, and destructive economic policies that have caused the poverty in the first place and continue to perpetuate it. Debt forgiveness and foreign aid to corrupt nations will often have the same effect: entrenching in power a corrupt government in that nation. Therefore debt forgiveness, though well-intended, has the potential of doing more harm than good.

---

43. United Nations Environment Programme, African Ministerial Conference on the Environment (A.M.CEN). Debt Cancellation, Nairobi (Oct. 26, 2005). www.unep.org/roa/docs/amcen/Brief_Debt_Cancellation.doc.

44. Enrique Carrasco, Charles McClellan, and Jane Ro,

"Forgiveness and Repudiation," *The University of Iowa Center for International Finance and Development* (April 2007). www.uiowa.edu/ifdebook/ebook2/contents/part4-I.shtml.

45. Ibid.

Who exactly are the nations that are receiving the benefits of such debt reduction programs? The International Monetary Fund lists thirty-five countries that have qualified for debt reduction. Twenty-six have reached what the IMF calls a "completion point," where they are eligible for the full measure of debt forgiveness that is being offered. Nine other countries are between the "decision point" and the "completion point" in the IMF reform program, and they have received partial debt forgiveness. Here is the list of countries:

Figure 12.1

LIST OF COUNTRIES THAT HAVE QUALIFIED FOR ... HIPC [HEAVILY INDEBTED POOR COUNTRIES] INITIATIVE ASSISTANCE (AS OF JULY 1, 2009)

Post-Completion-Point Countries (26)		
Benin	Guyana	Niger
Bolivia	Haiti	Rwanda
Burkina Faso	Honduras	Rwanda
Burundi	Madagascar	Senegal
Cameroon	Malawi	Sierra Leone
Central African Republic	Mali	Tanzania
Ethiopia	Mauritania	Uganda
The Gambia	Mozambique	Zambia
Ghana	Nicaragua	

Interim Countries (Between Decision and Completion Point) (9)		
Afghanistan	Democratic Republic of Congo	Guinea Bissau
Chad	Côte d'Ivoire	Liberia
Republic of Congo	Guinea	Togo [46]

What is distinctive about these countries? Even after completing the "reforms" required by the International Monetary Fund, they still are among the most unfree and oppressive countries in the world.

Here is the same list again, but with a number beside each country that shows where it ranks in economic freedom among the 179 nations of the world that are rated each year by the Heritage Foundation and the *Wall Street Journal*. In the scale, *1* indicates the most free country (Hong Kong) and *179* indicates the least free (North Korea).[47]

---

46. International Monetary Fund information, from www.imf.org/external/np/exr/facts/hipc.htm (accessed Feb. 4, 2010).

47. These rankings are taken from Terry Miller and Kim R. Holmes, eds., *2010 Index of Economic Freedom* (Washington, DC: Heritage Foundation, and New York: *Wall Street Journal*, 2010). The information here is taken from the summary chart inside the front cover.

Figure 12.2

Post-Completion-Point Countries (26)		
Benin 115	Guyana 153	Niger 129
Bolivia 146	Haiti 141	Rwanda 93
Burkina Faso 90	Honduras 99	São Tomé & Principe 149
Burundi 160	Madagascar 69	Senegal 119
Cameroon 132	Malawi 122	Sierra Leone 157
Central African Republic 152	Mali 112	Tanzania 97
Ethiopia 136	Mauritania 133	Uganda 76
The Gambia 118	Mozambique 111	Zambia 100
Ghana 87	Nicaragua 98	

Interim Countries (Between Decision and Completion Point) (9)		
Afghanistan N/A	Democratic Republic of Congo 172	Guinea Bissau 167
Chad 159	Côte d'Ivoire 123	Liberia 163
Republic of Congo 169	Guinea 134	Togo 161

The *2010 Index of Economic Freedom* is the current edition of a report that is published annually. It ranks countries in ten categories of economic freedom, including property rights, freedom from corruption, business freedom, investment freedom, and trade freedom, among others. All but one of the thirty-five countries receiving debt forgiveness were rated for this 2010 report. (Afghanistan was not ranked because of a lack of reliable data due to political and military instability.)

What is significant about this chart of countries receiving debt forgiveness is that they all rank quite low in terms of economic freedom. In fact, *thirty-one of the thirty-four countries* that were ranked *fell in the "unfree" or "repressed" categories.* (Any number higher than 89 indicates a country that is "mostly unfree"; any number higher than 144 indicates a country that is "repressed," the worst category.) This means that *91% of the countries receiving debt forgiveness are still governed by oppressive, corrupt governments.*

On this list of countries, only Ghana, Madagascar, and Uganda *even rank in the top half* of all the nations of the world with respect to these ten factors of economic freedom. Yet they all qualify for debt relief because they have carried out at least some of the "reforms" required by the IMF!

When I look at these statistics, it seems to me that a lot of the moral fervor that Christians have aimed against nations and banks that have made loans to poor countries should be redirected toward the corrupt governments of these repressive countries, where honest, skilled workers and business owners are not free to enjoy the fruits of their labors, and where bribery and routine violations of the law are accepted as a way of life.

Debt relief given to these countries is not going to change these underlying problems or provide any long-term solutions.

In addition, debt forgiveness is likely to increase the dependence of the poor nation on funds from other nations. Where is the evidence that debt forgiveness has ever reduced a country's dependence on other nations for economic aid?

In 2005, I received a copy of an email with evangelical megachurch pastor Rick Warren's plea for "The ONE Campaign: To Make Poverty History." This June 3, 2005, email urged people to write to President Bush, urging him to support a campaign to "cancel 100% of the debts owed by the poorest countries." A few days later, Gordon Brown, then the British Chancellor of the Exchequer (similar to America's Secretary of the Treasury), announced that the G8 finance ministers had "agreed to 100 per cent debt cancellation for Heavily Indebted Poor Countries."[48]

But did this 2005 campaign really "make poverty history"? No. The poor countries are still poor, more than four years after the world supposedly "made poverty history."

Therefore I have significant reservations about debt forgiveness for poor countries. At first it sounds like a good-hearted idea, and I'm sure that proponents can point to some specific development projects that seem like successful results in the short term. But where is the clear evidence that it will bring a country long-term economic good?

Finally, there is the question of fairness in forcing "contributions" from unwilling donors. Who actually pays for this debt forgiveness? Sometimes people imagine that it is just some rich banker somewhere who loses some money. But if the debt was from a bank, then *the stockholders of that bank*, including many retired people who have their pension plans or retirement savings in stock, have paid for that debt forgiveness. Do they really want to do this? On the other hand, if the forgiven loan was made by the United States government (or by the World Bank, which gets the largest amount of its funds from the US government), then debt forgiveness means that it is actually *the taxpayers of the United States* who have made a multimillion dollar "contribution" to this debt forgiveness. And if many of the benefits actually brought further power to corrupt governments in these poor countries (much of the money will go to the wealthy rulers and their friends in such countries), do Americans and citizens of other nations really want to pay more taxes for such a program?

5. Restrictions on foreign aid

It is important that the United States not give aid that will advance agendas in other nations that are morally wrong. For example, the Bush administration was correct when it refused to give foreign aid to any population control measures in China that would involve promoting abortions or forced abortions.

Nor should we give aid that will simply help oppressive totalitarian regimes stay in power (such as the horribly evil rule of Robert Mugabe in Zimbabwe).

---

48. *Fox News,* "G–8 Ministers OK $40B Debt Relief" (June 11, 2005). www.foxnews.com/story/0,2933, 159260,00.html.

6. The United States gives far more aid to other countries than any other nation

Earlier in this chapter I mentioned the statement of Lino J. Piedra, a member of the US Delegation to the United Nations Commission on Human Rights, that the United States was the origin of more than 70% of all financial flows reaching developing countries from the G–7 developed world, through private investment, private philanthropy, public aid, and private remittances (see p. 440).

D. ISRAEL

1. History of Israel: how did we get to this place?

The earliest recorded history of the people of the region of Palestine is that it was occupied by various Canaanite nations (see Gen. 10:15–19). But God promised that he would give this land to Abraham's descendants.

> On that day the LORD made a covenant with Abram, saying, "*To your offspring I give this land*, from the river of Egypt to the great river, the river Euphrates, the land of the Kenites, the Kenizzites, the Kadmonites, the Hittites, the Perizzites, the Rephaim, the Amorites, the Canaanites, the Girgashites and the Jebusites" (Gen. 15:18–21).

God also told Abraham something similar in Genesis 17:

> "And I will give to you and to your offspring after you the land of your sojournings, all the land of Canaan, for an everlasting possession, and I will be their God" (v. 8).

This promise found its initial fulfillment when the Jewish people, under the leadership of Joshua, entered the Promise Land and drove out the Canaanite people who had been living there but who came under God's judgment. God said to Joshua:

> "Moses my servant is dead. Now therefore arise, go over this Jordan, you and all this people, into the land that I am giving to them, to the people of Israel. Every place that the sole of your foot will tread upon I have given to you, just as I promised to Moses. From the wilderness and this Lebanon as far as the great river, the river Euphrates, all the land of the Hittites to the Great Sea toward the going down of the sun shall be your territory. No man shall be able to stand before you all the days of your life. Just as I was with Moses, so I will be with you. I will not leave you or forsake you. Be strong and courageous, for you shall cause this people to inherit the land that I swore to their fathers to give them" (Josh. 1:2–6).

The succeeding chapters in Joshua show how the people of Israel began to conquer the Canaanites and take possession of the land, but that process was not completed in Joshua's lifetime (see Josh. 13:1–7). Nevertheless, the nation of Israel was established in the land.

The remaining history of Israel in the Old Testament shows that its largest expansion of territory occurred under the kingships of David and Solomon (1 Sam. 16—2 Sam. 24 for David, and 1 Kings 1—11 for Solomon). Then the kingdom was divided and gradually diminished until the Babylonians finally conquered the last of the kingdom of Judah and carried the people off to Babylon in exile in 586 BC.

The history of the land of Israel from earliest times to the present may be summarized in the following chart:[49]

Figure 12.3

Before 1406 BC	Canaanite nation
1406 (or 1220) BC	Conquest by Israel
1010-971 BC	King David
971-931 BC	Solomon (followed by various Israelite kings)
586 BC	Babylonian Empire (beginning with Nebuchadnezzar)
539 BC	Persian Empire (beginning with Cyrus)
333 BC	Greece (beginning with Alexander the Great)
142 BC	Independent Israel (Maccabean revolt began in 167 BC)
63 BC	Roman Empire (beginning with Pompey)
330 BC	Byzantine Empire
636 AD	Muslim rule, then various Muslim or Christian (Crusader) rulers
1517 AD	Ottoman Empire (Turkish)
1917 AD	British rule
1948 AD	Israel as independent nation

One implication of this overview is that *there has never been a time in its entire history when an independent "Palestinian" nation existed in this land.*

On November 29, 1947, the United Nations passed General Assembly Resolution 181, which recommended *the establishment of two separate nations* in the land, the nation of Israel and an Arab nation, with specific boundary lines defined for each nation, a special power-sharing arrangement for the government of Jerusalem, and detailed arrangements for cooperation in economic, transportation, and agricultural matters. But the Arab residents of the land refused to accept this solution and refused to constitute themselves as a separate nation.

Israel, however, declared its independence on May 14, 1948, in accordance with the policy of the British government that had been declared November 2, 1917, in the Balfour

49. The dates in this chart prior to the first century are taken from *ESV Study Bible*, pp. 385, 1788–89.

Declaration, a formal statement of policy by the British government. The Balfour Declaration read as follows:

> His Majesty's Government view with favour the establishment in Palestine of a national home for the Jewish people, and will use their best endeavors to facilitate the achievement of this object, it being clearly understood that nothing shall be done which may prejudice the civil and religious rights of existing non-Jewish communities in Palestine, or the rights and political status enjoyed by Jews in any other country.[50]

The situation in Palestine in 1947–48 leading up to the declaration of independence was marked by considerable fighting between Arabs and Jews. Then the very day after that declaration—May 15, 1948—the armies of five Arab countries (Egypt, Syria, Jordan, Lebanon, and Iraq) attacked Israel. These were all four of the nations that bordered Israel to the north, northeast, west, and south, plus Iraq, which was farther east. To the surprise of much of the world, during the next year Israel increasingly took the offensive and became victorious in the war. Finally a cease-fire was declared and temporary new borders were established. Israel was admitted as a member of the United Nations on May 11, 1949.

Retired Princeton professor Bernard Lewis, who is one of the world's most widely recognized authorities on the history of Islam, notes that "during the fighting in 1947–1948" there was "an exchange of populations." He writes, "About three-fourths of a million Arabs fled or were driven (both are true in different places) from Israel and found refuge in the neighboring Arab countries.... A slightly greater number of Jews fled or were driven from Arab countries.... Most Jewish refugees found their way to Israel."[51]

But Lewis points out that what happened to these refugees was very different. The Jewish refugees from other countries—whether European or Middle Eastern—were accepted as citizens in Israel, but *the Palestinian Arab refugees were refused acceptance* in most of the surrounding Arab countries:

> The government of Jordan granted Palestinian Arabs a form of citizenship, but kept them in refugee camps. In the other Arab countries, they were and remained stateless aliens without rights or opportunities, maintained by U.N. funding. Paradoxically, if a Palestinian fled to Britain or America, he was eligible for naturalization after five years, and his locally-born children were citizens by birth. If he went to Syria, Lebanon or Iraq, he and his descendants remained stateless, now entering the fourth or fifth generation.
>
> The reason for this has been stated by various Arab spokesmen. It is the need to preserve the Palestinians as a separate entity until the time when they will return to reclaim the whole of Palestine; that is to say, all of the West Bank, the

50. The Balfour Declaration, November 2, 1917. www.mfa.gov.il/MFA/Peace%20Process/Guide%20to%20the%20Peace%20Process/The%20Balfour%20Declaration.

51. Bernard Lewis, "On the Jewish Question," *Wall Street Journal* (Nov. 26, 2007), A21.

Gaza Strip and Israel. The demand for the "return" of the refugees, in other words, means the destruction of Israel.[52]

2. Present-day negotiations

What about current "negotiations" between Israel and the Palestinians? Lewis writes frankly:

> The first question (one might think it is obvious but apparently not) is, "What is the conflict about?" There are basically two possibilities: that it is about the size of Israel, or about its existence.... If the issue is not the size of Israel, but its existence, negotiations are foredoomed. And in light of the past record, it is clear that is and will remain the issue, until the Arab leadership either achieves or renounces its purpose—to destroy Israel. Both seem equally unlikely for the time being.[53]

3. Arabs living in Israel

A number of Arabs chose to remain in the land that was governed by the new nation of Israel. These Arabs have citizenship rights and can vote in Israeli elections. In fact, Arab citizens of Israel in late 2009 held 12 of the 120 seats in the Israeli parliament (called the Knesset). There is a Christian Arab of Lebanese descent who is a permanent member of the Israeli Supreme Court. And there are Arab generals in the Israeli army.

By contrast, all Jews have been driven out of Arab lands since 1948, even though many of them and their families had lived peacefully in various Arab nations such as Israel, Syria, and Jordan for many centuries. The Arab nations of the Middle East (Egypt, Saudi Arabia, Yemen, Oman, United Arab Emirates, Qatar, Kuwait, Iraq, Jordon, Syria, Iran) include a total population of 266,807,498 and have a total land area of 6,336,746 sq. kilometers(2,446,631 sq. miles),[54] compared with the total population of 7,233,201 in Israel with a land area of 21,642 sq. kilometers (8,522 sq. miles).[55] Most of these Arab nations continue to insist that Israel has no right to exist. They have nearly forty times the population and nearly three hundred times the land area, but still claim the right to destroy the nation of Israel. In fact, Jordan[56] and Egypt[57] are the only Arab countries in the Middle East that have signed a peace treaty with Israel and recognize its existence. In addition, Iraq, since it recently established a democratic government, has not declared itself in favor of the destruction of Israel.

52. Ibid.

53. Ibid.

54. *The CIA World Factbook.* www.cia.gov/library/publications/the-world-factbook/region/region_mde.html.

55. Ibid.

56. Israel Ministry of Foreign Affairs, Israel-Jordan Peace Treaty, October 26, 1994. www.mfa.gov.il/MFA/Peace%20Process/Guide%20to%20the%20Peace%20Process/Israel-Jordan%20Peace%20Treaty.

57. Israel Ministry of Foreign Affairs, Israel-Egypt Peace Treaty, March 26, 1979. www.mfa.gov.il/MFA/Peace%20Process/Guide%20to%20the%20Peace%20Process/Israel-Egypt%20Peace%20Treaty.

I do not mean to say that Israel is without blame in its treatment of minorities within its borders. In particular, I have been concerned about reports of a lack of adequate protection of religious freedom within Israel. Sometimes Christians—particularly Palestinian Christians—have experienced hostile persecution from both Arabs and Israeli Jews.

Dr. Justus Weiner, a scholar in residence at the Jerusalem Centre for Public Affairs and a leading authority on Christian persecution in Palestine, says that the Christian population in Bethlehem has dropped from a high of 75–80% in the 1940s to approximately 12% today. He notes that the entire Christian population on the West Bank declined to 1.5 to 1.7% of the total population and is "practically close to disappearing."[58]

A 2006 report from the House International Relations Committee of the US Congress led to a letter from Congressman Henry J. Hyde, chairman of the committee, to President Bush on May 19, 2006, that contained the following statement:

> It is becoming increasingly difficult for Christians and Muslims living in the occupied territories to practice their faith. The security barrier, checkpoints, permit system, and segregated highway system render getting to religious services extremely difficult. In addition, the security barrier cuts through religious properties and impedes access to important holy sites. Consequently the fabric of religious life is being destroyed. The Christians in the area view the security barrier as something that is seriously damaging religious freedom in the Holy Land, impeding their access to important holy sites, and tearing at the social fabric of Christian life by destroying the important linkages between Bethlehem and Jerusalem, resulting in a decreasing Christian presence in both cities.[59]

Congressman Hyde also stated:

> There has been a decline of Christians in the Holy Land.... There are recent and very troubling indications that this decline will be exacerbated and accelerated by actions of the Israeli government and the ascendancy of Islamic fundamentalism.[60]

4. Suicide bombing and the Israeli security fence

For many years Israel sought to defend itself against Arabs who had the right to live in their cities but who would enter crowded buses or marketplaces and blow themselves up in suicide terrorist attacks, killing and wounding hundreds of Israeli Jews. The strategy was to intentionally target innocent civilians for death and thereby spread terror among the population.

58. Michelle Vu, "Persecution Fuelling Drastic Decline of Christians in Palestine," *ChristianToday.com* (July 23, 2007). www.christiantoday.com/article/persecution.fuelling.drastic. decline.of.christians.in.palestine/11791-2.htm.

59. "Staff Report on the Holy Land," in *Palestine—Israel Journal of Politics, Economics and Culture* 13:2 (2006), 114.

60. Ibid., 113.

Finally Israel decided that its only solution was to build a tall security fence that would separate areas that were dominantly Arab from those that were dominantly Jewish. The security fence was started in 2003[61] and is not yet complete. It is actually a series of concrete walls up to eight meters (twenty-four feet) high in some places. It is also called the "West Bank Barrier" in one area and the "Gaza Strip Barrier" in another.

There has been controversy over whether the placement of the fence is correct, but it has been without question a major factor in a significant reduction in the number of suicide bombings in Israel. The Israeli government therefore defends the fence as a necessary part of its essential self-defense. Palestinian Arabs, including Palestinian Christians, have objected that it has caused significant disruption in many of their lives because of its requiring much longer travel distances and delays at security checkpoints.

5. Controversy over Gaza

The Gaza Strip is a portion of land on the coast of the Mediterranean Sea located in the southwest corner of Israel. It is about 25 miles (41 kilometers) long and it varies in width from 4 to 7.5 miles (6–12 kilometers) wide. It has a total area of 139 sq. miles (360 sq. kilometers) and a population of 1.5 million people.

The Gaza Strip was intended to become part of the new Arab state, according to the 1947 partition plan passed by the United Nations General Assembly. But during the 1948 Arab-Israeli war, Egypt occupied the Gaza Strip, and it remained in effect under Egyptian control, yet never became an official part of Egypt. Then Israel took over the Gaza Strip after the Six-Day War in June 1967. Israel then created twenty-one new Jewish settlements, Jewish people built homes in the Gaza Strip, and Israel retained control of the area.

In 2005, pursuing the goal of "land for peace," Israel decided to withdraw from the Gaza Strip and remove all Israeli homes that were there. In an address to the UN General Assembly on September 25, 2009, Israeli Prime Minister Benjamin Netanyahu explained what happened:

> In 2005, hoping to advance peace, Israel unilaterally withdrew from every inch of Gaza. It was very painful. We dismantled 21 settlements, really, bedroom communities, and farms. We uprooted over 8,000 Israelis. We just yanked them out from their homes. We did this because many in Israel believed that this would get peace.
>
> Well, we didn't get peace. Instead we got an Iranian-backed terror base 50 miles from Tel-Aviv. But life in the Israeli towns and cities immediately next to Gaza became nothing less than a nightmare. You see, the Hamas rocket launches and rocket attacks not only continued after we left, they actually increased dramatically. They increased tenfold. And, again, the UN was silent—absolutely silent.[62]

61. Israel Ministry of Foreign Affairs, "Saving Lives: Israel's Security Fence." www.mfa.gov.il/mfa/mfaarchive/2000_2009/2003/11/.

62. Benjamin Netanyahu, transcript of remarks to the UN General Assembly, September 25, 2009 (accessed at washingtontimes.com Sept. 25, 2009).

The rockets fired from Gaza by Hamas forces had attacked Israeli civilian population centers in southern Israel, particularly the city of Sderot. Netanyahu said that Israel was faced with "an enemy committing a double war crime, of firing on civilians while hiding behind civilians."[63] The attacks had begun as early as 2000 from sections of the Gaza Strip, but when Israel completely pulled out of the Strip—hoping that giving up some land would lead to further concessions toward peace on the part of the Palestinians—they found that the attacks simply intensified. Israel's defense minister explained:

> After enduring eight years of ongoing rocket fire—in which 12,000 missiles were launched against our cities, and after all diplomatic efforts to stop this barrage failed—it was my duty as Defense Minister to do something about it. It's as simple and self-evident as the right to self-defense.[64]

What did Israel do to avoid killing civilians? The situation Israel faced was difficult because Hamas was "an enemy that intentionally deploys its forces in densely populated areas, stores its explosives in private homes, and launches rockets from crowded school yards and mosques."[65] Nevertheless, Israel attempted to target only military sites and warned civilians to move from the path of the attacks. General and former prime minister Ehud Barak says, "In Gaza, we reached out to the civilians via millions of leaflets, telephone calls and text messages, urging them to leave areas before we acted."[66]

On December 27, 2008, Israel sent fighter jets in a series of air strikes against specific targets in Gaza. This was followed by a ground invasion on January 3, 2009.

The United Nations Human Rights Council subsequently issued a report (the Goldstone Report) accusing Israel of carrying out war crimes in Gaza while mentioning nothing that condemned the 12,000 missiles that were launched indiscriminately against civilian targets over a period of eight years. In response, Prime Minister Netanyahu said to the UN General Assembly, "What a perversion of truth. What a perversion of justice."[67]

My own evaluation of these events is that I find it hard to see how Israel could have acted any differently and still have fulfilled its responsibility to defend its citizens from attack. In fact, when Barack Obama visited the city of Sderot while he was a presidential candidate, he said, "If somebody was sending rockets into my house where my two daughters sleep at night, I would do everything to stop them, and would expect Israel to do the same thing."[68] But now as President, he has given signs of increasing opposition to Israel, such as publicly demanding that they stop all settlement construction.[69]

---

63. Ibid.

64. Ehud Barak, "At the U.N., Terrorism Pays," *Wall Street Journal* (Sept. 25, 2009), A15.

65. Ibid.

66. Ibid.

67. Netanyahu, address to UN General Assembly, September 25, 2009.

68. "Israel's Gaza Defense," *Wall Street Journal* (Dec. 29, 2008), A12.

69. Chris McGreal and Rory McCarthy, "Obama: Halt to New Israeli settlements is in America's security interests," *guardian.co.uk* (May 29, 2009). www.guardian.co.uk/world/2009/may/28/barack-obama-jewish-settlements-israel-palestine-relations.

6. What is the solution to the Arab-Israeli conflict?

What is the solution to the current conflict? As long as the Palestinian Arab leaders and the surrounding Arab nations insist that their goal is the total destruction of Israel, and as long as they continue to insist that Israel has no right to exist as a nation, I see no point in negotiation between Israel and the Palestinians. There is no intermediate bargaining point between existing and not existing as a nation. Israel is not going to give up its right to exist or its right to defend itself, nor do I think it should ever give up those things. Therefore, until the most basic Palestinian position changes from this fundamental commitment, the only way to maintain a reasonable amount of peace in that region is for Israel to maintain a strong military force and use that force to defend itself when necessary. This seems to me to fit into the classic description of a just war (see pp. 389–90), because of the fundamental right of a nation to defend itself against an evil enemy who continues to attack and seek to destroy it.

Another way to explain the differences between the two sides is to say this: If the Palestinians would agree to lay down their arms and acknowledge the legitimate existence of Israel, they could have a separate Palestinian nation tomorrow and live in peace and increasing economic prosperity with their Jewish neighbors. But if Israel were to lay down its arms, it would be annihilated; it would cease to exist as a nation. That distinction shows the fundamental difference between the two sides in this conflict.

Therefore, if Western nations, including the United States, are serious about ending the Arab-Israeli conflict, *the first step* should be publicly demanding that Arab nations give up claiming that Israel has no right to exist and that they are going to destroy it. That is the root cause of the entire ongoing conflict and has been since 1948. The Arab states should immediately join the other 160 nations of the world that have recognized Israel as a nation.

7. Does God still give special favor and protection to the nation of Israel?

Evangelical Christians differ over the question of whether God gives special protection today to the nation of Israel. Those evangelicals who hold to a dispensational system of biblical interpretation say that God's promise of the land of Israel to the descendants of Abraham was an eternal promise and it will yet be fulfilled in even greater measure in a time yet to come.

On the other hand, non-dispensationalists (including me) argue that the Jewish people at the time of the New Testament rejected Jesus as their Messiah and thereby forfeited the promises to blessings from God that were to come as part of the new covenant in Christ. Non-dispensationalists place much more emphasis on the fact that *many of the promises made to Israel* in the Old Testament were seen by the New Testament authors to be *fulfilled in the church*.

For example, in Hebrews 8:8–13 the author takes a long quotation from Jeremiah 31:31–34, where God makes promises to "the house of Israel" and "the house of Judah" (Heb. 8:8), and he argues that *these are fulfilled in the new covenant*, which is now being experienced by the church of Jesus Christ, to whom the author was writing. Similarly,

1 Peter 2:1–10 sees many Old Testament promises to Israel *fulfilled in the church*. Therefore non-dispensationalists place much less expectation on the Jewish people receiving the fulfillment of God's *promise of the land* that was given in the Old Testament. While dispensationalists would argue that these promises of the land will be *literally fulfilled in a future time of great tribulation* after Christ returns to remove the church from the earth, non-dispensationalists like me do not think there will be such a time of tribulation when the church is removed from the earth. (They think that any future time of tribulation will happen before Christ returns and that Christians will still be on earth during that time.)

But even without resolving the differences between dispensationalists and non-dispensationalists, *is there anything that both sides in this discussion should be able to affirm about the future of Israel?*

First, both sides should clearly affirm that the Jewish people do not have a separate path to salvation apart from trusting in Jesus as their Messiah. Jesus said, "I am the way, and the truth, and the life. No one comes to the Father except through me" (John 14:6). Paul wrote, "There is one God, and there is one mediator between God and men, the man Christ Jesus" (1 Tim. 2:5). The New Testament teaches again and again that apart from trusting in Christ, no one can find forgiveness of sins and eternal salvation. There is no special "second path" of salvation for people just because they come from Jewish ancestry.

But it also seems clear that in the very section of Romans in which Paul expresses such sorrow that the Jewish people have rejected Jesus Christ as their Messiah (see Rom. 9:2–3, 6–8), he speaks about *a distinctive future for the very people of Israel who have rejected Christ*. Paul looks forward to a future time when the Jewish people will be fully included into the people of God, for he says:

> Now if *their trespass* means riches for the world, and if *their failure* means riches for the Gentiles, how much more will *their full inclusion* mean! (Rom. 11:12).

The phrases "their trespass" and "their failure" are speaking about the Jewish people's refusal to accept Jesus as their Messiah. During this present age (while Paul was preaching the Gospel) God had opened salvation to the Gentiles and there was great blessing for Gentiles; but this same verse looks forward to a still-future time that Paul calls "their full inclusion," a time when apparently a great majority of the Jewish people will become part of God's true people by trusting in Jesus as their Messiah.

Paul speaks of the same idea a few verses later:

> For if *their rejection* means the reconciliation of the world, what will *their acceptance* mean but life from the dead? (Rom. 11:15).

In speaking of a future time that Paul calls "their acceptance," he looks forward to a time of turning to Christ by large numbers of Jewish people.

Next, Paul uses the image of an olive tree to say that because the Jewish people had rejected Jesus as the Messiah, they were like branches that were "broken off" from the olive tree (representing God's true people, Rom. 11:17). Paul says they "were broken off because of their unbelief" (Rom. 11:20). Then he looks forward to a future time when he says, "How much more will these, the natural branches, be grafted back into their own olive tree" (Rom. 11:24). These "natural branches" are the Jewish people.

Paul speaks again of the Jewish people's rejection of Christ as temporary, for he says, "A *partial hardening* has come upon Israel, *until* the fullness of the Gentiles has come in. And in this way all Israel will be saved" (Rom. 11:25–26). Paul goes on to speak of ethnic Israel, the Jewish people, and says that "As regards the Gospel, *they* are enemies of God for your sake. But as regards election, *they* are beloved for the sake of *their* forefathers" (v. 28). The *same* Jewish people who are "enemies of God"—that is, who have rejected Jesus as the Messiah—are still the objects of some future purpose that God has in mind, for of these same people he says in the next sentence, "As regards election, *they* are beloved for the sake of their forefathers" (v. 28). Therefore, although they have rejected Christ and do not now have salvation, God still has a plan in mind for the Jewish people and in some sense (other than possessing salvation through Christ) he still counts them "beloved" and has a future purpose in mind for them, "for the gifts and the calling of God are irrevocable" (v. 29).

All of this shows that Paul still believes that *God views the Jewish people who have rejected Christ as a special ethnic group out of all the people of the earth*, a group that God still considers to be "beloved for the sake of their forefathers." And because of this, at some future time "all Israel will be saved" (v. 26), most likely referring to a future turning to trust in Jesus Christ on the part of a significant majority of the Jewish people on earth at that time.

Does God still give special favor and protection to the Jewish people today? Even if evangelical Christians do not agree on how many of the Old Testament promises to Israel will still be fulfilled among the ethnically Jewish people, all Christians should be able to agree that Romans 11 speaks of the Jewish people in the new covenant age, which is the age in which we presently live. Romans 11 still sees a special purpose and special love of God for the Jewish people, whom he will bring to salvation through Christ in great numbers in a future day. Therefore Paul can say that even today, "They are beloved for the sake of their forefathers" (v. 28).

I find it hard to read this as saying anything other than that God still has a kind of special favor and care for the people of Israel who are today "enemies" of God regarding the Gospel, but who will someday experience a "full inclusion" among the people of God and will "be grafted back into their own olive tree" (vv. 12, 24).

8. Should the United States give special protection and favor to Israel?

Regarding the United States' policy toward Israel today, I want to make it very clear, first, that we should never say about any nation that we will always support whatever it does, whether or not we agree with it. And clearly we should not say that about Israel. The vast majority of Jewish people in Israel today have made exactly the wrong decision on the most important question of all of life, namely, whether to trust in Jesus as their true Messiah and Savior and Lord. We cannot say they have made the right decision on that question!

Moreover, if Israel's military forces were to commit immoral acts, such as the intentional murder of innocent civilians rather than strictly attacking military forces and targets, then we should certainly criticize them for any such wrongdoing.

In September 2009, Israel's Defense Minister (and former Prime Minister) Ehud Barak agreed with this stance when he said:

> Israel is not perfect. As much as we as a society try to uphold the IDF's [Israeli Defense Force's] ethical code, mistakes sometimes happen.... And when we are told that things may not be right, we check it out and, when necessary, prosecute those involved. We are now pursuing two dozen criminal investigations regarding events that occurred in Gaza.[70]

Therefore our policy as a nation should never be "Israel is always right," any more than it should be "England is always right" or "Canada is always right" or "The United States is always right." We must be willing to hold even our closest allies and even our own nation up to criticism when we believe it has done something that is inconsistent with the moral standards of the Bible.

Having said that, I still believe that we should treat Israel as a very special and close ally. We should cooperate with and support it in many ways. We should be willing to defend it if attacked and also to defend and support it in diplomatic circles, especially in the United Nations. We should defend its right to exist and its right to defend itself. We should be seeking to find many ways in which we can help Israel grow and prosper as a nation, through free trade, cultural exchanges, educational and technological exchanges, access to military technology, the promotion of tourism, and so forth.

Therefore I disagree with Ron Paul's "noninterventionist" policy, which opposes any defense alliance with Israel and all foreign or military aid to Israel.[71]

I believe the United States should treat Israel as a favored ally for several reasons:

a. Israel is our most reliable ally out of the entire group of nations in the Middle East. From a military and strategic standpoint in terms of maintaining world peace and world commerce, Israel is crucial to our national interests.

b. Israel is now one of the most advanced nations in the world in terms of scientific and technological inventions, information processing, and financial management. When it finally decided to reject the socialistic economic system it had in place for several decades, it became one of the most successful entrepreneurial, free market economies in the world.[72]

These remarkable advances in the last ten years are described in fascinating detail in George Gilder's recent book *The Israel Test*.[73] Gilder's thesis is that the Jewish people as a whole have demonstrated throughout history amazing achievements far beyond their small numbers, especially in mathematics, science, military strategy, invention, and entrepreneurial and business success.

---

70. Barak, "At the U.N., Terrorism Pays."

71. See Ron Paul, *Revolution: A Manifesto* (New York: Grand Central Publishing, 2008), 10–17, 34–35.

72. Ron Paul incorrectly implies that Israel's economy lacks sufficient economic freedom to develop rapidly: see his *Revolution*, 35.

73. George Gilder, *The Israel Test* (Minneapolis: Richard Vigilante Books, 2009).

What Gilder calls "the Israel test" is the question of how the people of the world respond to the nation of Israel. He argues that nations and cultures that hate Israel fail this "Israel test" because they react out of envy and hatred for a nation that has achieved so much success in so many areas. But nations and cultures that appreciate Israel because of the contributions it makes to the entire world pass Gilder's "Israel test" and respond to the success of others in a morally right way.

Although I do not think that Gilder has fully explained the reasons for the hatred of Israel by some people and nations (he fails to consider sufficiently the high moral standards of historic Judaism and the spiritual component of opposition to God's plans for Israel), I think he is correct that envy of Israel's success is certainly a significant factor. The great value of Gilder's book is that he points out the immense benefits that have come to the entire world through Jewish intellectual achievements. (Gilder himself is not Jewish.)

c. We should support Israel because its establishment as a nation in 1948 was morally legitimate and was affirmed by a significant majority of countries in the United Nations at that time. The legitimacy of Israel's existence was again affirmed by its acceptance as a member of the United Nations in 1949, and so far 160 nations of the world have granted Israel diplomatic recognition.[74] The United States was the first nation to grant recognition, by an act of President Harry Truman eleven minutes after the Israeli Declaration of Independence was signed on May 14, 1948.[75]

It is important to remember that this establishment of Israel as a nation came in the aftermath of World War II and the attempt by Adolf Hitler and the Nazis to destroy the Jewish people. Jewish refugees had fled from persecution in many nations and were actively seeking a homeland that they could make their own—a place where they would be free from persecution in the future. The nations of the world largely agreed with this solution to the problem of where Jewish refugees could settle and be safe.

d. There are biblical reasons why Christians should support the continued existence and health of the nation of Israel. First, in a world filled with much moral relativism and confusion and also influenced by the harsh, totalitarian governments in strict Islamic nations, Israel provides a refreshing ally in terms of the similarity of its convictions to the moral standards held by Christian believers and taught in the Bible. Both Christians and Jews have moral values that trace their origin to the moral standards that God gave in the Ten Commandments in the Old Testament (Exod. 20:1–17). Therefore the nation of Israel can become a useful ally for Christians in seeking positive moral influence on the world.

Second, because the Bible clearly teaches God's sovereignty over the affairs of nations (see pp. 85–86) and also teaches that God has a future plan for the salvation of large numbers of Jewish people, it seems right to see the establishment of the nation of Israel in 1948 and the present gathering of 5.5 million Jews there as a significant preparation that God has made so that the future salvation of many Jewish people through trust in

74. Israel Ministry of Foreign Affairs, "Israel's Diplomatic Missions Abroad: Status of Relations," February 8, 2009. www.mfa.gov.il/mfa/about%20the%20ministry/diplomatic%20missions/Israel-s%20Diplomatic%20Missions%20Abroad.

75. "Press Release Announcing U.S. Recognition of Israel," May 14, 1948.

Jesus as Messiah will be evident to the entire world as a fulfillment of what Paul predicted in Romans 11. Throughout history God has worked through human means and human influences to implement his plans for history, and therefore it seems very likely that supporting Israel's continued existence and well-being as a nation is also a way of contributing to the preparation for the "full inclusion" of the Jewish people among the people of God at some time in the future.

Third, although I do not accept the dispensationalist system of interpretation of Scripture, and although I believe that many of the Old Testament promises to Israel have been fulfilled by God in the blessings given to the church in the new covenant, I think there is still legitimate room for *uncertainty about whether the promise of God to Abraham in Genesis 17 has been or will be completely fulfilled in the church.* There God promised Abraham the following:

> "And I will give to you and to your offspring after you the land of your sojournings, all the land of Canaan, for an *everlasting* possession, and I will be their God" (Gen. 17:8).

What does God mean when he says he will give to Abraham's offspring (that is, the Jewish people) "all the land of Canaan, for an *everlasting* possession"? Only the Mosaic covenant (beginning at Exod. 20) is ever called "the old covenant" in the New Testament, and that earlier covenant with Abraham is never called the "old covenant." Although I am somewhat uncertain about this, it seems to me quite possible that the establishment of the Jewish people as a nation in 1948 *in that same land that God had promised to Abraham before 2000 BC*(!) was one step that God made toward his eventual plan to fulfill this promise of the nation of Israel having that land "for an *everlasting* possession," and so, when they turn to Jesus as their Messiah, the last phrase of the verse will also come true: "and I will be their God" (Gen. 17:8).

Therefore it seems that even non-dispensational interpreters like me should at least retain a considerable measure of *uncertainty* about the question of God's present providential favor on Israel. I think we should consider it at least possible that God was even in recent times working to bring about steps leading to a fulfillment of Genesis 17:8 through the establishment of Israel in 1948. As Paul says about God's future plans for the very Israel that had rejected Jesus as Messiah, "For the gifts and the calling of God are irrevocable" (Rom. 11:29).

This line of thought also helps us understand a spiritual component behind the current Israel-Arab conflict. Because Romans 11 teaches that God has a future plan for salvation of large numbers of the Jewish people, Christians might well suspect that there is a deeper spiritual source behind the intense anti-Semitism, the often-violent and irrational hatred of the Jews, that has occurred in various areas throughout history. It seems reasonable to think, for example, that the spiritual source behind the horrendous evil in the attempt of Hitler and the Nazis to destroy the Jews was none other than Satan himself, who, according to Jesus, was "a murderer from the beginning" (John 8:44). It is not surprising that Satan would attempt to exterminate the Jewish people and prevent the fulfillment of God's plan to save large numbers of them in the future.

This same demonic hatred, then, seems to me to be the most likely source behind the inhuman evil of the suicide bombers who for years have blown themselves up in the midst of groups of Jewish civilians in Israel. This demonic opposition to God's plan for the Jews also helps to explain the irrational commitment of many Muslim nations today to destroy Israel at all costs.

As for how this affects the United States, it is, of course, our nation's support for Israel that is one of the primary reasons behind the terrorist attacks against us (see above, pp. 406–8). Our nation's steadfast resolve to be Israel's greatest defender in the world today leads naturally to the desire of radical jihadists to destroy the United States as well. In this way the opposition of Satan to the fulfillment of God's plans for the Jewish people can be seen as one of the deep spiritual causes behind the terrorist attacks on the United States.

For several reasons, therefore, it seems to me that the United States should count Israel as a close ally and, while not supporting Israel when it does wrong, should still give special favor and protection to that nation.

E. IMMIGRATION

What should be the policy of the United States (or any other nation) regarding the immigration of people from other countries?

1. Biblical teaching

The Old Testament has many verses that command the people of Israel to treat the "sojourner" (other versions say "alien") fairly and with kindness and love. For example,

> "You shall not wrong a *sojourner* or oppress him, for you were sojourners in the land of Egypt" (Exod. 22:21).

Is the "sojourner" in verses like this the same as a foreign immigrant in a nation today?

In his very perceptive book *The Immigration Crisis*, Old Testament scholar James Hoffmeier says that the word translated "alien" (NIV) or "sojourner" or "stranger" (ESV; sometimes NASB, KJV) in these Old Testament verses was "a person who entered Israel and followed legal procedures to obtain recognized standing as a resident alien."[76] Hoffmeier points out that there was a specific Hebrew word (*gēr*) used to refer to such an "alien" or "sojourner." In other words, Hoffmeier shows that these verses about the "sojourner" (Hebrew *gēr*) refer to "legal immigrants" into a country.[77] But other people who did not have this recognized standing were simply termed "foreigners"—using other Hebrew terms—and they did not have the same benefits or privileges that sojourners did.[78]

---

76. James Hoffmeier, *The Immigration Crisis: Immigrants, Aliens, and the Bible* (Wheaton, IL: Crossway Books, 2009), 52.
77. Ibid.

78. See Hoffmeier, 52, 89, 156, and elsewhere throughout the book.

Therefore Hoffmeier concludes that while "the legal alien ought to have most of the rights of citizenship," on the other hand,

> illegal immigrants should not expect these same privileges from the state whose laws they disregard by virtue of their undocumented status. The Bible clearly distinguishes between the status of a legal alien (*ger*) and a foreigner (*nekhar* and *zar*), and one consequence is that there really is a difference between the legal standing of a present-day documented alien and an illegal immigrant. Therefore it is legally and morally acceptable for government to deal with those in the country illegally according to the nation's legal provisions. The Christian insists, however, that they be dealt with in a humane manner.[79]

With this distinction in mind, we can notice other verses that command God's people to treat sojourners fairly and justly:

> "You shall not oppress a *sojourner*. You know the heart of a sojourner, for you were sojourners in the land of Egypt" (Exod. 23:9).

> "When a *stranger* sojourns with you in your land, you shall not do him wrong" (Lev. 19:33).

> "Love the *sojourner*, therefore, for you were sojourners in the land of Egypt" (Deut. 10:19).

Hoffmeier also emphasizes that nations in the world of the Old Testament clearly placed a high priority on protecting their borders and having the right to decide who would enter their nation and who would not: "Were ancient territorial borders taken seriously and was national sovereignty recognized? The answer is emphatically yes."[80] Hoffmeier also adds, after a survey of the biblical data, that

> Nowhere in the Old Testament is there any sense that a nation had to accept immigrants, nor was being received as an alien a right.[81]

Another important consideration from the Bible concerns the general responsibilities of governments to seek the good of the nations that they rule (Rom. 13:1–7; 1 Peter 2:13–14) and thereby truly serve as "God's servant for your good" (Rom. 13:4). This means that the immigration policies of a nation *should be designed to bring benefit to that specific nation.*

This purpose of seeking the good of the nation is also reflected in the opening paragraph of the Constitution of the United States, where the purposes of the new government included "ensure domestic tranquility" and "provide for the common defense" and "promote the general welfare." The government of the United States was established so that it would *do good for the nation* in these and other ways.

---

79. Ibid., 156–57.
80. Ibid., 32.
81. Ibid., 156.

Therefore, in the United States in particular but in nations generally, immigration policies should be designed to bring *benefit to the well-being of the nation as a whole.*

This would imply, for example, that *the United States should control all immigration processes* so that the country gives priority to accepting those people who will most likely make a positive contribution to US society. It is appropriate that *priority* in immigration be given, for example, to those who have sufficient education and training to support themselves and contribute well to American society, those who have demonstrated significant achievement in some area or another, *and all those who otherwise give evidence that they will make a positive contribution.* It is appropriate, also, to *exclude* those with a criminal record, those who have communicable diseases, or those who otherwise give indication that their overall contribution would likely be negative rather than positive in terms of advancing the well-being of the nation.

2. We have a historically different situation today

It is undoubtedly true that nearly everyone in the United States has some kind of immigrant background, so that we are a "nation of immigrants" (except for Native Americans). But there are two problems that have become acute within the last decade or so and make the present situation different from our entire history of past immigration.

(1) *Illegal immigrants:* There are many immigrants who have come here *illegally*, outside of the normal system for entering the United States. Estimates are that this number runs as high as 13 million or more[82] (or 4% of a nation of 307 million people).

(2) *Permanent lack of assimilation:* Too many immigrants who have come here *legally* within the last forty years do not seem to be assimilating well into American culture, but have formed their own ethnic communities in which their primary loyalty is not to the United States but to their nation of origin, and many remain as unskilled laborers, unable to rise above the lowest level of annual income. Many of these people (by some estimates) drain more resources from the nation than they provide to the nation.[83] That certainly is true if we include many illegal immigrants in that total.

According to the Center for Immigration Studies, households headed by illegal aliens imposed more than $26.3 billion in costs on the federal government in 2002 and paid only $16 billion in taxes, creating a net fiscal deficit of almost $10.4 billion, or $2,700 per illegal household. They found that the largest costs are Medicaid ($2.5 billion); treatment for the uninsured ($2.2 billion); food assistance programs such as food stamps, WIC (the Special Supplemental Nutrition Program for Women, Infants and Children), and free school lunches ($1.9 billion); the federal prison and court systems ($1.6 billion); and federal aid to schools ($1.4 billion).[84]

82. "How Many Illegal Immigrants?" Federation for American Immigration Reform, www.fairus.org/site/News2?page=NewsArticle&id=16859&security=1601&news_iv_ctrl=1007. Also see Center for Immigration Studies, Illegal Immigration, www.cis.org/Illegal.

83. See Mark Levin, *Liberty and Tyranny: a Conservative Manifesto* (New York: Threshold Editions, 2009), especially 154–70.

84. Steven A. Camarota, "The High Cost of Cheap Labor: Illegal Immigration and the Federal Budget," Center for Immigration Studies (July 2004). www.cis.org/node/54.

Some influential immigrant leaders actually *promote* the lack of assimilation into the United States. For example Raul Yzaguirre, former president of the Hispanic immigration advocacy group called La Raza, apparently wants to perpetuate the situation of people living in the United States for generations without being able to speak English, because he was quoted as saying, "U.S. English is to Hispanics as the Ku Klux Klan is to blacks."[85] Another advocate for Mexican immigrations into the United States, Juan Hernandez, said, "I want the third generation, the seventh generation, I want them all to think 'Mexico first.' "[86] Allowing such viewpoints to prosper is completely contrary to the best interests of the United States as a whole.

What is the solution to these two problems?

3. Step 1: Close the borders

Before any other solutions to the current immigration problems can be discussed, it is crucial to come to an agreement that the United States must take immediate action to immediately and effectively close its borders, especially the border with Mexico, from which most of the illegal immigrants originate.

It seems to me inexcusable that Congress has delayed so long in simply authorizing and clearing the way to build a secure fence that would effectively stop something like 99% of illegal immigration from Mexico. The United States as a nation must get control of its borders, as all strong nations throughout history have done. As long as the borders are ineffective, we have no control and no ability to keep criminals, terrorists, and others who would harm our nation from entering. Even those who enter with no intent of breaking any further laws but only of finding employment do this in a way that is unfair to thousands of others who decide to abide by the law and wait many years to be admitted as immigrants by legal means.

Then these illegal immigrants become part of a growing underground economy and a permanent "underclass" that is not really protected by the law because the legal system does not have a record that they exist! It means that they can be easily exploited because they won't seek legal help when wrong has been done against them, for fear they will be discovered and deported. On the other hand, it means that American citizens are not protected from the harm that illegal immigrants might do to others, because the legal system has no easy way to track them if they commit wrong.

These illegal immigrants have very little incentive to try to integrate into the society (as other immigrants from other nations have historically done when they came by legal means). Therefore illegal immigrants are much more likely to form isolated communities who think of their first national loyalty as to Mexico (or some other nation) rather than to the United States. Many of them do not feel themselves responsible to contribute to the well-being of society, as through military service or paying taxes or obedience to laws. Because their status here is already "illegal," their very presence generates disrespect for the rule of law in the nation as a whole.

---

85. Quoted by Mark Levin, *Liberty and Tyranny*, 162.
86. Ibid., 164.

In addition, these illegal immigrants are living in constant disobedience of Paul's command, "Let every person be subject to the governing authorities" (Rom. 13:1). It is not just that they have broken the laws of the United States by entering the country illegally, but they also continue living in the country in an undocumented status without the legal permission of the United States. They can hardly be subject to the governing authorities when those authorities do not even have a record that they exist. In this way, the continuing presence of a growing illegal minority *that is invisible to the entire legal recordkeeping system of the society* is a destructive force in the society itself—one that will increasingly bring negative consequences to the respect for law and the legal fabric of the nation.

It therefore astounds me that anyone in either party, whether Democrat or Republican, would oppose having Congress and the President take the necessary steps to *complete* a secure and impenetrable border fence immediately. This is not a high-tech problem, such as building a jet fighter or sending a rocket to the moon. A secure fence—that is, a double one with high-tech monitoring devices and a patrol road in between the two parts—that covers the entire 1,951-mile length of the border between the United States and Mexico could be built on an emergency basis within a few months, if the nation had the will to do this. But instead it has dragged on for years, with only partial individual sections being complete. Congress could pass special legislation, if it had the will, that would override environmental challenges to the building of the fence and override legal challenges to the use of eminent domain to obtain the right to build on the property all along the border. A secure fence could and should be built at once.

Closing the border is simply a matter of establishing the rule of law more effectively in a nation. I can see no valid reason to oppose it. I can see no valid argument to delay it. I can see no excuse for making it a bargaining chip for negotiations about other aspects of the immigration question. The United States should have the right to *determine* who enters the country and to *know* who enters the country.

4. Step 2: We should enact comprehensive reform of the immigration system

a. Stopping chain migration and exercising rational control over immigration

Prior to 1965, the United States had much more effective control over who would be allowed to enter the nation as an immigrant. Priority was rightfully given to those people *who would most clearly bring benefit to American society* as well as to their spouses and their immediate minor children.

But under pressure from President Lyndon Johnson, Congress passed the Hart-Celler Act of 1965. It established a new system by which citizens of the United States could sponsor not only a spouse and immediate children for immigration, but also *all of their brothers and sisters as well as their parents who are living in other countries.*

For example, let's say that a couple has eight children in Mexico and then enters the United States and has a baby daughter. Even if they were just here for a few days to give birth to her, she will automatically become an American citizen by virtue of being born here, and once she reaches the age of twenty-one, she becomes immediately able to sponsor her father, her mother, and all seven of her brothers and sisters to migrate to the United States (nine more persons). By that time the brothers and sisters, ranging in age from the early twenties to late thirties, are probably also married, so they can sponsor *their* spouses and also all of *their* children. (So now one person has been able to bring in maybe fifty more people, none of whom gained entry by demonstrating a willingness or ability to contribute to American society.)

Or if an adult aged forty, with six unmarried sons and daughters aged fifteen to twenty-five, comes to the United States legally and obtains permanent resident alien status (also legally, because of work, for example), he is able to sponsor all his unmarried sons and daughters as well as his spouse and parents to immigrate legally into the country. While this chain migration system is sometimes called the "family reunification" process, this pleasant-sounding name masks the reality of what is actually happening.

The differences in immigration patterns after this 1965 act became immense. There was *no limitation on the number of people who could become legal immigrants by this chain migration process*, so the number of *legal* immigrants into the United States, largely as a result of this law, soared from 2.1 million in the 1950s to 4.2 million in the 1970s to 6.2 million in the 1980s to about 9.7 million in the 1990s.[87] Some people may think this is a good thing (see discussion below on the benefits that immigrants bring), but the important point here is that the nation no longer even has control over the number.

Another problem traces back to 1986, when the Immigration Reform and Control Act (enacted under President Reagan) granted a one-time amnesty to about 3 million illegal immigrants who had entered the United States before January 1, 1982.[88] This act was supposed to be a one-time fix that would solve the problem of illegal immigrants in the United States, but it failed to do this, and in fact set a precedent that probably made future illegal immigrants hope that one day it would happen again, thereby giving added incentive to illegal immigration.

The problem with these immigration laws, and especially with chain migration prompted by the Hart-Celler Act, is that *the United States no longer has effective control over either the number of immigrants that come into the country or the qualifications that it can expect from immigrants*. With succeeding generations of immigrants who enter under this chain migration system, the problem will only multiply year after year into the future.

Therefore the United States no longer has the ability to decide on who can enter the nation *based on giving priority to those who show that they will contribute in the most positive way to the well-being of the nation as a whole*. Thousands upon thousands of immigrants come who do not speak English well and who do not have sufficient training for specialized jobs. They will continue to be an increasing burden to the US welfare

---

87. "Persons Obtaining Legal Permanent Resident Status: Fiscal Years 1820 to 2008," *Yearbook of Immigration Statistics*, U.S. Department of Homeland Security. www.dhs.gov/xlibrary/assets/statistics/yearbook/2008/table01.xls.

88. U.S. Citizenship and Immigration Services. www.uscis. gov/portal/site/uscis/menuitem.5af9bb95919f35e66f61417654 3f6d1a/?vgnextoid=04a295c4f635f010VgnVCM1000000ecd19 0aRCRD&vgnextchannel=b328194d3e88d010VgnVCM10000 048f3d6a1RCRD.

system, will make it harder and harder for teachers to teach using the English language, will provide an increasing burden to the medical care system of the nation, and will contribute to the growing size and increasing feelings of resentment of various isolated segments of society that do not really feel part of the nation and do not feel loyalty to the nation but feel primary loyalty to another country instead.

An even more dangerous result would occur if a single man from a Muslim country came to the United States, lived as an upstanding citizen, applied for citizenship, and obtained it. He could then sponsor for immigration five or six unmarried brothers and sisters, all of whom had trained as terrorists in a foreign nation and were coming to the United States for the purpose of bringing destruction to it.

Thus any immigration reform should repeal the chain migration system of the Hart-Celler Act and provide that a US citizen could *only* sponsor the immigration of a spouse or a minor child. Mark Levin wisely says, "No society can withstand the unconditional mass migration of aliens from every corner of the earth."[89]

b. The benefits of controlled immigration

On the other hand, we must recognize that *if it can be controlled with respect to who is allowed to enter, immigration is a great benefit to a nation.* Immigrants who want to come to the United States are, by and large, *producers* who bring benefit to the economy and *helpers* who bring other benefits to the society as a whole. The United States has immense land and resources, has the world's largest and most productive economy, and is able to accept and assimilate many thousands of people each year, all with beneficial results to the nation.

One of the great benefits of receiving immigrants was illustrated in October 2009, when the Nobel Prizes were announced. Nine people won Nobel Prizes in chemistry, physics, and medicine. Eight of them were American citizens, but of those eight, *four* were born outside the United States and came here only as graduate students or postdoctoral students or scientific researchers. In other words, nearly half of the Nobel Prizes in the scientific fields that year were won by American immigrants![90] Similar stories could be told hundreds of times in small businesses, medical research laboratories, and other ventures, where year after year recent immigrants have brought great benefits to the nation.

c. Needed patriotic and educational reforms in the schools and the immigration processes

The immigration process should also be accompanied by reform in the educational systems in the United States, so that the cultural ideals and values that have made America great are taught and passed down to each succeeding generation. In that way, children growing up in American schools can be taught the moral standards and ideals that have historically been true of the nation.

89. Levin, *Liberty and Tryanny*, 149.
90. See Susan Hockfield, "Immigrant Scientists Create Jobs and Win Nobels," *Wall Street Journal* (Oct. 20, 2009), A19.

In addition, the need to protect the well-being and security of the nation means that we should certainly continue to require that any new citizens must renounce allegiance to any other nation and swear allegiance to the United States. However, some have called for this requirement to be dropped! In an op-ed column for the *Wall Street Journal*, law professors Peter Shuck of Hofstra University and Peter J. Spiro of Yale called for dropping the "renunciation clause" from the Oath of Renunciation and Allegiance. They said immigrants should consider themselves to be "Mexican and American," for example, and basically have dual citizenship.[91]

Another reform is that we should place much greater emphasis on the need for all immigrants from every nation *to learn English well*. Out of a current US population of 307 million, current estimates are that 55 million (19.6%) now speak a language other than English at home.[92] More than 34 million of these (12.2% of the population) speak Spanish at home.[93]

If for no other reason than *care for the future well-being of Spanish-speaking people*, we should require that they speak English. I travel and teach in many countries of the world, and I can say from personal experience that *English is the one language that enables people to communicate in whatever nation they travel*. The leaders who are influencing the society in every nation largely speak English as a second language. I travel to China and find that little Chinese children are learning to speak English. I travel to a conference in Hungary attended by representatives of forty nations and find that they are all speaking English to each other. And that makes sense, because when the Swedes want to communicate with the Italians or the Czechs want to communicate with the Spaniards or the Bulgarians want to talk to the Dutch, the only language that they can all understand is English. Business conferences and scientific conferences around the world are conducted in English. English has now attained a status in the world similar to the status that Greek had in the first century, when the apostle Paul could travel to any country and speak Greek and find that he was understood. English is the second language of the whole world.

Therefore it is simply foolish and cruel to children to allow them to grow up without gaining an excellent knowledge of the English language. Lack of knowledge of English will seriously hinder their ability to achieve excellence and advancement in nearly any career field they choose.

There is another reason for requiring more English skill. The United States needs a population that speaks the same language so that people can communicate well with each other in all parts of the nation and gain a sense of being one nation and one society. If people from different national backgrounds stay in their own language group—that is, Somalis only speak to each other, Muslims only speak (in Arabic) to each other, and Mexicans only speak Spanish to each other—then we will forever remain a nation of small groups isolated from each other, and we will find it almost impossible to attain any kind of reconciliation or unity across ethnic lines.

91. Peter H. Shuck and Peter J. Spiro, "Dual Citizens, Good Americans," *Wall Street Journal* (March 18, 1998).

92. U.S. Census Bureau, "Language Spoken at Home." http://factfinder.census.gov/servlet/STTable?_bm=y&-geo_

id=01000US&-qr_name=ACS_2008_3YR_G00_S1601&-ds_name=ACS_2008_3YR_G00_.

93. Ibid.

d. Expanding the number of skilled workers who are admitted to the United States

Immigration reform should also expand the number of highly skilled people allowed into the country each year in various categories and from various countries. While we have vastly expanded the number of *unskilled* immigrants we admit through chain migration, we maintain restrictions that are far too severe on the visas granted to highly trained scientists, inventors, medical professionals, university researchers, and others with similar qualifications.

After September 11, 2001, the United States placed severe restrictions on individuals seeking visas. Officials with the National Academy of Science have said:

> Recent efforts by our government to constrain the flow of international visitors in the name of national security are having serious, unintended consequences for American science, engineering, and medicine. Ongoing research collaborations have been hampered.... Outstanding young scientists, engineers, and health researchers have been prevented from or delayed in entering this country, (and) important international conferences have been canceled or negatively impacted; and ... such conferences will be moved out of the United States in the future if the situation is not corrected.[94]

5. Step 3: Enforce tighter regulations on employers regarding illegal immigrants

There are two kinds of harm that come when employers hire illegal immigrants. First, they can exploit them, treat them unfairly, and pay them inadequately because they are quite confident that illegal immigrants will not appeal to any legal authority to correct any injustice done to them. Employers should not do this, because it is morally unjust, but to prevent it, there should be further enforcement of provisions that require employers to verify the immigration status of employees.

The second harm is that when illegal immigrants find jobs in the United States, this provides an incentive for other illegal immigrants to try to enter, thinking that they too will find jobs. This too would stop if more effective enforcement were carried out preventing employers from hiring illegal immigrants.

In Arizona (where I live), I have been told in private conversation that on January 1, 2008, the state began strict enforcement of the E-Verify program that requires employers to electronically verify the legal status of all their employees with the databases of the Social Security Administration and the Department of Homeland Security. But nationally this is still a voluntary program for most employers.[95]

---

94. Randolph Schmid, "U.S. Scientists Criticize Post–9/11 Visa Restrictions," Associated Press (Dec. 13, 2002). www.space. com/scienceastronomy/science_visas_021213.html.

95. "E-Verify," U.S. Citizenship and Immigration Services. www.uscis.gov/portal/site/uscis/menuitem.eb1d4c2a3e5b9ac8-9243c6a7543f6d1a/?vgnextoid=75bce2e261405110VgnVCM10 00004718190aRCRD&vgnextchannel=75bce2e261405110Vgn VCM1000004718190aRCRD.

6. Step 4: What should be done about illegal immigrants who are already here?

The most difficult problem with regard to immigration is what to do with illegal immigrants who are already in the United States.

I honestly do not think that any national consensus can develop on this question until the general public is persuaded not simply that politicians are *promising* to close the border, but that an effective border fence *has already been built and is effectively stopping the flow of illegal immigration into the United States* (see discussion above, pp. 473–74). At that point, the frustration, fear (sometimes well-grounded), and anger that people have, feeling that their country is being overrun by people who do not truly belong to this country, may cool down enough for a more rational discussion to occur. Once that happens, the following provisions would probably gain increasing assent:

a. Deport all known criminals

Political analyst and author Michael Medved rightly says:

> First, all parties to this debate agree that the 450,000 criminals and violators for whom outstanding deportation orders currently exist (but who the government finds it next to impossible to apprehend) must become the focus of an aggressive new effort to remove them from the country. These would include known gang members and others who have committed crimes. They constitute a real danger to the well-being of society, and I do not think that there is any reason why they should be allowed to stay within the country.[96]

b. Require immediate temporary registration of some kind for immigrants to receive any service from any facility in the United States

The first step in dealing with the remaining large number (perhaps 13 million or more) of illegal aliens should be that they must let the United States government know who they are and where they are. This would allow them to come out from the shadows and have some kind of temporary status that at least begins to put them within the legal system as long as they remain in this country. If that could be accomplished, it would take away their fear of participating in the legal system.

But how could they be persuaded to do this? It would require a national law saying that if they signed up to have temporary registration, they would not be immediately deported, and proof of such temporary registration would be required before they could receive *any* kind of benefits such as medical care or welfare or having their children attend schools or certainly working at any job.

This temporary registration would have to be coupled with a system by which they would have to seek full US citizenship or else permanent resident (green card) status or have their permission to stay in the country revoked after a certain number of years.

96. Michael Medved, "Immigration surprise: broad agreement, not polarization," *Townhall.com* (July 19, 2006). http:// townhall.com/columnists/MichaelMedved/2006/07/19/immigration_surprise_broad_agreement,_not_polarization.

(This required decision process could be a long time, such as five or ten years, and the temporary registration that they obtain could be subject to renewal if conditions and circumstances warrant it.)

c. A difficult but possible path to full citizenship

The United States discovered in 1986 that immediate amnesty given to about 3 million people was a mistake. It made the path to citizenship far too easy. However, for those who truly want to stay in the United States and also abide by the law, and *for those illegal immigrants who are contributing most positively to American society*, the biblical requirements of mercy and compassion, as well as the well-being of the nation, should make us want those immigrants to stay and continue to contribute positively to our society.

The requirements for citizenship should include a fine (which is an acknowledgment that the person has broken the law), some arrangement regarding back-taxes that need to be paid, the need to learn a good working knowledge of English, the need to swear allegiance to the United States above any other country, the need to learn the values of American society and culture, the need to show a record of employment that is continuing over time, and the need for a background check to show that they do not have a prior criminal record.

How much time should be required before they are allowed to obtain citizenship? This raises the question of fairness with respect to those who have been unable to enter the United States but have been waiting for many years for the right to enter it legally. Yet that consideration has to be balanced with the recognition that these people who want to stay and become citizens and meet these requirements have already been contributing in a very positive way to American society, and their contribution to society should be welcomed and encouraged. While it would be a question to be decided by the political process, it seems to me that a waiting period of something like five-to-ten years would be appropriate for obtaining full citizenship.

If this kind of immigration reform and this kind of path to citizenship were enacted, along with the immediate deportation of all known criminals who are illegal immigrants, then our difficult immigration problem would finally be solved, and the country would be stronger as a result. The United States would once again be opening its doors to a continual influx of citizens of many other nations who come here for the purpose of seeking a new and better life, but who also come because they admire and want to be a part of the kind of nation that we are. It seems to me that welcoming such people into our country would be all gain and no loss for the nation.

One objection that might be raised is that "foreign workers will take jobs away from Americans." However, this perspective is based on a misunderstanding of economics. The number of jobs in a society is never fixed, but is always changing. When talented new people come into a society, they may take some jobs, but they also create other jobs, because they produce goods and services that make the entire society wealthier, and their work also produces some demand for many products. In other words, they contribute to overall growth in the economy, which benefits the nation as a whole and leads to more jobs being created in the entire society. The number of jobs in the United

States has never been static—and is not now static—and the benefits that come from productive immigrants far outweigh the disadvantages.

7. What should American churches do about immigrants?

With this background, we can now ask, what should American churches do with regard to immigrants who are part of their congregations?

For immigrants who are here *legally*, churches should be a wonderful home away from home, a welcoming community that will work in many ways to help families from other nations adjust and adapt to life in this new country. (My wife, Margaret, and I remember with fondness and gratefulness the Baptist church that welcomed us, as foreign immigrants, to England from 1973 to 1976, and we also remember the Christians who have warmly welcomed us as temporary "sojourners" to many other countries.) Churches must remind employers to treat legal immigrants justly and fairly, never taking advantage of them because of their lack of language skills or lack of knowledge of American culture. All of the biblical verses regarding the "sojourner" ("alien" in the NIV) would apply to this situation.

But what about immigrants who are here *illegally?* Churches must kindly but honestly counsel such illegal immigrants that the Bible teaches that we are all to be "subject to the governing authorities" (Rom. 13:1). Therefore God requires us to be obedient to the laws of the nation in which we live. The current immigration laws of the United States require that people come here through an established legal process, and obeying that process does not require anyone to sin against God, so it does not fall under the category of the laws that we may in good conscience disobey (see above, p. 88). Illegal immigrants are obligated before God to obey the immigration laws of the United States.

In many cases it may be possible for churches to help illegal immigrants find an immigration lawyer who can help them work out a process to be able to stay in the United States legally. James Hoffmeier tells in his book about a church he was part of that did exactly this,[97] and he also speaks about a case where, with sadness, he counseled a good friend whose visitor's visa to Canada had expired, and he was fearing deportation. Hoffmeier rightly says, "My instincts told me he should do what was right and legal and trust that things would work out for him. So I helped him think through his options and encouraged him to leave Canada and apply for landed status [that is, a status that would enable him to stay in Canada permanently]." More than ten years later, Hoffmeier found out that this friend did exactly that and did eventually get his permanent resident status and was once again living in Canada. Hoffmeier says, "It was good to hear he did the right thing, followed the law, and things had worked out for him."[98]

But we must be honest and admit that there are times when this will not be possible and, in order to obey the law, illegal immigrants will have to leave and apply for entry into the United States on the same basis as everyone else, through proper legal channels.

---

97. See Hoffmeier, *The Immigration Crisis*, 159.
98. Ibid., 15.

In such cases, we must encourage them to trust God that obedience to him in the long run will be the path of greatest blessing in their lives, though they might not be able to see at the moment how that can be true.

Margaret and I had a similar situation that we encountered a few years ago. A wonderful, hard-working Hispanic woman had been coming to our home to clean it on a regular basis, and we liked her very much. But when our payments to her reached a total of $600 for the year, I asked her if she had a Social Security number. (A lawyer friend had told me that the law required me to begin making Social Security payments for her at the $600 point.) The woman said in broken English that she did not have an SSN, so with sadness we explained to her that we could not have her continue with us because we did not want to violate the laws of our country. We gave her a very generous severance check and told her, with tears, that we could not have her work for us again.

8. What about a guest worker program?

It does not seem to me that a temporary "guest worker" program would be a wise idea. Some people argue that seasonal agricultural workers should be allowed to come into the country (to California, for example) for temporary work and then exit afterward.

The difficulty—and I think the decisive objection—to such a program is that it seems almost impossible to get all such workers to abide by their agreements and return to their country of origin. Many of them simply fall beneath the radar and stay as a new group of illegal immigrants. So in this way a guest worker program becomes a pipeline for illegal immigration into a nation.

Peter Salins, political science professor at Stony Brook University, writes the following about the guest worker programs in Europe, where they have many years of experience in such a system:

> True enough, the guest workers in Germany, France, the Netherlands, Scandinavia did not assimilate; *but the majority have stayed, legally and illegally,* residing in alienated economic and cultural enclaves, resentful of and resented by their unwelcoming host citizenry. If we are determined to replicate Western Europe's full decade-old guest-worker experiment, we may soon reap the same civil discord it is experiencing today.[99]

In addition, I do not think that such a guest worker program is needed for American businesses. The economic system of supply and demand should provide enough labor even for agricultural work and should do so at a fair wage for people in the United States. There are certainly millions of *fully legal* recent immigrants who will stay in agricultural jobs.

In the future, if the market-determined wage level for agricultural workers in the United States is so low that it does not attract enough workers, employers will simply

---

99. Peter Salins, "The 'Guest-Worker' Folly," *Wall Street Journal* (June 6, 2007), A19.

have to raise wages to get enough workers to meet their needs, and the prices of the food products will have to go up accordingly. But then *the free market will be determining what the United States can produce*, and at what price, by employing people within its own borders to work at its own farms and factories.

Some people will object at this point, "But what if this means that some American farmers are driven out of business because they cannot compete with the cheaper food that is grown in other nations?" I do not think that this will happen in any significant measure, because American farmers are so resourceful and skillful that they are often able to find more productive ways to raise various crops with lower labor costs and more labor-saving machines used per worker. American farmers are the most productive farmers in the world. But if this happens to some degree, then this is simply a result of natural economic forces bringing about some shift in world markets.

Perhaps one day more strawberries will be grown in Mexico than in California. That will help Mexico and will also help ease pressure on our borders, and we should not think that American workers will then have nothing to do, because they did not want the jobs anyway at the pay that was offered. Historically, at one point about 60% of the American population was working in agriculture, but today only about 2% of the population works in agriculture. *What happened to the 58% that had to find jobs elsewhere, and their descendants (such as me—the first generation not connected at all to farming)?* They found more productive, generally higher-paying jobs in other fields, and the transition ultimately brought benefit to the economy as a whole.

13

FREEDOM OF SPEECH

A. BIBLICAL TEACHING

Several arguments from earlier chapters provide the biblical basis for a government to protect freedom of speech in a nation.

1. To prevent the abuse of power by government

Because of the tendency to sin that is in the heart of every human being (Rom. 3:23; see pp. 119–22), when rulers obtain government power, there is always a temptation for them to use that power not for the good of the people but for the benefit of the ruler himself or his friends or family. Thus government power tends to corrupt people (1 Sam. 8:11–17; 2 Sam. 11:1–27; see pp. 86–87, 125). But if a society safeguards freedom of speech, that tends to restrain government officials, because it makes them more accountable to the people. Freedom of speech allows people to speak out and criticize the government when they think it is doing something wrong.

2. To enable government to be chosen by the people

As I argued in chapter 3, there are significant reasons to hold that the Bible gives support to the idea that government should be chosen by the people themselves, which in practice means some kind of democracy (note the assumptions behind Gen. 1:27; Exod. 4:29–31; 2 Sam. 2:4; Rom. 13:4; see pp. 105–9).

If there is freedom of speech in a nation, then people are able to express their own ideas about what kind of government policy should be adopted and what candidates should be elected to office. Therefore freedom of speech in a society is necessary to protect the idea of democracy itself. Without freedom of speech (and freedom of the press), rulers could suppress any criticism of their actions and prohibit opposing candidates or any critics from being able to express their views in public. Then a true democracy would cease to exist in that society.

3. To protect human liberty

As I argued in another section in chapter 3, governments should also safeguard human liberty, which the Bible views as a highly valued privilege in the sight of God (Exod. 20:2; Lev. 25:10; Deut. 30:19; Isa. 61:1; see pp. 91–95). But one significant part of human liberty is the ability to express our ideas freely and attempt to persuade others of those ideas. Therefore this is another reason for governments to protect freedom of speech (and freedom of the press).

4. To protect religious speech

When freedom of speech in general is protected in a society, religious speech in particular will also be protected. This should be a very important value for Christians to defend, because it enables them to speak the Gospel message freely in public (and so obey Matt. 28:19–20) without fear of censorship or punishment.

5. To protect the ability of individuals to think and decide issues for themselves

I also argued above that the Bible places a high value on respecting human freedom of choice (Deut. 30:19; Josh. 24:15; Matt. 11:28; Rev. 22:17; see pp. 26–27, 91–92). But protecting people's ability to think and decide issues freely for themselves means that they must be able to have access to arguments on all sides of an issue. This can only happen if freedom of speech is permitted in a society and if all the different viewpoints on an issue are able to be freely expressed.

B. THE UNITED STATES CONSTITUTION

The founders of the United States realized that freedom of speech (along with its closely related idea of freedom of the press) is such an important protection that it was included in the First Amendment:

> Congress shall make no law respecting an establishment of religion, or prohibiting the free exercise thereof; *or abridging the freedom of speech, or of the press,* or the right of the people peaceably to assemble, and to petition the Government for a redress of grievances.[1]

---

1. Amendment 1, United States Constitution. www.law.cornell.edu/constitution/constitution.billofrights.html.

This amendment was important as a means of guarding against excessive power in the federal government, one of the primary goals of the framers of the Constitution as they sought to prevent the kind of abuse of government power that they had experienced from Great Britain.

This amendment was also a significant part of protecting human liberty, for the preface of the Constitution said that one of the purposes of the government and the Constitution was to "secure the blessings of liberty to ourselves and our posterity." Several years earlier, in the Declaration of Independence, the founders had listed "liberty" among the "certain unalienable rights" that had been given to each person "by their Creator." Therefore, protecting freedom of speech and freedom of the press was important because they were crucial components in protecting human liberty.

With this background, we can now consider some specific topics related to freedom of speech.

C. RESTRICTIONS ON FREEDOM OF SPEECH

Should any restrictions be placed on freedom of speech (and, similarly, on freedom of the press)?

For many years there have been four commonly accepted categories of speech that are still illegal and are not protected by the First Amendment. The first category is *defamation*—that is, speech that is false and wrongfully harms the reputation of another person. Laws against libel and slander fall under this category. The second category is *incitement to riot*—that is, it is illegal to shout, "Fire!" in a crowded theater, which would promote a panic and directly cause immediate harm to many people. The third and fourth categories are *obscenity* and *child pornography*.[2]

D. CAMPAIGN FINANCE RESTRICTIONS

1. The goal

The stated goals of legal restrictions on financial contributions to political campaigns are usually said to be (a) removing the corrupting influence of money from politics, and (b) giving every citizen an equal voice in political discussions.

But law professor Bradley Smith, who is also a former chairman of the Federal Election Commission and served on the FEC from 2000 to 2005, looks back at the historical record and sees a much more partisan goal:

> Campaign-finance reform is creating an intrusive regulatory regime on all levels of government. Its proponents, mostly on the left, have chiefly used it to bolster their own political fortunes and to undermine limited, constitutional

---

2. Henry Cohen, "Child Pornography: Constitutional Principles and Federal Statutes," *CRS Report for Congress* (Oct. 15, 2003). www.firstamendmentcenter.org/pdf/CRS.childporn1.pdf.

government.... From the mid-1960s on, opinion polls showed steady erosion in public support for big government and liberalism.... By 1970, Democrats feared—with reason—that their longstanding electoral majority was
in jeopardy.

To help prevent that outcome, the Democrats passed the Federal Election
Campaign Act (FECA) in 1971 (and amended it three years later), which would,
they hoped, strike at the heart of Republican political power—while leaving
untouched their own sources of influence, such as union-organized volunteers.
The law tightly limited both political contributions and any expenditure that
might "influence" an election....

Campaign-finance reform neatly accomplishes Democrats' goal of muffling
political speech on the right.[3]

Smith also points out that when supporters of such laws talk about removing "corrupting influences" from politics and giving every person an equal voice, they leave
alone "important sources of influence—including academia, and Hollywood, both
tilting to the left."[4] Then he points out that "the press" is also untouched by these
restrictions.

2. The real effects of campaign finance restrictions

The real effect of campaign finance restriction laws, therefore, is not to "level the playing
field" and give every person an equal voice. It is simply to remove much of the influence
of private citizens who want to use their own contributions to support candidates they
believe in. But if this kind of influence of average citizens is restricted by these laws, then
where does the remaining influence in politics come from? That is, is there any *advantage* that the restrictions give *to other groups*? Yes, there certainly is, for some remaining
groups are not affected by these laws, and therefore they gain influence.

Here are the real beneficiaries of campaign finance restriction laws:

(1) *Incumbents* benefit, because they already have the huge advantage of name
recognition.

(2) *The press* gains influence, because if there are spending limits on campaign advertising, then people will mostly get their information about candidates from what the
press writes and broadcasts. And it is unquestionable that the majority of the press (both
newspaper and TV) in the United States favors more liberal candidates. A May 2004 survey conducted by the Pew Research Center for the People in the Press of 547 journalists,
including 247 in the national media, found the following:

- Five times more national journalists identify themselves as "liberal" (34%) than
  "conservative" (just 7%).

---

3. Bradley Smith, "The Speech Police," *Wall Street Journal*
(Jan. 27, 2007), A13.
4. Ibid.

- The percentage of national reporters saying they are liberal has increased, from 22% in 1995 to 34% in 2004. The percentage of self-identified conservatives remains low, rising from 4% in 1995 to 7% in 2004.
- Liberals also outnumber conservatives in local newsrooms; 23% of the local journalists they questioned say they are liberals, while about half as many (12%) call themselves conservative.
- Fully 91% of those who work at national news organizations say it is *not* necessary to believe in God to be moral; 78% of local journalists agree.[5]

(3) *Labor unions* gain influence, because they are not subject to these finance restrictions, and they provide large amounts of funding and volunteer labor for more liberal candidates. In 2008, the Service Employees International Union spent $27 million through what are called "527 organizations" (more on that later) to elect candidates sympathetic to labor unions.[6]

(4) *Hollywood movies* gain influence, and they lean reliably to the left. One example is Michael Moore's *Fahrenheit 9/11,* which was a virulently anti-Bush movie. But because it was a movie, it was exempt from Federal Election Commission regulation. By contrast, there was an alternative movie that responded to much of what Michael Moore publicized in *Fahrenheit 9/11,* and that was produced by a conservative group called Citizens United. But when they tried to release the film, the FEC objected, saying it had to submit to the campaign finance regulation laws. This was because it was not produced by a Hollywood film studio that is "normally in the movie business."[7] (However, Citizens United won their case when they appealed this matter to the US Supreme Court. In a 5–4 decision in the case *Citizens United v. FEC,* announced January 21, 2010, the court overturned parts of the McCain-Feingold bill and declared that corporations and unions could purchase political ads (but not contribute directly to candidates) at any point in an election cycle. I see this decision, which also grants more freedom to nonprofit corporations, as a significant victory for freedom of speech in the United States.)

(5) *University faculty members* gain influence, and they have significant impact on young voters who are in or have recently graduated from universities. But university faculty members overwhelmingly tilt leftward in their political convictions. A 2005 poll of college and university faculty headed by Robert Lichter, a professor at George Mason University, found that 72% of the faculty described themselves as liberal, compared with only 15% who called themselves conservative. Some 50% said they were Democrats, compared with only 11% who said they were Republicans; 51% said that they rarely or never attended church. Lichter said, "What's most striking is how few conservatives there are in any field. There was no field we studied in which there were more conservatives than liberals or more Republicans than Democrats. It's

5. "How Journalists See Journalists in 2004," *Pew Research Center for the People and the Press,* 24. http://people-press.org/reports/pdf/214.pdf.

6. "Top 50 Federally Focused Organizations," Center for Responsive Politics. www.opensecrets.org/527s/527cmtes.php?level=C&cycle=2008.

7. Smith, "Speech Police," A13.

a very homogenous environment, not just in the places you'd expect to be dominated by liberals."[8]

(6) *Super-wealthy candidates* benefit, because the campaign finance laws still allow a candidate to contribute unlimited amounts of money to his own campaign. Therefore these laws have not "kept the money out of politics," but they have made it much more difficult for an ordinary citizen of modest means to enter a campaign on his own when an opponent can simply chip in millions or even tens of millions of dollars of his own money and far outspend any opponent of moderate means.

This is one reason why there are numerous multimillionaires now in prominent political offices in the United States. A report in November 2009 said there are now 237 millionaires in Congress![9] This includes many Democrats such as Herbert Kohl of Wisconsin (worth about $214.5 million through Kohl's discount clothing stores) and Senator John Kerry of Massachusetts (worth about $208.8 million and married to Theresa Heinz Kerry of the Heinz food fortune). House Speaker Nancy Pelosi was the twenty-second-wealthiest person in Congress ($31.4 million). There are also some wealthy Republicans, such as Darrell Issa of California ($251 million) and Vernon Buchanan of Florida ($142 million), but in 2008, eight of the ten wealthiest members of Congress were Democrats.[10]

Another effect of these campaign finance laws has been to make it much more difficult for ordinary citizens to run for office or even participate in a campaign. Former FEC Chairman Bradley Smith quotes several examples from a file of numerous letters he received from ordinary citizens who, without intending to violate any law, were tripped up by complex reporting requirements for campaign finances and were facing fines for doing what they thought was simply carrying out their civic duty of participating in a political campaign.

For example, when four men made a homemade sign that said "VOTE REPUBLICAN: NOT AL GORE SOCIALISM" and put it on the side of a trailer next to a Texas highway, the FEC spent nearly *eighteen months* investigating them for improper documentation![11] An experienced CPA who had served as an unpaid campaign treasurer on a volunteer basis, but who was being fined more than $7,000 for improper reporting, wrote to the FEC, "No job I have ever undertaken caused me more stress than this one. I was frightened and concerned every day that I would do something wrong."[12] Rather than enabling *ordinary citizens* to participate in the political process, these laws are frightening people away from participating in politics in any way. They are chilling and destroying ordinary freedom of speech in the nation.

---

8. Howard Kurtz, "College Faculties a Most Liberal Lot, Study Finds," *Washington Post* (March 29, 2005). www.washingtonpost.com/wp-dyn/articles/A8427–2005Mar28.html.

9. "Congressmen Lose Big Bucks in 2008, But Still Rank Among Nation's Richest," Center for Responsive Politics (Nov. 4, 2008). www.opensecrets.org/news/2009/11/congressmen-lose-big-bucks-in.html.

10. For a list, see the website of the Center for Responsive Politics at www.opensecrets.org/pfds/overview.php?type=W&year=2008 (accessed Nov. 10, 2009). The website cautions that the public disclosure forms required of members of Congress only list assets in broad ranges of value, so these estimates are approximate.

11. Ibid.

12. Ibid.

Finally, the real effect of these laws has *not* been to keep money out of politics. Hundreds of millions of dollars are still spent, first, because wealthy candidates contribute their own money to their campaigns, and second, because a loophole was discovered in the law by which so-called "527 organizations" could raise unlimited amounts of money and spend unlimited amounts of money to influence elections so long as they don't coordinate the activities with any specific candidate or party. For example, in the 2003–4 election campaign, currency speculator George Soros was reported to have donated more than $23.5 million to 527 organizations (such as MoveOn.org) that were dedicated to preventing the reelection of George W. Bush as President and Republicans to Congress.[13] If such a man can spend over $23 million to influence an election, then of what use are the current laws that place a $2,400 annual limit on personal contributions to a candidate? Soros contributed *10,000 times* that much! Our campaign finance laws greatly hinder ordinary citizens from giving more support to their candidate, but they simply have not been able to keep money out of politics.

3. Campaign finance laws have become a booby-trapped minefield that can destroy innocent people

Because the campaign finance laws have become so complex and confusing, it is remarkably easy for citizens and candidates who intend nothing wrong to find themselves accused of campaign finance violations.

A former commissioner on the Federal Election Commission, Hans A. von Spakovsky, explains:

> The Federal Election Campaign Act (FECA), passed in 1972, is 244 pages of restrictions and requirements. The regulations issued by the FEC are an additional 568 pages. The Federal Register is filled with 1,278 pages of explanations and justifications from the FEC for its regulation. The FEC has issued almost 1,800 advisory opinions since 1975, trying to explain to a confused regulated community the meaning of various provisions of FECA. The law and the regulations are a Byzantine labyrinth that burdens the ability to participate in political debate and federal elections.[14]

4. Restricting campaign contributions is restricting freedom of speech

In light of the preceding information, it seems clear that the United States should simply recognize that *restricting contributions to political campaigns is restricting freedom of speech* and is actually contrary to the First Amendment. In modern society it is impossible to get a message out to enough people to win an election unless you have the money to buy advertising on TV, on the Internet, and through print media and mailings. Simply saying that I have freedom of speech to knock on doors in my neighborhood is not sufficient,

13. "Going Out on Top," Center for Responsive Politics (Aug. 9, 2005). www.opensecrets.org/capital_eye/inside.php?ID=179.

14. Hans A. von Spakovsky, "What's Wrong with 'Hillary: the Movie'?" *Wall Street Journal* (Aug. 29, 2009), A13.

because it would be impossible for me or any other candidate to reach enough voters to get a message out effectively in the time available for any political campaign today other than at a very small, local level.

This is why eight former commissioners on the Federal Election Commission filed a brief that urged the Supreme Court to overrule two of its previous decisions and declare that the McCain-Feingold campaign finance law of 2002 is unconstitutional. One of these commissioners writes:

> It's clear to us that the D.C. Court's decision should be overturned on First Amendment grounds and McCain-Feingold ruled unconstitutional....[15]

The eight former commissioners argue that current campaign finance restrictions

> fundamentally violate the First Amendment and have chilled political speech.... The law and its accompanying regulations are so complex and so confusing that ordinary citizens, and even specialists, have a hard time understanding what's legally permissible and what's not.[16]

5. What is the solution?

It seems to me that the solution would be to abolish all these restrictions on campaign financing except for a requirement that all donations above a certain amount ($500? or $1,000?) be publicly reported, so that the public is aware of where the funding and the influence is coming from for various political advertisements.

Some may object that abolishing these finance restrictions will enable various people to "buy" elections. But they fail to realize that *unlimited amounts of money can already be spent by super-wealthy candidates on their own campaigns* (note all the millionaires in Congress). Still, while millions of dollars can help, sometimes wealthy candidates are defeated. On November 3, 2009, for example, Jon Corzine was defeated in his reelection attempt as governor of New Jersey, even though he had spent massive amounts of his own money to attempt to win the election. (Corzine was a former chairman and co-CEO of the investment firm Goldman Sachs.) Over the years he had spent $130 million in his bids for higher office, and in October 2009 alone, he "lent" his campaign $4.7 million dollars.[17] Also, Mitt Romney, who has an estimated net worth between $100 and $200 million, was unable to win the Republican presidential nomination, though he spent $42 million in his loss to John McCain.[18] In 1992 and 1996, Texas billionaire Ross Perot spent $63.5 million on his independent bids for President,[19] and Steve Forbes spent $38 million on his 1996 run for President. Both failed to win.[20]

---

15. Ibid.

16. Ibid.

17. Bill Pascoe, "Corzine's Self-Funded Campaign: Will Taxpayers Get Stuck with the Tab?" *CQ Politics* (Oct. 30, 2009). http://blogs.cqpolitics.com/in_the_right/2009/10/corzine.html.

18. "Romney Put in $42 Million of His Own Fortune," *Boston Globe* (Feb. 20, 2008). www.boston.com/news/politics/politicalintelligence/2008/02/romney_put_in_4.html.

19. Ibid.

20. Ibid.

E. CAMPUS "HATE SPEECH" CODES AND OTHER RESTRICTIONS OF FREE SPEECH ON COLLEGE CAMPUSES

In the past twenty years many colleges and universities in the United States (and even governments in other countries) have enacted policies that restrict freedom of speech in various ways. The Foundation for Individual Rights in Education (FIRE) has reported that 253 public universities have "speech code" policies that can be used to severely restrict free speech, including religious speech. This is 97% of all public universities![21] Whereas previous restrictions of freedom of speech were only because some speech could cause immediate harm to other people (such as slander or inciting to riot), these new "hate speech" regulations attempted to restrict speech that would cause "offense" to someone else. Therefore new rules have been adopted that prohibit or penalize speech that would offend people because of their race, gender, religion, disability, national origin, or "sexual orientation."

Various kinds of restrictions on the speech of Christians and others with conservative moral views have often been the result.

1. Censoring the Gospel and expressions of Christian moral values

Because of such "hate speech" codes, sometimes students have been penalized for expressing belief in the Gospel of Jesus Christ or attempting to share their faith with others. In other cases, Christians have been penalized for expressing Christian moral values, such as a conviction that homosexual conduct is contrary to Scripture or supporting California's Proposition 8, which defined marriage as between one man and one woman.

The good news is that in numerous cases Christian legal organizations such as the Alliance Defense Fund (ADF) have had remarkable success in challenging these policies, claiming that they are an unconstitutional violation of the First Amendment's guarantees of freedom of speech. They have launched a special litigation effort to defend the God-given First Amendment freedoms of students at public universities (www.speakupmovement.org). As of November 2009, they have never lost a case litigated to conclusion against these unconstitutional policies. For example:

- Georgia Tech University enacted a speech code that prohibited "acts of intolerance," engaged in viewpoint discrimination by defunding religious student groups, and fostered a state-approved religious view of homosexual behavior by informing students to shun religious groups that do not affirm homosexual behavior. A federal court ruled that the speech code be replaced, and it later found that the program denigrating religions that do not approve of homosexual behavior was unconstitutional.[22]

21. "FIRE's Spotlight on Speech Codes 2009," Foundation for Individual Rights in Education (2009), 4.

22. *Sklar v. Georgia Tech.*

- After ADF attorneys filed suit, officials at Savannah State University in Georgia quickly settled with a student group that had been dismissed from campus for engaging in "harassment," because they shared their faith with other students, and "hazing," because they engaged in the biblical practice of foot-washing. The group was restored to campus.[23]
- ADF attorneys in the state of Washington filed a lawsuit against officials of Community Colleges of Spokane and Spokane Falls Community College for violating the constitutional rights of pro-life students. SFCC officials threatened Beth Sheeran and members of a Christian student group with disciplinary measures, including expulsion, if they chose to hold a pro-life event on campus to share information with other students, because the message was "discriminatory" and did not include a pro-abortion viewpoint. The school eventually settled.[24]

But the bad news is that such legal challenges are necessary at all in the United States, with its historic legacy of freedom of speech. There are thousands of students who never know they can file a legal challenge, but just quietly submit to these misguided restrictions on their speech.

2. Discrimination against Christian organizations

In a number of cases, Christian organizations such as InterVarsity Christian Fellowship or the Christian Legal Society have been prohibited from meeting on university campuses or being recognized as a legitimate university organization along with other organizations. In other cases these groups have been pressured to accept leaders who do not affirm their beliefs, and if they refuse, they are denied the right to meet on campus or use campus facilities to promote their meetings.

ADF has been involved in numerous legal cases involving these so-called "nondiscrimination" policies, which are used only to discriminate against Christians! Here are some examples:

- Rutgers University used a "nondiscrimination" statement to require an InterVarsity Christian Fellowship to accept leaders who reject the group's Christian beliefs. After an ADF attorney filed suit, the school quickly dropped their effort.[25] Conservative commentator Laura Ingraham said, "One can only imagine if a group of devout Christians tried to join a Rutgers lesbian student group. The Christians would probably be brought up on disciplinary charges, accused of violating Rutgers' principle of community.'"[26] Alan Kors of FIRE commented that "if an evangelical Christian who believed homosexuality to be a sin tried to become president of the university's Bisexual, Gay, and Lesbian Alliance ... the administration would have led candlelight vigils on behalf of diversity and free expression."[27]

---

23. *Commissioned II Love v. Scott.*

24. *Sheeran v. Shea.*

25. "Rutgers University settles case fully in favor of the Rutgers InterVarsity Multi-Ethnic Christian Fellowship," *ADF Press*

Release (April 2, 2003). www.alliancedefensefund.org/news/pressrelease.aspx?cid=2931.

26. Laura Ingraham, "Universities Throwing Christians to the Lions," *Laura Ingraham E-Blast* (Jan. 6, 2003).

- Christian Legal Society chapters at Arizona State University,[28] Ohio State University,[29] and Southern Illinois University,[30] to name just a few, have had to file lawsuits with the help of ADF attorneys to successfully preserve their ability to reserve leadership positions for Christians.
- Officials at the University of North Carolina at Chapel Hill tried to force a Christian fraternity to open up its leadership to individuals who reject Christianity. ADF attorneys filed suit, and the school backed down.[31]

One recent high-profile case at the Supreme Court had the potential for a landmark ruling that would resolve such cases for the entire nation. The case *Christian Legal Society v. Martinez* involved a Christian Legal Society chapter that had been denied recognized student organization status at Hastings College of Law in San Francisco because it refused to agree to allow non-Christians to become officers and voting members. It also required its officers and voting members to refrain from unrepentant sexual conduct outside of marriage between one man and one woman. I was one of the authors of an *amicus curiae* ("friend of the court") brief in which evangelical scholars in Bible and theology argued that the CLS standards were necessary to their deeply held core religious beliefs and flowed directly and properly from their belief in the Bible as the inspired Word of God.[32] Unfortunately, CLS lost the case in a narrowly decided 5-to-4 ruling on June 28, 2010.

Other examples of discrimination against Christian groups on public university campuses are related to student fees. The University of Virginia denied a Christian newspaper equal access to student fees because of its "Christian perspective" even though it funded other student publications. The case, *Rosenberger v. Rector and Visitors of the University of Virginia*, eventually went all the way to the US Supreme Court, which ruled that the university had acted unconstitutionally when it denied the paper the same funding that all other groups received.[33] (This was a 5–4 decision announced June 29, 1995, with Rehnquist, Kennedy, O'Connor, Scalia, and Thomas in the majority and Souter, Stevens, Ginsburg, and Breyer in dissent.) This case set a legal precedent that has been used to reverse hundreds of unconstitutional actions denying Christians equal access to public facilities and funding.

---

27. John Leo, "Playing the Bias Card," *U.S. News and World Report* (Jan. 13, 2003).

28. "ADF and CLS Reach Settlement Agreement with Arizona State University," *ADF Press Release* (Sept. 5, 2005). www.alliancedefensefund.org/news/pressrelease.aspx?cid=3520.

29. "Ohio State University throws in the towel, agrees to change non-discrimination policy," *ADF Press Release* (Oct. 4, 2004). www.alliancedefensefund.org/news/pressrelease.aspx?cid=2811.

30. "Southern Illinois University settles lawsuit with Christian Legal Society, will recognize chapter," *ADF Press Release*

(May 22, 2007). www.alliancedefensefund.org/news/pressrelease.aspx?cid=4126.

31. "Federal court to UNC-Chapel Hill: Suspend your policy," *ADF Press Release* (March 5, 2005). www.alliancedefensefund.org/news/pressrelease.aspx?cid=3358.

32. See Evangelical Scholars brief at www.abanet.org/publiced/preview/briefs/pdfs/09-10/08-1371_PetitionerAmCuEvangelicalScholarsand2Grps.pdf.

33. Summary of *Rosenberger v. Rector and Visitors of the University of Virginia*, Alliance Defense Fund. www.alliancedefensefund.org/news/story.aspx?cid=2583.

These cases and many others demonstrate that the Alliance Defense Fund and other Christian legal groups have had remarkable success in protecting the rights of these organizations to have campus access equal to that of any other student organization.

3. Conclusion

Almost uniformly, such "hate speech" codes constitute a wrongful restriction of freedom of speech. For the twenty years or so that such speech codes were allowed to operate freely on American campuses, they no doubt contributed to a remarkable muzzling of conservative moral and religious ideas (and probably conservative political ideas as well). Therefore they effectively indoctrinated students in more liberal moral, political, and religious values. This was done in many state universities with the funding provided by taxpayer dollars, yet the policies were promoting views explicitly *contrary* to the views of large numbers of citizens paying those taxes and supporting those universities, and *contrary* to the views of parents who were paying thousands of dollars in tuition for their children to attend those universities. Some extensive documentation of this effect has been produced in printed form and on DVD.[34]

Such "hate speech" codes are wrong, both because they violate the biblical value of freedom of speech, which is grounded in a number of values mentioned in the first section of this chapter, and because, in the United States, they are violations of a basic constitutional right, the freedom of speech.

If the principle of freedom of speech does not protect speech that other people find offensive or objectionable, then it is not really freedom of speech at all. University campuses should especially be places where a wide diversity of viewpoints can be expressed freely without penalty and without fear of recrimination.

The argument that some speech might cause some people to *feel offended* might be an argument for personally advising the speaker to be more thoughtful in his speech, but it is certainly not an argument that any law or university policy should be used to bring penalties against the speaker.

Nor is it true that expressing *moral opposition* to a certain action *will inevitably lead to violence* against others. For instance, arguing that *abortion* is morally wrong does not *necessarily* or even *probably* lead people to take violent action against those who carry out abortions. Nor does arguing that *homosexual conduct* is morally wrong lead *necessarily* or even *probably* to others taking violent action against homosexuals.

Any speech, in order to be properly restricted by law, needs to *directly cause actual harm* to another person, as inciting to riot in a crowded theater would do. In fact, it is exactly *the free discussion of differences* regarding moral values and principles that is necessary to allow a democracy to work these questions out fairly and reasonably in the political process.

---

34. See the film *Indoctrinate U*, written by Evan Coyne Malloney, which is available for purchase on Amazon.com, but I have not been able to find it available on Netflix—which is remarkable considering the thousands of DVDs they carry. Another documentation of such bias in universities is *One-* *Party Classroom: How Radical Professors at America's Top Colleges Indoctrinate Students and Undermine Our Democracy*, by David Horowitz and Jacob Laskin (New York: Crown Forum, 2009).

Therefore it should be a cause for thanksgiving—especially by Christians, but also by everyone who values freedom of speech—that legal challenges to these "hate speech" codes have been successful time and again and are beginning to turn back this wrongful policy on American campuses.

Unfortunately, such wrongful restrictions of "hate speech" are still in force in many other nations, sometimes even as a matter of national law. In Sweden, Pastor Ake Green was sentenced to six months in prison for preaching in his church a sermon on sexual behavior, which was deemed to be hate speech. His case eventually went to the Swedish Supreme Court, where he was acquitted, but not before he was told by the prosecutor to "get a new Bible" that does not include sexual issues.[35] The law he was punished under read:

> Anyone who, through expression or other form of communication that is spread, *threatens* **or** *expresses disrespect* for a group of people or other such groups of persons with reference to race, color, national or ethnic origin, confession of faith or sexual orientation, is *sentenced for instigation* against a group of people to prison up to *two years* or, if the crime is minor, to fines. If the crime is major … *at least six months and up to four years* in jail. In the determination of whether the crime is major, consideration shall be given to whether the message has had an especially *threatening* **or** *offensive* content and whether the message has been spread to a great number of people in a way that is meant to generate considerable attention.[36]

In the Netherlands, Dutch authorities in 2000 attempted to prosecute Pope John Paul II on discrimination charges after he said that a homosexual advocacy march in Rome was "an offense to Christian values." They eventually realized that the Pope had "global immunity" because of his position as the head of the Vatican state, and therefore they could not pursue legal action against him.[37]

In 2003 the Canadian Parliament passed C–250,[38] which placed severe restrictions on the free speech of churches and ministries. For instance, Janet Epp of the Buckingham Evangelical Fellowship of Canada said, "Pastors are afraid. They're afraid to preach on this subject. Nobody wants the police to come to their door."[39] In addition, Focus on the Family cannot air radio programs in Canada on the topic of homosexual behavior without facing sanctions from the Canadian Communications Commission.

In December 2007 the Saskatchewan Human Rights Commission's imposition of a "lifetime" ban on a local man's freedom to publicly criticize homosexuality was upheld in its entirety by Saskatchewan Court of Queens Bench. Bill Whatcott was ordered to

---

35. Firsthand testimony of Benjamin Bull of the Alliance Defense Fund, who assisted with Pastor Green's defense and was present at his trial.

36. "Freedom of Religion on Trial in Sweden." www.akeg-reen.org.

37. "Dutch Will Not Prosecute Pope for Anti-Gay Remarks," *Reuters* (July 18, 2000).

38. C–250, Second Session, Thirty-seventh Parliament 51–52 Elizabeth II, 2002–2003, House of Commons of Canada, passed September 17, 2003.

39. "Canada's Anti-Gay Violence Law Worries Some," *Fox News* (May 18, 2004). www.foxnews.com/story/0,2933,120195,00.html.

pay $17,500 (Canadian) to four individuals who complained that their "feelings" and "self-respect" were "injured" by Whatcott's pamphlets that were critical of homosexual behavior.[40]

Several of these countries do not have the First Amendment protection that we have in the United States. Christians in those countries should oppose such wrongful restrictions on the basic right to freedom of speech in an open and democratic society.

F. THE "FAIRNESS DOCTRINE" AND TALK RADIO

In 1949 the Federal Communications Commission (FCC) introduced a policy called the "Fairness Doctrine," which required that radio stations broadcasting some discussion of controversial issues do so in a way that is honest, equitable, and balanced. In practice this meant that radio stations would often present speakers giving differing views of some political issue or other controversial public matter. But the policy was based on the idea that there were *a limited number of broadcast channels available,* so it was designed to give different sides an opportunity to get their views before the public.

The FCC abolished the Fairness Doctrine in 1987, reasoning that by that time there were so many radio stations and broadcasting channels open that it was no longer necessary to require every station to present differing sides of controversial issues, since that was being done by other stations that held different viewpoints. In this way the FCC was recognizing the principle that radio had become something like newspapers, for which any application of a fairness doctrine would be an obviously unconstitutional restriction of freedom of the press. At the time of the repeal of the Fairness Doctrine, the FCC stated the following:

> The intrusion by government into the content of programming occasioned by enforcement of [the Fairness Doctrine] restricts the journalistic freedom of broadcasters ... [and] actually inhibits the presentation of controversial issues of public concern to the detriment of the public and the degradation of the editorial prerogative of the broadcast journalist.[41]

The actual result of the *abolition* of the Fairness Doctrine has been *the proliferation of conservative talk radio.* Of course, liberal and conservative and Christian radio stations and stations with any other viewpoint are all free to go into business and broadcast as they wish. But as it turned out, conservatives discovered that there was finally a media outlet (talk radio) that on several stations quite consistently represented their own views (as opposed to the major TV networks or major newspapers), so political conservatives have supported conservative talk radio in overwhelming numbers.

Has this been a good development?

---

40. Hilary White, "Catholic Activist 'Banned for Life' from Publicly Criticising Homosexuality," *LifeSiteNews.net* (Dec. 13, 2007). www.lifesite.net/ldn/2007/dec/07121306.html.

41. John Shu, "Fairness Doctrine," Federalist Society (April 13, 2009). www.fed-soc.org/publications/pubID.1327/pub_detail.asp.

It seems to me that this development has been a wonderful and positive expression of freedom of speech and freedom of the press in the United States. There have been some liberal talk radio stations also, but in general they have not fared nearly as well, nor have many of them been able to attract sufficient advertising dollars to stay in business.

Now some liberal politicians have raised the question, "Should the Fairness Doctrine be reinstituted by the Federal Communications Commission?"

My response is, "Definitely not." If the Fairness Doctrine were reinstituted by the FCC, it would essentially destroy conservative talk radio and would leave American media once again dominated by the liberal journalists who control the major sources of TV and newspaper reporting as well as the government-supported National Public Radio.

How would the Fairness Doctrine destroy talk radio? It would mean that after every hour of Rush Limbaugh's broadcast, the station would have to broadcast an hour of an "alternative viewpoint" by some liberal commentator. And so it would be with every conservative talk show, such as those of Hugh Hewitt, Dennis Prager, Michael Medved, and Sean Hannity. Stations would be allowed to broadcast these conservative commentators only half of the time and would have to broadcast equally liberal commentators the rest of the time. Listeners would never know which viewpoint they were going to hear, and listening audiences would rapidly decline, cutting advertising revenue and making it impossible for these stations to stay in business.

Why would listenership decline? Because *liberal talk shows do not attract many listeners*, as the failure of many liberal radio networks such as Air America has demonstrated. For instance, even liberal *Vanity Fair* magazine reported, "At its height, the network's most popular program, *The Al Franken Show*, was carried by 92 affiliates and had 1.5 million weekly listeners. By contrast, *The Rush Limbaugh Show* is carried by more than 600 affiliates and has somewhere between 14 million and 20 million weekly listeners."[42]

In addition, radio stations would be subject to the large expense of legal fees for responding to regulators from the FCC who are challenging the amount of time given to one issue or another and challenging whether it is "fair" or not. In other words, this would result in *large-scale government regulation of the content* broadcast by radio stations, and thus would be a huge attack against freedom of speech.

Christians who are concerned about freedom of speech as well as any conservatives who are concerned about restricting the right of radio stations to exercise freedom of speech should be concerned about this threat and about any other attempt by liberal politicians to impose creeping new legislation that would further burden conservative stations with *more expenses* and *more restrictions* on the kind of content that they can carry.

---

42. Matt Pressman, "Whatever Happened to Air America?" *Vanity Fair* (March 12, 2009). www.vanityfair.com/online/politics/2009/03/what-ever-happened-to-air-america.html.

Chapter 14

FREEDOM OF RELIGION

A. BIBLICAL AND CONSTITUTIONAL BACKGROUND

The biblical basis for freedom of religion was explained in chapter 3 (see pp. 99–100). Jesus said, "Render to Caesar the things that are Caesar's, and to God the things that are God's" (Matt. 22:21). In this statement Jesus established the principle of a distinct realm of "things that belong to God" that should not be regulated or constrained by the government (or "Caesar"). Although Jesus did not specify what things belong to this realm that is outside of Caesar's control, certainly "the things that belong to God" must include decisions and actions regarding worship and doctrinal beliefs. This means that people's *religious convictions and religious activities* should clearly be an area in which government gives citizens complete freedom.

This principle was illustrated in the early history of the church when the governing authorities of the Jewish Sanhedrin attempted to prevent the early apostles from preaching the Gospel. But Peter and the other apostles refused to submit to this governmental restriction on freedom of religion, saying, "We cannot but speak of what we have seen and heard" (Acts 4:20), and then later, "We must obey God rather than men" (Acts 5:29).

I also argued in chapter 1 (pp. 23–29) that governments should not compel religion, because religious belief, if it is to be genuine, cannot be forced on people against their will. Therefore the government should not try to force compliance with any particular religious belief or practice, or compel people to support any particular religion.

These principles were rightly embodied in the First Amendment to the US Constitution, which says:

Congress shall make no law respecting an establishment of religion, or prohibiting the exercise thereof....[1]

With this simple statement the Constitution rightly established the proper boundaries for religions and for the state. It protected "free exercise" of religion but then also prohibited the government from making any one religion the "established" religion or the official religion of the government.

But subsequent Supreme Court rulings in the twentieth century significantly distorted the First Amendment from its original meaning. The First Amendment was not understood by anyone in 1787 (when the Constitution was adopted) to prohibit government officials from freely expressing their own religious beliefs in public and particularly at government functions, nor was it understood that way by the entire legal system of the United States for about the next two centuries.

For example, for many years the US Congress allowed Christian worship services to be conducted on Sundays in the Capitol itself. When Thomas Jefferson was President, church services were regularly held there. Jefferson not only attended the service, but made arrangements for the Marine band to play in it. Services were also held in the Supreme Court building. According to the Library of Congress, "Throughout his administration Jefferson permitted church services in executive branch buildings. The Gospel was also preached in the Supreme Court chambers."[2] After the Civil War, the First Congregational Church of Washington held services in the House of Representatives.[3]

Numerous presidential proclamations have made reference to God or even more specific reference to Christian beliefs. For instance, virtually every president since George Washington has issued a proclamation calling for a national Day of Thanksgiving. Washington's first proclamation read:

> WHEREAS it is the duty of all nations to acknowledge the providence of Almighty God, to obey His will, to be grateful for His benefits, and humbly to implore His protection and favor; and whereas both Houses of Congress have, by their joint committee, requested me "to recommend to the people of the United States a day of public thanksgiving and prayer, to be observed by acknowledging with grateful hearts the many and signal favors of Almighty God, especially by affording them an opportunity peaceably to establish a form of government for their safety and happiness...."[4]

In 1863 the US Senate requested President Abraham Lincoln to "designate and set apart a day for national prayer and humiliation." The request read:

> [S]incerely believing that no people, however great in numbers and resources or however strong in the justice of their cause, can prosper without His favor;

1. Amendment 1, United States Constitution. www.law.cornell.edu/constitution/constitution.billofrights.html.

2. "The State Becomes the Church: Jefferson and Madison," Part VI: Religion and the Federal Government. www.loc.gov/exhibits/religion/rel06–2.html.

3. Ibid.

4. "Proclamation—Thanksgiving Day 1789" (Oct. 3, 1789). www.wallbuilders.com/libissuesarticles.asp?id=3584.

and at the same time deploring the national offences which have provoked His righteous judgment, yet encouraged in this day of trouble by the assurances of His word to seek Him for succor according to His appointed way through Jesus Christ, the Senate of the United States do hereby request the President of the United States, by his proclamation, to designate and set apart a day for national prayer and humiliation.[5]

Lincoln complied with their request, issuing the following proclamation:

It has pleased Almighty God to hearken to the supplications and prayers of an afflicted people and to vouchsafe to the Army and the Navy of the United States victories on land and on the sea so signal and so effective as to furnish reasonable grounds for augmented confidence that the Union of these States will be maintained, their Constitution preserved, and their peace and prosperity permanently restored. But these victories have been accorded not without sacrifices of life, limb, health, and liberty, incurred by brave, loyal, and patriotic citizens. Domestic affliction in every part of the country follows in the train of these fearful bereavements. It is meet and right to recognize and confess the presence of the Almighty Father and the power of His hand equally in these triumphs and in these sorrows: Now, therefore, be it known that I do set apart Thursday, the 6th day of August next, to be observed as a day for national thanksgiving, praise, and prayer, and I invite the people of the United States to assemble on that occasion in their customary places of worship and in the forms approved by their own consciences render the homage due to the Divine Majesty for the wonderful things He has done in the nation's behalf and invoke the influence of His Holy Spirit to subdue the anger which has produced and so long sustained a needless and cruel rebellion, to change the hearts of the insurgents, to guide the counsels of the Government with wisdom adequate to so great a national emergency, and to visit with tender care and consolation throughout the length and breadth of our land all those who, through the vicissitudes of marches, voyages, battles, and sieges, have been brought to suffer in mind, body, or estate, and finally to lead the whole nation through the paths of repentance and submission to the divine will back to the perfect enjoyment of union and fraternal peace.[6]

In 1944 President Franklin Roosevelt went on national radio and offered the following prayer for the soldiers who had landed on the Normandy Beaches to commence D-Day operations:

And so, in this poignant hour, I ask you to join with me in prayer: Almighty God: Our sons, pride of our Nation, this day have set upon a mighty endeavor, a struggle to preserve our Republic, our religion, and our civilization, and to

---

5. *Journal of the Senate of the United States of America, Being the Third Session of the Thirty-Seventh Congress* (Washington, DC: Government Printing Office, 1863), 378–79.

6. "Proclamation—Day of Thanksgiving, Praise, and Prayer, August 6, 1863." www.presidency.ucsb.edu/ws/index.php?pid=69897.

set free a suffering humanity. Lead them straight and true; give strength to their arms, stoutness to their hearts, steadfastness in their faith.... And for us at home—fathers, mothers, children, wives, sisters, and brothers of brave men overseas—whose thoughts and prayers are ever with them—help us, Almighty God, to rededicate ourselves in renewed faith in Thee in this hour of great sacrifice. Many people have urged that I call the Nation into a single day of special prayer. But because the road is long and the desire is great, I ask that our people devote themselves in a continuance of prayer. As we rise to each new day, and again when each day is spent, let words of prayer be on our lips, invoking Thy help to our efforts.... And, O Lord, give us Faith. Give us Faith in Thee; Faith in our sons; Faith in each other; Faith in our united crusade...."[7]

Therefore, as I explained in more detail in chapter 5 (p. 137), recent Supreme Court decisions that have had the effect of *excluding religious expression from the public square* cannot be justified by the original intention or original meaning of the First Amendment. None of the original authors of the Constitution, and none of the national officials first elected under the Constitution, gave any indication that they intended that exclusion to be the meaning of the Constitution, nor did any of the states that approved the Constitution.

Thus the modern concept of "separation of church and state," by which people argue that no government property or government function should contain any religious expression, has no legitimate basis in the original meaning of the Constitution.

What, then, is its basis? This idea of such a strict "separation of church and state" is based on a modern myth that the Constitution legally requires it, whereas those words are found nowhere in the Constitution and nowhere in any subsequent national laws that were passed by Congress. This myth is sustained by endless repetition in the press today, but it finds no legitimate basis in the laws or in the actual Constitution of the United States.

How, then, did this myth of "separation of church and state" acquire its power in our government? As I explained in chapter 5 (pp. 136–37), it acquired its power simply because it was imposed on the country by certain decisions of the Supreme Court, especially the decision *Everson v. Board of Education* (1947) and also the decision *Lemon v. Kurtzman* (1971). These decisions have led to numerous other legal controversies as well as to actions such as the prohibition of prayers before high school graduation ceremonies, the removal of crosses or other religious symbols from state seals, the prohibition of the teaching of intelligent design as an alternative to evolution, or (in some places) stopping the teaching of abstinence as part of a sexual-education curriculum.[8]

But if we return to the basic biblical principle that government should allow *freedom of religion* and *freedom of religious expression*, and if we go back to the original meaning

---

7. Franklin Delano Roosevelt, Prayer on D-Day, June 6, 1944. www.presidency.ucsb.edu/ws/index.php?pid=16515.

8. See "Abstinence Scofflaws" at www.villagevoice.com/2002–08–20/news/abstinence-scofflaws/.

of the First Amendment, then we will reach some different conclusions about questions related to freedom of religion in the United States today.

B. RELIGIOUS EXPRESSION IN THE PUBLIC SQUARE

Once we base our reasoning on the more sure grounds of biblical teaching and the original meaning of the First Amendment, a proper conclusion is that the government in the United States today should allow much more space in the public square for a wide variety of religious expression. In fact, in some areas this principle still works quite well.

For example, with regard to the armed forces, there is an allocation of chaplains that is in a broad way representative of the many different religious groups in the United States as a whole and in the military services. Until recently, for example, the Navy used a formula dividing its chaplains into thirds: one-third consisting of liturgical Protestant denominations (such as Methodists, Lutherans, Episcopalians, and Presbyterians); another third consisting of Catholics; and a third consisting of nonliturgical Protestant denominations (such as Baptists, evangelicals, Bible churches, and Pentecostals and charismatics) as well as other faiths.[9] Such a system does not constitute an "establishment of religion," because it does not compel anyone to follow a particular religion. But it does give support to *religious practices in general,* because the society has concluded that this makes a positive contribution to the work of the military services and therefore to the public good.

So then, what should a *city council* be able to do? It seems appropriate that some kind of reasonably proportioned representation among various religious groups in the community should be allowed to give opening prayers for city council meetings, with each local council having wide discretion in exactly how they carry this out. Allowing someone to open a city council meeting with prayer is far from *compelling* anyone to *accept* a particular religion, so there should be no question that this is not a violation of the original meaning of the First Amendment.

The Alliance Defense Fund has prepared model constitutional prayer policies for state and local governments in all fifty states.[10] ADF Senior Legal Counsel Mike Johnson says:

> The practice of opening public meetings with prayer is and always has been lawful. The Constitution does not ban citizens or elected officials from invoking divine guidance and blessings upon their public work. It's a practice that is part of our nation's religious heritage, and the Constitution does not prevent public officials today from doing the same thing America's founders did.[11]

---

9. "Accomodating Faith in the Military," *Pew Forum on Religion and Public Life* (July 3, 2008). http://pewforum.org/events/?EventID=191.

10. "Model Prayer Policies." www.alliancedefensefund.org/adfresources/default.aspx?cid=4134.

11. "Tangipahoa Parish School Board votes unanimously to adopt ADF model prayer policy,"*ADF Press Release* (Aug. 22, 2007). www.alliancedefensefund.org/news/story.aspx?cid=4210.

Moreover, such a policy contradicts no other law that has been passed by Congress or by any state.

On the other hand, if a local city council decided it did *not* want to have any opening prayer at its city meetings, then it should be free to enact this as well. Freedom of religion should include the freedom not to participate in any religious activity.

What about *Christmas displays on public property*? These do not *compel* anybody to *believe in or follow* the Christian religion, nor do they compel individuals to *support* the Christian religion. When they are simply a way of giving expression to widely held beliefs in the community, I cannot see any good constitutional or moral reason why they should not be allowed. It would also be appropriate, if there are Jewish people in the community, to allow the placement of appropriate Jewish symbols in the same area during Jewish holidays. The same would be true for Muslim symbols for Muslim holidays if there were a significant number of Muslim believers in the community.

What possible harm could come from that? It would allow communities to give *free expression* to the celebration of various religious beliefs represented in the community. It would allow the "free exercise" of religion in a way that would bring benefit to the entire community.

The Supreme Court has been somewhat more restrictive than allowing the freedom for different kinds of religious displays I am suggesting here, but they have definitely never ruled out religious displays, such as a manger scene at Christmas, in general. Two Supreme Court cases in the 1980s, *Lynch v. Donnelly* (1984) and *County of Allegheny v. ACLU Greater Pittsburgh Chapter* (1989), looked at holiday displays in Rhode Island and Pittsburgh, and the court's rulings resulted from what is now known as the "Three Reindeer Rule." Essentially, public displays of religious symbols are permissible only when the inclusion of other decorations makes it clear that the government is not endorsing a religious message. According to the ADF:

> The "Three Reindeer Rule" used by the courts requires a municipality to place a sufficient number of secular objects in close enough proximity to the Christmas item (such as a crèche) to render the overall display sufficiently secular. Although the overall display must not convey a message endorsing a particular religion's view, Christmas displays are not banned as some people believe.[12]

What is important is that all religions have the same opportunities that other religions have, or "equal access."

In recent years the American Civil Liberties Union (ACLU) and other secular groups have launched legal attacks on *Ten Commandments displays on public property*. So far, the courts have issued conflicting opinions on the constitutionality of these monuments, with the possibility of another case involving a display in Haskell County, Oklahoma, to be heard soon by the US Supreme Court. However, in 2005 the US Court of Appeals

12. "ADF attorneys: U.S. Constitution does not require Christmas to be removed from Mustang holiday play," *ADF Press Release* (Dec. 9, 2004). www.alliancedefensefund.org/news/story.aspx?cid=3254.

for the 6th Circuit issued a ruling affirming the constitutionality of a Ten Commandments monument in Mercer County, Kentucky, and the court's ruling was critical of the attempts by the ACLU to remove these memorials:

> The ACLU's argument contains three fundamental flaws. First, the ACLU makes repeated reference to "the separation of church and state." This extra-constitutional construct has grown tiresome. The First Amendment does not demand a wall of separation between church and state.... Second, the ACLU focuses on the religiousness of the Ten Commandments. No reasonable person would dispute their sectarian nature, but they also have a secular nature that the ACLU does not address.... Third, the ACLU erroneously—though perhaps intentionally—equates recognition with endorsement. To endorse is necessarily to recognize, but the converse does not follow.
>
> Because nothing in the display, its history, or its implementation supports the notion that Mercer County has selectively endorsed the sectarian elements of the first four Commandments, we fail to see why the reasonable person would interpret the presence of the Ten Commandments as part of the larger "Foundations" display as a governmental endorsement of religion. We will not presume endorsement from the mere display of the Ten Commandments. If the reasonable observer perceived all government references to the Deity as endorsements, then many of our Nation's cherished traditions would be unconstitutional, including the Declaration of Independence and the national motto. Fortunately, the reasonable person is not a hyper-sensitive plaintiff.... Instead, he appreciates the role religion has played in our governmental institutions, and finds it historically appropriate and traditionally acceptable for a state to include religious influences, even in the form of sacred texts, in honoring American legal traditions.[13]

What, then, should be done about the controversial topic of *prayer in public schools*? Various studies have noted destructive trends in the nation that began about the time the Supreme Court ruled prayer in public schools unconstitutional in *Engel v. Vitale* (1962)[14] and *School District of Abington Township v. Schempp* (1963).[15] Once that happened, then, by implication, other decisions began to prohibit teachers from expressing belief in God at all or expressing their belief that there were moral standards that came from God and should be followed. Once such changes in the public schools began to take effect, crime and other destructive forces in society began to increase year after year.

In his book *America: To Pray or Not To Pray?"* historian David Barton documented the negative effects of removing school prayer, by contrasting the top seven leading problems in schools in 1940 with those in 1990. Here is what he found:

13. *American Civil Liberties Union of Kentucky v. Mercer County*, No. 03–5142, U.S. Court of Appeals for the 6th Circuit p.14 (2005). www.telladf.org/UserDocs/ACLUvMCopinion.pdf.

14. *Engel v. Vitale*, 370 U.S. 421, 436, United States Supreme Court (1962).

15. *Abington School District v. Schempp*, 374 U.S. 203, 226–227, United States Supreme Court (1963).

Figure 14.1

1940	1990
Talking out of turn	Drug Abuse
Chewing Gum	Alcohol Abuse
Making noise	Pregnancy
Running in the halls	Suicide
Line Cutting	Rape
Dress Code Violations	Robbery
Littering	Assault [16]

In the book Barton documents the dramatic rise in teen pregnancy rates, teen suicides, and drug abuse since prayer was removed from public schools.[17]

This is a tragic change in our nation, but it makes perfect sense. When children are not allowed to be taught that there is a God or that God has moral standards that they should obey, and when that teaching is *excluded from the classroom* every hour of the day for thirteen of the most formative years of a child's life, then it is little wonder that children grow up with fewer internal moral convictions and an overall pattern of behavior that is increasingly immoral and destructive in society. I realize that schools today still try to teach some "character development" for children—encouraging them to be trustworthy, honest, respectful, tolerant, and such. But merely affirming these qualities—and even cheering loudly for them—provides a far weaker basis for moral conduct than teaching that there is a God who holds us responsible for our conduct.

I see no valid constitutional reason and no valid biblical principle to exclude the use of prayer in public schools or to exclude teaching children that there is a God who watches our conduct and will hold us accountable for our actions. It would be a wonderful benefit for our nation if the Supreme Court could be persuaded that its earlier decisions establishing such a strict "wall of separation" between church and state were not based in any valid way on the Constitution itself and should be overturned. And if some basic ethical standards (approved by the local school district) with divine authorization could once again be taught to children in our schools, it would begin to reverse much of the moral decline seen since the Supreme Court removed God from the classroom in 1962.

To return to the question of prayer in public schools: I would like this to be decided by individual local school districts, which are ultimately responsible to voters in each

---

16. David Barton, *America: To Pray or Not to Pray?* (Aledo, TX: Wallbuilder Press, 1988), 35.
17. Ibid., 23–46 and 57–84.

district. Prayer in school could be solved in various ways that would not involve compelling anyone to believe in any particular religion. For example, school districts could authorize various nonsectarian prayers that could be used by teachers (as was widely done in the United States prior to 1962), or they could ask representatives of various religious groups to open a school day or a school week with prayers, or they could establish a moment of silence where students would be encouraged to pray silently in their own way. (Unfortunately—and I think incorrectly—the US Supreme Court in *Wallace v. Jaffree* in 1985 ruled that laws allowing moments of silence of voluntary prayer or meditation were unconstitutional.)[18]

If the Supreme Court were ever to overturn its prohibition of prayer or moments of silence, what would be the harm in allowing local school districts to decide this question as they thought best? It would clearly promote the public good, what the Constitution calls "promote the general welfare." It would not be compelling anyone to believe in any particular religious view. Also, it would teach children that the great majority of people in their community do believe in God and do believe that prayer to him is appropriate. (Even children who did not or whose parents did not believe in God would not be compelled to endorse or support any particular religious viewpoint, but would only be expected to be present while these viewpoints are being expressed, unless parents requested that they be excused.)

Yet today, when the courts operate by a misguided principle that "nobody should be offended" by any religious expression in public, then *freedom of religion and freedom of speech are severely curtailed* in a wrongful way. The government is actually violating the original sense of the Constitution because it is "prohibiting" the "free exercise" of religion! In this way, the will of a tiny minority, sometimes even one person, can be used to frustrate and nullify the wishes of the large majority. And this is done, not in a way of preserving a fundamental human right, but only under the principle that no one should have to feel "offended." There is no constitutional or moral "right" not to feel offended! This is a clearly wrong standard and should be overturned by the courts or outlawed by legislatures and Congress.

In 2009 the so-called "Freedom from Religion Foundation" (FFRF) filed suit against Shirley Dobson, the wife of Focus on the Family founder Dr. James Dobson, and President Obama, in an effort to bring an end to government support for the annual National Day of Prayer, which has been observed by every president since 1952. The FFRF claims that the National Day of Prayer creates a "hostile environment" for nonbelievers and that it violates the First Amendment.[19] Attorneys with the Alliance Defense Fund are defending Mrs. Dobson in her role as chairman of the National Day of Prayer Task Force, which coordinates the Christian observance of the national prayer day each year. The attorneys are asking the federal court to dismiss the lawsuit.[20]

---

18. *Wallace v. Jaffree*, 472 U.S. 38, 61, United States Supreme Court (1985).

19. *Freedom from Religion Foundation et al. v. President Bush et al.* (now Obama), filed October 3, 2008.

20. *Freedom from Religion v. Obama*, U.S. District Court for the Western District of Wisconsin.

C. "FAITH-BASED" PROGRAMS

On January 29, 2001, shortly after he became President, George W. Bush established the White House Office of Faith-Based and Community Initiatives (OFBCI). This office was intended to improve the ability of so-called faith-based organizations to obtain federal funding for the social services that they carry out, such as job training, drug rehabilitation, alcoholism rehabilitation, prison ministries, and free housing and food for the poor and homeless. There was much controversy about this initiative, with some Christian conservatives thinking it provided a dangerous precedent for government intrusion into religious activities and many others arguing that it was a wrongful use of government funds to support religious activities.

I will give my own evaluation of such programs here, along with the reasons I find persuasive, but I realize that others, both conservative and liberal, both Republican and Democrat, will decide that they disagree with me on this issue.

In my own judgment, much good can come from government financial assistance to these organizations as they carry out social service functions that "promote the general welfare" of the nation. These activities advance the common good in many ways and actually save tax dollars that would otherwise need to be spent to help the people who are cared for by these religiously based institutions. And these activities help these organizations carry out the work they were set up to do. In addition, there are significant benefits to the people who are helped to learn a new job skill or to overcome drug addiction or to have a changed life so that they will not end up back in prison a few months after being released. *Everybody wins* from such a program—government, the society, the ministry, and the people receiving aid.

Yes, I agree that government funding always carries the danger of increased government control, and both the government and the religious organizations need to continually guard against this. But I do not think that this danger is significant enough to be a reason for the groups to refuse to participate.

It is important that government funds be clearly used for the specific social welfare benefit that the organization receives the funds for and not simply to finance the religious worship activities of that organization, for example. Therefore, if a Christian group runs a homeless shelter, they should be able to show through their recordkeeping that the government funds were used directly for the purpose intended—that is, for providing food and shelter for homeless people, not for buying hymnbooks or Bibles and not for paying a Bible teacher to lead Bible studies. (These activities would have to be funded by separate, private contributions.) That is simply a matter of honoring "donor intent," something that churches and other charities do all the time. In this case the government is the donor of some of the organization's funds.

If religious groups clearly keep the funds for these social services separate from other funds, then, if the government in the future started to try to exercise control over the entire content of the programs used by these religious groups, the groups could relinquish the funds without any wrongful government intrusion into their specifically religious activities.

Since the use of any of these social services is entirely voluntary on the part of the recipient, it does not seem to me that such a program comes anywhere near to having the government "compel religion" with respect to all its citizens or even any single citizen.

Of course, such government aid should be open to *any* religious *or nonreligious* group that is carrying out these services. Roman Catholic, Protestant, Mormon, Muslim, and Jewish groups and so forth should all be eligible based simply on an ability to provide the social services for which the funds are being requested. Such a program is certainly not a violation of the First Amendment as the authors originally intended it.

Should the government, in giving faith-based funds, be able to require that ministries *refrain* from any specifically religious activities or conversations in carrying out these social services? Should they insist, for example, that Catholics not have a crucifix on the wall or that evangelicals not hold a Bible-teaching time in a prison or homeless shelter? Should government require that evangelical Christians *refrain* from encouraging drug-addicted people to trust in Jesus as their personal Savior for forgiveness of sins and a change of heart?

No, I do not think that government should ever make such restrictions regarding faith-based organizations. That would be a wrongful prohibition of the "free exercise" of religion. For these groups, the religious component is an essential part of the ministry that they carry out. People who give food and clothing to the poor do it "in the name of Jesus" and out of obedience to him and as a means of witness to him. I do not think governments should ever object to this. The government funding is given to carry out the social welfare function (feeding and sheltering the homeless, or helping people to escape from drug addiction, for example). If that is accomplished by the faith-based organization, then the government should not object to these ministry-related components of what the organization does in fulfilling its functions. The groups must not be prohibited from their "free exercise" of religion, but those specific activities should be funded by private donations.

The principle is still preserved that the *choice to participate* in the program is voluntary on the part of the recipient, and the choice to accept or reject what he hears is also voluntary. There is no government compulsion forcing people to give support to any particular religion, so there is no genuine violation of the original meaning of the First Amendment.

D. POLITICAL ADVOCACY BY CHURCHES AND THEIR TAX-EXEMPT STATUS

In 1954 the US Congress amended (without debate or analysis) Internal Revenue Code §501(c)(3) to restrict the speech of nonprofit tax-exempt entities, including churches, requiring that they refrain from any advocacy of or opposition to any specific political candidates by name. The amendment, offered by then-Senator Lyndon Johnson, stated that nonprofit tax-exempt entities could not "participate in, or intervene in (including the publishing or distributing of statements), any political campaign on behalf of or in opposition to any candidate for public office."[21] Apparently Johnson had proposed this amendment, which passed on a voice vote, to "get back" at two nonprofit organizations that had vocally opposed his candidacy for the Senate.[22]

The penalty for violating this policy is a revocation of the tax-exempt status of the church. Churches in the United States have generally followed this restriction since the enactment of the so-called "Johnson amendment" in 1954 that authorized the IRS to make this restriction.

But before the amendment was passed, *there were no restrictions* on what churches could or couldn't do with regard to speech about government and voting, except for a 1934 law preventing nonprofits from using a substantial part of their resources to lobby for legislation. However, since the passage of the 1954 amendment, the IRS has steadfastly maintained that *any* speech by churches about candidates for government office, including sermons from the pulpit, can result in loss of tax exemption. But that has turned out to be a hollow threat, because the IRS has never actually revoked the tax-exempt status of any church for violating this policy.[23]

Of course, many pastors and other church leaders understand that it is often *unwise* for a church to support or oppose a particular candidate. Specific political positions are not required for people to join a church. Every church probably has members who would support different candidates in any given election. Therefore, when churches refrain from endorsing individual candidates, they also avoid offending their members who have different political convictions. I suspect that nearly all Christians and all churches would recognize the wisdom of *exercising considerable caution and restraint* with regard to advocating specific political positions from the pulpit of the church.

But that still does not answer the question, Is it right for the Internal Revenue Service to prohibit *all* recommendations for or against specific candidates in *all* elections in *all* circumstances? Should such a decision be made by the government, or should such decisions be left to individual churches and pastors to decide according to what they think is wise in each situation?

The Alliance Defense Fund has recently begun to question the validity of this IRS policy because they have concluded that the policy is actually an unconstitutional violation of freedom of speech and freedom of religion. ADF attorneys believe the Johnson amendment is unconstitutional because (in their words):

- The amendment violates the Establishment Clause by requiring the government to excessively and pervasively monitor the speech of churches to ensure they are not

---

21. "The Pulpit Initiative Executive Summary for Sermons Addressing Candidates for Office and Their Issues." www.alliancedefensefund.org/userdocs/Pulpit_Initiative_executive_summary_candidates_2009.pdf.

22. Karla Dial, "Aiming at Goliath," *Focus on the Family Citizen* (Aug. 2009), 25–29.

23. "The Pulpit Initiative: White Paper," Alliance Defense Fund (May 11, 2009). www.alliancedefensefund.org/userdocs/Pulpit_initiative_white_%20Paper_candidates_2009.pdf. The

IRS recently investigated the tax-exempt status of All Saints Episcopal Church in Pasadena, California, over a sermon delivered by a guest speaker who maintained that Jesus would not vote for President Bush because of the Iraq War. After the church refused to cooperate with the IRS investigation, the IRS closed the examination without penalizing the church, even though the IRS claimed in the closure letter that the sermon constituted direct campaign intervention.

transgressing the restriction in the amendment. The amendment allows the government to determine when truly religious speech becomes impermissibly "political." The government has no business making such decisions.

- The amendment violates the Free Speech Clause because it requires the government to discriminate against speech based solely on the content of the speech. In other words, some speech is allowed, but other speech is not. The Supreme Court has invalidated this type of speech discrimination for decades.

- The amendment also violates the Free Speech Clause by conditioning the receipt of a tax exemption on refraining from certain speech. Put simply, if a church wants the tax exemption, it cannot speak on any and all relevant issues addressed by Scripture. This is an unconstitutional condition on free speech.

- The amendment violates the Free Exercise Clause because it substantially burdens a church's exercise of religion. The government does not have a compelling reason to burden religion in this way.[24]

The ADF is *not* arguing that pastors *should* routinely endorse or oppose various candidates in political elections. Rather, it contends that there are times when the moral and religious issues on which candidates differ are so blatant and so clearly supported or opposed by biblical principles that *pastors should have the freedom to speak out on various candidates when they think it wise to do so.* The ADF recognizes that pastors will want to be careful in exercising this freedom and would be wise to consult their elder boards or other leaders well in advance, but the ADF holds that such decisions should be made by individual churches or denominations, not by the government.

Therefore, on the last Sunday in September prior to the 2008 presidential election and also prior to the November 2009 elections, the Alliance Defense Fund found a number of pastors around the United States who were willing to preach sermons *publicly endorsing or opposing specific candidates* and stating from the pulpit why there were biblical moral grounds on which they based these recommendations. The sermons were actually carefully constructed with legal advice from the ADF so that they would constitute a clear challenge to the IRS regulations.[25] The sermons were sent to the IRS well in advance with a notification that this was the intention of the pastors! It was the hope of the ADF that the IRS would actually revoke the tax-exempt status of at least one of these churches, to provide a test case by which the principle of the policy could be tested in court. The ADF actually believes that if this policy ever does come to trial, it has a very strong likelihood of winning on appeal to the Constitution's protection of freedom of speech.[26] ADF Senior Legal Counsel Erik Stanley says, "Our hope is that the IRS will respond by opening church tax inquiries against them, and then we'll file multiple law-

---

24. "The Pulpit Initiative," op. cit.

25. Laurie Goodstein, "Challenging the IRS," *New York Times* (June 23, 2008); Dale Buss, "Provoking the IRS, Preachers Address the Bully Pulpit," *Wall Street Journal* (Oct. 3, 2008). Pulpit Freedom Sunday was held on September 28, 2008.

26. See Allan J. Samansky, *Tax Consequences When Churches Participate in Political Campaigns*, Political Law and Legal Theory Working Paper No. 76, Center for Interdisciplinary Law and Policy Studies Working Paper No. 49, Ohio State Univ. College of Law (Aug. 2006), http://ssrn.com/abstract=924770; Shawn A. Voyles, *Choosing Between Tax-Exempt Status and Freedom of Religion: The Dilemma Facing Politically Active Churches*, 9 REG. U. L. REV. 219 (1997).

suits in federal jurisdictions and seek to have what the IRS is doing declared unconstitutional. That's why we started this initiative—to end 50 years of intimidation."[27]

Until the passage of the law in 1954, pastors and churches had often made statements for and against individual candidates. The ADF writes:

> Historically, churches had frequently and fervently spoken for and against candidates for government office. Such sermons date from the founding of America, including sermons against Thomas Jefferson for being a deist; sermons opposing William Howard Taft as a Unitarian; and sermons opposing Al Smith in the 1928 presidential election. Churches have also been at the forefront of most of the significant societal and governmental changes in our history including ending segregation and child labor and advancing civil rights.[28]

For example, in 1800 the Rev. William Linn of Pennsylvania said, "It is well understood that the Honorable Thomas Jefferson is a candidate for the Chief Magistracy of the United States, and that a number of citizens will give him all their support. I would not presume to dictate to you who ought to be president, but entreat you to hear with patience my reason why he ought not."[29]

In 1864 Pastor O. T. Lanphear told his parishioners why he supported the re-election of Abraham Lincoln, stating, "The man who casts his vote in the election now pending in favor of a peace not won by the conquests of our enemies does the rebel cause more service, if possible, than he could by joining the rebel army."[30]

It seems to me that the Alliance Defense Fund is right in this argument. Decisions about what is preached from the pulpit of a church should not belong to the government, but to the individual pastor and the church itself. Any government control of what is said from a pulpit constitutes a wrongful violation of religious freedom and a wrongful violation of freedom of speech. It is the government—the realm of "what is Caesar's"—attempting to intrude into a realm where it does not belong—the realm of "what is God's." So I hope that the ADF will prevail against the IRS and that the courts will rule that this policy is unconstitutional.

---

27. Dial, "Aiming at Goliath."
28. Ibid.

29. The Rev. William Linn: cited in Dial, "Aiming at Goliath."
30. Pastor O. T. Lanpher: cited in Dial, "Aiming at Goliath."

15

SPECIAL GROUPS

A. WHY THE TOPICS IN THIS CHAPTER ARE DIFFERENT FROM EARLIER CHAPTERS

In this final chapter dealing with specific political issues, I adopt a somewhat different approach.

First, the treatment of each issue is shorter, simply giving a general overview of the questions that are at stake.

Second, these issues all involve the general question, "What is the best way to do good for the nation in this area of its life?" Therefore the answers I give do not come directly from moral principles of the Bible or from biblical teachings that speak directly to the issue, but instead come from an evaluation of whether a certain policy truly fulfills the government purpose of doing good for the nation as a whole. This chapter discusses issues where a proper decision depends on *evaluating the results* of certain policies and actions.

The biblical justification for this approach is the basic responsibility of those in authority to use their office as "God's servant *for your good*" (Rom. 13:4). The government is supposed to give encouragement and "approval" to those who "do what is good" (Rom. 13:3) and "to praise those who do good" (1 Peter 2:14). I also argued in chapter 3 that the purpose of civil government, according to the Bible, is *to serve the people*, not to be served by the people (see pp. 80, 86–87). Therefore Samuel was a model of a good ruler in his term as judge over Israel, because he had not "defrauded" or "oppressed" anyone or taken things from the people for his own benefit, and he had not "taken a bribe" from anyone (1 Sam. 12:3–4). By contrast, Samuel warned that a king would become corrupt and would "take ... take ... take ... take ... take" from the people again and again for his own benefit rather than for the good of the nation (see 1 Sam. 8:11–17).

I also contended in chapter 3 (see pp. 91–95) that governments should safeguard human liberty, which God values highly because it respects the ability of human beings to make choices regarding their own well-being apart from the burden of government restrictions on what they can do (except that government should prevent people from committing crimes and doing evil to others).

Therefore this chapter covers topics in which even Christians who fully believe the Bible will probably find that they have more sincerely held differences of opinion. When I argue for or against a policy based on the *results* of that policy, people will differ about exactly what the results are, how helpful or harmful they are, and what the results would be from changing the policy. In the nature of that kind of argument, there are going to be different evaluations and different proposed solutions.

To put it briefly, these topics are less directly based on specific teachings of Scripture, and therefore I think that in churches, people should be willing to hear and evaluate arguments from different sides, all within the broad parameters of encouraging government to seek the good of the nation as a whole.

Finally, nearly all of the topics that I cover in the chapter have one characteristic in common: They deal with laws and policies that *give special government benefits to certain special groups* rather than giving benefits to the nation as a whole. Now, people might think this is a good thing. For example, we have a system of farm subsidies that gives special government benefits to farmers who raise certain kinds of crops. Perhaps people think it is a good thing for the nation to give benefits to these farmers, because their crops are useful to the nation as a whole, or because people want to do what they can to preserve family farms that raise these crops. That is certainly a legitimate kind of argument to make. But the results of the policy *for the nation as a whole* also need to be evaluated.

My argument in this chapter in general is going to be that *the United States should abolish several laws and policies that give benefits to special groups*—laws and policies that cost the nation much more than the benefits they bring to the nation.

B. REGULATORS: INVISIBLE BUREAUCRATS WHO REGULATE PEOPLE'S LIVES

Few Americans realize the extent to which our daily lives are controlled by a vast army of bureaucrats at various governmental agencies who exercise immense influence over the way we live. Such agencies include the Environmental Protection Agency (EPA), the Occupational Safety and Health Administration (OSHA), the Food and Drug Administration (FDA), the Equal Employment Opportunity Commission (EEOC), the Consumer Product Safety Commission (CPSC), and many other agencies. These agencies control what products are allowed to be sold in the United States, what hiring and firing practices companies must have, what medicines we are allowed and not allowed to buy, what kind of packaging must be put on goods that are sold, and even what kinds of toilets and light bulbs are allowed to be sold in stores.

Some of these regulations imposed on us come as a result of direct passage of laws by Congress (such as the vehicle mileage standards and the kinds of light bulbs we will be able to buy). Others are simply the result of rulings by regulators within these various government agencies.

Of course, certain product control standards and certain standards for safety and justice in the workplace are necessary and should be enforced by such government agencies. But the problem is that too often an agency that starts out as a good and necessary protection against harm (thus fulfilling the government responsibility "to punish those who do evil," as 1 Peter 2:14 says) can become overly powerful and overly intrusive into people's lives. Legislators too often shine a spotlight on a small problem that would probably be fixed by the free market anyway, and they enact massive legislation that, in effect, uses a sledgehammer to kill a mosquito.

The classic explanation of this excessive regulatory process in the United States is found in the remarkable book by Manhattan attorney Philip K. Howard, *The Death of Common Sense: How Law Is Suffocating America*.[1] (This is such a significant book that I think every citizen in America should read it!) Howard argues that the problem with government regulations is not the idea of government in itself, but recent commitments to *detailed regulatory law* that prevents people from making individual judgments about what is best in each situation. Mountains of paperwork are used to define more and more detailed procedures that are required in each kind of situation, so that government agencies no longer have any flexibility to *make judgments* based on the need and specific circumstances in an individual situation, but must apply the regulations in a blind and often harmful manner.

Thus we have a system of "governing by excruciating detail, dictating every result in advance,"[2] rather than allowing people to have freedom and exercise common sense to make their own best decisions in each situation according to broad guidelines. The result is that people end up paying hundreds of thousands of dollars in fines for violating rules they didn't know existed and for doing things that were causing no harm, and they end up spending hundreds of hours per year filing forms showing that they comply with hundreds of such detailed regulations. What is lost is human freedom. US government regulators have produced "the death of common sense." Howard's book has dozens of humorous and tragic stories that illustrate this consequence.

For example, Howard describes a brick factory, Glen-Gery Brick, near Reading, Pennsylvania. Inspectors from OSHA (a division of the US Department of Labor) have visited the brick factory several times and required detailed compliance with their safety rules. This means that even piles of sand have to be labeled as "poison"! Howard explains:

> Warnings are posted everywhere. A large POISON sign dominates one side of a storage shed filled with bags of something hazardous: it turns out to be sand. OSHA categorizes sand as poison because sand, including the beach sand you

1. Philip K. Howard, *The Death of Common Sense: How Law Is Suffocating America* (New York: Random House, 1994).
2. Ibid., 21.

and I sunbathe on in blissful ignorance, contains a material called silica. Some scientists believe that silica, in conditions found nowhere except in certain grinding and mining operations, might cause cancer.[3]

Howard explains how OSHA also decided that special "Material Safety Data Sheets" (MSDS) had to be supplied with every package or container that workers used in factories. Of course, this made sense with dangerous substances such as hydrochloric acid or other dangerous chemicals, but OSHA, in all its wisdom, set its regulators loose and decided that piles of bricks needed warnings against brick poisoning. Yes, brick poisoning! Howard explains,

> Bricks can fall on people, but never have bricks been considered poisonous. In 1991, the OSHA regional office in Chicago, after visiting a construction site, sent a citation to the brick maker for failing to supply a MSDS form with each pallet of bricks. If a brick is sawed, OSHA reasoned, it can release small amounts of the mineral silica. The sawing of bricks however, does not release large amounts, and bricklayers don't spend much time sawing bricks.... Brick makers thought the government had gone crazy.... Brick manufacturers dutifully began sending out the MSDS form, which describes, for the benefit of workers, how to identify a brick (a "hard ceramic body ... with no odor") and giving its boiling point (above 3500° F). The problem, at least as seen by the brick manufacturers, was not just the paperwork, but the necessary implication that the material is, in fact, hazardous. In our litigation-crazy society, these forms were an invitation to lawsuits.
>
> In 1994, after several years of fighting, the brick industry succeeded in reversing OSHA's designation of bricks as poisonous. But thousands of other common substances are still on the list.[4]

Howard goes on to point out that a company in Florida was cited for not having MSDS forms for the Windex cleaning solution it was using. "Another employer was cited for not putting a warning label on table salt. All these things can be bad for you. The law is just trying to treat every potentially harmful substance uniformly."[5]

Sometimes different bureaucrats end up giving conflicting or contradictory guidelines, and in a society where there are so many thousands of rules, when you keep one rule you can easily end up violating another one without even knowing it. Howard explains what happened to some friends:

> A colleague of mine and his wife worked hard for several years to renovate the kitchen and bathroom of their Brooklyn brownstone. All plans were duly filed. Inspectors came periodically to see the work. They finally finished, got sign-offs from the inspectors, and went to get the certificate of occupancy. It was refused on the ground they had been living in the home. Of course they had been living

---

3. Ibid., 13.
4. Ibid., 37.
5. Ibid., 37–38.

there; it is, after all, their home. But, they were told, the law prohibits "habitation" in a dwelling under renovation. No inspector, in all their visits, had ever told them of the rule.... [The rule] can't distinguish between a gutted home, which probably would not be appropriate to live in, and one being spruced up by the family living there. But that didn't matter to the bureaucrat at the desk. My colleague had broken the rule. It took him and his wife months ... to get the problem straightened out.[6]

Sadly, Howard tells many stories of people who have simply shut down their businesses or had to move out of their homes because of arbitrary enforcement of inflexible rules that do not take into account specific unique situations.

In England, the classic description of this regulatory process was published in 1944 in the book *The Road to Serfdom*[7] by F. A. von Hayek, an Austrian economist and eventual Nobel Prize winner. Hayek had fled his native Austria to escape from Nazism and Hitler, and he took up residence in England, where he taught economics at the University of London. He watched creeping socialism begin to take over every aspect of British life, eroding more and more individual freedom. Hayek concluded that excessive government laws and regulations were essentially turning England into a nation of "serfs"—that is, people who were living a life of servitude that was completely regulated by the central government, similar to the lives of the farm servants on feudal estates in the Middle Ages who were called serfs. Hayek's argument is that governments have a tendency to nibble away at freedom more and more every year, until freedom is lost.

My point in this section is that citizens, and especially legislators, must continually be on guard against such increasing government regulation. It is anti-democratic, because it does not allow people to make their own choices even about what kinds of light bulbs they want to buy, for example. And it is increasingly anti-free market, because government regulators rather than the wants of the economy as a whole determine the economic activity of large segments of the nation. Therefore human liberty is continually being reduced in incremental steps.

For example, government regulations have created major havoc with the automobile industry. Murray Weidenbaum, director of the Center for the Study of American Business at Washington University in St. Louis, wrote:

> The fuel efficiency standards applied to cars made in the United States after 1990 are estimated to result in over 2,200 additional traffic deaths every year [because consumers are forced into smaller, lighter vehicles]. Overall, safety and emissions requirements add more than $2,500 to the price of the average new automobile. That's a stiff hidden tax on the American motorist.
>
> In turn, the higher cost of new automobiles resulting from the hidden regulatory tax means that many people are driving their old cars longer because they cannot afford to replace them. As a result, the nation is not getting the

---

6. Ibid., 33.

7. F. A. von Hayek, *The Road to Serfdom* (Chicago: University of Chicago Press, 1944; new ed. with introduction by Milton Friedman, 1994).

intended benefits of the host of expensive safety-environmental-energy regulations that have been promulgated.[8]

Weidenbaum also describes how government regulations actually make cars *heavier* because of the features automakers are forced to include, therefore defeating the attempts to make them lighter for better fuel economy. He writes:

> Specific regulations cover almost every aspect of the vehicle, including design, production, and operation. Government is directly involved in setting standards for such basic items as engines, bumpers, headrests, seat belts, door latches, brakes, fuel systems, and windshields, as well as the type of fuel that can be used. Yet among this vast array of government paperwork and directives there is no coordination of the various regulatory agencies administering them. The regulations, and the regulators, often work at cross-purposes.
>
> For example, the law to control emissions reduces fuel efficiency. The government's requirements concerning side-door guard beams, energy-absorbing steering columns, and other safety features have added about 200 pounds to the weight of an automobile. These government actions lower fuel economy—and generate more pollution in the process.[9]

The result is that consumers ultimately get less safe but more expensive vehicles.

It is easy to find other examples of foolish government regulations. In 2008, Eli Lehrer of the Competitive Enterprise Institute published a report on "The Five Dumbest Product Bans." Among his examples were these:

> Louisiana's unique-in-the-nation florist licensing statute makes it illegal for anybody to arrange two or more types of flowers without passing a largely subjective state licensing exam. In theory, a child could face a fine for picking a bouquet of flowers and selling it at a roadside stand.... Louisiana's floral licensing law serves no valid public purpose. Flower shops have faced fines or threats of fines for not having "licensed florists" on duty. The law stops many florists from practicing their chosen profession, and, just as importantly, restricts consumer choice.
>
> The Cardio-Pump. No one has ever contended that anybody could do harm using this American-designed device intended to help resuscitate heart attack victims, which may actually help save lives. Although it has found wide use in other countries—the Food and Drug Administration bans its use in the United States.... The Food and Drug Administration ... ruled that the device should be considered a "significant risk device" and therefore its use required "informed consent"—something that is literally impossible to get for a device that is used only on those suffering heart attacks.[10]

---

8. Murray Weidenbaum, "Government Regulation of the Automobile," *The Heartland Institute* (Jan./Feb. 1999). www.heartland.org/policybot/results/381/Government_Regulation_of_the_Automobile.html.

9. Ibid.

10. Eli Lehrer, "The Five Dumbest Product Bans: An Overview of Regulatory Absurdity," *Competitive Enterprise Institute*, No. 130 (Feb. 26, 2008).

In California, new regulations will strictly reduce the types of televisions individuals can purchase, because high-density TVs (HDTVs) require more energy usage. The new regulations are so stringent that only one-quarter of all the televisions on the market could meet the new standards. TV manufacturers say that the new regulations will "cripple innovation, limit consumer choice, and harm California retailers" because consumers will purchase their TVs out of state or order them online, bypassing retailers who are already suffering because of the recession.[11]

The most recent example of excessive government regulation is the Consumer Product Safety Improvement Act of 2008, which was an overreaction by Congress to the fear of lead poisoning from some toys, because of a few toys imported from China. (In 2008 only one child in the entire United States was injured by lead poisoning from toys.)

The law was written so broadly that it devastated much of the toy industry in the United States, especially small companies who were makers and resellers of specialty products for children. Thrift shops had to clear out and get rid of all of their supplies of secondhand children's toys and even books, not because these things contained any dangerous lead, but because the government required that *massively expensive testing and labeling had to be carried out* to prove that the books did not have any wrongful lead content in them! Books and used toys and used children's clothing all were foolishly made subject to these regulations. Many thrift shops and individual toy manufacturers simply could not comply and were driven into bankruptcy.[12]

Thrift store operators like Goodwill and the Salvation Army predicted that they would have to destroy more than $100 million worth of inventory. That is a direct loss of value in the overall wealth of a nation and a direct loss of the availability of many toys, especially for lower-income families who would have bought them. Toy stores expected that some $600 million worth of toys would have to be discarded. Motorcycle and ATV makers predicted a loss of around $1 billion to the total industry because of inventory that would have to be destroyed. (They are sold to older "children," and testing all the various components would cost far too much.) Children's clothing stores "suffered huge losses." All of this is not because any of these products contained any lead, but because the manufacturers could not afford to have independent third-party testing and labeling to demonstrate that they did not have any lead! No one had shown that any of these products had ever been a problem before this draconian law. But Congressman Henry Waxman, a Democrat from California and chairman of the House Energy and Commerce Committee, refuses even to hold hearings to consider reforming the law.[13]

Such examples show that government bureaucrats who regulate people's lives have obtained far too much power, and the nation as a whole is poorer as a result.

---

11. Samantha Young, "California Targets TV's to Lower Electricity Demand," Associated Press (Nov. 18, 2009). http://apnews.myway.com/article/20091118/D9C1S1080.html.

12. See "Toys R Congress," *Wall Street Journal* (April 3, 2009),

A16; also "Consumer Product Destruction," *Wall Street Journal* (Aug. 12, 2009), A14.

13. "Consumer Product Destruction."

C. EARMARKS

In the United States, earmarks are spending directives inserted by members of Congress into laws and congressional committee reports. Through this process, individual members of Congress, without any accountability to the public, can direct many millions of government dollars to pet projects. Earmarks can be inserted anonymously so that members of Congress don't have to identify which ones they have put into bills. According to the Sunlight Foundation, a watchdog organization that tracks earmarks,

> It's not so much any single earmark that is the problem, but rather the entire process. There is no transparency or accountability in the system; members can secure hundreds of millions of dollars of funding for a project without subjecting it to debate by their colleagues in the Congress, or to the scrutiny and oversight of the public. Because earmarks are hard to identify, some members use them to secretly award their biggest campaign contributors or ... exchange them for bribes. The secrecy of the earmarking process invites backroom deals and unethical—or even corrupt—behavior, part of a pay-to-play culture where lobbyists and contractors and well-connected individuals give campaign contributions to legislators in return for federal funding.... Generally the more powerful members of Congress get more earmarks. The surest way to become a leader in earmarking is to sit on the Appropriations Committees in the House and Senate. Members of these committees, and especially the chairs of their subcommittees, are in the best position to secure earmarks. They can insert them into spending bills during closed committee meetings, with no public scrutiny. Earmarks are also offered to members to entice them to vote for a bill they otherwise would not vote for. Sen. Tom Coburn calls earmarks the "trading currency" of Congress.[14]

This gives immense power to direct funds to more senior members of Congress and especially members of appropriations committees in the House and Senate. As the Sunlight Foundation reports, earmarks often serve as a means for a member of Congress to reward his or her large contributors with federal funds directed to some pet project or other.

Some reforms of the earmark process were instituted in the 110th Congress (2007–9), but the earmark process is still the basis for widespread funding of pet projects and special interests. Earmarks account for up to 2% of the federal budget, which is an amazingly large number. Citizens for Government Waste reported that in 2009 there were 10,160 earmarks, totaling $19.6 billion. Some examples were the following:

- $3.8 million for the Old Tiger Stadium Conservancy in Detroit;
- $1.9 million for the Pleasure Beach water taxi service in Connecticut;
- $1.8 million for swine odor and manure management research in Ames, Iowa;

---

14. "Earmarks FAQ," Sunlight Foundation. www.sunlight-foundation.com/earmarksFAQ/.

- $380,000 for a recreation and fairgrounds area in Kotzebue, Alaska;
- $143,000 for the Greater New Haven Labor History Association in Connecticut;
- $95,000 for the Canton Symphony Orchestra Association in Ohio; and
- $71,000 for Dance Theater Etcetera in Brooklyn for its Tolerance through Arts initiative.[15]

The major problem with the earmark process in Congress is that it allows individual members, rather than the entire Congress voting on a budget bill, to designate many millions of dollars of government money to projects that benefit certain groups within their own states. This is not the process of budget direction that was intended for the US government. Congress has the responsibility to pass the overall budgets, but after that, it should be the responsibility of the executive branch, under the direction of the President and the agencies that report to him, to decide how funds should be allocated within those budget categories. In that way the executive branch would carry out what the Congress has passed into law with its budget. That process should not be allowed to be taken over secretly and with no vote and with no accountability by individual members of Congress who have the power to insert these earmarks in bills as they wish.

D. AFFIRMATIVE ACTION

The phrase "affirmative action" is used to refer to government policies that give preferential treatment to members of certain minorities in education, in employment, and in awarding of government contracts to businesses. Such preferences require, for example, that blacks or other racial minorities be awarded a certain percentage of jobs in certain businesses or in admissions to certain education programs. Some affirmative action programs also require that certain jobs or contracts be given to women or to companies run by women. (I will treat gender-based preferences in the next section.)

The arguments in favor of these policies are that (a) they promote more diverse representation of all segments of society in different areas, and (b) they are needed to overcome past discrimination against certain minority groups.

But are such affirmative action policies really good for a society as a whole? Any evaluation of these policies must consider not only the benefits, but also the costs and disadvantages that come with them.

One disadvantage of affirmative action policies is that they are inherently discriminatory against the groups that are not favored by the policy. For example, in New Haven, Connecticut, the fire department gave a test in late 2003 to see which firefighters would qualify for a promotion. Of the 118 applicants who took the two tests for promotion to lieutenant or captain, 56 earned passing scores. However, there was a very limited number of vacancies, so it was decided that only the top scorers were eligible for promotion—17 whites and 2 Hispanics. None of the 27 black firefighters with passing scores

---

15. "Earmarks Rise to $19.6 Billion in CAGW's *2009 Pig Book*," Citizens for Government Waste Press Release (April 14, 2009). www.cagw.org/site/News2?page=NewsArticle &id=11994.

was eligible. Therefore the city invalidated the test results, because not enough black firefighters had qualified, and the city then used other means to decide on promotions, with the result that some black firefighters were also promoted.[16]

The nineteen firefighters who filed a lawsuit against New Haven claimed that they had been discriminated against because of their race and therefore had not gotten the promotions. Their case went all the way to the US Supreme Court in the case *Ricci v. DeStefano*. The decision was announced on June 29, 2009, in which the court (by a 5–4 vote) ruled that New Haven was wrong to ignore the test results.[17]

The details of the case illustrate the difficulties involved with affirmative action. If the test was a fair measure of ability to do the job, then the affirmative action policy of New Haven, by which they eventually gave hiring preferences to black firefighters who had lower scores, actually ended up *hiring less qualified people* to be promoted within the fire department. Whereas in previous years American society had wrongfully discriminated *against blacks*, now this kind of affirmative action decision was wrongfully discriminating *against whites and Hispanics*. But if all human beings are created in the image of God (Gen. 1:27) and all have equal status before him, then employment selections should be entirely free of racial considerations—there should be no discrimination against blacks *or* whites *or* Hispanics *or* any other ethnic group. And in this case that is exactly what the Supreme Court (by a very narrow majority) decided.

Another difficulty with affirmative action is that it tends to cast a doubt on the qualifications of *all* members of the minority who are appointed to a position. Did they get the position because they were genuinely qualified for it, or because of their racial background? Such policies therefore tend to perpetuate the separation of American society into different racial groups, with the not-favored group likely to feel resentment and unfairness in the process, and the favored group always wondering if their qualifications really would have been enough to win them the position anyway. Thus affirmative action simply perpetuates racial division and divisiveness in US society.

Sadly, another result of affirmative action policies in law schools, for example, is that there are actually fewer black attorneys today than there otherwise would have been. This is because (1) affirmative action policies allow more black students to enter law school than would have entered based on grades and test scores alone; (2) those additional students have lower academic skills than the rest of their law school classmates and do not do as well in their studies; and then (3) they subsequently fail bar exams at a higher rate after graduation. The final result is that (4) fewer of them become lawyers. This is the finding of a significant study, "A Systemic Analysis of Affirmative Action in American Law Schools," published in 2004 by law professor Richard Sander of the University of California at Los Angeles (UCLA).[18]

16. Suzanne Sataline, Jess Bravin, and Nathan Koppel, "A Sotomayor Ruling Gets Scrutiny," *Wall Street Journal* (May 29, 2009). http://online.wsj.com/article/SB124354041637563491.html.

17. *Ricci v. DeStefano*, 557 U.S. 1, (2009).

18. Richard Sander, "A Systemic Analysis of Affirmative Action in American Law Schools," *Stanford Law Review* 57 (Nov. 2004), 367–482. www.law.ucla.edu/sander/Systemic/final/SanderFINAL.pdf.

Sander says that because of affirmative action, the top-tier, elite law schools actually admit some black applicants who otherwise would not have qualified based on their academic records alone. As a result, the second-tier and third-tier law schools have to do the same, also admitting students whose academic records are lower than would ordinarily be required for admission. The result is that there are harmful consequences that follow for the black students admitted in this way. Sander's study showed that "when black and white students with similar academic credentials compete against each other at the same school, they earn about the same grades," and "when black and white students with similar grades from the same tier school take the bar examination, they pass at about the same rate."[19] But when black students are admitted to schools for which they would not otherwise qualify in terms of academic background, the consequences are very discouraging: "In elite law schools, 51.6% of black students had first-year grade point averages in the bottom 10% of their class as opposed to only 5.6% of white students." The consequences later are similarly discouraging:

> Under current practices, only 45% of blacks who enter law school pass the bar on their first attempt as opposed to over 78% of whites. Even after multiple tries, only 57% of blacks succeed. The rest are saddled with significant debt, routinely running as high as $160,000, not counting undergraduate debt.... 43% of black law students never became lawyers.[20]

The recommendations of Richard Sander are simple: Abolish affirmative action admissions so that law school students are matched with the law schools to which their academic abilities would gain them admission. Sander estimates that the following consequences would result:

> Because the cascade effect principally reshuffles black applicants among law schools rather than expanding the pool, about 86% of blacks currently admitted to some law school would still gain admission to the system without racial preferences. Those who would not be admitted at all have, under current practices, very small chances of finishing school and passing the bar. The 86% admitted to a race-blind system would graduate at significantly higher rates, and pass the bar at substantially higher rates, than they do now. Under a range of plausible assumptions, race-blind admissions would produce an *increase* in the annual number of new black lawyers. It is clear beyond any doubt that a race-blind system would not have severe effects on the production of black lawyers, and that the black lawyers emerging from such a system would be stronger attorneys as measured by bar performance.[21]

---

19. These quotations come from a summary of Sander's study by a member of the U.S. Commission on Civil Rights. See law professor Gail Heriot, "Affirmative Action Backfires," *Wall Street Journal* (Aug. 24, 2007), A15; also Sander, "A Systematic Analysis," 454.

20. Heriot, "Affirmative Action Backfires," A15.
21. Sander, "A Systemic Analysis," 374.

Gail Heriot summarizes these findings of Sander by equating them to numerical equivalents:

> If law schools were to use color-blind admissions, fewer black law students would be admitted to law schools (3,182 students instead of 3,706), but since those who were admitted would be attending schools where they have a substantial likelihood of doing well, fewer would fail or drop out (403 vs. 670). In the end more would pass the bar on their first try (1,859 vs. 1,567) and more would eventually pass the bar (2,150 vs. 1,981) than under the current system of race preferences.[22]

Sander concluded:

> … blacks are the victims of law school programs of affirmative action, not the beneficiaries. The programs set blacks up for failure in school, aggravate attrition rates, turn the bar exam into a major hurdle, disadvantage most blacks in the job market, and depress the overall production of black lawyers. Whites, in contrast, arguably benefit from preferences in a number of ways. Whites have higher grades because blacks and other affirmative action beneficiaries fill most of the lower ranks; whites are the most obvious beneficiaries of the diversity produced by affirmative action programs; it is even plausible to argue that bar passage rates are kept high to avoid embarrassingly high failure rates by minority exam-takers. The next legal challenge to affirmative action practices by law schools could very plausibly be led by black plaintiffs who were admitted, spent years and thousands of dollars on their educations, and then never passed the bar and never became lawyers—all because of the misleading double standards used by law schools to admit them, and the schools' failure to disclose to them the uniquely long odds against their becoming lawyers.[23]

I agree that the United States must not forget that we have a tragic history of racial discrimination against blacks in particular. But programs of affirmative action just prolong another type of racial discrimination and perpetuate racial divisiveness and animosity along with a sense of insecurity and questions about their own abilities on the part of those who do qualify for such positions. It seems to me that a crucial step toward overcoming remaining racial differences in US society is the complete abolition of all affirmative action policies in law and business and government once and for all.

In other words, *actual instances of discrimination* against any person or group should be illegal, but there should be no policies based on any *"presumed" discrimination* that is based on numerical quotas or just attempting to achieve desired outcomes in terms of how many numbers of each group are accepted for each position.

One final reason against affirmative action policies is that they are (according to a common-sense reading of the original meaning) contrary to the Constitution itself.

22. Heriot, "Affirmative Action Backfires," A15.
23. Sander, "A Systemic Analysis," 481–82.

The 14th Amendment to the Constitution, ratified July 9, 1868, was intended to abolish racial discrimination in the United States. It provided that no state may "deny to any person within its jurisdiction the equal protection of the laws." If this amendment is understood according to the plain sense of the words as they were originally intended, it means that there can be no preferences or exclusions based on racial differences in the laws of the United States. Affirmative action policies are inherently discriminatory because they deny to the group that is not favored the "equal protection of the laws."

E. GENDER-BASED QUOTAS

A similar analysis to that for race-based affirmative action can be made with respect to gender-based quotas that require a certain percentage (sometimes an equal percentage) of women and men in government-based employment, business contacts, or college sports activities.

The difficulty with these policies is that they can end up artificially imposing an arbitrary number of women that *must* be enrolled in some program rather than allowing these numbers to be determined by individual choices and preferences on the part of the people involved.

One example is Title IX, passed by Congress in 1972. This federal law bars sex discrimination by schools that receive federal money. Schools must offer scholarship opportunities and general program funding in athletics, for example, roughly equal to the school's overall male and female populations. According to the Department of Education, a school may demonstrate compliance by meeting any one of the three parts:

1. Whether the institution provides opportunities for participation in intercollegiate sports for male and female students in numbers that are substantially proportionate to their respective enrollments; or
2. Whether the institution can show a history and continuing practice of program expansion that is demonstrably responsive to the developing interests and abilities of the members of the sex that is underrepresented among intercollegiate athletes; or
3. Whether the institution can show that the interests and abilities of the members of that sex have been fully and effectively accommodated by the present program.[24]

But what if more men than women *want* to be in university sports programs? And what if more men than women *decide to actively participate* in university sports programs? *Do their preferences matter*, preferences of the men and the women to emphasize activities of their own choosing? Not according to Title IX.

The result of this policy has been that for many years universities have had to arbitrarily cancel popular sports programs for men (such as wrestling or gymnastics) simply

---

24. See www.ed.gov/about/bdscomm/list/athletics/qsandas.html.

to *reduce* the number of men until it is equal to the number of women who are involved in official university sports programs (in proportion to the total number of men and women in the university). This is government-mandated social engineering *attempting to force people to behave in certain ways* rather than allowing people's different preferences and tendencies to work themselves out in accordance with human liberty. In 2002, for example, San Jose State University in California dropped its nationally ranked male soccer team. It had previously cut its men's gymnastics and tennis programs because of the equity and money situations, because too much money had to be spent on non-revenue-generating or revenue-losing female sports in order to provide equal opportunities. The National Wrestling Coaches Association reported that 350 men's programs have been cut nationwide as a result. The losses have been in sports such as swimming, wrestling, track-and-field, and gymnastics.[25] In 2003 the University of Toledo, which had already eliminated men's wrestling, had to drop swimming and track-and-field. Bowling Green University had to drop several men's sports as well.[26]

Is it really possible, if people are completely free to follow their own preferences and desires, that more men than women will choose to be involved in competitive sports at the university level? Yes, that is entirely possible. Admitting this is just recognizing that there might be different distributions of preferences, in general, between men and women.

It cannot be denied that there is far more spectator interest in watching men's sports than women's sports, both at the university level and at the level of professional sports. (Note the weekend sports programming on TV or the number of spectators in the stands at college sports.) Both men and women will give substantially more time and money to watching men's sports than women's sports. I do not think this difference is the result of any wrongful discrimination or wrongful societal conditioning. It is simply the result of a statistical difference in preferences for sports activities as opposed to other kinds of activities among men and women. It is neither better nor worse to have that preference. It just is. Government bureaucrats should not try to force men and women into artificial compliance with their preconceived policies that are essentially anti-democratic and anti-liberty.

It is important, of course, that universities devote substantial funding and attention and facilities to women's sports programs as well as to men's. That is not the question. The question is whether the government should force the universities to have an absolutely equal number of men and women enrolled in these sports programs, even if that is not what the students themselves want. This is simply not right. It is another example of government discrimination against individual human preferences.

Another harmful effect of government assumptions about no inherent differences between men and women is *allowing girls to compete in boys' wrestling teams* and wrestle against boys or to compete on boys' football teams in high schools.

---

25. Larry D. Hatfield, "Coaches charge anti-male bias: Title IX causes cuts in men's college sports," *San Francisco Chronicle* (Jan. 17, 2002). www.sfgate.com/cgi-bin/article.cgi?file=/c/a/2002/01/17/MN47748.DTL&type=printable.

26. Matt Markey, "UT eliminates swimming, track for male athletes; state cuts, Title IX figure in decision," *Toledo Blade* (April 23, 2003). www.toledoblade.com/apps/pbcs.dll/article?Date=20030422&Category=NEWS21&ArtNo=104220092&Ref=AR.

The problems are particularly evident with regard to wrestling. If a boy in a wrestling match is assigned to wrestle against a girl, he faces an impossible choice. If he loses to a girl, it is a badge of shame that will (properly, I think) challenge his feelings of masculine strength and his sense of physical ability to protect others, perhaps for years to come, and certainly among his peers in the high school. But if he wins, he has become guilty of physically overpowering a woman against her will, and doing so in a way that is never appropriate for a man to do against a woman under any circumstance at all (except perhaps to stop a woman from committing a violent crime). In the wrestling match, he is forced to act in violation of a deep-seated and God-given instinct that his role in the world is to be a protector and defender and respecter of the wonderful gift of woman-hood as embodied in the women to whom he relates. Encouraging violence against a woman and the aggressive attitude that the violence must entail in order to be successful is encouraging him to have exactly the wrong attitude toward women, an attitude that biblical standards of manhood would direct him not to have. And the contest likewise encourages in young women a physically aggressive, hostile, violent attitude toward a man that will hinder the development of healthy relationships with men in the future.

In addition, the intensely close physical contact that is required in wrestling, even with the genital area and a woman's breasts, means that on another level a boy wrestler is compelled to violate standards of decency and physical touch in areas where, outside of marriage, he has no right to be, and a girl wrestler has to engage in a contest where this kind of contact is expected and considered normal. This is again the result of a government-sponsored attempt to deny the distinctive sexuality of men and women and to deny the essential differences between men and women as given by God. My own view is that Christian coaches of wrestling teams—and in fact all coaches of wrestling teams, who respect and honor the goodness of masculinity and femininity given to us by God—should resign rather than allow themselves to be compelled to endorse this kind of activity. Christian parents of both boys and girls pushed into such situations should likewise withdraw their children from participation rather than forcing them at such a young age, and often without mature understanding of differences between men and women, to violate the moral patterns of Scripture.

With regard to football, the conflict is not quite as blatant, but the physical wrong involved is just as significant when a boy is required to use violence to tackle a girl or block her with all his strength. Having a girl on a boys' football team also hinders the unique camaraderie and sense of unity in gender identity that is so crucial for develop-ing a proper sense of manhood among boys. Similarly, involving boys in all-girl sports or having a few girls participate in an all-boys sport also denies to the girls the unique opportunity to develop a healthy sense of womanhood and gender-based unity and identity that are essential to adolescent development. These policies can only bring con-tinuing harm to American society. Such policies flow from a secular philosophy that attempts to use the power of law to compel people to deny the wonderful differences between men and women as created by God, and to deny plain old, ordinary common sense. Men and women are equal in God's sight (see Gen. 1:27), and men and women have equal value before God, yet men and women are not the same, and no laws will ever be able to make them the same.

F. FARM SUBSIDIES

Farm subsidies are fees paid to farmers by the government for two types of reasons. In the first case, the government promises to buy a farmer's crops at a certain "support price" (or price floor) even if the market price for that crop drops lower than that support price. These policies were put in place during the Great Depression, but were never halted after prosperity returned. In the second case (discussed below), the government pays a farmer *not* to produce a certain kind of crop but to let a field lie uncultivated or, through the "Conservation Reserve Program," keeps farmers from cultivating certain areas in the name of environmental protection.[27]

1. Support-price policy

Here is how the first type of farm subsidies works: The government might promise to pay $6 per bushel of wheat as the *support price*. If it is a good year for wheat and the world market has a lot of wheat to sell, then the world price for wheat might drop to $4, but the wheat farmer in the United States doesn't care, because the government has already promised to buy his crop at $6 per bushel.[28] The result of this support price is that farmers will plan to produce a lot of wheat (rather than hedging their bets and planting a few other crops that might be in greater demand) because they know they have a great deal going—they can sell it all to the government and make a tidy profit. So US farmers will raise more wheat than the world market demands, more than the forces of supply and demand and the world price would normally encourage them to produce. If we multiply this by the incredible number of bushels of wheat produced in the United States every year, the result of this farm subsidy is that the nation will produce far more wheat than the world market would normally require and pay for. And this happens for many other crops as well.

Bruce Babcock, a professor at Iowa State University, wrote in the *Iowa Agricultural Review*:

> Farmers who sign up for ACRE (Average Crop Revenue Election) are protected against corn prices below $3.75/bu, soybean prices below $8.75/bu, and wheat prices below $6.00/bu. Farmers who buy subsidized revenue insurance receive revenue guarantees based on $4.04 for corn, $8.80 soybeans, and $6.20 spring wheat. Farmers who sign up for both ACRE and crop insurance will receive double compensation if harvest prices fall dramatically. Why should farmers use the private sector and hedge against low prices when taxpayers are providing heavily subsidized price protection?

---

27. David Streitfeld, "As Prices Rise, Farmers Spurn Conservation Program," *New York Times* (April 9, 2008). www.nytimes.com/2008/04/09/business/09conserve.html?_r=2&ex=1365480000&en=ce91b80157d8e73c&ei=5090&partner=rssuserland&emc=rss&oref=slogin.

28. Bruce A. Babcock, "ACRE: Price Support or Crop Insurance?" *Iowa Agricultural Review* 15, no. 2 (Spring 2009). www.card.iastate.edu/iowa_ag_review/spring_09/article3.aspx.

The private sector simply cannot compete with the heavily subsidized risk management programs offered by the government. The question then becomes whether taxpayers are getting anything in return for their investment or whether the subsidies are really just a hidden means of transferring money to farmers and the crop insurance industry.[29]

What does the government do with this excess wheat, far beyond what the world market demands? It can store it for a time in huge surplus grain storage bins. But the wheat cannot keep forever without spoiling, so the US government is forced either to *sell it* or to *give it away* in the world market, in either case at a price that is *below* that year's normal market price. (If it were not at a lower price, nobody would buy it.) The US government therefore "dumps" millions of bushels of cheap wheat into the world supply of wheat. What is the result? The price drops dramatically. Wheat farmers in other countries—some of them often very poor and just on the edge of survival in their businesses—see that the world price of wheat responds to this huge extra supply, and with dismay they see that they can sell their wheat only at the new, lower world market price.

In this way, the United States' policy of "dumping" wheat onto the world market *artificially depresses prices below what they would otherwise be,* and other countries find it harder to sell their own wheat on the world market and get the price they had expected and otherwise would have received.

Who are the *winners* and who are the *losers* in this system of farm subsidies? The first winner is the wheat farmer in the United States. He has produced more wheat than the world market would ordinarily desire, but he doesn't care, because the government has paid him a price that is above the world market price. Moreover, he is protected whether the price goes up or down, for if there is a poor wheat crop the next year and the price per bushel goes up, he will simply sell his smaller crop at that high market price, and he is just fine. The American taxpayers have given a great benefit to this wheat farmer.

Some people might think that the poor wheat farmer needs this help. But in fact the farm subsidies paid out by the US government often go to gigantic companies that own millions of acres and therefore receive huge amounts of money. In 2002 the Cato Institute reported:

> Figures from the U.S. Department of Agriculture (USDA) show that the average farm household income was $61,307 in 2000. This is 7.5 percent higher than the average U.S. household income of $57,045 in 2000. Commercial farms, as defined by the USDA, get about half of all farm subsidies, had average household incomes of $118,450 in 2000, and received an average subsidy of $43,379. When large-scale federal farm subsidies began in the 1930s, farm incomes were just half of the national average.... Farm subsidy recipients include Fortune 500 companies, members of Congress, and millionaires such as Ted Turner.[30]

29. Bruce A. Babcock.."Should Government Subsidize Farmers' Risk Management?" *Iowa Agricultural Review* 15, no. 2 (Spring 2009). www.card.iastate.edu/iowa_ag_review/ spring_09/article1.aspx.

30. Chris Edwards and Tad DeHaven, "Farm Reform Reversal," *Cato Institute Tax & Budget,* No. 2 (March 2002). www.cato. org/pubs/tbb/tbb–0203–2.pdf.

Other wealthy recipients, according to Cato, were the Westvaco Corporation, Chevron, John Hancock Mutual Life Insurance, DuPont, and Caterpillar—hardly struggling family farms.[31]

There is one other "winner" in this whole scheme, and that is the people in other countries who like to eat a lot of wheat and prefer wheat over other grains such as rice or corn or barley or oats. For them, the US taxpayers have provided a nice bonus because the US government has used US taxpayers' money to drive down the price of these people's favorite commodity. They get wheat for a lower price, and they are happy. Bakers in other countries who use a lot of wheat in their products are also winners in this scheme.

So who are the losers? First, the US taxpayers are losers. They have paid the wheat farmer to produce a lot of wheat that the world really didn't want (according to what it indicated through its demand and the resulting world price of wheat).

Another loser is any American who buys *any other kind of food product* in the grocery store. That is because, when the wheat farmer chose to produce *more wheat* because of the generous support price, he also had to choose to produce *less corn or rye or oats or barley,* or less broccoli or beans or tomatoes or peas, or whatever else he could have grown on that land. Or he has chosen to raise fewer cattle or sheep or hogs for meat, or to graze fewer cows for milk.

Therefore the wheat support price has artificially distorted the market in another way. It has *reduced the supply of the other commodities* below what the market would normally produce, and that simply drives up the price of these other commodities to some degree. Maybe it is only by a few cents for each thing that is bought, but multiply a few cents by 307 million consumers in the United States and you see that US consumers have also paid a significantly higher price for the other things that they eat besides wheat—things that are not subsidized by the support price. But the wheat farmer doesn't care, because he has earned a tidy profit. In other words, the situation is this: *The few profit, and the many pay.*

There is still another loser: the wheat farmer in other countries. When I travel to other countries and speak about economic development, I am often asked why the United States continues its destructive policy of "dumping" commodities on the world market and depressing world commodity prices so that farmers in poor countries can hardly stay in business and sometimes hardly earn enough income to feed their families. I have no answer to these questions except to say that the political forces in the United States are such that no one seems able to do away with the broken system of subsidies that are still being paid by the United States (and by countries of the European Union; see below) to support their own agricultural industries—subsidies that less developed nations see as highly unfair to them.

What is the political reason for this? If we dig a bit deeper, we discover that the American system of government has a built-in bias toward protecting farmers in this way. That is because the US Senate is made up of two senators from every state, no matter how many or how few people the state has. Therefore large agricultural states

31. Ibid.

with very few people still have two senators. Montana has two senators, and so does Wyoming, Nebraska, Kansas, Colorado, and so forth. These senators are very sensitive to the farm vote, because it often means the difference between getting elected and not getting elected. So farmers from wheat-producing states are never going to find it easy to vote against farm subsidies for wheat.

But the story does not stop there. *Other states* have farm subsidies to support other crops. In fact, there are only a few states that do not have a large number of farm producers and a very influential farm lobby. Therefore the senators from Georgia might not care much about the support price for wheat, but they do want the vote of the senators from Nebraska when it comes to *peanut* support prices, and the senators from Wisconsin want the Georgia senators' votes when it comes to support prices for *dairy products*. And so in this way, though only 2% of the American population is involved in farming, the farm lobby has immense influence in the US Senate.

One strength of the US system of government, and one protection against the majority trampling on the rights of the minority, is the wonderful system of electing two senators from every state. But one consequence is that farmers tend to have immense political influence, far beyond their numbers. And so it is, when farm support prices apply not just to wheat but to dozens of commodities, that there are multiple market distortions, and the US taxpayer ends up paying a lot of money for the benefit of a very small group of people—not only small farmers, but also often huge agribusinesses that profit immensely from these farm subsidies.

2. Uncultivated fields policy

A second kind of farm subsidy is paying farmers *not* to produce certain kinds of crops but to leave fields uncultivated. The purpose for this is to reduce the supply of a certain crop to keep prices higher for those farmers who are still producing the crop or, through the "Conservation Reserve Program," to keep farmers from cultivating certain areas for the purpose of environmental protection.

Once again, this policy simply increases costs for *the many* (taxpayers in general) while giving reward to *the few*. The winners are the farmers who are paid to do nothing with the land and the farmers who raise a certain crop and get higher prices because there is less supply. The losers are the rest of the nation and the world, who have less of that crop and higher prices for what they can still buy.

Those who support such a policy say that it is necessary to keep certain kinds of agriculture within the United States, and if the nation did not keep domestic prices high in this way, the prices would drop so low that many farmers would be driven out of business.

But if the purpose of government is to support the good of the nation in general, then this policy of paying farmers to produce *nothing* on some of their land is completely foolish. The total amount of farm products produced in a year is *less* because of this policy rather than *more*! How can it make a nation better off when it spends money to get *less* of something? It makes the nation poorer, not richer overall. It just brings financial benefit to farmers that have the political clout needed to maintain this subsidy.

Such subsidies should be abolished, and the normal forces of supply and demand should be allowed to determine the price for a crop and the amount produced. If this drives the price down for a certain crop (say peanuts), then all the consumers in the nation who eat peanuts are better off as a result! If some inefficient farmers are driven out of business because of the lower price, then that is good for the nation. Those farmers need to switch to some other crop that they could grow more profitably, or else they need to leave agriculture and work in some other area of the economy.

In fact, in some cases individuals are receiving farm subsidies because they purchased land that was *previously* used for farming! The *Washington Post* reported in 2006:

> Even though Donald R. Matthews put his sprawling new residence in the heart of rice country, he is no farmer. He is a 67-year-old asphalt contractor who wanted to build a dream house for his wife of 40 years.
>
> Yet under a federal agriculture program approved by Congress, his 18-acre suburban lot receives about $1,300 in annual "direct payments," because years ago the land was used to grow rice.
>
> Matthews is not alone. Nationwide, the federal government has paid at least $1.3 billion in subsidies for rice and other crops since 2000 to individuals who do no farming at all, according to an analysis of government records by *The Washington Post*. Some of them collect hundreds of thousands of dollars without planting a seed. Mary Anna Hudson, 87, from the River Oaks neighborhood in Houston, has received $191,000 over the past decade. For Houston surgeon Jimmy Frank Howell, the total was $490,709....
>
> The checks to Matthews and other landowners were intended 10 years ago as a first step toward eventually eliminating costly, decades-old farm subsidies. Instead, the payments have grown into an even larger subsidy that benefits millionaire landowners, foreign speculators and absentee landlords, as well as farmers. Most of the money goes to real farmers who grow crops on their land, but they are under no obligation to grow the crop being subsidized. They can switch to a different crop or raise cattle or even grow a stand of timber—and still get the government payments. The cash comes with so few restrictions that subdivision developers who buy farmland advertise that homeowners can collect farm subsidies on their new back yards.
>
> The payments now account for nearly half of the nation's expanding agricultural subsidy system, a complex web that has little basis in fairness or efficiency. What began in the 1930s as a limited safety net for working farmers has swollen into a far-flung infrastructure of entitlements that has cost $172 billion over the past decade. In 2005 alone, when pretax farm profits were at a near-record $72 billion, the federal government handed out more than $25 billion in aid, almost 50 percent more than the amount it pays to families receiving welfare.[32]

32. Dan Morgan, Gilbert M. Gaul, and Sarah Cohen, "Farm Program Pays $1.3 Billion to People Who Don't Farm," *Washington Post* (July 2, 2006). www.washingtonpost.com/wp-dyn/content/article/2006/07/01/AR2006070100962.html.

One final argument for farm subsidies is an argument from the perspective of national security. Some people say that if the United States does not have farm subsidies, all agricultural production will move overseas and we will be dependent on foreign nations for our entire food supply. Therefore we need these subsidies to protect our domestic food production, which is important for our national security.

It seems to me that this argument is overstated. With modern farming methods and high-yield crops and huge farm machinery, American farmers are the most productive farmers in the world. According to the American Farm Bureau Association, each American farmer feeds an average of 143 people, compared with just 19 people in 1940.[33] Also, shipping costs for food from domestic farms are much less than for food imported from distant countries. Removing agricultural subsidies is not going to destroy American agriculture. And even if foreign competition and lower prices began to bring about a great decline in the percentage of food produced in the United States, new programs could be introduced to retain some agriculture here if that became necessary in the future. But that seems to me unlikely.

G. TARIFFS

A tariff is a tax or fee imposed on goods when they enter or leave a country. In this section I will focus on the most common kind of tariff, that on goods at the time they enter the United States from another country.

To take a simple example, imagine that a certain size and quality of automobile tire that is manufactured in the United States costs $80. Suppose that a Chinese company can manufacture that exact same tire, with exactly the same quality of rubber and exactly the same specifications, and ship it to the United States and sell it for $60. Of course, most of the customers are going to buy the $60 dollar tire from China rather than the $80 tire from the United States. (There might be a slight preference for the tire made in the United States, but if customers are convinced that the quality is the same, they will mostly decide not to "waste" the extra $20 so that they can spend the money on something else.)

That is the way the world market works for thousands of items that are imported and exported around the world every year. Different countries find that they can manufacture products more efficiently or with better qualities than other countries can, and they export them to those other countries. In fact, in terms of high-precision manufacturing, the United States is still a huge exporter of goods, shipping $1.84 trillion in goods and services to other countries in 2008,[34] everything from Boeing airplanes to Caterpillar tractors to semiconductors. According to the latest US Department of Commerce figures, the top US exports are nuclear reactors and machinery, electronic machinery, and various forms of vehicles.[35]

---

33. "Statement by Bob Stallman, President, American Farm Bureau Federation, Regarding the Obama Family Planting a White House Garden," *The Voice of Agriculture* (March 23, 2009). www.fb.org/index.php?fuseaction=newsroom.newsfocus&year=2009&file=nr0323.html.

34. December 2008 Export Statistics Released February 11, 2009, U.S. Department of Commerce. http://trade.gov/press/press_releases/2009/export-factsheet_021109.pdf.

35. See http://ese.export.gov/NTDChartDisplay.aspx?UniqueURL=2xnzg145n4dtikunk1aj1hj0–2009–11–18–12–57–44.

In economics, the principle of comparative advantage teaches that—because no country can manufacture everything for the whole world, and because countries end up specializing in things they can do quite well, and because consumers' wants for more and higher-quality things will never be satisfied—*all countries will always have some things that they can manufacture advantageously* and from which a profit can be made.

But there is one group of people in the United States that is upset about these $60 tires from China, namely, US tire manufacturers, and especially the union workers at those manufacturing plants. These companies and workers complain that it is "unfair" that these Chinese companies can sell products in the American market for such a low cost. In this way labor unions often put the greatest pressure on the US government to impose tariffs on imports of foreign goods.

For example, if the United States suddenly imposes a $20 tariff on Chinese tires, then the Chinese tire will cost $80, the same price as the American tire. Now the American tire workers still have a job, and they are happy.

But what has happened? Once again, *the many* have paid for a benefit that goes to *the few*. Drivers now have to buy tires at $80 instead of $60 (and similar considerations would apply to other tires in other price ranges). Now the American consumer has just lost the $20 that he thought he was going to save to use however he wanted. The "winners" in this arrangement are the rubber workers in the tire plant, whose jobs are suddenly protected, and the owners of the tire companies. But the economy as whole has become the loser because of higher prices in imported tires.

On September 14, 2009, President Obama announced that he was increasing the tariffs on Chinese-made tires to 35%, to the delight of unions who had lobbied for this increase. Roy Littlefield, executive director of the Tire Industry Association, which represents the non-manufacturing aspects of the tire industry, said:

> It's a very disappointing decision.... This is not going to bring a single job back into America. The companies that are manufacturing tires overseas are going to continue doing so. The manufacturers will simply reroute shipping, so instead of coming from China the tires will come in from Brazil and India. From a consumer angle, obviously these tires are going to cost more.[36]

This process, of course, is not limited to tires. Tariffs can spread to all sorts of other goods, multiplying higher prices for everybody in the economy.

There is another consequence as well. The Chinese tire companies do not like the penalty that they have to pay to the American government. Therefore they will often pressure the Chinese government to place a retaliatory tariff on some American goods that are being imported into China, such as cars and trucks or high-end electronic

---

36. Aaron Smith, "Tariff could flatten cheap tires from China," *CNN.com* (Sept. 14, 2009). http://money.cnn.com/2009/09/14/news/companies/china_tire_tariff/index.htm.

equipment. This then cuts into the sales of the US company that manufactures these items. So American producers of exports suffer as well.

Does the US government get some revenue from the tariffs that it charges? Yes, it does get $20 per tire in revenue from all of the Chinese tires that continue to be imported. But American consumers are also paying that extra $20 when they buy a tire!

In that way, tariffs are simply a form of tax on American consumers. Yet they are an invisible tax because American consumers in general do not realize that a tariff has been imposed on the imported tire. They just see that tires cost $80, and they do not even realize that the government has quietly raised the cost of tires by $20 and pocketed the $20 for its own purposes. In this way, *tariffs take away the freedom of American consumers to spend their money as they wish,* and they transfer more of an individual's money into the hands of the government, which then decides how the money should be spent rather than allowing consumers the freedom to decide how they think the money should be spent.

The overall result of tariffs on hundreds and thousands of goods is to drive up the prices of everything that consumers buy if it is imported from other countries. Tariffs also prop up higher prices on products made within a country (such as US-made tires) that would have been imported for a lower cost from other countries if the high tariff had not made the cost of the imports prohibitively high.

Therefore a government that seeks to be faithful to God's purpose in Romans 13:4, "To be God's servant *for your good,*" should seek to reduce tariffs and eventually eliminate them altogether and thus bring lower prices and more freedom and more "good" to the people of a nation.

This is why the "free trade" agreements that the United States has entered into with other countries are so valuable to the entire American population. Under presidents Ronald Reagan and George H. W. Bush, the United States adopted the Canada-U.S. Free Trade Agreement of 1987 and then began to push for the adoption of the North American Free Trade Agreement (NAFTA), which was eventually signed into law by President Bill Clinton with strong Republican support. (The agreement had been signed by Bush in December 1992, but was not ratified by Congress until Clinton came into office.) President Clinton also gave China "most favored nation" trading status in 2000 that provided low tariffs on trade between the United States and China.

Today the World Trade Organization (WTO) promotes lower tariffs and freer trade arrangements between various countries of the world. However, recent negotiations among some countries, currently called the Doha Round of negotiations, have not been able to come to agreement on various proposals to move toward further freedom in trade among nations. These negotiations began in the city of Doha, Qatar, in November 2001, but progress has been slow. One sticking point in negotiations has been the agricultural subsidies that are still being paid by the United States and countries of the European Union to support their agricultural industries, subsidies that less developed nations contend are highly unfair to them. Policies that maintain high tariffs are called "protectionist" policies because they tend to "protect" certain industries and groups within a nation from competition coming from other countries.

Since Democrats gained majorities in Congress in 2006, the United States has adopted a much more protectionist policy regarding foreign trade. This is because the Democratic Party receives strong support from labor unions, and unions in general have been avid opponents of free trade. They think free trade will destroy their jobs. The result of Democratic political power is that "America is leaving itself behind as the rest of the world tries to liberalize trade."[37] The European Union has made free trade agreements with South Korea "by copying the trade deal the Bush Administration negotiated with Seoul but that Congress refuses to ratify."[38] Another recent agreement means that Canadian exporters, even farmers, will be able to sell their products in Columbia tariff-free, while "farmers in Iowa or Nebraska will be stuck with tariffs of between 5% and 80%"[39] because Congress refuses to ratify the free trade agreement that the Bush administration negotiated with Columbia. Worldwide, "the U.S. is a party to only five of the 64 trade pacts that have taken effect since 2005."[40]

My own evaluation of this issue is that countries should move toward abolishing nearly all tariffs on imports, because this means that consumers in various nations of the world can purchase thousands of items at lower prices and therefore have more freedom to decide how to spend the rest of their own money.

However, there are probably certain industries that a nation would consider essential to its well-being or defense, and for this reason (not simply to raise money or protect workers in a certain industry) a country might legitimately decide to impose tariffs on imports. One example might be agricultural products in Switzerland—though the cost of dairy products might be higher, the Swiss people might reason that preserving and protecting its small dairy farms in mountain regions is essential to the historic traditions, cultural values, and beauty of the nation. Or the United States might argue that national security dictates that it continue to produce its own military armaments and fighter planes, so it would impose various restrictions on imports of these things from other nations (or it might specify that the United States must buy large percentages of its weapons from American companies). In such cases the purpose of the tariff (or other kinds of restriction of trade) is not simply to raise money for the government or to protect some workers in some industry, but *to protect something else that the nation thinks to be important.* These are the only reasons for which I could see that tariffs would be good for the nation as a whole.

In general, it seems to me beneficial to a nation to promote free trade without any barriers from tariffs.

H. TRIAL LAWYERS, MEDICAL MALPRACTICE AWARDS, AND REFORM OF TORT LAW

Many people in the United States believe that their legal system is defective because it allows trial lawyers to win tens of millions and sometimes hundreds of millions of

37. "America Leaves Itself Behind," *Wall Street Journal* (Nov. 11, 2009), A20.
38. Ibid.
39. Ibid.
40. Ibid.

dollars when individuals sue a company or another person for allegedly harming them. Many of these multimillion dollar awards are given in medical malpractice cases, as when a person is seriously harmed during surgery or when a doctor misdiagnoses a case of cancer. At other times these huge awards come when a lawyer claims that his client was injured by negligent action on the part of some company. One example is when a customer sued McDonald's because the cup of coffee that she bought was too hot, and it spilled and burned her when she tried to add cream and sugar while holding it between her legs while sitting in the passenger seat of her automobile. She sued and received a jury award of $2.86 million.[41] (A judge later reduced the punitive damages amount to $480,000.)

Philip K. Howard, writing in the *Wall Street Journal*, talked about the ramifications of outrageous lawsuit awards on nonprofit organizations, including churches:

> Sooner or later, Americans will realize that sue-for-anything justice erodes their freedom. First it was diving boards that disappeared, then seesaws. Businesses stopped giving references, and doctors started quitting. Like a lake receding from its shores, the area of our freedom continues to diminish with each new theory of liability. The latest casualty is volunteerism. Last month, a jury in Milwaukee found the Catholic Archdiocese liable because a volunteer for a Catholic lay organization, driving her own car, ran a red light and caused an accident while delivering a statue of the Virgin Mary to an invalid. Although the church does not direct the activities of this group, called the Legion of Mary, its meetings are held on church property. The jury decided the Archdiocese should pay $17 million to the paralyzed victim, an 82-year-old semi-retired barber. The chill on volunteer activities will be immediate. Volunteers often drive here and there for their charities. Religious institutions are particularly vulnerable, because they allow their premises to be used for a wide range of volunteer activities, including the Boy Scouts and Alcoholics Anonymous. What are the contours of liability? Why take the risk?[42]

Howard concluded:

> The harm is not that crazy verdicts will sink our economy. Extreme verdicts are relatively rare, and usually reduced on appeal. The harm is to the fabric of freedom. People no longer feel comfortable doing what's right and good. Legal fear now infects social dealings throughout society.[43]

The legal category under which most of these cases fall is called *tort law*, where the word "tort" refers to the damage or injury that party A does to party B through negligence

41. Gayathri Vaidyanathan, "Ten Ridiculous Lawsuits Against Big Business," *Business Insider Law Review* (Nov. 11, 2009). www.businessinsider.com/the-ten-dumbest-lawsuits-against-big-business–2009–11#mcdonalds-coffee-case–1.

42. Philip K. Howard, "Charity Case," *Wall Street Jour-* *nal* (March 17, 2005). http://online.wsj.com/article/SB111102341720581903.html?mod=opinion_main_commentaries.

43. Ibid.

or an intentional act, but the harmful action was not a violation of a legal contract (which would be covered by *contract law* rather than tort law). Tort law also is distinguished from *criminal law,* in which a person has broken a law of the state and the state will bring prosecution against him.

I fully realize that genuine victims of harmful behavior need to be protected and compensated, and for that to happen the nation needs to have effective, skilled trial lawyers to represent the victims, often to gain fair compensation for damages done by a large company or by a doctor with greater economic resources than the patient. I am not opposed to trial lawyers in general! Nevertheless, several problems can be seen in the current legal system in the United States that allows trial lawyers to gain such large awards from filing such lawsuits.

1. Awards too high

Many people feel that the huge awards that trial lawyers sometimes win from jury trials seem for too high in comparison with the benefits that such lawyers bring to society. The Institute for Legal Reform, part of the US Chamber of Commerce, estimates that personal injury lawsuits and tort claims cost $260 billion a year,[44] which is more than $3,300 for every family of four.[45] The institute commissioned a study in 2007 that found small businesses alone pay $98 billion a year to cover the cost of America's tort system—money that could otherwise be used to hire additional workers, expand productivity, and improve employee benefits.[46]

2. Large costs paid by innocent parties to avoid going to court

Because the potential for losing millions of dollars in a lawsuit is so great, many times companies will simply reach a "settlement" with the trial lawyer and his client to avoid going to trial. Even when a company or individual is innocent, insurance companies often decide that it is better to pay the $1 million and get the lawyer off its back instead of risking the loss of $10 million or more in an unpredictable jury decision. This is especially true in the medical field, where insurance companies would rather settle a malpractice lawsuit, even if the doctor is innocent, than leave it to the whims of a jury. Unfortunately, the doctor then receives a black mark on his or her record—including possible revocation of the license to practice medicine—because he or she has not been cleared of the charges.[47]

The result of this is that innocent people and innocent companies will spend huge amounts of money to avoid a trial, simply because they do not want to risk getting an unfavorable jury that is just anti-business and simply wants to punish them.

44. "Lawsuit Abuse Impact," *Institute for Legal Reform.com.* www.instituteforlegalreform.com/component/ilr_issues/29/item/LAI.html.

45. "A Tangled Tale," *Institute for Legal Reform.com.* www.triallawyerearmarks.com/.

46. "Lawsuit Abuse Impact."

47. George F. Indest III, J.D., M.P.A., LL.M. and Jason L. Harr, J.D., M.P.A. "The NPDB and Legal Ramifications of Settling Your Medical Malpractice Lawsuit," The Health Law Firm. ttp://www.thehealthlawfirm.com/npdb.asp.

But who really pays for this? *The American consumer ultimately pays for this,* because companies have to raise prices to offset the extra costs of such a settlement. The fear of defending against a lawsuit is so great that lawyers have a high incentive to bring even frivolous lawsuits against a business, knowing that there is a likelihood that they will be able to get *some* payment out of even an innocent company.

For example, in 2005, Roy Pearson, a judge in Washington, DC, brought a lawsuit against a Korean immigrant couple running a dry-cleaning business. He said they had lost the pants to a suit that he was going to wear and sued them for $67 million (eventually reduced to $54 million), even though the couple had been willing to pay him up to $12,000 to replace the pants and eventually found the pants. ABC News reported that the judge said in court papers that he had "been through the ringer over a lost pair of prized pants he wanted to wear on his first day on the bench" and that he had endured "mental suffering, inconvenience and discomfort" because "he was unable to wear that favorite suit on his first day of work." As part of the lawsuit, he sued for $500,000 in emotional damages and $542,500 in legal fees (even though he represented himself), as well as ten years of weekend car rentals so he could transport his dry cleaning to another store! He also cited the District's consumer protection laws, and he claimed he was entitled to $1,500 per violation per day.

Soo Chung, the co-owner of the dry-cleaning business with her husband, said, "I would have never thought it would have dragged on this long, I don't want to live here anymore. It's been so difficult. I just want to go home, go back to Korea."[48]

Although the judge lost the lawsuit, the damage was done. In September 2007 the couple was forced to sell its dry-cleaning store. Their attorney said, "This is a truly tragic example of how devastating frivolous litigation can be to the American people and to small businesses. This family has poured its heart and soul into their dry cleaning stores, only to have their dreams crushed by Roy Pearson's lawsuit."[49]

A trial lawyer might object to my bringing up this dry-cleaning case or the McDonald's case, saying that these are rare cases and unrepresentative of our actual tort law system, which for the most part works quite well. I agree that we should not think these rare cases represent most tort cases in the U.S. In fact, I have also heard of settlements that are far too small for the damage suffered. (I was actually part of a jury several years ago in which the majority voted for a paltry damage award that seemed to me far too low.) But it seems to me that the reason these large-settlement cases resonate with the American people is that today *we all live with a vague fear of being hit by such a huge lawsuit ourselves,* even when we have done nothing wrong. The *potential* for the legal system to ruin someone's life unfairly just seems too great to the majority of the American public. We have heard too many such stories, and many of us even know personally some of the innocent victims of a tort system that needs somehow to be corrected.

---

48. Jim Avila, Chris Francescani, and Mary Harris, "The $67 Million Pants," *ABCNews.com* (May 2, 2007). http://abcnews.go.com/TheLaw/Story?id=3119381&page=1.

49. "Dry cleaner in infamous pants lawsuit sells 2nd shop," *CNN.com* (Sept. 19, 2007). http://money.cnn.com/2007/09/19/news/pants_suit/.

When the possibility of winning or getting a huge settlement payment is so great, it provides individuals and trial lawyers with incentives for bringing frivolous lawsuits, and these end up costing a lot of money that is ultimately paid by an innocent company, or by their innocent customers who have not done anything wrong but have to pay higher prices as a result. Maybe "only a few" lawyers do this, but a few do, and the bar associations and the legal system have not prevented this from happening, so we all live in fear of frivolous lawsuits.

In other famous cases of class-action lawsuits, entire companies have been driven to bankruptcy because of producing a product for which no harm or damage had ever been proven. For example, the Dow Corning company was driven to bankruptcy because of multiple lawsuits over silicone breast implants they had produced. The company fought off many lawsuits beginning in 1984, but in 1998 it finally conceded to a multi-billion-dollar class-action settlement. These lawsuits drove the company into bankruptcy for nine years, from 1995 to 2004.

Why do I see a problem with this? Because no reputable scientific study has ever shown that silicone breast implants cause breast cancer or any other identifiable diseases such as lupus or arthritis, for which the company was sued.[50] Does it matter that Dow Corning was driven to bankruptcy? It is a large company providing more than 7,000 products and services in silicones, adhesives, lubricants, solvents, and other household and industrial products. It has over 8,000 employees. It does much good for the economy and provides many jobs. It does not seem right to me that a company like this should be driven to bankruptcy by trial lawyers when it has done nothing wrong.

3. Higher medical costs

Because doctors constantly face the threat of lawsuits for medical malpractice, they have to pay huge fees to insurance companies who bear the risk of defending them against the suits. For example, a 2005 study found that obstetrician/gynecologists (or ob-gyns) could be expected to pay $250,000 or more every year on malpractice insurance premiums.[51] This means that the cost of medical care from these doctors is higher, because they have to charge more to cover their fees.

According to Kenneth Thorpe, chair of the Department of Health Policy and Management, Rollins School of Public Health, Emory University, in Atlanta, Georgia, malpractice insurance rate increases in Pennsylvania in 2003 alone ranged from 26% to 73%.[52] In addition, doctors will often order many more tests than they would normally think appropriate for certain symptoms, simply to guard against the possibility of being sued later for not checking out every possible cause for the symptoms, no matter how unlikely it might seem. This also drives up medical costs because insurance

50. "Dow Corning emerges from bankruptcy," Associated Press (June 1, 2004). www.usatoday.com/money/industries/manufacturing/2004–06–01-dow-corning_x.htm.

51. Joseph Brownstein, "New York Doctors Frustrated Over Malpractice Insurance Hike," ABCNews.com (July 4, 2007). http://abcnews.go.com/Health/story?id=3344926&page=1.

52. Kenneth E. Thorpe, "The Medical Malpractice 'Crisis': Recent Trends and the Impact of State Tort Reforms," Health Affairs (Jan. 21, 2004). http://content.healthaffairs.org/cgi/content/full/hlthaff.w4.20v1/DC1?maxtoshow=&HITS=25&hits=25&RESULTFORMAT=&author1=thorpe&andorexactfulltext=and&searchid=1&FIRSTINDEX=0&resourcetype=HWCIT.

companies then have to pay for many more tests than doctors would normally think necessary.

How much money is wasted in this way? According to the *Wall Street Journal:*

> Consulting firm Tillinghast Towers-Perrin has suggested the direct cost of medical tort litigation is … $30 billion *annually.* PriceWaterhouseCoopers estimates that last year $240 billion in health expenditures were the result of doctors ordering unnecessary procedures to protect against the risk of lawsuits.[53]

4. Costs of defending against lawsuits

The cost of defending against lawsuits is a huge expense for many companies, and this is therefore a deterrent to economic growth. If a company is sued, it has to hire skilled trial lawyers to defend itself, and their fees are often $500 or more per hour, with some earning as much as $30,000 per hour![54] This is a large expense to any firm and results in higher product prices for all consumers.

5. Fear of lawsuits leading to a fear-driven society and preventing many good activities

The fear of lawsuits drives many people and groups in the United States to make decisions based on fear rather than reason and common sense. For example, diving boards at public swimming pools have almost completely disappeared in the United States. Steve Moore, writing in the *Wall Street Journal,* noted:

> The insurance industry says that most pool-construction companies won't even install the boards anymore out of fear of lawsuits. Texas lawmakers earlier this year enacted a de facto prohibition on diving boards by making the safety standards so stringent that few existing pools can meet them without spending millions of dollars….
>
> Diving accidents may be rare, but when they occur, lawyers become relentless in their quest for a jackpot jury verdict. In one famous 1993 case, a 14-year-old boy in Washington state took a "suicide dive"—headfirst with no arms out for protection—off the board of a neighbor's pool. He was tragically paralyzed from the neck down when he hit his head on the bottom of the pool. Despite the boy's own unsafe behavior, the parents' legal team sued every imaginable party—the neighbors, the pool-construction company, the diving-board manufacturer, the pool industry—and the family won a $10 million jury award….
>
> Ever since, it's been off to the races. Even cases in which there is no negligence on anyone's part can lead to jury awards of $5 million or more. The

---

53. "And a Buried Tort Bomb," *Wall Street Journal* (Nov. 12, 2009), A24.

54. "The New Billionaires," Center for Legal Policy at the Manhattan Institute (2008). www.triallawyersinc.com/html/part03.html.

plaintiff attorneys often walk off with up to half the loot. "This day and age, you can pretty much sue anyone for anything if there's an injury involved," a spokesman from the Pool and Spa Institute tells me.[55]

I can remember from childhood, and also from when our children were young, what a challenge it was for children to work up the courage even to jump off a low diving board, and then when they were a little older to jump or dive off a high diving board. It was a great part of the fun and challenge of childhood! But now every swimming pool owner is afraid of a lawsuit in case of an injury, and the result is that people have stopped building diving boards on swimming pools and have removed many of those that were there. The whole nation is worse off as a result, because these decisions were made not because of common sense or reason, but out of fear that a lawsuit could drive someone to bankruptcy.

Similarly, one of the most enjoyable playground toys in my childhood memory is an old-fashioned merry-go-round. Children could sit on wooden benches on any of eight sides in the circular merry-go-round, and then other children (on the inside and outside of the circle) would push it so it would spin fast, and then everybody would jump on and ride it. It was exhausting, but it gave great exercise, strength development, and a challenge to a lot of different physical skills. But now merry-go-rounds have completely disappeared from most playgrounds. Why? Because playground owners and school districts are afraid of lawsuits from a rare case where someone receives a serious injury. So rather than common sense and reasonableness driving a decision, our country has become a fear-driven society where everything has to be excessively safe. And our children are growing fatter and lazier and less adventuresome every year as a result.

Writing in the *Wall Street Journal*, Philip K. Howard said:

> There is nothing left in playgrounds that would attract the interest of a child over the age of four. Exercise in schools is carefully programmed, when it exists at all. Some schools have banned tag. Broward County, Fla., banned running at recess. (How else can we guard against a child falling down?) Little Leagues forbid sliding into base. Some towns ban sledding. High diving boards are history, and it's only a matter of time before all diving boards disappear.[56]

I remember another example of fear of lawsuits driving a foolish decision when we lived in Libertyville, Illinois. Our house was about a half-mile from the place where a railroad track crossed Milwaukee Avenue, the main street in Libertyville. Whenever a train approached the crossing, the gates would go down and stop traffic, several bright red lights would begin flashing, and a loud bell would ring to warn cars and pedestrians that a train was coming. Those safety measures were more than adequate to prevent anyone from straying onto the tracks.

55. Steve Moore, "Off the Deep End," *Wall Street Journal* (June 23, 2006). www.opinionjournal.com/taste/?id=110008555.

56. Philip K. Howard. "Why Safe Kids Are Becoming Fat Kids," *Wall Street Journal* (Aug. 13, 2008). http://online.wsj.com/article/SB121858701285435131.html.

But that wasn't enough for some federal government regulators. In some office in Washington, DC, someone instituted a regulation that every train approaching a crossing had to sound its train whistle. Therefore, in the middle of the night, sometimes at two or four o'clock, an incredibly loud train whistle would pierce the neighborhoods surrounding that intersection, waking up hundreds of people or at least interrupting their sleep. It wasn't too difficult for us, being about a half mile away, but it was still loud enough that it kept me from having our bedroom windows open at night in the middle of the summer. For the people who lived closer to the train tracks, the noise must have been terrible, as it caused regular disturbances to every night of sleep.

When I approached the city council members about a remedy for this—namely, passing a "no whistle/quiet zone" ordinance that would have stopped trains from disturbing everyone's sleep in Libertyville—I was told that they could not do this because they had been given legal advice that if they took this action and then someone went through the barrier gate and ignored the bells and the red lights, the city would be "possibly liable to a lawsuit." Therefore, year after year, in our fear-driven society, thousands of people across the United States have their sleep disturbed every night because of a foolish regulation and because of the fear of lawsuits by aggressive trial lawyers who are looking for large rewards.

6. Solutions

The most obvious needed reform seems to me to be some kind of legal limits on awards in medical malpractice suits and other tort cases. Many states have recently passed legislation that places such limits on damage awards. I need to make it clear that I do not think these limits should be unreasonably low, because true victims of medical malpractice should be fairly compensated for their loss. The law should still allow for adequate compensation in the case of serious, long-term disability that results from a doctor's mistake. But some limits are necessary because the current system has simply become far too expensive.

Many states have decided to set reasonable limits on such compensation, to limit the size of awards that can be given to lawyers, and also to limit or prohibit the punitive damages being paid in addition to the penalties that compensate for the specific loss that was suffered. In this way, says the *Wall Street Journal*, "30 states have adopted caps on awards as the core of their reform, with huge success. Texas imposed malpractice caps in 2003, and the state has been rewarded with fewer lawsuits, a 50% drop in malpractice premiums, and a flood of new doctors."[57]

When states have passed such restriction on medical malpractice awards, it has immediately resulted in lower insurance premiums for doctors practicing in those states and lower insurance costs for medical insurance bought by individuals. Kenneth Thorpe found that insurance premiums in states with a cap on awards were 17.1% lower than in

---

57. "And a Buried Tort Bomb."

states without such caps.[58] But in states that still allow exceptionally high damages in medical malpractice claims, the costs of buying insurance have become so high that in some communities doctors have simply been driven out of business and moved to other states or decided to retire. Thorpe cited a Georgia survey of physicians that found that a third of ob-gyns and a fifth of family practitioners stated that they would stop performing high-risk procedures. Another 12% noted that they would not cover the emergency room in the future.[59] When action like this happens, it indicates that the cost to society that comes from these excessive malpractice awards is far too great and that some reform is needed.

Unfortunately, the Democratic Party has tried to block such reforms. In the health care reform bill that the US House passed on November 7, 2009, states will only qualify for special "incentive payments" if they adopt a new "medical liability law" that "does not limit attorneys' fees or impose caps on damages."[60] This is an attempt to use the immense power of federal funding to force states to revoke their limits on excessive malpractice awards—exactly the wrong solution, for it will drive the malpractice insurance rates even higher! (Trial lawyers each year bounce between being the largest and second-largest contributors to the Democratic Party.)

Another very helpful reform that is already practiced in several countries is a "loser pays" system, in which there is a penalty for bringing an accusation against an innocent person. That way the cost of defending against a frivolous charge does not have to be borne by the innocent person or company, but by the person who brought the false accusation. A "loser pays" system would have stopped Roy Pearson from suing the Korean dry cleaners for $67 million for losing a pair of pants!

In the Old Testament legal code there was a penalty for false accusation:

> If a malicious witness arises to accuse a person of wrongdoing, then both parties to the dispute shall appear before the Lord, before the priests and the judges who are in office in those days. The judges shall inquire diligently, and if the witness is a false witness and has accused his brother falsely, then you shall do to him as he had meant to do to his brother. So you shall purge the evil from your midst. And the rest shall hear and fear, and shall never again commit any such evil among you (Deut. 19:16–20).

In other words, the penalty for false accusation was severe. Accusing an innocent person of wrongdoing was a serious wrong within Israel. A "loser pays" system in the United States would be a great benefit and would solve many of the difficulties of frivolous lawsuits that cause significant harm to society.

But is it likely that any such reforms will be passed in the current political climate? While between 70% and 80% of Americans "believe the country suffers from excess litigation"[61] and would support some kind of reform in tort law, the situation is complicated

---

58. Thorpe, "The Medical Malpractice 'Crisis.'"
59. Ibid.
60. Ibid.

61. Kimberley Strassel, "The President's Tort Two-Step," *Wall Street Journal* (Sept. 11., 2009), A17.

by the fact that trial lawyers as a group are one of the top contributors to Democratic candidates and the Democratic Party. Therefore the Democratic Party is committed to protecting the trial lawyers. The *Wall Street Journal* reported that during committee hearings on a proposed health-care bill in 2009, "Republicans offered eleven tort amendments that varied in degree from mere pilot projects to measures to ensure more rural obstetricians. On a party line vote, Democrats killed every one."[62]

I. THE NATIONAL EDUCATION ASSOCIATION

The National Education Association (NEA) is the largest labor union in the United States, with 3.2 million members.[63] The NEA has significant political influence, particularly at the state level. It also has great power because in many states and cities teachers have to pay dues to it, even if they don't join. For example, in Bedford, Ohio, teachers have to pay $713 in yearly dues to the union, regardless of membership.[64]

The problem with the NEA is that its leadership and activities have increasingly moved to the left side of the political spectrum. It has never endorsed the Republican candidate for President, for example, and in 2009 it endorsed same-sex marriage.[65] It makes campaign contributions to candidates, but a large percentage of those contributions go to Democratic candidates at both the local and national level. In 2008 the Center for Responsive Politics reported that 82% of the NEA's money went to Democrats and only 18% to Republicans.[66]

My largest objection against the NEA is that it consistently opposes any proposals that would give greater choice to parents in sending their children to public or private schools.

For example, in April 2007, the state legislature of Utah approved a statewide school voucher program that was signed by the governor and became law. This was the first time a state had endorsed a program that would give parents all over an entire state the opportunity to have vouchers that they could use to pay for sending their children to public schools or to private schools.[67] But the NEA waged an immense public relations battle against this law, bringing it to a state referendum and expending $3.2 million and thousands of hours of volunteer time. The result was that the NEA was able to defeat the voucher proposal through this referendum so that it never was able to go into practice.[68] (See the discussion of school vouchers on pp. 250–56 above.)

---

62. Ibid.

63. See www.nea.org/home/1704.htm.

64. Robert Nozar, "Teachers contract approved," *The Bedford* (OH) *Sun* (Sept. 25, 2008). www.cleveland.com/bedford-sunbanner/news/index.ssf?/base/news–0/1222349921279880.xml&coll=4.

65. William McGuiness, "ABA, NEA Come Out for Gay Rights," *The Advocate* (Aug. 11, 2009). http://advocate.com/News/Daily_News/2009/08/11/ABA,_NEA_Come_Out_for_

Gay_Rights/.

66. "Education: Long-Term Contribution Trends." www.opensecrets.org/industries/indus.php?ind=W04.

67. Robert C. Enlow, "Utah Adopts Universal Vouchers," *Buckeye Institute for Public Policy Research* (April 5, 2006). www.buckeyeinstitute.org/article/944.

68. "Utah Voters Defeat Measure to Create U.S. First Statewide School Voucher Program," Associated Press (Nov. 7, 2007). www.foxnews.com/story/0,2933,308936,00.html.

In this way the NEA prevented a greater opportunity for school choice by parents and prevented the competition that the public schools so desperately need in order to do a better job of educating children. In most places in the country, NEA-staffed public schools have a monopoly on public education, and parents who want to send their children to other schools have to pay for it themselves, which means that only parents with substantial incomes are able to do this.

What is the reason why children from public elementary and secondary schools in the United States do so poorly compared with children from other nations? And why do children from inner-city schools in particular do so poorly in academic achievement, trapping generation after generation in poverty, with low job skills and little ability to advance? Should not most of the blame fall to the NEA, which controls an effective monopoly on government-funded education?

Again and again when parents are given the opportunity to receive vouchers to send their children to alternative private schools, they eagerly do so. The voucher program for children from poor families in Washington (DC) schools provides an excellent recent example. The US Department of Education reported in March 2009 that "After 3 years, there was a statistically significant positive impact on reading test scores. Overall, those offered a scholarship were performing at statistically higher levels in reading equivalent to 3.1 months of additional learning."[69]

Private schools do a better job, because when such schools are free of burdensome government direction and union regulation, teachers do a much better job of simply teaching children what they need to learn. This has been shown in study after study. For example, the *New York Times* reported in 2002 that state officials found that by eighth grade, private and religious schools outperformed public schools by a significant margin—7 percentage points in math and 11 percentage points in English.[70] The US Department of Education reported in July 2006 that by eighth grade, the average private school mean reading score was 18.1 points higher than the average public school mean reading score, and the mean mathematics score was 12.3 points higher.[71]

I am not saying that all public schools do a poor job of training children. My own three sons all went to an outstanding public high school in Libertyville, Illinois. But it was an upper-middle-class neighborhood with high property taxes, high salaries paid to teachers, and high parental involvement and expectations for the schools. It also had a measure of competition from an excellent Roman Catholic high school that was nearby (although parents and church members had to fund that school).

69. "Evaluation of the DC Opportunity Scholarship Program: Impacts After Three Years," U.S. Department of Education (March 2009). http://ies.ed.gov/ncee/pubs/20094050/pdf/20094050.pdf.

70. Anemona Hartocollis, "Public Schools Lag in Test Scores," *New York Times* (March 15, 2002). www.nytimes.com/2002/03/15/nyregion/public-schools-lag-in-test-scores.html.

71. Henry Braun, Frank Jenkins, and Wendy Grigg, "Comparing Private Schools and Public Schools Using Hierarchal Linear Modeling," National Assessment of Educational Progress (July 2006). http://nces.ed.gov/nationsreportcard/pdf/studies/2006461.pdf.

But in many communities in the country, especially in lower-middle-class or poorer neighborhoods, schools are not nearly that good. When private schools are established in those neighborhoods, they can often train children for only a fraction of the cost of the public schools. And where parents in those areas are allowed to receive vouchers to pay for sending their children to an alternative school, the educational achievement in these private schools is still much better and also provides strong competition that drives improvement in public schools.

Why does the NEA oppose such a system that would bring benefit to the children of the nation and thus to the nation as a whole? It is another case of *a few people* benefiting (the teachers who are part of the NEA), while the costs are being borne by *the many*—the entire population of the nation. (In this case the cost is both higher expenses and a lower quality of education for the children.)

J. NATIVE AMERICANS (AMERICAN INDIANS)

Native Americans (also called American Indians) number about 4.3 million[72] and constitute about 1.5% of the population of the United States.[73] (This includes both people who claim only Native American ethnic background and people who claim a mixed ethnic background of Native American and some other group.)

Many Native Americans live on Indian reservations. There are about 310 Indian reservations[74] in the United States, comprising 55.7 million acres (225,410 km).[75] This represents 2.3% of the country's area. These reservations fall under the management of the US Department of the Interior and specifically under the Bureau of Indian Affairs. However, Native American tribes have a degree of national sovereignty over these reservations, and thus they have their own laws and legal systems, including their own courts.

While the history of these reservations is long and complex, any impartial evaluation of the *results* of the system today must honestly admit that it is a broken, failed system that traps most Native Americans in perpetual poverty and perpetual alienation from the rest of American society. While a few Native American leaders derive vast wealth from the gambling casinos that are allowed to operate on these lands, 32% of Native Americans still live below the poverty line. There are few jobs, with unemployment rates 2.5 times the national average,[76] and levels of alcoholism and drug abuse are tragically high. According to the Indian Health Service, alcoholism death rates are seven times the

72. The 2006–2008 American Community Survey 3-Year Estimates. http://factfinder.census.gov/servlet/DTTable?_bm=y&-geo_id=01000US&-ds_name=ACS_2008_3YR_G00_&-mt_name=ACS_2008_3YR_G2000_B02001.

73. "Key Statistics: American Indians and Alaska Natives," Graduate Management Admission Council (2008).

74. See www.census.gov/geo/www/GARM/Ch5GARM.pdf.

75. National Atlas of the United States, U.S. Department of the Interior. www.nationalatlas.gov/mld/indlanp.html.

76. "Unemployment rates for persons ages 16 and over, by race/ethnicity: 1994 to 2003," U.S. Department of Commerce, Census Bureau, March Current Population Survey (CPS), 1994 to 2003: cited in "Status and Trends in the Education of American Indians and Alaskan Natives," National Center for Education Statistics, U.S. Department of Education. http://nces.ed.gov/pubs2005/nativetrends/ind_8_2.asp.

national average.[77] Education levels are also tragically low. A 2003 study by the Manhattan Institute found that a national average of only 54% of Native American students graduate from high school. The 2003 National Assessment of Educational Progress reported that Native American students' scores were considerably lower than those of their white counterparts. In fourth-grade math, for instance, 20% of American Indians and Alaskan natives scored at or above proficiency, compared with 44% of whites.[78]

What is the solution to this tragic situation?

The most necessary change, without which no genuine reform will occur, is to enable private ownership of individual parcels of land on the Indian reservations. Currently the land is held by a system of tribal ownership, managed under the broad oversight of the US Bureau of Indian Affairs, so no one individual has responsibility for the land, and there is almost no incentive for individuals to improve the land or develop economic benefit from it.

The lack of personal property rights is highly significant, because the study of economic development in world history shows that the key to economic growth among any people in any part of the world is *enabling individuals to be able to obtain clearly documented ownership to their own property*. This has been abundantly demonstrated by Peruvian economist Hernando de Soto.[79] When *individuals* can own a piece of land that belongs to them and nobody else, then they care for it, improve it, and develop it, and some eventually use its value as the basis for borrowing money to start a business. In that way, through documented private ownership of property, an economy grows and people lift themselves out of poverty, find meaningful employment, and develop opportunities for providing their children and grandchildren with better education and further economic opportunities.

Exactly how Native Americans could move from a system of tribal ownership of land to a system of private ownership (the system of the rest of the United States), I cannot specify in detail. This would have to be worked out by tribes themselves in cooperation with the Bureau of Indian Affairs and the individual states in which the reservations are located. Probably some system of giving an initial allocation of property to individual Native Americans who are on these reservations would have to be worked out. But after an initial allocation to Native American individuals and families, the system would have to provide the right for individuals to sell their land *to anyone to whom they wanted to sell it*, whether Native American or not, or else it would not be possible to integrate into the economic wealth of the rest of the American economy.

Would this, then, mean the end of the Indian reservations as they now exist in the United States? Over time, yes, it probably would. Of course, individual tribes could certainly set aside some portion of their land to uphold as their own tribal area for commemorating and preserving their own cultural traditions. But unless a system of private

77. American Psychological Association, "statistics show mental health services still needed for native populations," *APA Monitor on Psychology* 35, no. 9 (Oct. 2004). www.apa.org/monitor/oct04/services.html.

78. Stacy A. Teicher, "America's first students get a second look," *Christian Science Monitor* (March 22, 2005). www.csmonitor.com/2005/0322/p11s01-legn.html.

79. See Hernando de Soto, *The Mystery of Capital: Why Capitalism Triumphs in the West and Fails Everywhere Else* (New York: Basic Books, 2000).

ownership of property can be instituted, American Indian tribes will simply continue trapping their people in poverty forever.

Some Indians might object that moving from a system of *tribal ownership* to *private ownership* of property would be "acting contrary to our historic tribal traditions." But as I argued in chapter 9 (see pp. 261–68), the Bible teaches a system of private ownership of property, not tribal ownership or government ownership. So in this case I think it is right to recognize that these tribal traditions are in direct conflict with the teaching about property in the Word of God. The words of Jesus are appropriate here:

> "And why do you break the commandment of God for the sake of *your tradition?*" (Matt. 15:3)

> "For the sake of *your tradition* you have made void the word of God" (Matt. 15:6).

> "You have a fine way of rejecting the commandment of God in order to establish *your tradition!*" (Mark 7:9)

Similarly, the apostle Paul wrote this to the church in Colossae:

> See to it that no one takes you captive by philosophy and empty deceit, according to *human tradition*, according to the elemental spirits of the world, and not according to Christ (Col. 2:8).

Another reform needed is that the tribal court system on reservations must be placed under the jurisdiction of the state in which the reservation exists, and this must include the ability to appeal to state appellate courts in legal cases. This already happens on some reservations (according to changes adopted in 1953), but many reservations remain essentially outside the judicial system of their state. This means that business investors simply decide not to invest in businesses on tribal lands, because they have no assurance that contracts will be enforced fairly by the tribal court system. Many people who live near tribal lands refuse even to drive through them, for fear that they might get into an accident and fail to receive justice from the tribal courts, beyond which there is no appeal. Terry L. Anderson, a researcher with expertise in law and economics, writes that "a stable judicial system is crucial for investment, and tribal courts have not provided this."[80]

Once again, this reform would remove some measure of tribal sovereignty over the areas in which Native Americans live. But once again, the choice is clear: Will Native Americans cling to their traditions—which are trapping their people in poverty and economic despair, and in alienation from the prosperous society that surrounds them—or will they abandon some of these traditions for the good of their people? If they take seriously the Bible's statement that a civil government ruler should be "God's servant *for your good*" (Rom. 13:4), then they should implement these reforms, because they clearly would bring good to their people.

---

80. Terry L. Anderson, "Native Americans Need the Rule of Law," *Wall Street Journal* (March 16, 2009), A19.

K. GAMBLING

Gambling is a significant economic activity in the United States. In 2007 the total gross revenue for legal gambling businesses in the United States was $92.27 billion. This figure is the total amount that people spent on gambling minus the "winnings" they received in return, and it is calculated before businesses pay their expenses of salaries, taxes, and overhead.[81] This is approximately 0.66% of the total US gross domestic product for that year of about $14 trillion. In very approximate terms, this means that money spent on gambling accounts for one-half of 1% of the US economy.

Supporters of gambling argue that it brings benefits to society. It allows people to be free to enjoy the entertainment value that comes from spending money at casinos or buying lottery tickets or betting on horseracing and so forth. Informal gambling through raffles is also a popular way of raising money for charities when they sell raffle tickets to raise money for certain events. And supporters of gambling claim that it provides jobs and tax revenue to states where gambling is allowed, and that this tax revenue is often used for improving the educational systems in those states.

However, serious objections can be brought against gambling, or at least commercial gambling as a business. A number of studies have shown that gambling brings negative effects in a society, and these must be seriously considered. First, it is socially harmful because the largest number of gamblers comes from the poorest segments of the population, who make unwise decisions and trap themselves deeper and deeper in debt. Second, the existence of gambling businesses leads to an addiction to gambling on the part of a certain percentage of the population, and this addiction destroys marriages, families, and any hope for career advancement, and it increases societal breakdown in this way. Third, studies have shown that where gambling businesses are established, crime rates increase. Finally, even if gambling provides some tax revenue to states, it functions as a heavy tax on the poorest people in the state, those who can least afford to pay it. Therefore, it is a socially undesirable form of raising tax revenue.

All US states now permit gambling of some type except for Hawaii and Utah. Many states have lotteries, and many also now have Indian gaming casinos on Indian reservations, while some also allow commercial casinos to operate on private property.

Lotteries are especially tempting for states to adopt, thinking it will be a harmless way of generating revenue. But the advertising for such lotteries is remarkably misleading, because it does not state fairly and clearly, in terms most buyers can understand, the remarkably small odds of winning any significant award.

What should a Christian approach be to the question of gambling? While I am not aware of any specific Bible verses that directly prohibit participating in gambling, I think that churches should teach their people that gambling is a very unwise use of their money. If people place their hope of economic advancement in winning the lottery rather than developing job skills and working hard and saving money, they are acting foolishly and will experience economic loss—perhaps significant loss—as a result. In addition, there is

---

81. Information from website of American Gaming Association: americangaming.org (accessed Nov. 7, 2009).

the danger of becoming addicted to gambling, something that happens to a certain percentage of people. Gambling addicts lose their rational judgment and end up thousands of dollars in debt, destroying their lives and the lives of those around them for years to come.

Therefore, while I cannot find biblical basis for absolutely insisting that it is wrong to participate in a charity raffle (where you understand that you are essentially giving money to the charity rather than giving the money in hope of winning something) or in an office pool that is betting on a sports event, my personal practice for many years has been to avoid gambling (except for an occasional raffle ticket to help a charity) and avoid the foolish expense and the danger of addiction that can come with it.

In addition, my own judgment is that large commercial gambling outlets such as casinos and state-sponsored lotteries bring much more harm to a society than the benefits they generate (as explained above). Therefore I personally would vote against allowing a lottery in the state or allowing Indian casinos or commercial business casinos to operate in a state. The social damage seems to me to be much greater than any good that comes from these activities.

But I admit that this is a judgment call based on observing the *consequences* of gambling, not an issue that I would put in the category of a clear moral right and wrong (as I would with regard to abortion, for example, or freedom of religion or freedom of speech or preserving marriage as between one man and one woman).

Part 3

CONCLUDING OBSERVATIONS

Chapter 16

THE PROBLEM OF MEDIA BIAS: WHEN THE WATCHDOGS FALL ASLEEP

A. PUBLIC PERCEPTIONS OF MEDIA BIAS

Numerous surveys have demonstrated that the American public, by a significant margin, thinks of mainstream media outlets as politically biased in a liberal direction. For instance, the nonpartisan Pew Research Center reported in October 2008 that 70% of the general public believed that the media wanted Barack Obama to be elected President.[1]

Surveys on the political beliefs of the media give credence to this perception of bias. In 2006, the Pew Research Center for Excellence in Journalism reported:

> ... 40% of journalists described themselves as being on the left side of the political spectrum (31% said they were "a little to the left" and 9% "pretty far to the left").... According to 2002 Gallup data in "The American Journalist," only 17% of the public characterized themselves as leaning leftward, and 41% identified themselves as tilting to the right. In other words, journalists are still more than twice as likely to lean leftward than the population overall.[2]

So-called "mainstream media" outlets would include the three major television networks (ABC, CBS, NBC) plus two other networks, CNN and MSNBC. The mainstream media also include the most influential newspapers (*New York Times*, *Washington Post*, *Los Angeles Times*, *Chicago Tribune*, and *USA Today*, all of which have

---

1. "Most Voters Say News Media Want Obama to Win," *Pew Research Center for the People and the Press* (Oct. 22, 2008). http://pewresearch.org/pubs/1003/joe-the-plumber.

2. "Politics and Party Affiliation," *Pew Research Center's Project for Excellence in Journalism* (Oct. 6, 2006). www.journalism.org/node/2304.

articles that are then picked up and published in hundreds of other newspapers); the Associated Press, which similarly supplies articles to thousands of news outlets every day; and *Time* and *Newsweek*, the two largest news magazines. (Fox News is generally still thought of as a newcomer and an outsider to mainstream media. The *Wall Street Journal*, which has been published continually since 1889, is in one sense old enough and influential enough to be considered part of the mainstream media, but its editorial policies so clearly favor the free market that it is not thought of as part of the "liberal mainstream media.")

Partly as a result of this public perception of bias, there has also been a huge decline in how much trust people have in mainstream media outlets. In September 2009, Pew reported that just 29% of Americans said that news organizations generally get the facts straight, while 63% said that news stories are often inaccurate.[3] In a 2005 report chronicling public perceptions of the press over a seventeen-year period, Pew reported that the number of Americans who thought news organizations were highly professional declined from 72% to 49%; the number who thought news organizations were moral dropped from 54% to 39%; the number who felt news organizations tried to cover up their mistakes rose from 13% to 67%; and the number who felt that news organizations were politically biased rose from 45% to 59%.[4]

In part because of this perception of bias (coming at a time when many people are already getting more news from the Internet), there has also been a huge decline in newspaper circulation, with the most liberal newspapers (*New York Times* and *Los Angeles Times*) experiencing surprising losses of subscribers. By contrast, the *Wall Street Journal*, whose motto is "free markets and free people," has not experienced a decline in circulation, but has continued to increase and currently has the widest circulation of any newspaper in the United States. The editorial pages of the *Wall Street Journal* provide a generally conservative analysis of world and national events, one that has no overt religious viewpoint but is usually quite consistent with a Christian worldview.

In October 2009 the *New York Times* reported on the latest circulation reports:

> Among the nation's largest newspapers, *The San Francisco Chronicle* reported the biggest decline, 25.8 percent on weekdays, to about 252,000—less than half what it was six years earlier—and 23 percent on Sundays, to about 307,000. For *The Star-Ledger* of Newark and *The Dallas Morning News*, circulation dropped more than 22 percent on weekdays, and about 19 percent on Sundays.... *The Los Angeles Times,* which dropped 11 percent in weekday sales, has fallen from 1.1 million in early 2000 to 657,000. *The New York Daily News* fell 14 percent to 544,000 and *The New York Post* 19 percent to 508,000.... *USA Today,* the Gannett newspaper published only on weekdays,

3. "Press Accuracy Rating Hits Two-Decade Low," *Pew Research Center for the People and the Press* (Sept. 14, 2009). http://pewresearch.org/pubs/1341/press-accuracy-rating-hits-two-decade-low.

4. "The State of the News Media: 2005," *Pew Research Center's Project for Excellence in Journalism.* www.stateofthemedia.org/2005/narrative_overview_publicattitudes.asp?cat=7&media=1.

fell from almost 2.3 million to 1.9 million, a 17.1 percent fall, losing the top spot in weekday circulation for the first time since the 1990s, to *The Wall Street Journal*. The Journal's circulation, just over two million, rose 0.6%. At *The New York Times*, which has repeatedly raised its prices in recent years, weekday circulation fell 7.3%, to about 928,000, the first time since the 1980s that it has been under one million.[5]

Fortunately, some of that liberal bias today has been offset by alternative sources of information, especially conservative talk radio and the Internet. On television, the Fox News Channel has gained a large following as many people have realized that it provides a more conservative perspective on the news and yet also provides articulate liberal representatives so that both sides can be represented on an issue. In Washington, DC, the conservative newspaper *Washington Times* provides a responsible alternative source of news to the influential *Washington Post*. In addition, some conservative news magazines form an alternative to *Time* and *Newsweek*. Particularly influential have been the *National Review*, the *Weekly Standard*, *First Things*, *Townhall*, and *World* magazine. (*World* is written from an evangelical Christian viewpoint.) But all of these alternative sources of media still fail to come close to capturing the amount of influence that the mainstream media have in American life.

B. SURVEYS OF JOURNALISTS

Various academic studies and media reports on the political views of mainstream journalists have confirmed this perception of bias. There are many more news reporters on the national scene who personally voted for Democratic candidates rather than Republican candidates, and this is a trend that has continued for at least the last thirty years. Even liberal *New York Times* columnist Nicholas Kristof agrees, writing on the 2008 presidential election:

> Conservatives are utterly convinced that the mainstream news organizations have been deeply unfair to the Republican ticket, and they have some points they can cite as evidence. For example, the Project for Excellence in Journalism found that there were twice as many favorable Obama stories after the convention as favorable McCain ones. Conversely, twice as many McCain stories were negative. The Center for Media and Public Affairs found that network TV coverage of Obama was 65 percent positive, compared to 31 percent positive for McCain.... Then there's also the well-known fact that national reporters for major news organizations are disproportionately likely to vote Democratic. Slate.com polled its staff and found that Barack Obama won 55 votes, and John McCain 1.[6]

5. Richard Perez-Pena, "U.S. Newspaper Circulation Falls 10%," *New York Times* (Oct. 26, 2009). www.nytimes.com/2009/10/27/business/media/27audit.html?_r=1.

6. Nicholas Kristof, "On Media Bias," *New York Times* (Nov. 4, 2008). http://kristof.blogs.nytimes.com/2008/11/04/on-media-bias/?pagemode=print.

In 2007, Bill Dedman of MSNBC reported:

> MSNBC.com identified 143 journalists who made political contributions from 2004 through the start of the 2008 campaign, according to the public records of the Federal Election Commission. Most of the newsroom checkbooks leaned to the left: 125 journalists gave to Democrats and liberal causes. Only 16 gave to Republicans. Two gave to both parties.[7]

An editor for the *Seattle Times* said:

> If we wore our politics on our sleeves in here, I have no doubt that in this and in most other mainstream newsrooms in America, the majority of those sleeves would be of the same color: blue. Survey after survey over the years have demonstrated that most of the people who go into this business tend to vote Democratic, at least in national elections. That is not particularly surprising, given how people make career decisions and that social service and activism is a primary driver for many journalists.[8]

In 2004, then-*New York Times* public editor Dan Okrent asked the question, "Is the *New York Times* a liberal newspaper?" His answer was:

> Of course it is. The fattest file on my hard drive is jammed with letters from the disappointed, the dismayed and the irate who find in this newspaper a liberal bias that infects not just political coverage but a range of issues from abortion to zoology to the appointment of an admitted Democrat to be its watchdog. (That would be me.) ... These are the social issues: gay rights, gun control, abortion and environmental regulation, among others. And if you think *The Times* plays it down the middle on any of them, you've been reading the paper with your eyes closed.[9]

The following list gives some examples of the type of bias in reporting that makes the American public feel that the mainstream media are not impartial in their reporting. Many additional examples were given by former CBS journalist Bernard Goldberg in *Bias: A CBS Insider Exposes How the Media Distort the News*[10] and then in other subsequent books on the same theme, such as *Give Me a Break: How I Exposed Hucksters, Cheats, and Scam Artists and Became the Scourge of the Liberal Media* by John Stossel[11] and *Slander: Liberal Lies about the American Right* by Ann Coulter.[12]

---

7. Bill Dedman, "Journalists Dole Out Cash to Politicians (Quietly)," *MSNBC.com* (June 25, 2007). www.msnbc.msn.com/id/19113485/.

8. Brent Baker, "Top Seattle Times Editor Admits Majority of Newsroom Votes 'Blue,' Driven by 'Activism,'" *NewsBusters.org* (Aug. 16, 2007). http://newsbusters.org/node/14898/print.

9. Dan Okrent, "The Public Editor: Is the New York Times a Liberal Newspaper?" *New York Times* (July 25, 2004). www.nytimes.com/2004/07/25/opinion/the-pub-lic-editor-is-the-new-york-times-a-liberal-newspaper.html?sec=&spon=&pagewanted=all.

10. Bernard Goldberg, *Bias: A CBS Insider Exposes How the Media Distort the News* (Washington, DC: Regnery, 2002).

11. John Stossel, *Give Me a Break: How I Exposed Hucksters, Cheats, and Scam Artists and Became the Scourge of the Liberal Media* (New York: Harper Collins, 2004).

12. Ann Coulter, *Slander: Liberal Lies about the American Right* (New York: Random House, 2002).

1. Biased selection of material to favor liberal causes

In the economic crisis of 2008–9, media reports frequently blamed the stock market crash, the plunge in housing prices, and the failure of many financial institutions on the greed of bankers or "market failure" or "deregulation" as the reasons for the economic crisis. But there was seldom any mention of the real causes of the inflated housing prices and the collapse of financial institutions that had made subprime mortgage loans. The three government policies that caused these things were largely ignored.

(a) There were hardly any reports of the involvement of Barney Frank, Massachusetts congressman, in propping up *Fannie Mae and Freddie Mac*, the quasi-government agencies that guaranteed that they would stand behind these loans to people who had no ability to repay them. And there was little if any mention of the Democrats' blocking of any Republican attempts to reform Fannie Mae and Freddie Mac in previous years, or of the repeated warnings in the *Wall Street Journal* month after month that these agencies were leading the country into a severe financial crisis.

(b) Nor was there much reporting of the *government requirements*, imposed by Congress, *that banks make a certain percentage of their loans to people whose financial ability would not allow them to qualify for loans!* But banks were forced to do this by government policy, backed up by the threat of lawsuits and fines. Ralph R. Reiland, an associate professor of economics at Robert Morris University, traced the roots of the mortgage crisis to this policy that was instituted by the Democrats in the late 1970s. He wrote:

> The roots of today's mortgage-based financial crisis can be traced back to the Community Reinvestment Act (CRA), which Jimmy Carter signed in 1977. Seeking to address complaints from anti-poverty activists and housing advocates about banks allegedly discriminating against minority borrowers and "redlining" inner-city neighborhoods, the CRA decreed that banks had "an affirmative obligation" to meet the credit needs of victims of discrimination in borrowing.
>
> To add a government stick to the process, the CRA decreed that federal banking regulators would consider how well banks were doing in meeting the goal of more multiculturalism in loaning when considering requests by banks to open new branches or to merge.
>
> A good "CRA rating" was earned by way of increasing loans in poor neighborhoods. Conversely, lenders with low ratings could be fined.
>
> The Fed, for instance, warned banks that failure to comply with government guidelines regarding the delivery of "equal credit" could subject them to "civil liability for actual or punitive damages in individual or class actions, with liability for punitive damages being as much as $10,000 in individual actions and the lesser of $500,000 or 1 percent of the creditor's net worth in class actions."
>
> However well-intentioned in terms of delivering "economic justice," this push for more government-directed social engineering produced a widespread weakening of long-established industry standards for credit worthiness.[13]

13. Ralph R. Reiland, "Roots of rotten mortgages," *Pittsburgh Tribune-Review* (Sept. 29, 2008). www.pittsburghlive.com/x/ pittsburghtrib/opinion/columnists/reiland/s_590330.html.

Why did the media persist in calling this "banker's greed" rather than government policy foolishness?

(c) Nor was there much reporting of the third major component leading to the financial crisis, namely, the irresponsible policy of *the Federal Reserve Board* throughout many years of the Bush administration in keeping interest rates so low that they encouraged millions of people to borrow much more than would be financially responsible in ordinary circumstances, thus leading to an excess amount of credit on the market and driving up housing prices year after year in a bubble that was eventually going to burst. During this time, interest rates went as low as 4.25%.[14]

But I wonder how many people reading these pages were previously even aware of those three primary causes of the economic crisis? Probably very few. There was a failure of mainstream media to give a balanced perspective.

2. Repeated and prolonged attention to conservative wrongdoing, but minimizing or ignoring wrongdoing by liberals

Media reports frequently mention "anger" at conservative or Republican rallies, but seldom point out any "anger" at liberal or Democratic rallies.

Another example is the relentless personal attacks that were made against Sarah Palin, with the endless repetition of any slight misstatements she made under immense media pressure or unfounded negative gossip about her personal life, while promoting the family values of Barack Obama, even though there were so-called "skeletons" in his family closet as well.[15]

At the same time, the widespread corruption of Louisiana Congressman William Jefferson, who had sixteen federal charges filed against him accusing him of using his political office to bribe businessmen and influence foreign officials, went underreported. The federal indictment against him said that Jefferson received more than $500,000 in bribes and sought millions more in separate schemes to enrich himself by using his office to broker business deals in Africa. The charges came almost two years after investigators raided Jefferson's home in Washington and found $90,000 in cash stuffed in his freezer.[16] Eventually, Jefferson was convicted (August 11, 2009) on bribery and racketeering charges and was sentenced to thirteen years in prison.[17]

Until recently, the news media have been fairly silent on the tax-evasion problems of Congressman Charles Rangel, a liberal Democrat and chairman of the House Ways and Means Committee, which sets the tax policy of the United States![18]

14. Thorsten Polleit, "Manipulating the Interest Rate: A Recipe for Disaster," *Mises Daily* (Dec. 13, 2007). http://mises.org/story/2810.

15. Matthew Balan, "CNN: Palin Family Issues Like Soap Opera; Downplays Obama Relatives' Troubles," *NewsBusters.org* (April 17, 2009). http://newsbusters.org/blogs/matthew-balan/2009/04/17/cnn-palin-family-issues-soap-opera-downplays-obama-relatives-troubles.

16. "Congressman William Jefferson's Corruption Charges Lead to Political Uproar on Capitol Hill," *FoxNews.com* (June 6, 2007). www.foxnews.com/story/0,2933,278080,00.html.

17. "Ex-Rep. Jefferson Sentenced to 13 Years for Bribery," *FoxNews.com* (Nov. 13, 2009). www.foxnews.com/politics/2009/11/13/ex-rep-jefferson-sentenced-bribery-friday.

18. Joseph Henchman, "Congressman Rangel's Tax Woes," Tax Foundation (Sept. 23, 2008). www.taxfoundation.org/blog/show/23647.html.

3. Reporting unfounded liberal claims without fact-checking

Sometimes media reporters simply hear unfounded or questionable liberal claims on some subject and report them as true without ever checking on them, which is irresponsible journalism.

One of the most blatant examples of this was the media passing along false statements about Rush Limbaugh when it was discovered that he was part of a group seeking to buy the Saint Louis Rams football team. Widespread media reports claimed that Limbaugh had once supported slavery and that he had praised James Earl Ray, the murderer of Martin Luther King Jr. CNN's Rick Sanchez reported the slavery comment as fact, as was pointed out by the daily editor of the *London Telegraph*.[19]

Sanchez eventually retracted the statement on Twitter, writing, "i've know rush. in person,i like him. his rhetoric, however is inexcusably divisive. he's right tho. we didn't confirm quote. our bad" (sic).[20]

Then, after *St. Louis Post-Dispatch* sports columnist Bryan Burwell printed these quotes in a blistering attack on Limbaugh, the paper had to post the following retraction:

> A quote in Bryan Burwell's column Oct. 7 attributed to Rush Limbaugh about the merits of slavery in the United States cannot be verified, and its use did not meet the Post-Dispatch's standards for sourcing. Limbaugh said he did not make the statement. Burwell's column did not identify the source of the quote, which was Jack Huberman's 2006 book "101 People Who Are Really Screwing America." The book provided no details about the origin of the quote. When contacted by the Post-Dispatch, Huberman said that he had a source for the quote but declined to reveal it on advice of counsel. The book's publisher, Nation Books, did not return calls to the Post-Dispatch. The Post-Dispatch found references attributing the quote to Limbaugh in other publications and on Internet blogs as far back as 1993, but none of those cited a source. The Burwell column on this page is an edited version in which the quote has been removed.[21]

Snopes.com, a well-known Internet website that refutes so-called "urban legends" and false quotations, says about the Ray quote: "This statement is attributed to Limbaugh (without sourcing) in *101 People Who Are Really Screwing America*. Although it is often cited as something he said on the radio on 23 April 1998, we haven't turned up any references to this quote from earlier than 2005."[22]

Nobody checked the facts. As Limbaugh wrote on October 16, 2009, in the *Wall Street Journal*, "I never said I supported slavery and I never praised James Earl Ray. How sick

---

19. Toby Harnden, "The Rush Limbaugh media lynch mob," *Telegraph.co.uk* (Oct. 14, 2009). http://blogs.telegraph.co.uk/news/tobyharnden/100013647/the-rush-limbaugh-media-lynch-mob/.

20. See http://twitter.com/ricksanchezcnn/status/4901464014.

21. Bryan Burwell, "NFL should think twice on Rush Limbaugh," *St. Louis Post-Dispatch* (Oct. 7, 2009). www.stltoday.com/stltoday/sports/columnists.nsf/bryanburwell/story/E196145D807 64B2F86257648000EF26B?OpenDocument.

22. See www.snopes.com/politics/quotes/limbaugh.asp.

would that be? Just as sick as those who would use such outrageous slanders against me or anyone else who never even thought such things."[23]

But the damage was already done. Limbaugh was slandered in the public media, and the investor who had invited him to join the group purchasing the Saint Louis Rams dropped Limbaugh from the group.[24] Many sports writers, CNN, and MSNBC simply took Jesse Jackson, who had made the accusations against Limbaugh, at his word. But where were the transcripts of any such statements? Where were the tapes showing that Limbaugh had made such a statement? They were nowhere to be found, because they did not exist and Limbaugh had never made these statements. The mainstream media yawned and went on to other stories, after slandering Limbaugh. Many of them never corrected their errors.

In the meantime, not a peep had been made about the rabid leftist political commentator Keith Olbermann, who is allowed to be a co-host on NBC's NFL football pregame show. The *Wall Street Journal* pointed out this hypocrisy:

> What happened here, and is happening elsewhere in American life, is that Mr. Limbaugh's outspoken political conservatism is being deemed sufficient reason to ostracize him from polite society. By contrast, MSNBC's Keith Olbermann, who fires off his own brand of high-velocity, left-wing political commentary but lacks Mr. Limbaugh's sense of humor, appears weekly as co-host of NBC's "Football Night in America." We haven't heard anyone on the right say Mr. Olbermann's nightly ad-hominem rants should disqualify him from hanging around the NFL. Al Franken made it all the way to the U.S. Senate on a river of political vitriol....
>
> It is no secret that this country's politics has become intense across the ideological spectrum. Rush Limbaugh lets his listeners blow off steam and then get on with the rest of their day. But if the people who claim to worry about such things want to see a truly angry right develop in this country, they should continue to remain silent while the left tries to drive Rush Limbaugh and others out of American political life. If that happens, the NFL by comparison will look like an afternoon tea.[25]

Another example is the media reporting of the costs of President Obama's health care plan. As writer Ramesh Ponnuru reports in some detail, when the Congressional Budget Office released some estimates of the cost of a Democratic health care bill on October 7, 2009, the report said that the government would actually gain $81 billion from the plan over ten years, *provided certain assumptions were made*, which the report itself said were unrealistic assumptions. But reporters at CBS and in the *Washington Post* simply reported the "$81 billion savings" as fact, without doing any investigation of

---

23. Rush Limbaugh, "The Race Card, Football and Me," *Wall Street Journal* (Oct. 16, 2009). http://online.wsj.com/article/SB1 0001424052748704322004574477021697942920.html.

24. "Checketts Group Drops Limbaugh from Rams' Bid," Associated Press (Oct. 15, 2009). http://msn.foxsports.com/ nfl/story/10219272/Checketts-group-drops-Limbaugh-from-Rams-bid.

25. "Leveling Limbaugh," *Wall Street Journal* (Oct. 16, 2009). http://online.wsj.com/article/SB100014240527487043220045 74475681181683914.html?mod=rss_opinion_main.

the (unrealistic) assumptions that had been built into that evaluation.[26] Ponnuru points out that the bill actually will "almost certainly increase the deficit."[27]

Still another blatant example of media bias happened less than two months prior to the 2004 presidential election, when, on September 8, 2004, veteran CBS news anchor Dan Rather reported a sensational story of allegations of wrongdoing by George W. Bush in 1972–73 when he was a member of the Texas Air National Guard.[28] The story reported the discovery of memos purportedly from Bush's commander (the late Lt. Col. Jerry B. Killian), alleging that Bush had received preferential treatment to be accepted into the National Guard and also that he (Lt. Col. Killian) was being pressured to cover up poor evaluations of Bush's performance and his failure to take a required physical exam.[29]

The allegations were immediately picked up by other mainstream media outlets, and the story had the clear potential of throwing the election to Bush's opponent, John Kerry. But the validity of the documents was soon questioned by many Internet forums and eventually by mainstream media sources other than CBS.[30] However, Dan Rather and CBS simply repeated the accusations again and again.

Finally, more than two weeks after the report (on Sept. 20), CBS publicly repudiated the story and admitted it had not treated the sources of the memo with adequate suspicion or required appropriate authentication. The CBS website story now has this disclaimer: "A report issued by an independent panel on Jan. 10, 2005, concluded that CBS News failed to follow basic journalistic principles in the preparation and reporting of this broadcast."[31] CBS News President Andrew Hayward said, "CBS News cannot prove that the documents are authentic, which is the only acceptable journalistic standard to justify using them in the report."[32]

An independent report was conducted and issued that documented CBS News' negligence in checking the facts.[33] Producer Mary Mapes and some others were fired,[34] and many suspect that Dan Rather was forced into premature retirement.[35] (Rather's lawsuit against CBS regarding their handling of this incident was dismissed by a New York state appeals court on September 29, 2009.)[36]

The alarming aspect of this story is that even when it was pointed out that the type font of the alleged memo from 1973 had not even been *designed* until many years later,

26. Ramesh Ponnuru, "Media Malpractice," *National Review* (Nov. 2, 2009), 26–28.

27. Ibid.

28. "New Questions on Bush Guard Duty," *CBS Evening News* (Sept. 8, 2004). www.cbsnews.com/stories/2004/09/08/60II/main641984.shtml.

29. Ibid.

30. "CBS can't vouch for Bush Guard memos," *CNN.com* (Sept. 20, 2004). www.cnn.com/2004/ALLPOLITICS/09/20/cbs.documents/.

31. Ibid.

32. Ibid.

33. Dick Thornburgh and Louis D. Boccardi, "Report of the Independent Panel Review on the September 8, 2004 *60 Minutes II Segment 'For the Record' Concerning President Bush's Texas Air National Guard Service*" (Jan. 5, 2005). www.cbsnews.com/htdocs/pdf/complete_report/CBS_Report.pdf.

34. "CBS ousts four over Bush Guard story," *CNN.com* (Jan. 11, 2005). www.cnn.com/2005/SHOWBIZ/TV/01/10/cbs.guard/.

35. Jacques Steinberg, "Rather Leaves CBS," *New York Times* (June 21, 2006). www.nytimes.com/2006/06/21/business/media/21rather.html?ei=5090&en=c8a0cb004f516f4a&ex=1308542400&adxnnl=1&partner=rssuserland&emc=rss&adxnlx=1258225806-/Dj0s3JTvQyyWqeVEJVQcw.

36. "Court Tosses Dan Rather's Lawsuit Vs. CBS," *CBSNews.com* (Sept. 29, 2009). www.cbsnews.com/stories/2009/09/29/business/main5350915.shtml.

and that the exact spacing of letters and words must have been generated by a modern computer and could not have been produced on any typewriter available in 1973 (but the memo could easily be reproduced with 2004-era default settings from MS Word),[37] CBS and Dan Rather stood by their story for more than two weeks. They were so convinced that they had found wrongdoing by George W. Bush that they would not admit that they themselves had been duped.

4. Reporting on war

Too often media reports simply repeat anti-American claims about "US bombs killing children"[38] or killing many civilians, reporting the wildly exaggerated numbers claimed by terrorist groups such as al-Qaeda or the Taliban without verifying the legitimacy of these claims or getting alternative estimates from American forces, and without putting the claims in the larger context of terrorists hiding missile launchers and weaponry in the homes of civilians or in children's schools or mosques.[39] In May 2007, CNN reported one example of such terrorist strategy:

> American soldiers discovered a girls' school being built north of Baghdad had become an explosives-rigged "death trap." The plot at the Huda Girls' school in Tarmiya was a "sophisticated and premeditated attempt to inflict massive casualties on our most innocent victims," military spokesman Maj. Gen. William Caldwell said. The military suspects the plot was the work of al Qaeda, because of its nature and sophistication.[40]

Another example is the widespread media reporting in which "the U.S. and its coalition partners were routinely blamed for the destruction of Iraq's heritage—from allowing the National Museum in Baghdad to be overrun by looters, to neglect of sundry archaeological sites, including the most revered ancient site of Babylon."[41] But now, several years after the idea of wanton rampaging by US troops has been fixed in the public mind, alternative facts have come to light. A *Wall Street Journal* editorial on November 14–15, 2009, reported, "a June 2008 trip by top Western archeologists to southern Iraq's eight most important sites found little or no post-Saddam damage, much to the archeologists' surprise." In addition, an eyewitness who watched what was happening as US troops entered Babylon gives an entirely different picture from a recent UNESCO report:

> Neither the [UNESCO] report's authors nor those in the media who repeated their accusations, it seems, bothered to read Emilio Marrero's memoir "A Quiet

37. Thornburgh and Boccardi, "Report of the Independent Panel Review," 12.

38. For example, see Tom Coghlan, "Seven children die as US bombs Afghan school," *TelegraphUK.com* (June 19, 2007). www.telegraph.co.uk/news/worldnews/1555005/Seven-children-die-as-US-bombs-Afghan-school.html.

39. For a detailed look at how Iraq had an elaborate plan to conceal weapons, see Ibrahim al-Marashi, "How Iraq Conceals and Obtains Its Weapons of Mass Destruction," *Middle East Review of International Affairs Journal* 7, no.1 (March 2003). http://meria.idc.ac.il/journal/2003/issue1/jv7n1a5.html.

40. "Military: New Iraqi School Had Bombs Built In," *CNN.com* (May 3, 2007). www.cnn.com/2007/WORLD/meast/05/03/iraq.school.bomb/index.html.

41. Melik Kaylan, "Myths of Babylon," *Wall Street Journal* (Nov. 14–15, 2009), A15.

Reality" published this April by FaithWalk, nor attempted to contact him. As chaplain of the Marine Expeditionary Force that first secured Babylon from looters during the Marines' three-month stint there in 2003, he records how they worked conscientiously to protect the site, ejecting looters, undertaking repairs to the perimeter and establishing ground rules for the war's duration. Chaplain Marrero saw the site immediately after Saddam's forces evacuated. It was in poor condition then.[42]

As for the National Museum in Iraq, Melik Kaylan writes,

> The National Museum is again open to the public, with the majority of its greatest treasures back on display. Moreover, we've long known that much of the pillaging had already occurred in Saddam's time, along with the substitution of fakes for many objects. Many of the museum's most valuable items were locked away in a vault, untouched by looters.[43]

But how much of that vindication of American troops has been reported in mainstream media, even as an alternative view of what happened, or (even better) as part of an extensive investigative report as to what actually happened? Essentially nothing. The media yawns and goes on its way issuing other reports that malign the American military and undermine our pride in our country.

5. Global warming

Although there is widespread disagreement about the theory that human carbon dioxide emissions are causing significant increases in the earth's temperature, and although this disagreement has been expressed in responsible articles and books and petitions signed by hundreds of competent scientists, the mainstream media simply continue to treat the idea of manmade global warming as a "proven fact," giving the public a biased viewpoint of the opinions of scientists on an immensely complex issue (namely, predicting the weather for many years into the future!). (See the discussion in chap. 10 above, pp. 361–83.)

6. Media bias in favor of Barack Obama

Probably the most blatant example of media bias in at least the last thirty years was the unquestioning support of the mainstream media for Barack Obama and his policies during the 2008 presidential campaign and for much of 2009 as well. Consider some examples:

Even though Obama got his political start working with admitted and unrepentant terrorist bomber Bill Ayers, who still holds strongly anti-American views, there was almost no mainstream media investigation of Ayers and his connection to Obama.

---

42. Ibid.
43. Ibid.

When conservative investigative reporters sought access to archived information regarding the earlier connection between these two men and the Annenberg Fund, the access was denied and there was no media protest or army of lawyers claiming access and the American public's "right to know." Stanley Kurtz, senior fellow at the Ethics and Public Policy Center, made several attempts to access the documents in the Richard J. Daly special collections section at the University of Illinois-Chicago library and was repeatedly stonewalled,[44] yet the media remained suspiciously silent, with the exception of Fox News.[45] I am not saying that President Obama agrees with the views of Ayers, but rather that the lack of journalistic investigation of the entire relationship was uncharacteristic of American media, which usually pursue any such story relentlessly. But Obama was given a pass. Why?

There were other, similar topics that could have been the subject for detailed journalistic investigations, but they were never pursued. For example, convicted felon Tony Rezko in Chicago provided much of the money behind Obama's early political career. The *Chicago Sun-Times* reported in December 2006 that Obama had deep, long-standing ties to Rezko, reporting that "Obama and Rezko have been friends since 1990, and the Wilmette businessman had raised as much as $60,000 in campaign contributions for him. After Rezko's indictment, Obama donated $11,500 to charity —the amount Rezko contributed to the senator's federal campaign fund." Obama also bought property from Rezko that enlarged his personal real estate. In addition, the *Sun-Times* reported that a former Obama intern, "Individual D" in Rezko's indictment, allegedly received a $250,000 kickback tied to a scheme to steer lucrative state pension deals to firms and consultants that donated to disgraced Illinois Rod Blagojevich.[46]

But once the presidential campaign had started, there was no journalistic investigation of Rezko's connection to Obama, and the legitimate, hard questions about that connection were never asked in any way that gained traction in the mainstream media. Perhaps President Obama was innocent of wrongdoing in any of these situations, but there was no determined media investigation to allow the public to know. The situations were mostly just ignored.

Another example of a journalistic investigation that never happened was President Obama's early connection with ACORN (Association of Community Organizations for Reform Now), for whom he had worked as a community organizer and then represented as a lawyer. The *Wall Street Journal* reported:

> In 1992 he [Obama] led voter registration efforts as the director of Project Vote, which included Acorn. This past November, he lauded Acorn's leaders for being "smack dab in the middle" of that effort. Mr. Obama also served as a lawyer for Acorn in 1995, in a case against Illinois to increase access to the polls.

---

44. Stanley Kurtz, "Chicago Annenberg Challenge Shutdown?" *National Review* (Aug. 18, 2008). http://article.nationalreview.com/print/?q=MTgwZTVmN2QyNzk2MmUxMzA5 OTg0ODZlM2Y2OGI0NDM=.

45. "Newly Released Documents Highlight Obama's Relationship with Ayers," *FoxNews.com* (Aug. 26, 2008). www.foxnews.com/politics/elections/2008/08/26/newly-released-documents-highlight-obamas-relationship-with-ayers/.

46. Frank Main, "Obama's Rezko Ties Deeper Than Land Deal," *Chicago Sun-Times* (Dec. 23, 2006).

During his tenure on the board of Chicago's Woods Fund, that body funneled more than $200,000 to Acorn. More recently, the Obama campaign paid $832,000 to an Acorn affiliate. The campaign initially told the Federal Election Commission this money was for "staging, sound, lighting." It later admitted the cash was to get out the vote.[47]

In the same article, the *Wall Street Journal* thoroughly documented ACORN's long record of political corruption, writing:

Acorn is spending $16 million this year to register new Democrats and is already boasting it has put 1.3 million new voters on the rolls. The big question is how many of these registrations are real.

The Michigan Secretary of State told the press in September that Acorn had submitted "a sizeable number of duplicate and fraudulent applications." Earlier this month, Nevada's Democratic Secretary of State Ross Miller requested a raid on Acorn's offices, following complaints of false names and fictional addresses (including the starting lineup of the Dallas Cowboys). Nevada's Clark County Registrar of Voters Larry Lomax said he saw rampant fraud in 2,000 to 3,000 applications Acorn submitted weekly.

Officials in Ohio are investigating voter fraud connected with Acorn, and Florida's Seminole County is withholding Acorn registrations that appear fraudulent. New Mexico, North Carolina and Missouri are looking into hundreds of dubious Acorn registrations. Wisconsin is investigating Acorn employees for, according to an election official, "making people up or registering people that were still in prison."

Then there's Lake County, Indiana, which has already found more than 2,100 bogus applications among the 5,000 Acorn dumped right before the deadline. "All the signatures looked exactly the same," said Ruthann Hoagland, of the county election board. Bridgeport, Connecticut estimates about 20% of Acorn's registrations were faulty. As of July, the city of Houston had rejected or put on hold about 40% of the 27,000 registration cards submitted by Acorn.

That's just this year. In 2004, four Acorn employees were indicted in Ohio for submitting false voter registrations. In 2005, two Colorado Acorn workers were found to have submitted false registrations. Four Acorn Missouri employees were indicted in 2006; five were found guilty in Washington state in 2007 for filling out registration forms with names from a phone book.[48]

This shows a consistent, intentional organizational pattern to commit election fraud and rig election results with thousands of votes from dead or non-existent people all

---

47. "Obama and ACORN." *Wall Street Journal* (Oct. 14, 2008). http://online.wsj.com/article/SB122394051071230749. html?mod=djemEditorialPage.

48. Ibid.

over the country. Such actions would effectively nullify the legitimate votes of thousands of citizens. Why was Obama so closely tied to an organization such as ACORN in the past? The mainstream press just yawned and let it pass. Why?

Another uninvestigated and largely unreported topic is the huge campaign contributions that President Obama had received from Fannie Mae—the second-largest amount of any US senator in spite of his very short tenure in the Senate.[49] Did then-Senator Obama have any complicity in supporting the reckless loan-guarantee polices at Fannie Mae that led to the collapse of the housing market in 2008? (See p. 559 above.)The press showed no interest in this at all.

President Obama has also targeted news networks that are critical of him, such as Fox News, which the White House tried to blackball and shut out of White House coverage.[50] Perhaps some people think it is legitimate to criticize conservative news outlets, but that is not my question. My question is why there was no press outrage at President Obama about this as there was when it was discovered in 1973 that President Nixon had an "enemies list"? Why the different kind of treatment?

Similar concerns can be raised about the reporting of economic statistics. Why did unemployment climb from 6.7%[51] in November 2008—when President Obama was elected—to 10.2% in October 2009, creating a huge national problem? The October 2009 report showed that just 58.5% of adults were working, the lowest level since 1983 and down from about 63% before the recession.[52] MarketWatch.com reported that "an alternative gauge of unemployment, which includes discouraged workers and those forced to work part-time, rose to 17.5%, the highest on record dating to 1995."[53]

The jobless rate for men rose to 10.7% and for adult women to 8.1%. The jobless rate for blacks rose to 15.7%, compared with 9.5% for whites and 13.1% for Hispanics.[54] Actually, when the number of discouraged job-seekers who have simply given up looking for work is counted, the Bureau of Labor Statistics reported that in August 2009 there were roughly 758,000 discouraged workers nationally, compared with 349,000 in November 2007, the month before the recession officially began.[55] The true unemployment rate as of June 2009 was higher than 20%.[56]

With so many people unable to find work, why have the mainstream media not loudly emphasized this huge national problem day after day, and why have they not laid any blame for this directly at the feet of President Obama's failed "stimulus plan" that

49. Lynn Woolley, "Obama's Friends at Fannie Mae," *Human Events* (Oct. 1, 2008). www.humanevents.com/article.php?id=28797.

50. Jonathan Karl, "Obama, in Media Blitz, Snubs 'Whining' Fox," *ABCNews.com* (Sept. 19, 2009). http://abcnews.go.com/Politics/obamas-media-tour-include-fox-news/story?id=8621065.

51. "The US Unemployment Rate January 1948 to September 2009." www.miseryindex.us/urbymonth.asp.

52. Rex Nutting, "Unemployment Rate Hits 10.2%, A 26-Year High," *MarketWatch.com* (Nov. 6, 2009). www.marketwatch.com/story/unemployment-rate-hits–102-in-october–2009–11–06–83100.

53. Ibid.

54. Ibid.

55. Michael Luo, "Out of Work, and Too Down to Search On," *New York Times* (Sept. 7, 2009). www.nytimes.com/2009/09/07/us/07worker.html?_r=1.

56. Anthony Mirhaydari, "True Unemployment Rate Already at 20%." http://blogs.moneycentral.msn.com/topstocks/archive/2009/07/06/true-unemployment-rate-already-at-20.aspx.

was supposed to create so many new jobs? (The American Recovery and Reinvestment Act of 2009, popularly called the "stimulus plan"—or "recovery plan"—was passed with no Republican votes in the House and only three Republican votes in the Senate [Susan Collins, Olympia Snowe, and Arlen Specter] and was signed by President Obama on February 17.)

A chart showing the *projected* success of the stimulus plan in creating jobs was used by the Obama administration to illustrate why the plan was needed, but the predictions differed widely from what actually happened:[57]

Figure 16.1

UNEMPLOYMENT RATE WITH AND WITHOUT THE RECOVERY PLAN

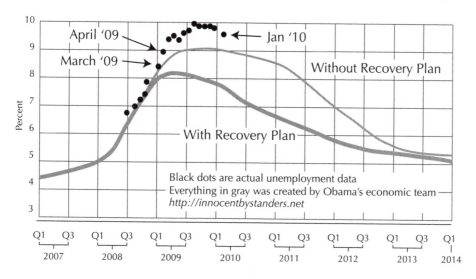

But in fact, this did not happen, because the unemployment rate shot straight up when the $787 billion stimulus plan was passed in February and continued at its tragic high level throughout most of 2009. As mentioned earlier, in October 2009 the unemployment rate was 10.2%.[58] (Business owners saw the huge increase in government spending and realized it had to be paid for somehow by more taxes that would fall on them. They also saw the likely passage of President Obama's health care proposal and knew it would require additional massive increases in their required health insurance costs. So they decided not to hire, but to cut back their work forces.) Here is the actual unemployment rate, month by month, after the passage of the stimulus plan:

---

57. The graph was taken from http://campaignspot.nationalreview.com/post/?q=YTVmZGYxMDJkNDJkZTU1NWMyMDMyMDFhNTRhZDZiZjU= and has been adapted for presentation in this book. Reprinted with permission of National Review online.

58. U.S. Department of Labor, Bureau of Labor Statistics. www.bls.gov/eag/eag.us.htm and http://data.bls.gov/PDQ/servlet/SurveyOutputServlet.

Unemployment

Feb 2009	8.2%
March 2009	8.6%
April 2009	8.9%
May 2009	9.4%
June 2009	9.5%
July 2009	9.4%
August 2009	9.7%
September 2009	9.8%
October 2009	10.1%
November 2009	10.0%
December 2009	10.0%
January 2010	9.7%[59]

My question here is this: Why has there been no ongoing media outrage, no ongoing focus on this prolonged national tragedy of high unemployment? Why have the failed Democratic tax-and-spend policies been given a pass by the mainstream national media?

7. Health care reform

The media have been so sympathetic to the Democratic proposals for health care reform that there have been few if any reports that show in a simplified chart or graph exactly what these plans would cost typical American families over the next year or over the next five years, and so forth. Why no clear coverage of the enormous costs?

Why has there been no media outrage at the secret congressional committee meetings in which countless amendments were added, but where the Republicans were locked out of the amendment-making process?

Why has there been so little objection to the fact that bills are brought to the House or Senate floor and voted on before there is any time for anyone even to read them, to say nothing about considering them carefully and debating them?

C. WHAT HAPPENS TO A NATION WHEN ITS WATCHDOGS ARE SILENT?

The founders of the United States realized that the press has an incredibly important role in protecting the nation. This is why in the First Amendment to the Constitution they said:

---

59. Ibid.

Congress shall make no law ... abridging the freedom of speech, or of the press....

This guarantee of a free press allows people to criticize the government and call it to account and to have their criticisms reported in press reports that reach the general public. When the press carries out its proper function and warns people of government wrongdoing, it provides accountability for the government. If government leaders begin to do something wrong, at least what they are doing can be pointed out by the press and made known to the public.

But what happens if the press is silent? What happens if the press just gives a certain viewpoint or a certain party or a certain politician a "pass" on anything that is done, not questioning or calling it into account in any appropriate way? It is like having a country protected by watchdogs that cannot bark.

The Hebrew prophet Isaiah knew this had happened with the nation of Israel long ago. He said:

His watchmen are blind; they are all without knowledge; *they are all silent dogs; they cannot bark*, dreaming, lying down, loving to slumber (Isa. 56:10).

When this happens—when the watchdogs "cannot bark"—they fail to call the leaders to account. Then the people of a nation do not have adequate information to make wise decisions about their leaders and about the direction in which the nation is going.

When the watchdogs are silent, a nation will soon be led astray by its leaders, who no longer have sufficient accountability to the public.

Chapter 17

APPLICATION TO DEMOCRATIC AND REPUBLICAN POLICIES TODAY

At the end of this extensive survey of biblical teachings about civil government, a Christian worldview, and specific political issues today, it is now time to look back at our study to draw some conclusions about the way in which these biblical teachings compare to the current policies favored by the Democratic and Republican parties in the United States. (Readers in countries other than the United States can take this list of policy questions and consider how the various political parties in their own nation measure up to these conclusions as well.)

When I was writing this book, some people told me that they hoped it would be "nonpartisan." They hoped I would simply look at the issues and not at the individual parties. They hoped that the book would evenhandedly support Democrats where their policies were more consistent with biblical teaching and support Republicans where their policies were more consistent with biblical teaching.

But the policies favored by Democrats and Republicans today are so different that it is unlikely that anyone with a consistent worldview and a consistent view of the purpose of government will support Democratic policies about 50% of the time and Republican policies about 50% of the time. This is because the parties' basic views of the role of government are so different, and their fundamental principles are so different.

That is why, for example, Jim Wallis's book *God's Politics: Why the Right Gets It Wrong and the Left Doesn't Get It*[1] is not at all nonpartisan. The title makes people think that

---

1. Jim Wallis, *God's Politics: Why the Right Gets It Wrong and the Left Doesn't Get It* (San Francisco: HarperSanFrancisco, 2005).

Wallis is going to criticize both Republicans and Democrats equally, but the book actually turns out to be an extended argument for supporting Democratic candidates and positions and opposing Republican ones.

Wallis ends up supporting Democratic policies regarding war, the economy, and capital punishment and (for the most part) even giving mild support to a more liberal view of same-sex marriage, as I have documented in several sections above. With regard to abortion, Wallis refuses to support the Republican position that we should have *laws* prohibiting abortion (except to save the life of a mother). Rather, he tells Democrats that they should be more tolerant of pro-life Democrats within the party[2] and also tells them they should do more to reduce teen pregnancy and to support low-income women who are at greater risk for unwanted pregnancies.[3] Then he tells readers that the differences between Democrats and Republicans on abortion are not enough reason to support Republicans, because Republicans do not support "a consistent ethic of life" regarding other issues, since they support capital punishment and nuclear weapons and do not do enough to eradicate poverty and racism, all of which are "critical components of a consistent ethic of life."[4] (See discussion above, pp. 196–97.)

In other words, Wallis gives readers no reason that they should support Republican policies and makes the entire book an argument to support Democrats and policies favored by the Democratic Party. The entirety of *God's Politics* ends up saying, in essence, that God supports the Democratic Party.

Why does Wallis reach these conclusions? They are strongly informed by (1) his pacifist convictions regarding war and military power and international relations, (2) his view that the primary solution to poverty is more government redistribution of income from the rich to the poor, and (3) his decision that biblical standards regarding abortion and homosexual conduct should not be the determining factor regarding the kinds of laws that governments should make.

Although Wallis says that "God is not a Republican or a Democrat," and he and his organization Sojourners supported a campaign with that slogan,[5] his book in actuality ends up arguing "God's politics" are the politics of the Democratic Party. I encourage readers to read Wallis's book if they want to hear an argument that God supports the Democrats and their positions.

I have come to quite different conclusions in this book, for the reasons discussed in the preceding sixteen chapters. Although I have disagreed with Republican policies at some points (for instance, regarding the widespread and unnecessary increase in federal spending in George W. Bush's administration, even when Republicans had majorities in both the House and the Senate), I have concluded in most of the preceding chapters that the policies endorsed by the leadership of the Republican Party have been much more consistent with biblical teachings.

Wallis and others say that God supports the positions of the Democrats. I think that the teachings of the Bible, as I understand them, mostly support the current policies

2. Ibid., 298–99.
3. Ibid., 300.

4. Ibid., 301.
5. Ibid., 9.

of the Republicans. How can people decide between these two views? They can decide in the way people have always decided: by reading the arguments, reading their Bibles (where biblical arguments are used), and then deciding which arguments are the most persuasive. They can discuss their thinking about these matters with others, and when they disagree, they can do so while maintaining a respectful attitude toward the other person. This is a healthy process, and it is essential to a well-functioning democracy.

Sometimes people say they "vote for the candidate, not the party." I think this view is naïve. It simply fails to recognize how decisions are actually made in our current political system. Because only parties—not individuals—can get bills passed in Congress and confirm or reject judicial appointments, *every vote for every candidate is a vote for the candidate's party as much as it is for the candidate.* It is impossible today to vote for a candidate and not also vote for and give support to that candidate's party. And the party in power will determine the course of the nation.

The Democratic and Republican parties have come to represent very different basic positions today, and the elected officials of those parties support those positions, both by their individual votes (usually along party lines) and by the votes they bring to electing the leaders in the House and Senate—leaders who determine the course of all legislation. In the current situation in the United States (early 2010), the policies favored by the Democratic and Republic parties have moved far apart on dozens of very important issues.

The Republican Party has been dominated by people favoring smaller government, lower taxes, strong defense, traditional moral standards regarding abortion and marriage, the promotion of democracy, and the promotion of free market economies. These stances seem to me to be consistent with biblical teachings on government and a biblical worldview, as I explained in chapters 3 and 4.

By contrast, the Democratic Party has come to be dominated by people favoring larger government, higher taxes, more reliance on negotiations rather than superior military force in dealing with enemies, opposition to biblical moral standards on abortion and homosexual "marriage," and promotion of a more Socialist-leaning economy that is highly controlled by the government. These policies seem to me to be at odds with a biblical worldview and with biblical teachings regarding government (see chaps. 3 and 4).

In this chapter I summarize the earlier discussions in the book and compare my policy conclusions with the policies favored by the majority of Republicans and the majority of Democrats, or by those who have determined the policy decisions in their respective parties.

A. THE COURTS AND ULTIMATE POWER IN A NATION

In chapter 5 we considered the question of the courts and the ultimate power in a nation. The American system of government as forged by the Founding Fathers gave the ultimate power in the nation, not to any person or group of persons, but to a document: the United States Constitution (which could be changed by the people of the nation, but only with great difficulty). Subject to that Constitution, power was divided among the legislative, executive, and judicial branches of government and was also divided among national, state, and local governments. In this way no one was given excessive power. The laws were to be made by the legislative branch and interpreted and applied by the judicial branch (the courts).

But the system no longer functions in the way it was set up to function, because judges—especially the justices of the US Supreme Court—have increasingly begun to base their decisions, not on the actual wording of the Constitution or the original meaning of the words when they were written, but on the justices' own ideas of what should be done in a society. In this way they have begun to "make laws" rather than just interpret and evaluate laws that have been made by the Congress. By this process the Supreme Court has become the most powerful group in the nation, usurping to itself powers that the Constitution never intended it to have.

The result is that the Supreme Court has imposed on the nation a whole series of left-leaning or liberal-leaning policies that have not been approved by a majority of the people themselves—policies that give legal protection to abortions, exclude religion from much of public life, take away private property and give it to other private parties, restrict the use of the death penalty, and in many other ways override the right of the people to decide their own laws through their democratically elected representatives.

Chapter 5 concluded that the excessive power of the Supreme Court is the most serious problem facing the United States of America today. The American system of government is "broken"—no longer functioning as the Constitution directed that it should function.

Democrats favor appointing Supreme Court justices who will continue in this direction of *making* laws and policies rather than just *interpreting* and *applying* them. By contrast, Republicans have almost uniformly favored appointing state judges, federal judges, and Supreme Court justices who will judge according to the original intent of the laws and the federal and state constitutions to which they are subject.

I argued that the only way to change this situation in the United States would be the consistent election of Republican candidates for state and national offices, so that the entire judicial system will increasingly be staffed by judges who will judge according to the original intent of the law and the Constitution.

B. PROTECTION OF LIFE

In chapter 6 I argued that abortion is the intentional taking of an innocent human life and that this should be prohibited by law in all cases except to save the life of the mother. On this question Democrats in general (not every single Democrat, but uniformly in their national leadership positions) favor "a woman's right to choose," which means they do not favor any enactment of laws that would restrict a woman's right to take the life of her own preborn child. By contrast, Republicans in general (not every single Republican, but uniformly in their top national leadership) have favored laws that protect the life of preborn children. I also argued, however, that no significant change to laws regarding abortion can ever happen in the United States until the Supreme Court overrules its 1973 decision *Roe v. Wade*. This will only happen when there is a sufficient number of "original intent" justices to overturn that decision. And they will only be appointed by Republican presidents and confirmed by a sufficient number of Republican senators in the US Senate.

Chapter 6 also concluded that euthanasia, in the sense of actively taking steps to put an old or very ill patient to death, is prohibited by the biblical commands against murder. More liberal Democrats have tended to favor the liberalization of laws regarding euthanasia, but some Democrats have opposed this. Nearly all Republicans, at least on the level of national leadership, have opposed giving people the legal right to take the life of a terminally ill or very old patient.

Regarding capital punishment, I argued that the Bible supports the government's right to carry out capital punishment, at least in the case of premeditated murder. The viewpoints of Democrats and Republicans are not entirely predictable on this question, but a significantly larger number of Republicans would favor the use of capital punishment, at least for premeditated murder, and a significant proportion of Democrats would oppose the use of capital punishment in all cases. In 2008 the Gallup Poll found that only 52% of Democrats support the use of capital punishment, compared with 78% of Republicans and 66% of Independents.[6]

Finally, I argued in chapter 6 that governments should allow people to have some effective means of self-defense, and in nations where there are already many gun owners, this would mean permitting private citizens to own guns for the purpose of self-defense (with reasonable restrictions preventing convicted felons and mentally ill people, for example, from owning guns).

Republicans candidates in general, by a large proportion, have favored the right of citizens to own guns. On the other hand, as of April 2009, 60% of Democrats would support stricter gun-control laws, compared with 13% of Republicans and 17% of Independents.[7] Opposition to all gun ownership has been a consistent pattern of more liberal political groups in other nations as well.

C. MARRIAGE

In chapter 7 I argued that biblical teachings restrict marriage to the union of one man and one woman. On this issue, Republicans have almost uniformly supported such a definition of marriage in the laws of individual states and the laws of the United States. Some Democrats have supported this position, but the party as a whole—through the judges that it has supported and through the votes of senators and congressmen on the Defense of Marriage Act, for example—has shown that it is far more supportive of

6. Lydia Saad, "Americans Hold Firm to Support for Death Penalty," *Gallup.com* (Nov. 17, 2008). www.gallup.com/poll/111931/Americans-Hold-Firm-Support-Death-Penalty.aspx.

7. Bill Schneider, "Poll: Fewer Americans Support Stricter Gun Control Laws," *CNN.com* (April 8, 2009). www.cnn.com/2009/POLITICS/04/08/gun.control.poll/.

same-sex "marriage" in the United States. In October 2009 the Pew Research Center for the People and the Press found that more than seven-in-ten liberal Democrats (72%) favor same-sex marriage, while eight-in-ten conservative Republicans (81%) oppose it.[8]

I also argued that biblical teachings on marriage indicate that the ideal for marriage is the union of one man and one woman for life. This would lead to the support of laws that aim at protecting marriage by making it much more difficult to divorce than is currently true in most states. Generally speaking, it has primarily been Democrats who have favored the liberalization of divorce laws, thus making it easy for people to get divorced and end their marriage. Republicans, on the other hand, have sometimes supported easy divorce laws, but many times have opposed the liberalization of divorce laws in their states.

Finally, I argued that the production and distribution of pornography brings significant harm to marriages and to society as a whole, and that both national and local governments in the United States should much more aggressively use current anti-pornography laws and court-defined standards to prosecute those who produce and distribute material that is clearly pornographic and outside the protection of the law. I also showed how Republican-appointed Justice Department officials and local prosecutors have been far more likely than Democratic-appointed officials to pursue anti-pornography prosecutions.

D. THE FAMILY

In chapter 8 I argued that the Bible views the bearing of children as a positive blessing from God and something that is to be encouraged and approved. I also argued that the right to determine the kind of education a child receives should ultimately belong to the parents (within certain broad guarantees of educational competence that the state might require).

This led me to conclude that there should be much more involvement of parents (as opposed to teachers) in deciding what knowledge children are taught and what moral and behavioral standards children are taught in schools.

I also reasoned that the state should not remove the right of parents to discipline their children, even to use physical discipline (such as spanking) so long as there is no actual physical harm that comes to the children (and this of course means that actual abuse of children should be punished by law).

I also argued that a widespread system of school vouchers given to parents, by which they could pay for their children's schooling at any private or public school of their choice, would lead to much higher quality in the educational system, much greater

8. "Majority Continues to Support Civil Unions," *Pew Research Center for the People and the Press* (Oct. 9, 2009). http://people-press.org/report/553/same-sex-marriage.

choice and competition among schools, and a much better educational outcome for the children.

With regard to the positions that I advocated in this chapter, by far the most common approach of Democrats is to place the views of the government and the teachers regarding what is right for children above the views of parents. Republicans, by contrast, largely believe that the views of parents must take priority over the viewpoints of government officials.

The opposition to the ability of parents to use physical discipline with their children comes almost entirely from Democrats, who would often support laws outlawing spanking of children completely. Opposition to the use of vouchers for parents to choose their children's schools comes almost entirely from Democrats, especially because of the political clout the National Education Association has in the Democratic Party. Republicans, by contrast, tend to favor the protection of parents' rights regarding raising their children, tend to favor protecting the right to exercise physical discipline, and tend to favor programs that would give vouchers to parents for school choices.

E. ECONOMIC POLICIES

In chapter 9 I argued that the teachings of the Bible support a system of private ownership of property and an emphasis on a free market as opposed to extensive government regulation of the economic decisions in any nation.

With regard to these questions, Democrats have commonly tended to favor much more government regulation of people's use of private property and government regulation to direct how the economy works and how income is distributed. Democrats have generally favored higher taxes, in part because this is one way they can redistribute income from the rich to the poor. Republicans, by contrast, have tended to favor more protection of property rights and more emphasis on allowing the free market and free competition between businesses to solve the problems of allocating goods and services in the economy.

I argued also that businesses, in general, are the primary means by which wealth is created and increased in the economy, and therefore businesses should be viewed as basically "good" in what they are trying to carry out (although businesses can do evil things, for which they should be punished by the law).

In recent US history it is primarily Democrats who have been in favor of placing higher taxes and increasing government regulation on businesses, while Republicans have generally (but not uniformly) favored lower taxes and fewer regulations on businesses.

Concerning the rich and the poor, Democrats have often tended to use rhetoric that portrays "the rich" as evil and to support policies that tend to take money from the rich and give it to the poor—in other words, income redistribution policies. Democrats have favored tax laws that strongly trend in this direction. On the other hand, Republicans have tended to favor allowing individual freedom and allowing everyone in the economy, whether rich or middle-class or poor, to keep the fruits of their labors. And

Republicans have tended to think of wealthy people, in general, as those who have created much economic good for a society and who have rightfully gained personal benefit from those actions.

I also argued that lower taxes are, in general, beneficial for an economy and, in addition, lower taxes have the great benefit of giving individuals much more freedom to decide how to use their own money. On this issue, the consistent goal of Democrats in state and national government has been to increase taxes more and more (as seen particularly in the Democratic-controlled states of California and New York, for example). But Republican positions (not uniformly, but generally) have tended to *decrease* tax rates, not temporarily but permanently, and not for just certain favored groups, but for the entire nation, thus promoting greater economic growth and prosperity throughout the economy.

Regarding health care, I argued that a competitive free market is a much better provider of health care than any government-run and government-managed system. I also argued for steps that would encourage the free market, such as eliminating state mandates for expensive "all-inclusive" policies, allowing consumers to buy insurance across state lines, limiting medical malpractice awards, and giving private individuals the same tax breaks that are given to individuals working for large companies when buying insurance. All of these actions would bring down health care costs, improve health care coverage, and avoid having the government take over and ruin the system that now provides Americans with the best health care in the world.

Republicans generally are in support of policies such as the ones I favored, while Democrats generally favor much more government control of the entire health care segment of the economy (as shown in President Obama's 2009 health care bill).

F. THE ENVIRONMENT

In chapter 10 I argued that God has created a wonderfully resourceful earth in which there are abundant resources of every kind, a viewpoint in contrast to the fear-generating rhetoric of much modern media coverage of the environment.

I also argued that we should develop and use energy resources from many types of sources (wind, hydroelectric, oil, coal, natural gas, nuclear power, and solar energy). God has placed in the earth abundant energy sources for us to use for our benefit. In particular, there are huge energy resources remaining in oil, coal, natural gas, and nuclear power, and we should wisely make use of these abundant energy resources while we continue to work on developing alternative forms of energy as well. The great value of energy for human use is that it saves us work, saves us time, and makes our lives more enjoyable and more comfortable. Therefore we should see the earth's abundant energy resources as a blessing from God that he put there for our benefit.

Again and again, it has been Democrats who have blocked the development of these energy resources, preventing further drilling of abundant oil on America's own land (whether they are offshore sources of oil or the abundant sources found in the Alaskan National Wildlife Refuge). Democrats have also stood in the way of enabling new nuclear power stations to be built and sensible nuclear storage facilities to be opened. Therefore, Democrats (in general) have hindered the development of energy resources again and again in the United States. By contrast, most Republicans (nearly all) have favored the development of such energy resources, all of which would make products less expensive for everyone and would make the cost of living less for everyone, thus promoting more individual freedom. All these things can be done without any significant danger of doing harm to the earth in the long term.

I also argued that it is highly doubtful that human production of carbon dioxide is having any significant effect on the earth's temperature, and that the alarmist predictions of massive global warming heard so commonly in the media are without substantial basis in fact. It does not seem to me to be likely that God would set up the earth to work in such a way that we would destroy it by doing morally good things that he wants us to do, such as building a fire to keep warm or to cook food, or driving a car or a truck (with appropriate pollution controls, but carbon dioxide is not a pollutant), or flying in an airplane, or running a factory to produce goods for people.

Democrats have by and large supported the "man-made global warming" hypothesis and have therefore strongly favored proposals that would actually *reduce* our carbon output each year until it is far below the current level. This would require either substantial reductions in our standard of living (we would no longer have enough energy to do many things) or else the largest increases in the cost of living that we have ever seen (because of huge increases in costs due to using much more expensive alternative energy sources). Republicans have claimed that these government plans to force us to reduce our carbon energy usage are prohibitively expensive, are harmful to the poor more than anybody else, create a massive increase in government control of our lives, and are an entire waste of money and effort because carbon dioxide is not to be considered a pollutant, but something that occurs naturally in the earth that God made for us. Carbon dioxide has no demonstrated danger of causing people or the earth any harm, and it actually does much good (enabling plants and crops to grow larger).

Finally, I argued that the fuel efficiency (CAFE) standards for automobile mileage, strongly supported by Democrats (with some exceptions in car-producing states like Michigan) but generally opposed by most Republicans (but not all), have done much more harm than good to the nation, forcing people to drive smaller and more dangerous cars than they would otherwise choose to drive, and resulting in far more injuries and fatalities in auto accidents than otherwise would have happened.

G. NATIONAL DEFENSE

In chapter 11 I argued that a strong military defense is a moral obligation that God places on nations so that they will be able to protect their national sovereignty and protect their citizens from attacks coming from the outside. Therefore a strong US military force should be seen as a *good* thing and not as something evil in the world. US military power increases peace because it deters any potential enemy from thinking it can benefit from attacking our nation. This promotes peace in the world.

All Republicans of national prominence and some (but not all) Democrats agree with this perspective. But the Obama administration and its more liberal supporters in the Democratic Party have, like President Jimmy Carter before them, pressed for massive reductions in defense spending, even canceling further production of the greatest fighter plane ever produced, the F-22 ("Raptor") fighter. President Obama insisted on killing authorization for any further production of this remarkable aircraft, something I argued was a significant mistake. But it comes from a mentality that believes that military conflicts are caused by weapons rather than by evil in the hearts of people.

I argued that Islamic Jihadism (international Islamic terrorism) is fundamentally a religious movement and is based on a strong religious belief, namely, a small minority view within worldwide Islam that argues that the rule of Islamic law should be promoted by military conquest and terrorist attacks in various nations of the world, and then, once nations are conquered, Islam should be imposed on nations by the application of superior military power. The cause of such terrorism, therefore, is not poverty, or any perception of oppression of certain nations by the United States, or any failure to negotiate adequately with terrorists, but is rather a profoundly evil and deeply held religious view. I argued that Islamic Jihadism will only be overcome, from a human perspective, by the use of superior military force to find and imprison or otherwise defeat those who would promote it.

Republicans in general have agreed with this position, while Democrats generally have minimized the religious component behind Islamic Jihadism, have tended to downplay the need for the use of superior military force, and have emphasized instead the hope that more negotiation in good faith, more money, and more apologies for supposed US misconduct could lead us to come to terms with those who are opposed to the United States and its policies.

I argued that the war in Iraq and the war in Afghanistan were necessary and morally right in terms of traditional just war theory, because they were founded on the need to defend ourselves against international terrorist attacks. However, we need to have sufficient resolve and sufficient commitment of military forces to pursue those conflicts until the national governments within those countries are well established and secure in their democratic processes, and until they voluntarily decide, on their own accord, that they can take care of themselves and would like American forces to leave.

Republicans have in general agreed with this policy and supported the approach of President George W. Bush to these wars. Most Democrats, by contrast, have continued to push for immediate withdrawal from these countries, an approach that, it seems to me, recklessly risks losing everything we have gained in those countries and risks allowing them to be overrun once again by the terrorist forces of al-Qaeda and the Taliban. However, it is good that President Obama, in late 2009, did commit to sending an additional 30,000 troops to Afghanistan.

I argued that it is hopeless and wishful thinking to imagine that the world will ever be free of nuclear weapons, because world history shows that once new weapons are developed, they are never subsequently abandoned. Therefore the United States and other major peace-loving nations that now have nuclear weapons must maintain a strong nuclear arsenal in order to guarantee their ability to defend against attack by any other nations.

While it is true that President Reagan, a Republican, supported some reduction of the US nuclear arsenal, Republicans generally have tended to support a strong nuclear force, while Democrats have in general sought to impose greater and greater reductions in the nuclear arsenal and greater restrictions on the development and testing of these weapons. (This has been the recent policy of President Obama, for example.)

With regard to missile defense systems that would destroy enemy missiles before they could reach the United States, it seems to me that this is a wonderful idea that no impartial, thinking person should oppose. That is because they provide an excellent, life-saving alternative to defending ourselves by sending massive numbers of nuclear weapons against an attacking country. They allow us, instead, to destroy an incoming missile before it can reach our country or do any harm to anyone.

Republicans have favored further development and deployment of such systems, which were first begun by President Reagan. Democrats, by contrast, have opposed and even mocked such systems from the beginning (calling President Reagan's plans a hopeless "Star Wars" scheme based in fiction, not reality). But these systems have proven increasingly accurate in test after test. Unfortunately, President Obama canceled the planned deployment of such anti-missile systems in Poland and the Czech Republic in 2009.

I also argued that a spy network such as the CIA is necessary to gain intelligence against enemies who would attack us, and that Americans should, in general, support the CIA and not automatically assume (from the influence of a biased media and enter-tainment industry) that it is constantly doing evil things. The CIA performs a necessary function in defending the nation. Republicans in general have supported the activities of the CIA, but many Democrats have attempted to investigate and restrict it with the goal of limiting its ability to carry out its task.

I argued that the use of the word "torture" is not helpful in the discussion of the treat-ment of enemy prisoners, because it has so many different meanings for people. It seems to me that the best policy for the United States would be to treat prisoners humanely and with significant care, never to attempt to punish them. But in exceptional cases where an enemy was captured who had knowledge of a "ticking bomb" or other likely terrorist attack, I argued that coercive measures, stopping short of anything that would actually be immoral, should be applied to extract information from such prisoners, and that abundant evidence indicates that this kind of treatment actually worked with regard to some high-ranking captured terrorists after 9/11.

Republicans have generally tended to support such coercive interrogation methods (within strict guidelines), but not entirely. For instance, Senator John McCain, among others, expressed opposition to any such use of "coercive interrogation"—but he later backtracked on this somewhat. On the other hand, Democrats have been much more insistent that no such means should ever be used, and Obama issued an executive order banning the use of such means of interrogation within a day after becoming President.

H. RELATIONSHIPS WITH OTHER NATIONS

In chapter 12, with respect to other nations, I argued that the purpose of our foreign policy should be to seek the good of the United States and the protection of its citizens in relationships with other nations, but also that we should attempt to give help to other nations and do good for them where we are able to do so. For example, it is right to give various kinds of foreign aid to other nations, both through government sources and through private channels and private charitable organizations.

With regard to Israel, I argued that the United States should continue to support that nation as a close ally, both because it is the most dependable ally for the United States in the Middle East, and because it is a functioning democracy and a growing economy with which we have multiple, mutually beneficial relationships.

Another reason to support Israel is an argument from the Bible that God still has a future purpose for the Jewish people, in which he will bring many of them back to a personal relationship with himself through trust in Jesus as the Messiah (Rom. 11). It seems likely to me that the establishment of the nation of Israel in 1948 and the gathering of millions of Jewish people in that land are one providential step toward the realization of that future plan of God. This is a further reason why, it seems to me, the United States should support Israel. It also seems to me that this plan of God in Romans 11 probably explains the deep spiritual reason why many Muslim nations surrounding Israel are so adamantly opposed to the very existence of Israel as a nation.

What is the origin of the Arab-Israeli conflict in the Middle East? It goes back to the establishment of Israel as a nation in 1948. The same United Nations resolution (in 1947) that authorized the nation of Israel also authorized the establishment of a separate Arab nation alongside Israel, and specified boundaries for each nation, so that two nations would have been created in 1948. But the Arab nations surrounding Israel and the Palestinian-Arab people themselves rejected this two-state solution and refused to acknowledge the legitimacy of Israel as a nation or to establish the separate Arab nation in Palestine that had been authorized by the United Nations. In addition, the surrounding Arab nations also refused to accept any Palestinian refugees as permanent citizens in their own countries, such as Egypt and Jordan. Therefore, it is ultimately the refusal of Arab nations to accept even the legitimacy of the existence of Israel as a nation that is the unsolvable barrier to peace in the Middle East.

Up to this point in history, both Democrats and Republicans have largely been supportive of Israel as a nation and supportive of Israel's right to defend itself and our obligation to act as an ally toward Israel. Some recent statements of President Obama have begun to call into question his commitment to this policy, but no major change in policy has yet come about.

With regard to immigration, I argued that the Bible requires us to treat immigrants from other nations with love and respect and equality before the law, so long as they fall in the category of the "sojourner" or "alien" that is talked about quite often in the Old Testament. But we must understand that these were people who came into another nation with the full knowledge and permission of the host nation. They were not the same as illegal immigrants who enter a nation today.

With respect to illegal immigration, I argued the following:

(1) A complete and secure border fence must first be built before the nation is ready to work toward any other kind of solution to this problem.

(2) The system must be reformed to stop the pattern of "chain migration" that allows huge extended families to multiply their presence many times over in the United States. In addition, the teaching of English and American traditions and values should be required for people who want to become American citizens.

(3) With regard to illegal aliens who are already in the country, those who are criminals or who have outstanding warrants for their arrest should immediately be deported (about 450,000 people). For the rest, there should be a program of registration plus a difficult but clearly attainable path to citizenship for those who desire it, with appropriate fines, learning of English, and a waiting period that would not unfairly preempt people who have already been in the citizenship process for a long time.

(4) Finally, it does not seem to me that a "guest worker" program would be appropriate, because too many would fall beneath the radar again and create another large illegal-immigrant problem.

Many Republicans have been supportive of plans such as the general policies that I have explained here, but unfortunately, among Republican ranks there have been some hyper-conservative people who have opposed any elements of a plan that would allow any path to citizenship whatsoever for the illegal aliens who are now here in the United States. Democrats, on the other hand, have tended to favor much more liberal policies that would lead to much quicker citizenship (and therefore, they hope, more Democratic votes) for those who are here illegally. Moreover, Democrats have tended to block efforts to carry out a quick completion of a totally secure fence along the border with Mexico. This seems largely to be because of the thought that the larger the immigrant population that comes into the United States, the more political power Democrats and their candidates will have. This is putting concerns for their own political power ahead of the good of the nation.

I. FREEDOM OF SPEECH

In chapter 13 I argued that freedom of speech is an essential policy for any free nation.

With regard to campaign finance restrictions, I argued that they are mostly wrongful restrictions on freedom of speech. They have not kept money out of politics, but have given unfair advantage to incumbents and to independent candidates who are extremely wealthy. It seems to me appropriate that all campaign finance restrictions should be abolished, with only the requirement that contributions above a certain amount be made public.

Democrats have tended to favor these campaign finance restrictions, because it seems that they give to Democrats (who are largely favored by the media and Hollywood) an advantage in the political system. Such restrictions also provide an endless maze of regulations by which candidates can be inadvertently tripped up and then held liable for breaking the law. Unfortunately, some Republicans have also supported these campaign finance restrictions (the most prominent being John McCain), but a number of Republicans have also opposed them.

I argued that the "hate speech" codes on university campuses are a wrongful and also unconstitutional restriction on freedom of speech and are often used to give privileged status to liberal policies and ideas and to criticize the speech of Christians defending biblical values or promoting the Gospel.

Democrats and political liberals in the academic community have tended much more strongly to support such hate speech codes. This has not been much of an issue among Republicans in politics.

Finally, with regard to the Fairness Doctrine that would require equal time for broadcasting alternative viewpoints on controversial issues, I argued that it would be a wrongful restriction on freedom of speech and would basically be used to try to destroy conservative talk radio, which is the primary media outlet available to conservatives in the United States today. Some Democrats have supported the idea that the FCC should reimpose the Fairness Doctrine; Republicans uniformly oppose this.

J. FREEDOM OF RELIGION

In chapter 14, regarding freedom of religion, I argued that neither the Bible nor the US Constitution (in its original intent) excludes individual people or even government agencies from giving expression to particular religious views or beliefs in the public square. It has been a morally and legally mistaken promotion of the myth that the Constitution requires a complete "separation of church and state," promoted particularly by some mistaken Supreme Court decisions, that has led to an increasing exclusion of religious speech in the public square in the United States.

These inappropriate restrictions on religious expression in the public square have largely been imposed on the nation and on the individual states by the decisions of more liberal judges who have been appointed (largely but not exclusively) by Democratic governors to the various state courts and by Democratic presidents to the federal judicial system. Republicans, by contrast, have generally (but not always) appointed judges who rule more consistently according to the original intent of the US Constitution or the various state constitutions.

I also argued that faith-based programs, by which religious organizations receive government funding to carry out social welfare programs, seem to me to be legitimate in terms of both biblical teaching and the US Constitution. It also seems to me that they do not pose any significant danger to a loss of religious freedom on the part of these organizations.

Republicans (but not uniformly) have tended to favor allowing government funding to be given to such faith-based programs (such as shelters for the homeless, job training, drug rehabilitation, and prison ministries), while Democrats have largely (but not entirely) been much more reluctant to support them.

Finally, I argued that the Internal Revenue Service's prohibition against political advocacy by churches and religious organizations seems to me to be an unconstitutional restriction on freedom of speech by churches. The decision of whether to express a viewpoint for or against an individual candidate should be left to the individual church and the individual pastor or priest or rabbi, not made by the government. I do not think that many Republicans or Democrats have expressed an opinion about this question (although the restrictions were first put into place under the leadership of then-Congressman Lyndon Johnson, a Democrat who later became President).

K. SPECIAL GROUPS WITHIN THE NATION

In chapter 15 I argued that there are many policies, laws, and programs in the United States that end up favoring certain small groups at the expense of the good of the nation as a whole. These include the policies behind thousands of regulations imposed by government regulators who had never been elected by the people, earmarks directing how to spend about 2% of our national budget, affirmative action programs with regard to racial quotas, gender-based quotas for school sports programs, farm subsidies, tariffs, the essential monopoly possessed by the National Education Association, laws that reward wealthy trial lawyers, special reservations and legal systems for Native Americans, and laws that promote gambling in the United States.

With regard to many of these policies, much more support and defense of them has come from Democrats than from Republicans. However, with respect to farm subsidies, it seems that there has been bipartisan support on the part of members of both parties who represent agricultural states. Also, both Republicans and Democrats have been guilty of inserting earmarks into bills and thus designating government money to be spent on pet projects that they favor (or spent on the interests of people who have made contributions to them).

But by far the strongest support for affirmative action, gender-based quotas, the teachers' unions, and the trial lawyers has come from Democrats. Republican opposition to laws that favor such groups has been unable to bring an end to such laws.

L. MEDIA BIAS

In chapter 16 I argued that there is a strong media bias in favor of more liberal policies and in favor of Democratic policies and candidates in the United States today. This means that the "watchdog" function that should be played by a free press is largely missing from the national media, and this is especially evident with regard to the Obama administration.

M. WHY DO THE TWO PARTIES ADOPT THESE DIFFERENT POLICIES?

Is there a reason why Republicans have far more often ended up supporting policies that are consistent with biblical teachings, whereas Democrats have far more frequently ended up opposing these policies? I suggest that there are several factors that account for this difference. I have listed them here in an order that moves from the obvious political differences that anyone can see to the deeper factors that involve a person's entire worldview and deeper spiritual commitments.

(1) *Liberal versus conservative views of government:* The Democratic Party has attracted and has come to represent people who favor much more government control of individual lives and much more government-enforced equality of income among people. The Republican Party, on the other hand, has tended to attract people who believe in much smaller and more limited government and believe in allowing people to keep the fruits of their labors as long as they have been earned legally. This is a classic difference between a "liberal" and a "conservative" view of government. Thus there is a basic policy difference between those who believe in *big government* and *making everybody equal* and those who believe in *small government* and *allowing greater individual differences among people and greater individual freedom.*

Because of the Bible's emphasis on individual freedom and a limited role for government (see chap. 3), this means that Republicans have tended to favor policies that seem to be more consistent with biblical teachings.

(2) *Abortion:* Beginning in the 1970s, the Democratic Party became increasingly dominated by people who favor the protection of abortion rights for women. Behind this commitment is a conviction that we cannot know any absolute moral standards for human conduct, particularly sexual conduct, and if unwanted pregnancies result from sexual intercourse outside of marriage or within marriage when a child is not "wanted," then the more liberal commitment to moral relativism means that there is an unwillingness to have the government say that taking the life of this preborn child is wrong. Protecting people's sexual freedom has become, for the Democratic Party, a much higher value.

Thus the Democratic Party's increasingly uniform support for abortion rights (at least on the national leadership level, among national candidates, and in national judicial appointments) means that the Democrats have committed themselves to a position that is fundamentally opposed to the biblical teachings on the value of the preborn child.

Republicans, by contrast, have more and more become a party in which, on the national level and increasingly on the level of most states, no significant leadership positions can be held by people who favor the continuation of a legal right to abortion (except to save the life of the mother). This means that, on the question of laws to regulate abortion, Republicans and Democrats have strayed further and further apart, and the biblical values are clearly on the side of the Republican position on this issue.

This difference regarding sexual moral standards has then naturally led to differences about the question of homosexual "marriage." Since the abortion controversies started and pro-abortion people gravitated to the Democratic party, that resulted in a large number of Democrats who were convinced that no one could know any universal moral standards with regard to sexual conduct between consenting adults. Therefore, once the issue of homosexual "marriage" came up, Democrats tended almost uniformly to favor "equal rights for homosexuals" and therefore homosexual "marriage."

Most Republicans, whether because of the Bible's teachings or because of an instinctive sense of moral right and wrong, have held that marriage should be limited to a union between one man and one woman. Therefore Republicans have also largely ended up on the side of the Bible's teachings on homosexuality and marriage.

(3) *Individual human responsibility for good and evil:* With regard to the existence of good and evil in the heart of every individual, and therefore the rightness of holding people accountable for the choices they make, it seems to me that Republicans have, in general, come down on the biblical side of this fundamental question as well. Therefore they have tended to favor stronger military forces (to defend against evil from other nations), stronger police forces, and stronger enforcement of criminal laws (to defend against evil deeds done by people within the nation). Democrats, on the other hand, have been more likely to blame the evil things that people do on forces outside the individual, such as family or society or guns or corporations or national governments. This tends to minimize an emphasis on individual accountability for one's own actions, and this, in turn, makes people think that those who do wrong can simply be persuaded to change their minds with more conversation and more negotiation, whether it be with a criminal within the nation or with leaders who attempt evil things from outside the nation.

(4) *Beliefs about the relationship between the human race and the natural world:* Belief that mere chance has brought about the origin of all living things through evolution leads a person to believe that human beings are just a higher form of animal that has evolved from the material universe. Then it is an easy step to reason that we should not think of human beings as deserving any kind of special role with regard to the earth or the animal kingdom. Because of this belief, people who hold to materialistic evolution as the explanation of all life tend to assume that all development of the earth's resources will cause damage to the environment, and such people will likely support the stricter environmentalist policies of the Democratic Party. They will also be more likely to fear that, since random processes *created* human life on earth, random or careless events in the future might cause the *destruction* of the earth and the human race.

Yet there is still something in human nature that makes people seek to serve a cause greater than themselves. If people do not think it is possible to know God as a person, then that longing to serve a cause greater than themselves can easily propel people toward a "save the earth" campaign. (What could be a greater cause than saving the whole earth, especially if you do not think anyone can know about God?) In this way, people who tend toward having environmentalism as their substitute religion would also gravitate toward the Democratic Party.

But people who take the Bible as their reliable guide for life tend to believe that God has created a good earth, a resourceful earth, and one that he wants us to develop and use wisely for our own benefit (according to Genesis 1:28). These people will tend to think that development of the earth's resources is a good thing, something that God wants us to do. Even apart from such a religious basis for this view of the earth, mere observation and common sense have led many people to think that human beings are obviously far superior to any other living creature, and this has led these people to think that the earth's resources and the plant and animal kingdoms should rightfully be developed and used (but in a wise and nondestructive way) for the benefit of mankind. Such people have gravitated toward the Republican Party, whose policies have more strongly favored "wise use" of the environment for the benefit of mankind.

(5) *Beliefs about whether we can know right and wrong:* If a person does not believe that absolute truth and absolute right and wrong can be known, then it follows that one person's views are just as good as another's. There is no way to know whether someone is right or wrong. Once a person reaches that conviction, he or she no longer feels accountable to any moral standard, or any standard of truth that is higher than any other, and certainly not to any God (who probably can't be known anyway, even if he does exist).

It follows that if there is no right and wrong that can be known, the people who are *most dangerous* are those who have strongly held religious convictions (such as fundamentalist Muslims and fundamentalist Christians!). These people must not be allowed to have their viewpoints influence the society.

Taking this reasoning one step further, if there is no absolute right and wrong, then the people who can have the most beneficial influence on society (according to what they personally think is "good" for society) are simply those who have the most power. It follows, then, that if you think there is no absolute right and wrong, it is right to seek more and more power, and that power comes, in most nations, through the attaining of political office and the power of the government. Therefore the Democratic Party tends to attract to itself people for whom gaining power through the government, and then increasing that power, is the best way they know to do something "good" with their lives (as they understand what is "good"). That is why Democrats seek to continually increase government power over individual lives.

Republicans, by contrast, have many more people who believe that there are absolute moral standards (as found in the Bible, or for some conservatives in traditional Jewish teaching, or the Bible plus Roman Catholic Church tradition, or the Book of Mormon, and so forth). These people also tend to think that they will be held accountable for their actions to a personal God who will one day judge them. This means that they believe there are absolute moral standards, and the *attainment of power* is not the ultimate goal, but rather *being obedient to the moral code that God has given to us.* They will tend to resist increases in government power, thinking that God has given to government a limited role.

In addition, these people tend to think that the religious system on which they base their beliefs places a high value on individual responsibility and individual freedom of choice. This is another reason why they tend to want smaller government—government that allows more individual freedom. But this individual freedom should be limited to prevent evil people from harming others through murder or rape or theft or breaking contracts and so forth. Therefore Republicans tend to emphasize individual freedom (within certain boundaries of the law).

(6) *Religious beliefs:* There is a significant difference in the religious beliefs of Republicans and Democrats taken as a whole. Conservative evangelicals, who tend to believe

that the Bible is God's Word in its entirety, have tended to align with Republican principles. So have others whose religious views lead them to believe in absolute moral right and wrong, such as Roman Catholics, Mormons, and more traditional Jews.

But people who have no religious belief at all, or who do not believe that we can know what God has told us with regard to moral standards, tend to be moral relativists, and this aligns them much more closely with the Democratic Party and its emphasis on allowing people to choose abortion or choose homosexual marriage and so forth.

(7) *Conclusion:* The differences between Democrats and Republicans today have great significance. These differences are not accidental, but stem from differing convictions about several moral and theological issues.

Chapter 18

FAITH AND WORKS, AND TRUSTING GOD WHILE WORKING IN POLITICS AND GOVERNMENT

How can we have deep faith in God's sovereignty over history while we work to influence the laws and policies of a nation for good?

Is there any contradiction or any tension between our "faith" and our "good works" in the political realm?

This chapter will be addressed more specifically to Christian believers, and it will attempt to place the concerns of this book into the larger biblical perspective of how Christians should live their entire lives—continually *trusting* in God while also *obeying* him and living lives filled with "good works" (Eph. 2:10).

A. WHAT DOES IT MEAN TO TRUST GOD'S SOVEREIGNTY OVER THE DIRECTION OF WORLD HISTORY?

Trusting God regarding his sovereignty over the direction of world history simply means believing what God says about his rule over the nations and having a settled confidence and peace in our hearts that this is true.

1. God rules over the rulers and destinies of nations

Consider the following passages of Scripture:

> For kingship belongs to the LORD, and *he rules over the nations* (Ps. 22:28).

> Who rules by his might forever, *whose eyes keep watch on the nations*—let not the rebellious exalt themselves (Ps. 66:7).

> For not from the east or from the west and not from the wilderness comes lifting up, but *it is God who executes judgment, putting down one and lifting up another* (Ps. 75:6–7).

> The LORD has established his throne in the heavens, and *his kingdom rules over all* (Ps. 103:19).

> The *king's heart* is a stream of water in the hand of the LORD; he turns it wherever he will (Prov. 21:1).

> "*The Most High rules the kingdom of men* and gives it to whom he will and sets over it the lowliest of men" (Dan. 4:17).

> Jesus answered him, "You would have no authority over me at all unless it had been *given you from above*" (John 19:11).

> "And *he made from one man every nation* of mankind to live on all the face of the earth, *having determined allotted periods and the boundaries of their dwelling place*" (Acts 17:26).

> Let every person be subject to the governing authorities. For *there is no authority except from God*, and those that exist have been instituted by God (Rom. 13:1).

In the summer of 2008 I realized the truth of these verses in a new way. I had been speaking at a conference in Rome, and the day before it ended I was standing on the roof of a hotel that was on a hill overlooking the entire city of Rome. As I gazed at that incredible city, I realized that this was a city that had ruled the known world for more than five centuries. Emperors had walked those streets. Armies had marched out from Rome and returned victorious. Laws had gone forth from Rome to govern many nations. And it was all under the sovereign, invisible providence of God, working out his purposes in history—for in the year 4 BC, the emperor Caesar Augustus issued a decree from this city:

> In those days a decree went out from Caesar Augustus that all the world should be registered. This was the first registration when Quirinius was governor of Syria. And all went to be registered, each to his own town. And Joseph also went up from Galilee, from the town of Nazareth, to Judea, to the city of David, which is called Bethlehem, because he was of the house and lineage of David, to be registered with Mary, his betrothed, who was with child. And while they

were there, the time came for her to give birth. And she gave birth to her first-born son and wrapped him in swaddling cloths and laid him in a manger, because there was no place for them in the inn (Luke 2:1–7).

Caesar Augustus in his palace in Rome along with the mighty Roman armies whose soldiers began to enforce that decree had no idea that God in heaven was using them to fulfill his plan, so that "when the fullness of time had come, God sent forth his Son, born of woman, born under the law, to redeem those who were under the law" (Gal. 4:4–5).

Caesar Augustus thought he ruled the entire civilized world. But far above him, reigning eternally, was the Lord, who "rules over the nations" (Ps. 22:28). So it was throughout all ages, and so it is today. Although God has allowed much evil to continue in the world without yet bringing it into judgment, he is still ruling over the rulers and the destinies of nations.

Therefore these words of Scripture should plant faith in God's sovereignty over history deep in our hearts.

2. God will accomplish his good purposes on the earth

a. God will accomplish his good purposes for Christian believers and for his church

The Bible gives multiple assurances that God will accomplish his good purposes for those who have trusted in Christ for salvation:

> And we know that for those who love God all things work together for good, for those who are called according to his purpose (Rom. 8:28).

God will also build his church and cause it to grow throughout the earth, further advancing his good purposes and bringing blessing to millions of people and to many nations:

> "And I tell you, you are Peter, and on this rock I will build my church, and the gates of hell shall not prevail against it" (Matt. 16:18).

The church of Jesus Christ therefore will not be destroyed, and it will not be defeated. It will continue its growth throughout all nations and all peoples, bringing the "good news" of forgiveness of sins, teaching peace and love and justice and righteousness, and breaking down all the weapons of the enemy and shattering even the "gates of hell" if they should stand in its way.

Jesus Christ, who is now exalted and enthroned in heaven, continues to work on earth to bring about the progressive realization of his purpose for his church:

> Husbands, love your wives, as Christ loved the church and gave himself up for her, that he might sanctify her, having cleansed her by the washing of water with the word, *so that he might present the church to himself in splendor, without spot or wrinkle or any such thing*, that she might be holy and without blemish (Eph. 5:25–27).

The Lord who reigns over both heaven and earth still proclaims today, "I will build my church, and the gates of hell shall not prevail against it" (Matt. 16:18).

b. God's plans for all of history

God's plans for all of history will stand, and they will not be defeated. He promises through the prophet Isaiah:

> "Remember the former things of old; for I am God, and there is no other; I am God, and there is none like me, declaring the end from the beginning and from ancient times things not yet done, saying, *'My counsel shall stand, and I will accomplish all my purpose'*" (Isa. 46:9–10).

In the New Testament, after Christ has risen from the dead, he makes this promise regarding the course of history and nations:

> "The one who conquers and who keeps my works until the end, *to him I will give authority over the nations*" (Rev. 2:26).

When I read such verses, I think of some Christian lawyers whom I have met from many nations, who argue faithfully for human freedom and justice and righteousness before the courts of many nations. Sometimes they are successful, but in some nations they almost always lose due to the oppressive nature of the judicial system there. These verses make me realize that I would not be surprised, after Christ returns, to see many of those same courageous lawyers sitting as judges over cities and states and nations. "You have been faithful over a little; I will set you over much" (Matt. 25:21).

c. Christ will return and will one day rule over the nations

Who will ultimately gain ruling authority over the entire world? Not Caesar Augustus. Not Nero. Not Hitler. Not the President of the European Union or the President of the United States. No, Christ will someday return to earth and will rule over all the nations:

> For the Lord himself will descend from heaven with a cry of command, with the voice of an archangel, and with the sound of the trumpet of God (1 Thess. 4:16).

> Then the seventh angel blew his trumpet, and there were loud voices in heaven, saying, "The kingdom of the world has become the kingdom of our Lord and of his Christ, and he shall reign forever and ever" (Rev. 11:15).

Therefore, in light of all these verses, we as Christians can do all of our work in politics and government in an atmosphere of deep faith and tremendous hope. Our fundamental disposition regarding politics and government should never be one of anxiety or fear, but rather deep trust in God. Our heart should be filled with a calm and quiet peace.

> You keep him in perfect peace whose mind is stayed on you, because he trusts in you (Isa. 26:3).

Therefore, no matter what happens, no matter whether we win or lose individual elections and individual political battles, we should never despair, for our God is on the throne, and he will certainly accomplish his good purposes in all of history, his good purposes for his church, and his good purposes for each of us.

3. God works through human actions to bring about his purposes

If we only focused on biblical verses about God's sovereignty in history, we would have a mistaken picture, because we would have only half of the total biblical teaching regarding human history. The other half of the biblical picture is that there is still much evil in the world. God has not yet chosen to remove it from the earth:

> But understand this, that *in the last days there will come times of difficulty.* For people will be lovers of self, lovers of money, proud, arrogant, abusive, disobedient to their parents, ungrateful, unholy, heartless, unappeasable, slanderous, without self-control, brutal, not loving good, treacherous, reckless, swollen with conceit, lovers of pleasure rather than lovers of God (2 Tim. 3:1–4).

> Indeed, all who desire to live a godly life in Christ Jesus will be persecuted, while evil people and impostors will go on from bad to worse, deceiving and being deceived (2 Tim. 3:12–13).

The great evil that remains in the world does immense harm to people who have been created in the image of God. In America alone, 49 million preborn babies have been killed.[1] Children's sense of sexual innocence and modesty and purity are destroyed. Children's developing sexual self-awareness is tampered with and distorted. All sense of moral accountability to God has been removed from much of government and much of the public square. Terrorist bombs still kill hundreds and sometimes thousands of innocent civilians.

Christians in North Korea and China and many Muslim nations are put to death for their faith. Christians are mocked and ridiculed and slandered and sued and persecuted in various ways for their faith. The rich and powerful oppress the poor and weak. Powerful media outlets earn huge fortunes by glorifying immoral conduct of the worst sort. Marriages and families and individual lives are ruined through alcoholism, drug abuse, and sexual immorality and through addictions to gambling and violence and dishonesty. Above all this, the name of God, the eternal and infinitely good and wise and powerful Creator, is slandered rather than being honored or praised by millions of people on the earth.

In order to oppose and overcome such evils in the world, God calls his people to serve him in many ways. He gives us the privilege of being involved in the struggle to overcome evil. In this way God works through our human actions to bring about the fulfillment of his purposes in history. He calls us to pray (see Matthew 6:10). He calls

---

1. See www.nrlc.org/abortion/facts/abortionstats.html.

us to evangelize through sharing the good news of the Gospel with others (see Matthew 28:19–20). He calls us to act in obedience to him each day.

God does not often change the world miraculously without also using a good deal of human work. William Wilberforce had to work for his entire lifetime before he could persuade the British parliament to abolish the slave trade and then slavery. Tens of thousands of Christians have worked now for more than thirty-five years to give legal protection to preborn children in the United States, and their efforts have not yet succeeded. But I believe one day they will succeed. God calls us to work for good laws and good government in the nations of the earth because civil government is one of the primary means he uses to restrain evil on the earth. The civil ruler "is the servant of God, an avenger who carries out God's wrath on the wrongdoer" (Rom. 13:4).

We do not need to do this work in the midst of confusion or uncertainty. We know that the final goal is that people on earth will live in accordance with the moral laws of God in Scripture and so bring honor to him. Therefore we know that it is pleasing to God when we work in various ways toward that final goal even now. We are to pray and to act in such a way that God's kingdom will come and his will will be done "on earth as it is in heaven" (Matt. 6:10).

B. THE FUTURE: WILL THE UNITED STATES BECOME A BETTER OR WORSE NATION IN THE NEXT FEW DECADES?

Will the work of Christians to bring "significant Christian influence" to government have success? Or will it fail? No one knows for sure. God alone knows the future.

1. Negative signs pointing to God's impending judgment

I look at my own nation, the United States of America, and I see signs of increased evil. I am concerned that God in heaven, "whose eyes keep watch on the nations" (Ps. 66:7), might bring judgment on the nation for its evil, just as he has on other nations in the past—judgment in terms of economic collapse, an incurable disease epidemic, a military attack from powerful enemies, the imposition of a totalitarian government, or some other means.

I am concerned about Hollywood movies and TV shows that blatantly and proudly glorify adultery, premarital sex, homosexual conduct, murder, violence, and demonic perversion of all that God has created good. I am concerned about a flood of pornography that is consumed by our nation both in print media and through the Internet. I am concerned about the imposition of same-sex "marriage" on the citizens of Massachusetts, Iowa, Vermont, and New Hampshire. I am concerned about massive, irresponsible consumer debt. I am concerned about much complacency toward the continuing threat of radical Islamic terrorism and the increasing threat of nuclear weapons in the hands of North Korea and perhaps Iran.

I am concerned about the number of high-profile evangelical Christians who have been exposed for sexual immorality of various sorts, such as Ted Haggard, former president of the National Association of Evangelicals;[2] Governor Mark Sanford of South Carolina;[3] Senator John Ensign of Nevada;[4] and Senator David Vitter of Louisiana.[5] When I see these things, I wonder whether they are representative of a wider trend in the evangelical world that wrongly assumes that obedience to God's moral standards really doesn't matter, since we are all "forgiven" anyway!

I am concerned about millions of Americans who claim to be Christians but have simply come to adopt "Christianity lite." They live together outside of marriage. They consume pornography. They give almost nothing out of their earnings to their church or other charitable work. They spend all of their income on themselves. They habitually lie throughout the day.

I am concerned that we have a presidential administration that is aggressively pushing a far-left agenda, including an increase in abortion rights, the promotion of the legitimacy of homosexual conduct, the appointment of activist judges at every level of the federal judicial system, and a historically unprecedented swallowing up of whole sections of the economy and our personal income by a federal government that never thinks it has enough control of our lives.

2. Positive signs pointing to God's continued blessing and perhaps even to a revival of the church

By contrast, I see many encouraging signs as well, and I wonder if they indicate that God is about to pour out increased blessing on his people and on this nation.

I am encouraged to see a remarkable growth in the home-schooling movement and the number of private Christian schools that are teaching moral standards and truth consistent with the Bible.

I am encouraged to see an evangelical scholarly community in biblical studies and in theology (especially the Evangelical Theological Society) that is vibrant, active, and amazingly prolific as well as strongly supportive of protecting marriage between one man and one woman.

I am encouraged to see more than a dozen strong, biblically faithful evangelical seminaries in the United States that are growing and thriving. I am encouraged to see several good, reliable recent Bible translations in English. I am encouraged to see numerous

2. "Evangelical confesses to 'sexual immorality' in letter," *CNN.com* (Nov. 6, 2006). www.cnn.com/2006/US/11/05/haggard.allegations/index.html.

3. David Saltonstall, "Love letter for Argentine mistress outed Gov. Mark Sanford's affair to wife Jenny," *New York Daily News* (June 26, 2009). www.nydailynews.com/news/national/2009/06/26/2009–06–26_gov_mark_sanford_apologizes_to_staff_for_affair_wife_jenny_reveals_she_.html.

4. Paul Kane and Chris Cillizza, "Sen. Ensign Acknowledges an Extramarital Affair," *Washington Post* (June 17, 2009). www.washingtonpost.com/wp-dyn/content/article/2009/06/16/AR2009061602746.html.

5. Joel Roberts, "Senator Caught in 'D.C. Madam' Scandal," *CBSNews.com* (July 10, 2007). www.cbsnews.com/stories/2007/07/09/national/main3037338.shtml.

strong parachurch and mission organizations growing and thriving. I am encouraged to see the remarkable Christian influence that exists on the Internet.

I am encouraged to see increasing signs of unity and life and spiritual power in some churches. One example is the churches of California that united in prayer and fasting and work to support the amazing passage of Proposition 8, which reversed the actions of the California Supreme Court that had imposed same-sex "marriage" on the state's citizens earlier in the year and established the truth of marriage between one man and one woman as law in that state. On November 4, 2008, over seven million Californians (more than 52%) voted to restore marriage in the state despite what seemed to be over-whelming odds.[6] Churches throughout California played a pivotal role in mobilizing Christians to take a stand for marriage.[7]

I am encouraged to see a younger generation of Christians filled with courage and deep commitment, with thousands of them attending conferences with solid, strong biblical teaching.

I am both saddened but also encouraged to see that numerous high-profile Christians have not been able to hide their sin but have been publicly exposed for sexual immoral-ity. I wonder whether this is the beginning of a revival where God begins first to expose sin and bring discipline upon his own people: "For it is time for judgment to begin at the household of God" (1 Peter 4:17).

I am encouraged to see Christian legal organizations such as the Alliance Defense Fund, Liberty Legal Institute, Liberty Counsel, the Christian Legal Society, and the American Center for Law and Justice winning victory after victory to protect freedom of speech, freedom of religion, and marriage and human life. I am encouraged by the Blackstone Legal Fellowship, a ministry of the Alliance Defense Fund, which trains first- and second-year law students each summer in a Christian worldview and constitutional law, so that they can become the legal leaders of tomorrow. (As of November 2009, 813 students have graduated from this program, and many have already assumed influential positions in the nation's legal system.)

I am encouraged to see an outpouring of new worship songs in churches wherever I go. I am encouraged to see the remarkable growth of Bible-believing evangelical churches in Africa and Asia and Latin America, unlike anything that has ever happened in the history of the world.

And many more things could be added.

Therefore, although I do not know for certain what will happen, I still have a strong expectation that revival rather than God's judgment is in store for the United States, and perhaps even for Europe. (North America, Europe, and Australia are the only continents that still remain untouched by a revival of the church that seems to be sweeping the rest of the world.)

6. Source: California Secretary of State. www.sos.ca.gov/elections/sov/2008_primary/ssov/ballot_measures_all.pdf.

7. "Pastors Unite to Protect Marriage," *Christian NewsWire* (Oct. 2, 2008). www.christiannewswire.com/news/931758112.html.

C. THE DETAILS OF REVIVAL: WHAT MIGHT IT LOOK LIKE IF GOD BROUGHT ABOUT A REVIVAL OF THE CHURCH AND A TRANSFORMATION OF THE NATION FOR GOOD?

If God does indeed bring about a revival in his church in the United States and elsewhere, what might that look like?

1. Preliminary steps

If God does bring revival, one of the first indications will be much evidence of deeper love for God and commitment to prayer on the part of God's people. "Draw near to God, and he will draw near to you" (James 4:8).

Another step will be a deeper sense of repentance for sin and commitment to personal holiness among God's people. "Strive for peace with everyone, and for the holiness without which no one will see the Lord" (Heb. 12:14).

Simultaneously, another preliminary step will be the turning of many individuals to Christ for the first time, and the returning to Christ of many who had once expressed faith in him but had strayed away. Churches will begin to see many thousands of new Christians flocking to them for fellowship and teaching and ministry to various kinds of needs.

Personal evangelism that has been carried out faithfully over many years will suddenly begin to bear much fruit. Perhaps even at the highest levels of government—in the Supreme Court, in Congress, and among the Executive Branch—many will find themselves turning to Jesus Christ in faith for the first time. University presidents and senior professors will begin to publicly profess faith in Christ and repentance from sin. Hollywood movie directors and network news anchors, one after another, will begin to profess genuine personal faith in Christ and repentance from sin. And so it will be through all levels of society.

If such a remarkable increase in genuine conversions to Christ does come about, I expect it will follow the pattern of events in the New Testament Gospels and Acts, where the Gospel message was proclaimed along with many miraculous manifestations of the truth of the Gospel, with God himself bearing witness "by signs and wonders and various miracles and by gifts of the Holy Spirit distributed according to his will" (Heb. 2:4). In imitation of the entire ministry of the apostle Paul, I expect that this will happen as the good news of Jesus Christ is proclaimed "by the power of signs and wonders, by the power of the Spirit of God" (Rom. 15:19). There will be many immediate and visible miracles along with the clear and powerful presentation of the Gospel, for that is always the New Testament pattern.

2. Next steps (part 1): the church

Within the church, a genuine revival will soon be followed by a great increase of solid teaching to Christian believers regarding God's moral standards for conduct of life as taught in the Bible. Jesus Christ is seeking a mature church that will no longer consist of "children, tossed to and fro by the waves and carried about by every wind of doctrine," but one filled with Christians who are continually "speaking the truth in love" (Eph. 4:14–15), walking in maturity of faith and holiness of life.

In addition, churches will be filled with sound teaching regarding the Bible's standards and principles as they apply to civil government, so that Christians will be able to think with mature wisdom regarding how they should vote in each election and for each candidate. If churches regularly teach about these standards, then a new Christian who joins the US Senate or the US Supreme Court or a local school board or a state legislature will know and understand what God expects government to do and for what reasons and for what goals. In that way, government will more and more become "God's servant for your good," as God intends it to be (Rom 13:4).

3. Next steps (part 2): the society

In past times of great revival in various countries of the earth, there has been not only personal renewal but also, eventually, a remarkable transformation of societies for good, as Christian believers began to put biblical principles into practice in all their conduct and all their decisions.

If this happens, the courts in the United States might return in overwhelming numbers to the proper role of interpreting and not creating law. The Congress, by a vast majority, might begin truly seeking the good of the nation far more than their own political power. And Christians at all levels of government would realize that government must never be used as a tool by which people attempt to compel religious belief of any kind, but instead should always protect genuine freedom of religion throughout the nation.

The President and the Executive Branch might come to follow the teachings of Scripture more and more in their policies regarding the protection of the life of the preborn, the protection of marriage between one man and one woman, the protection of individual freedom and liberty, and the protection of the nation from those who would attack it.

The news media might become more and more filled with responsible reporters who promote both genuine truthfulness and the good of the nation and who delight in and thereby encourage the goodness of moral standards of conduct that are consistent with the teachings of the Bible.

The entertainment industry might find that more and more Christians can work in it to purify it and call it to holiness of life. It might once again begin producing truly great films that reflect an awareness of the great conflict that exists between good and evil in human conduct.

Universities might find that Christians can continually work to bring to bear greater influence on faculty and books and courses that are grounded in truthfulness about the world and that respect the truthfulness of God's Word. In the public schools, Christians might be continually working for increased school choice and increased parental control of education, so that children throughout the nation will once again be taught that God exists, that he created the universe, and that he has moral standards to which he holds all people accountable (both in this life and in the future). But these things would be taught while always respecting the individual religious viewpoints that parents and children might hold.

Businesses might find that the entire world of commerce is increasingly becoming a model of integrity, honesty, productivity, and innovation. Families might begin to experience more and more the wonderful permanence of marriage and the joy of respectful obedience on the part of children and the inexpressible joy of experiencing the various stages of life together.

4. Working now for such revival and transformation

Until such a revival comes, the work of Christians today at all levels of society—and especially at all levels of political influence—is essential in order to protect the freedoms necessary to bring about such changes. In particular, the work of Christian lawyers in defending freedom of religion, defending freedom of speech, protecting marriage, and protecting life is necessary to provide the legal "space" in which others can act to bring influence in these areas and also to nullify hostile forces that will attempt to stop such revival and transformation at every stage if it begins to happen.

We simply do not know what measure of success God will grant to our efforts. But God may allow us to be pleasantly surprised at what he does through these efforts!

Still, no matter what happens, at the end of our days—whether we find ourselves, like Paul, in prison in a place like Rome, or find ourselves in the midst of great revival and societal transformation—it is important for us to continue to pray and act in faith, trusting in God's power for any success that might come. We must continually put forth our utmost efforts to move the history of our nation in the right direction, according to the wise and wonderful standards found in the Bible. We must continually be mindful of Jesus' admonition:

> "I am the vine; you are the branches. Whoever abides in me and I in him, he it is that bears much fruit, *for apart from me you can do nothing*" (John 15:5).

This verse reflects an attitude of faith in God that is rightfully combined with hard work in politics and government, because faith in God and hard work are not contradictory. God works *through* our human actions to bring about good in our world and to advance his kingdom.

And then at the end of the days we might be able to say with the apostle Paul:

> I have fought the good fight, I have finished the race, I have kept the faith. Henceforth there is laid up for me the crown of righteousness, which the Lord, the righteous judge, will award to me on that Day, and not only to me but also to all who have loved his appearing (2 Tim. 4:7–8).

SCRIPTURE INDEX

INDEX OF NAMES

Note: Biblical names, ancient names, authors, and modern names are all contained in this single index of names.

SUBJECT INDEX

Systematic Theology

An Introduction to Biblical Doctrine

Wayne Grudem

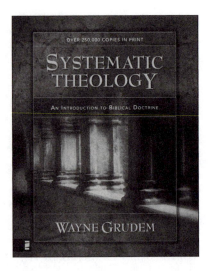

The Christian church has a long tradition of systematic theology, that is, studying theology and doctrine organized around fairly standard categories such as the Word of God, redemption, and Jesus Christ. This introduction to systematic theology has several distinctive features:

- A strong emphasis on the scriptural basis for each doctrine and teaching
- Clear writing, with technical terms kept to a minimum
- A contemporary approach, treating subjects of special interest to the church today
- A friendly tone, appealing to the emotions and the spirit as well as the intellect
- Frequent application to life
- Resources for worship with each chapter
- Bibliographies with each chapter that cross-reference subjects to a wide range of other systematic theologies.

Every Christian 'does theology.' With over 300,000 copies in print *Systematic Theology: An Introduction to Biblical Doctrine* is a proven, trusted resource for introducing biblical doctrine and instructing theological application.

Christian Beliefs

Twenty Basics Every Christian Should Know

Wayne A. Grudem, Edited by Elliot Grudem

Christian Essentials Made Plain and Simple

God doesn't call every Christian to go off to seminary, but there are certain matters of doctrine—that is, the church's teaching—that every Christian simply must know. If you're a relatively new believer in Jesus, or if you're a more mature Christian looking for a quick brush-up on basics of the faith, *Christian Beliefs* is for you.

This readable guide to twenty basic Christian beliefs is a condensation of Wayne Grudem's award-winning book on systematic theology, prized by pastors and teachers everywhere. He and his son, Elliot, have boiled down the essentials of Christian theology and made them both clear and applicable to life. You will learn about the Bible, the characteristics of God, what it means that we are created in the image of God, what God has done for us in Christ, the purpose of the church, and much more. Each chapter includes questions for personal review or group discussion.

> Based on Systematic Theology, *this summary will certainly help beginners with Christ to get the hang of their faith.*
> —J. I. Packer, Regent College, Vancouver, British Columbia

> *As Wayne Grudem's* Systematic Theology *contracts into a compact book, I do not lose my enthusiasm for the truth he loves and the clarity of his words.*
> —John Piper, Bethlehem Baptist Church, Minneapolis, Minnesota

Available in stores and online!

ZONDERVAN

Share Your Thoughts

With the Author: Your comments will be forwarded to
the author when you send them to *zauthor@zondervan.com*.

With Zondervan: Submit your review of this book
by writing to *zreview@zondervan.com*.

Free Online Resources at

www.zondervan.com

Zondervan AuthorTracker: Be notified whenever your favorite authors publish new books, go on tour, or post an update about what's happening in their lives at www.zondervan.com/authortracker.

Daily Bible Verses and Devotions: Enrich your life with daily Bible verses or devotions that help you start every morning focused on God. Visit www.zondervan.com/newsletters.

Free Email Publications: Sign up for newsletters on Christian living, academic resources, church ministry, fiction, children's resources, and more. Visit www.zondervan.com/newsletters.

Zondervan Bible Search: Find and compare Bible passages in a variety of translations at www.zondervanbiblesearch.com.

Other Benefits: Register yourself to receive online benefits like coupons and special offers, or to participate in research.